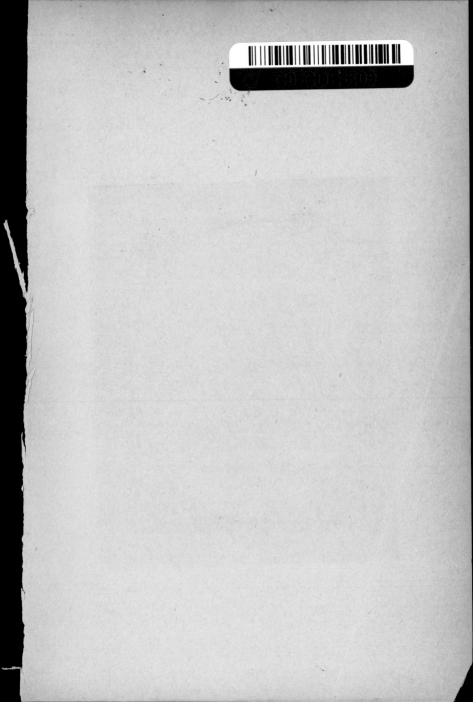

READINGS IN MODERN EUROPEAN HISTORY

*A collection of extracts from the sources chosen with the
purpose of illustrating some of the chief phases
of the development of Europe during
the last two hundred years*

BY

JAMES HARVEY ROBINSON

PROFESSOR OF HISTORY IN COLUMBIA UNIVERSITY

AND

CHARLES A. BEARD

ADJUNCT PROFESSOR OF POLITICS IN COLUMBIA UNIVERSITY

VOLUME II

EUROPE SINCE THE CONGRESS OF VIENNA

GINN AND COMPANY

BOSTON · NEW YORK · CHICAGO · LONDON
ATLANTA · DALLAS · COLUMBUS · SAN FRANCISCO

The Athenæum Press

GINN AND COMPANY · PRO-
PRIETORS · BOSTON · U.S.A.

PREFACE

This volume agrees precisely with the previous one in purpose and arrangement. It has, however, been necessary, on account of the ever-increasing diffuseness of the material upon which we have had to draw, to resort more frequently to condensation. Parliamentary speeches, state papers, pamphlets, books of travel, magazine articles, and treatises on important phases of our modern life rarely yield their best in the succinct form essential, considering the space at our disposal. Moreover, with the class of readers we have in view it seemed wise to avoid all digressions and obscure allusions which could hardly fail to increase the difficulties in the student's path. We have, however, always plainly indicated in the margin those cases in which a speech, treaty, constitution, or extract from a book or article is "condensed" or "much condensed." While we have struck out sentences and paragraphs where there was not space for them, and they could be spared, we have only in the rarest instances ventured to change a word, excepting always in the case of translations, which commonly solicit amelioration either from the standpoint of sense or taste. The critical student who suspects that he is missing something can always, by means of our Table of Contents and List of Citations, readily turn to the text upon which we have relied.

J. H. R.
C. A. B.

COLUMBIA UNIVERSITY
NEW YORK CITY

CONTENTS AND LIST OF CITATIONS

VOLUME II

CHAPTER XVII — EUROPE AFTER THE CONGRESS OF VIENNA

PAGE

CHAPTER XX — REVOLUTION OF 1848 — AUSTRIA, GERMANY, ITALY

Section 60. The Fall of Metternich

Section 61. Failure of the Revolution in Bohemia and Hungary

Section 62. Austria regains her Power in Italy

CHAPTER XXIV — FRANCE UNDER THE THIRD REPUBLIC

CHAPTER XXVII — THE BRITISH EMPIRE IN THE NINETEENTH CENTURY

ction 88. The Extension of British Dominion in India

ction 89. The Dominion of Canada

n 90. The Australasian Colonies

CHAPTER XXVIII — THE RUSSIAN EMPIRE IN THE NINETEENTH CENTURY

READINGS IN MODERN
EUROPEAN HISTORY

VOLUME II
EUROPE SINCE THE CONGRESS OF VIENNA

READINGS IN MODERN EUROPEAN HISTORY

CHAPTER XVII

EUROPE AFTER THE CONGRESS OF VIENNA

Section 49. The Restoration in France and the Revolution of 1830

Although the Bourbon line of kings, in the person of Louis XVIII, was restored after the downfall of Napoleon, absolute monarchy in France had been destroyed for all time by the Revolution. Accordingly, Louis XVIII found it necessary to issue a constitutional charter in which he enumerated many of the rights of citizens that had been proclaimed in the Declaration of the Rights of Man of 1789, and also provided for a legislature of two houses. This document is especially important because it furnishes an expression of the permanent results produced by the Revolution, and these are not at all obscured by the king's pretense that he is merely reviving ancient institutions. This charter served France for a long period, for, although modified on the accession of Louis Philippe, it was retained in its essential form until 1848.

185. Extracts
from the
French
Charter of
1814
*Louis, by the grace of God king of France and Navarre, to all
those to whom these presents come, salutation :*

Divine Providence, in recalling us to our estates after a long
absence, has imposed grave responsibilities upon us. Peace was
the first necessity of our subjects, and with this we have unceas-
ingly occupied ourselves. That peace so essential to France and
to the rest of Europe has been signed.

Reasons
which led
Louis XVIII
to grant a
constitution

A constitutional charter was demanded by the existing condition of the kingdom ; we promised this and now publish it.
We have taken into consideration the fact that, although the
whole authority in France resides in the person of the king,
our predecessors have not hesitated to modify the exercise of
this in accordance with the differences of the times. It was
thus that the communes owed their enfranchisement to Louis
the Fat, the confirmation and extension of their rights to St.
Louis and Philip the Fair, and that the judicial system was
established and developed by the laws of Louis XI, Henry
II, and Charles IX. It was in this way, finally, that Louis
XIV regulated almost every portion of the public administration by various ordinances which have never been surpassed
in wisdom.

Louis recog-
nizes that the
world has
changed

We, like the kings our predecessors, have had to consider
the effects of the ever-increasing progress of knowledge, the
new relations which this progress has introduced into society,
the direction given to the public mind during half a century,
and the serious troubles resulting therefrom. We have perceived that the wish of our subjects for a constitutional charter
was the expression of a real need ; but in yielding to this wish
we have taken every precaution that this charter should be
worthy of us and of the people whom we are proud to rule.
Able men taken from the highest official bodies of the State
were added to the commissioners of our council to elaborate
this important work.

While we recognize that the expectations of enlightened
Europe ought to be gratified by a free monarchical constitution,
we have had to remember that our first duty toward our people
was to preserve, for their own interest, the rights and prerogatives of our crown.

We hope that, taught by experience, the nation may be convinced that the supreme authority alone can give to institutions which it establishes the power, permanence, and dignity with which it is itself clothed ; that, consequently, when the wisdom of kings freely harmonizes with the wish of the people, a constitutional charter may long endure, but that when concessions are snatched with violence from a weak government, public liberty is not less endangered than the throne itself.

We have sought the principles of the constitutional charter in the French character and in the venerable monuments of past centuries. Thus we perceived in the revival of the peerage a truly national institution which binds memories to hope by uniting ancient and modern times. We have replaced by the Chamber of Deputies those ancient assemblies of the March Field and May Field, and those chambers of the third estate which so often exhibited at once proof of their zeal for the interests of the people and fidelity and respect for the authority of kings.

Louis pretends to be merely reviving ancient institutions

In thus endeavoring to renew the chain of time which fatal excesses had broken, we effaced from our memory, as we would we might blot out from history, all the evils which have afflicted the country during our absence. Happy to find ourselves again in the bosom of our great family, we could only respond to the love of which we receive so many testimonies by uttering words of peace and consolation. The dearest wish of our heart is that all Frenchmen may live like brothers, and that no bitter memory should ever trouble the tranquillity which should follow the solemn decree which we grant them to-day.

Confident in our intentions, strong in our conscience, we engage ourselves, before the assembly which listens to us, to be faithful to this constitutional charter; with the intention, moreover, of swearing to maintain it with added solemnity before the altars of Him who weighs in the same balance kings and nations.

The king binds himself to observe the charter

For these reasons we have voluntarily, and by the free exercise of our royal authority, granted and do grant, concede, and accord, as well for us as for our successors forever, the Constitutional Charter as follows :

Public Rights of the French [1]

Article 1. All Frenchmen are equal before the law, whatever may be their title or rank.

2. They contribute without distinction to the impositions of the State in proportion to their fortune.

3. They are all equally eligible to civil and military positions.

4. Their personal liberty is likewise guaranteed; no one can be prosecuted or arrested except in the cases and in the manner prescribed by law.

5. All may with equal liberty make profession of their religion and enjoy the same protection for their worship.

6. Nevertheless the Roman Catholic and apostolic religion is the religion of the State.

7. The ministers of the Roman Catholic and apostolic religion, and those of other Christian forms of worship only, shall receive subsidies from the royal treasury.

8. All Frenchmen have the right to publish and cause their opinions to be printed, if they conform to the laws destined to check the abuse of this liberty.

9. All property is inviolable; that known as *national* property forms no exception, since the law recognizes no difference between that and other property.

10. The State may demand the surrender of property in the interest of the public when this is legally certified, but only with previous indemnification.

11. All investigation of opinions expressed or of votes cast previous to the Restoration is prohibited; oblivion of these is imposed upon the courts and upon citizens alike.

12. The conscription is abolished; the method of recruiting both for the army and the navy shall be determined by law.

Form of the Government of the King

Position of the king

13. The person of the king is inviolable and sacred; his ministers are responsible. In the king alone is vested the executive power.

[1] This list of rights should be compared with the Declaration of the Rights of Man drawn up in 1789 (see Vol. I, pp. 260 *sqq.*).

14. The king is the supreme head of the State ; he has command of the land and naval forces, declares war, concludes treaties of peace, alliance, and commerce, appoints all the officials of the public administration, and issues the regulations and ordinances necessary for the execution of the laws and the safety of the State.

15. The legislative power is exercised jointly by the king, the Chamber of Peers, and the Chamber of Deputies of the departments. System of lawmaking

16. The right of initiating legislation belongs to the king.

17. Proposed laws are submitted, at the option of the king, either to the Chamber of Peers or to the Chamber of Deputies, except laws for raising taxes, which must be submitted to the Chamber of Deputies first.

18. Every law must be discussed and passed freely by a majority of each of the two houses.

19. The chambers have the right to petition the king to submit a law relating to any subject and to indicate what they deem the law should contain. [1] . . .

Louis XVIII's intentions of restoring harmony and prosperity to the long distracted nation were sadly hindered by the bitterness and discontent which the Revolution and the Napoleonic wars had engendered. The nobles and clergy, who had left France or had been driven out, came back with the determination to recover their ancient privileges; and distinguished soldiers of Napoleon found themselves rudely thrust aside by the returning emigrants, many of whom had borne arms against France. Chancellor Pasquier (see above, Vol. I, p. 349), with his usual insight, gives in his *Memoirs* the following picture of the strained relations in France after the Restoration of the Bourbons.

[1] The succeeding sections on the Chamber of Peers, the Chamber of Deputies, the judiciary, etc., are omitted here. The whole document may be found in *Translations and Reprints*, Vol. I, No. 3, or Anderson, *Constitutions and Documents*, pp. 456 *sqq.*

186. Difficult position of Louis XVIII and his government.

Vanquished on the 10th of August, 1792, immolated on the 21st of January, 1793, the Bourbon monarchy had returned after twenty-two years, which had seen a republic, a directorial government, a consulate, and an empire. It came back not in a blaze of glory, since not a single victory had been won in the past twenty years either by it or in its name, but bringing with it the blessings of a necessary peace. Peace abroad, peace at home, was all that was expected of it; but for this dual peace to be lasting it must be an honorable one. No longer could any ambitious daydreams be indulged in; we could revel no more in the enjoyment of the brilliant victories which had become so dear to the French heart. Care must be taken the while to respect the memory of them, and to be considerate in the treatment of those who had risen to an illustrious and glorious prominence, all the more precious in that it alone had survived the shipwreck. Yet fate and the force of circumstances rendered these memories — cherished by so large a majority of Frenchmen — a painful subject to the king, the royal family, and almost all those who had returned in their wake.

Strained relations between the returned *Émigrés* and the Napoleonic nobility

The situation was a delicate one, for hardly any one dared to give frank expression to his natural sentiments. Some there were who, in spite of the caution enjoined by policy, necessarily found their prestige dimmed. Accustomed as they had been for fifteen years to hold first rank both in the army and at court, they now found themselves forced to share their power with men the greater number of whom had hitherto remained unknown to fame, and who suddenly assumed an attitude characterized by a superiority which displayed itself with that ease which usually belongs only to a possession of long date. . . .

Napoleon's former generals slighted

It not unfrequently occurred that the most illustrious among generals heard people ask in the salons of the Tuileries who they were. These names, which had so often resounded in the bulletins of the *Grande Armée*, were known in Vienna, in Berlin, and in the many capitals through which their bearers had passed as conquerors. On the other hand, those who in their own country, and in its very capital, involuntarily put this slight upon them, were perpetually exasperated at heart by the consideration and respectful treatment which policy dictated should be shown to men of the empire, and which seemed to the returned royalists excessive. . . .

There was an ever-present and ill-concealed feeling of antagonism between the throng of officers who had won their promotion in the wars of the Revolution and the noblemen of all ages who were in so great a hurry to wear their old epaulets once more or to procure fresh ones.

Notwithstanding these conflicting elements, the moderation and indifference of Louis XVIII prevented any serious disturbances during his reign, but his death in 1824 brought to the throne a man of decidedly reactionary notions, — his brother, Charles X. The new ruler, who was known as "King of the Emigrants," was especially favorable to the clergy, whom he regarded as the main support of the monarchy, but his efforts to aid them in regaining their former influence really helped to prepare the way for his own overthrow. De Tocqueville, whose work on *Democracy in America* gave him a permanent place among the noted publicists of the nineteenth century, thus describes the religious situation after the Restoration, as he remembered it, in a letter to an Englishman, Lord Radnor, bearing the date of May, 1835.

. . . When Napoleon reëstablished the exercise of the Catholic religion, he did not restore their property to the clergy, but assigned to them part of the revenue of the State. From proprietors they became pensioners. This was not the only blow struck by him at their independence. . . . He gave up the inferior clergy to the uncontrolled jurisdiction of the bishops, for the emperor thought, rightly or not, that he would always be able to manage easily a few bishops, and that by controlling them he would be master of all the clergy. This was the position of the ministers of our religion at the Restoration.

187. De Tocqueville's account of clerical influence in politics after the Restoration

The Bourbons returned resolved to support the monarchy by the Church; and the Charter of 1814 announced that the

The Church used to support the monarchy Catholic religion was the religion of the State, although it did not dare to define the words "the religion of the State." The property of the clergy was not restored to them, nor, I believe, were even their salaries increased. But they were allowed an indirect share in the government. The parish priest, from the weight given to his recommendations, became a sort of political authority. Offices were filled with more regard to religious opinions than to capacity—so, at least, it was generally thought. As the Restoration became more firmly established, the union between Church and State became more and more evident. A law was passed punishing with the utmost rigor all sacrilegious profanation of sacred objects and theft from churches. The archbishops and some of the bishops obtained seats in the House of Peers. The nation was governed, or thought that it was governed, by the priests; their influence was felt everywhere.

The spirit of Voltaire revived Then reappeared what we call in France the Voltairian spirit: the spirit of systematic hostility and sarcasm directed not only against the ministers of religion but against religion itself,—against Christianity in all its forms. The books of the eighteenth century were reprinted in cheap editions. Plays, songs, and caricatures were filled with bitter satires against religion. The hatred of a portion of the population against the clergy became inconceivably violent. At that time I held a judicial post; and I noticed that whenever a priest was accused of any offense whatever, the jury, in general very indulgent, almost invariably and unanimously condemned him. Under the empire the Church took no part in politics; after the Restoration it became a political party in itself. It joined the most ardent votaries of absolute monarchy, and often declaimed from the pulpit in its favor.

Impiety a form of opposition to the king's policy The result was fatal. Almost all the Liberal party, that is, the great majority of the nation, became irreligious on political grounds. Impiety was a form of opposition. Excellent men were furious when religion was mentioned; others, notoriously immoral, talked incessantly of restoring altars and of inculcating reverence toward God. I do not think, my lord, that there is a single Frenchman of any party whatever, who at this day does not consider the religious hatred brought about by the Restoration as the chief cause of the downfall of the Bourbons. If it had stood alone, the elder branch would have sustained itself with difficulty ; united to the clergy, and exposed to the intense animosity excited by the political influence of the priests, its fall was inevitable.

In addition to the controversy about the political power of the clergy, France was agitated by a conflict over the liberty of the press which (subject to laws designed to check its abuse) had been guaranteed by the eighth article of the Charter. The opponents of the royal policy had seized the opportunity to criticise the government in the most extravagant terms and had rudely caricatured the clergy and nobles. To Charles X's ministers this seemed deplorable, and extremely dangerous to the established order, and accordingly, in the following memorandum, they gave him their view of the situation, urging him to make use of the power which he enjoyed under article fourteen of the Charter to regulate and control the liberty of the press.

Notwithstanding a real prosperity such as France never enjoyed before, signs of disorganization and symptoms of anarchy manifest themselves at almost every point in the kingdom. The successive causes which have concurred to weaken the authority of monarchical government tend now to impair and debase it. **188. Charles X's ministers advise him to check the licentiousness of the press (July, 1830)**

The press has excited confusion in the most upright minds, — has shaken the firmest convictions, and produced, in the midst of society, a confusion of principles which lends itself to the most fatal enterprises. Its anarchical theories pave the way for anarchy in the State. It is worthy of remark, sire, that the periodical press has not even fulfilled its most essential condition, — that of publicity. Strange as it may seem, it is none the less true that there is no publicity in France, taking this word in its correct sense. In this state of things, facts, even **Facts are distorted by the press** when they are not entirely fictitious, do not come to the knowledge of several millions of readers, except mutilated and disfigured in the most odious manner. A thick cloud, raised by the journals, conceals the truth, and in some manner intercepts the light between the government and the people.

Even the king's speeches are distorted

The kings, your predecessors, sire, always loved to communicate with their subjects; this is a satisfaction which the press has not thought fit that your Majesty should enjoy. A license which has passed all bounds has, in fact, not respected, even on the most solemn occasions, either the express will of the king or the words pronounced from the throne. Some have been misunderstood and misinterpreted; others have been the subject of perfidious commentaries, or of bitter derision. . . .

The press endeavors to influence the Parliament

This is not all. The press tends to nothing short of subjugating the sovereignty and invading the powers of the State. The alleged organ of public opinion, it aspires to direct the debates of the two chambers; it is incontestable that it brings to bear upon them an influence no less fatal than decisive. This domination has assumed in the Chamber of Deputies, especially within these two or three years, a manifest character of oppression and tyranny. In this interval of time we have seen the newspapers pursue with their insults and their outrages the members whose votes appeared to them uncertain or suspected. Too often, sire, the freedom of debate in that chamber has sunk under the reiterated blows of the press. . . .

Religion is not spared by the newspapers

The periodical press has not displayed less ardor in pursuing, with its poisoned darts, religion and its priests. Its object is, and always will be, to root out of the heart of the people the very last germ of religious sentiments. Sire, do not doubt that it will succeed in this, by attacking the foundations of the press, by poisoning the sources of public morals, and by covering the ministers of the altars with derision and contempt. . . .

Upright men look to the king for relief

Give ear, sire, to the prolonged cry of indignation and of terror which rises from all points of your kingdom. All peaceable men, the upright, the friends of order, stretch out their suppliant hands to your Majesty. All implore you to preserve them from the return of those calamities which so grievously afflicted their fathers or themselves. These apprehensions are too real not to be attended to; these wishes are too legitimate to be disregarded. . . .

The right as well as the duty of assuring its own maintenance is the inseparable attribute of sovereignty. No government on earth would remain standing, if it had not the right to provide for its own security. This power takes precedence of the laws, because it is in the nature of things. These, sire, are maxims which have in their favor the sanction of time and the assent of all the publicists of Europe. But these maxims have another sanction still more positive, — that of the Charter itself. The fourteenth article has invested your Majesty with a sufficient power, not undoubtedly to change our institutions but to strengthen them and render them more stable. Circumstances of imperious necessity do not permit the exercise of this supreme power to be longer deferred. The moment has come to have recourse to measures which are in the spirit of the Charter, but which are beyond the limits of the existing laws, the resources of which have been exhausted in vain.

The king has power to act alone

Sire, your ministers, who are to secure the success of these measures, do not hesitate to propose them to you, convinced as they are that right will prevail.

We are, with the most profound respect, sire, your Majesty's most humble and most faithful subjects.

Sunday, July 25, 1830

In response to the recommendations of his ministers, Charles X, on July 25, 1830, issued three important ordinances: one (given below) against the press, another dissolving the newly elected Chamber of Deputies before it could hold its first session, and a third altering the qualifications of voters in favor of the more conservative classes. These decrees were the signal for the Revolution of 1830.

189. Charles X's ordinance against the press

Charles, &c. To all to whom these presents shall come, greeting.

On the report of our Council of Ministers, we have ordained and ordain as follows:

ARTICLE 1. The liberty of the periodical press is suspended.

2. The provisions of articles 1, 2, and 9 of the first section of the law of the 21st of October, 1814, are again put in force, in consequence of which no journal, or periodical, or semiperiodical work, regardless of the character of the matters therein treated, established, or about to be established, shall appear either in Paris or in the departments, except by virtue of an authorization first obtained from us by the authors and the printer respectively. This authorization shall be renewed every three months. It may also be revoked.

3. The authorization shall be provisionally granted and provisionally withdrawn by the prefects from newspapers and periodicals, or semiperiodical works, published or about to be published in their departments.

4. Newspapers and writings published in contravention of article 2 shall be immediately seized. The presses and types used in the printing of them shall be placed in a public warehouse under seals, or rendered unfit for use.

5. No work of less than twenty printed pages shall appear, except with the authority of our Minister-Secretary of State for the Interior, at Paris, and of the prefects in the departments. Every work of more than twenty printed pages, which shall not constitute one single publication, must be likewise issued under authorization only. Writings published without authorization shall be immediately seized ; the presses and types used in printing them shall be placed in a public warehouse, and under seals, or rendered unfit for use.

6. Reports of legal proceedings and transactions of scientific and literary societies must be previously authorized if they treat in whole or in part of political matters, in which case the measures prescribed by article 5 shall be applicable.

Given at Chateau St. Cloud, the 25th of July, of the year of grace 1830, and the sixth of our reign.

(Signed)   CHARLES

This ordinance against the press was immediately met by a protest from the Paris journalists, who declared that they would attempt to print their papers without the royal authorization required in the decree. The Paris deputies to the Chamber, which had been dissolved, likewise denounced the king's arbitrary action, and in a short time an uprising in the capital overthrew Charles X. Thereupon the Chamber of Deputies declared the throne vacant and offered the crown to Louis Philippe.

The Chamber of Deputies, in view of the imperative necessity resulting from the events of July 26, 27, 28, and 29, and the following days, and the general situation of France due to the violation of the Constitutional Charter; **190. The Chamber of Deputies summons Louis Philippe to the throne**

In view also of the fact that, in consequence of this violation and of the heroic resistance of the citizens of Paris, his Majesty Charles X and his Royal Highness Louis Antoine, the dauphin, and all the members of the older branch of the royal house are at this moment leaving French territory, declares that the throne is vacant in fact and of right, and that it is indispensable to provide therefor. **The throne declared vacant**

The Chamber of Deputies declares, secondly, that, in accordance with the wish and in the interest of the French people, the preamble of the Constitutional Charter [1] is suppressed as wounding the national dignity, since it appears to *grant* to Frenchmen the rights which are inherently theirs, and that the following articles of the same character must be suppressed or modified in the manner below indicated.

[Here follows a series of modifications in the Charter intended to preclude the illiberal construction which Charles X had placed upon it.]

On condition of the acceptance of these arrangements and propositions, the Chamber of Deputies declares that the general and pressing interest of the French people summons to the throne his Royal Highness Louis Philippe of Orleans, duke of Orleans, lieutenant general of the kingdom, and his descendants forever, from male to male, in order of primogeniture, to **Louis Philippe invited, under certain conditions, to become king of France**

[1] See above, p. 3

the perpetual exclusion of women and their descendants. Accordingly his Royal Highness Louis Philippe of Orleans shall be invited to accept and swear to the clauses and engagements above enumerated, and to the observation of the Constitutional Charter including the modifications indicated, and, after having done this in the presence of the assembled chambers, to take the title of King of the French.

Section 50. Establishment of the Kingdom of Belgium

In the general European settlement of 1815 the old Austrian Netherlands had been united with the Dutch provinces under the kingship of the prince of Orange, who took the title of William I. From the very outset the inhabitants of the southern districts chafed under this forced union with Holland, and shortly after the overthrow of Charles X a revolution was started in Brussels with the cry, "Let us do as the French have done." A provisional government was later set up, independence declared, and a national congress called to draft a constitution for the new state. At the opening of this congress, October 10, 1830, the causes for the separation from Holland were stated by the provisional government in the following address.

191. Reasons which led to the creation of the kingdom of Belgium

In the name of the Belgian people, the provisional government opens an assembly of the representatives of the nation. The nation has confided to these representatives the august mission of founding, on the broad and solid basis of liberty, the edifice of the new social order which will be the beginning and the guarantee of durable happiness to Belgium.

Grievances of the Belgian provinces against Holland

You are aware, gentlemen, that at the time of our union with Holland a Fundamental Law was presented to an assembly of notables, chosen by the government, not to examine, discuss, modify, and finally to accept it and make it the condition of a compact between the people and the head of the State, but either to submit to it unconditionally or to reject it altogether. It was rejected, as might have been expected from the good sense and integrity of the Belgians; but by an unparalleled subterfuge it was nevertheless declared to be accepted, and thus it came about that our country was oppressed by a constitution imposed by Holland.

If this Fundamental Law had at least been properly executed in all its provisions, in time, perhaps, and with the aid of the progress which the arbitrary conduct of the ministers compelled us daily to make in the career of constitutional opposition, it might have become the hope of Belgian liberty.

But far from this being the case, freedom of conscience was violated, education fettered, the press condemned to be nothing more than an instrument of the government or forced into silence, . . . and the right of petition was disregarded. The despotic imposition of a privileged language, . . . and an enormous debt and expenditure, were the only portion which Holland brought to us at the time of our deplorable union. Add to these grievances taxes, overwhelming by their amount and still more by the manner in which they were apportioned, laws always voted by the Dutch for Holland only and always against Belgium, . . . and, lastly, the most offensive partiality in the distribution of civil and military appointments by a government in whose eye the name of Belgian was a disgrace; in a word, all Belgium treated as a conquered province, as a colony, — everything, in short, conspired to render a revolution necessary and inevitable and hastened its approach. Such just and real grievances could only lead to one result.

We rose against despotism to reconquer our rights, and we were treated by tyranny as rebels. Our cities were burned; the most barbarous treatment was inflicted even upon old men and upon women; the rights of humanity, the laws of war, were trampled underfoot. Such conduct testifies to the ferocity of our enemy and calls down blessings on the victory of the people which has cleared our territory of them.

The fruit of this victory has been independence. The people have proclaimed it through us, and have called you together, gentlemen, as the organ of its wishes to establish it forever.

Section 51.   *Germany and the Reaction after 1814*

The German liberals came out of the struggle against
Napoleon with high hopes. They desired that the many
German states might be bound together into a really
firm national union, under a constitutional government.
Prussia favored this plan at the Congress of Vienna, but
Austria opposed it for obvious reasons, and the German
Act of Confederation, drawn up by the Congress, established a very loose union of sovereign princes, who dealt
with one another almost like independent rulers. Nevertheless this constitution lasted Germany from 1815 to
1866, and formed a transition from the ancient Holy
Roman Empire, which Napoleon had destroyed, to the
present German Empire.

In the name of the Most Holy and Indivisible Trinity :

**192. The
German Act
of Confeder-
ation
(June 8,
1815)**

The sovereign princes and free towns of Germany, animated
by the common desire to carry into effect Article VI of the
Peace of Paris of May 30, 1814, and convinced of the advantages which would result for the security and independence of
Germany and for the repose and equilibrium of Europe from
a firm and lasting union, have agreed to unite themselves in a
perpetual confederation, and have for this purpose invested
their envoys and deputies at the Congress of Vienna with full
powers, viz. :

**Metternich's
grandeur**

His Imperial and Royal Apostolic Majesty ; the Sieur Clement
Wenceslas, Prince of Metternich-Winneburg-Ochsenhausen,
Knight of the Golden Fleece, Grand Cross of the Royal Order
of St. Stephen of Hungary, Knight of the Order of St. Andrew,
of the Order of St. Alexander Newsky and of St. Anne of the
First Class ; Grand Cordon of the Legion of Honor ; Knight
of the Order of the Elephant, of the Order of the Annunciation,
of the Black Eagle, of the Red Eagle, of the Seraphim, of St.
Joseph of Tuscany, of St. Hubert, of the Golden Eagle of Würtemberg, of the Fidelity of Baden, of St. John of Jerusalem,

and of several others; Chancellor of the Military Order of Maria Theresa; Curator of the Imperial and Royal Academy of Fine Arts; Chamberlain and Active Privy Councilor of his Majesty the emperor of Austria and king of Hungary and Bohemia; his Majesty's Minister of State and of Conferences, as well as Minister of Foreign Affairs and first plenipotentiary at the Congress, — and the Sieur John Philip, baron of Wessenberg; Grand Cross of the Royal Sardinian Order of St. Mauritius and St. Lazarus, and of the Royal Order of the Crown of Bavaria, etc.; Chamberlain and Active Privy Councilor of his Imperial and Royal Apostolic Majesty, and his Majesty's second plenipotentiary at the Congress.

His Royal Majesty of Prussia; the Prince Hardenberg, his Chancellor of State.[1] . . .

GENERAL PROVISIONS

ARTICLE I. The sovereign princes and free towns of Germany, including their Majesties the emperor of Austria and the kings of Prussia, of Denmark, and of the Netherlands; to wit, the emperor of Austria and the king of Prussia, for all of their possessions formerly belonging to the German Empire[2]; the king of Denmark for Holstein; and the king of the Netherlands for the grand duchy of Luxemburg, — unite in a perpetual union which shall be called the German Confederation.

II. The aim of the same shall be the maintenance of the external and internal safety of Germany and of the independence and inviolability of the individual German states.

III. All members of the union have, as such, equal rights. They all engage alike to maintain inviolate the Act of Confederation.

IV. The affairs of the Confederation shall be confided to a Diet of the Confederation, in which all members of the union shall vote through their plenipotentiaries, either individually

Voting in the Diet

---

[1] It has not been deemed necessary to give the names of all the plenipotentiaries. All the states enumerated in Article IV were represented at the Congress.

[2] I.e. the Holy Roman Empire.

or collectively, in the following manner, without prejudice to their rank.

	Votes			Votes
1. Austria	1	12.	The grand ducal and ducal houses of Saxony	1
2. Prussia	1	13.	Brunswick and Nassau	1
3. Bavaria	1	14.	Mecklenburg-Schwerin and Mecklenburg-Strelitz	1
4. Saxony	1			
5. Hanover	1	15.	Holstein-Oldenburg, Anhalt, and Schwarzburg	1
6. Würtemberg	1			
7. Baden	1	16.	Hohenzollern, Liechtenstein, Reuss, Schaumburg-Lippe, Lippe, and Waldeck	1
8. Electoral Hesse	1			
9. Grand duchy of Hesse	1			
10. Denmark, for Holstein	1	17.	The free towns, Lübeck, Frankfort, Bremen, and Hamburg	1
11. The Netherlands, for the grand duchy of Luxemburg	1			

Total votes 17

V. Austria shall preside in the Diet of the Confederation. Each member of the union has the right to make and support propositions, and the presiding state is bound within a determined period to bring them under deliberation.

System of voting on special occasions

VI. Whenever fundamental laws of the Confederation are to be enacted or amended, or measures are to be adopted relative to the Act of Confederation itself or organic institutions of the Confederation, or other arrangements of common interest are under consideration, the Diet shall form itself into a general assembly (*Plenum*), in which the distribution of the votes, based upon the respective extent of the individual states of the union, has been arranged as follows : [1]

	Votes		Votes
1. Austria	4	14. Nassau	2
2. Prussia	4	15. Saxe-Weimar	1
3. Saxony	4	16. Saxe-Gotha	1
4. Bavaria	4	17. Saxe-Coburg	1
5. Hanover	4	18. Saxe-Meiningen	1
6. Würtemberg	4	19. Saxe-Hildburghausen	1
7. Baden	3	20. Mecklenburg-Strelitz	1
8. Electoral Hesse	3	21. Holstein-Oldenburg	1
9. Grand duchy of Hesse	3	22. Anhalt-Dessau	1
10. Holstein	3	23. Anhalt-Bernburg	1
11. Luxemburg	3	24. Anhalt-Cöthen	1
12. Brunswick	2	25. Schwarzburg-Sondershausen	1
13. Mecklenburg-Schwerin	2	26. Schwarzburg-Rudolstadt	1

[1] The system of voting which now prevails in the Federal Council (*Bundesrath*) of the German Empire is based on this plan of 1815.

VOTES		VOTES
27. Hohenzollern-Hechingen . . 1	33. Schaumberg-Lippe 1
28. Liechtenstein 1	34. Lippe 1
29. Hohenzollern-Sigmaringen . . 1	35. The free town Lübeck . . . 1
30. Waldeck 1	36. The free town Frankfort . . 1
31. Reuss, Elder Branch 1	37. The free town Bremen . . . 1
32. Reuss, Younger Branch . . . 1	38. The free town Hamburg . . . 1

Total votes 69

The Diet of the Confederation, in deliberating on the organic laws of the union, shall take into consideration whether the mediatized estates of the former empire shall be granted any collective votes in the *Plenum*. . . . Reference to the great readjustment of 1803

VIII. When the organic laws shall have been drawn up, the Diet of the Confederation shall take into consideration the future permanent order of voting to be adopted. In so doing they shall deviate as little as possible from the regulations of the former Diet, especially as based upon the provisions of the Decree of the Imperial Commission of 1803.

IX. The Diet of the Confederation shall sit at Frankfort-on-the-Main. The first meeting is fixed for the 1st of September, 1815.

XI. All members of the Confederation pledge themselves to protect Germany as a whole, as well as every single confederated state, against attack, and mutually guarantee their entire possessions, so far as those are included within the Confederation.

When war is once declared on the part of the Confederation no member shall negotiate separately with the enemy, or conclude an armistice or make peace.

XII. The members of the Confederation reserve to themselves the right of forming alliances of all kinds. They pledge themselves, however, to contract no engagement which shall be directed against the safety of the Confederation or that of any individual state within the union. Members reserve the right to form alliances

The members of the Confederation pledge themselves likewise not to make war among themselves upon any pretense, or to follow up their contentions with force, but to submit these to the Diet. It shall devolve upon this body to attempt arbitration by means of a commission. Should this fail and a judicial decision become necessary, the same shall be effected through a well-organized court of arbitration, to the decision of which the conflicting parties shall forthwith submit.[1]

The extreme phase in the spirit of reaction was reached in Germany when the laws given below were enacted by the Diet. Using the murder of Kotzebue as an excuse, Metternich called a conference of the larger states of the Confederation at Carlsbad (Bohemia) in August, 1819. Here a series of resolutions were drawn up, with the aim of checking the free expression of opinions hostile to existing institutions and of discovering and bringing to justice conspirators, who were supposed to exist in dangerous numbers. These Carlsbad Resolutions were laid before the Diet, which, under Austria's influence, reluctantly ratified them.

193. Chief provisions of the Carlsbad Resolutions as ratified by the Diet (September 20, 1819)

1. A special representative of the ruler of each state shall be appointed for each university, with appropriate instructions and extended powers, and shall reside in the place where the university is situated. This office may devolve upon the existing curator or upon any other individual whom the government may deem qualified.

Law providing for a supervision of the university professors and students

The function of this agent shall be to see to the strictest enforcement of existing laws and disciplinary regulations; to observe carefully the spirit which is shown by the instructors in the university in their public lectures and regular courses, and, without directly interfering in scientific matters or in the methods of teaching, to give a salutary direction to the instruction, having in view the future attitude of the students. Lastly, he shall devote unceasing attention to everything that may promote morality, good order, and outward propriety among the students. . . .

[1] The "special provisions" which follow are omitted. The most important of these, and one which later caused much discussion, was Article XIII, which read: "A constitution based upon the system of estates shall take place (*statt finden*) in all the states of the union."

2. The confederated governments mutually pledge themselves to remove from the universities or other public educational institutions all teachers who, by obvious deviation from their duty, or by exceeding the limits of their functions, or by the abuse of their legitimate influence over the youthful minds, or by propagating harmful doctrines hostile to public order or subversive of existing governmental institutions, shall have unmistakably proved their unfitness for the important office intrusted to them. . . .

No teacher who shall have been removed in this manner shall be again appointed to a position in any public institution of learning in another state of the union.

3. Those laws which have for a long period been directed Students' against secret and unauthorized societies in the universities societies shall be strictly enforced. These laws apply especially to that association established some years since under the name Universal Students' Union (*Allgemeine Burschenschaft*), since the very conception of the society implies the utterly unallowable plan of permanent fellowship and constant communication between the various universities. The duty of especial watchfulness in this matter should be impressed upon the special agents of the government.

The governments mutually agree that such persons as shall hereafter be shown to have remained in secret or unauthorized associations, or shall have entered such associations, shall not be admitted to any public office.

4. No student who shall be expelled from a university in virtue of a decision of the university senate ratified or prompted by the agent of the government, or who shall have left the institution in order to escape expulsion, shall be received in any other university. . . .

1. So long as this decree shall remain in force no publica- Press law tion which appears in the form of daily issues, or as a serial not exceeding twenty sheets of printed matter, shall go to press in any state of the union without the previous knowledge and approval of the state officials.

Writings which do not belong to one of the above-mentioned classes shall be treated according to the laws now in force, or which may be enacted, in the individual states of the union. . . .

(4. Each state of the union is responsible, not only to the state against which the offense is directly committed, but to the whole Confederation, for every publication appearing within the limits of its jurisdiction in which the honor or security of other states is infringed or their constitution or administration attacked. . . .

(6. The Diet shall have the right, moreover, to suppress on its own authority, without being petitioned, such writings included in Article 1, in whatever German state they may appear, as, in the opinion of a commission appointed by it, are inimical to the honor of the union, the safety of individual states, or the maintenance of peace and quiet in Germany. There shall be no appeal from such decisions, and the governments involved are bound to see that they are put into execution. . . .

7(When a newspaper or periodical is suppressed by a decision of the Diet, the editor thereof may not within a period of five years edit a similar publication in any state of the union.)

Establishment of an investigating committee at Mayence

1. Within a fortnight, reckoned from the passage of this decree, there shall convene, under the auspices of the Confederation, in the city and federal fortress of Mayence, an extraordinary commission of investigation to consist of seven members, including the chairman.

2. The object of the commission shall be a joint investigation, as thorough and extensive as possible, of the facts relating to the origin and manifold ramifications of the revolutionary plots and demagogical associations directed against the existing constitution and the internal peace both of the union and of the individual states; of the existence of which plots more or less clear evidence is to be had already, or may be produced in the course of the investigation. . . .

10. The central investigating commission is to furnish the Diet from time to time with a report of the results of the investigation, which is to be carried out as speedily as possible. . . .

Section 52. Restoration in Spain and Italy

Shortly after Napoleon set aside the ruling Bourbon line in Spain in 1808, and placed his brother Joseph on the throne, a national Cortes was summoned by a committee in the name of those Spaniards who resisted the dominion of the foreigner. Only the liberals responded to the call, and the Cortes, while nominally loyal to their king, Ferdinand VII, whom Napoleon had deposed along with his father, Charles IV, completed a constitution in 1812 on the model of the French Constitution of 1791, expressly declaring that sovereignty resided in the nation and reducing the royal power to a mere shadow. When Ferdinand returned to Spain in 1814, after the expulsion of the French, he did all he could to restore the old régime and began by declaring this constitution of 1812 null and void.

This form of legislation, so foreign to the Spanish nation, consigns to oblivion the laws which have rendered it so happy and respected in former times. In fact, all the foundations of the ancient monarchical constitution have been overturned, while all the revolutionary and democratic principles of the French Constitution of 1791 have been copied. . . . Thus are promulgated not the fundamental laws of a limited monarchy, but those of a popular government presided over by a chief or magistrate, who is only a clerk, not a king. He is given the name of king, it is true, but this is only to allure and deceive shortsighted and credulous men. . . .

194. Manifesto of Ferdinand VII abolishing the constitution of 1812 (May 1814)

In order to dispose the minds of men to receive without suspicion such dangerous innovations, especially relating to the royal personage and to the prerogatives of the crown, use is made of some of the newspapers with which most of the deputies in the Cortes are themselves connected. The attempt is made to render the royal power odious by giving to all of the rights of the crown the name of despotism, by viewing the

How the title of king has been degraded in Spain by the innovators

titles of king and despot as synonymous, and by calling tyrants kings. At the same time those who have the courage to combat these innovations and object to this anarchical and seditious language are prosecuted in the most cruel manner. Wherever democracy appears, all is changed which recalls the name of king; the armies, the institutions which for a long time have been honored by the title of royal, are called "national," and thus the people are deceived, who, nevertheless, in spite of so many perfidious intrigues, have preserved their natural loyalty and nobleness of character.

The newspapers have dared to criticise the king

I have learned of all this since my happy return to the realm, both from my own observations and from the newspapers in which many articles have been impudently printed up till this very day about my character and return, so gross and infamous that they would constitute a grave offense against any other person than myself and would merit the severest punishment. Unexpected insults have also filled my heart with bitterness. I have only been consoled by the evidences of the love of my faithful subjects, who longed for my arrival in the hope that my presence would put an end to the evils and oppression under which those who preserved the memory of my person and desired the true welfare of the country, groaned.

Ferdinand abhors despotism

I promise you and I swear to you, true and loyal Spaniards, that since I sympathize with the evils which you have suffered, you will not be in the least deceived in your hopes. Your sovereign wishes to live for you; he makes his glory consist in being the sovereign of a heroic nation which by immortal exploits has won the admiration of all other peoples, and has maintained its liberty and its honor. I detest, I abhor despotism; it cannot be reconciled either with civilization or with the enlightenment of the nations of Europe. Kings have never been despots in Spain; neither the kings nor the constitution of the realm has ever authorized despotism, although unfortunately we have seen at times, here as everywhere, certain abuses of power which no human constitution could ever entirely prevent because there are certain abuses in all that is human; but if this has occurred in Spain, it is not the fault of the constitution but the fault of persons and circumstances. . . .

Conforming myself to the general demonstration of good will on the part of my people, which I believe to be well founded, I declare that my royal intention is not only to refuse to swear to or accept their constitution or any decree of the General and Extraordinary Cortes and of the ordinary Cortes now actually assembled ; and particularly the decrees which attack the rights and prerogatives of my sovereignty established by the constitution and the laws which have governed the nation for so long a time ; but also declare their constitution and their decrees null and void now and forever ; that my subjects, of whatsoever rank or condition, are not bound to observe them ; and that those who seek to uphold them in opposition to my royal intentions in this matter shall be regarded as having made an attack on the prerogatives of my sovereignty and the well-being of the nation. The constitution declared void

I declare guilty of lese-majesty, and as such punishable by death, whoever ventures either by act, by writing, or by word of mouth to excite or engage any one to observe or execute the decrees and constitution. . . . Death penalty for supporting the constitution

I declare that whoever opposes the execution of the present decree in any way whatsoever is guilty of lese-majesty and as such is punishable with death. All suits brought before one of the tribunals of the realm involving a violation of the constitution are herewith quashed. All persons detained for the same cause shall be immediately set at liberty. Such is my will, consistent with the good and well-being of the nation. Death for opposing this decree

THE KING

Signed at VALENÇAY, the 4th of May, 1814

PEDRO DE MACANAZ, Secretary of the King

A few weeks after abolishing the liberal constitution of 1812, Ferdinand VII restored the tribunal of the Inquisition which Napoleon has suppressed.

The glorious title of Catholic, by which the kings of Spain are distinguished amongst other Christian princes, as a result of their not tolerating any one in the kingdom who professes any other than the Roman Catholic apostolic religion, has 195. Decree restoring the Inquisition in Spain (July, 1814)

powerfully inclined my heart to employ all the means which
God has placed in my hands, in order to make myself worthy
of that title. The past disturbances ; the war which, for the space
of six years, has afflicted all the provinces of the kingdom
(there having remained in it during all this time foreign troops
composed of various sects, almost all of whom were infected
with abhorrence and hatred for the Catholic religion), and the
disorder which invariably follows these evils, in conjunction
with the careless manner in which everything relating to the
affairs of religion has been conducted, — all these things have
given complete license to the wicked to live according to their
free will, and have permitted the introduction and establishment in the kingdom of many pernicious opinions, by the same
means through which they are propagated in other countries.

Being desirous, therefore, of providing a remedy for so serious an evil, and of preserving in my dominions the holy religion of Jesus Christ, which my people love, and in which they
have lived and continue to live happily ; on account of the duty
which the fundamental laws of the kingdom impose upon the
prince who reigns, and which I have sworn to observe and to
fulfill ; and as a measure best adapted to the preservation of my
subjects from domestic dissensions, and for their maintenance
in quiet and tranquillity, I have thought that it would be proper
under existing circumstances that the tribunal of the Holy
Office should be restored to the exercise of its jurisdiction.

Spain saved
from disaster
by the
Inquisition

Wise and virtuous prelates, many corporations, and many
persons of weight, both ecclesiastical as well as secular, have
represented to me that Spain owes to this tribunal immunity
from contamination, in the sixteenth century, by the errors
which have caused such great affliction to other kingdoms ;
the nation flourishing at the same time in every kind of literature, in great men, and in sanctity and virtue.

Its abolition
was designed
by Napoleon
to sow corrup-
tion and
discord

One of the principal measures adopted by the Oppressor of
Europe, to sow corruption and discord, from which he derived
such great advantages, was to destroy this tribunal, under the
pretext that the state of knowledge would not longer admit of
its existence ; and afterwards the Cortes, called the General and
Extraordinary, under the same pretext, and the constitution

which they tumultuously drew up, abolished this tribunal, to the regret of the nation.

Wherefore the reëstablishment of this tribunal has been earnestly entreated of me; and acceding to the prayers and desires of the people, who, out of love to the religion of their fathers, have restored of their own accord some of the subordinate tribunals to their functions, I have resolved that the Council of the Inquisition and the other tribunals of the Holy Office should return to and continue in the exercise of their ecclesiastical jurisdiction, which the popes granted at the request of my august ancestors. . . . *Former jurisdiction of the Inquisition restored*

I am, moreover, desirous that, as soon as the Council of Inquisition is assembled, two of its members, with two members of my Royal Council, all of them to be named by myself, should examine the form and mode of proceeding of the Holy Office in respect to the cases brought before it, and the established mode of censuring and prohibiting books; and if in these forms they should find anything contrary to the welfare of my subjects and the upright administration of justice, or which ought to be changed, they may propose it, and consult with me, that I may order that which is proper. *Reformation of procedure to be undertaken*

THE KING

AT THE PALACE, 21 July, 1814
DOM PEDRO MACANAZ

The settlement of 1815 left Italy in a sadly distracted condition. All of the petty states that existed before Napoleon's revolutionary work, except Genoa and Venice, were reëstablished, and Austrian instead of French predominance prevailed once more, for none of the diplomats at the Congress of Vienna regarded Italy as worthy of independence, or desired to see unity established there. As in Spain, moreover, the restored rulers sought to return to the ancient state of things, but finding it impossible to overturn all the French innovations, they set up old institutions again in the midst of the new, thus adding greater confusion than ever to their domestic administration. The general disorder of the time is indicated by Farini, an Italian patriot and historian of the period.

196. Farini's description of Italy after the Restoration (condensed)

In her days of hope Italy has ever been the object of envy to the stranger, and in her periods of misfortune she has been his merchandize and spoil. In the twenty years of the French Revolution and the wars attending it, this our wretched land was trampled by aliens of every race, until at last it both lost the ancient liberties of some of its noblest provinces, and saw dragged under the yoke of Austria, Lombardy, the whole Venetian territory, and some places and fortresses of the Papal States.

Italian rulers vassals of the Austrian emperor

When the Austrian sway had thus been strengthened and extended, our own princes came, as matter of course, into the position of those ancient lords whom the Holy Roman Emperors regarded as vassals. The communes were in servitude, the states were fiefs, and the sovereigns were Austrian prefects.

Spirit of independence at Rome

If at that period there was any token of a spirit of independence, it appeared to proceed from the court of Rome, which made complaints against the seizure of its territory beyond the Po and against the occupation of its fortresses at Ferrara and Comacchio. It is the peculiar nature of the Roman court that it can acquiesce upon occasion but never bends in mind before either violence or adverse fortune, and never forgets its claims through length of time.

Exalted position of the Pope in Italy

The venerable Pius VII had brought back from exile an ample stock of personal influence; and the court of Rome enjoyed a rare and marvelous opportunity to turn it to account and establish a good and popular government. In the people there was great acuteness of mind; a nature somewhat rude, I grant, yet generous; a longing for repose, favorable to study, to trade, and to commerce; a love of civil equality; and an anxiety, enhanced by military rule, for honorable freedom. In their ruler were combined the most exalted and revered majesty in all the earth and a sanctity of mind corresponding with that of his name and his office, while he wore the crown of a martyr, brighter than that of mere earthly glory.

Nevertheless, on the restoration of the Pope, the clerical party came back to power with the ideas it had when it fell, and with passions not tempered, but inflamed, by calamity. In spite of the Pope, the most hot-headed and fanatical persons prevailed at court; and these persons, who counted the very moments until they could get full power to overthrow all that had been accomplished, did and said the strangest and maddest things in the world. Restoration of clerical administration in the Papal States

When Consalvi returned to Rome he endeavored, in the discharge of his duty as Secretary of State, to stem the current, but with incomplete success. The state was neither thoroughly reorganized nor was the ancient order of things reestablished as a whole. What was newly introduced was not adapted to the peculiar circumstances of the States of the Church, or to the new needs and altered conditions of society. In general the returning clergy maintained or restored the bad rather than the good, or, at any rate, what was hateful, rather than what was agreeable, to the people. There were unbounded promises of civil and criminal codes, but only some cardinals' proclamations and papal bulls were actually issued, with a few new and yet conflicting laws. There were taxes and duties in the French fashion, general administration in the Roman; no rules for a military conscription, troops picked up at random on the highways; as for commerce and industry they were discouraged by that legal interference which some economists call protection and encouragement. Instruction was impoverished, the censorship was meddlesome; all the men who had been distinguished in the time of Napoleon were suspected and in disfavor. General disorder in the Roman provinces

In the other Italian states, likewise, obstacles were encountered, and false steps of a retrograde character were taken; but in the lay principalities there was no such palpable necessity for extensive changes as in the ecclesiastical. In the first, the administrative and civil institutions had already been in part reformed before the French Revolution; in Lombardy, at Naples, and in Tuscany, the excessive encroachment of the Church upon the State had at that period been checked. Nor did the sovereigns, when restored, think of destroying all that Reaction in other Italian states

they themselves or their fathers had effected. At Rome, on
the contrary, the reactionary movement tended towards those
methods of administration, of legislation, and of policy, which
reflected the Middle Ages, — a matter which was the cause of
serious discontent, especially in those provinces that for many
years had formed part of the kingdom of Italy created by
Napoleon.

Sudden change in officers

In the secular States the public functionaries were changed,
and perhaps, too, — as is the custom of revolutions and of
restorations, — without any restraint of justice or humanity ;
but in the pontifical State the havoc was much greater, inasmuch as the ecclesiastics returned to the exercise of those civil
offices which in former times, when society was in infancy, they
had filled not without distinction to themselves and advantage
to the public, but which now they resumed by mere privilege
of caste. It is manifest how much evil this must have caused
to the laity, how much jealousy towards the clergy. Add that,
the philosophical doctrines which take their name from the
Encyclopædists had penetrated among us during the sway of
the French, so that the authority of Rome had greatly declined
among the educated classes ; moreover, the meretricious tongue
of the conquerors had deformed our own ; men both thought
and wrote in the French manner.

Section 53. *The Spanish-American Colonies and the Revolution of 1820*

The vigorous efforts of Ferdinand VII of Spain and
the various Italian rulers to stamp out all signs of liberalism, instead of succeeding, only made the radical reformers all the more determined. In 1820 some bold
officers in the Spanish army started an insurrection
against the absolutist policy of Ferdinand, and the
movement was taken up with such energy in the most
important towns that the king, at Madrid, fell into the
power of the liberals and was compelled to issue the

following manifesto restoring the constitution of 1812, which he had so contemptuously rejected six years before (see above, pp. 23 *sqq.*). The tone of the document shows how completely Ferdinand was under the control of the triumphant liberals.

When, by your heroic exertions, an end was put to the captivity in which I had been detained by the most unheard-of perfidy, I had scarcely set my foot on my native soil before all that I saw and learned tended to convince me that the nation wished to see its ancient form of government restored; and this conviction led me to comply with that which appeared to be the almost unanimous wish of a generous people, who, after having triumphantly contended against a foreign enemy, dreaded the still more horrible results of internal discord.

197. Manifesto of Ferdinand VII restoring the constitution of 1812 (March, 1820)

I did not fail to perceive, however, that the rapid progress of European civilization, the general diffusion of knowledge, even among the less enlightened classes, the more frequent intercourse between the different countries of the globe, and the wonderful events which had been reserved for the present generation, had inspired ideas and wishes unknown to our ancestors, and had created new and imperious wants; nor was it less obvious to me that it was indispensable to mold our political institutions conformably to those elements, in order to establish between the people and the laws that harmony upon which depend the stability and repose of society.

But whilst I was maturely deliberating, with the solicitude peculiar to my paternal heart, upon the changes to be introduced into our fundamental system of government, as most suitable to the national character and to the present state of the different parts of the Spanish monarchy, and at the same time the best adapted to the organization of an enlightened people, you expressed to me your anxious desire for the reëstablishment of that constitution which, amidst the clash of hostile arms, was promulgated at Cadiz in the year 1812, at a period when, to the admiration of the world, you were fighting for the liberty of your country. I have listened to your wishes, and, as a tender father, have consented to that which my

Ferdinand is made to say that he had been meditating reforms before the revolution

children think conducive to their happiness. I have sworn to that constitution for which you were sighing, and I will ever be its firmest supporter. I have already taken the necessary measures for the early convocation of the Cortes. Coöperating with your representatives, I shall then rejoice in promoting the great work of building up national prosperity.

Spaniards, your glory is the only ambition of my heart. My soul desires only to see you united around the throne in peace and harmony. Trust to your king, then, who addresses you with the sincere feelings inspired by the circumstances in which you are placed at this moment, and with a deep sense of the exalted duties imposed upon him by Providence. . . . Avoid the effervescence of the passions which too often transform into enemies those who ought to live as brothers, united by affection, as they are by religion, language, and habits. . . . Let us follow openly, myself the first, the path of the constitution, and, holding out to Europe an example of wisdom, order, and perfect moderation, at a crisis which, in other nations, has been attended with tears and misfortunes, let us excite admiration and reverence for the Spanish name at the same time that we establish for ages to come our own happiness and glory.

FERDINAND

PALACE OF MADRID, 10th March, 1820

During the disorders that had followed the establishment of Joseph Bonaparte on the throne of Spain, the Spanish colonies in America had taken occasion, one after the other, to throw off the rule of the mother country. However, after the revolution of 1820 in Spain, the liberals thought that the colonists would, on learning of the restoration of constitutional government at home, return to their ancient allegiance, and accordingly they induced Ferdinand VII to issue a lengthy address to the inhabitants of Spanish America, from which the following brief extract is taken.

Spanish Americans!

. . . . You, who have strayed from the right path, have now gained that which you have been so long seeking, but at the expense of immense toils, of endless sufferings, of sanguinary wars, of horrible desolation, and of the most frightful destruction of life. Your lamented separation has been productive to you of nothing but tears and grief, disappointment and bitterness, turbulence, rancor, deadly feuds, famine, incendiarism, devastation, and unheard-of horrors; the recital alone of your miseries will be sufficient to terrify future generations.

198. Ferdinand's appeal to the Spanish Americans to return to their allegiance (March, 1820)

What, then, do you desire? Hear the tender voice of your king and father; let the restless and jealous fears which agitate you cease, and let rancor end with the circumstances in which it originated, and give place to tender and generous sentiments. Let not vengeance be regarded as a virtue, nor hatred as a duty. The two hemispheres, formed to esteem one another, need only come to a proper understanding to be forever inseparable friends, affording mutual aid, instead of seeking opportunities for injuring one another. Nor is it possible that those should be enemies who are in truth brothers, who speak the same language, who profess the same religion, who are ruled by the same laws, who observe the same customs, and who are, above all, adorned with the same virtues, — virtues which are the offspring of valor, of generosity, and of the elevated sublimity of great souls.

Spaniards in both hemispheres are united by blood, language, religion, and laws

Let those relations with the mother country be renewed which, after the toils and sacrifices of three centuries, were established by our ancestors, the favored sons of victory; and let others be created which the enlightened state of the age and the nature of a representative government require. Let arms be laid aside, and let the barbarous war come to an end, which has been the cause of events so disastrous as to be recorded in letters of blood on the page of history. The quarrels of members of the same family should not be fought out or adjusted by arms; let us, therefore, lay them aside, in order to avoid despair and the risk of oppression and hatred.

Reform in Spain especially favors the restoration of harmony with the colonies

The whole nation entertains this wish, and will give me the means of overcoming, without the use of force, the obstacles which have stood in the way of our happiness during the period of domestic calamity. We have adopted a system more generous in its principles, and in harmony with those which you have yourselves laid down; let the distinguishing feature of our character be to observe reciprocally a frank and loyal conduct, rejecting the maxims and suggestions of that erring and crooked policy which the false combinations of fortune may perhaps have once smiled upon with ephemeral favor. The parent State sets you the example; follow it, Americans, for upon this depends your present and future happiness. Give to the mother country a day of joy, at a period so productive of calamitous events; and let the love of order and the general good make us one in our wishes and opinions.

The colonists are asked to send representatives to confer with the Cortes on terms of reunion

The Cortes, whose name alone is to all Spaniards a sweet memorial of portentous events, are about to assemble. Your brethren of the Peninsula are anxiously waiting with open arms the arrival of those who may come deputed by you to confer with them, as their equals, upon the measures required by the misfortunes of their country and of your own in particular. The security of their persons has for its guarantee the national honor, and that long-wished-for constitution to which, in the face of the world, I have sworn and which I will religiously observe. The fathers of their country, the wise and chosen favorites of the people, will, united, save the State, and fix forever the destinies of both hemispheres; and, as a reward of their wisdom, their contemporaries will prepare the immortal crown to be bestowed upon them by the gratitude of posterity. What happiness, what blessings will this desired union produce! . . .

FERDINAND

The revolutions which broke out in Spain and Italy in 1820 had been anticipated by Metternich, who was the soul of the reactionary policy, and who was bent upon setting up a permanent barrier to "revolution," — under which terrible term he included all tendencies toward constitutional government. As early as November, 1815, Austria, Russia, Prussia, and England had concluded a

treaty in which they agreed to continue their alliance
against any new attempt on the part of France to disturb the repose of Europe. Furthermore, in Article VI
of the treaty they arranged for periodical meetings of
representatives from the powers, as follows :

To facilitate and secure the execution of the present treaty
and to strengthen the bonds which at the present moment so
closely unite the four sovereigns for the happiness of the world,
the high contracting parties have agreed to renew their meetings at fixed periods, either under the immediate auspices of
the sovereigns themselves or of their respective ministers, for
the purpose of consulting upon their common interests and
for the consideration of the measures which, at each of these
periods, shall be considered most salutary for the repose and
prosperity of nations and for the peace of Europe.[1]

Metternich arranges a system of international congresses to deal with " revolution "

Though it was by no means clear from the language of
this clause to what extent the powers should interfere
in the domestic affairs of European nations, Metternich
held that they were bound to strike at revolution wherever it appeared, and especially in Italy, where Austria
had so many interests at stake. Accordingly a congress
of the powers [2] was called at Troppau in 1820. There a
system of intervention in the internal affairs of those
countries threatening the repose of Europe was agreed
upon, and was justified in a circular note which casts
much light on the policy of the reactionary monarchs
who were under Metternich's influence.

[1] For the whole of this interesting document, see Anderson, *Constitutions and Documents*, pp. 482 *sqq.*

[2] France was admitted to the councils of the powers at a congress
held at Aix-la-Chapelle in 1818. England, while participating formally or
informally in these congresses, never committed herself to the doctrine
of general intervention, but was inclined to regard interference as justifiable only when the territorial settlement of 1815 was threatened.

199. Circular note of Troppau setting forth Metternich's theory of intervention

Having been informed of the false and exaggerated rumors which have been circulated by ill-intentioned and credulous persons in regard to the results of the conferences at Troppau, the allied courts deem it necessary to transmit authentic explanations to their representatives at foreign courts, in order to enable them to refute the erroneous ideas to which these rumors have given rise. The brief report here annexed will enable them to do this. . . .

TROPPAU, December 8, 1820

BRIEF REVIEW OF THE FIRST RESULTS OF THE CONFERENCES AT TROPPAU

The events which took place in Spain March 8 and at Naples July 2, as well as the catastrophe in Portugal, could not but arouse a feeling of the deepest indignation, apprehension, and sorrow in those who are called upon to guard the tranquillity of the nations; and, at the same time, it emphasized the necessity of uniting in order to determine in common the means of checking the misfortunes which threaten to envelop Europe. It was but natural that these sentiments should leave a deep impression upon those powers which had but lately stifled revolution and which now behold it once more raise its head.

Nor was it less natural that these powers, in encountering revolution for the third time, should have recourse to the same methods which they had employed with so much success in the memorable struggle which freed Europe from a yoke she had borne for twenty years. Everything encouraged the hope that that alliance, formed in the most ·critical circumstances, crowned with the most brilliant success, and strengthened by the conventions of 1814, 1815, and 1818, as it had prepared the way for, established, and assured the peace of the world, and delivered the European continent from the military representatives of revolution, so it would be able to check a new form of oppression, not less tyrannical and fearful, namely, that of revolt and crime. Such were the motives and the aim of the meeting at Troppau.

. . . The powers are exercising an incontestable right in taking common measures in respect to those States in which the overthrow of the government through a revolt, even if it be considered simply as a dangerous example, may result in a hostile attitude toward all constitutions and legitimate governments. The exercise of this right becomes an urgent necessity when those who have placed themselves in this situation seek to extend to their neighbors the ills which they have brought upon themselves and to promote revolt and confusion around them. . . . *Right of the powers to interfere in the internal affairs of States threatened by revolution*

Nothing could menace more directly the tranquillity of the neighboring States than the revolution at Naples, gaining ground as it did daily. In view of the fact that the allied courts could not be attacked so promptly and immediately as these neighboring States, it was deemed expedient to proceed, in regard to the Kingdom of the Two Sicilies, according to the principles above enunciated. *Danger to the Italian States from the revolution at Naples*

In order to prepare conciliatory measures toward this end, the monarchs convened at Troppau resolved to ask the king of the Two Sicilies to meet them at Laibach, with the single aim of freeing him from all external compulsion and placing him in the position of mediator between his erring people and the States whose tranquillity they threaten. . . .

[It is needless to prove that the resolutions taken by the powers are in no way to be attributed to the idea of conquest, or to any intention of interfering with the independence of other governments in their internal administration, or, lastly, to the purpose of preventing wise improvements freely carried out and in harmony with the true interests of the people. Their only desire is to preserve and maintain peace, to deliver Europe from the scourge of revolution, and to obviate or lessen the ills which arise from the violation of the precepts of order and morality. . . .

The Italian affairs were settled by the two congresses of Troppau and Laibach, and Austrian troops restored the king of Naples to his throne. Spain next received the attention of the powers at the congress of Verona in

1822, but the Spanish question was not so easily settled
as the Italian, for England refused to join in intervention, and France, remembering the troubles of Napoleon
in the Peninsula, hesitated. The three eastern powers,
however, — Austria, Russia, and Prussia, — sent out a
circular which seemed to indicate that they might intervene in Spain, although there was slight probability that
they would find it possible to do so.

200. Circular of Austria, Russia, and Prussia on affairs in Spain (Verona, 1822)

. . . Events have called the attention of the monarchs to
the pitiable condition of the Western Peninsula. Spain is now
undergoing the fate which awaits all States unfortunate enough
to seek what is good, in a way in which it can never be found.
It is passing through the fateful circle of its revolution, a revolution which deluded or evil-disposed men represent as a benefit,
or indeed a triumph, of the enlightened century. All governments are witnesses of the zeal with which these men seek to
persuade their comrades that this revolution is the necessary
and wholesome fruit of advanced civilization, and the means
by which it acts ; and that it is furthermore supported by the
noblest flight of enthusiastic love for the fatherland. If civilization can have for its aim the destruction of human society,
and if it were possible to admit that the armed force which is
only meant for the preservation of peace in the kingdom can
seize the government of the kingdom unpunished, certainly the
Spanish revolution may claim the admiration of the age, and
the military rising of the island of Leon may serve as a pattern
for reformers. But truth has soon asserted her rights, and
Spain only presents another sad example (at the cost of her
happiness and her fame) of the inevitable consequences of
such transgressions of the eternal laws of the moral order of
the world.

The sad plight of Spain

Legitimate power fettered and turned into an instrument for
the overthrow of all rights and all lawful liberty ; all classes of
the people drawn into the stream of revolutionary agitation ;
caprice and oppression exercised under the guise of laws ; a
whole kingdom given up to disorders and convulsions of every

kind ; rich colonies preparing to set themselves free by the same maxims upon which the mother country has just based its constitution, and which it vainly condemns in another hemisphere ; the last resources of the country destroyed by civil war, — this is the picture which Spain now presents ; these are the vexations with which a noble people worthy of a better fate is afflicted ; lastly, these are the grounds of the just anxiety which such a concurrence of the elements of discontent and confusion must awake in the countries contiguous to the Peninsula. If ever a power was raised in the very heart of civilization hostile to all conservative principles, to all the principles on which the European alliance rests, that power is Spain in its present state of decomposition.

Can the monarchs look with equanimity on the evils heaped on one country which are accompanied with so many dangers for others? Dependent only on their own judgment and their own conscience in this grave juncture of affairs, they must ask themselves whether it is longer permissible to remain quiet spectators of calamities which threaten to become more dangerous and more horrible ; or even, by the presence of their representatives, to give the false appearance of a silent consent to the measures of a faction ready to do anything to maintain and support their pernicious power. The decision of the monarchs cannot be doubtful. Their ambassadors have received orders to leave the Peninsula.

The three powers withdraw their ambassadors from revolutionary Spain

Whatever may be the result of this step, the monarchs declare before Europe that nothing can move them to waver in a resolution approved by their most heartfelt convictions. The greater the friendship they entertain for the king of Spain, the livelier their interest in the well-being of a nation which has ever been distinguished for its virtues and its grandeur, and the more strongly do they feel the necessity of taking the measures on which they have decided, and which they will know how to carry out.

The English foreign secretary, Canning, protested at Verona against interference with the internal government of Spain, and declared that the mutual guarantee of 1815 related only to the territorial settlement, — not to the domestic affairs of the European countries. The reason for this decided stand of England is not to be found in any theories about non-intervention held by her statesmen, but rather in the fact that England had built up powerful commercial interests with the revolted Spanish-American possessions, which would have been destroyed if the mother country could have recovered her authority over them and restored the ancient monopolistic policy. The grounds for the English attitude toward the whole Spanish colonial situation is revealed by the following petition addressed to the House of Commons by a large number of London merchants.

201. Petition of English merchants on Spanish-American trade

Showeth — That your petitioners are engaged in trade with the countries in America, formerly under the dominion of Spain.

That the entire extinction of Spanish authority in the greater part of that continent, and the encouragement by the government at home, induced your petitioners to embark in that extensive commerce, with full confidence that it would receive the most complete protection, and ultimately prove most beneficial to themselves and the country at large. The measures adopted by the government most decisively demonstrated the anxiety to acquire and secure this intercourse.

Parliament authorizes trade with the revolted Spanish colonies

In the session of 1822 an act of Parliament was passed (cap. 43), authorizing the importation of goods, the growth, production, or manufacture of "any country or place in America, being or having been a part of the dominions of the king of Spain," either in British ships, or in ships the build of those countries. In the following year consuls were appointed to proceed to the ports thereof, and subsequently there has been made public the declaration of his Majesty's government, that, in its opinion, "the recognition of such of the new States as have established, *de facto*, their separate political existence cannot be much longer delayed."

Your petitioners further humbly represent that many millions of capital have already been embarked in this trade ; that large commercial establishments have been formed both in South America and at home ; and that past experience affords the strongest ground for believing that this commercial intercourse will admit of great extension, the reciprocal demand for the productions of the respective countries being constantly increasing.

Millions already invested in South America by Englishmen

Your petitioners consequently find themselves greatly embarrassed by those countries remaining " without any recognized political existence." Not a week passes but they are assailed with rumors of the most alarming kind, involving their proceedings in doubt, hesitation, and distraction, and grievously destructive of that confidence so essential to the success of all commercial undertakings. Your honorable House must be well aware that no commercial intercourse can be permanently carried on with security and advantage to those concerned, if it is rendered liable to fluctuation by constant alarms of political changes, necessarily producing sudden and excessive alterations in the value of the property embarked.

Security of trade demands recognition of independence

That your petitioners are enabled to state, and to prove unequivocally to your honorable House, that, in the several States of Colombia, Buenos Ayres, and Chili there does not remain the smallest vestige of Spanish dominion in any shape, each State enjoying its own government, separate and independent from all interference of a hostile force. That the revolution which has produced this alteration in the political condition of these countries has now been in progress fifteen years. In Buenos Ayres there has not been a Spanish soldier in hostility for eight years. In Chili there has been none for four years ; and in Colombia the third annual Constitutional Congress is now sitting. In none of these States does there exist any party, or persons in possession of power or authority, excepting the constituted executive government.

Spanish dominion is really at an end

Your petitioners therefore humbly submit that these States have established, *de facto*, their separate political existence, and are, according to the practice of nations in former instances, entitled to be recognized as independent governments; but they would not have presumed to have addressed your honorable House on a question of this nature, if the continued delay in recognizing this political existence did not produce the most detrimental consequences to the commercial transactions in which they are concerned.

Your petitioners, therefore, most humbly pray that your honorable House will take this question into its serious consideration, and adopt such measures, as to its wisdom may seem fit, for promoting the immediate recognition of the independence of such of the States of South America as have, *de facto*, established the same. And your petitioners, as in duty bound, will ever pray.

Like England the United States had excellent reasons for not wishing the restoration of Spanish dominion over the revolted American colonies. The possibilities of commerce with independent States were considerable, and as the United States was a new and comparatively weak country, its citizens regarded as dangerous to their liberties the reëstablishment of Spanish power on their southern borders by the aid of the more reactionary rulers of Europe. American statesmen did not realize how remote such a contingency was, and accordingly they regarded as ominous the congress at Verona. Therefore President Monroe, in his presidential message of December, 1823, defined the attitude of the United States toward the Spanish-American colonies and European intervention, thus enunciating the principles which were destined to become famous as the Monroe Doctrine.

202. President Monroe's message on foreign intervention in Spanish America (December, 1823)

It was stated at the commencement of the last session that a great effort was then making in Spain and Portugal to improve the condition of the people of those countries, and that it appeared to be conducted with extraordinary moderation. It need scarcely be remarked that the result has been so far very different from what was then anticipated. Of events in that quarter of the globe, with which we have so much intercourse and from which we derive our origin, we have always been anxious and interested spectators. The citizens of the United States cherish sentiments the most friendly in favor of the liberty and happiness of their fellow-men on that side of the Atlantic. In the wars of the European powers, in matters relating to themselves, we have never taken any part, nor does it comport with our policy so to do. It is only when our rights are invaded or seriously menaced that we resent injuries or make preparations for our defense.

With the movements in this hemisphere we are of necessity more immediately connected, and by causes which must be obvious to all enlightened and impartial observers.

The political system of the allied powers is essentially different in this respect from that of America. This difference proceeds from that which exists in their respective governments ; and to the defense of our own which has been achieved by the loss of so much blood and treasure, and matured by the wisdom of their most enlightened citizens and under which we have enjoyed unexampled felicity, this whole nation is devoted. We owe it, therefore, to candor and to the amicable relations existing between the United States and those powers, to declare that we should consider any attempt on their part to extend their system to any portion of this hemisphere as dangerous to our peace and safety. *The political system of the allied powers is un-American*

With the existing colonies or dependencies of any European power we have not interfered and shall not interfere. But with the governments who have declared their independence and maintained it, and whose independence we have, on great consideration and on just principles, acknowledged, we could not view any interposition for the purpose of oppressing them, or controlling in any other manner their destiny, by any European power in any other light than as the manifestation of an unfriendly disposition towards the United States. *Interference by European powers regarded as unfriendly*

In the war between those new governments and Spain we declared our neutrality at the time of their recognition, and to this we have adhered, and shall continue to adhere, provided no change shall occur which, in the judgment of the competent authorities of this government, shall make a corresponding change on the part of the United States indispensable to their security.

The late events in Spain and Portugal show that Europe is still unsettled. Of this important fact no stronger proof can be adduced than that the allied powers should have thought it proper, on any principle satisfactory to themselves, to have interposed by force in the internal concerns of Spain.

The United States does not interfere in European politics

To what extent such interposition may be carried, on the same principle, is a question in which all independent powers whose governments differ from theirs are interested, even those most remote, and surely none more so than the United States. Our policy in regard to Europe, which was adopted at an early stage of the wars which have so long agitated that quarter of the globe, nevertheless remains the same, which is, not to interfere in the internal concerns of any of its powers; to consider the government *de facto* as the legitimate government for us; to cultivate friendly relations with it, and to preserve those relations by a frank, firm, and manly policy, meeting in all instances the just claims of every power, submitting to injuries from none.

But it cannot be indifferent to European intervention in the New World

But in regard to these continents, circumstances are eminently and conspicuously different. It is impossible that the allied powers should extend their political system to any portion of either continent without endangering our peace and happiness; nor can any one believe that our southern brethren, if left to themselves, would adopt it of their own accord. It is equally impossible, therefore, that we should behold such interposition in any form with indifference. If we look to the comparative strength and resources of Spain and those new governments, and their distance from each other, it must be obvious that she can never subdue them.

It is still the true policy of the United States to leave the parties to themselves, in the hope that other powers will pursue the same course.

CHAPTER XVIII

THE INDUSTRIAL REVOLUTION

Section 54. Invention of Machinery for Spinning and Weaving

A civil engineer, in giving testimony before a committee of the House of Lords in 1857, stated that the spinning machinery then in existence was supposed to combine over eight hundred different patents. Whether this estimate is exact or not, there can be no doubt that every great inventor builds upon the successes of a multitude of preceding workers. Nevertheless there stand out in the history of textile inventions four great names, — Hargreaves, Crompton, Arkwright, and Cartwright, — and the study of their lives and times affords an insight into the actual process by which was begun the great industrial revolution that has transformed the world and its problems. A biographer of Lancashire worthies has given the following brief account of Hargreaves and the difficulties which he encountered in his efforts to introduce his spinning jenny.

In the first decade of the second half of the eighteenth century James Hargreaves was a weaver at Standhill, near Blackburn. He is sometimes described as a carpenter, and probably he combined both trades. He was "a stout, broadset man, about five feet ten inches high, or rather more "; and this is all that is known of him personally. The Blackburn of the well-to-do Peel and of the humble Hargreaves was a town of some 5000 inhabitants. It was noted for the production of

203. Hargreaves's invention of the spinning jenny (Condensed)

"Blackburn greys," cloths of linen warp and cotton weft, which, before the introduction of calico printing into Lancashire by the first Robert Peel and others, were generally sent to London to undergo that decorative operation. Doubtless, in the district of the "Blackburn greys," Hargreaves must have seen and heard much about the demand for cotton yarn outstripping the supply, and about schemes to supersede or improve the rude and sluggish old one-thread spinning wheel.

How Hargreaves contrived the jenny

Hargreaves is said to have received the original idea of his machine from seeing a one-thread wheel overturned upon the floor, when both the wheel and spindle continued to revolve. The spindle was thus thrown from a horizontal into an upright position ; and the thought seems to have struck him that if a number of spindles were placed upright, and side by side, several threads might be spun at once. He contrived a frame, in one part of which he placed eight rovings in a row, and in another part a row of eight spindles. The rovings, when extended to the spindles, passed between two horizontal bars of wood, forming a clasp, which opened and shut somewhat like a parallel ruler; when pressed together this clasp held the threads fast. A certain portion of roving being extended from the spindles to the wooden clasp, the clasp was closed and was then drawn along the horizontal frame to a considerable distance from the spindles, by which the threads were lengthened out and reduced to the proper tenuity. This was done with the spinner's left hand, and his right hand at the same time turned a wheel which caused the spindles to revolve rapidly, and thus the roving was spun into yarn. By returning the clasp to its first situation, and letting down a presser wire, the yarn was wound upon the spindle.[1]

The jenny causes rapid increase in productive power

All, and more than all, that Kay's shuttle [2] had done for the weaver, the jenny did for the spinner. If the fly shuttle doubled the productive power of the weaver, the jenny at once octupled the spinner's. The number of spindles in the jenny was at first eight ; when Hargreaves obtained a patent it was sixteen ; it soon rose to be twenty or thirty ; and no less than one hundred

[1] See illustration in *Development of Modern Europe*, Vol. II, p. 35.
[2] Ibid. p. 34.

and twenty have since been used. The jennies could be worked
by children as well as, nay, better than, by adults. The awkward posture required to spin on them was discouraging to
grown-up people, who saw with surprise children from nine to
twelve years of age manage them with dexterity, whereby plenty
was brought into families overburdened with children, and the
poor weavers were delivered from the bondage in which they
had lain from the insolence of spinners.

Nevertheless the usefulness of the jenny was of a restricted *Limitations*
kind. It did not make the rovings, which had still to be spun *of Har-*
on the ordinary wheel, and to be supplied to the jenny for *greaves's*
conversion into yarn. Above all, the yarn spun by the jenny *jenny*
was fit only for weft, and unless a yarn hard enough for warp
had been produced in other ways afterwards, there would have
been no cotton manufacture strictly so called. But the revolution which the spinning jenny produced in the manufacture
as it then existed was, of course, immense.

Hargreaves is supposed to have invented the jenny about *Hargreaves's*
1764, and certainly by 1767 he had so far perfected it that a *machine*
child could work eight spindles at once with it. When first *broken up*
invented it was doubtless a rude machine, and Hargreaves is *by his*
said to have kept it a secret, and to have used it merely in his *neighbors*
own family and his own business, to supply himself with weft
for his looms. It was, of course, a secret which could not long
be kept. If the jenny came into general use, the weaver would
no longer be at the mercy of the spinner; the production of
yarn would be multiplied, and its price would fall. The spin-
sters of Blackburn, their fathers, brothers, sweethearts, were
not students of political economy, and did not reflect that
increased supply at a lower price would produce an increased
demand. They looked only to the probable immediate effect
of the jenny on the number of the persons employed in spinning and on the price of yarn. The very weavers were dis-
satisfied, being afraid, it seems, "lest the manufacturers should
demand finer weft woven at the former prices." The Black-
burners rose upon Hargreaves, broke into his house, destroyed
his jenny or jennies, and made the town and neighborhood
too hot for him.

Hargreaves
migrates to
Nottingham

Hargreaves shook the dust from off his feet and fled the ungrateful district. He made for Nottingham, as a chief seat of the manufacture of silk and worsted stockings, and where that of cotton hosiery, though much valued, had languished for the want of suitable yarn.

Richard
Arkwright's
invention

This Hegira of Hargreaves took place in 1767, in which very year Mr. Richard Arkwright, barber, of Bolton, had his earliest conferences with one Kay, a clock maker at Warrington, respecting the bending of some wires and the turning of some pieces of brass for a spinning machine he was building. Two years later, warned by the fate of Hargreaves, Mr. Arkwright, too, quietly migrated to Nottingham, and in the July of 1769 he "enrolled" the specification of his famous first patent for spinning by rollers.

Hargreaves
patents his
jenny (1770)

Poor Hargreaves was to have no such successful career as that of the Bolton barber. After his arrival in Nottingham he worked for a while in the employment of Mr. Shipley, for whom he made some jennies secretly in his house. It was probably with the assistance of a Nottingham joiner by the name of James that Hargreaves was enabled, in the July of 1770, to take out a patent for his spinning jenny. Finding that

Lancashire
manufacturers
make use of
the jenny

several of the Lancashire manufacturers were using the jenny, Hargreaves gave notice of actions against them. The manufacturers met, and sent a delegate to Nottingham, who offered Hargreaves £3000 for permission to use the machine; but he at first demanded £7000, and at last stood out for £4000. The negotiations being broken off, the actions proceeded; but before they came to trial Hargreaves's attorney was informed that his client, before leaving Lancashire, had sold some jennies to obtain clothing for his children (of whom he had six or seven); and in consequence of this, which was true, the attorney finally gave up the action in despair of obtaining a verdict.

Moderate
success of
Hargreaves

Hargreaves, however, did not, like Kay, die in a foreign land, and in misery or poverty. The partnership business was carried on "with moderate success" until the death of Hargreaves on the 22d of April, 1778, the year before that in which Samuel Crompton invented the mule.

One of the most attractive, but certainly one of the least successful of the inventors, from a financial point of view, was Samuel Crompton, of Bolton. An intimate friend of Crompton's, especially in the days of his misfortunes, Mr. John Kennedy, has left an interesting account of the inventor in a paper which he read before the Manchester Literary and Philosophical Society in 1830.

Samuel Crompton was born on the 3d of December, 1753, at Firwood, near Bolton, in Lancashire, where his father held a farm of small extent; and, as was customary in those days, employed a portion of his time in weaving, carding, and spinning. During the infancy of Samuel Crompton the family removed to Hall-in-the-Wood, which was the scene of his early inventions. **204. An account of Crompton's life by a friend**

His parents were very respectable in their station of life, and taught him to read and write. His father died when he was very young; his mother was a prudent and virtuous woman, and this circumstance, together with the sequestered situation in which they lived, induced a contemplative turn of mind. He had taken various views of the Christian religion, but finally preferred the Swedenborgian faith, without adopting the restrictions it imposes on certain kinds of food. In all his dealings through his life he was strictly honest, patient, and humane. In politics he took little interest, but regretted the waste of life and property which war occasions. **Crompton's many virtues**

When about sixteen years old he learnt to spin upon a jenny (of Hargreaves's make), and had occasionally woven the yarn which he had spun. This, being but indifferent work, led him to reflect how it might be improved, and set him to construct the machine which we are about to describe. He was only twenty-one years of age when he commenced this undertaking, which took him five years to effect, — at least before he could bring his improvements to maturity. As he was not a regular mechanic, and possessed only such tools as he purchased with his little earnings acquired by labor at the loom or jenny **Crompton sets to work to improve Hargreaves's jenny** and as he had also to learn the use of those simple tools, we may be justly surprised that even in five years he succeeded so far as to make his machine practically useful.

Crompton annoyed by his neighbors He often said that what annoyed him most was that he could not get leave to enjoy his little invention to himself in his garret; for, the product of his machine obtaining a better price than other yarns of those times, a report soon got abroad that he had constructed a new machine for the purpose of improved spinning, and people from the neighborhood, for miles round, came and climbed up at the windows to see him at his work. He erected a screen to prevent this, but the annoyance was so great that he could not proceed advantageously with his ingenious labor; and finally he was induced to lay the whole thing before a number of gentlemen and others, who subscribed a guinea each to look at it. On this as on every other occasion, the late Mr. Pilkinton, of Bolton, gave him his steady and friendly support. These sums amounted to about £50, which enabled him to construct another machine still further improved and of larger dimensions. When relating this little history to Mr. G. A. Lee and myself, Mr. Lee having observed "it was a pity he had not kept the secret to himself," he replied, "that a man had a very insecure tenure of a property which another could carry away with his eyes.". . .

A subscription is raised for the inventor About the year 1802 Mr. Lee and myself set on foot a subscription for him, which amounted to about £500; and with this he was enabled to increase his little manufacturing establishment in Bolton, namely of spinning and weaving. He was prevailed upon also to sit to a London artist for his portrait, which is now in my possession. He was left a widower when his children were very young, and his only daughter kept his little cottage in King Street, Bolton, where he died and where she is now living. Being a weaver, he erected several looms for the fancy work of that town, in which he displayed great ingenuity. Though his means were but small, his economy in living made him always in easy circumstances. He was fond of music, and built for himself an organ, which he had in his little cottage.

In 1812 he made a survey of all the cotton districts in
England, Scotland, and Ireland, and obtained an estimate of
the number of spindles then at work upon his principle, which
amounted to between four and five millions. On his return
he laid the result of his inquiries before Mr. Lee and myself,
with a suggestion that Parliament might grant him something.
With these data before him, Mr. Lee, who was a warm friend
to genius of every kind, with his usual energy entered fully
into his merits, and made an appointment with the late George
Duckworth, Esq., of Manchester, who also took a lively interest in the scheme, and gratuitously offered to draw up a memorial to Parliament in behalf of Mr. Crompton. This was signed
by most of the principal manufacturers in the kingdom who
were acquainted with his merits. . . . A bill was passed [by
Parliament] for a grant of £5000 in full, without fees or
charges. *(marginal note: Parliament aids Crompton)*

Mr. Crompton was now anxious to place his sons in some
business, and fixed upon that of bleaching; but the unfavorable state of the times, the inexperience and mismanagement
of his sons, a bad situation, and a misunderstanding with his
landlord, which occasioned a tedious lawsuit, conspired in a
very short time to put an end to this establishment. His
sons then dispersed, and he and his daughter were reduced to
poverty. Messrs. Hicks and Rothwell of Bolton, myself, and
some others, in that neighborhood and in Manchester, had in
1824 recourse to a second subscription, to purchase a life
annuity for him, which produced £63 per annum. The amount
raised for this purpose was collected in small sums, from one
to ten pounds, some of which were contributed by the Swiss
and French spinners, who acknowledged his merits and pitied
his misfortunes. At the same time his portrait was engraved
for his benefit, and a few impressions were disposed of. He
enjoyed this small annuity only two years. He died January
26, 1827, leaving his daughter, his affectionate housekeeper,
in poverty. *(marginal note: The inventor's financial troubles and sad end)*

Many of the inventors have been men of slight education, and have not commonly left to later generations

accounts of their own achievements. Cartwright, the inventor of the power loom, was, however, a clergyman and a man of considerable literary attainments, and in a few paragraphs he has told just how he happened to think about contriving a loom, and also how he set about the work of building one.

205. Cartwright's narrative concerning his invention of the power loom

Happening to be at Matlock in the summer of 1784, I fell in company with some gentlemen of Manchester, when the conversation turned on Arkwright's spinning machinery. One of the company observed, that as soon as Arkwright's patent expired so many mills would be erected, and so much cotton spun, that hands never could be found to weave it. To this observation I replied that Arkwright must then set his wits to work to invent a weaving mill. This brought on a conversation on the subject, in which the Manchester gentlemen unanimously agreed that the thing was impracticable; and, in defense of their opinion, they adduced arguments which I certainly was incompetent to answer, or even to comprehend, being totally ignorant of the subject, having never at that time seen a person weave. I controverted, however, the impracticability of the thing by remarking that there had lately been exhibited in London an automaton figure which played at chess. Now you will not assert, gentlemen, said I, that it is more difficult to construct a machine that shall weave than one which shall make all the variety of moves which are required in that complicated game.

Cartwright's first crude loom

Some little time afterwards, a particular circumstance recalling this conversation to my mind, it struck me that, as in plain weaving, according to the conception I then had of the business, there could only be three movements which were to follow each other in succession, there would be little difficulty in producing and repeating them. Full of these ideas, I immediately employed a carpenter and smith to carry them into effect. As soon as the machine was finished I got a weaver to put in the warp, which was of such material as sailcloth is usually made of. To my great delight, a piece of cloth, such as it was, was the product. As I had never before turned my thoughts to anything mechanical, either in theory or practice, nor had ever seen a loom at work, or known anything of its construction, you will readily suppose that my first loom was a most rude piece of machinery. The warp was placed perpendicularly, the reed fell with the weight of at least half a hundredweight, and the springs which threw the shuttle were strong enough to have thrown a Congreve rocket. In short, it required the strength of two powerful men to work the machine at a slow rate, and only for a short time. Conceiving, in my great simplicity, that I had accomplished all that was required, I then secured what I thought a most valuable property by a patent, 4th of April, 1785.

This being done, I then condescended to see how other people wove ; and you will guess my astonishment when I compared their easy modes of operation with mine. Availing myself, however, of what I then saw, I made a loom, in its general principles nearly as they are now made. But it was not till the year 1787 that I completed my invention, when I took out my last weaving patent, August 1st of that year. . . .

Baines, in his *History of Cotton Manufacture in Great Britain,* gives the following description of the tedious methods by which calico was formerly printed by hand, and of the way in which the old processes were supplanted by the cylinder printing machine.

Calico printing has been the subject of modern improvements which may be compared in importance with those in cotton spinning and bleaching ; and most of these improvements have either originated or been matured and perfected in Lancashire. The old method of printing, still continued for certain parts of the work, was by blocks of sycamore, about ten inches long by five broad, on the surface of which the pattern was cut in relief, in the common method of wood engraving. On the back of the block was a handle, by which the workman held it ; the surface was applied to a woolen cloth, stretched over a vessel containing the color, and in contact with that color, so as to be saturated by it, and was then

206. How machinery supplanted calico printing by hand

laid upon the piece of cloth (there being wire points at the corners of the block, to enable the workmen to apply it with exactness), and struck with an iron mallet. Thus the figure was impressed upon the cloth, one color only being used at once ; and if other colors were required to complete the pattern, it was necessary to repeat the operation with different blocks. In order to produce more delicate patterns than could be engraved on wood, copper plates were introduced in the neighborhood of London, and the cloth was thus printed from flat plates, with the kind of press used in copper-plate printing. Each of these modes was tedious, as no more of the cloth could be printed at once than was covered with the wooden block or copper plate ; and a single piece of calico, twenty-eight yards in length, required the application of the block 448 times.

Bell introduces cylinder printing in Lancashire about 1785   The grand improvement in the art was the invention of cylinder printing, which bears nearly the same relation, in point of dispatch, to block printing by hand as mule spinning bears to spinning by the one-thread wheel. This great invention is said to have been made by a Scotchman of the name of Bell, and it was first successfully applied in Lancashire about the year 1785, at Mosney, near Preston, by the house of Livesey, Hargreaves, Hall & Co., celebrated for the extent of their concerns, and the magnitude of their failure in 1788, which gave a severe shock to the industry of that part of the country.

This new mode of printing may be thus described : a polished copper cylinder, several feet in length (according to the width of the piece to be printed), and three or four inches in diameter, is engraved with a pattern round its whole circumference, and from end to end. It is then placed horizontally in a press, and, as it revolves, the lower part of the circumference passes through the coloring matter, which is again removed from the whole surface of the cylinder, except the engraved pattern, by an elastic steel blade, placed in contact with the cylinder, and reduced to so fine and straight an edge as to take off the color without scratching the copper. This blade has received the name of the *doctor,* which may be a workman's abbreviation of the word "abductor," applied to it from the purpose which it answers; or may have been given from a vulgar use of the words "to doctor," meaning to set to rights. The color being thus left only in the engraved pattern, the piece of calico or muslin is drawn tightly over the cylinder, which revolves in the same direction, and prints the cloth. After the piece is printed it passes over several metallic boxes, six feet long, ten inches broad, and six inches deep, heated by steam, which dry it.

A piece of cloth may be thus printed and dried in one or two minutes, which by the old method would have required the application of the block 448 times. Nor is this all. Two, three, four, and even five cylinders may be used at the same time in one press, each cylinder having engraved upon it a different portion of the pattern, and being supplied with a different color. The piece passes over them successively, and receives the entire pattern almost in the same moment. To produce the same effect by hand block printing would have required 896, 1344, 1792, or 2240 applications of the block, according as two, three, four, or five cylinders may have been employed. The saving of labor, therefore, is immense : one of the cylinder printing machines, attended by a man and a boy, is actually capable of producing as much work as could be turned out by one hundred block printers and as many tear boys. In consequence of the wonderful facility given to the operation, three fourths of all the prints executed in this country are printed by the cylinder machine. . . .

Hand and cylinder printing compared

One of the striking facts of the Industrial Revolution is the way in which inventions in one branch of industry stimulate and make necessary inventions in many other branches. For example, machinery has constantly to be devised to make machinery until there seems to be no end to the process. This inherent tendency of machinery to conquer all industries was early noted by Karl Marx,[1] who was an acute observer of the industrial progress which

---

[1] See *The Development of Modern Europe*, Vol. II, pp. 396 *sqq.*

he saw going on around him in England during his residence there from 1848 to his death in 1883.

207. The way in which machinery invades all industries (Condensed)

A radical change in the mode of production in one sphere of industry involves a similar change in other spheres. This happens at first in such branches of industry as are connected together by being distinct steps in the manufacture of a single article, cloth for instance, and yet are separated by the division of labor in such a way that at each step an independent commodity is produced. Thus spinning by machinery made weaving by machinery a necessity, and both together made imperative the mechanical and chemical revolution that took place in bleaching, printing, and dyeing. So too, on the other hand, the revolution in cotton spinning called forth the invention of the gin for separating the seeds from the cotton fiber; it was only by means of this invention that the production of cotton became possible on the enormous scale at present required.

Modern industry makes a revolution in transportation necessary

But more especially, the revolution in the modes of production of industry and agriculture made necessary a revolution in the means of communication and of transportation. These, in the form in which they had been handed down from the earlier period, became unbearable trammels on modern industry, with its feverish haste of production, its enormous extent, its constant flinging of capital and labor from one sphere of production into another, and its newly established connections with the markets of the whole world. Hence, apart from the radical changes introduced in the construction of sailing vessels, the means of communication and transportation became gradually adapted to the modes of production of mechanical industry, by the creation of a system of river steamers, railways, ocean steamers, and telegraphs. But the huge masses of iron that had now to be forged, to be welded, to be cut, to be bored, and to be shaped, demanded, on their part, monster machines, for the construction of which the methods of the manufacturing period were utterly inadequate.

Modern industry had therefore itself to take in hand the machine, its characteristic instrument of production, and to

construct machines by machines. It was not till it did this, The use of machinery to make machinery
that it built up for itself a fitting technical foundation and stood
on its own feet. Machinery, simultaneously with the increasing
use of it, in the first decades of this century, appropriated by
degrees the fabrication of machines proper. But it was only
during the decade preceding 1866 that the construction of
railways and ocean steamers on a stupendous scale called into
existence the cyclopean machines now employed in the construction of " prime movers," or motors.

The most essential condition for the production of machines The slide rest for the turn-ing lathe
by machines was a prime mover capable of exerting any amount
of force, and yet under perfect control. This condition was
already supplied by the steam engine, but at the same time it
was necessary to produce the geometrically accurate straight
lines, planes, circles, cylinders, cones, and spheres, required in
the detail parts of the machines. This problem Henry Mauds-
ley solved in the first decade of this century by the invention
of the slide rest, a tool that was soon made automatic, and in
a modified form was applied to other constructive machines
besides the lathe, for which it was originally intended. This
mechanical appliance replaces not some particular tool but
the hand itself, which must, in order to produce a given form,
hold and guide the cutting tool along the iron or other material
operated upon. Thus it became possible to produce the individual parts of machinery with a degree of ease, accuracy, and
speed that no accumulated experience of the hand of the most
skilled workman could give.

Thus when we fix our attention on the machinery employed The machine only a giant tool
in the construction of machines, we find the manual imple-
ments reappearing, but on a grand scale. For instance, the
cutting part of the boring machine is an immense drill driven
by a steam engine ; without this machine, the cylinders of large
steam engines and of hydraulic presses could not be made.
The mechanical lathe is only a gigantic reproduction of the
ordinary foot lathe ; the planing machine, an iron carpenter,
that works on iron with the same tools that the human carpenter employs on wood ; the instrument that, on the London
wharves, cuts the veneers, is a gigantic razor ; the tool of the

shearing machine, which shears iron as easily as a tailor's scissors cut cloth, is a monster pair of scissors; and the steam hammer works with an ordinary hammer head, but of such a weight that not even the god Thor himself could wield it. These steam hammers are an invention of Nasmyth, and there is one that weighs over six tons and strikes with a vertical fall of seven feet, on an anvil weighing thirty-six tons. It is mere child's play for it to crush a block of granite into powder, yet it is no less capable of driving, with a succession of light taps, a nail into a piece of soft wood.

Section 55. The Steam Engine

James Watt, who brought the steam engine to such perfection that it could be used economically for mechanical industries, was a man of many interests and striking personal characteristics, and his good temper and versatility won for him the profound admiration of many warm friends. One of these, Lord Jeffrey, editor of *The Edinburgh Review* and a man of literary distinction, wrote the following charming account of the inventor when he received the news of his death in 1819.

208. Lord Jeffrey's account of his friend James Watt, the inventor of the steam engine

. . . We have said that Mr. Watt was the great *improver* of the steam engine; but, in truth, as to all that is admirable in its structure, or vast in its utility, he should rather be described as its *inventor*. It was by his inventions that its action was so regulated as to make it capable of being applied to the finest and most delicate manufactures, and its power so increased as to set weight and solidity at defiance. By his admirable contrivance it has become stupendous alike for its force and its flexibility; for the prodigious power which it can exert, and the ease, and precision, and ductility with which it can be varied, distributed, and applied. The trunk of an elephant, that can pick up a pin or rend an oak, is as nothing to it. It can engrave a seal and crush masses of obdurate metal before it; draw out, without breaking, a thread as fine as a gossamer, and lift a ship of war like a bauble in the air. It can embroider muslin and forge anchors, cut steel into ribbons and impel loaded vessels against the fury of the winds and the waves.

It would be difficult to estimate the value of the benefits which these inventions have conferred upon this country. There is no branch of industry that has not been indebted to them ; and, in all the most material, they have not only widened most magnificently the field of its exertions, but multiplied a thousandfold the amount of its productions. . . . It has increased indefinitely the mass of human comforts and enjoyments, and rendered cheap and accessible, all over the world, the materials of wealth and prosperity. It has armed the feeble hand of man, in short, with a power to which no limits can be assigned ; completed the dominion of mind over the most refractory qualities of matter ; and laid a sure foundation for all those future miracles of mechanic power which are to aid and reward the labors of after generations. It is to the genius of one man, too, that all this is mainly owing ; and certainly no man ever bestowed such a gift on his kind. The blessing is not only universal, but unbounded ; and the fabled inventors of the plow and the loom, who were deified by the erring gratitude of their rude contemporaries, conferred less important benefits on mankind than the inventor of our present steam engine.

The manifold results of the steam engine

This will be the fame of Watt with future generations ; and it is sufficient for his race and his country. But to those to whom he more immediately belonged, who lived in his society and enjoyed his conversation, it is not, perhaps, the character in which he will be most frequently recalled, most deeply lamented, or even most highly admired. Independently of his great attainments in mechanics, Mr. Watt was an extraordinary, and in many respects a wonderful, man. Perhaps no individual in his age possessed so much and such varied and exact information, had read so much, or remembered what he had read so accurately and well. He had infinite quickness of apprehension, a prodigious memory, and a certain rectifying and methodizing power of understanding, which extracted something precious out of all that was presented to it.

Watt's remarkable mental faculties

The wide
range of
Watt's
interest

His stores of miscellaneous knowledge were immense, and
yet less astonishing than the command he had at all times over
them. It seemed as if every subject that was casually started
in conversation with him had been that which he had been
last occupied in studying and exhausting; such was the copi-
ousness, the precision, and the admirable clearness of the
information which he poured out upon it without effort or
hesitation. Nor was this promptitude and compass of knowledge confined in any degree to the studies connected with his
ordinary pursuits. That he should have been minutely and
extensively skilled in chemistry and the arts, and in most of
the branches of physical science, might perhaps have been
conjectured; but it could not have been inferred from his
usual occupations, and probably is not generally known, that
he was curiously learned in many branches of antiquity, meta-
physics, medicine, and etymology, and perfectly at home in
all the details of architecture, music, and law. He was well acquainted, too, with most of the modern languages and familiar
with most of recent literature. Nor was it at all extraordinary
to hear the great mechanician and engineer detailing and expounding, for hours together, the metaphysical theories of the
German logicians, or criticising the measures or the matter
of the German poetry.

His power of
getting at the
heart of things

His astonishing memory was aided, no doubt, in a great
measure, by a still higher and rarer faculty, by his power of
digesting and arranging in its proper place all the information
he received, and of casting aside and rejecting, as it were in-
stinctively, whatever was worthless or immaterial. Every conception that was suggested to his mind seemed instantly to take
its place among its other rich furniture, and to be condensed
into the smallest and most convenient form. He never appeared,
therefore, to be at all encumbered or perplexed with the verbi-
age of the dull books he perused, or the idle talk to which he
listened ; but to have at once extracted, by a kind of intellectual alchemy, all that was worthy of attention, and to have
reduced it, for his own use, to its true value and to its simplest
form. And thus it often happened that a great deal more was
learned from his brief and vigorous account of the theories

and arguments of tedious writers than an ordinary student could ever have derived from the most painful study of the originals ; and that errors and absurdities became manifest from the mere clearness and plainness of his statement of them, which might have deluded and perplexed most of his hearers without that invaluable assistance.

It is needless to say that, with those vast resources, his conversation was at all times rich and instructive in no ordinary degree ; but it was, if possible, still more pleasing than wise, and had all the charms of familiarity, with all the substantial treasures of knowledge. No man could be more social in his spirit, less assuming or fastidious in his manners, or more kind and indulgent towards all who approached him. . . . The delight of his conversation

His talk, though overflowing with information, had no resemblance to lecturing or solemn discoursing, but, on the contrary, was full of colloquial spirit and pleasantry. He had a certain quiet and grave humor, which ran through most of his conversation, and a vein of temperate jocularity which gave infinite zest and effect to the condensed and inexhaustible information which formed its main staple and characteristic. There was a little air of affected testiness, and a tone of pretended rebuke and contradiction, with which he used to address his younger friends, that was always felt by them as an endearing mark of his kindness and familiarity, and prized accordingly, far beyond all the solemn compliments that ever proceeded from the lips of authority. His voice was deep and powerful, though he commonly spoke in a low and somewhat monotonous tone, which harmonized admirably with the weight and brevity of his observations, and set off to the greatest advantage the pleasant anecdotes which he delivered with the same grave brow and the same calm smile playing soberly on his lips. . . . The unaffected charm of his manner

His health, which was delicate from his youth upwards, seemed to become firmer as he advanced in years ; and he preserved, up almost to the last moment of his existence, not only the full command of his extraordinary intellect but all the alacrity of spirit and the social gayety which had illumined his happiest days. His friends in this part of the country never saw him more full of intellectual vigor and colloquial animation His vigorous old age

— never more delightful or more instructive — than in his last visit to Scotland in the autumn of 1817. Indeed, it was after that time that he applied himself, with all the ardor of early life, to the invention of a machine for mechanically copying all sorts of sculpture and statuary, and distributed among his friends some of its earliest performances, as the productions of a young artist just entering on his eighty-third year.

The tranquillity of his last days   This happy and useful life came, at last, to a gentle close. He had suffered some inconvenience through the summer, but was not seriously indisposed till within a few weeks from his death. He then became perfectly aware of the event which was approaching, and, with his usual tranquillity and benevolence of nature, seemed only anxious to point out to the friends around him the many sources of consolation which were afforded by the circumstances under which it was about to take place. · He expressed his sincere gratitude to Providence for the length of days with which he had been blessed, and his exemption from most of the infirmities of age, as well as for the calm and cheerful evening of life that he had been permitted to enjoy, after the honorable labors of the day had been concluded. And thus, full of years and honors, in all calmness and tranquillity, he yielded up his soul, without a pang or struggle, and passed from the bosom of his family to that of his God.

Section 56. The Factory System

Beginnings of the factory system were made, even before the invention of machinery, by those wealthy merchants who collected several looms in one building and employed workmen to operate them. But the extensive modern factory, with its thousands of machines, was not introduced until after the astounding inventions of Hargreaves, Arkwright, and Crompton. It so happened that one of these men, Arkwright, who is accused, with good reasons, of having taken some of his leading ideas from other inventors, was a shrewd business man and foresaw the possibilities of industry on a large scale. The rise of the factory system and the labors of Arkwright are fully described by Baines, an early student of the cotton industry, from whose writings the following extract is made.

Hitherto the cotton manufacture had been carried on almost entirely in the houses of the workmen ; the hand or stock cards, the spinning wheel, and the loom required no larger apartment than that of a cottage. A spinning jenny of small size might also be used in a cottage, and in many instances was so used ; when the number of spindles was considerably increased adjacent workshops were used. But the water frame, the carding engine, and the other machines which Arkwright brought out in a finished state required both more space than could be found in a cottage and more power than could be applied by the human arm. Their weight also rendered it necessary to place them in strongly built mills, and they could not be advantageously turned by any power then known but that of water. 209. Arkwright's establishment of the factory system

The use of machinery was accompanied by a greater division of labor than existed in the primitive state of the manufacture ; the material went through many more processes, and, of course, the loss of time and the risk of waste would have been much increased if its removal from house to house at every stage of the manufacture had been necessary. It became obvious that there were several important advantages in carrying on the numerous operations of an extensive manufacture in the same building. Where water power was required it was economy to build one mill, and put up one water wheel rather than several. This arrangement also enabled the master spinner himself to superintend every stage of the manufacture ; it gave him a greater security against the wasteful or fraudulent consumption of the material ; it saved time in the transference of the work from hand to hand ; and it prevented the extreme inconvenience which would have resulted from the failure of one class of workmen to perform their part, when several other classes of workmen were dependent upon them. Another circumstance The advantage of manufacturing on a large scale which made it advantageous to have a large number of machines in one manufactory was, that mechanics must be employed on the spot to construct and repair the machinery, and that their time could not be fully occupied with only a few machines.

The beginnings of the factory system

All these considerations drove the cotton spinners to that important change in the economy of English manufactures, the introduction of the *factory system;* and when that system had once been adopted, such were its pecuniary advantages that mercantile competition would have rendered it impossible, even had it been desirable, to abandon it. The inquiry into the moral and social effects of the factory system will be made hereafter. At present we observe that although Arkwright, by his series of machines, was the means of giving the most wonderful extension to the system, yet he did not absolutely originate it. Mills for the throwing of silk had existed in England, though not in any great number, from the time of Sir Thomas Lombe, who, in 1719, erected a mill on the river Derwent, at Derby, on the model of those he had seen in Italy.

Early use of water power

It has been seen that Wyatt's first machines, at Birmingham, were turned by asses, and his establishment, at Northampton, by water. So Arkwright's first mill, at Nottingham, was moved by horses; his second, at Cromford, by water. "During a period of ten or fifteen years after Mr. Arkwright's first mill was built (in 1771), at Cromford, all the principal works were erected on the falls of considerable rivers; no other power than water having then been found practically useful. There were a few exceptions, where Newcomen's and Savery's steam engines were tried. But the principles of these machines were defective and their construction bad, the expense in fuel was great, and the loss occasioned by frequent stoppages was ruinous." . . .

Arkwright's extensive business

Arkwright was now rapidly making a large fortune, not merely by the sale of his patent machines and of licenses to use them, but much more by the profits of his several manufactories, for, having no less enterprise than judgment and skill, and being supported by large capital and very able partners, he greatly extended his concerns, and managed them all with such ability as to make them eminently prosperous. He offered the use of his patents by public advertisements, and gave many permission to use them on receiving a certain sum for each spindle. In several cases he took shares in the mills erected; and from these various sources he received a large annual tribute. . . .

Arkwright continued, notwithstanding, his prosperous career. Wealth flowed in upon him with a full stream from his skillfully managed concerns. For several years he fixed the price of cotton twist, all other spinners conforming to his prices. His partnership with the Messrs. Strutt terminated about 1783, and he retained the works at Cromford, still carried on by his son; whilst Messrs. Strutt had the works at Belper, which also are yet conducted by the surviving members of their family. In 1786 Arkwright was appointed high sheriff of Derbyshire; and having presented an address of congratulation from that county to the king on his escape from the attempt of Margaret Nicholson on his life, Arkwright received the honor of knighthood. Sir Richard was for many years troubled with a severe asthmatic affection; he sunk at length under a complication of disorders, and died at his house at Cromford, on the 3d of August, 1792, in the sixtieth year of his age.

Arkwright knighted

I have found myself compelled to form a lower estimate of the inventive talents of Arkwright than most previous writers. In the investigation I have prosecuted, I have been guided solely by a desire to ascertain the exact truth. It has been shown that the splendid inventions, which even to the present day are ascribed to Arkwright by some of the ablest and best-informed persons in the kingdom, belong in great part to other and much less fortunate men. In appropriating those inventions as his own, and claiming them as the fruits of his unaided genius, he acted dishonorably, and left a stain upon his character, which the acknowledged brilliance of his talents cannot efface. Had he been content to claim the merit which really belonged to him, his reputation would still have been high, and his wealth would not have been diminished.

Arkwright profited by the labor of others

That he possessed inventive talent of a very superior order has been satisfactorily established. And in improving and perfecting mechanical inventions, in exactly adapting them to the

purposes for which they were intended, in arranging a comprehensive system of manufacturing, and in conducting vast and
complicated concerns, he displayed a bold and fertile mind
and consummate judgment, which, when his want of education
and the influence of an employment so extremely unfavorable
to mental expansion as that of his previous life are considered,
must have excited the astonishment of mankind. But the marvelous and " unbounded invention " which he claimed for himself, and which has been too readily accorded to him, — the
creative faculty, which devised all that admirable mechanism,
so entirely new in its principles, and characteristic of the
first order of mechanical genius, — which has given a new
spring to the industry of the world, and within half a century
has reared up the most extensive manufacture ever known, —
this did *not* belong to Arkwright. It is clear that some of the
improvements which made the carding engine what it was
when he took out his second patent were devised by others;
and there are two prior claimants to the invention of spinning
by rollers, one of whom had undoubtedly made it the subject
of a patent thirty-one years before the patent of Arkwright. ...

The most marked traits in the character of Arkwright were
his wonderful ardor, energy, and perseverance. He commonly
labored in his multifarious concerns from five o'clock in the
morning till nine at night; and when considerably more than
fifty years of age, — feeling that the defects of his education
placed him under great difficulty and inconvenience in conducting his correspondence, and in the general management
of his business, — he encroached upon his sleep in order to
gain an hour each day to learn English grammar, and another
hour to improve his writing and orthography! He was impatient
of whatever interfered with his favorite pursuits; and the fact
is too strikingly characteristic not to be mentioned, that he
separated from his wife not many years after their marriage,
because she, convinced that he would starve his family by
scheming when he should have been shaving [it will be remembered that he was a barber], broke some of his experimental models of machinery. Arkwright was a severe economist
of time; and that he might not waste a moment, he generally

traveled with four horses and at a very rapid speed. His concerns in Derbyshire, Lancashire, and Scotland were so extensive and numerous as to show at once his astonishing power of transacting business and his all-grasping spirit. In many of these he had partners, but he generally managed in such a way that, whoever lost, he himself was a gainer. So unbounded was his confidence in the success of his machinery, and in the national wealth to be produced by it, that he would make light of discussions on taxation, and say that *he* would pay the national debt ! His speculative schemes were vast and daring ; he contemplated entering into the most extensive mercantile transactions and buying up all the cotton in the world, in order to make an enormous profit by the monopoly ; and from the extravagance of some of these designs his judicious friends were of opinion that if he had lived to put them into practice, he might have overset the whole fabric of his prosperity ! . . .

The progress of the Industrial Revolution in England was greatly promoted by the large and steady demands for goods which English traders had developed in the four corners of the earth. Long before the coming of machinery these traders had accumulated vast fortunes and built up great enterprises. They competed with the landed gentry in politics and were the forerunners of the capitalists like Arkwright, who established the new industries on a large scale. Defoe (1661–1731), the author of *Robinson Crusoe*, tells in his charming fashion how tradesmen of his time were already contributing toward the industrial and commercial supremacy of England.

210. Defoe's description of eighteenth-century merchant princes

Having thus done justice to ourselves, in the value we put upon trade and tradesmen in England, it reflects very much upon the understandings of those refined heads who pretend to depreciate that part of the nation which is so infinitely superior in wealth to the families who call themselves gentry, and so infinitely more numerous.

As to the wealth of the nation, that undoubtedly lies chiefly among the trading part of the people; and though there are a great many families raised within few years, in the late war, by great employments and by great actions abroad, to the honor of the English gentry, yet how many more families among the tradesmen have been raised to immense estates, even during the same time, by the attending circumstances of war, such as the clothing, the paying, the victualing, and furnishing, etc., both army and navy. And by whom have the prodigious taxes been paid, the loans supplied, and money advanced upon all occasions? By whom are the banks and companies carried on, and on whom are the customs and excises levied? Have not the trade and tradesmen borne the burden of the war? And do they not still pay four millions a year interest for the public debts? On whom are the funds levied, and by whom the public credit supported? Is not trade the inexhausted fund of all funds, and upon which all the rest depend?

Tradesmen often richer than " gentlemen "

As is the trade, so in proportion are the tradesmen; and how wealthy are tradesmen in almost all the several parts of England as well as in London? How common is it to see a tradesman go off the stage, even but from mere shopkeeping, with from ten to forty thousand pounds' estate to divide among his family! When, on the contrary, [we] take the gentry in England from one end to the other, except a few here and there, what with excessive high living, which is of late grown so much into a disease, and the other ordinary circumstances of families, we find few families of the lower gentry, that is to say, from six or seven hundred a year downwards, but they are in debt and in necessitous circumstances, and a great many of greater estates also.

Tradesmen secure old family estates

On the other hand, let any one who is acquainted with England look but abroad into the several counties, especially near London, or within fifty miles of it; how are the ancient families worn out by time and family misfortunes, and the estates possessed by a new race of tradesmen, grown up into families of gentry, and established by the immense wealth gained, as I may say, behind the counter; that is, in the shop, the warehouse, and the counting house!

How many noble seats, superior to the palaces of sovereign princes, in some countries, do we see erected within few miles of this city by tradesmen, or the sons of tradesmen, while the seats and castles of the ancient gentry, like their families, look worn out and fallen into decay! Witness the noble house of Sir John Eyles, himself a merchant, at Giddyhall, near Romford; Sir Nathanael Mead, near Weal green, his father a linen draper; with many others, too long to repeat; and, to crown all, the Lord Castlemain's, now earl of Tilney, at Wanstead, his father, Sir Josiah Child, originally a tradesman. . . . *(Merchants' homes finer than old country seats)*

This being the case in England, and our trade being so vastly great, it is no wonder that the tradesmen in England fill the lists of our nobility and gentry; no wonder that the gentlemen of the best families marry tradesmen's daughters, and put their younger sons apprentices to tradesmen; and how often do these younger sons come to buy the elder sons' estates and restore the family, when the elder and head of the house, proving rakish and extravagant, has wasted his patrimony and is obliged to make out the blessing of Israel's family, where the younger son bought the birthright and the elder was doomed to serve him! *(Gentlemen marry tradesmen's daughters)*

Trade is so far from being inconsistent with a gentleman that, in short, trade in England makes gentlemen, and has peopled this nation with gentlemen; for, after a generation or two, the tradesman's children, or at least their grandchildren, come to be as good gentlemen, statesmen, parliament men, privy counselors, judges, bishops, and noblemen as those of the highest birth and the most ancient families, as we have shown. Nor do we find any defect either in the genius or capacities of the posterity of tradesmen, arising from any remains of mechanic blood, which, it is pretended, should influence them; but all the gallantry of spirit, greatness of soul, and all the generous principles that can be found in any of the ancient families, whose blood is the most untainted, as they call it, with the low mixtures of a mechanic race, are found in these; and, as is said before, they generally go beyond them in knowledge of the world, which is the best education. *(Tradesmen in every way as good as gentlemen of old families)*

Tradesmen
seek pedigrees

We see the tradesmen of England, as they grow wealthy, coming every day to the herald's office to search for the coats of arms of their ancestors, in order to paint them upon their coaches and engrave them upon their plate, embroider them upon their furniture, or carve them upon the pediments of their new houses; and how often do we see them trace the registers of their families up to the prime nobility or the most ancient gentry of the kingdom! In this search we find them often qualified to raise new families, if they do not descend from old; as was said of a certain tradesman of London, that if he could not find the ancient race of gentlemen from which he came, he would begin a new race, who should be as good gentlemen as any that went before him. . . .

Trade makes
England great

These things prove abundantly that the greatness of the British nation is not owing to war and conquests, to enlarging its dominions by the sword, or subjecting the people of other countries to our power; but it is all owing to trade, to the increase of our commerce at home and the extending it abroad. It is owing to trade that new discoveries have been made in lands unknown, and new settlements and plantations made, new colonies planted, and new governments formed, in the uninhabited islands and the uncultivated continent of America; and those plantings and settlements have again enlarged and increased the trade, and thereby the wealth and power of the nation by whom they were discovered and planted.

We have not increased our power, or the number of our subjects, by subduing the nations which possess those countries, and incorporating them into our own, but have entirely planted our colonies and peopled the countries with our own subjects, natives of this island; and, excepting the negroes, which we transport from Africa to America as slaves to work in the sugar and tobacco plantations, all our colonies, as well in the islands as on the continent of America, are entirely peopled from Great Britain and Ireland, and chiefly the former; the natives having either removed further up into the country, or, by their own folly and treachery in raising war against us, been destroyed and cut off.

An immediate result of the Industrial Revolution was an enormous increase in the amount of goods manufactured and exported. This remarkable increase in production is described in the following extract.

To show the expansion of trade following the new inventions it is necessary to give a few statistics. When machinery was introduced into the textile industries the output of manufactured goods increased by leaps and bounds. In 1764 the cotton imported into England amounted to about 4,000,000 pounds; in 1841 it had increased to nearly 500,000,000 pounds. In 1792 the amount of cotton imported into Lancashire alone from the United States was 138,000 pounds; in 1800 it was 18,000,000 pounds. The wool imported into England in 1766 was only about 2,000,000 pounds; in 1830 the amount had risen to more than 32,000,000 pounds. In 1788 the iron output was 61,000 tons; in 1839 it was over 1,250,000 tons. One hundred years after Crompton invented his spinning mule there were in Lancashire 2655 cotton mills running a total of nearly 38,000,000 spindles and 463,000 power looms; in the twenty-two years from 1793 to 1815 English exports, according to official valuation, rose from £17,000,000 annually to £58,000,000, in spite of the depression caused by the Napoleonic wars.

211. Efficiency of modern industrial methods (from C. A. Beard's *The Industrial Revolution*)

These figures give an inkling of the industrial transformation which followed the great inventions. Now let us turn to the real increase in the productive capacity of the individual. In other words, let us see whether productive capacity has grown more rapidly than the population. Unfortunately careful statistics are only of recent date, but we know that Hargreaves's jenny worked, originally, only eight spindles. The number was gradually increased to one hundred and twenty, and by the beginning of the nineteenth century to two hundred. The jenny now has more than a thousand spindles, each revolving at the rate of ten thousand revolutions per minute. A man and two boys can tend two thousand spindles.

The hand-loom weaver used to make from sixty to eighty throws of the shuttle per minute. Fifty years ago the best power loom made only one hundred throws; to-day the highest-grade loom runs at the rate of about four hundred per minute, and along with the increase of the productive capacity of the machine there is a decrease in the amount of human labor required in the operations. Formerly one weaver tended but one loom; now one worker tends from two to ten looms, according to the grade of goods. So great has been the increase in the efficiency of textile machinery that a single operative can supply two hundred and fifty persons with the necessary cotton garments, or three hundred persons with woolen clothing.

In every branch of industry attention has been devoted to increasing productive power, until almost marvelous results have been attained. In the continuation of the construction of the Cologne cathedral in 1870, two men with a steam crane lifted as much stone in a day as three hundred and sixty men could have done in the same time in the Middle Ages. The old craftsman produced at best a couple of pairs of shoes per day; the modern worker with machinery can turn out five hundred pairs a day. In one year six English workmen can produce enough bread to supply a thousand people for the same length of time. This includes all the labor from the breaking up of the soil to the delivery of the bread to the consumer.

The extent to which mechanical power can be substituted for hand labor depends upon the ability of man to contrive machinery. Here is the material key to man's spiritual progress. The plowing of a furrow, the sowing of the seed, the reaping of the grain, its transportation from one market to another, the weaving of a fabric, and the making of a coat, all represent in the final analysis the application of so much power to matter. The past achievements of inventors have shown us that there are no limits to the ways in which the exhaustless forces of nature can be applied to do man's work. If we look back, we see man struggling to maintain life by sheer strength of muscle; but if we look forward along the centuries of the future, we see the struggle for existence taking only a small portion of man's energy, leaving all the remainder of his powers of heart and brain free for the enlargement and enriching of life.

CHAPTER XIX

THE REVOLUTION OF 1848 IN FRANCE

Section 57. Unpopularity of Louis Philippe's Government

Louis Philippe was called to the throne of France by a small minority of political leaders at Paris, and no serious attempt was made to render the Orleans monarchy popular by the extension of the right to vote or by social reforms. Consequently the new government became the object of the severest criticism on the part of many discontented persons of all shades of opinion. The following bitter attack on the monarchy, selected from among innumerable similar diatribes, is not to be taken as a fair description of Louis Philippe's government, but merely as an illustration of how it appeared to a decided opponent who was instrumental in overthrowing it in the Revolution of 1848.

Until the opening of the year 1847 the monarchical power in France seemed to gain strength steadily, and to the superficial observer appeared to be firmly established. Success had apparently crowned all its efforts. With a single exception, — the sudden death of the heir to the throne, — fortune had in no way thwarted the projects of the aged monarch, whom his courtiers, anticipating history, ventured to designate by the most glorious titles. Even his own ministers, in the curious letters discovered in February, 1848, place Louis Philippe far above Louis XIV and Napoleon.

212. A partisan criticism of Louis Philippe's government (condensed)

Family
interests
govern Louis
Philippe's
policies

Thus the "system," as it was first called, grew apace, and by degrees the mask was withdrawn that concealed its ulterior aims. Audacious impudence took the place of the wily policy of the preceding fifteen years. At home, dynastic interests controlled every transaction, while abroad this selfish conspiracy seconded the schemes of an absolutist diplomacy directed against the real interests of the nation. To compensate for the Spanish marriages, which brought to the House of Orleans an immediate dowry of thirty millions, with a probable crown in reversion, the other European powers were allowed to efface the last vestiges of Poland, and French arms were freely given to the Jesuits of the *Sonderbund*.[1]

Corruption
reigns in
high places

At the same time the court, the ministers, the inferior functionaries, and the aristocrats devoured the financial resources of the nation. The civil list laid a heavy hand on the public domains, and carved broad acres out of the state forests; the budget was so adjusted as to satisfy the cravings of the minions of the government. The public offices, commissariat, national institutions, were made the objects of shameful corruption; and thus venality, which had its source in the cabinet of the ministers, spread in many streams through all the ministerial branches, and only stayed its course at the extreme verge of this political hierarchy. The most scandalous appointments, the monopoly of public offices by privileged families, and an almost hereditary claim, favored by the government, in the higher elective offices, — everything tended to encourage, at the center of the official world, corruption, sordid passions, and vulgar instincts.

The immoral-
ity of the
court

The princes had revived the frightful morals of the Regency and of the Directory. Each of them was surrounded by his own petty court of schemers and *roués*. There were royal hunts and races at Chantilly and Compiègne; days of gallantry and nights spent at the card table. And on the morrow all these sons of sin went to receive the communion at St. Roch, with the devotees of the old régime. Hypocrisy was the bosom friend of Immorality; and never did the juggleries of the old faith stand higher in favor than in these days of dissolution.

[1] See *The Development of Modern Europe*, Vol. II, p. 73, note 2.

The youth of the Faubourg St. Germain aped the court, and crowded round the priests and Jesuits; and Paris, to its great astonishment, once more beheld monks of all kinds proposing to confess the women, guide the men, and educate the children.

The deputies speculated with their political functions; peers of France gambled with the public securities; bankers monopolized the newspapers, which had been already decimated by the laws of September. The Jew of kings and king of Jews had won over the leading periodicals, and the voice of journalism was stifled at the same time as that of the French tribune.

The higher classes dominated by spirit of gain stifling of the press

The evil suddenly manifested itself externally, and attacked those who had hoped to profit by it. A terrible financial crisis and the obviously impending ruin of every branch of industry aroused at once capitalists, speculators, manufacturers, and merchants from their lethargy. The result of the most desperate gambling in railway scrip, which renewed the follies of the Rue Quincampoix in the time of John Law, was the total ruin of most persons involved. With the exception of two or three directors of the Northern Railway, who had doubled their capital, and of Madame Adelaide, who, if report speaks true, cleared twenty millions, the remainder of the railway speculators were sooner or later involved in utter ruin by the varying chances of the game. The provinces, too, were deeply compromised; Lyons was a loser to the amount of something like fifty millions, whilst Bordeaux, Albi, and other cities of the south were unable to meet their engagements. All the great centers of commercial activity were depressed. The manufactories of Lyons, Nîmes, Mühlhausen, Rouen, etc., found themselves overstocked in consequence of the depression of commerce in general, without any home market for their goods, while the export market was closed to them by foreign competition.

General demoralization ends in a financial crash

Louis Philippe's government not only found opponents among those who thought that it was corrupt, but also among the politicians who wanted to turn the officials out in order to find places for themselves. It was especially unpopular among workingmen, who had many schemes of social reform to put through in their own favor and yet were excluded from voting. Great definiteness was given to these aspirations for reform by Louis Blanc's programme for social reorganization, which deserves careful study both because it was a prominent feature of the Revolution of 1848 and because it enjoys an important place among the various socialistic schemes of the nineteenth century.

213. Louis Blanc's labor programme

ARTICLE 1. A ministry of progress should be created, whose business would be to consummate our social revolution, and gradually, peaceably, without injury to any one, bring about the abolition of poverty.

ART. 2. To effect this end, the ministry of progress should be directed : first, to buy up with the public revenue all mines and railways ; second, to transform the Bank of France into a national bank ; third, to have but one grand national insurance office, to the great advantage of individuals and of the government ; fourth, to establish, under the direction of responsible officers, large public warehouses, where producers and manufacturers could deposit their merchandise and provisions, for which they would have negotiable receipts of an estimated and determinate value, which should serve the purpose of paper money and be guaranteed to the full amount by the merchandise thus deposited ; fifth, to open shops which would supply the place of our retail dealers, just as the public warehouses or magazines would take the place of the present system of wholesale business.

The labor budget

ART. 3. The ministry of progress would make out their special budget, the "labor budget," comprising the profits arising from the warehouse dues, railways, mines, insurance, and the bank ; all of which are now employed in private speculation, but would, in the new system, be appropriated by the government.

ART. 4. The interest and the gradual repayments on the sums borrowed for the above-mentioned operations having been deducted from the labor budget, the rest would be employed : first, in establishing associations of workmen; second, in founding agricultural colonies.

ART. 5. In order to be entitled to the assistance of the government, every association must be established on the principle of community of interests, so as to be able to acquire in its progressive development an *inalienable*, *ever-increasing*, *common* capital, which is the only means of destroying all kinds of usury, and of preventing capital from continuing an instrument of tyranny, the possession of the implements of labor a privilege, money dealing a trade, happiness an exception, and idleness a right.

ART. 6. Consequently every association that would desire government aid must embody the following regulations in its constitution. After deducting wages, interest of capital, and expenses of management, the profits should be thus divided into four parts : (1) one quarter to pay off the capital borrowed by the government for the association; (2) one quarter to be appropriated as a fund for the assistance of the aged, the sick, the disabled, etc.; (3) one quarter to be divided as profits among the members in a manner to be stated below; (4) the remaining quarter to form a reserve fund, the object of which will be explained further on. Such would be the constitution of a single association. *[margin: Regulations controlling establishment of workshops]*

The next thing would be to connect all the associations of the same trade, so that they might be bound up in one common interest. Two conditions would be enough : first, to determine the cost price; the amount of legal profits would then be fixed above the cost price, always considering the state of the industrial world, so that we might establish a uniform price and prevent competition between establishments of the same trade; next, there would be established throughout all the associations of the same trade not an equality of salaries but a proportional scale of salary, because the material wants of life are not the same in all parts of France. *[margin: All associations of the same trade to be united]*

Having thus established solidarity, or community of interests, among all the associations of the same trade, it would be necessary to give the crowning touch to our edifice whereby we should establish order on an everlasting basis and prevent *[margin: Establishment of general solidarity among all trades]* the possibility of war, hatred, and revolution. This would be done by establishing solidarity, or community of interest, between all the various trades and all the members of society.

In order to effect this, two conditions are requisite. Ascertain the sum total of the profits of each trade, and divide it equally among all the operatives. Then make a mutual assistance fund of the various reserve funds mentioned above, so that any branch of trade that was prosperous one year would, by this means, assist any other that might be in distress. This would furnish a certain amount of capital belonging to all the members collectively. The distribution of this capital would be intrusted to an administrative council regulating the affairs of the whole body of united branches.

The government would gradually develop this plan by a series of successive measures. No one need be injured. The government would have its model institution, and private associations would be carried on at the same time. But so great would be the advantages of the government system that all private undertakings would be gradually attracted to it by the all-powerful influence of its superiority, so that it would form a center from which all other associations would diverge, as the stone thrown into the water becomes the center of innumerable circles that continue to spread and enlarge themselves indefinitely.

ART. 7. The agricultural colonies would be founded with the same object and based upon the same principles.

Section 58.   *The Second French Republic*

The various elements of opposition to Louis Philippe's government finally forced the king to dismiss his unpopular minister, Guizot, and later the more radical republicans succeeded in February, 1848, in overthrowing the monarchy altogether. The provisional government, which was then set up to manage affairs until the new constitution could be established, immediately issued the following proclamation.

In the name of the French people:

A reactionary and oligarchical government has just been over-thrown by the heroism of the people of Paris. That government has fled, leaving behind it a trail of blood that forbids it ever to retrace its steps.

The blood of the people has flowed as in July; but this time this noble people shall not be deceived. It has won a national and popular government in accord with the rights, the progress, and the will of this great and generous nation.

A provisional government, the result of pressing necessity and ratified by the voice of the people and of the deputies of the departments, in the session of February 24, is for the moment invested with the task of assuring and organizing the national victory. It is composed of Messieurs Dupont (de l' Eure), Lamartine, Crémieux, Arago (of the Institute), Ledru-Rollin, Garnier-Pagès, Marie, Armand Marrast, Louis Blanc, Ferdinand Flocon, and Albert (a workingman).

These citizens have not hesitated a moment to accept the patriotic commission which is imposed upon them by the pressure of necessity. With the capital of France on fire, the justification for the present provisional government must be sought in the public safety. All France will understand this and will lend it the support of its patriotism. Under the popular government which the provisional government proclaims, every citizen is a magistrate.

Frenchmen, it is for you to give to the world the example which Paris has given to France; prepare yourselves by order and by confidence in your destiny for the firm institutions which you are about to be called upon to establish.

The provisional government wishes to establish a republic, — subject, however, to ratification by the people, who shall be immediately consulted.

The unity of the nation (formed henceforth of all the classes of citizens who compose it); the government of the nation by itself; liberty, equality, and fraternity, for fundamental principles, and " the people " for our emblem and watchword; — these constitute the democratic government which France owes to itself, and which our efforts shall secure for it.

214. The overthrow of the Orleanist monarchy is proclaimed by the provisional government (February 24, 1848)

Provisional government desires a republic

The formal proclamation of the second French republic is very characteristic of the momentary situation.

In the name of the French people :

215. The second French republic is proclaimed (February 26, 1848)

Citizens : royalty, under whatever form, is abolished ; no more legitimism, no more Bonapartism, no regency.

The provisional government has taken all the measures necessary to render impossible the return of the former dynasty or the advent of a new dynasty.

The republic is proclaimed.

The people are united.

All the forts which surround the capital are ours.

The brave garrison of Vincennes is a garrison of brothers.

Let us retain that old republican flag whose three colors made with our fathers the circuit of the globe.

Let us show that this symbol of equality, of liberty, and of fraternity is at the same time the symbol of order, — of order the more real, the more durable, since justice is its foundation and the whole people its instrument.

The people have already realized that the provisioning of Paris requires a freer circulation in the streets, and those who have erected the barricades have already in several places made openings large enough for the passage of wagons and carts. Let this example be imitated everywhere. Let Paris reassume its accustomed appearance and trade its activity and confidence. . . .

216. Decrees of the provisional government relating to the working-men (February 25, 1848)

The workingmen and their leaders played an important part in the February revolution. This fact is emphasized by the decrees in the interest of the laboring classes which were issued by the provisional government on the day following its creation.

The provisional government of the French republic decrees that the Tuileries shall serve hereafter as a home for the veterans of labor.

The provisional government of the French republic pledges itself to guarantee the means of subsistence of the workingman by labor.

It pledges itself to guarantee labor to all citizens.

It recognizes that workingmen ought to enter into associa- Labor unions
tions among themselves in order to enjoy the advantage of sanctioned
their labor.

The provisional government returns to the workingmen, to Suppression
whom it rightfully belongs, the million which was about to fall of the civil
due upon the civil list. list

The provisional government of the French republic decrees Return of
that all articles pledged at the pawn shops since the first of Feb- pawned
ruary, consisting of linen, garments, clothes, etc., upon which articles
the loan does not exceed ten francs, shall be given back to those
who pledged them. The minister of finance is ordered to meet
the payments incidental to the execution of the present edict.

The provisional government of the republic decrees the Establish-
immediate establishment of national workshops. The minister ment of
of public works is charged with the execution of the present national
decree. workshops
(February 26)

On account of the financial crisis that accompanied
the Revolution, the provisional government found it necessary to provide employment for idle workmen in order
to keep them contented during the crucial period of reorganization. Furthermore, owing to the assistance which
the workingmen had rendered in carrying out the actual insurrection in February, it was also found necessary to permit them to be represented on the provisional government.
However, the republican members of that government
wanted no labor reforms. So, while they appointed the
two labor representatives, Louis Blanc and Albert, a committee to meet at the Luxemburg palace to deliberate
upon labor's demands, they appropriated no money to
establish workshops in order to give employment to the
idle in accordance with Blanc's plan. The only thing that
was seriously attempted by the provisional government
itself was the employment of the idle in breaking stones

and building roads and fortresses. It has been so often stated that Louis Blanc's scheme was tested in 1848, that it seems worth while to give at some length his own account of the matter.

217. Louis Blanc's version of the work-shops experiment of 1848 (condensed)

The situation of Paris immediately after the great shock of February is well known. The immediate consequences of so violent and unforeseen a crisis were, of course, a disturbance of industrial operations, a panic among capitalists, and a considerable multitude of workingmen thrown upon the streets, starving for want of work, and armed. Such a state of things could not but cause uneasiness to the government. Consequently, on the twenty-seventh of February, 1848, during the first days of the Revolution, before the experiment of the Luxemburg was thought of, the provisional government decreed the establishment of national workshops, and the minister of public works, M. Marie, was charged with the execution of the decree.

An opponent of Louis Blanc's scheme put in charge of the national workshops

But what were these national workshops to be? A mere hazardous expedient, or a noble and vigorous experiment in the organization of labor ; — a temporary resource to meet the serious problem of the unemployed, or a starting point for social regeneration ? M. Marie knew my opinions better than any one else ; for only a few days before the Revolution of February, in a rather numerous gathering of deputies and journalists in his own house, I had clearly explained them ; and I may add, they had encountered no more decided opponent than M. Marie himself. And yet it was to him, who totally misunderstood and dreaded socialism, who had sworn in his heart to resist it, *à l'outrance*, that the organization of the national workshops was to be committed. The actual direction of the workshops, moreover, was intrusted to M. Émile Thomas, whom I did not even know by sight ; and one of the claims which recommended that person was his ardent, indefatigable opposition to my doctrines. Later he officially testified, "I have never spoken to M. Louis Blanc in my life ; I don't know him." Again, "While I was at the head of the workshops I saw M. Marie daily, sometimes twice a day ; never once M. Ledru Rollin, M. Louis Blanc, nor M. Albert."

Nor let it be objected that, though these national workshops
were not organized with my concurrence, they were, at all
events, in conformity with my principles. The truth is precisely the reverse. In point of fact, it is monstrous to com-
found the industrial system developed in my *Organization of
Labor* with the system of the national workshops managed by
M. Émile Thomas, under the sanction of M. Marie.

Blanc
distinguishes
the national
workshops
from his
plan

The *social workshops*, such as I had suggested, were each of
them to consist of workmen belonging to the same trade. The
national workshops, as put in operation by M. Marie, consisted
in a collection of workmen got together pellmell, and yet —
absurd as it was ! — all put to the same kind of work. In the
social workshops, as suggested by me, the workmen were to
pursue their business, the State lending them capital, to be repaid according to certain stipulations ; they, working exclusively
for their own profit, with a view to a joint benefit, that is to
say, with all the stimulus of personal interest, combined with
the *esprit de corps* engendered by the pursuit of a common
object.

In the *national workshops*, as managed by M. Marie, the
State interfered simply as a contractor ; the operatives worked
only as paid instruments. Now, as the kind of labor in these
workshops was utterly unproductive and absurd, besides being
such as the greater part of the men were unaccustomed to, the
State was simply squandering the public funds ; its subsidies
were a premium upon idleness ; its wages, alms in disguise.
The *social workshops*, as suggested by me, consisted of groups
of workingmen, united by the most intimate ties and identity
of interest ; groups, therefore, seriously concerned in being in-
dustrious and in the highest degree productive. The *national
workshops*, as managed by M. Marie, were nothing more than
a rabble of paupers, whom it was enough to feed, since no one
knew how to employ them, and who had to live together without any other ties than a military organization, and under chiefs
who bore the name, at once so strange and yet so characteristic, of sergeant majors.

The national workshops emptied the exchequer at a dead
loss; they humiliated the workingman, who was reduced to

accept the bread which he desired to *earn;* they discredited
State interference in industrial matters. In the place of associations of workmen they got together battalions of paid idlers,—
a strange army, sooner or later to be disbanded at the risk of
civil war! The believers in the doctrine of *laissez faire* had,
of course, every reason for attempting to fix upon us the
responsibility for all this mischief. What luck for the disciples
of the old political economy, if they could succeed in playing
a trick on public opinion; if they could contrive to pass off as
the highest practical form of the organization of labor those
"national workshops," which were nothing more than its
ignoble travesties!

Section 59. *Louis Napoleon and the Second French Empire*

After the National Assembly, called by the revolutionary government in 1848, completed the republican constitution, and it became necessary to choose a president,
public attention centered on Louis Napoleon, a nephew
of Napoleon I. For some years he had been preparing
the mind of the French people for his establishment in
power by writing on social questions and especially about
his distinguished uncle. In a work entitled *Napoleonic
Ideas*, published in 1839, he represented Napoleon I as
the savior of France against European tyrants, the champion of the people, the Messiah of the Revolution, the
friend of the poor.

218. Louis
Napoleon's
view of
Napoleon I's
ideals

Napoleon, advancing upon the stage of the world, saw that
it was his part to be the *testamentary executor* of the Revolution. The destructive fire of parties was extinct; and when
the Revolution, dying but not vanquished, bequeathed to
Napoleon the accomplishment of its last wishes, it should have
addressed him as follows: "Establish upon solid foundations
the results of my efforts; reunite the divided people of France;
repulse feudal Europe, leagued against me; heal my wounds;

enlighten the nations; extend in breadth that which I have done in depth. Be for Europe what I have been to France; and even though you water the tree of civilization with your blood, though you see your projects misinterpreted, and your family wandering about the world without a native land to own them, never abandon the sacred cause of the French people, but lead it to triumph by all the means to which genius gives birth and humanity approves."

The emperor Napoleon contributed more than any other man to accelerate the reign of liberty by preserving the moral influence of the Revolution, and by diminishing the fears which it inspired. But for the Consulate and the Empire the Revolution would have been merely a grand drama, leaving behind it great memories but few achievements. The Revolution would have been drowned in the counter-revolution; whereas the precise contrary has taken place, because Napoleon rooted in France and spread throughout Europe the principal advantages of the grand crisis of '89, and because, to employ one of his own expressions, *he sobered the Revolution, consolidated the dynasties of kings, and ennobled the people.* . . . <aside>Napoleon I saved the moral influence of the Revolution</aside>

It was this reflecting of popular sentiments, instincts, and will, which constituted the whole force of the emperor. It were a grave fallacy to suppose that a great man is omnipotent, and that he derives his strength solely from himself. The capacity to foresee, to act upon that foresight, and to lead, — such are the first qualities of a superior genius. "I am not inclined," said Napoleon, "to fall into the error of regarding myself as representing in my own person and ideas the wisdom of nations. The genius of the workman consists in knowing how to make use of the materials at his disposal."

The emperor, while restoring the old forms, rested his authority altogether upon a new and firm basis, — the new conditions and interests. Consequently the transformation of the republic into a monarchy and the reëstablishment of public worship, instead of awakening fear, gave additional confidence to men's minds; since, so far from injuring any interest, it fulfilled political and moral requirements, and represented the wishes of the majority. In fact, if these changes had not been <aside>Napoleon reflected the wishes of the majority</aside>

demanded by the sentiments of the majority, Napoleon would
not have accomplished them, for he possessed accurate
powers of divination, and it was his aim to augment and not
to weaken his moral power. Never, accordingly, were such
changes effected with so little effort. Napoleon had but to
say, "Let the churches be opened," and the faithful rushed
to the churches in crowds. He said to the nation, "Do you
desire an hereditary monarchy?" and the nation replied in
the affirmative, by four millions of votes. . . .

The emperor
desired to
improve the
condition of
the poor

The improvement of the condition of the poor classes was one
of the first considerations of the emperor. In a letter to the
Minister of the Interior, dated 2d November, 1807, he says
that he attached great glory to the idea of the abolition of men-
dicancy. He had workhouses established; forty-two already
existed in 1809. In order to ascertain the effectual means
of relieving the misery of the people, he sought information
from all the public writers. He instituted the Maternal Society,
which was to have an administrative council in all the large
towns of the empire. The institution of Sisters of Charity
was reëstablished with all its old advantages, but without the
abuses which had diverted their purposes. Six houses destined
to receive the orphan daughters of the Legionaries of Honor,
to the number of six hundred, were created in 1810. The
Hôtel des Invalides was reorganized in 1803, and several
branches were added to it in different places. Napoleon created homes for the veterans, where each of those who were
admitted had a rural dwelling and a portion of land with a net
revenue, equal to his retiring pension. . . .

The emperor desired that everything connected with worship should be gratuitous, and that, for the people, the burial
of the poor should be gratuitous and respectable. "We have
no right," said he, "to set a tax on the dead; we ought not to
deprive the poor, because they are poor, of that which consoles
them for their poverty." He ordered that the churches should
be opened free to the public; that if the church was hung in
black for a rich man, the black should not be taken down
until after the service of a poor man. He had intended to have
the prices of the pit seats in the Theatre Français reduced

on Sundays to one franc, in order that the people might enjoy the masterpieces of our literature. . . .

Let us repeat in conclusion : the Napoleonic idea is not an idea of war, but a social, industrial, commercial idea — an idea of humanity. If to some men it seems still to threaten new conflicts, the reason is that it was, indeed, long enveloped in the smoke of cannon and the dust of battles. But now the clouds have dispersed and men discern, through the effulgent glory of arms, a civil glory, greater and more enduring. Let the ashes of the emperor repose in peace ! His memory spreads wider and wider every passing day. Each wave that breaks on the rock of St. Helena brings with the breath of Europe a homage to his memory, a regret to his ashes ; and the breezes of Longwood repeat over his tomb, " *The free nations of the earth everywhere labor to carry on thy work !* "

Napoleonic idea — an idea of humanity

Louis Napoleon by no means contented himself with writing books which kept his name and policies before the French people. Twice before the Revolution of 1848 he attempted in vain to make himself ruler of France, and the overthrow of Louis Philippe finally afforded him the opportunity which he had long been waiting. He returned to France from England where he had been in exile, and when the time approached to elect a president of the new republic, he announced his candidacy in an adroitly worded manifesto.

Louis Napoleon to his fellow-citizens:

In order to recall me from exile, you have elected me a representative of the people ; on the eve of choosing a chief magistrate for the republic my name presents itself to you as a symbol of order and security.

Those proofs of so honorable a confidence are, I am well aware, addressed to my name rather than to myself, who, as yet, have done nothing for my country ; but the more the memory of the Emperor protects me and inspires your suffrages, the more I feel compelled to acquaint you with my

219. Louis Napoleon explains his position to the voters of France (November 29, 1848)

sentiments and principles. There must be no equivocation between us. I am moved by no ambition which dreams one day
of empire and war, the next of the application of subversive
theories. Brought up in free countries, disciplined in the
school of misfortune, I shall ever remain faithful to the duties
which your suffrages and the will of the Assembly impose
upon me.

If elected president, I shall shrink from no danger, from
no sacrifice, in the defense of society, which has been so
outrageously assailed. I shall devote myself wholly and without reservation to the consolidation of the republic, so that it
may be wise in its laws, honest in its aims, great and strong
in its deeds. My greatest honor would be to hand on to my
successor, after four years of office, the public power consolidated, its liberties intact, and genuine progress assured. . . .

LOUIS NAPOLEON BONAPARTE

After the expiration of three years of the four for
which he had been elected president, Louis Napoleon
determined to secure a new lease of power by the following revolutionary appeal to the people, calling for the
reconstruction of the government and an extension of
his term. In this proclamation the legislature, which he
had just dissolved, was the object of his attack, and he
made political capital by promising to restore universal
suffrage which it had seriously restricted.

Frenchmen :

220. Louis Napoleon's appeal to the French people (December, 1851)

The present state of things can last no longer. Every day
that passes aggravates the danger of the country. The Assembly, which ought to be the firmest support of order, has become
the center of plots. The patriotism of three hundred of its
members has not been able to arrest its fatal tendencies. Instead of making laws for the general interest, it forges arms
for civil war. It attacks the power which I hold directly from
the people. It encourages all bad passions. It compromises

the repose of France. I have dissolved it; and I make the whole people the judge between it and myself.

The Constitution, as you know, was made with the object of weakening in advance the power which you were about to confide to me. Six millions of votes were a signal protestation against it ; and yet I have faithfully respected it. Provocations, calumnies, outrages, have found me unmoved; but now, when the fundamental compact is no longer respected even by those who incessantly invoke it, and since the men who have already overturned two monarchies wish to tie my hands that they may destroy the republic, it is my duty to baffle their perfidious projects, to maintain the republic, and to save the country, by invoking the solemn judgment of the only sovereign whom I recognize in France, — the people.

I make, therefore, a loyal appeal to the entire nation ; and I say, if you wish to continue this state of confusion, which degrades us and compromises our future, choose another in my place ; for I no longer wish for a power which is impotent for good, which renders me responsible for acts which I cannot prevent, and which chains me to the helm when I see the ship rushing towards the abyss. If, on the contrary, you still have confidence in me, give me the means of accomplishing the great mission which I hold from you.

This mission consists in closing the era of revolutions, in satisfying the legitimate wants of the people, and in protecting them against subversive passions. It consists, especially, in creating institutions which can survive men, and which will be foundations upon which one can build something durable. Persuaded that the instability of power and the preponderance of a single Assembly are the permanent causes of trouble and of discord, I submit to your suffrages the following fundamental bases of a constitution which the Assemblies will hereafter develop : *Louis Napoleon's propositions for a stable government*

1. A responsible chief appointed for ten years.

2. Ministers dependent upon the executive power alone.

3. A council of state, composed of the most distinguished men, drafting the laws, and supporting them in the discussion before the legislative body.

4. A legislative body, to discuss and vote the laws, elected by universal suffrage, not, however, on a general ticket, which violates the principle of popular election.

5. A second assembly, composed of the most distinguished men of the nation; a preponderating power, guardian of the fundamental compact and of the public liberties.

This system, created by the First Consul at the commencement of the century, has already given France repose and prosperity; it will guarantee them still. Such is my profound conviction. If you share it, declare it by your suffrages; if, on the contrary, you prefer a government without power, monarchical or republican, borrowed from I know not what chimerical past or future, reply negatively.

Thus, then, for the first time since 1804, you will vote with a knowledge of the case, knowing well for whom or for what. If I should not obtain the majority of your suffrages, then I shall bring about the meeting of a new assembly, and shall surrender to it the commission I have received from you; but if you believe that the cause of which my name is the symbol — that is, France regenerated by the Revolution of 1789, and organized by the emperor — is still your cause, proclaim it by sanctioning the powers which I ask of you. Then France and Europe will be preserved from anarchy; obstacles will be removed; rivalries will have disappeared; for all will respect in the decision of the people the decree of Providence.

Given at the Palace of the Élysée, the 2d of December, 1851.

LOUIS NAPOLEON BONAPARTE

Although Louis Napoleon, by the *coup d'état* of December, 1851, secured an extension of his presidency for ten years, he was not satisfied until he had won the title of Emperor. In September, 1852, he undertook a tour through the southern provinces in order to test public opinion. Many suggestions had reached him, encouraging him to assume the imperial crown, and frequently on his journey he was received with the cry, "Long live the emperor!" In his speech at Bordeaux, October 9, 1852, he definitely announced his belief that France was ready for the abolition of the second republic.

The purpose of this journey, as you know, was to see for myself our beautiful provinces of the south and familiarize myself with their needs. It has, however, given rise to a much more important result. Indeed, — and I say it with a candor as far removed from arrogance as from false modesty, — never has a people testified in a manner more direct, spontaneous, and unanimous, the longing to be freed from anxiety as to the future by concentrating in a single person an authority which shall accord with their desires. They realize now both the false hopes with which they have been deluded and the dangers which threaten them. . . .

221. Louis Napoleon's Bordeaux address (October 9, 1852)

France to-day encompasses me with her sympathies because I do not belong to the group of dreamers. In order to benefit the country it is not necessary to resort to new systems, but, above all, to establish confidence in the present and security for the future. This is why France seems to wish to revert to the empire.

There is, nevertheless, one apprehension, and that I shall set at rest. A spirit of distrust leads certain persons to say that the empire means war. I say, the empire means peace. France longs for peace, and if France is satisfied, the world is tranquil. Glory is rightly handed down hereditarily, but not war. . . .

Napoleon's policy of peace

I concede, nevertheless, that, like the emperor, I have many conquests to make. I would, like him, conquer, for the sake of harmony, the warring parties and bring into the great popular current the wasteful and conflicting eddies. I would conquer, for the sake of religion, morality, and material ease, that portion of the population, still very numerous, which, in the midst of a country of faith and belief, hardly knows the precepts of Christ; which, in the midst of the most fertile country of the world, is hardly able to enjoy the primary necessities of life. We have immense uncultivated districts to bring under cultivation, roads to open, harbors to construct, rivers to render navigable, canals to finish, and our network of rail-roads to bring to completion. . . .

This is what I understand by the empire, if the empire is to be reëstablished. These are the conquests which I contemplate, and all of you who surround me, who, like myself, wish the good of our common country, you are my soldiers.

Many interpretations have been given of the character of Napoleon III, but there is none more interesting than that by his close friend and warm admirer, Dr. Evans (his American dentist), from whose work on *The Second French Empire* this extract is taken.

222. Dr. Evans's characterization of Napoleon III

The Emperor wished to see France great and prosperous. But the dream he cherished was that Europe and the world might be at peace; and his hope, his ambition, was that it might be his destiny to lay the foundations of a future reign of justice among men. In 1854 he said : "France has no idea of aggrandisement ; I love to proclaim it loudly ; the time of conquests has passed never to return, for it is not by extending the limits of its territory that a nation is to be henceforth honored and to become powerful ; it is by making itself the leader of generous ideas and by causing the sentiment of right and justice to prevail everywhere." And he continued to say these things to the end of his life — striving all the while to make real what he was profoundly convinced ought to be governing principles in a well-ordered State. . . .

Napoleon III's solicitude for the common people

His philanthropy manifested itself in innumerable ways, and in his dealings with every one, no matter how humble his station in life. His grandeur never weighed heavily with him. A democrat at heart, he loved to talk with the common people — the soldier, the peasant, the workingman ; he was always willing to listen to their complaints and ready to relieve them when he could.

One day, when he was inspecting some buildings that were being erected by his direction, an aide-de-camp informed him that the workmen seemed to be discontented. "What is the matter?" said the Emperor. "Well," replied the officer, after hesitating a moment, " they say that you and everybody about are drinking champagne, while beer is thought to be good enough for them." The Emperor made no reply, but slowly and alone walked forward, and, approaching a number of the men who were standing together in a group, said, " Good morning, my friends." Then, after a few pleasant words, he continued : " Ah, they have given you beer, I see. Come, let us have a glass of champagne ! " And when the champagne, which he then ordered, had been brought and the glasses of all had been filled, calling out to the foreman, and touching glasses with him, he said, " My best wishes," and, turning to the others, " Your good health, my friends ! "

All of this was done and said with such perfect ease and naturalness, such entire sincerity, that it went straight to the hearts of these men, who felt that the Emperor was not like other emperors and kings, but was, as they expressed it, " one of us." And yet, although approachable at all times and absolutely free from haughtiness, when he was most familiar there was in his manner a dignity which caused those with whom he was speaking to understand that he was still the Emperor.

Never was a ruler judged more falsely than Napoleon III. He loved mankind and was always thinking of ways in which he could benefit the people or make some one happy. On one occasion, after he had spoken of the condition of the laboring classes in France, and the measures that ought to be taken to raise the standard of living among the people generally, I ventured to say to him, " Why ! your Majesty is almost a socialist, your sympathies are always with the poor ; their welfare would seem to concern you more than anything else." " It ought to," he replied. Was he not worthy of the title given to him by the people — " L'Empereur des Ouvriers "? Napoleon
loved
mankind

But it must not be supposed that the Emperor, deeply interested as he was in ameliorating the condition of the poor, sought to find in fanciful speculations and theories remedies for the want and suffering which he deplored. " No amelioration of the lot of the laboring classes is possible," he said, " except under a firmly established government, and where there is a sense of absolute social security."

The Emperor has been bitterly denounced by his political
adversaries, who have applied to him nearly every name in
the vocabulary of ineptitude and of crime. These names, however, are not to be taken seriously; they never were by those
who uttered them. They are not characterizations. They
merely indicate the state of mind of those who made use of
them; for, as Paul Louis Courier has told us, "imbecile,"
"rascal," "thief," "assassin," are in France the conventional
epithets which writers and speakers apply to a person when
they simply wish to say they do not agree with him. But very
few of the Emperor's calumniators have failed to recognize
the amiable character of the man.

CHAPTER XX

REVOLUTION OF 1848 — AUSTRIA, GERMANY, ITALY

Section 60. The Fall of Metternich

The February revolution in France was speedily followed by an uprising of the Liberal party in Vienna, which, on March 13, forced Metternich to resign the influential position which he had held for so many years. The next day he wrote an account of the affair to Tsar Nicholas, who, he well knew, would heartily sympathize with him.

Sire, the most invincible of forces, that of circumstances, has put an end to my long political life. Your Imperial Majesty has always deigned to honor me with that form of esteem which has the highest value in my eyes, namely, confidence in my principles and such encouragement as the upright man should seek in his own conscience. To-day once more my conscience impels me as a duty to lay before your Imperial Majesty the expression of my profound gratitude for the sympathy which I believe that I have merited on your part, and of which, during the whole course of your Majesty's glorious reign, you have deigned to give me so many proofs. 223. Metternich informs the Tsar of the March revolution in Vienna

Europe, sire, is involved in a crisis which much exceeds the bounds of political movements. It is a crisis in the social body. I foresaw the event; I have combated it consistently during a ministry of well-nigh forty years. To check the torrent is no longer within the power of man. It can only be guided. ·

My efforts have been in vain. And as I do not know how to steer a middle course, or to remain in a situation repugnant to my moral sense, I have retired from the scene. Too advanced in years to hope to witness the events which, according to my views, may ultimately put an end to the present crisis, it only remains for me to offer to my master and to my country the good wishes which I shall not cease to entertain for their inseparable happiness. . . .

Condescend, sire, to retain a kind remembrance of me and permit me to assure you of the most profound respect. I remain, your Majesty, etc., etc.

METTERNICH

VIENNA, March 14, 1848

Two months before the overthrow of Metternich and a month before the February revolution in France, it was clear that the Austrian government was likely to have trouble with its subjects in Italy. The English consul general writes from Venice, January 18, 1848:

224. The signs of revolt in Venetia and Lombardy (January, 1848)

Though the Venetian provinces have hitherto been much more tranquil than the provinces of Lombardy, they appear now disposed to make common cause with the latter, and it is surprising to see the change that a short time has brought about.

The Austrians ostracized in northern Italy

When I left Venice, early in November last, everything was perfectly quiet, and although some little excitement had been produced by the speeches delivered by a few persons during the sitting of the Scientific Congress, society was upon its accustomed footing. Now, however, it is quite different; the Venetians have adopted the system of the Milanese, and there is hardly a Venetian house into which an Austrian is admitted. This determination has been come to very unwillingly by many, but they act under a system of intimidation that is carried on to a degree scarcely credible. Persons supposed to have a leaning towards the government are held up to public execration, and their names are written upon the walls as traitors to their country. . . .

Should a collision ensue between the troops and the people, — and a very slight thing may bring it on, — the consequences, I fear, would be extremely serious.

The government at Vienna, however, had been warned by disturbances in Milan early in the month, and Marshal Radetzky, the Austrian commander, encouraged his troops by the following declaration issued in Milan on the same day that the above letter was written from Venice by the English consul.

MILAN, January 18, 1848

225. **Marshal Radetzky encourages his soldiers**

His Majesty the emperor, being determined according to his rights and duties to defend the Lombardo-Venetian kingdom, as well as every other part of his dominions, against all attacks of an enemy, either from without or from within, has permitted me to make this, his resolve, known to all the troops of the army stationed in Italy. He is persuaded that his intentions will meet with the firmest support in the valor and fidelity of the army.

Soldiers, you have heard the words of the emperor; I am proud to make them known to you. Against your fidelity and your valor the efforts of fanaticism and the infidel spirit of innovation will be broken like brittle glass against solid rock. The sword which I have borne with honor in so many battles during sixty-five years is still eager for action. I shall know how to make use of it to defend the tranquillity of a country a short time since most happy, and which a mad faction now seeks to plunge into misery.

Soldiers, our emperor relies upon you ; your old general trusts you : let this suffice. Let them not force us to unfold the banner of the double-headed eagle, for the strength of its talons is yet unimpaired. Let our motto be : Defense and tranquillity to faithful and friendly citizens and destruction to the enemy who shall dare with a treacherous hand to disturb the peace and welfare of nations.

The present order of the day shall be announced to all the corps in their respective languages.

On March 22, 1848, Radetzky, in spite of his boasts, was forced to evacuate Milan, and the provisional government which had been established there appealed to the king of Sardinia for aid.

MILAN, March 23, 1848

Sacred Majesty :

226. Milan, after revolting from Austria, appeals to the king of Sardinia for aid (March 23, 1848)

We have vanquished the enemy who occupied the city. He left the castle last night and marched towards Verona, but he is not yet far from the capital and is marking every step with slaughter and plunder. Our citizens have made heroic efforts, and with very few resources they have repulsed the pride of an enemy confident in his strength. . . .

Although the city is now free, the speedy and potent aid of your Majesty is none the less important. The provisional government therefore implores your Majesty to hasten to assist us by every means. Your Majesty will thus be a benefactor to the sacred cause of Italian independence and brotherhood, and will surely receive the applause and gratitude of this people. We would willingly add more, but our position as a provisional government does not allow us to anticipate the wishes of the nation, which are, without doubt, all directed toward the furtherance of the cause of Italian unity.

While the northern Italians were preparing to resist to their utmost the rule of Austria, the Pope was entering upon a serious conflict with the republicans at Rome. The latter demanded that a constitutional convention be convoked, and were ready to seize the government by force of arms, when the Pope fled from the city. The Convention was then elected, and on February 9, 1849, it abolished the temporal authority of the Pope and proclaimed the short-lived Roman Republic in the following decree.

ART. I. The Papacy has forfeited in fact and of right the temporal government of the Roman State.

II. The Roman pontiff shall have all the guarantees necessary to secure his independence in the exercise of his spiritual power.

III. The form of the government of the Roman State shall be a pure democracy, and it shall take the glorious name of the Roman Republic.

IV. The Roman Republic shall maintain such relations with the rest of Italy as our common nationality may require.

February 9, 1849, 1 o'clock in the morning.

G. GALETTI, *President*

GIOVANNI PENNACCHI
ARIODANTE FABRETTI
ANTONIO ZAMBIANCHI
QUIRICO FILOPANTI BARILI, *Secretaries*

227. Decree establishing the Roman Republic (February, 1849)

The decree establishing the republic was immediately followed by a proclamation to the people.

LONG LIVE THE ROMAN REPUBLIC!

ROME, February 8, [1849]

It is 1 o'clock, after midnight, and we issue at this moment from the hall where the convention has been assembled since 11 o'clock A.M. Who can describe the commotions which have agitated us? The great word has been pronounced.

Democracy has won the day. After a serious, animated, but free and conscientious discussion, at a quarter past 11 P.M., amidst the applause of the people assembled in crowds in the galleries, the Roman Republic was proclaimed, after the fall of the temporal power of the Pope had been declared. Out of more than 140 representatives of the people only some twenty were against the propositions that were passed.

In this manner religion has been purified. Italy has recovered Rome, and Rome has opened to itself a glorious future. The majority of the representatives agreeing in this great proclamation demonstrates fully that the desire of the people to be emancipated from a theocratic government could no longer be repressed.

228. Proclamation announcing the Roman Republic (February, 1849)

Nevertheless, we admire the firmness of those who have voted to the contrary, desirous of leaving it in the power of the Italian Constituent Assembly to establish the form of government for our State. They have at least fulfilled a great function, — that of causing a question of such vital importance to be discussed seriously and quietly.

It is impossible to describe the general applause and the enthusiasm with which the word, full of hope, has been received by the public. Long may we be grateful in deed and in word to the redeeming Assembly, have a firm hope in the future, and trust that this resolution has been taken at a proper time, and that it will be hereafter unchangeable.

With the intention of giving to-morrow a fuller account of the important acts that have taken place to-day, we conclude, as we began, with the cry of " Long live the Roman Republic ! "

While Lombardy and Venetia were trying vainly, with the help of the king of Sardinia, to free themselves from the yoke of Austria, the Germans were busy drawing up a new constitution, which they trusted would at last make a nation out of the various German States so loosely united by the union of 1815. On the occasion of the opening of the National Assembly at Frankfort, the diet of the old Confederation sent to the new Assembly the following graceful, if rather forced, message of congratulation.

229. Message of the diet to the new National Assembly at Frankfort (May 18, 1848)

The force of extraordinary events, the ardent desire which has loudly manifested itself throughout our whole fatherland, together with the summons on the part of the several German governments which these have called forth, have combined to bring into being in this momentous hour an Assembly such as has never before been seen in all our history.

Our old political life has been stirred to its very depths, and, greeted by the acclamations and confidence of the entire German people, the German parliament, new and grand, emerges into life.

The German governments and their common organ, the diet, united with the German people in a common love for our great fatherland, and gladly yielding to the spirit of the time, extend a hand of welcome to the representatives of the nation and wish them happiness and prosperity.

Section 61. Failure of the Revolution in Bohemia and Hungary

After a few months' triumph the revolutionary government in Vienna was overthrown by the bombardment and capture of the city, October, 1848, by Windischgrätz, the emperor's general, who had just suppressed the Bohemian revolution. The city had decided to surrender, when it was encouraged to a last futile resistance by the arrival of an army from Hungary ready to forward the revolution. An Englishman, an eyewitness, stationed outside the city, published the following narrative in the English newspapers.

The beautiful street leading to the Prater [a park] had been the scene of the hardest fighting of all, as it had been fortified by a succession of barricades, built up to the first-floor windows in a half-moon shape, with regular embrasures and planted with cannon. This was strewn with the dead bodies of men and horses; but they, and the pools of blood all about, did not strike us so much as the horrid smell of roast flesh arising from the half-burned bodies of rebels killed in the houses fired by Congreve rockets, which we saw used by the troops with terrible effect. Half of the houses in this beautiful suburb are thus burned down, while the other half are riddled with shot and shell. On every side we may see weeping wives, sisters, and daughters, picking, literally piece-meal, out of the ruins the half-consumed bodies of their relatives.

On Sunday evening, the 29th, the city, dreading a bombardment from the Belvedere, agreed to surrender; but

230. Vienna retaken by the emperor's troops under Windisch-grätz (October 31, 1848)

the capitulation was shamefully violated when early the next morning the approach of the Hungarians to raise the siege was signaled from the tower of the cathedral. Then came the real crisis. . . . We were fired upon continually from the ramparts; and I for the first time literally tasted blood, which was dashed over my face and clothes, when a round shot carried off the head of an artilleryman by my side.

All this time the roar of cannon, the whizzing of rockets, and the roll of musketry in our rear told us that the Hungarian army had joined battle; while in our front, from all the ramparts, tops of houses, and churches, the rebels were firing signal guns and waving flags to cheer them on. It was a beautiful, clear, sunshiny autumn day; and all felt that there were trembling in the balance not only the fate of the•grand old Austrian empire (*an Seigen und an Ehren reich*), — the monarchy of Charles V and Maria Theresa, and so long the bulwark of Christendom against the Turk, — but with it the peace and safety of Europe.

At length the firing behind us gradually slackened and then died away; and towards sunset the victorious imperialists marched back from the field of battle, having utterly routed the Hungarians and driven three thousand of them into the Danube, which will roll their bodies down to Pesth, a fearful tiding of their defeat. You may fancy what cheers arose from the imperialists and what yells of despair from the rebels, whose offers of a conditional surrender were now scornfully rejected.

Louis Kossuth, leader in the struggle for constitutional government in Hungary and later in the war for independence, issued in 1850, from his place of exile in Turkey, a long address to the people of the United States, giving his version of the recent conflict. During the revolution the Secretary of State at Washington had instructed an agent of the United States to proceed to Hungary, and, if he found that country able to maintain the independence which had been declared, to assure the new

State that the United States desired to be the "very first to congratulate her and welcome her entrance into the family of nations." Before the American representative could reach Hungary, however, the revolt had been suppressed by Austria, but for a long time the United States manifested a sympathetic interest in Hungarian affairs and heartily welcomed Kossuth on the occasion of a visit which he afterwards made to the United States in 1851.

ADDRESS OF KOSSUTH TO THE PEOPLE OF THE UNITED STATES

BRUSA, March 27, 1850

Two years ago, I, by God's providence, who would be only an humble citizen, held in my hands the destiny of the reigning House of Austria. Had I been ambitious, or had I believed that this treacherous family were so basely wicked as they afterward proved themselves to be, the tottering pillars of their throne would have fallen at my command, and buried the crowned traitors beneath their ruins, or I would have scattered them like dust before a tempest, — homeless exiles, bearing nothing but the remembrance of their perfidy.

231. Kossuth's address to the people of the United States (slightly condensed)

However, I did not take advantage of these favorable circumstances, though the entire freedom of my dear native land was the only wish of my heart. My requests were of that moderate nature which, in the condition of Hungary and Europe, seemed best fitted for my countrymen. I asked of the king not the complete independence of my beloved country — not even any new rights or privileges — but simply these three things :

Hungary's first requests were moderate

1. That the inalienable rights, sanctioned by a thousand years and by the constitution of my fatherland, should be guaranteed by a national and responsible administration.

2. That every inhabitant of my country, without regarding language or religion, should be free and equal before the law, — all classes having the same privileges and protection from the law.

3. That all the people of the Austrian empire that acknowledged the same person as emperor whom we Hungarians recognized as king, and the same laws of succession, should have
restored to them their ancient constitutional rights, of which
they had been unjustly despoiled, modified to suit their wants
and the spirit of the age.

Independence
and constitu-
tional govern-
ment ancient
Hungarian
rights

The first demand was not for any new grant or concession,
but simply a fresh guarantee. In the arrangement made with
our ancestors, when, by their free will, they elevated the House
of Hapsburg to the throne, a condition was made that the king
should preserve the independence and constitution of the
country. This independence and this constitution were the
very vitality of our national being. During three centuries
twelve kings of the House of Hapsburg had sworn in the presence
of the eternal God, before ascending the throne, that they
would preserve our independence and the constitution ; and
their lives are but a history of perpetual and accursed perjury.
Yet such conduct did not weaken our fidelity. No nation ever
manifested more faithfulness to their rulers ; and though we
poor Hungarians made endless sacrifices, often at the expense
of our national welfare ; though these kings, in times of peace,
drew their support from us, and in times of war or danger
relied upon the unconquerable strength of our army ; [1] though
we have ever trusted in their words, they deceived us a thousand times and made our condition worse. . . .

The second demand was still less for any political right.
We asked for nothing more than a reform in the internal
administration of the State, — a simple act of justice which the
aristocracy owed the people ; and in this how much the king
would have gained ! The strength of his throne would have
been increased tenfold by thus winning the affections of his
faithful people.

Hungary
wished consti-
tutional
liberty for
all peoples
under the
House of
Hapsburg

The third demand was prompted by humanity and fraternal
feeling. It was the proper and holy mission of our nation as
the oldest member of the empire, and possessing a constitutional form of government, to raise its voice in behalf of those

[1] Maria Theresa's appeal to Hungary will be remembered. *The Development of Modern Europe*, Vol. I, p. 65.

sister nations under the same ruler, and that were united to us by so many ties of relationship. . . .

The king and royal family granted these requests, appealing to the sanctity of their oaths as a guarantee of their fulfillment; and I, weak in myself, but strong through the confidence of my countrymen and the noble sympathy of the Austrian people, proclaimed everywhere, amid the raging storm of revolution, that " the House of Austria should stand; for by the blessing of the Almighty it had begun to move in the right direction, and would be just to its people." It stood; and stood, too, at a time when, whatever might have been the fate of Hungary, the revolutionary tempest, under my direction, would have blown away this antiquated and helpless dynasty like chaff before the winds of heaven. . . . *The king made promises*

On the very day they signed the grant of these moderate demands of the Hungarian people, and solemnly swore, before God and the nation to maintain them, they secretly resolved and planned the most cruel conspiracy against us. They determined to break their oaths, to desolate the land with insurrection, conflagration, and blood, till, feeble and exhausted under the burden of a thousand miseries, Hungary might be struck from the roll of living nations. Then they hoped by the power of the bayonet, and, if necessary, by the arms of Russia, to erect a united and consolidated empire, like the Russian, of sixteen various nations; they hoped to realize their long-conceived purpose of making themselves an absolute power. . . . *And then proved false*

We desired an honorable peace, and were willing to submit to any reasonable terms. We many times tendered the olive branch. We asked the constitutional governments of Europe to interpose. They heard us not. The haughty imperial family, forgetting that they were the real traitors, rejected every proposition with the defiant expression that they "did not t eat with rebels." Ay, more, — they threw our ambassadors into prison, and one of them, the noblest of Hungary's sons, they cowardly and impiously murdered. Still we hesitated to tear asunder forever the bonds that united us. Ten months we fought, and fought victoriously, in defense; and it was only *Independence declared only as a last resort* when every attempt to bring about an honorable peace failed; when Francis Joseph, who was never our king, dared, in his manifesto of the 4th of March, 1849, to utter the curse "that Hungary should exist no longer"; when there was no hope of arresting the Russian invasion by diplomacy; when we saw that we must fight to save ourselves from being struck off the earth as a nation; when the House of Austria, by its endless acts of injustice and cruelty, and by calling in the aid of a foreign power, had extinguished, in the heart of the Hungarian people, every spark of affection — then, and then only, after so much patience, the nation resolved to declare its absolute independence. Then the National Assembly spoke the words which had long been uttered by every patriotic tongue: "Francis Joseph, thou beardless young Nero! thou darest to say Hungary shall exist no more! We, the people, answer, we do and will exist; but you and your treacherous House shall stand no longer! You shall no more be kings of Hungary! Be forever banished, ye perfidious traitors to the nation!" . . .

The powers refused aid to Hungary

Oh, that Hungary had received but a slight token of moral support from the European powers, — from those powers whose dreams are troubled with fears of the advance of the Cossack. Had only an English or a French agent come to us during our struggle, what might he not have done! He too would have seen and estimated our ability to sustain ourselves; he would have observed the humanity, the love of order, the reverence for liberty, which characterized the Hungarian nation. Had these two powers permitted a few ships to come to Ossara, laden with arms for the noble patriots who had asked in vain for weapons, the Hungarians would now have stood a more impregnable barrier against Russia than all the arts of a miserable and expensive diplomacy.

There was a time when we, with the neighboring Poles, saved Christianity in Europe. And now I hesitate not to avow before God that we alone — that my own Hungary — could have saved Europe from Russian domination. As the war in Hungary advanced its character became changed. In the end the results it contemplated were higher and far more important; nothing less, in fact, than universal freedom, which was not thought of in the beginning. This was not a choice; it was forced upon us by the policy of the European nations, who, disregarding their own interests, suffered Russia to invade and provoke us. . . .

In vain fell the bravest of men in this long war; in vain were the exertions of my countrymen; in vain did the aged father send, with pious heart, his only son, the prop of his declining years, and the bride her bridegroom; in vain did all private interests yield to the loftiest patriotism; in vain arose the prayers of a suffering people; in vain did the ardent wishes of every friend of freedom accompany our efforts; in vain did the genius of liberty hope for success. My country was martyred. Her rulers are hangmen! They have spoken the impious words that the liberty-loving nation "lies at the feet of the Tsar!" Instead of the thankful prayers of faith, of hope, and of love, the air of my native land is filled with the cries of despair; and I, her chosen leader, am an exile. . . .

The heroic struggles of the Hungarians

Before you I assert that the accusation that the Magyar race was unjust to the other races — by means of which a portion of the Servians, Wallachians, Slavonians, and Germans dwelling in Hungary was excited against us — is an impious slander, circulated by the House of Hapsburg, which shrinks from no crime to weaken the united forces of our united army, to conquer one race after another, and thus bring them all under the yoke of slavery.

The Magyars not unjust to other races

It is true, some of the races in Hungary had reason to complain; but these subjects of complaint were the inevitable consequences of the preëxisting state of things and the Austrian interference. But the Croatians had no reason to complain. This race of half a million, in a separate province, had a national assembly of its own and enjoyed greater privileges than even the Hungarians. They contributed proportionally but half as much in taxes. They possessed equal rights with Hungary; whilst the Hungarian Protestants, on account of their religion, were not suffered to hold lands in Croatia. Their grievances and ours were the same, in the perpetual violation of the constitution by the imperial government. But their own peculiar grievances arose from the evils of former times, and from the

Austrian system of government, which forcibly placed the
Slavonian, Servian, and Wallachian boundary districts on the
German military footing. . . .

In America people of different languages dwell, but who says
that it is unjust for senators and representatives to use the
English language in their debates, and to make it the official
language of the government? . . .

Louis Kossuth, *Governor of Hungary*

Section 62. *Austria regains her Power in Italy*

The Austrian government was able, as we have seen,
to put down, in October, 1848, the revolt in Vienna, and
then had a free hand to reconquer its Italian provinces.
The intervention of Charles Albert was unsuccessful,
and after his final defeat at Novara, March 23, 1849,
his abdication was proclaimed in the following manner:

*Proclamation of Eugene, prince of Savoy-Carignan, lieutenant
general of his Majesty:*

232. Proclamation of Charles Albert's abdication (March 26, 1849)   I have a sad message to communicate to you. The king,
Charles Albert, after having faced with intrepidity the bullets
of the enemy, would not consent, in view of the reverses of
our armies, to bow to ill fortune. He has preferred to crown
his life by a new sacrifice. On March 23 he abdicated in
favor of the duke of Savoy. The gratitude of his people
toward him will know no end, nor our respectful attachment.
Let us rally around our new king, in battle a worthy rival of
the paternal virtues, and the stanch guardian of the constitutional liberties granted by his august father. Long live the
king, Victor Emmanuel !

Turin, March 26

Although Charles Albert failed in his attempt to free
Italy from the dominion of Austria and was compelled
to lay down his crown, he nevertheless left as a legacy to
the people of Sardinia a charter establishing constitutional

government. This is a lengthy document, but it was summed up by the king in the following preliminary statement of its leading principles. His successor, Victor Emmanuel, maintained this new constitution in the midst of the general reaction that followed, and it later became the fundamental basis for the government of united Italy.

233. The bases of the Constitutional Charter of Sardinia (1848)

We have much pleasure in declaring that, with the advice and approval of our ministers and the principal advisors of our crown, we have resolved and determined to adopt the following bases of a fundamental statute for the establishment in our States of a complete system of representative government.

ART. 1. The Catholic, apostolic, and Roman religion shall be the sole religion of the State. Other forms of public worship at present existing shall be tolerated in conformity with the law.

ART. 2. The person of the sovereign is sacred and inviolable. His ministers are responsible.

The Executive

ART. 3. The executive power is vested in the king alone. He is the supreme head of the State. He commands all the forces, both naval and military ; declares war, concludes treaties of peace, alliance, and commerce ; nominates to all offices, and gives all the necessary orders for the execution of the laws, without, however, suspending them or dispensing with the observance thereof.

ART. 4. The king alone shall sanction and promulgate the laws.

ART. 5. All justice emanates from the king, and is administered in his name. He may grant pardons and commute punishment.

The legislature

ART. 6. The legislative power shall be collectively exercised by the king and by two chambers.

ART. 7. The first of these chambers shall be composed of members nominated by the king for life ; the second shall be elective, on a basis to be determined later.

ART. 8. The proposal of laws shall be vested in the king and in each of the chambers, but with the distinct understanding that all laws imposing taxes must originate in the elective chamber.

ART. 9. The king shall convoke the two chambers annually; he may prorogue their sessions, and may dissolve the elective chamber; but in this case he shall convoke a new assembly at the expiration of four months.

ART. 10. No tax may be imposed or levied unless approved by the chambers and sanctioned by the king.

ART. 11. The press shall be free, but subject to laws for its control.

ART. 12. Individual liberty shall be guaranteed.

Section 63. Outcome of the Revolution of 1848 in Germany

The members of the Frankfort Assembly, which met in the spring of 1848, laboriously worked out a constitution, but before they had finished it, conditions became highly unfavorable to their hopes of a political regeneration of Germany. Austria once more regained its former influence, and when, a year later, the Assembly offered the imperial crown to the timid Frederick William of Prussia, he naturally declined it. He proposed, nevertheless, that Prussia should join the other German States in preparing a revision of the constitution drawn up by the deputies at Frankfort, who had been very generally discredited by the conduct of the radical and republican factions.

To my People :

Taking as a pretense the interests of Germany, the enemies of the fatherland have raised the standard of revolt, first in the neighboring Saxony, then in several districts of south Germany. To my deep chagrin, even in parts of our own land some have permitted themselves to be seduced into following this standard and attempting, in open rebellion against the legal government, to overturn the order of things established by both divine and human sanction. In so serious and dangerous a crisis I am moved publicly to address a word to my people.

I was not able to return a favorable reply to the offer of a crown on the part of the German National Assembly, because the Assembly has not the right, without the consent of the German governments, to bestow the crown which they tendered me, and, moreover, because they offered the crown upon condition that I would accept a constitution which could not be reconciled with the rights and safety of the German States.

234. The king of Prussia refuses the crown tendered him by the Frankfort Assembly (May 15, 1849)

I have exhausted every means to reach an understanding with the German National Assembly. . . . Now the Assembly has broken with Prussia. The majority of its members are no longer those men upon whom Germany looked with pride and confidence. The greater part of the deputies voluntarily left the Assembly when they saw that it was on the road to ruin, and yesterday I ordered all the Prussian deputies who had not already withdrawn to be recalled. The other governments will do the same.

A party now dominates the Assembly which is in league with the terrorists. While they urge the unity of Germany as a pretense, they are really fighting the battle of godlessness, perjury, and robbery, and kindling a war against monarchy; but if monarchy were overthrown, it would carry with it the blessings of law, liberty, and property. The horrors committed in Dresden, Breslau, and Elberfeld under the banner of German unity afford a melancholy proof of this. New horrors are occurring and are in prospect.

Conduct of the republican radicals

While such crimes have put an end to the hope that the Frankfort Assembly can bring about German unity, I have, with a fidelity and persistence suiting my royal station, never lost hope. My government has taken up with the more important German States the work on the German constitution begun by the Frankfort Assembly. . . .

This is my method. Only madness or deception will dare, in view of these facts, to assert that I have given up the cause of German unity, or that I am untrue to my earlier convictions and assurances. . . .   FREDERICK WILLIAM

CHARLOTTENBURG, May 15, 1849

The uprising in Berlin in 1848 had led to the assembly of a Prussian national convention, which set to work to draft a constitution, but was dissolved by the king before it completed its labors. The king thereupon proclaimed on his own authority a constitutional charter, which he later submitted to the revision of the two chambers for which it provided. He then solemnly swore to observe this charter; and on taking the oath, February, 1850, he gave the following explanation of his conduct to the Prussian parliament.

Gentlemen :

235. Speech of king of Prussia on taking oath to observe the new constitution (February, 1850)

I ask your attention. The words I am about to speak are entirely my own, for I appear before you to-day as I never have done before, and never shall do hereafter. I am here, not to exercise the innate and hereditary sacred duties of the royal office (which are exalted high above the opinions and wishes of parties) ; above all, not sheltered by the responsibility of my highest counselors, but as myself alone, as a man of honor, who is about to give that which is dearest to him — his word, his yea ! — firmly and deliberately. Therefore a few words by way of introduction.

The work which I am this day about to sanction took its beginning during a year which the loyalty of coming generations will wish in sorrow, but in vain, to blot from our history. In the form in which it was first submitted to you it was indeed the outcome of the devoted loyalty of men who have saved this throne, — men to whom my gratitude will only be extinguished with my life ; but it originated during a period when, in the strictest sense of the word, the very existence of the fatherland was threatened. It was the work of the moment, and bore the broad stamp of its origin.

It is a legitimate question, How can I, with this in mind, give my sanction to this work? Yet I do it because I can ; and it is, thanks to you alone, gentlemen, that I can. You have laid an improving hand upon it. You have removed objectionable points from it, and have introduced improvements in it; by your admirable labors, and by the adoption of my last proposals, you have given me a pledge that you will not, after my sanction, abandon the perfecting work already begun, so that our united, honest endeavors may succeed in rendering it, in a constitutional manner, ever more conformable to the vital requirements of Prussia. I am in a position to sanction this work because I can do it with hope. I acknowledge, with the warmest thanks to you, gentlemen, — and I say it with joyful emotion, — that you have deserved well of the fatherland. And so I declare, God being my witness, that my oath to the constitution is sincere and without reserve. But the continued existence and success of the constitution, as you and all noble hearts in our country feel, depend upon the fulfillment of essential conditions.

You, gentlemen, must help me, as well as the diets after you; the loyalty of my people must help me against those who would use the freedom thus granted by the monarch as a cloak for malice and for an attack on its originators and the authority appointed by God; you and they must help me against those who would wish to regard this document as taking the place of even God's blessed providence, of our history, and of the old sacred loyalty. All the good people of the country must unite in loyal respect for the monarchy and for this throne, which rests upon the victories of our armies, on the observance of the laws, on a faithful fulfillment of the oath of allegiance, as well as of the new oath of loyalty and obedience to the king, and on the conscientious observance of the constitution, — in a word, the condition of the constitution's continued existence is that government may be rendered possible to me under this new fundamental law; for in Prussia the king must govern; and I govern, not because it is my pleasure, God knows it, but because it is God's ordinance; therefore I am determined to continue to govern. A free people under a free king; that has been my watchword for ten years, so it is still to-day, and will so remain as long as I breathe. *The divine nature of the Prussian monarchy*

Before I proceed to the ceremony of the day I will renew before you two former pledges in view of the ten years of my government which have elapsed.

First, I repeat and confirm, solemnly and expressly, the pledges which I took before God and man at Königsberg and here. Yes, so help me God.

Secondly, I repeat and confirm, solemnly and expressly, the sacred vow which I pronounced [at the opening of the Prussian Estates General] on the 11th of April, 1847, "With my House to serve the Lord." Yes, yes, that I do, so help me God! That vow stands above all others; it must be contained in every one, and, like the pure water of life, must run through all other pledges, if they are to be of any value.

Now, moreover, as in virtue of my royal sovereignty I hereby sanction the Constitution, I vow solemnly, truly, and expressly, before God and man, to maintain the Constitution of my country and realm firmly and inviolably, and to govern in conformity with it and the laws. Yes, yes, that I will, so help me God!

And now I commit the law thus sanctioned into the hands of God Almighty, whose providence in the history of Prussia can plainly be recognized, in order that, out of this work of man, he may make an instrument for the salvation of our dear fatherland, namely, for giving effect to his holy will and decrees. So be it.

CHAPTER XXI

THE UNIFICATION OF ITALY

Section 64. Cavour and Italian Unity

When Italian patriots contemplated the unhappy state of their disunited country, governed by absolute rulers and subjected to the tutelage of Austria, they determined that some remedy must be found. On two things they were agreed: Italy must be united and a constitutional government established; but as to the methods of achieving these aims they were sadly at variance. Some believed that unity should be achieved under the leadership of the Sardinian monarchy, by diplomacy, and war if necessary. Others believed in proclaiming an Italian republic and appealing to the patriotic instincts of the people to support it. To this latter group belonged Mazzini, who founded in 1832 a society known as Young Italy, designed to achieve unity and establish a democratic government for Italy. In the following paper Mazzini set forth the ideals of his new organization.

LIBERTY — EQUALITY — HUMANITY — INDEPENDENCE — UNITY

236. Mazzini's instructions to members of Young Italy

Young Italy is a brotherhood of Italians who believe in a law of *progress* and *duty*, and are convinced that Italy is destined to become one nation, convinced also that she possesses sufficient strength within herself to become one, and that the ill success of her former efforts is to be attributed not to the weakness, but to the misdirection of the revolutionary elements within her, —

that the secret force lies in constancy and unity of effort. They join this association with the firm intention of consecrating both thought and action to the great aim of reconstituting Italy as one independent sovereign nation of free men and equals. . . .

The wish of Young Italy

The aim of the association is *revolution ;* but its labors will be essentially educational, both before and after the day of revolution ; and it therefore declares the principles upon which the national education should be conducted, and from which alone Italy may hope for safety and regeneration. . . .

Why Young Italy should aim at a republic

Young Italy is *republican* and *unitarian*,[1] — republican, because theoretically every nation is destined, by the law of God and humanity, to form a free and equal community of brothers ; and the republican government is the only form of government that insures this future : Because all true sovereignty resides essentially in the nation, the sole progressive and continuous interpreter of the supreme moral law ; . . . because the monarchical element being incapable of sustaining itself alone by the side of the popular element, it necessarily involves the existence of the intermediate element of an aristocracy, — the source of inequality and corruption to the whole nation ; because both history and the nature of things teach us that elective monarchy tends to generate anarchy, and hereditary monarchy tends to generate despotism ; because, when monarchy is not — as in the Middle Ages — based upon the belief, now extinct, in right divine, it becomes too weak to be a bond of unity and authority in the State ; because the inevitable tendency of the series of progressive transformations taking place in Europe is toward the enthronement of the republican principle, and because the inauguration of the monarchical principle in Italy would carry along with it the necessity of a new revolution shortly after.

Our Italian tradition is essentially republican ; our great memories are republican ; the whole history of our national progress is republican ; whereas the introduction of monarchy amongst us was coeval with our decay, and consummated our ruin by its constant servility to the foreigner and antagonism to the people as well as to the unity of the nation.

[1] That is, opposes a *federal* system.

While the populations of the various Italian states would cheerfully unite in the name of a principle which could give no umbrage to local ambition, they would not willingly submit to be governed by one man, — the offspring of one of those States ; and their several pretensions would necessarily tend to federalism.

If monarchy were once set up as the aim of the Italian insurrection, it would, by a logical necessity, draw along with it all the obligations of the monarchical system, concessions to foreign courts, trust in and respect for diplomacy, and the repression of that popular element, by which alone our salvation can be achieved. By intrusting the supreme authority to monarchists whose interest it would be to betray us, we should infallibly bring the insurrection to naught. . . .

Young Italy is *unitarian*, because, without unity there is no true nation ; because, without unity there is no real strength ; and Italy, surrounded as she is by powerful, united, and jealous nations, has need of strength above all things ; because federalism, by reducing her to the political impotence of Switzerland, would necessarily place her under the influence of one of the neighboring nations ; because federalism, by reviving the local rivalries now extinct, would throw Italy back upon the Middle Ages ; . . . because federalism, by destroying the unity of the great Italian family, would strike at the root of the great mission Italy is destined to accomplish for humanity ; because Europe is undergoing a progressive series of transformations, which are gradually and irresistibly guiding European society to form itself into vast and united masses ; because the entire work of internal civilization in Italy will be seen, if rightly studied, to have been tending for ages toward unity.

Young Italy is for complete unity, not federation

The means by which Young Italy proposes to reach its aim are education and insurrection, to be adopted simultaneously and made to harmonize with each other. Education must ever be directed to teach, by example, word, and pen, the necessity of insurrection. Insurrection, whenever it can be realized, must be so conducted as to render it a means of national education. Education, though of necessity secret in Italy, will be public outside of Italy. . . .

The aims of Young Italy are education and insurrection

Insurrection, by means of guerrilla bands, is the true method of warfare for all nations desirous of emancipating themselves from a foreign yoke. This method of warfare supplies the want — inevitable at the commencement of the insurrection — of a regular army ; it calls the greatest number of elements into the field, and yet may be sustained by the smallest number. It forms the military education of the people and consecrates every foot of the native soil by the memory of some warlike deed. Guerrilla warfare opens a field of activity for every local capacity, forces the enemy into an unaccustomed method of battle, avoids the evil consequences of a great defeat, secures the national war from the risk of treason, and has the advantage of not confining it within any defined and determinate basis of operations. It is invincible, indestructible. The regular army, recruited with all possible solicitude and organized with all possible care, will complete the work begun by the war of insurrection.

All the members of Young Italy will exert themselves to diffuse these principles of insurrection. The association will develop them more fully in its writings, and will explain from time to time the ideas and organization which should govern the period of insurrection.

In direct opposition to Mazzini's idealistic policy and unlimited faith in the people stood Cavour, who, though no less desirous of unity, was convinced that it could only come through diplomacy and the extension of the authority of the Sardinian king. Cavour was for a time uncertain amidst the confusion that existed among the reformers, but at last he fixed upon a definite programme and followed it consistently to the end. As early as 1833 he had settled down into a cautious yet firm liberal policy, as he explains in a letter to a friend.

As for myself, I have long been undecided in the midst of these conflicting movements. Reason inclines me toward moderation ; an immoderate desire to make the conservatives move impels me toward action ; finally, after numberless and violent agitations and oscillations, I have ended like the pendulum by fixing myself at the golden mean. However, I assure you that I am an honest Moderate, desiring, hoping, and laboring for social progress with all the forces at my command, but determined not to purchase it at the cost of a general political and social revolution. My state of moderation, however, will not hinder me from desiring; as soon as possible, the emancipation of Italy from the barbarians who oppress her, and consequently from foreseeing that a crisis is inevitable, however slight may be the violence which accompanies it ; but I wish that crisis to be accompanied by all the precautions which are consistent with the circumstances ; and I am, moreover, thoroughly persuaded that the mad attempts on the part of the men of the movement will only hinder it and render the outcome more doubtful. After you have read my confession of faith permit me to ask whether it conforms to your point of view. . . .

Despite Cavour's early determination to free Italy from the "barbarians," the real situation was most discouraging, for there seemed to be no way of arousing Italy to the supreme effort. Nevertheless he was not disheartened, and when many of his compatriots were in exile for their hostile demonstrations against the existing Italian governments or had fled in disgust from their native land, he refused to give up hope. In 1835, when the realization of his ideal seemed entirely out of the question, he refused to be allured to Paris, and in a letter to a lady announced his determination to remain in the land of his birth, and labor there for the welfare of Italy.

238. Cavour's letter to Countess de Circourt, refusing an invitation to reside in Paris

No, madame, I cannot leave my family or my country. Sacred obligations prevent that, and hold me near a father and a mother who have never given me the least occasion for complaint. No, madame, I will not plunge a poniard into the bosom of my parents ; I will never be an ingrate toward them,

I will only leave them when the tomb separates us. And why, madame, should I abandon my country, in order to go to Paris to seek a reputation in letters, in order to run after a little renown, a little glory, without ever being able to attain the object of my ambition? What good can I do for humanity outside of my own country? What influence can I exert in favor of my unhappy brethren, among strangers and exiles, in a country where selfishness occupies all of the principal social positions? What do they accomplish at Paris, all that crowd of foreigners whom misfortunes or inclinations have carried far away from their native land? Who among them is rendered really useful to his kind? Who among them has been able to make a great career, to win an influence in society? Not one. Those who would be great in the land that nourished them vegetate obscurely in the midst of the vortex of Parisian life.

The poor achievements of men who have left Italy   The political troubles which have desolated Italy have forced her noblest sons to flee from her. The most distinguished men of my country have left it, and most of these noble exiles have gone to Paris. Not one of them has realized the brilliant hopes which he had conceived. All those whom I have known personally have been grieved to the depths of their hearts by the spectacle of great talents left sterile and powerless. A single Italian has made a name in Paris, and gained a position there : this is the criminal lawyer, Rossi. But such a place ! such a position ! The cleverest man in Italy, the most versatile genius of the period, the most practical spirit in the world, perhaps, has succeeded in obtaining a chair in the Sorbonne and another at the Academy, the highest goal to which his ambition was able to attain in France. This man, who has abjured his country, who will never again be anything to us, would have been able in a more or less distant future to play a tremendous rôle in shaping the destinies of his country, and would have aspired to guide his compatriots along the new paths which civilization opens every day, in place of having to teach intractable pupils.

Italy is to have Cavour's life   No, no, it is not in escaping one's country because it is wretched that one attains a glorious end. Woe to him who abandons with scorn the land that has given him birth, who disowns his brothers as unworthy of him! As for me, I am determined never to separate my fate from that of the Piedmontese. Happy or unhappy, my country shall have my whole life; I will never be disloyal, even though I were certain to find elsewhere a brilliant future.

But leaving aside the question of duty, forgetting my qualities of a citizen and a son, let us see what I should gain by leaving Italy for a future in France. What would I do in France? How should I find a reputation and fame? The only means within reach would be literature. Now, madame, I confess to you frankly that I do not feel any literary genius; my head is practical and not imaginative. I would seek in vain to develop in myself the faculty of imagination; I possess no germ of it. I have never in my life succeeded in inventing the most trifling tale, the slightest story, to amuse a child. In spite of all the efforts I might make, I should never be more than a mediocre littérateur,— a man of letters of the third rank. Now, madame, here is a prospect which does not fascinate me. In point of art I can conceive of but one tenable position, namely, the first order.

Cavour not attracted by letters or science

But if literature could not be my refuge, would there not be for me all the vast domain of science? It is true, I could become a *savant*, a profound mathematician, a great physician, indeed even a distinguished chemist. I could make a name in the academies of Europe and win a reputation in the world of scholars. One way of obtaining glory is as good as another; only there is little attraction in it for the Italian with a rosy complexion and the smile of a child. . . .

The Revolution of 1848 at last afforded Cavour the opportunity he had so ardently desired; it gave to Sardinia a constitutional government and offered him a career as political leader. In 1852 he became head of the ministry and set about the work which he had long pondered upon. He knew that Italy could not be united until Austria was driven out, and that the aid of some foreign power was necessary to the accomplishment of this design. Accordingly he brought Sardinia prominently to the front in European affairs by joining England and France in the war against Russia, and at the 'conference at Paris in 1856, which closed the Crimean War, Cavour brought the condition of Italy vividly to the attention of Napoleon III. The French emperor was not averse to winning fame by a successful conflict, and in 1859 he joined Sardinia in a war against Austria, announcing his motives in the following proclamation of May 3, 1859.

239. Napoleon III justifies his intervention in Italy

Frenchmen, Austria in ordering her army to invade the territory of the king of Sardinia, our ally, has declared war upon us. She has thus violated treaties and justice and threatens our frontiers. All the great powers have protested against this aggression.

Piedmont having accepted conditions which should have maintained peace, one cannot but inquire what can be the reason for this sudden invasion on Austria's part. It is because Austria has brought matters to such a pass that either she must dominate as far as the Cottian Alps, or Italy must be freed to the Adriatic ; for every corner of territory which remains independent in that whole region is a menace to her authority.

Hitherto moderation has been the rule of my conduct ; now an aggressive policy becomes my duty. Let France arm herself and say to Europe with determination : " We do not wish for conquest, but we are resolved to maintain without flinching our national and traditional policy ; we observe treaties on condition that they shall not be violated to our disadvantage ; we respect the territory and the rights of neutral powers, but openly avow our sympathy for a people whose history is bound up with ours, and who groan under foreign oppression."

France has shown her hatred of anarchy ; she has been pleased to give me an authority strong enough to render powerless the abettors of disorder and the incorrigible members of former factions who have not hesitated to form alliances with our enemies ; but she has not, on that account, abandoned her function as a civilizing power. Her natural allies have always been those who desire the improvement of humanity, and when she draws her sword it is not in order to domineer, but to liberate.

The purpose of this war is, then, to restore Italy to herself, not simply to change her master; and we shall have upon our frontiers a friendly people who will owe their independence to us. We are not going into Italy to foment disorder, nor to disturb the authority of the Holy Father, whom we have replaced upon his throne, but to protect him against that foreign oppression which weighs upon the whole peninsula, and to participate in establishing order there which shall satisfy all legitimate interests. We are, in short, about to enter that classic land rendered illustrious by so many victories. We shall find there traces of our forefathers, of whom God grant we may prove ourselves worthy. . . .

NAPOLEON

PALACE OF THE TUILERIES, May 3, 1859

Although Napoleon III abruptly withdrew from the war and left Austria in the possession of Venetia, he had given an impetus to Italian movement toward unity which could not be checked. Modena, Parma, and the Romagna — a portion of the Papal States — voted to join Sardinia and accept the Sardinian king as their common sovereign. On the outbreak of the war the people of Tuscany had forced their grand duke to leave his realm, and a provisional government had been formed. A representative assembly was convoked, and in September, 1859, the final acceptance of the sovereignty of Victor Emmanuel was announced as follows:

240. The Tuscan proclamation declaring Victor Emmanuel king

FLORENCE, September 29, 1859

Tuscans:

The Assembly of your lawful representatives has declared it to be the firm desire of Tuscany to form a part of a strong constitutional kingdom under the scepter of King Victor

Emmanuel of the House of Savoy. The Assemblies of Modena, Parma, and the Romagna have unanimously issued similar declarations. The king-elect has accepted the free act of subjection on the part of the people of Tuscany, Modena, Parma, and the Romagna, and has declared that the first act of his sovereignty should be formally to sanction the rights which had been conferred on him by those peoples.

The people act for themselves These acts of the several peoples and of the king-elect constitute the strongest and most legitimate bond that can unite the ruler and the subject. This bond has been formed by justice, — for it is not by force that thrones are established, but by the just national will, — and the peoples who were abandoned by the bad governments of foreigners, or of those friendly to foreigners, have therefore felt the necessity and the right of providing for themselves by securing the independence of the nation.

The Tuscans have fought for national emancipation The war undertaken by Napoleon and Victor Emmanuel was a solemn recognition of that right, since it was undertaken to liberate Italy from Austrian dominion and to constitute Italian nationality. All Italians were called on to profit by the great occasion, and the people of central Italy flew to arms. The Tuscans had the double honor of fighting under the glorious Italian banner and under the invincible eagles of the French empire. This coöperation in a war not of conquest but of national emancipation authorized the formation of a new kingdom of Italy, which the other European States may recognize, but to which they cannot give legitimacy. The latter is the result of the spontaneous consent of the peoples electing and of the king-elect. For them the compact is complete and irrevocable; a strong kingdom is a thing established; the king-elect is their king.

But if the present government is to govern for his Majesty until the king-elect assumes personal rule over the Tuscans, it should also glory in and strengthen itself under his august name. In this way the new settlement of the Italian nation will proceed with security, every obstacle will gradually disappear, and Europe will be indebted for its tranquillity and its true equilibrium to the union and firmness of the Italians.

Tuscans! Your government proclaims that it will for the future exercise its power in the name of his Majesty Victor Emmanuel of Savoy, the king-elect.

Given at FLORENCE, the 29th of September, in the year 1859

In order to give popular sanction to all of the annexations made as a result of the Austrian war, the people of each province were called upon to vote on the question, in March, 1860. The majority in favor of unification was of course overwhelming, and on April 2, 1860, an Italian parliament was opened at Turin, composed of representatives from the provinces so united. In his opening address Victor Emmanuel reviewed the achievements of the past year.

The last time that I opened this parliament, in the midst of the travails of Italy and dangers to the State, faith in divine justice encouraged me to prophesy a happy issue for us. In a very short space of time an invasion has been repelled; Lombardy has been freed, thanks to the glorious exploits of our heroes, and central Italy has been delivered, thanks to the remarkable courage of its inhabitants; and to-day the representatives of right and of the hopes of the nation are assembled about me. 241. Victor Emmanuel reviews the events of 1859–1860

We owe many benefits to a magnanimous ally, to the bravery of his soldiers as well as of ours, to the self-abnegation of the volunteers, and to the harmony of the various peoples; and we render thanks to God, for without superhuman aid these enterprises, memorable not only for our own generation but for ages to come, could not have been achieved.

Out of gratitude to France for the services she has rendered to Italy, and in order to consolidate the union of the two nations, which have a community of origin, of principles, and of destiny, some sacrifice was necessary; I have made that one which costs most to my own heart. Subject to the vote of the people and the approbation of the parliament, . . . I have agreed to a treaty providing for the reunion of Savoy and of the district of Nice to France. Cession of Savoy and Nice to France

We still have many difficulties to overcome, but, sustained by public opinion and by the love of the people, I will not permit any right or liberty to be infringed or diminished.

Victor
Emmanuel's
attitude
toward the
Church

Although I am as consistent in my respect toward the supreme head of our religion as the Catholic rulers, my ancestors, have always shown themselves, nevertheless, should the ecclesiastical authority resort to spiritual arms in support of its temporal interests, I will, relying upon a pure conscience and the traditions of my forefathers, find strength to maintain civil liberty and my authority, for the exercise of which I owe an account only to God and to my people. . . .

In spite of the great advance toward unity made before the opening of the parliament at Turin, it was clear that the Italians were not yet satisfied. During the Austrian war the subjects of the king of Naples showed that they were discontented with their ruler and their isolated position. Taking advantage of this discontent, and undoubtedly with the approval of Sardinia, Garibaldi, with about a thousand volunteers, landed in Sicily in May, 1860, and in a short time had possession of the island. He then went over to the mainland and soon completed what he called the "annihilation of Bourbonism in the Two Sicilies." The spirit of Garibaldi is clearly seen in his own account, here much condensed, of his departure for Sicily with his thousand warriors, and of his capture of Naples.

242. Garibaldi describes his Sicilian expedition and the capture of Naples (from his *Memoirs*)

Once more, Sicily, it was thine to awaken sleepers, to drag them from the lethargy in which the stupefying poison of diplomatists and doctrinaires had sunk them, — slumberers who, clad in armor not their own, confided to others the safety of their country, thus keeping her dependent and degraded.

Austria is powerful, her armies are numerous ; several formidable neighbors are opposed, on account of petty dynastic aims, to the resurrection of Italy. The Bourbon [1] has one hundred

---

[1] I.e. the king of Naples.

thousand soldiers. Yet what matter? The hearts of twenty-five millions throb and tremble with the love of their country. . . .

O noble Thousand! In these days of shame and misery I love to remember you. Turning to you, the mind feels itself rise above this mephitic atmosphere of robbery and intrigue, relieved to remember that, though the majority of your gallant band have scattered their bones over the battlefields of liberty, there yet remain enough to represent you, ever ready to prove to your insolent detractors that all are not traitors and cowards — all are not shameless self-seekers, in this land of tyrants and slaves!

Yet sail on, sail on fearlessly, " Piemonte " and " Lombardo," — noble vessels, manned by the noblest of crews. History will remember your illustrious names in spite of calumny. Sail on, sail on; ye bear the Thousand who in later days will become a million, — in that day when the blindfolded masses shall understand that the priest is an impostor and tyrannies a monstrous anachronism. How glorious were thy Thousand, O Italy, fighting against the plumed and gilded agents of despotism and driving them before them like sheep! glorious in their motley array, just as they came from their offices and workshops at the trumpet call of duty, in the student's coat and hat or the modest garb of the mason, carpenter, or smith. . . . *(Garibaldi's dislike of Church and monarchy)*

After their successful operations in Sicily, Garibaldi led his troops to the mainland.

The first of October dawned on the plains of the ancient capital of Campagna upon a hideous tumult, a fratricidal conflict. On the side of the Bourbons, it is true, foreign mercenaries were numerous, — Bavarians, Swiss, and others belonging to the nations who for centuries had been accustomed to look upon this Italy of ours as their pleasure ground. This crew, under the guidance and with the blessings of the priest, have always been accustomed, by sheer right of the strongest, to cut the throats of the Italians, trained from childhood by the priest to bow the knee to them. But it is only too certain that the greater number of the men who fought on the slopes of *(Victory over the Bourbons)*

Tifata were sons of this unhappy country driven to butcher one another, — one side led by a young king, the child of crime, the other fighting for the sacred cause of their country. . . .

The enemy, after an obstinate combat, were routed all along the line and retired in disorder within the walls of Capua about five P.M., their retreat being covered by the guns of that fortress. About the same time Bixio announced to me the victory of his right wing over the Bourbon troops, so that I was able to telegraph to Naples, " Victory all along the line."

[The next day] the Bourbon troops, taken unawares, offered but little resistance and were driven back almost at a run, hotly pursued by the brave Calabrians as far as Caserta Vecchia. A few of them held this village for a short time, firing from the windows and from behind the cover afforded by some ruined walls; but these were quickly surrounded and made prisoners. . . .

The Sardinian government sends an army to check Garibaldi

With the victory of Caserta Vecchia, October 2, the glorious period of our campaign of 1860 closes. The Italian army of the north, sent by Farini and Company to combat the " revolution personified " in us, found us brothers; and to this army fell the task of completing the annihilation of Bourbonism in the Two Sicilies. In order to regulate the position of our gallant fellow-soldiers, I asked for the recognition of the army of the south as a part of the national army; and it was a piece of injustice not to grant my request. They resolved to enjoy the fruits of conquest while banishing the conquerors.

Magnanimous retirement of Garibaldi

When I understood that this was the case, I handed over to Victor Emmanuel the dictatorship conferred upon me by the people, and proclaimed him King of Italy. To him I recommended my gallant comrades, the thought of whom was the only painful element of my departure, eager as I was to return to my solitude.

On the 18th of February, 1861, the new Italian parliament met at Turin in a large hall temporarily built of wood. King Victor Emmanuel opened proceedings with the following address, in which he alludes to the recent important events.

Senators and Deputies:

Free and almost entirely united by the wonderful aid of Divine Providence, the harmonious coöperation of the people, and the splendid valor of the army, Italy confides in our uprightness and wisdom. Upon you it devolves to give her uniform institutions and a firm foundation. In extending greater administrative liberty to peoples that have had various usages and institutions, you will take care that political unity, the aspiration of so many centuries, may never be diminished.

The opinion of civilized nations is favorable to us. The just and liberal principles now prevailing in the councils of Europe are favorable to us. Italy herself will in turn become a guarantee of order and peace, and will once more be an efficient instrument of universal civilization.

The emperor of the French, firmly upholding the maxim of nonintervention, — a maxim eminently beneficial to us, — nevertheless deemed it proper to recall his envoy. If this fact was a cause of chagrin to us, it did not change our sentiments of gratitude toward him or diminish our confidence in his affection for the Italian cause. France and Italy, with their common origin, traditions, and customs, formed on the plains of Magenta and Solferino a bond that will prove indissoluble.

The government and people of England, that ancient country of freedom, warmly sanction our right to be the arbiters of our own destinies; and they have lavishly bestowed upon us their good offices, the grateful remembrances of which will be imperishable.

A loyal and illustrious prince having ascended the throne of Prussia, I dispatched to him an ambassador in token of respect for him personally and of sympathy with the noble German nation, which I hope will become more and more secure in the conviction that Italy, being established in her natural unity, cannot impair the rights or interests of other nations. . . .

Valiant youths, led on by a captain who has filled with his name the most distant countries, have made it evident that neither servitude nor long misfortune has been able to weaken the fiber of the Italian peoples. These facts have inspired

243. Victor Emmanuel's address at the opening session of the Italian parliament (February 18, 1861)

Accession of William as king of Prussia

Appreciative allusion to Garibaldi's band

the nation with great confidence in its own destinies. I take pleasure in manifesting to the first parliament of Italy the joy that fills my heart as king and soldier.

The first measure proposed was a bill declaring Victor Emmanuel king of Italy; this passed almost unanimously, there being only two votes in the negative. Against this act the papal government protested.

244. Pope Pius IX's attitude toward the unification of Italy

A Catholic king, forgetful of every religious principle, despising every right, trampling upon every law, after having, little by little, despoiled the august head of the Catholic Church of the greatest and most flourishing portion of his legitimate possessions, has now taken to himself the title of King of Italy; with which title he has sought to seal the sacrilegious usurpations already consummated, — usurpations which his government has already manifested its intention of completing to the detriment of the patrimony of the apostolic see. Although the Holy Father has solemnly protested against the successive attacks made upon his sovereignty, he is nevertheless under the obligation of issuing a fresh protest against the assumption of a title tending to legitimize the iniquity of so many deeds.

It would here be superfluous to recall the sacred character of the possessions of the Church's patrimony and the right of the supreme pontiff to it, — an incontestable right, recognized at all times and by all governments. Therefore the Holy Father will never be able to recognize the title of King of Italy, arrogated to himself by the king of Sardinia, since it is opposed to justice and to the sacred property of the Church. On the contrary, he makes the most ample and formal protest against such an usurpation.

A few words uttered a short time after by the prime minister of Italy, Baron Ricasoli, showed that the Pope's apprehensions were by no means ill-founded. During a debate in the parliament, Ricasoli, after repudiating the idea that Italy would ever surrender an inch of Italian land, said:

But the king's government sees a territory to defend and a territory to recover. It sees Rome ; it sees Venice ! To the Eternal City and to the Queen of the Adriatic it directs the thoughts, the hopes, and the energies of the nation. The government feels the heavy task that lies before it ; with God's help it will fulfill it. Opportunity matured by time will open our way to Venice. In the meantime we think of Rome.

245. The Italian government looks forward to winning both Venice and Rome

Yes, we will go to Rome. Shall Rome, politically severed from the rest of Italy, continue to be the center of intrigue and conspiracy, a permanent threat to public order? To go to Rome is for the Italians not merely a right ; it is an inexorable necessity. The king's government will be frank and clear upon this matter, even more than upon any other subject. We do not wish to go to Rome through insurrectional movements, — unreasonable, rash, mad attempts, — which may endanger our former acquisitions and ruin the national enterprise. We will go to Rome hand in hand with France !

Section 65. The Kingdom of Italy since 1861

The opportunity of securing Venetia was offered by the war between Prussia and Austria in 1866, in which the new kingdom of Italy joined, securing as a reward the possession of the long-coveted territory through the mediation of Napoleon III. The Pope was able to hold Rome only with the aid of the French garrison there, and this Napoleon was compelled to withdraw on account of the war with Prussia in 1870. Shortly after the battle of Sedan the Italian army entered papal territory, and on September 20 the city of Rome was taken without a serious battle. The representative of the British government in Italy dispatched to London a brief narrative of the event.

246. The English ambassador's account of the taking of Rome

FLORENCE, September 22, 1870

All efforts at a pacific arrangement with the commander of the papal troops having failed, orders were sent to General Cadorna on the 19th instant to take possession of Rome by force; and accordingly, at 5 o'clock on the morning of the 20th instant, a cannonade was opened, two breaches were effected at half past 8, and at 10 o'clock the Italian troops entered the city between the Porta Pia and Porta Salara. The white flag was then hoisted by command of the Pope, hostilities ceased, and a capitulation was signed between General Kanzler, commander of the papal troops, and General Cadorna. There was no fighting in the streets. According to the terms of the capitulation, the papal forces had to lay down their arms. They are, or will be, sent to Civita Vecchia, — the natives to form a depot without arms, while the foreigners having no means to defray their expenses will be sent back to their own countries.

Slight resistance offered

On the special demand of the Pope, transmitted through General Kanzler, General Cadorna has furnished two battalions for the purpose of maintaining order in the Leonine City. Castel St. Angelo was occupied for strategical reasons after the assault. The loss on the Italian side amounts to somewhat over one hundred in killed and wounded. A proof that the Pope ordered the defense, and that it was not, as erroneously asserted, the military element which was master of the situation and imposed its will on his Holiness, is that, as stated above, it was on the Pope's order that the firing ceased from the town, and that the garrison surrendered. . . .

I am informed that, since the entry of the troops, some of the foreign representatives in Rome have expressed to the Italian general their satisfaction at the conduct and bearing of the soldiers, as well as with the measures which have been taken for the preservation of order. The reception of the Italian army is described as having been enthusiastic.

A republican uprising

The occupation was scarcely effected when the party of action, Mazzinists, etc., commenced their usual operations. They were speedily put down, and several arrests were made; but many more will still have to be made before the cause of order will be secured.

A vote on the annexation

A plebiscite is to take place in the Roman Provinces on the 2d of October; whether it can take place on the same day in Rome itself must depend upon the condition of the city at that time. . . . The great object of the government now is to reassure the Pope and Europe as to their intentions; and General La Marmora's appointment is the best guarantee which could be given in this respect.

The news of the entry into Rome has been received through-out Italy with the utmost enthusiasm. In every town the streets have been hung with flags; there have been processions, bands of music, shoutings, illuminations, and, not the least remarkable of these demonstrations, considering their occasion, the bells of all the cathedrals and churches have been ringing out merry peals in honor of the deathblow inflicted upon the temporal power of the Holy Father. General rejoicing over the entry into Rome

The cry now is to transfer the capitol to Rome at once; and the 15th of October is spoken of by the press as the day when the Chamber is to meet to vote upon this subject. I doubt, however, if any decision in this sense has been taken by the government. Many things have to be arranged before the Chamber can be consulted on this subject; and, amongst them, communications with the Catholic powers would appear to be a necessary preliminary step. The demand for the trans-ference of the capitol from Florence to Rome

To judge by the general tone of public opinion, one might suppose that with the acquisition of Rome all the difficulties of the Roman question had been solved; but there is room for very grave doubts on this subject, and those who reflect cannot but foresee that the establishment, in one and the same city, of a constitutional and excommunicated king by the side of an infallible Pope, of a representative parliament by the side of an absolute authority, of a liberty of the press and freedom of discussion by the side of the Inquisition, — without mentioning other anomalies, — is giving a legal sanction to a state of things which can hardly be expected to work harmoni-ously, or, indeed, without creating very serious embarrassment, confusion, and misunderstandings. What has been gained by the occupation of Rome by Italy is, that the temporal power has at last and forever come to an end; and upon this result not only Italy but the world in general, including the Pope himself, may well be congratulated. But having attained this result, I believe that there are many serious men — in fact, at Possible troubles ahead one time there was certainly the majority of the Moderate party in this country — who would be in favor of pausing here, of maintaining the capital of Italy where it now is,[1] and leaving Rome as the exclusive residence of the Pope.

I am bound, however, to add my belief that, when it comes to a vote in the Chamber, there will be very few who will venture to go counter to what is the general feeling of the masses on this subject. But in any case, supposing the transfer of the capital were to be voted to-morrow, I do not see how it will be practically possible to carry it into effect for some little time to come.

I have, etc.,

EARL GRANVILLE   A. PAGET

In his address at the opening of the first parliament after the achievement of unity, Victor Emmanuel rejoiced with the senators and deputies in the completion of the work which had so long occupied the best efforts of the Italian people, and then foreshadowed the new issues which were to come before the nation.

Senators and Deputies, gentlemen :

247. The address of Victor Emmanuel to the new Italian parliament (1871)

The work to which we consecrated our life is accomplished. After long trials of expiation Italy is restored to herself and to Rome. Here, where our people, after centuries of separation, find themselves for the first time solemnly reunited in the person of their representatives ; here where we recognize the fatherland of our dreams, everything speaks to us of greatness ; but at the same time it all reminds us of our duties. The joy that we experience must not let us forget them. . . .

The Church-State question

We have proclaimed the separation of Church and State. Having recognized the absolute independence of the spiritual authority, we are convinced that Rome, the capital of Italy, will continue to be the peaceful and respected seat of the Pontificate. In this way we shall succeed in reassuring the consciences of men. It is thus, by the firmness of our resolutions, and by the moderation of our acts, that we have been

---

[1] The capital had been transferred from Turin to Florence.

able to hasten the national unity without altering our amicable relations with foreign powers. . . .

Economic and financial affairs, moreover, claim our most careful attention. Now that Italy is established, it is necessary to make it prosperous by putting in order its finances ; we shall succeed in this only by persevering in the virtues which have been the source of our national regeneration. Good finances will be the means of reënforcing our military organization. Our most ardent desire is for peace, and nothing can make us believe that it can be troubled. But the organization of the army and the navy, the supply of arms, the works for the defense of the national territory, demand long and profound study. The future will demand a severe accounting for any negligence on our part. You will examine the measures which will be presented to you to this end by my government. . . . Economic and financial problems

Senators and deputies, a vast range of activity opens before you ; the national unity which is to-day attained will have, I hope, the effect of rendering less bitter the struggles of parties, the rivalry of which will have henceforth no other end than the development of the productive forces of the nation.

I rejoice to see that our population already gives unequivocal proofs of its love of work. The economic awakening is closely associated with the political awakening. The banks multiply, as do the commercial institutions, the expositions of the products of art and industry, and the congresses of the learned. We ought, you and I, to favor this productive movement while giving to professional and scientific education more attention and efficiency, and opening to commerce new avenues of communication and new outlets. Commercial advance

The tunnel of Mont Cenis is completed ; we are on the point of undertaking that of the St. Gotthard. The commercial route, which, crossing Italy, terminates at Brindisi and brings Europe near to India, will thus have three ways open to railway traffic across the Alps. The rapidity of the journeys, the facility of exchanges, will increase the amicable relations which already unite us to other nations, and will make more productive than ever the legitimate competition of labor and the national rivalry in advancing civilization.

A brilliant future opens before us. It remains for us to respond to the blessings of Providence by showing ourselves
worthy of bearing among the nations the glorious names of
Italy and Rome.

Pius IX very reasonably regarded the forcible seizure
of Rome as a violent and unwarranted usurpation of his
rights and authority. He accordingly refused to recognize the legitimacy of the newly established political
system and protested vigorously against the "imprisonment" which he was forced to endure at the hands of
the government.

248. The encyclical of Pius IX to all patriarchs, archbishops, etc., protesting against the conduct of the Italian government (May, 1871)   . . . We deem it an obligation imposed upon us by our Holy
Apostolic office solemnly to declare through you to the entire
world that not merely the so-called "guarantees,"[1] perversely fab-
ricated through the machinations of the Sub-alpine government,
but all the titles, honors, immunities, and privileges of whatever
nature which may be included under the name of securities or
"guarantees" can in no way suffice to maintain the free and
unrestricted exercise of the powers which God has granted
us and preserve the freedom which is essential to the Church.

We, therefore, in accordance with the duty which our office
imposes upon us, do once more declare — as we have repeatedly declared and made known — that we cannot, without
violating our most sacred pledges, agree to any form of reconciliation that shall in any degree destroy or diminish our rights,
which are at the same time the rights of God and of the Apostolic See. We can, accordingly, never in any manner acknowledge or accept those securities or "guarantees" devised by
the Sub-alpine government, however they may be stated, nor
any others, no matter how sanctioned, which may be offered us
under the false pretense that they will serve as a protection
for our sacred authority and our independence, and will take
the place of, and compensate us for, our temporal dominion
with which it has pleased Divine Providence to fortify and
strengthen the Holy See, — a dominion to which our right is

[1] See *The Development of Modern Europe*, Vol. II, p. 101.

confirmed by an uninterrupted series of valid legal titles as well as by eleven hundred years and more of possession.

For it must be clearly evident to all that the Roman Pontiff, if he be subjected to the dominion of another prince and is no longer actually in possession of sovereign power himself, cannot escape (whether in respect to his personal conduct or the acts of his apostolic office) from the will of the ruler to whom he is subordinated, who may prove to be a heretic, a persecutor of the Church, or be involved in war with other princes. Indeed, is not this very concession of guarantees in itself a clear instance of the imposition of laws upon us, — upon us on whom God has bestowed authority to make laws relating to the moral and religious order, — on us who have been designated the expounder of natural and divine law throughout the world? And do not these laws imposed upon us by the secular government affect the entire Church, and yet under the present circumstances their enforcement depends entirely upon the will of this secular power. *The result of the subordination of the Pope to a secular power*

Touching the relation of the Church and civil society, venerable brethren, you are well aware that we have received, through the person of St. Peter, directly from God himself all the powers and authority necessary for the government of the entire Church ; nay more, that these prerogatives and rights, as well as the freedom of the Church, were won and redeemed by the blood of Jesus Christ and are to be cherished and revered in proportion to the infinite preciousness of that divine blood. Of this we should render ourselves unworthy should we consent to accept from princes of this world these our rights, diminished and dishonored in the form they are tendered us. For Christian princes are sons, not rulers, of the Church. . . . *Dishonor in surrender*

God grant that the princes of the earth (who are vitally interested in taking measures to prevent such an act of usurpation as that from which we now suffer, from being perpetrated, to the destruction of all law and order) may combine with unanimous wills and hearts and endeavor to allay the dissensions and disorder to which rebellion has given rise, and put an end to the fatal machinations of faction in order that the Holy See may be restored to its rights, the visible head of the *An appeal to the Catholic powers*

Church once more enjoy his complete freedom, and civil society again rejoice in the peace for which it has so long yearned.

The most important problems in Italy to-day are economic in their nature and relate principally to emigration, taxation, and poverty. The intimate connection of all these questions is admirably shown by an Italian writer in an article dealing principally with emigration, but including also the problems of poverty and taxation.

249. A review of the economic situation in Italy, 1906 (condensed)

The official Bulletin on Emigration establishes the fact that during the year 1904 the number of emigrants was about 506,731. In 1903 it was 507,976; in 1902, 531,509; in 1901, 533,245; in 1900, 352,782. This exodus does not represent a total loss of population, because a considerable number of emigrants do not leave the country for good; a part of them — more than half — return. The general emigration commission of Italy has accurately distinguished two separate categories of emigrants, — those who belong to the permanent type and those who belong to the temporary. The proportion existing between the two categories is, according to official figures, about 45 per cent for the permanent emigration and 55 per cent for the temporary. Temporary emigration is that which is directed principally toward the other European countries, and is composed largely of agriculturists, masons, and laborers going to foreign places periodically to do work of short duration. The temporary emigration is also directed to countries across the sea, especially to South America, and in this case it is almost exclusively composed of peasants engaged for agricultural work. These peasants leave their fields during the winter, reaching the Argentine Republic in springtime, remaining there for three months, and returning then to their own homes where their labor is once more required.

In rough figures there is an average of 2000 emigrants annually per 100,000 inhabitants in southern Italy, or two per cent. These figures would naturally alarm us if the excess of births over deaths did not make up the loss, at least in most of the provinces of the south. This excess was 1114 per 100,000 in 1902 for the entire peninsula, while the average immigration for the same year was 907 per 100,000. It is also true, however, that the average loss of population in the south reaches almost double the excess of births for the whole of Italy. Nearly all of the southern emigrants who go without any intention of returning to Italy, at least in the near future, belong to the peasant class. Statistics show, in fact, that the peasants represent about 80 per cent of the permanent emigration.

Nevertheless, in spite of this astounding rate of emigration, the increase in population has not only been constant since 1871, but has surpassed for some years the average annual increase of the other states of continental Europe which are the most prolific. The density of the population in Italy at present is about 115 inhabitants to the square kilometer, whilst it was but 99.28 in 1881. In France the density is about 73; in Germany, 104; in Austria, 87. To maintain this enormous and constantly increasing population, it would be necessary for the wealth of the country to increase in the same proportion and at the same rate. But this does not happen. The wealth of Italy does not keep pace with the increase of the population; and the nourishing earth, becoming powerless, sends forth her people to the four corners of the world.

According to statistics, the following is, approximately, the wealth per inhabitant in 1900 in the different European countries : **Wealth per inhabitant**

England	6600 francs
France	5560 "
Germany	2840 "
Austria-Hungary	1960 "
Italy	1600 "

Applying the same calculation to the sum total of wages apportioned among families of five persons living by their own work, it can be estimated that a family of five persons would earn annually, on the average, as follows : **Family incomes**

England	3310 francs
France	3415 "
Germany	2700 "
Austria	1250 "
Italy	835 "

Population
increases
more rapidly
than wealth

The total wealth of Italy, valued in francs at forty-six thousand millions in 1880, rose to fifty-two thousand millions in 1900; but this increase loses all importance if it is placed beside the increase in population, which was about four million inhabitants during the same period, — a large increase in spite of the already considerable exodus of emigrants.

No one will question the economic advance of Italy, I least of all. However, I am obliged to state that the supply of workmen in this country still exceeds the limit of the demand, that is to say, the power of absorption of available capital. This fact is the more evident since the agricultural development is not far behind the progress of industrial capitalism. In the north where industry is implanted in the midst of the fields, the question has been settled; the peasants go elsewhere to supplement their wages, and then return. But in the south the problem assumes a gravity quite different, for the lack of capital has prevented, up to the present time, a rational transformation, and on a sufficiently vast scale, of the methods of agricultural exploitation.

Contrast between northern and southern Italy

To the south of Tuscany there commences a new world, the southlands of Italy, under conditions of sadness and misery. The Roman Campagna with the Pontine Marshes and the Maremmes, which unite them geographically, constitute the first evidence, — how eloquent, alas! — of the profound differences which mark the two portions of Italy. In one there is a feverish activity, a prosperity that time and labor will undoubtedly assure; in the other there is veritable desolation. A first characteristic of the southlands from the point of view of agriculture is the immense extent of marshy land or land imperfectly cultivated. The great landed property dominates there; and, except in Apulia, is almost everywhere devoid of the necessary farming equipment. The untilled lands in Italy extend over a surface of 3,774,000 hectares. They are divided into 2,500,000 hectares of dry land, and 1,274,000 hectares of swampy land, and nine tenths of this waste area belongs to southern Italy, where untilled lands cover one fifth of the territory.

In spite of this, or rather because of these extremely distressing conditions in the south, taxation, oppressive in the north, literally exhausts agriculture in the south. The Italian land tax is, on the average, about 6.48 francs per hectare. It is about 3.41 francs in the Netherlands; 3.17 in France; 1.51 in Austria; 1.39 in Prussia; and 0.89 in England. If, on the other hand, one considers, instead of the tax on land, the tax on incomes, one finds that it rises to 11 per cent in France; in Prussia to 15 per cent; in Belgium to 18 per cent; in England to 22 per cent; in Italy to 24 per cent. Italy is only surpassed by Austria, where the tax on landed income is about 30 per cent. Unfortunately this lower rate of Italy in comparison with its neighbor, Austria, is made up by the additional charges levied for the communes and the provinces, the amount of which never exceeds 25 per cent of the State tax in other countries, including Austria, although in Italy it attains at times 100 per cent. In 1871 the Italian government received 128,487,480 francs of land tax, which fell to 106,625,456 francs in 1897. It has wavered, since that year, around 106,000,000. But the local taxes rose during the same period (1871–1897) from 55,000,000 to 81,000,000 for the communes, and from 29,000,000 to 54,000,000 for the provinces. Thus if, on the one hand, the State has diminished its tax on landed income about 22,000,000, the local administrations have, on the other hand, increased it about 50,000,000. And this increase has not been abandoned since.

I have calculated myself, with the official statistics as a basis, about 5,000,000,000 francs, as the value of the annual agricultural produce of Italy. The [net] revenue, properly speaking, taking account of the average of the costs of farming would not exceed the fifth part of that sum, namely 1,000,000,000. Thus, to speak very moderately, we have the following fiscal charges which burden this income, for a country essentially agricultural, possessing superficially about 28,000,000 hectares and a population of 34,000,000 inhabitants:

State tax	106,000,000 francs
Additional communal taxes	81,000,000 "
Additional provincial taxes	54,000,000 "
Total	241,000,000 francs

corresponding to 24 per cent of the income from the land.

CHAPTER XXII

FORMATION OF THE GERMAN EMPIRE AND THE AUSTRO–HUNGARIAN UNION

Section 66. *Prussia assumes the Leadership in Germany*

250. Bismarck's view of the constitutional crisis in Prussia (condensed) King William I of Prussia and his chief minister, Bismarck, who became the head of the Prussian ministry in 1862, were firmly convinced that the long-desired union of Germany could only come by force of arms; accordingly they bent every effort to increase the army for the conflict which they believed inevitable. In this they were stoutly opposed by the liberal members of the Prussian diet, which had been created under the Prussian constitution of 1850. Although the king dissolved the diet several times, the opposition steadily continued. So the king and Bismarck determined to proceed with the increase of the army and the levy of money without the consent of the diet. The following extracts from two of Bismarck's speeches give his view of the Prussian constitution and the right of the king, under the law of necessity, to do what he deemed best in the matter of preparing his country for the impending conflict.

This conflict has been viewed too tragically, and taken too seriously by the press; the government seeks no conflict. Could the crisis be avoided with honor, the government would gladly welcome it. . . . But Prussia must keep her strength intact for the favorable moment, which is too often missed. Prussia's boundaries are not favorable to the development of a strong body politic. Not through fine speeches and majority resolutions will the questions of the hour be decided — that was the mistake of 1848 and 1849 — but by Iron and Blood. . . .

The policy of Iron and Blood

If you [gentlemen of the Prussian lower House] had the right to determine by your own resolutions the total budget and its individual items; if you had the right to demand from his Majesty the dismissal of those ministers who do not have your confidence; if you had the right to determine by your resolutions relating to the budget, the organization of the army and duration of military service; if you had the right, which you do not constitutionally possess, to control absolutely the relation of the executive power to its officers, then you would be in full possession of sovereignty in this country. You formulate your demands in such a manner as to intimate that the constitution is violated in so far as the crown and House of Lords do not bend to your will; you bring the charge of violating the constitution against the ministry, not against the crown, whose fidelity to the constitution you do not question at all. Against this distinction I protested in the sessions of the committee. You know as well as anybody in Prussia that the ministry in Prussia acts in the name and at the command of his Majesty, and that just the very measures of the government in which you profess to see violations of the constitution, were carried out on this principle.

Attacks on the ministry are really on the crown

You know that the Prussian ministry in this respect stands in a different position from the English ministry. An English ministry, whatever it may be called, is a parliamentary one, a ministry of a majority of Parliament. We, however, are ministers of his Majesty the king. In denying the separation of the ministry from the crown I am not moved by a desire to make the authority of the crown a shield with which to cover the ministry. We do not need this cloak; we stand fast on the ground of our good right. I reject this doctrine of separation because by it you conceal the fact that you find yourselves actually in a contest with the crown itself for the sovereignty of this land — not in a struggle with the ministry.

Ministerial systems of Prussia and England contrasted

Necessity
justifies col-
lecting taxes
without sanc-
tion from the
diet

As to what is the law when no budget is voted, many theories
are advanced, the justification of which I will not consider here.
The necessity that the State shall exist is enough for me ; necessity alone is authoritative ; we have taken this necessity into
account and you yourselves would not wish us to stop paying
officers' salaries and interest on the debt. The Prussian monarchy has not yet fulfilled its mission ; it is not yet ready to
form a mere ornament for your constitutional structure, — to
be no more than a useless wheel in the mechanism of parliamentary government.

Section 67.   War of 1866 and the Formation of the North German Federation

Bismarck availed himself of the complications involved
in the disposal of Schleswig-Holstein to put Austria in the
wrong. On June 14, 1866, the king of Prussia declared
that Austria had violated the principles upon which the
union of 1815 was founded, and that the union had, accordingly, ceased to exist. A few days later William issued a summons to the Prussian people ("*An mein Volk*").

251. King
William ex-
plains to his
people the
cause of the
war with
Austria
(June 18,
1866)

At the instant when Prussia's army is advancing to a decisive
conflict I am moved to address my people, — the sons and
grandsons of those brave forefathers to whom half a century
ago my father (now resting in God) spoke the never-to-be-
forgotten words, "The country is in danger." Austria and a
great part of Germany are armed against us.

It is but a few years since, when there was a question of
freeing a German land from foreign domination, I voluntarily,
and without a thought of previous grievances, extended to the
emperor of Austria the hand of friendship. From the blood
shed together on the field of battle I hoped that a brotherhood
in arms would spring which might in turn lead to a firmer union
resting upon mutual respect and gratitude. This, I trusted,
would bring with it that coöperation which should have as its
fruit the domestic welfare of Germany and the increase of its
prestige among the nations.

But this hope has been disappointed. Austria will not forget that its princes once ruled Germany. In the more youthful but powerfully developing Prussia she refuses to perceive a natural ally, but sees only a hostile rival. Prussia — so Austria reasons — must be opposed on every occasion, since what is good for Prussia is bad for Austria. The old, unhappy jealousy has again blazed up. Prussia shall be weakened, annihilated, dishonored. With Prussia no treaties are to be observed; the confederated princes have not only been roused against Prussia; they have been induced to dissolve the confederation. Wherever we look throughout Germany we are surrounded by enemies, whose war cry is, "Down with Prussia!"

But the spirit of 1813 still lives in my people. Who can rob us of a single foot of Prussian soil, if we are firmly resolved to protect the acquisitions of our fathers; if king and people are united more firmly than ever by the danger to the fatherland, and hold it to be their highest and most sacred duty to risk blood and treasure for her honor? In anxious expectation of what has now happened, I have for years regarded it as the first duty of my royal office to prepare Prussia's military resources for a powerful manifestation. And no Prussian can fail to view, as I do, with confidence and satisfaction the military forces which now protect our boundaries. With their king at their head the Prussian people feel themselves, in truth, a nation in arms. Our enemies are deceived when they imagine that Prussia is paralyzed by internal discord. Over against the enemy the nation is a single powerful unit. In the face of the enemy all differences disappear and we stand united, whether it be for good or evil fortune. *The nation in arms against Austria*

I have done all that I could to spare Prussia the burden and sacrifices of a war: my people know this; God, who searches all hearts, knows it. Up to the last moment I have, in combination with France, England, and Russia, sought and kept open the way for a peaceful settlement. Austria, however, was averse to this, and other German states have openly taken their place at her side. *Austria responsible for the conflict*

Let it be so. The fault is not mine should my people have hard battles to fight and mayhap heavy burdens to bear. No alternative is any longer left us. We must fight for our very existence. We must engage in a life-and-death struggle with those who would cast down the Prussia of the Great Elector, of Frederick the Great; the Prussia which emerged victorious from the War of Liberation, from the position to which the skill and strength of her princes and the bravery, devotion, and character of her people have raised her.

Let us petition Almighty God, the director of the history of nations, the disposer of battles, to bless our arms. Should he grant us the victory, we shall then be strong enough to renew, in a firmer and more beneficent manner, the bonds which have so loosely bound the German lands together, in name rather than in fact, and which have now been torn asunder by those who fear the right and might of the national spirit.

May God be with us.

WILLIAM

BERLIN, June 18, 1866

Count Bismarck was able to write to his wife on July 9, three days after the great and decisive victory of Prussia at Königgrätz, as follows:

HOHENMAUTH, Monday, July 9

252. Bismarck writes to his wife about the battle of Königgrätz

. . . It goes well with us — at least, if we are not excessive in our demands and do not think that we have conquered the world, we shall achieve a peace that is worth while. But we are as easily elated as we are cast down, and I have the thankless task of pouring water into the intoxicating wine, and making it plain that we do not live alone in Europe but with three neighbors.

The Austrians have taken a stand in Moravia, and we are at present so rash as to propose that to-morrow our headquarters shall be on the spot they now occupy. Prisoners are still coming in, and one hundred and eighty cannon have arrived since the 3d. If they bring on their southern army, we shall, with God's gracious aid, beat that, too. Confidence is everywhere. Our soldiers are dears [*Unsere Leute sind zum Küssen*], — every one of them so heroic, quiet, obedient, and decent, though with empty stomachs, wet clothes, wet camp, little sleep, and no soles to their shoes! They are friendly to all, with no plundering or burning, but paying what they can, and eating moldy bread. There must be a goodly stock of fear of God among our common men, otherwise things could not be as they are. It is hard to get news of acquaintances; we are scattered miles apart, and do not know where to send, and have no one to send. There are men enough, of course, but no horses. . . .

The king exposed himself a great deal on the 3d, and it was a good thing that I was with him, for the warnings of others did not influence him, and no one else would have dared to talk to him as I did the last time, — and it did the job, — when a knot of ten cuirassiers and fifteen horses of the sixth cuirassier regiment were trampling about us in bloody confusion and the shells buzzed around disagreeably near his Majesty. The worst of them happily did not go off. I should, however, rather have had him too venturesome than to have him show himself overprudent. He was delighted with his troops, and with good reason, so that he did not seem to notice the whizzing and din about him. He was as composed as if he were on the Kreuzberg, and kept finding a new battalion to thank and say good-night to, until we were nearly within the firing line again. But so much was said to him of his recklessness that he will be more careful in the future, so your mind may be at rest on that score. I can hardly believe yet that the battle has really taken place. . . .

Conduct of William in the battle

Bismarck's fears that the king and his advisers would be intoxicated by the brilliant victory over Austria and would wish to press on, and perhaps lose much in the end, were justified. He tells in his memoirs how, although outvoted in the council, he had his own way after all.

253. How
Bismarck
held Prussia
in check
after the
victory of
Königgrätz

On July 23, under the presidency of the king, a council of
war was held, in which the question to be decided was whether
we should make peace under the conditions offered or continue
the war. A painful illness from which I was suffering made it
necessary that the council should be held in my room. On this
occasion I was the only civilian in uniform. I declared it to be
my conviction that peace must be concluded on the Austrian
terms, — but remained alone in my opinion ; the king supported
the military majority.

My nerves could not stand the strain which had been put
upon them day and night ; I got up in silence, walked into
my adjoining bedchamber, and was there overcome by a violent
paroxysm of tears. Meanwhile I heard the council dispersing
in the next room. I thereupon set to work to commit to paper
the reasons which, in my opinion, spoke for the conclusion of
peace, and begged the king, in the event of his not accepting
the advice for which I was responsible, to relieve me of my
functions if the war were continued.

Hazard of
continuing
the war

I set out with this document on the following day to explain
it by word of mouth. In the antechamber I found two colonels
with a report on the spread of cholera morbus among their
troops, barely half of whom were fit for service. These alarming figures confirmed my resolve to make the acceptance of
the Austrian terms a cabinet question. Besides my political
anxieties, I feared that by transferring operations to Hungary,
the nature of that country, which was well known to me, would
soon make the disease overwhelming. The climate, especially
in August, is dangerous ; there is great lack of water ; the
country villages are widely distributed, each with many square
miles of open fields attached ; and, finally, plums and melons
grow there in abundance. Our campaign of 1792 in Champagne
was in my mind as a warning example ; on that occasion it
was not the French but dysentery which caused our retreat.
Armed with my documents I unfolded to the king the political and military reasons which opposed the continuation of
the war.

We had to avoid wounding Austria too severely ; we had
to avoid leaving behind in her any unnecessary bitterness of

feeling or desire for revenge; we ought rather to reserve the possibility of becoming friends again with our adversary of the moment, and in any case to regard the Austrian State as a piece on the European chessboard and the renewal of friendly relations as a move open to us. If Austria were severely injured, she would become the ally of France and of every other opponent of ours; she would even sacrifice her anti-Russian interests for the sake of revenge on Prussia. *Bismarck's reasons for treating Austria leniently*

On the other hand, I could not see any guarantee for us in the future of the countries constituting the Austrian monarchy, in case the latter were split up by risings of the Hungarians and Slavs or made permanently dependent on those peoples. What would be substituted for that portion of Europe which the Austrian state had hitherto occupied from Tyrol to Bukowina? Fresh formations on this territory could only be of a permanently revolutionary nature. German Austria we could neither wholly nor partly make use of. The acquisition of provinces like Austrian Silesia and portions of Bohemia could not strengthen the Prussian State; it would not lead to an amalgamation of German Austria with Prussia, and Vienna could not be governed from Berlin as a mere dependency. *Prussia has nothing to gain from destroying the Austrian power*

. . . To all this the king raised no objection, but declared the actual terms as inadequate, without, however, definitely formulating his own demands. Only so much was clear, that his claims had grown considerably since July 4. He said that the chief culprit could not be allowed to escape unpunished, and that, justice once satisfied, we could let the misled backsliders off more easily; and he insisted on the cessions of territory from Austria which I have already mentioned.

I replied that we were not there to sit in judgment, but to pursue the German policy. Austria's conflict and rivalry with us were no more culpable than ours with her; our task was the establishment or foundation of German national unity under the leadership of the king of Prussia.

Passing on to the German States, the king spoke of various acquisitions by cutting down the territories of all our

opponents. I repeated that we were not there to administer
retributive justice, but to pursue a policy; that I wished to
avoid in the German federation of the future the sight of mutilated territories, whose princes and peoples might very easily
(such is human weakness) retain a lively wish to recover their
former possessions by means of foreign aid.

After the close of the short war between Prussia and
Austria, a constitutional convention was summoned to
draw up a plan of federation for Prussia and her neighbors north of the river Main. The constitution of the
North German Federation was the result. The Assembly did its work so well that when, four years later, the
southern States, Bavaria, Baden, and Würtemberg, came
into the union after the war with France, the constitution did not have to be materially altered, and still remains that of the present German Empire. Sybel, the
distinguished historian, was a member of the Assembly
in 1867, and well describes in a speech the peculiar
difficulties of devising a union which should meet at once
the demands of Prussia (as a European power) and those
of the various German monarchs, who had long regarded
themselves as sovereigns and were fearful of being made
the subjects of the king of Prussia.

254. Three
forces pro-
vided for in
the German
federation   Gentlemen, we must now take up what is obviously the
most important and characteristic part of our task. Now
that we have sketched out in general the powers which the
proposed federal government is to enjoy, we must reach a
decision in regard to the organization of the union, — perhaps the most difficult question that any statesman has
faced during the course of the century, — namely, the formation of a practicable and enduring central authority for
Germany, strong enough to fulfill the various functions which
devolve upon a modern State, and yet so far limited that the

German princes and the individual States will not feel that they have been completely subordinated and mediatized. The central government must also be so far dependent upon the parliament that the political sentiments of the nation at large shall not be violated. Surely no task could be more difficult than ours. . . .

The plan of a federation now before us, whatever may be its nature, is in no way a constitutional monarchy, nor is it a federation according to the traditional theories which have been developed in the universities. . . . Indeed, those who have drawn up the plan have unmistakably struck into a path diametrically opposed to that which has been hitherto followed in Germany. They have not taken a treatise upon political theory, I care not how good it may be, and copied out the features of a constitutional state as they are described therein ; they have not, after arranging their plan, divided and distorted the real forces in our country in order to fit them into it. On the contrary, they have searched out in the long-standing chaos of German conditions the actually existing forces; they have endeavored to give them a legal basis and a form adjusted to the strength and importance of each; they have supplied each with its proper organ, and defined its scope and activity.

Neither a constitutional monarchy feasible nor a federation as commonly conceived

The forces to be considered were, as every one here well knows, the strong, victorious Prussia, whose traditions of a glorious past, whose present might, and, above all, whose future power combine to render her far too big to be fitted into that academic federation of the Göttingen professors. [*Laughter.*] In the situation of Europe at the present moment she necessarily enjoys in some respects a dictatorial power. Then, on the other hand, there are the other German States, who in the war against Prussia certainly won no laurels. Even those who were her allies were thrown sadly into the shade by the gigantic increase of Prussia's power. Yet, in spite of their relation with Prussia, the various German States have exhibited marked vitality and in some instances enjoy a strong support from outside. Moreover, — and that weighed most heavily, — in spite of the efforts of the cultivated class toward unity, the individual States each retains the very real sympathy of its own people on its own soil.

Thirdly and lastly, there was liberal public opinion, — in Prussia, in Germany, in Europe. In Prussia, indeed, it seemed that public opinion had been worsted in the unsuccessful opposition to Bismarck's ministry and had been forced to give up many of its positions. Yet in spite of this, by and large, and in the whole range of European relations, this public opinion has grown stronger and stronger, until not even the strongest of military monarchies can permanently resist the attacks of this moral power. . . .

It was necessary, then, to reckon with these three forces, — (1) with the military demands of the great Prussian State, (2) with the various individual German States, the demands of which were supported by local sentiment, and (3) with the strength of public opinion. The draft of the constitution, as it lies before us, provides for an organ for each of these forces : to Prussia — to the crown of Prussia — is assigned the presidency of the federation ; to the smaller States, the Federal Council (*Bundesrath*) ; to public opinion, the Imperial Diet (*Reichstag*).[1]

On the outbreak of the war in 1866 several German States had taken up arms against Prussia, but they were forced to yield before they could join forces with the Austrians. Accordingly, Prussia by right of conquest annexed three States and the city of Frankfort, and this action was announced to the Prussian diet on August 16, 1866, in a message from the king.

255. William I's announcement of the annexations after the war of 1866   We, William, by the grace of God king of Prussia, etc., hereby declare and make known : The governments of the kingdom of Hanover, of the electorate of Hesse, and of the duchy of Nassau, as well as the free town of Frankfort, have,

[1] For an account of the peculiarities of the present German federation, especially of the Federal Council, which is a species of *corporate monarch*, in whom the sovereignty is vested, *not in the emperor*, see J. H. Robinson, *The German Bundesrath*, Philadelphia, 1891.

by their participation in the hostile conduct of the former federal diet, placed themselves in a state of open war with Prussia. They declined the neutrality as well as the alliance repeatedly offered to them by Prussia, even at the last moment, with a guarantee of the integrity of their territory ; they took an active part in Austria's war against Prussia, and appealed to the decision of war for themselves and their countries. This decision, according to God's decree, has been against them. Political necessity obliges us to refuse to restore to them the power of government of which they have been deprived by the victorious advance of our army.

In case they should be permitted to maintain their independence, the aforesaid countries, on account of their geographical position, could create difficulties and obstructions, by a hostile or even uncertain attitude toward Prussian policy and her military operations, far out of proportion to the extent of their actual power and importance. Not from a desire of acquiring territory, but a conviction that it is our duty to protect our inherited States from a recurrence of the danger and to give a broader and surer foundation to the national reorganization of Germany, — these are the reasons which force us to unite with our monarchy forever the kingdom of Hanover, the electorate of Hesse, the duchy of Nassau, and the free town of Frankfort. *Necessity compels the annexation*

We know very well that only a part of the people of those States share with us the conviction of this necessity. We respect and honor the feelings of loyalty and devotion which bind the inhabitants of those countries to their princely Houses, and to their independent political institutions, but we trust that the share to be accorded them in the progressive development of the national welfare, together with a careful attention to the special legal interests involved, will facilitate their inevitable expansion into the new and more extensive commonwealth.

BERLIN, August 16, 1866

The States which were seized by Prussia naturally protested strongly against what they deemed a most outrageous and high-handed confiscation. In a lengthy manifesto the king of Hanover solemnly denounced the Prussian government and declared, in vain, that he would never surrender his rights to the kingdom from which he had been driven.

256. Protest of the king of Hanover against the annexation of his territories by Prussia (condensed) The only ground that the Prussian government alleges as a justification for this arbitrary act [of annexation], unheard of in the annals of German history, is that which it claims to find in the right of conquest. Now the right of conquest presupposes a war made in conformity to the principles of international law. But there has never been between us and the king of Prussia a war of that nature. Besides, it could not take place except in violation of the fundamental laws of the Germanic Confederation, and it ought to be morally impossible on the part of one of our near relations, of a sovereign friend, of a German prince. Consequently we find ourselves, purely and simply, in the position of legitimate defense in the face of an aggression which nothing justifies and which we have by no means provoked.

Grievances against Prussia In view, then, of the facts which we have just presented, we protest solemnly : against the unjustifiable invasion that some regiments of the army of the king of Prussia were allowed to make into our territory, June 15, 1866, and on the following days ; against the occupation of our realm by the same military regiments ; against the damages that we and our royal House have sustained or that we may have yet to sustain on the part of Prussia with regard to our property, our revenues, or our goods of whatsoever nature ; against the spoliations that the public treasury of Hanover has suffered under the Prussian administration, and against those which it will have to endure in the future. . . . Finally we protest in the presence of the world against the seizure of our realm and against its incorporation with Prussia, declaring that this incorporation is an unworthy usurpation and an odious spoliation, a flagrant violation of European treaties and of all principles of international law.

An appeal to the powers for aid We pray for the support of all the powers who have recognized our sovereignty and the independence of our realm, persuaded that, like ourselves, they will never recognize anything but the supreme rights of justice, in view of the fact that the principle applied by Prussia would menace the existence of all the monarchies and of all the legitimate States of the world.

We declare that we shall never renounce our rights of sovereignty over our States; and that we shall consider always as illegal, null, and void all the acts that the Prussian government or its agents have committed or shall commit in consequence of that usurpation, the responsibility for which we throw back on the one who is the author of it. Let all those who may be interested stand then as warned. We await future events full of confidence in the justice of our cause and animated by the firm hope that the Divine Providence will not delay in making an end of the machinations, iniquities, and violences (of which so many States and so many peoples are victims at this moment) among us and among our brave Hanoverians. GEORGES REX

HIETZING, near VIENNA, September 23, 1866

(L.S.)

Acts of the Prussian government declared void

The formation of the North German Federation, and the prospect that the States to the south of the river Main would sooner or later join it, seemed to indicate that the final unification of Germany was at hand which it had been the policy of French statesmen since the days of Richelieu to resist. Two alternatives were presented to the government of Napoleon III : frank recognition of the new nation and the establishment of cordial relations with it ; or, on the other hand, the continuance of a policy designed to prevent the southern States from joining the northern union, — perhaps even to disrupt the new union. In an interesting pamphlet, said to have been inspired officially at Paris and to have been the expression of Napoleon III's own personal views, the former policy was eloquently urged, but unhappily for the two nations events worked against its execution.

257. Extracts from a pamphlet, *Napoleon III and Europe in 1867*

Germany is made! The North German Federation, the customs' treaties and military conventions between Prussia and the South German States, the tendencies of the deliberative assemblies, the intentions of the cabinet of Berlin, and the manifest aspirations of the immense majority of the German people, — all these symptoms and facts compel every impartial mind to agree to the correctness of this affirmation — Germany is made!

The river Main, already lost sight of in the unity of commercial interests and military command, is nothing but an imaginary frontier. From the promontories of Schleswig to the mountains of the Tyrol, and possibly beyond; from the bridge of Kehl to the confines of the grand duchy of Posen, there exists a people with a common nationality, with common interests, forces, and language. Unity exists in its most decisive and most substantial shape. If we behold elsewhere the name without the fact, here, in Germany, we clearly have the fact without the name.

The slightest aggression from without would suffice to create one of those floods which disappoint all calculations and carry away all the barriers erected by conventionality, skill, might, and events. Yes, Germany is made! and the slightest breath may suffice to raise the wave which will place the sovereign crown of Germany upon the forehead of the chief of the House of Hohenzollern.

German unity inevitable

Superficial or systematically hostile observers see in the battle of Sadowa the sole cause of German unity; but to us who know the past of the German nation, the tendencies of its genius, the spirit of its schools, the dreams of its youth, the songs of its poets, the breath of its literature, and its practical requirements and material interests, — to us, acquainted with all this, the battle of Sadowa was nothing but an event conceived long since in the mysterious womb of the past, and finally brought into the world, into the daylight of history, at the prophetic hour of its completed formation.

It is certain, or at least probable, that this formation might have been retarded; but it is also certain that it could not have been prevented. For if, upon the one hand, facts engender events, events, upon the other hand, predispose facts. Interference, which tries to delay what must be accomplished, serves only to produce a catastrophe where, in the natural course of things, a change might have been developed, if not entirely without a commotion, at least without one of those earthquakes which shake the bases of European order and hold in suspense for an indefinite period the destinies of peoples and the fate of crowns.

Germany is made! but this Germany in process of formation, of unification upon our very frontier, is she a threat to us or a danger? Does there exist a duty, or indeed a right, that obliges or authorizes us to interfere in this solemn drama of the formation of a great people upon our frontier? Ought France to prevent Germany from becoming united? Can France prevent Germany from becoming united? *Ought France to interfere in Germany?*

To this twofold question thus plainly put, we reply without hesitation, "No." France ought not; France cannot. Let us hasten to add that when we say France cannot oppose herself to the formation of the German nationality, we do not assuredly intend to speak of physical and material want of power. We wish to say that France cannot do so because she ought not. She cannot, because she must not be false to her democratic and liberal mission. She ought not and she cannot, lastly, because she must not make what is illogical and unjust the pivot of her policy. *Intervention unjust*

Ardent spirits, more impatient than reflecting, might retort that France is not in the habit of counting her enemies. But, to tell the truth, we dread a victory quite as much as a defeat. In a war undertaken to prevent the unification of Germany, — a war which would be as sacred to our patient and tenacious neighbors as is the idea of unity itself, — in such a war ten battles gained or lost would never bring about anything but truces, falsely called treaties of peace. The imprudent hand that should desire to prevent Germany from remaining or becoming a nation would kindle a war destined to ravage Europe for an incalculable period, sacrificing successive hecatombs of victims. Let the arbiters of the destinies of Germany also reflect upon this! *Even a successful war to be dreaded*

Section 68. The Franco-Prussian War and the Foundation of the German Empire

Bismarck describes in his memoirs the way in which he claimed to have precipitated what he believed to be an unavoidable war with France. The Prussian king was at Ems, a well-known watering place, when the French ambassador, Benedetti, approached him and demanded that the king should pledge himself never to permit the Hohenzollern prince to become a candidate again for the Spanish throne. This William refused to do, and as his patience was worn out by the importunities of the French ministry, he sent word to Benedetti that he would not see him again. He telegraphed the news of this to Bismarck, with permission to publish it in the newspapers if he wished. Upon the receipt of the message, Bismarck says :

258. How Bismarck cut down the Ems telegram so as to assure war with France

All considerations, conscious and unconscious, strengthened my opinion that war could only be avoided at the cost of the honor of Prussia and of the national confidence in her. Under this conviction I made use of the royal authorization communicated to me through Abeken to publish the contents of the telegram ; and in the presence of my two guests [General Moltke and General Roon] I reduced the telegram by striking out words, but without adding or altering anything, to the following form :

Ems dispatch as published by Bismarck

"After the news of the renunciation of the hereditary prince of Hohenzollern had been officially communicated to the imperial government of France by the royal government of Spain, the French ambassador at Ems made the further demand of his Majesty the king that he should authorize him to telegraph to Paris that his Majesty the king bound himself for all future time never again to give his consent if the Hohenzollerns should renew their candidature. His Majesty the king thereupon decided not to receive the French ambassador again, and sent to tell him, through the aid-de-camp on duty, that his Majesty had nothing further to communicate to the ambassador."

The difference in the effect of the abbreviated text of the Ems telegram as compared with that produced by the original was not the result of stronger words, but of the form, which made this announcement appear decisive, while Abeken's version would only have been regarded as a fragment of a negotiation still pending and to be continued at Berlin.

After I had read out the concentrated edition to my two guests, Moltke remarked: "Now it has a different ring; in its original form it sounded like a parley; now it is like a flourish of trumpets in answer to a challenge." I went on to explain: "If, in execution of his Majesty's order, I at once communicate this text, which contains no alteration in or addition to the telegram, not only to the newspapers, but also by telegraph to all our embassies, it will be known in Paris before midnight, and not only on account of its contents, but also on account of the manner of its distribution, will have the effect of a red rag upon the Gallic bull.

"Fight we must if we do not want to act the part of the vanquished without a battle. Success, however, depends essentially upon the impression which the origination of the war makes upon us and others; it is important that we should be the ones attacked, and the Gallic insolence and touchiness will bring about this result if we announce in the face of Europe, so far as we can without the speaking tube of the Reichstag, that we fearlessly meet the public threats of France."

This explanation brought about in the two generals a revulsion to a more joyous mood, the liveliness of which surprised me. They had suddenly recovered their pleasure in eating and drinking and spoke in a more cheerful vein. Roon said, "Our God of old still lives, and will not let us perish in disgrace." Moltke so far relinquished his passive equanimity that, glancing up joyously toward the ceiling and abandoning his usual punctiliousness of speech, he smote his hand upon his breast and said, "If I may but live to lead our armies in such a war, then the devil may come directly afterwards and fetch away the old carcass."

Bismarck and his companions rejoice at the prospects of war

Bismarck, in a letter to his wife written immediately after the battle of Sedan, describes the capture of Napoleon III.

VENDRESS, September 3, 1870

259. Bismarck describes the surrender of Napoleon III at Sedan

Day before yesterday before daybreak I left my quarters here; to-day I am returning, and have in the meantime experienced the great battle of Sedan on the 1st; in which we made towards thirty thousand prisoners and forced back the rest of the French army (which we have been pursuing all the way from Bar-le-Duc) into the fortress, where they must surrender themselves along with the emperor. Yesterday morning at five o'clock, after I had been discussing until one o'clock in the morning with Moltke and the French generals the terms of the capitulation, General Reille, whom I know, awoke me to tell me that Napoleon wished to speak with me.

I rode, without washing and with no breakfast, towards Sedan, and found the emperor in an open carriage with three officers of high rank and three others on horseback on the highroad near Sedan. I dismounted, greeted him as politely as if we were in the Tuileries, and asked what were his Majesty's commands. He wished to see the king. I told him, as was the truth, that his Majesty had his quarters three miles from there, at the place where I am now writing. On Napoleon's asking whither he should go, I offered him, since I was unfamiliar with the region, my quarters at Donchéry, a little place in the neighborhood close to Sedan. He accepted my invitation, and, accompanied by his six Frenchmen, myself, and Karl,[1] who had in the meantime followed me, drove, in the silence of the morning, toward our forces.

Before we reached the place he began to be apprehensive lest he might encounter a number of people, and he asked me whether he could not get out at a lonely laborer's cottage on the road. I had the place inspected by Karl, who reported that it was miserable and dirty. "*N'importe*," said Napoleon; and I ascended with him a narrow, rickety stairway. In a room ten feet square, with a deal table and two rush-bottomed

---

[1] Bismarck's son.

chairs, we sat an hour, while the others remained below, — a singular contrast to our last interview in '67 in the Tuileries.

Our negotiations were difficult, unless I consented to touch upon matters which could not but be painful to one who had been so cast down by God's mighty hand. I had summoned officers, through Karl, from the town and had asked Moltke to come. We then sent out one of the former to reconnoiter, and discovered, half a mile away, in Fresnois, a little villa with grounds.

Thither I accompanied the emperor, with an escort from the king's cuirassier regiment, which had been called up in the meantime ; and there we concluded, with the French general Wimpffen, the capitulation, according to which forty to sixty thousand French, — I cannot be more accurate at this time, — with all that they had, became our prisoners. Day before yesterday and yesterday cost France one hundred thousand men and an emperor. This morning the latter started with all the members of his court, his horses and carriages, for Wilhelmshöhe, near Cassel.

This has been an event of vast historic importance, — a victory for which we must thank the Lord in humbleness of heart. It decides the conflict, although we must still carry on the war against an emperorless France. . . .

Good-by, my sweetheart. Love to the children.

Your v. B.

The republic was declared in France on September 4, 1870. Jules Favre, the minister of foreign affairs under the new provisional government, two days later issued a remarkable circular to the French diplomatic agents abroad, explaining the situation in France.

260. The French minister of foreign affairs on the downfall of the second empire (September 6, 1870)

Sir, the events which have just taken place in Paris are so well explained by the inexorable logic of facts that it is needless to dwell upon their meaning and bearing. In ceding to an irresistible impulse which had been but too long restrained, the population of Paris has obeyed a necessity superior to that of its own safety. It did not wish to perish with the criminal government which was leading France to her ruin. It has not pronounced the deposition of Napoleon III and of his dynasty; it has simply registered it in the name of right, justice, and public safety; and the sentence was so completely ratified beforehand by the public conscience that no one, even among the most noisy defenders of the power that was falling, raised a voice to uphold it. It collapsed of itself under the weight of its faults and amid the acclamations of the entire nation, without a single drop of blood being shed, without one individual being deprived of his personal liberty.

. . . Rescued from the shame and the danger of a government which has proved a traitor to all its duties, every one now comprehends that the first act of national sovereignty, reconquered at last, must be one of self-control, — the seeking for strength by respecting right. Moreover, no time must be lost; our enemies are at our very gates; we have but one thought, — their expulsion from our territory.

The emperor responsible for the war

But this obligation, which we resolutely accept, we did not impose upon France. She would not have been in her present position if she had listened to our voice. We have energetically defended the policy of peace even at the cost of our popularity. We still maintain the same opinion. We are heartbroken at the sight of these human butcheries consuming the youth of two nations, whom a little good sense and a great deal of liberty would have preserved from such frightful catastrophes. We cannot find any adequate expression of our admiration for our heroic army, sacrificed through the incapacity of its supreme commander, but showing itself greater in defeat than in the most brilliant victory.

I would explain our position in a few words and submit my statement to the judgment of my country and of Europe. We loudly condemned the war, and, while proclaiming our respect for the rights of nations, we asked that Germany should be left mistress of her own destinies. We wished that liberty should be at the same time our common bond and our common protection. We were convinced that these moral forces would forever insure peace. But we claimed arms for all citizens and the right to elect our leaders. Had this been conceded, we should have remained invincible on our own soil. The government of the emperor, which had long since divorced its interests from those of the country, opposed that policy. We revert to it with the hope that, taught by experience, France will have the wisdom to put it into practice.

The king of Prussia has declared that he made war not against France but against the imperial dynasty. The dynasty has fallen. France is free. Does the king of Prussia wish to continue an unholy struggle, which will be at least as fatal to him as to us? Does he wish to give to the nineteenth century the cruel spectacle of two nations destroying one another, and, forgetful of humanity, reason, and culture, heaping corpse upon corpse, and ruin upon ruin? He is free to assume this responsibility in the face of the world and of history.

If it is a challenge, we accept it. We will cede neither an inch of our territory nor a stone of our fortresses. A disgraceful peace would mean a war of extermination at an early date. We will treat only for a permanent peace. In this respect our interest is that of the whole of Europe, and we have reason to hope that, divested of all dynastic considerations, the question will thus present itself to the cabinets of Europe. But even should we stand alone, we shall not yield. We have a resolute army, well-provisioned fortresses, a strong cordon of troops, and, above all, the hearts of three hundred thousand combatants determined to hold out to the bitter end.

France will yield no territory

The following is the official account of the reëstablishment of the German Empire, January 18, 1871.

In the palace of Louis XIV, in that ancient center of a hostile power which for centuries has striven to divide and humiliate Germany, the solemn proclamation of the German Empire was made on January 18, exactly one hundred and seventy years after the assumption of the royal dignity by the Prussian sovereigns at Königsberg. Though the German people, owing to the necessities of the times, were represented at the ceremony only by the German army, the eyes of the entire nation were gratefully turned to the place where, surrounded

261. How the German Empire was proclaimed in Versailles (January 18, 1871)

by sovereigns, generals, and soldiers, King William announced to the world the assumption by himself and his heirs of a title for the reëstablishment of which we have been yearning during the sixty long years it has been in abeyance.

As yet the infatuation of the enemy does not permit us to throw aside the weapons we have taken up in self-defense ; and as our unity arose out of the first part of the campaign, so will our empire be strengthened by the remaining feats of arms. By the self-sacrificing devotion of all classes of society, the nation has proved that it still possesses that warlike prowess which distinguished our ancestors. It has recovered its ancient position in Europe ; and, neither fearing an adversary nor envying any neighbor, discreet and temperate in its acts and aims, it accepts the destiny prophesied for it in the proclamation of its new emperor. This destiny is to add to its power not by conquest but by promoting culture, liberty, and civilization. As far as the German people are concerned, there will be no more wars in Europe after the termination of the present campaign. . . .

Ceremony at Versailles

Owing to the unfavorable weather, the festive procession which was to conduct his Majesty from the prefecture to the palace did not take place. The crown prince, with Lieutenant General Blumenthal, his chief of staff, and an escort of Prussians, Würtembergers, Badeners, and Bavarians, drove to the palace to receive his royal father at the eastern portal in front of the Princes' Stairway. In the courtyard of the palace a company of the king's own troops was drawn up as a guard of honor. . . .

At a quarter past twelve his Majesty entered the hall, when a choir consisting of men of the Seventh, Forty-Seventh, and Fifty-Eighth regiments intoned the choral, " Let all the world rejoice in the Lord." . . . When the choir ceased, the congregation sang one verse of the choral, " Praise and honor unto the Lord." The ordinary military liturgy was then read by the clergymen and a sermon preached by the Reverend A. Rogge. Alluding to the well-known inscription on the ceiling of the hall, "*Le roi gouverne par lui-même,*" the preacher observed that the kings of Prussia had risen to greatness by adopting a different and more religious motto, namely, "The kings of the earth reign under me, saith the Lord." The *Te Deum Laudamus* closed the service.

The king then walked up to where the colors were displayed, and, standing before them, read the document proclaiming the reëstablishment of the German Empire. Count Bismarck having read the king's proclamation to the German nation, the grand duke of Baden stepped forth and exclaimed, "Long live his Majesty the emperor!" The cheers of the assembly were taken up by the bands playing the national anthem.

Section 69. Austria-Hungary since 1866

The dominions of the emperor of Austria and king of Hungary underwent, after the war of 1866, a transformation no less revolutionary than that of Germany. The relations between Austria and Hungary, which had been the source of so much trouble between the two countries, were settled in a manner fairly satisfactory to a large majority by the "Compromise" of 1867, from which the following important provisions are taken.

262. **Extracts** from the Compromise (Ausgleich) of 1867, which forms the basis of the constitution of Austria-Hungary

Law of December 21, 1867, concerning the matters common to all the countries of the Austrian monarchy and the manner of treating them.

ART. I. The following affairs are declared common to the realms and countries represented in the *Reichsrath*, and to the countries under the crown of Hungary :

Affairs common to the whole empire

(*a*) Foreign affairs, comprising the diplomatic and commercial representation in foreign countries as well as measures relating to international treaties, reserving the right of the ratification of the said treaties by the bodies representing each of the two halves of the empire (i.e. the Austrian *Reichsrath* and the Hungarian *Reichstag*), in so far as this approbation is constitutionally required.

(*b*) Military affairs, including the navy but excluding the determination of the quotas of troops and legislation regulating the military service.

(*c*) Finances, relating to those expenses for which it is necessary to provide in common.

Affairs to be settled by joint agreement

Art. II. The following matters are not to be treated in common, but are, from time to time, to be settled on the same basis by joint agreements.

1. Commercial matters, particularly tariff legislation.

2. Legislation on indirect taxes closely connected with industrial production.

3. The regulation of the monetary system and the system of coinage.

4. Arrangements affecting railway lines which concern both portions of the empire.

5. The establishment of a system of defense for the country.

Joint expenses

Art. III. The common expenses are to be met by the two parts of the monarchy according to a ratio fixed by periodical agreements between the respective parliaments of the two parts of the empire, and approved by the emperor. The ways and means of raising the portion charged to each of the two parts of the empire remain the exclusive affair of each.

The joint ministry

Art. V. The administration of the common affairs shall be vested in a joint responsible ministry, which is prohibited from managing, during the same period, the affairs peculiar to either of the two parts of the empire.

Arrangements concerning the management, conduct, and internal organization of the entire army belong exclusively to the emperor.

The " Delegations "

Art. VI. The parliaments of the two portions of the empire [to wit, the Austrian Reichsrath and the Hungarian Reichstag] shall exercise their legislative powers, which relate to common matters, through Delegations.

Art. VII. The Delegation of the Reichsrath numbers sixty members, one third to be chosen from the House of Lords, two thirds from the lower house.[1]

Mode of choosing Austrian Delegation

Art. VIII. The House of Lords shall choose from its own body, by absolute majority vote, the twenty members of the Delegation whom it has a right to elect.

[1] The Delegation of the Hungarian Reichstag, numbering sixty, is also chosen by the two chambers composing that body.

The forty members left to the choice of the lower house shall be elected by the deputies of the various provincial diets, either from their own number or from the entire Chamber, by an absolute majority of votes according to the following apportionment:

From the kingdom of Bohemia	10 delegates
From the kingdom of Dalmatia	1 "
From the kingdom of Galicia and Lodomeria with the grand duchy of Cracow	7 "
The arch duchy of Austria below the Enns . .	3 "
The grand duchy of Austria above the Enns . .	2 "
The duchy of Salzburg	1 "
The duchy of Styria	2 "
The duchy of Carinthia	1 "
The duchy of Carniola	1 "
The duchy of Bukovina	1 "
The margravate of Moravia	4 "
The duchy of upper and lower Silesia	1 "
The county principality of Tyrol	2 "
The territory of Vorarlberg	1 "
The margravate of Istria	1 "
The county-principality of Goertz and Gradiska	1 "
The city of Trieste with its territory	1 "
	40 delegates [1]

Art. X. The choice of delegates and their alternates shall be renewed each year by the two chambers of the Reichsrath. Members of the Delegation are reëligible.

Art. XI. The Delegations shall be convoked each year by the emperor, who fixes the place of meeting.

Art. XIII. The authority of the Delegations shall extend to all matters concerning common affairs. All other subjects are beyond their sphere of action.

Art. XIV. The proposals of the government shall be transmitted by the common ministry to each of the two Delegations separately.

The way the Delegations conduct business

Each Delegation shall have an equal right to present projects with reference to matters within its jurisdiction.

[1] This provision, which has now been supplanted by direct election of representatives by the Austrian parliament, serves to show the several ancient political subdivisions of the Austrian Empire.

Art. XV. For the passage of every law within the powers of the two Delegations, the approval of both is necessary, or, in case of disagreement, a vote of the two bodies assembled in joint session ; in both cases the approval of the emperor is necessary.

Art. XIX. Each Delegation acts, deliberates, and decides in separate session on matters which concern it.

Art. XXX. The two Delegations shall communicate their decisions to each and, whenever it is necessary, the motives for these decisions.

This communication shall be made in writing in the German language on the part of the Delegation from the Reichsrath, and in the Hungarian language on the part of the Delegation from the Reichstag ; in each case there shall be annexed to the text an authentic translation into the language of the other Delegation.

Art. XXXI. Each Delegation has the right to propose that a question shall be decided by a vote taken in common, and that proposition cannot be rejected by the other Delegation after there has been an exchange of three written communications which have produced no result.

The two presidents shall fix by mutual agreement the time and place of a joint session for taking the common vote.

263. Extract from the papal allocution condemning the Austrian constitution (June 22, 1868)

While the Compromise was being reached with Hungary, the entire government of Austria was being reorganized by the adoption of fundamental laws establishing a legislature and political and religious liberty. This action was in flat contradiction to the Concordat with the Pope, agreed upon in 1855, which recognized Catholicism as the exclusive state religion, and gave to the clergy all the rights and privileges which they claimed as theirs. Accordingly the Pope condemned the new Austrian constitution in the following terms :

By our apostolic authority we reject and condemn the above-mentioned laws in general and in particular, together with all that has been ordered, done, or enacted in these or other matters affecting the rights of the Church by the Austrian government or its subordinates; by the same authority we declare these laws and all their implications to have been and to be for the future null and void. We exhort and adjure their authors, especially those who boast of the name of Catholics, who have dared to propose, to accept, to approve, and to execute them, to remember the censures and spiritual penalties incurred *ipso facto*, according to the apostolic constitutions and decrees of the Ecumenical Councils, by those who violate the rights of the Church.

The following year Count Beust, the Austrian Imperial Chancellor, made it clear, however, in his instructions to the Austrian ambassador at Rome, that there was no hope for the restoration of the old authority of the Church, and that he deemed it necessary for the Pope to recognize the fact.

In the mind of every true patriot it was clear in 1866 that the stability of the State could only be secured through a fundamental regeneration establishing the great principles of constitutional liberty. Accordingly the encouragement of the free evolution of all the living forces of the nation became the leading idea of the government. It must be regretted that the Austrian bishops and the messages dispatched by them to the Holy See did not take into account this irresistible force which was responsible for the sudden change in Austrian affairs. This oversight furthermore allowed more than one mistaken view to be entertained in Rome. Had the representatives of the Church understood that in face of a complete revolution — the result of imperative necessity — there was no longer any question of making fruitless attempts to recover decaying privileges, but that it was their duty to turn the new order of things as far as possible to the advantage of the Church (as when the Belgian clergy, for instance, grasped this fact and accepted the constitution of the year 1831), they surely would not have made that stubborn opposition to the projected reforms, which raised against them the reproach of being enemies to the constitutional organization of the monarchy. It is this reproach

264. Beust's instructions to the Austrian ambassador at the papal court (July 2, 1869)

which makes the position of the clergy so difficult, and which, to the great regret of the Imperial and Royal government, often imbitters differences of opinion relating to unimportant and simple questions of detail.

The foregoing also makes it partially clear how it comes about that the interference of the Holy See can still further aggravate the conflict in a lamentable fashion. . . . Painful as it may be for the Roman Court to be compelled to hear these words, we cannot conceal from it the following truths :

The existing provisions of the Concordat can no longer be enforced in Austria. The privileged position which this act conceded to the clergy can no longer exist for them, and would only injure them in the future. It is illusory to hope that this state of affairs is only transitory and can be modified by a change of ministers. It is as far as possible from the desire of the Imperial and Royal government to seek conflict with the Church ; it wishes, on the contrary, nothing more earnestly than agreement. In the midst of the difficulties with which it has to struggle, it did not for a moment renounce its calmness and impartiality. It has given to all parties counsel of wisdom and moderation, and has steadily taken into consideration the possibility of restoring better relations with the papal court in the future. The evidence for these statements may be found in two facts : that the Imperial and Royal government most carefully refrained from pronouncing upon the legal continuation of the Concordat within its boundaries ; and that precisely in those questions which caused the greatest uproar in Rome — that is, in regard to the reforms relating to the solemnization of marriage and the conduct of schools — it showed great reserve.

If one adds to this that circumstances, as well as the principles which these reforms had introduced, did not warrant the government in longer assuming the position of an exclusively Catholic State, and that, on the contrary, it was bound to bring its legislative activities into harmony with the principle of equality of religions before the law, one must do the Imperial government the justice of recognizing that it endeavored to spare as far as possible the Catholic interests. . . .

The Concordat cannot be enforced in Austria

Rome must, above all, bring herself to the conclusion that Austria is not to be regarded as a land which is exclusively appointed to hold the same views as the Holy See ; as a result it is necessary to place the Austro-Hungarian monarchy in the class of modern constitutional States, and accordingly it is also necessary not to require the Imperial and Royal government to approve demands which one would not think of making upon such countries as France and Belgium, because it would be known in advance that such claims would meet refusal there and would compromise the Holy See in vain. What can happen in other lands without bringing about on that account a breach with Rome must also be possible in Austria. This is the first fundamental principle on which the government as well as the people are firmly determined not to weaken. . . . {Rome has no special claim on Austria}

The Austrian constitutional settlement of 1867 excluded a large proportion of the people from all participation in political life by causing the members of the lower house to be elected by the local diets of the many provinces into which Austria was divided.[1] This indirect election was later supplanted by a class system similar to that in vogue in Prussia. At last, in 1906, after prolonged agitation, a very democratic measure establishing practically universal suffrage was passed, and shortly afterwards a general election was held under the new law, the results of which (as described by a former member of the Austrian parliament in an article in the *Fortnightly Review*, from which this extract is taken) clearly shows the extraordinary and bewildering number of parties in Austria. {265. The Austrian election of 1906}

The result of the elections of May 14, which has, it is true, been considerably modified by the supplementary elections, was very startling. Overwhelming successes of the socialist candidates were reported from all parts of the country. If we

[1] See above, p. 167

Bohemia

turn first to Bohemia, the most important part of the western division of the monarchy and at all times the cockpit of Austrian political warfare, we find that the discomfiture of the Young Czech party was the most important feature of the first pollings. . . . There seems little doubt that on May 14 many electors in Bohemia who were not socialists gave their votes to the socialist candidates, moved by a general feeling of discontent caused by the unjust treatment of Bohemia in the electoral bill to which

Young and Old Czechs

most of the Young Czechs had given their assent. The elections of May 23 in Bohemia, as in other parts of the empire, witnessed the rally of the nonsocialist parties; as already mentioned, a considerable number of the members of the formerly dominant Young Czech party now obtained seats, as well as some men belonging to the more ancient, more conservative party known as the Old Czechs. A few seats were also won by the Radical party, whose platform included the reëstablishment — in a modified form — of the ancient Bohemian constitution.

The agrarians

The party, however, that achieved the greatest success at the elections of May 23 was that known as the "agrarians," and it is to this party that the largest number of the representatives of Bohemia in the new parliament of Vienna will belong. Land is overtaxed in Austria to an almost incredible degree, and the peasants have succeeded in returning a considerable number of members specially pledged to protect the interests

German party in Bohemia

of landowners. The fate of the German deputies of Bohemia was yet more disastrous; their places were almost everywhere taken by socialists. An interesting feature of the election was the complete discomfiture of the so-called "Pan-Germanic" party, most of whose representatives were returned by the Germans of Bohemia. These men had attempted to establish, in a manner they were never able clearly to define, a closer connection between Austria and Germany. They had rendered themselves ridiculous by their abject devotion to Germania, who somewhat contemptuously rejected the wooing of her uncouth lovers. . . .

Moravia and Silesia

The "sister lands" of Bohemia — that is, Moravia and Silesia, both countries which have a mainly Slavic population — voted in a manner not dissimilar from that of Bohemia. It should, however, be noted that in Moravia a considerable number of the clericals were elected, — a fact that may not inconsiderably influence the state of parties in the new parliament.

As regards the German parts of Austria, the elections of Vienna, the capital of the empire, of course attract the most attention. That city had formerly held liberal views, but gradually became clerical through the almost unlimited influence which Dr. Karl Lueger acquired over the Viennese. This somewhat second-rate Cleon began life as a Liberal, but soon became a Jew-baiter or Anti-Semite. Through the indomitable energy of Lueger, his party, which afterward assumed the name of Christian Socialists, — though it is really conservative or rather clerical, — widely extended its influence and power. As one of its leaders stated at a recent public meeting, this party now has " adherents among all Germany from the Lake of Constance to the Bukovina ! " At the Vienna elections the Christian Socialists were successful, but hardly to so great an extent as had been anticipated. The liberals indeed only secured three seats, but the Christian Socialists, to whom the absence of Dr. Lueger through illness was very harmful, found more dangerous antagonists in the members of the socialist party. That party has been very ably organized by Dr. Adler, a man of exceptional talent, and one of the many brilliant leaders whom, from the time of Lassalle downward, the Semitic race has given to the socialists. Besides winning many seats in Vienna, the socialists have also won seats in provincial towns of Lower Austria, while they have won a seat even at Innsbruck and have captured the entire parliamentary representation of Linz, the capitol of Upper Austria, and of Trieste, the great seaport of the empire. The former German Liberal party has been long split up into various factions, and has at the election lost largely both to the clericals and to the socialists. . . .

The Slovenes, who inhabit parts of Styria, Carinthia, and Carniola, have mainly elected representatives who, though favorable to the claims of the Slavic populations which they represent, will consider it their principal duty to further the clerical policy which finds favor among the agricultural populations of the districts which elected them. In Galicia, which

German Austria

The Christian Socialists

The Slovenes

Galicia

sends about a hundred representatives to the parliament of Vienna, the elections have only just ended. As already mentioned, the new electoral law greatly favored the Polish majority of the population at the expense of the Ruthenian minority.

The Poles The Poles were therefore, on the whole, successful, though a certain number of Ruthenians obtained seats in the new parliament. Two Zionists elected by the Galician Jews will be members of the new parliament of Vienna.

The socialists Hardly ever, perhaps, in the annals of parliamentary government, have elections resulted in so complete a surprise as did those just held in Austria. The recent defeat of the socialists in Germany led even experienced statesmen to believe that they would be far more unsuccessful in Austria, which, rightly or wrongly, has always been considered a very conservative country. The extreme moderation hitherto displayed by the socialists largely contributed to their victory. It is a proof of the universal veneration with which all Austrians look on their sovereign, that not a single disloyal cry was heard during the recent elections, — and the socialists formed no exception in this respect.

During recent years the leading issues in Hungarian politics have been the question of extending the suffrage, which is now very restricted, and the readjustment of relations with Austria. The character of the suffrage, which is the source of so much agitation, is described as follows by an ardent advocate of reform.

266. The un-democratic government of Hungary Bismarck once said that a more absurd and wretched electoral system than the Prussian three-class suffrage could not be devised in any State. Bismarck was evidently unacquainted with the Hungarian electoral system, which, in absurdity and infamy, outranks the Prussian. In a population numbering almost 17,000,000, the number of voters amounts to 970,841; that is, 5.23 per cent of the population; while the corresponding figures for England are 16.3 per cent, for the German Empire 21.5 per cent, and for France 26.5 per cent. The economic and social condition of this voting population is apparent from the following data : 795,628 (82 per cent) belong to the property classes; 127,102 (13.1 per cent) to the peasantry and the petty bourgeoisie ; 48,111 (4.9 per cent) to the working class. In this reckoning the intellectuals, — the higher and middle-grade state and private officials, — are placed in the first category, and the lower officials in the second category.

If one considers, however, the reverse of the medal, — the number and class position of the disfranchised elements, — one discovers the following astounding facts: On a basis of the twenty-year age limit, the number of males amounts to 4,322,-960. Of this number 970,841 (22.4 per cent) have the right to vote ; 3,352,119 (77.6 per cent) are excluded from the suffrage. In this last group the proletariat predominates, with the enormous number of 2,131,279. If one compares with this the number, given above, of the working class entitled to vote, it is seen that only 2.2 per cent of the entire Hungarian proletariat are enfranchised.

The number of the disfranchised

One must not think, however, that this most atrocious injustice contributes to the maintenance of the so-called Magyar predominance, and that accordingly the Hungarian people have an interest in retaining it. The people who are related by blood to the ruling class suffer from it in the same degree as the remaining races of Hungary. The above-stated number of males over twenty years of age can be distributed in the following way: Hungarians, 2,248,166, of which 542,417 (24 per cent) are voters; the non-Hungarian peoples, 2,074,794, of whom 428,424 (20.8 per cent) are voters.

The composition of the Hungarian parliament corresponds to the social composition of the electorate. After the last election the composition of the lower house was as follows : 142 landlords, 114 lawyers, 66 executive or administrative officials, 56 great landlords (counts and barons), 22 clergymen, 5 merchants, 5 doctors, and 2 capitalists. Out of an electorate and a parliament so composed, there necessarily results a class absolutism which corresponds to the needs and interests of the landed classes, and which for forty years has actually dominated in Hungary all questions of domestic policy.

Composition of the Hungarian parliament

CHAPTER XXIII

THE GERMAN EMPIRE

Section 70. The German Constitution

{Germany did not introduce the cabinet system of England. The chief minister of the emperor, the Imperial Chancellor, was made responsible by the constitution to the emperor himself, not to the diet. In a speech before the Reichstag, made in 1878, Bismarck gave his reasons for thinking that the English system of parliamentary government, which had many advocates, could never work in Germany, owing to the existence of numerous hostile parties, which did not readily form strong, enduring alliances with one another.[1])

267. Bismarck on cabinet government (condensed) The parliamentary system works easily, and, so to speak, with elegance when there are but two parties, as in England where there are only the Whigs and Tories. If the same conditions prevailed with us, the course of events would be clear enough. One of the two parties would always have a majority. There was a time in England when one could say that five factions existed, which, it must be admitted, did not harbor the animosity for one another that the Germans contract through their affiliations in the army, the university, or in the parties of the Reichstag. These English groups never reach the point of cherishing mutual hatred; they always place the interests of their country in the front rank. It was this same reason which led the English to have no more than two parties of any importance

[1] Very recently the Imperial Chancellor has recognized his dependence on the will of the majority in the Reichstag. But the German Empire is still a long ways off from the English cabinet system.

— for the other minor parties, which I may call the English nihilists, I need not take into account.(In reality, there are in England but two great parties, of which one always has of necessity the majority in Parliament.)

If there were similarly with us a party composed of a majority, it would always be a pleasure for the minister in power to attach himself to it, if not openly, at least by a secret alliance, and thus to work in harmony with it. But we are still far from this ideal. We have here something like eight factions; the German holds strictly to the spirit of his party and keeps aloof from others.

Many factions in German politics

It is true that on all occasions during recent years we have found ourselves confronted by a compact association of the Progressive party, the Center, the Poles, and the Guelphs; but if these associations were in a majority for a single day, and if it were necessary for them to form a government on their side, would the Progressives join with the Center and would the Poles join the Guelphs?

We of the government find ourselves in the sad situation of having three sevenths of the Chamber absolutely against us. It is like maneuvering without having any ground on which to put one's feet. From the Progressive party, from the Center, from about one hundred and fifty deputies who are grouped in these two parties, we are not to expect the least support under any circumstances or for any project of law we are able to present, — on this point we harbor not the least doubt. Our base of operations is reduced to four sevenths of the Reichstag, composed of three groups of National Liberals and two groups of Conservatives.

The government's dependence on five groups

But I can do no more than address a prayer to the three parties, the National Liberals and the two Conservative groups, urging that their members may consent to render, not only to the government but to their country and their compatriots, the service of coming to terms with one another, and that all those who desire above all things the political development of the empire on sound lines may unite and never divide, except on fundamental questions which inevitably produce divergences, — certainly never on mere questions of precedence or rivalry.

Section 71. Kulturkampf

It so happened that during the decade in which the conflict for German unity was brought to a conclusion, the Pope, profoundly disturbed by the revolutionary political events taking place in Europe, especially in Germany, Austria, and Italy, sought to stay the triumph of the secular powers over the Church by a series of extraordinary declarations which helped to precipitate in Germany the conflict between the government and the Church, known as the *Kulturkampf*. In one of these documents, known as the "Syllabus of Errors," issued in 1864, Pope Pius IX stated in a condensed form what he regarded to be the leading errors of his time, among which the following, pertaining principally to affairs of government and to religious freedom, may be given as examples. It must be remembered that each statement is the exact *contrary* of the belief sanctioned by the Pope.

The syllabus of the principal errors of our time, which are stigmatized in the consistorial allocutions, encyclicals, and other apostolical letters of our Most Holy Father, Pope Pius IX :

268. Pius IX's list of errors in the Syllabus of 1864

15. Every man is free to embrace and profess the religion he shall believe true, guided by the light of reason.

16. Men may in any religion find the way of eternal salvation, and obtain eternal salvation.

18. Protestantism is nothing more than another form of the same true Christian religion, in which it is possible to be equally pleasing to God as in the Catholic Church.

20. The ecclesiastical power must not exercise its authority without the permission and assent of the civil government.

24. The Church has not the power of availing herself of force, or any direct or indirect temporal power.

39. The commonwealth is the origin and source of all rights, and possesses rights which are not circumscribed by any limits.

41. The civil power, even when exercised by an unbelieving sovereign, possesses an indirect and negative power over religious affairs.

42. In the case of conflicting laws between the two powers, the civil law ought to prevail.

43. The civil power has a right to break, and to declare and render null, the conventions (commonly called *Concordats*) concluded with the Apostolic See, relative to the exercise of rights pertaining to the ecclesiastical immunity, without the consent of the Holy See, and even contrary to its protests.

44. The civil authority may interfere in matters relating to religion, morality, and spiritual government.

47. The most approved theory of civil society requires that popular schools open to the children of all classes, and, generally, all public institutes intended for instruction in letters and philosophy, and for conducting the education of the young, should be freed from all ecclesiastical authority, government, and interference, and should be completely subject to the civil and political power, in conformity with the will of rulers and the prevalent opinions of the age. *Secular education*

48. This system of instructing youth, which consists in separating it from the Catholic faith and from the power of the Church, and in teaching exclusively, or at least primarily, the knowledge of natural things and the earthly ends of social life alone, may be approved by Catholics.

53. The laws for the protection of religious establishments, and securing their rights and duties, ought to be abolished; nay, more, the civil government may lend its assistance to all who desire to quit the religious life they have undertaken, and to break their vows. The government may also suppress religious orders.

55. The Church ought to be separated from the State, and the State from the Church.

63. It is allowable to refuse obedience to legitimate princes; nay, more, to rise in insurrection against them.

79. Moreover, it is false that the civil freedom granted to every mode of worship, and the full power given to all of overtly and publicly manifesting their opinions and their ideas, *Freedom of worship*

whatsoever their nature, conduce more easily to corrupt the morals and minds of the people, and facilitate the propagation of the pest of indifferentism.

80. The Roman Pontiff can and ought to reconcile himself to, and agree with, progress, liberalism, and civilization, as lately introduced.

Six years after the publication of the "Syllabus of Errors" the Vatican Council, a great ecclesiastical assembly convoked from Catholic Christendom, solemnly recognized the doctrine of papal infallibility, and confirmed the Pope in the possession of those ancient powers and the superiority over all churches and governments of the world, which had been claimed in the Middle Ages. A portion of this famous enunciation of papal supremacy and infallibility is given here.

269. The doctrine of papal supremacy and infallibility as enunciated by the Vatican Council of 1870

Wherefore, resting on plain testimonies of the Sacred Writings, and adhering to the plain and express decrees both of our predecessors, the Roman Pontiffs, and of the General Councils, we renew the definition of the ecumenical council of Florence, in virtue of which all the faithful of Christ must believe that the holy Apostolic See and the Roman Pontiff possess the primacy over the whole world, and that the Roman Pontiff is the successor of blessed Peter, Prince of the Apostles, and is the true vicar of Christ, and head of the whole Church, and father and teacher of all Christians; and that full power was given to him in the blessed Peter to rule, feed, and govern the universal Church by Jesus Christ our Lord; as is also contained in the acts of the General Councils and in the sacred Canons.

The subordination of clergy and laity to the Roman Pontiff

Hence we teach and declare that by the appointment of our Lord the Roman Church possesses the primacy in virtue of the power of an "ordinary"[1] over all other churches, and that this power of jurisdiction of the Roman Pontiff, which is truly episcopal, is immediate; to which all, of whatever rite

[1] That is, of a bishop's power.

and dignity, both pastors and faithful, both individually and collectively, are bound, by their duty of hierarchical subordination and true obedience, to submit not only in matters which belong to faith and morals, but also in those that appertain to the discipline and government of the Church throughout the world, so that the Church of Christ may be one flock under one supreme pastor through the preservation of unity both of communion and of the profession of the same faith with the Roman Pontiff. This is the teaching of Catholic truth, from which no one can deviate without loss of faith and of salvation. . . .

Further, from this supreme power possessed by the Roman Pontiff of governing the universal Church, it follows that he has the right of free communication with the pastors of the whole Church, and with their flocks, that these may be taught and ruled by him in the way of salvation. Wherefore we condemn and reject the opinions of those who hold that the communication between this supreme head and the pastors and their flocks can lawfully be impeded ; or who make this communication subject to the will of the secular power, so as to maintain that whatever is done by the Apostolic See, or by its authority, for the government of the Church, cannot have force or validity unless it be confirmed by the assent of the secular power. *Freedom of the Pope to communicate with his flock*

And since by the divine right of Apostolic primacy the Roman Pontiff is placed over the universal Church, we further teach and declare that he is the supreme judge of the faithful, and that, in all cases, the decision of which belongs to the Church, recourse may be had to his tribunal, and that none may reopen the judgment of the Apostolic See, than whose authority there is no greater ; nor can any lawfully review its judgment. Wherefore they err from the right course who assert that it is lawful to appeal from the judgments of the Roman Pontiffs to an ecumenical council, as to an authority higher than that of the Roman Pontiff. *The Pope is the supreme judge of the faithful*

If, then, any shall say that the Roman Pontiff has the office merely of inspection or direction, and not full and supreme power of jurisdiction over the universal Church, not only in

Condemnation of those who dispute the Pope's authority

things which belong to faith and morals, but also in those which relate to the discipline and government of the Church scattered throughout the world; or assert that he possesses merely the principal part, and not all the fullness of this supreme power; or that this power which he enjoys is not ordinary and immediate, both over each and all the churches, and over each and all the pastors and the faithful, let him be anathema. . . .

Definition of the doctrine of infallibility

. . . Therefore, faithfully adhering to the tradition received from the beginning of the Christian faith, for the glory of God our Savior, the exaltation of the Catholic religion, and the salvation of Christian people, the sacred Council approving, we teach and define that it is a dogma divinely revealed: that the Roman Pontiff, when he speaks *ex cathedra*, that is, when in discharge of the office of pastor and teacher of all Christians, by virtue of his supreme Apostolic authority, he defines through the divine assistance promised to him in the blessed Peter, a doctrine regarding faith or morals to be held by the universal Church, is possessed of that infallibility with which the divine Redeemer willed that his Church should be endowed for defining doctrines regarding faith or morals; and that therefore such definitions of the Roman Pontiff are unalterable in themselves, and not in virtue of the sanction of the Church.

But if any one — which may God avert — presume to contradict this our definition, let him be anathema.

The dogma of papal infallibility was rejected by some members of the Church in Germany, who formed themselves into a separate sect known as "The Old Catholics"; and the assertion of the supremacy of the Church over the secular government aroused the deep displeasure of Bismarck. The great body of Catholic clergy in Germany, however, were loyal to the Pope, and, as they viewed with some apprehension the ascendancy of Protestant Prussia in German imperial affairs, they sought to increase their influence by organizing a political party (the Center). Bismarck met the opposition of the clergy with decided measures of repression, and not until after he became apprehensive of the growing power of the socialists, was he willing to come to terms with Rome. He thus expressed himself in a speech before the Prussian House of Lords.

270. Bismarck on the Church-State conflict (condensed)

The question before us is misrepresented and viewed in a false light if it is considered as a denominational or ecclesiastical question. It is really a political issue.

Contrary to the contention of one of our Catholic fellow-citizens, this is not a war carried on by a Protestant dynasty against the Catholic Church; there is no question of a conflict between belief and unbelief. It is at bottom the ancient struggle for power which is as old as the human race,—the contest between kingship and priesthood, which is far older than the advent of our Savior in this world; the contest, which under the name of the conflict between the German kings and the popes, filled the history of the Middle Ages until the dissolution of the German Empire; the contest which came to its end as the last representative of the illustrious Swabian imperial line died on the scaffold under the ax of a French conqueror who joined in an alliance with the Pope.

Supremacy the goal of the popes

The Papacy has always been a political power which has intervened in the affairs of the world with the greatest confidence and the most important results. The goal which continually appears before the papal power, the programme which, in the time of the mediæval emperors, was near realization, is the subjection of the temporal to the spiritual power, an eminently political project.

The contest of the priesthood with the kingship, the contest of the Pope with the German emperors as we have seen it in the Middle Ages, is to be judged as any other fight for power. It has its alliances, its treaties of peace, its temporary lulls, its truces. There have been peaceful popes and warlike, conquering popes. It has not always been the case in the struggles of the Papacy that the Catholic powers have been exclusively the allies of the Pope; and the clergy have not always stood by the side of the popes. We have had cardinals as ministers of great powers at times when the powers were carrying out a strong anti-papal policy, extending even to acts of violence. We have found bishops in the army of the German emperor arrayed against papal interests.

The contest is for political power

This contest for power, then, is subject to the same conditions as every other political struggle; and when presented as if it were a question of persecuting the Church, it is mere subterfuge calculated to impress people incapable of forming their own judgments. It is really a question of protecting the State, it is a question of fixing the boundary line between the priesthood and the kingship, and this line of demarcation must be so placed that the State can maintain its existence. For in the kingdom of this world the State must have both precedence and command.

The origin of the Center party

When we were in Versailles it surprised me somewhat to learn that an appeal was issued to the Catholic members of legislative bodies, asking them to declare whether they were ready to form a sectarian group, such as we recognize to-day in the Center party, and whether they would agree to work for and vote for the propositions which we are considering to-day, in order to secure their embodiment in the Constitution. This programme did not then frighten me, — in general I was peaceably inclined. However, when I returned here I saw for the first time how strong was the organization of the Church party in warfare against the State. What called my attention to the danger was the power which this newly formed group exerted. Representatives who had resided in their districts and had been repeatedly re-elected for a long time were set aside by orders from Berlin and the election of new representatives prescribed, whose names were not even known to their constituents before. This happened not only in one election district; it happened in many.

The State must be protected against Rome

This is really an attempt to establish two States within one nation, — States, moreover, which would have to assume a hostile attitude toward each other, — one of whose sovereigns is a foreign ecclesiastical prince with his seat of power at Rome; an ecclesiastical prince who, through the most recent modifications in the constitution of the Catholic Church, has become more powerful than ever before. This situation is simply intolerable for the government; it is in duty bound to protect the State against this danger. In its struggle to protect the State the government turns to the House of Lords with an appeal for support and aid in strengthening the State and defending it against the assaults and undermining which endanger its peace and its future.

Section 72. Bismarck and State Socialism

Bismarck encountered far bitterer opposition on the part of the Social Democrats than the clergy had offered, for the socialists aimed at a reconstruction of the Prussian and the Imperial governments along decidedly democratic lines, and they furthermore proposed that all the great industries should be taken over and operated by the governments so revolutionized. The Chancellor, therefore, believed that the best way to deal with these new agitators was to suppress their meetings and newspapers, and in a speech made while his proposition was being considered in the Reichstag, he stated his reasons for regarding the Social Democrats as the enemies of the fatherland.

271. Bismarck's speech on the Anti-Socialist law (condensed)

For eleven years we have had the advantage of associating here with Social Democrats, and do you remember, Gentlemen, of hearing, amid all the long speeches delivered in this place by socialists, a single one in which it was possible to discover the slightest shadow of a concrete idea or of a project for future action indicating what they actually intend to do when they shall have made a breach in the existing social system? I recall nothing of the sort, and I believe I know the reason why these gentlemen are so carefully silent about the manner in which they intend to refashion the world when they are masters. It is because they do not know themselves. They can never keep the promises with which they have misled the people.

Bismarck
criticises
socialists
for attacking
sacred things

That these gentlemen with their obscure promises should have been able to seduce some people is not astonishing to any one who is discontented with his situation, particularly when he resents it and makes the most of his discontent with Germanic energy. When socialism is presented to the people who know how to read, but who can form no judgment on what they have read (the ability to read is much more extensive with us than in France or England, though perhaps the ability to form a judgment on what is read is less common in Germany than in these two countries), when one makes such people brilliant promises, and, moreover, contemptuously derides as rubbish and fiction everything formerly held sacred ; when the glorious motto "With God for King and for Country," which has filled with enthusiasm and guided and sustained our fathers and ourselves, is represented as a hollow phrase, a mere dupery ; when one takes away from such people faith in God, faith in our royalty, attachment to the country, belief in family relations, in property, in the transmission by inheritance of what has been acquired for the children ; — when one takes away all this, it is then not very difficult to carry the half-educated man to the point of finally crying out with Faust : "Cursed be hope, cursed be faith, and cursed be patience particularly." If I had myself arrived at this state of unbelief which is taught to these people, if I had lost what the poet calls "Faith in God and in a better future," nothing could make me desire to live a day longer. (Loud applause.) Take away this faith from the poor man to whom you can assure no compensation, and you produce in him a disgust with life.

Recent advent
of the
socialists

It is only since 1867 that we have been able to recognize officially the leaders of Social Democracy by the presence in Parliament of Messrs. Bebel, Liebknecht, Fritsche, Schweitzer, and Mende. At the period of which I speak these gentlemen presented themselves with a certain timidity still, although they carefully announced that they were not tractable people like Lassalle and his kind, and proclaimed themselves true Social Democrats. But the ambition which animates them to-day, namely, to seize the power of the State and use it for their own interest and ideas, has really taken its rise since 1870.

Before 1870, while the leaders of the International lived in London and Geneva, France was the real home of their endeavors; France was the real field of their operations; it was only in France that the socialists had an army all ready, able to give battle for the Commune and render itself effectually the master of the situation for a short time.[1] At that moment, when they found themselves in the possession of authority, did they work out a definite programme, indicating how they could employ their power for the advantage of the needy classes? They were able to write Utopian phrases in their journals, but with authority in their hands they made no attempt in Paris to show by example what they really wanted. They did nothing but assassinate, burn, give themselves up to cruelty of every sort, destroy national monuments; and even when they had transformed Paris into a heap of ashes, in the face of this destruction they did not know any more about what they wanted: "We are malcontents; things ought to be otherwise; but how? We do not know." They went no further.

Bismarck takes the Paris Commune as an example of socialism

The method suggested by Bismarck for suppressing social-democratic agitation met the approval of the Reichstag, and an elaborate law was passed against the socialists. The following are some of the principal provisions of the measure.

Associations which aim, by social-democratic, socialistic, or communistic agitation, at the destruction of the existing order in State or society are forbidden. The same holds of associations in which such activity makes its appearance in a manner to endanger the peace, in particular, the harmony between different classes of the population. . . .

272. Provisions of the Anti-socialist law (1878)

Meetings in which social-democratic, socialistic, or communistic tendencies, directed to the destruction of the existing order in State or society, make their appearance are to be dissolved. Such meetings as appear to justify the assumption that they are destined to further such tendencies are to be

Meetings

[1] Compare with the account given in *The Development of Modern Europe*, Vol. II, pp. 155-156.

forbidden. Public festivities and processions are placed under the same restrictions.

Publications   All printed matter, in which appear social-democratic, socialistic, or communistic tendencies, directed to the destruction of the existing order in State and society in a manner dangerous to the peace and, in particular, to the harmony between different classes of the population, is to be forbidden. In the case of periodical literature, the prohibition can be extended to any further issue, as soon as a single number has been forbidden under this law.

Collections   The collection of contributions for the furthering of social-democratic, socialistic, or communistic endeavors, directed toward the destruction of the existing order in State or society, as also the public instigation to the furnishing of such contributions, are to be forbidden by the police. . . . The money seized [by the police] from forbidden collections, or the equivalent of the same, is to fall to the poor-relief fund of the neighborhood.

Special precautions   For districts or localities which are, owing to the above-mentioned agitation, threatened with danger to the public safety, the following provisions can be made, for the space of a year at most, by the central police of the State in question, and subject to the permission of the Bundesrath.

(1) That public meetings may only take place with the previous permission of the police; this prohibition does not extend to meetings for an election to the Reichstag or the diet.

(2) That the distribution of printed matter may not take place in public roads, streets, squares, or other public localities.

(3) That residence in such districts or localities can be forbidden to all persons from whom danger to the public safety or order is to be feared.

Bitter as was Bismarck's hatred for Social Democracy, he was by no means averse to government interference on behalf of the working classes. Indeed, it was largely for the purpose of destroying the discontent of the workingmen, which he regarded as largely responsible for socialist gains in elections, that he proposed that the government should secure them against that poverty caused by sickness, accidents, and old age. Before his resignation in 1890, Bismarck was able to carry through a series of insurance laws for the benefit of the working classes. In an elaborate report published in 1904 the German government gives a full account of the nature and results of these famous measures.

The minimum of relief in case of sickness entitles the beneficiary to free medical treatment and medicine for 26 weeks; and in case of incapacity for work, financial assistance to the extent of one half of the average daily wage, or to free hospital nursing, besides one half of the allowance for those dependent on the sick person. Further, it entitles sick women to relief for six months after their confinement; and in case of death, burial money amounting to twenty times their average daily wage.

273. How the working classes are insured in Germany (condensed from a government report)

The necessary means are raised by weekly contributions (not higher than four per cent of the average wage), two thirds of which is borne by the insured and one third by the employer. The administration is carried out through sickness clubs organized according to trades or localities, whose presiding officers are chosen from the insured and the employers according to the ratio of the contributions. The insurance against sickness embraces (inclusive of the miners' clubs) about ten million persons in more than twenty thousand clubs, and involves an annual expenditure of about 200 million marks.

Insurance against accidents replaces the old law of Employers' Liability (its many defects being equally harmful to employer and employed) by a legal provision, which also insures the person injured, or his survivors, in cases of casual accidents, or such as have occurred through the fault of his co-workers, or through his own carelessness. The personal liability of the employer is thus changed into an economical charge upon the entire trade concerned, which is apportioned to single establishments according to the measure of their risk.

Accident insurance

The minimum indemnity against accidents comprises : (1) in the case of wounded persons (from the commencement of the fourteenth week after the accident, that is to say, as a supplement to the sickness insurance) the expenses of medical treatment, and a payment during the period of incapacity for work up to two-thirds of the annual earnings, or free nursing in an institute until medical treatment is no longer necessary, and the same allowance to those dependent on the injured person as in case of death ; (2) in case of death, funeral money to the amount of the fifteenth part of annual salary, but in any case not less than fifty marks, and for those dependent on the deceased an allowance amounting to 60 per cent of the annual wage for widow and children, and to 20 per cent of same for necessitous parents. Up to the end of 1903 more than 1,000,-000,000 marks were paid in indemnities for accidents.

Insurance against disablement and old age, which was introduced on the first of January, 1891, by an imperial law (revised in 1899), completes the system of workmen's insurance. The administrators of the insurance, which includes all branches of trade, are territorial insurance institutions, guaranteed by the State, whose self-administration is shared equally by the employer and employees. The insurance entitles those incapable of work to pensions without regard to age, and gives old-age pensions to septuagenarians regardless of working ability. Further it assures return of subscriptions paid by insured women who marry before receiving a pension, to widows or orphans of those insured persons who die before receiving an allowance, and to those insured who are disabled through accidents, but who do not receive a disablement allowance because of their higher accident-insurance allowance.

The funds necessary for this insurance are raised through a yearly contribution from the government of fifty marks for each pension, together with weekly contributions to an equal amount from employer and employed. The amount of the same for a definite period is so estimated in advance that the capital value of the pensions which the insurance institution must bear is covered, as well as the reimbursements of contributions and the other expenses of insurance.

The disablement-insurance scheme comprises about 13.5 million persons insured, or almost the whole of the working classes.

To the initiative of imperial social policy the blessing is therefore due that in Germany nearly all workmen are insured in case of sickness, accident, and disablement. Every day 1,250,000 marks are spent for this branch of workman's protection alone. In countries without compulsory insurance scarcely one tenth of the workmen enjoy a similar protection, and this, moreover, falls considerably short of the German workman's insurance in certainty and scope.

In one year over five million persons in need of help received about 370,000,000 marks; during the whole period of seventeen years (1885–1901) 50,000,000 persons in round numbers (sick and injured persons, the incapacitated and their families) received indemnities amounting to 3,000,000,000 marks as a result of the legislation for the insurance of workmen, although the most far-reaching clauses of the law (insurance against disablement) only came into force on January 1, 1891. The workmen have only paid the smaller part of the contribution, and have already received about 1,000,000,000 marks more in compensation than their contributions amount to. *Some statistics on the amount of aid rendered*

The significance of this insurance for German workmen extends far beyond a simple financial one, for it has become a social-political school for the whole nation. The importance of German workmen's insurance towers far above its financial aspect. Through the mutual participation of the employer and employee in the administration and payment of contributions, the workman is himself daily reminded of the moral duty of making provision for the future from his own resources, the employers of their social duties to their employees, and both parties of their common interest in their calling. Thereby social reconciliation is effected where otherwise special organizations would array themselves against each other as antagonists. It is of great importance, moreover, that the cure of sick and disabled workmen is more rapidly effected through the erection of special institutions. Owing to the success reached through these measures, public sanitation has been directed into *Moral benefits of working-class insurance* entirely new channels. Above everything else, the coöperation of these organizations with those of voluntary charity, especially with the Red Cross Society and the National Women's Club, has made it possible for even the smallest and poorest country parish to systematically cure the sick, and to undertake an organized campaign against that frightful national pestilence, — tuberculosis of the lungs.

Instead of smothering the free initiative of self-helping bodies, as many had feared workmen's insurance would do, it has, on the contrary, enabled them to develop to their highest powers.

Use of reserve fund for public improvements   The reserve capital of 1,500,000,000 marks has furnished the means for solving the most important social economical questions.

Up to the end of 1902 over 400,000,000 marks had been expended from the funds of disablement-insurance institutions for the construction of workmen's dwellings, sick and convalescent houses, sanatoriums, public hospitals, homes for traveling workmen, public baths, blind asylums, kindergartens, slaughterhouses, systems of water works, sewerage and draining plants, street paving, savings banks, coöperative stores, and similar institutions for public welfare, as well as for the payment of agricultural loans (mortgages, light railroads, land and road improvement, development of cattle breeding, etc.), all measures the final aim of which is to cause the masses of the people to participate to an ever-increasing degree in the advance of civilization.

Summary of advantages   The advantages of German workmen's insurance, in distinction to other systems, is that :

1. It guarantees the support required by necessitous persons immediately, and as a well-earned right;

2. It gives both employer and employee common interests in their duties, and thereby acts in a way as an instrument of social reconciliation ;

3. It awakens a feeling of social duty throughout the nation ; and

4. It strengthens the working and defensive power of the nation.

Section 73. Germany's Policy of Protection and Colonization

Under the newly established imperial government Germany's industry and commerce advanced with astonishing rapidity, especially after the new protective tariffs introduced in 1879.

It was not long, therefore, before the German home markets were glutted, and German merchants began to look abroad for suitable places to invest their money and develop their trade. In 1897 the murder of some German missionaries in China led the imperial government to demand that China should make reparation for the wrong, and in a speech made on the occasion of the departure of the fleet for the East, under the command of Prince Henry, the Kaiser announced that the government was ready to protect German interests in every part of the world.

The voyage on which you are starting and the task you have to perform have nothing essentially novel about them. They are the logical consequences of the political labors of my late grandfather and his great Chancellor, and of our noble father's achievements with the sword on the battlefield. They are nothing more than the first effort of the reunited and reëstablished German Empire to perform its duties across the seas. In the astonishing development of its commercial interests the empire has attained such dimensions that it is my duty to follow the new German Hansa, and to afford it the protection it has a right to demand from the empire and the emperor. Our German brethren in holy orders, who have gone out to work in peace, and who have not shrunk from risking their lives in order to carry our religion to foreign soil and among foreign nations, have placed themselves under my protection, and we have now to give permanent support

274. William II's speech on German world policy (1897)

and safety to these brethren, who have been repeatedly harassed and often hard pressed.

Rights of German traders will be protected

For this reason, the enterprise which I have intrusted to you, and which you will have to carry out conjointly with the comrades and the ships already on the spot, is essentially of a defensive and not of an offensive nature. Under the protecting banner of our German war flag, the rights we are justified in claiming are to be secured to German commerce, German merchants, and German ships, — the same rights that are accorded by foreigners to all other nations. Our commerce is not new, for the Hansa was, in old times, one of the mightiest enterprises the world has ever seen, and the German towns were able to fit out fleets such as the broad expanse of the sea had hardly ever borne before.

The Hansa decayed, however, and could not but decay, for the one condition, namely imperial protection, was wanting. Now things are altered. As the first preliminary condition, the German Empire has been created. As the second preliminary condition, German commerce is flourishing and developing, and it can develop and prosper securely only if it feels safe under the power of the empire. Imperial power means naval power, and they are so mutually dependent that the one cannot exist without the other.

Use the mailed fist if necessary

As a sign of imperial and of naval power, the squadron, strengthened by your division, will now have to act in close intercourse and good friendship with all the comrades of the foreign fleets out there, for the protection of our home interests against everybody who tries to injure Germany. That is your vocation and your task. May it be clear to every European out there, to the German merchant, and, above all, to the foreigner whose soil we may be on, and with whom we shall have to deal, that the German Michael has planted his shield, adorned with the eagle of the empire, firmly on that soil, in order, once for all, to afford protection to those who apply to him for it. May our countrymen abroad, whether priests or merchants or of any other calling, be firmly convinced that the protection of the German Empire, as represented by the imperial ships, will be constantly afforded them.

Should, however, any one attempt to affront us, or to infringe our good rights, then strike out with mailed fist, and, if God will, weave round your young brow the laurel which nobody in the whole German Empire will begrudge you.

Prince Henry replied to his august imperial brother in the following exalted strain:

Most Serene Emperor, most powerful King and Lord, illustrious brother, — as children we grew up together. Later on it was granted to us as men to look into each other's eyes and stand faithfully at each other's side. To your Majesty the imperial crown has come with thorns. I have striven in my restricted sphere and with my scanty strength, as man, soldier, and citizen, to help your Majesty. We have reached a great epoch, an important epoch for the nation, an important epoch for your Majesty and the navy. Your Majesty has made a great sacrifice, and has shown great favor to myself in intrusting this command to me. I thank your Majesty from the bottom of a loyal, brotherly, and humble heart. I well understand your Majesty's feelings. I know what a heavy sacrifice you made in giving me so fine a command. It is for this reason, your Majesty, that I am so much moved, and that I so sincerely thank you. I am further deeply indebted for the confidence which your Majesty reposes in my weak person, and I can assure your Majesty of this: I am not allured by hopes of winning glory or laurels, I am only animated by one desire, — to proclaim and preach abroad to all who will hear, as well as to those who will not, the gospel of your Majesty's anointed person. This I will have inscribed on my banner, and will bear it wherever I go.

These sentiments with which I set out are shared by my comrades. I raise my glass, therefore, and call upon those who with me enjoy the happy privilege of being permitted to go forth, to remember this day, to impress the person of the emperor on their minds, and to let the cry resound far out into the world — Our most Serene, Mighty, Beloved Emperor, King and Master, for ever and ever. Hurrah! hurrah! hurrah!

In addition to opening up markets for trade and investment in other countries, the German government in 1884 joined in the general European scramble for African territory, and secured four enormous colonies which it hoped to develop into profitable trading centers. The African natives, however, on several occasions, broke out in rebellion against German rule, and enormous sums of money were required for the suppression of these uprisings. The cost of these commercial and colonial enterprises has, of course, greatly increased the German budget, and the whole policy of Imperialism was made the leading question of German politics in the election of 1907. The chief opposition has come from the Social Democrats, and thus Imperialism and Socialism have become the leading issues. The attitude of the Conservatives is shown in their election proclamation issued in 1906.

275. Conservative election manifesto on Imperialism and Socialism (1906)

The Reichstag has been dissolved because it did not grant the government the troops and supplies demanded for the energetic and complete suppression of the uprisings in German Southwest Africa. For the first time the Reichstag has been dissolved for reasons which belong to the sphere of foreign policy, and which spring from the necessity of defending our rapidly growing interests beyond the seas. With just indignation at the triumphant vote of the opposition, the Chancellor exclaims: "Shall the German nation show itself weaker than other nations, and acknowledge itself weaker?" That is the great question which the German people must answer at the polls on January 25. For the German nation, which for thirty years has been restricted to its position of a great power in Europe, has to-day to direct its attention not only to its colonial possessions but also to its oversea trade, mounting upward into the billions.

A firm colonial policy demanded

We Conservatives, for our part, cannot and will not leave the government in the lurch in its task of guarding and maintaining the honor, power, and national dignity of our country, whether it be to protect the German Empire itself or the colonies dearly bought and boldly defended by the life blood of thousands of German soldiers; for their economic development and settlement are attainable only under this preliminary condition. Only thus can we expect a conscious, well-directed, and orderly administration conformable to the conditions of each colony; and only thus can we hope that the government, taking into account our financial resources, will guard and advance the development of our colonies in the interests of the German nation, and yet with due regard for the principle of constitutional responsibility. . . .

We choose for the Reichstag only those men who remain true to our national mission of maintaining a strong military power on land and sea in order to secure peace for us and protect us against all enemies. We choose furthermore only those men who are determined to support the interests of agriculture and commerce, — in short, the entire middle class, with due consideration for their financial abilities, — and who are also determined to promote a tariff and commercial policy which will take this class into account. We support, furthermore, a sound social policy as understood by William I; we desire, however, a simpler, cheaper, and better administration, taking greater care for the interests of the middle class and for the preservation of the strength and prosperity of the employer as well as the workingman.

In the conflict for our national possessions and ideals as well as for our social and political institutions, sorely threatened by Social Democracy, we expect from the imperial authority energetic and effective measures which will oppose more vigorously than ever before the endeavors of those unpatriotic socialists who are in open opposition to the Christian culture of the German Empire. *Dangers of Social Democracy*

And now to the election campaign for German honor, courage, and reputation against all enemies.

THE COMMITTEE OF THE GERMAN CONSERVATIVE PARTY

BERLIN, December 18, 1906

Section 74. The Reign of William II

On his accession to the throne in 1888, the new emperor, William II, in a speech to the Reichstag, announced the policies which he intended to follow.

Gentlemen :

276. William II's first address to the Reichstag, 1888 (condensed)

It is with deep sorrow in my heart that I greet you, and I know that you mourn with me. The grievous sufferings of my father, who has entered into his rest, still fresh in the minds of all, the momentous fact that, three months after the decease of his Majesty Emperor William, I should have been called upon to ascend the throne, exercise a like effect upon the hearts of all Germans, and our grief has found warm sympathy in all the countries of the world. With the weight of this burden upon me, I pray that God may give me strength to fulfill the lofty duties to which his will has called me.

In obeying this call I have before my eyes the example which the Emperor William left to his successors, of peaceful rule succeeding to wars of grave issue, — an example to which the government of my lamented father also conformed, in so far as the execution of his intentions was not prevented by sickness and death.

William promises to follow his grandfather's example

I have summoned you, Gentlemen, that I may make my declaration before you to the German people, that I am resolved, as emperor and king, to walk in the same path in which my late illustrious grandfather won the confidence of his federal allies, the love of the German people, and the good will of other countries. Whether I also shall succeed in this rests with God, but I will earnestly and laboriously endeavor to attain this end.

The most important duties of the German emperor consist in assuring the military and political security of the empire abroad, and in watching over the execution of the imperial laws at home. Of these laws, the chief is the imperial Constitution itself; to guard and protect this, including all the rights which it guarantees to the two legislative bodies of the nation and to every German subject, but no less those which it guarantees to the emperor, to each of the federal States, and to their sovereigns, is the emperor's most exalted right and duty.

In the legislation of the empire I have, according to the Constitution, to coöperate rather in my capacity as king of Prussia than in that of German emperor; but in both capacities it will be my endeavor to carry on the work of imperial legislation in the same spirit in which it was begun by my late illustrious grandfather. Especially I appropriate to myself his message of the 17th of November, 1881, in its full extent, and shall continue to strive, in the sense of that declaration, to secure imperial legislation which will afford to the working population in a still higher degree that protection, based on the principles of Christian morality, which it is able to guarantee to the weak and distressed in the battle for existence. *Legislation for the working classes*

I hope that it may become possible in this way to modify unsound social contrasts, and I confidently trust that I shall meet with the unanimous support of all true members of the empire and of the federated governments, without division or party difference, in this solicitude for our internal welfare. I consider it necessary, however, to keep our national and social development within the strict limits of legality, and firmly to oppose all movements which have for their aim and tendency the undermining of public order.

In foreign politics I am resolved, so far as in me lies, to maintain peace with all men. My affection for the German army, and the position I hold toward it, will never lead me into the temptation of jeopardizing for my country the benefits of peace, unless war be a necessity forced upon us by an attack upon the empire or its allies. Our army is meant to maintain peace, and to be in a position, if peace is broken, to win it back with honor. That it will be able to do with the help of God, through the strength which your recent unanimous vote has guaranteed to it. To use this strength for wars of aggression is very far from my heart. Germany requires neither added martial glory nor any fresh conquests, now that she has definitely won the right in war to exist as a united and an independent nation. . . . *Peace to be maintained*

Our existing agreements with Austria-Hungary and Italy
permit me, to my satisfaction, to cultivate my personal friendship for the emperor of Russia, and those friendly relations to
our Russian neighbors which have existed for hundreds of
years, and with which my own feelings and the interests of
Germany are equally in harmony. . . .

With trust in God and in the defensive power of our nation
I feel confident that it will be granted to us to defend, and
to confirm by peaceful labor, what was won in arms under the
leadership of my two predecessors on the throne, now resting
in God.

Shortly after his accession to the throne William II
found great difficulty in coöperating with Bismarck in
the conduct of the government. The Iron Chancellor,
quite naturally, both from his long experience and his
services to the State, regarded himself as best fitted to
manage affairs of State. The new emperor, however,
had a will of his own, and he differed fundamentally
from his chancellor on some of the policies to be pursued. His version of the troubles which led to the withdrawal of Bismarck is given in the following extract
from the *Memoirs* of Prince Chlodewig of Hohenlohe-
Schillingfürst.

STRASSBURG, April 26, 1890

277. The
causes of
friction be-
tween Wil-
liam II and
Bismarck
(condensed)

. . . I drove with the emperor to the shooting box at
Sufflenheim. It was about an hour's drive, and during this
time the emperor related the whole story of his difference
with Bismarck without interruption. He said that relations
had become strained as early as December. The emperor
then desired that something should be done upon the question
of the workingmen. The chancellor objected. The emperor's
view was that, if the government did not take the initiative,
the Reichstag — in other words, the Socialists, the Center, and
the Progressives — would take the matter in hand and that the
government would be forced to follow them. The chancellor

desired to bring the Socialist Law, including the provisions for the expulsion of offenders, before the new Reichstag, to dis- solve the Reichstag if it rejected the law, and to take energetic measures in the event of a revolt. The emperor objected to this policy, saying that, if his grandfather had been forced to deal with rebels after a long and glorious reign, no one would have thought the worse of him. But he was himself in a different position, for he had as yet achieved nothing. He would be reproached with beginning his reign by the slaughter of his subjects. He was ready enough to act, but he wished to be able to act with a clear conscience, and first to make an attempt to satisfy the legitimate grievances of the workingmen, and at least to do everything that was possible to fulfill their justifiable demands. . . .

This friction had considerably disturbed the relations be- tween Bismarck and the emperor, and these were further strained by the question of the cabinet regulation of 1852. Bismarck had often advised the emperor to grant the ministers access to himself, and this was done. But when communication between the emperor and his ministers became more frequent, Bismarck took offense, became jealous, and revived the cabinet regulation of 1852 in order to interrupt communications between the emperor and the ministers. The emperor protested and demanded the repeal of the regulation ; Bismarck made a show of consent, but nothing was done in the matter. The emperor therefore demanded that he should either issue an order repealing the regulation, or hand in his resignation. This decision the emperor communicated to Prince Bismarck through Hahnke. The prince hesitated, but gave in his resignation on March 18.

It must be added that as early as the beginning of February Bismarck had told the emperor that he should retire. He afterwards explained that he had changed his mind and would stay, at which the emperor was not pleased, but offered no remonstrance until the affair of the cabinet regulation arose. . . . In any case the last three weeks of Bismarck's administration were occupied by unpleasant discussions between the emperor and himself. It was, as the emperor expressed it, " a beastly

time," and the question at issue was, as the emperor went on
to say, whether the Hohenzollern dynasty or the Bismarck
dynasty should reign.

In a formal letter accepting the resignation of Bismarck,
William II gives due recognition to the services which
that great statesman had rendered to the German nation.

My dear Prince,

278. William II's letter to Bismarck on his resignation

I was deeply moved to learn from your request on March 18
that you had determined to lay down the offices which you
have held with unparalleled success for so many years. I had
hoped that during our lifetime I should never be compelled
even to think of our separation. If, however, with full consciousness of the serious import of your resignation, I am compelled to reconcile myself to the thought of our separation,
I do so with a sad heart to be sure, but nevertheless in the
firm assurance that the granting of your request will contribute
to preserving and sparing your indispensable life and strength
as long as possible to the fatherland. The reasons advanced
for your decision convince me that further efforts to induce
you to withdraw your proposal would be fruitless. I therefore
comply with your wishes, since I grant you the requested discharge from your offices of Imperial Chancellor, President of
the Cabinet, and Minister of Foreign Affairs under pleasant
circumstances and in the firm assurance that your advice and
energy, your loyalty and devotion will not fail me and the
fatherland in the future.

I have considered it one of the most fortunate events in
my life that I was able to have you by my side as my first
counselor on my accession to the throne. What you have
sought and accomplished for Prussia and Germany, what you
have been to my House, my predecessors, and myself will remain to me and to the German people a grateful and imperishable remembrance. Moreover foreign nations will forever
regard with distinguished recognition your wise and forceful
policy of peace, which I have firmly decided to make my sure
guide in the future.

It is not within my power to reward you worthily for your services. I must therefore content myself with assuring to you the immortal gratitude of myself and the fatherland. As a sign of this regard I bestow upon you the dignity of Duke of Lauenburg. I will also transmit to you a life-size portrait of myself.

God bless you, my dear prince, and vouchsafe to you many years of a happy old age, cheered by consciousness of duty loyally discharged.

In these sentiments I shall remain in the future your duty-bound and grateful

Emperor and King,
WILLIAM, R. I.

The year following his coronation William II showed his interest in measures designed to improve the condition of the laboring classes by calling an international congress to consider practical propositions of reform. In the following letter to the new Imperial Chancellor he set forth the reasons why he deemed coöperation among the nations indispensable to the progressive improvement of the condition of workingmen in each.

To the Imperial Chancellor:

I am resolved to assist, so far as the limits fixed by the necessity of keeping German industry in condition to compete with the world's markets permit me, in ameliorating the lot of the German workingman. Serious losses, of course, of our home industries by reason of a decrease in our exports would not only injure the employers, but would also deprive their employees of the means of existence. The difficulties created by international competition when trying to improve the condition of our laboring classes can only be partially overcome by international agreement among those countries most interested in the world's markets. In the conviction, therefore, that other governments are also animated by the desire to examine jointly those efforts made even now by the laboring classes of these different countries, I direct that my

279. **William II's call for an international labor conference**

representatives in France, England, Belgium, and Switzerland make official inquiry whether these governments are inclined to associate themselves with us for the purpose of an international agreement as to the possibility of meeting those desires and requirements of the laboring classes which have been enunciated by them on the occasion of strikes during the last few years. As soon as these foreign governments have acceded in principle to my proposal, I shall instruct you to invite the cabinets of all those governments taking a common interest in the labor question to a conference as to the main points entering into this question.

WILLIAM

Notwithstanding the belief of Bismarck and the Kaiser that reforms on behalf of workingmen would prevent an increase in the socialist vote, their hopes were disappointed. The social-democratic party steadily perfected its organization, increased its number of newspapers, and spread its propaganda broadcast. Finally, in the election of 1907 the government declared open war on socialism, and sought to unite all factions against the "red specter." Though the supporters of the government were unable to prevent an actual increase in the number of socialist votes, they did succeed by effective combination in reducing the number of socialist members in the Reichstag from seventy-nine, at the time of dissolution, to forty-three. The following announcement of this significant election is taken from an article by Herr Bernstein, one of the most distinguished of the socialist leaders in Germany.

280. Socialism in the election of 1907 (condensed)

In the course of the six weeks which elapsed between the dissolution of the Reichstag and the day of the election a significant shifting of the line of battle took place. At first in the outcry against "the black and the red," the accent lay on the word "black." The Center, with its "backstairs government," was the enemy,—Social Democracy only the associate.

But the further the battle proceeded the more it became a war to destroy the "red," in which the "black" were expected to join in the end. For the Center party had only to defend seats and had very few to conquer. . . .

Quite the contrary was the case with the Social Democrats. They had not only to defend seats but meant also to conquer a good many. They fight everywhere and all parties alike. Sanguine members of the party counted upon an increase of seats from seventy-nine — the number when the Reichstag was dissolved — to one hundred or more, and there was nothing fantastic in this. The party is spread all over the empire; wherever modern industry has changed sleepy rural districts into communities with an alert working-class population, there Social Democracy has its adherents organized into branches of the party or of trade unions led in the spirit of the party. Never before had the state of Social Democracy in regard to its organization, press, and finances, been even approximately so prosperous as on the eve of this battle. It is no exaggeration to say that since 1903, when the party achieved a surprising electoral success, its membership and the circulation of its press had increased by more than 25 per cent. At the Mannheim congress held in September, 1906, the treasurer of the party, Herr Gerisch, gave the number of paying members at 400,000, and the circulation of their newspapers (i.e. the number of *subscribers*, for of street sale there is very little), at 840,000.

To this must be added the membership of the centralized trade unions and their press, for these unions are almost without exception led by Social Democrats, and their papers — all have their own papers, mostly compulsory to members — are frankly written in the social-democratic spirit. The centralized unions have made most wonderful progress and they now rank with the strongest British trade unions. They count over one million and a half members, and if we make a deduction for double membership, we may estimate the proletarian army represented by the social-democratic and trade union members as at least 1,600,000. A very large percentage of these are vigorous enthusiasts in the prime of life, and ready to take

The extensive organization of the Social Democrats

Rôle of the trade unions

upon themselves any work necessary for the distribution of the electoral literature of the party and the working up of the electors. Clubs of socialist cyclists exist in large numbers and train their members for efforts in rural districts. As to finance, the war chest of the party was well filled, and, besides, many of its papers make a good surplus; and, as they are party property, hand over their profits to the party funds. All this considered, it was very natural to conclude that the increase in the votes of the party would correspond to the increase in its organized force, in which case the vote would have come up to about 4,000,000 and an increase in seats would have been inevitable.

Socialist losses in the election

The facts have not justified this expectation. The party vote obtained on January 25 showed an advance which would have been regarded as quite creditable, namely from 3,011,000 to 3,259,000, i.e. just a quarter of a million. But as, on the whole, 1,767,000 more electors went to the poll than in 1903, the share of the social-democratic party, which in that year had received about 32 per cent of the whole vote, should have been this time about 560,000 new votes. Accordingly the party was 300,000 behind its normal increase. And thus only twenty-nine of its candidates were elected at the first ballot; whilst in 1903 the number had been fifty-six, and with those elected at the second ballot the total of this parliamentary group is now forty-three instead of seventy-nine at the time of the dissolution, and eighty-one on the morning after the election of 1903.

Causes of the losses

There are many causes to explain this retrogression. Thus, the intimate connection of the Social Democracy with the centralized trade unions has in some places led such workers as belonged to other unions to vote against the party. This has been the case particularly with members of the Christian Catholic trade unions, which in several places had candidates of their own, half a dozen of whom have been elected. The connection of the Social Democracy with the most militant trade unions and the tremendous growth of the latter have also induced many small masters who formerly had voted for social-democratic candidates to vote against them this time. The same has been the case with a number of small traders because of the promotion of coöperative societies by the Social Democracy. In rural districts small farmers have turned against it (as well as against advanced Radicals) because of the movement for the repeal of the duties on pigs and pork. They were delighted with the rise in price of the animal they fed, and would not hear of the change. To use Prince Bülow's words, it was in many districts the *brave swine* that saved the State. And similar examples of an estrangement of sections of the popular classes from the Social Democracy were found elsewhere.

But the main reason of the failure is to be found in the strong combined action of almost all nonsocial democratic parties and their agencies against the party of socialism, which is based on the class-war theory. Never before have these parties displayed such activity as at this time, and never have they been so united in their opposition. It was indeed a great social reaction. Bismarck at his best succeeded in getting a political combination formed that included the two Conservative parties and the National Liberals. The National Combine of 1906 embraced all these and advanced liberalism, besides including the South German Radical Democracy. It was, so to speak, a united effort of all the upholders of the present state of society against social revolution. With a zeal never displayed before, all these parties canvassed the electors and fetched them up in conveyances of all sorts to the polling places.

Union of forces against the socialists

CHAPTER XXIV

FRANCE UNDER THE THIRD REPUBLIC

Section 75. The Establishment of the Third French Republic

The opening months of the Third Republic were filled with anxiety, humiliation, and disaster for France. The empire of Napoleon III came to an end with his defeat at Sedan in September, 1870, but the Germans pressed on in spite of the protestations of the new provisional government at Paris, which declared that the war had been begun by the emperor, not by the French people. The victorious Germans surrounded Paris and subjected the great city to a terrible siege, lasting from September, 1870, to January 28, 1871, when the French were at last compelled to surrender and see the Prussians march in and occupy portions of their capital. The conditions are vividly portrayed by an Englishman, Mr. Whitehurst, who was in the city during the bombardment.

281. The siege of Paris described by an eyewitness

Thursday, December 29 [1870]. The bombardment is going on in a desultory fashion, but the two days have cost the French about a hundred and fifty killed and wounded. It seems that the officers suffer out of all proportion. At Avron the loss was considerable, and four officers were killed. A horrible episode marked the history of the bombardment of the opening day. A Colonel Heintzler and his wife were giving breakfast at Avron to several friends, a servant being in the room. One of the guests was laughing with the hostess, and said, " No butter, certainly, but there may be a shell in its place, and —" As he spoke a shell burst in the room, killed six of the party, wounded severely the host and hostess, and only the doctor of the regiment and the servant got off unscathed. The remains of the six came just now to the Val de Grâce hospital, but it was such a human ruin that no individuality could be recognized. The Prussians are firing with eighty guns, some of them being 112-pounders, and ranging from three miles and a half to four miles.

More curious facts of this startling siege : Mr. Geisling, one of the great "scullers" of the Seine, and well known here in connection with Church and Charity, is in [the regiment known as] the Mobiles of the Seine. On Christmas Eve he was on duty within five or six hundred yards of the Prussian lines, and the rifle shots — odd compliments of the season — were mutually passing like good wishes at a friendly party. At midnight he left the trenches, advanced to the Prussian lines, and sang a Christmas hymn. The Prussians ceased firing, and did not recommence till the Anglo-Frenchman finished and coolly retreated into his own lines. . . .

A gentleman sent yesterday to his butcher's for any possible scraps for his two favorite cats; the answer was this : "We will give no food to any cats, but we will buy any cats to sell for food." M. Deboos, the butcher of the Boulevard Haussmann, has just paid one thousand and eighty pounds for three of the elephants of the Jardin des Plantes, which he proposes to kill, cut up, and sell at sixteen and eightpence a pound as "bœuf de siège." This will keep certain cooks of certain capitalists employed perhaps for ten days, but it certainly will not benefit the poor and needy; and had the government been that which they are not, they would really have taken all meat, normal and abnormal, to themselves and served out "rations"; as it is, their system is absurd and the result a failure. If we are really reduced to kill the elephants, the omnibus horses, and cut down the trees on the boulevards, Champs-Elysées, and the Bois de Boulogne and the Bois de Vincennes, is it not time (having little else) to eat humble pie? Why not do on the 1st of January what you must do on the 1st of March, and so save two months' battle, murder, starvation, and sudden death? . . .

Paris on the verge of starvation

How the Germans entered Paris, March 1, 1871

[*March 1, 1871.*] The troops were to enter Paris at 10 A.M., but at 8.30 A.M. five-and-twenty of those wonderful Uhlans approached the celebrated Arc de Triomphe, and the leader, waving his sword, jumped the chain and took possession of Paris. Later two thousand men of all arms came and held the Palais d'Industrie and the Place de la Concorde, where French absurdity had veiled with black "crêpe" the faces of the "Cities of France," which caused them exactly to resemble the widows of nigger melodists, and ridiculous enough to make an angel weep under the circumstances. When the absurdity was exhibited to one Prussian it did, through some operation by the surgeon of his regiment, cause him to smile !

" Woe to the conquered "

Then occurred several hours of most unnecessary cruelty. It is needless to say that the French no more stayed at home, as they "proclaimed" others should do, then Favre kept his inch of earth or Ducrot his promise to conquer or die. In fact, there were more French in the Champs-Elysées than there had been since the fatal Fourth ! Now Prussia must have known that the wild "red" blood of Paris was mad with an impotent and insane desire to go on fighting, and as North Germany was so utterly triumphant she might have spared irritation to an already much tried and overexcited people. But no ! *Vae victis !* was the order of the day, and so for hours little billeting parties paraded the quarter of Paris bordered on one side by the Seine, and on the other by the Rue du Faubourg-St.-Honoré, with maps and ready-made billet papers displayed with unnecessary ceremony. Small sections of men, too, were posted just wherever the Parisians *must* see them, and every now and again three Uhlans — or an Hussar with his orderly — walked past, saluting a line officer who swaggered about with a victorious and most trying assumption of dignity. . . .

The splendid German army

Of course I ought to be very enthusiastic or very downcast about this fall of Paris, but I was neither. Any military spectacle is splendid to a man who is as fond of soldiers as I am, and I will admit that since I saw the army of Sadowa defile before the Sultan, I have not looked on such good, well-drilled, military machines, — none of your republican independence here !

On the surrender of Paris to the Germans it was
arranged that a general election should be held throughout France to choose representatives to a National
Assembly which should succeed the merely provisional
"Government of the Public Defense," hastily set up in
the previous September after the downfall of Napoleon
III. This new assembly proved to be conservative, and
a majority of its members professed themselves believers
in monarchy of one kind or another. This disgusted the
Parisians, who had no confidence in monarchy, and the
capital refused to recognize the authority of the National
Assembly. Republicans, socialists, anarchists, commu-
nists, and the discontented generally, of whom there were
great numbers in the great city, joined in defying the
Assembly, which had taken up its sittings at Versailles.
A bitter civil war ensued between the army of the
Assembly and the troops which the Parisians had organized, ending in the capture of the city by the forces
of the Versailles government. Early in the struggle the
National Assembly made the following appeal to the
people of Paris.

The Government of the French Republic to the Parisians:

France, freely consulted by universal suffrage, has elected a
government, which is the only legal one ; the only one that
can command obedience if universal suffrage is not an empty
word. This government has given you the same rights as those
enjoyed by Lyons, Marseilles, Toulouse, and Bordeaux ; and,
except by repudiating the principles of equality, you cannot
demand more rights than are possessed by the other cities of
our country.

In spite of this government, the Commune — that is to say,
the minority which oppresses you, and which dares to hoist
the infamous red flag — presumes to impose its will upon
France. By its works you will be able to judge of the régime

282. The National Assembly calls on the Parisians to avoid a terrible civil war

to which it would destine you. It violates property, imprisons citizens to make hostages of them, turns your streets and your public places, once throbbing with the commerce of the world, into deserts; suspends labor in Paris, paralyzes it throughout France; arrests the prosperity which was about to revive, retards the evacuation of territory by the Germans, and exposes you to fresh attacks on their part, which they are prepared to execute without mercy, unless we ourselves come and suppress the insurrection.

We have listened to all the deputations which have been sent to us, and not one has offered a condition that did not involve the abasement of national sovereignty in the face of revolt, and the sacrifice of every liberty and every interest. We have repeatedly declared to these deputations that we will spare the lives of those who lay down their arms, and that we will continue the subsidy to needy workmen. We have promised this, and we promise it again; but this insurrection must cease, for France must perish if it be prolonged.

Force will be used only to open gates to the city

The government that speaks to you would have desired that you should, through your own efforts, have freed yourselves from the tyrants who have made sport of your liberties and your lives. Since you cannot do this, the members of the government must make it their own business, and it is for this that the government has brought together under your walls an army which comes at the risk of its blood, not to conquer but to deliver you. Up to the present time the attack has been limited to the outworks; the moment has now come when to shorten your sufferings the walls must be attacked. Paris will not be bombarded, as the people of the Commune and the Committee of Public Welfare will not fail to say is our intention. A bombardment menaces the safety of a whole town, renders it uninhabitable, and has no other aim than to intimidate the citizens and compel them to a capitulation. The government will fire no cannon, except to force one of your gates, and will make every effort to limit this war, of which it is not the author, to the point of attack.

The government is well aware, from many sources, that as soon as the soldiers have entered the walls you will rally

round the national flag and assist our army in the destruction
of a sanguinary and cruel tyranny.

It depends upon yourselves to avert the disasters inseparable from an assault. You are a hundred times more numerous than the followers of the Commune. Join, then, and in a
body open the gates to us, which they have closed against
law, against order, against your own prosperity and that of
France. The gates once open, the guns will be silenced at
once; quiet, order, prosperity, and peace will return within
your walls; the Germans will evacuate your territory, and the
traces of your misfortunes will rapidly disappear.

But if you do not act, the government will be obliged to
take the surest and promptest measures for your deliverance.
It owes this to you, but it owes it above all to France, because
the evils that weigh on you weigh on her, the paralysis of business that ruins you extends to and equally ruins her. She has
the right to be saved, even if you do not know how to save
yourselves. Parisians, think seriously; in a very few days we
shall be in Paris. France will make an end of civil war. She
will, she should, she can. She comes to deliver you, you can
contribute to your own safety by rendering the assault needless,
and by once more taking your place amongst your brethren.

Nevertheless
Paris will be
taken at all
costs

As time went on it became clear that neither the
Orleanists, the Legitimists, nor the Republicans could
obtain a majority in the National Assembly. Under the
circumstances M. Adolphe Thiers, who was elected president by the Assembly on its meeting at Bordeaux, though
an Orleanist in principle, came to the conclusion that, in
view of the contending parties, the establishment of a
republic was the only solution for the deadlock. His
reasons for arriving at this conviction were set forth in
a manuscript, found on his death among his papers, from
which the following extract is taken.

283. Thiers's
reasons for
favoring a
republic

In 1873, when the country saw the administrative system,
the army, and the finances reëstablished, and the foreign enemy

departed from our soil, a universal demand arose for the abandonment of the provisional form of government, and for the establishment of a permanent constitution, which meant, to give to each party, weary of waiting, the government of its choice. But there were three monarchical parties, and but one throne. The idea of gratifying them all had, therefore, to be abandoned. As for myself, my mind was made up. In the presence of these three competitors, monarchy was impossible. A republic was difficult without doubt, but possible if prudence and wisdom were exercised. Under a republic France had just been revived.

How Thiers resigned

I should have preferred that the question had not been brought up, but it could no longer be evaded. As a simple deputy, elected president of the republic by my colleagues, I stated the question without allowing myself to solve it. I could do neither more nor less. The three monarchical parties, united in the common design of resisting the establishment of a republic, proposed to the Assembly that it separate itself from me, and, as I was not less desirous of separating myself from it, I handed in my resignation, for which my successor did not have to wait ten minutes. . . .

Neither Bourbon, Orleanist, nor Bonapartist can secure the crown

Now I ask every honest man, to whatever party he may belong, if the Count de Chambord could be placed on the throne, with the opinions that he professes and with the flag that he unfurls, or if it is hoped that he may some day be acceptable after he has modified his views? We respect him too much to believe that he will do so. I will say nothing of the Orleans princes, who wish to be mentioned only after the Count de Chambord, according to their hereditary rank; but I ask if the country is ready to receive the Prince Imperial [son of Napoleon III], who, though innocent of the misfortunes of France, suggests them so keenly that the nation still shudders at the bare mention of his name? . . .

Delay is ruinous to business

Must France wait until her future masters are ready; until one candidate is brought over to other ways of thinking, until another has made an advance in his right of succession, and until a third has finished his education? In the meanwhile everything will be in suspense,—commerce, industry, finances,

State affairs. How can business men be asked to engage in great industrial enterprises, and financiers to negotiate loans, when the future threatens fresh political troubles? And how can foreign cabinets be expected to strengthen their relations and form alliances with us, when French policy is liable to be directed by new chiefs and influenced by new ideas? . . .

We persistently ask if there be any other alternative than the following: either the monarchy, which is impossible, because there are three claimants and but one throne; or a republic, difficult to establish without doubt, not because of itself, but because of the opposition of the monarchical parties, but, nevertheless, possible, for it is supported by an immense majority of the people. *The republic has many supporters*

It is the duty, therefore, of this immense majority of the people to consult together, to unite and to vote against those who resist the establishment of the only government possible. Monarchy to-day, after the three revolutions that have overthrown it, would mean immediate civil war, if it were established now; and if put off for two years, or three years, the civil war is only postponed until that epoch. A republic is an equitable participation of all the children of France in the government of their country, according to their abilities, their importance, and their callings, — a possible and practical participation, excluding nobody except those who announce that they will govern only by revolution. A republic is absolutely necessary, for everybody who is not blind or lying must admit that it alone is possible. . . . *A republic alone is possible*

Section 76. The Third French Republic since 1875; the Dreyfus Affair

The government of the Third Republic had scarcely settled down to steady work before its existence seemed to be threatened by General Boulanger, who was charged with aiming to put himself in power in somewhat the same fashion as Napoleon III. He did win great popularity by urging preparation for defense against Germany, if not a war of revenge; also by demanding a revision of the constitution, and by attacks on the parliament for neglecting desirable reforms. Although he was charged with threatening the safety of the State, found guilty, and only escaped punishment by fleeing to Belgium where he committed suicide, General Boulanger had many able defenders, among whom was the radical journalist, Henri Rochefort. The following extracts from an article by him give a lively idea of some of the chief issues in France in 1888.

284. Rochefort's defense of Boulanger

The Boulangist movement has in reality a twofold character : it is at once patriotic and anti-parliamentary. France understands perfectly well the necessity incumbent upon her at present of fortifying herself against all attacks from the outside, and also the impossibility of continuing to keep alive a republic founded upon monarchical institutions. It has been said repeatedly — and no insinuation or suggestion, however vile, has been neglected which might press the statement home — that General Boulanger was the representative in France of the desire for an immediate revenge upon Germany, and that he was eager for war at all risks. That is simply a calumny borrowed from the German press, which Prince Bismarck keeps alive out of his " reptile fund." Even when he was minister of war, General Boulanger issued the following declaration, which those who know him know to be his real and characteristic opinion : " If I wished war I should be a fool ; if I did not prepare for war I should be a vile traitor." And those who saw him at work as minister for war are able to testify that he did prepare for war with a well-directed energy, of which, unfortunately, none of his predecessors had set the example, and of which his successors seem to have lost the secret. . . .

Boulanger popular for strengthening the defenses of France

General Boulanger is popular because he has always worked for the defense of the fatherland, while the Opportunists have all labored for their own personal advancement ; and his popularity is so deep-rooted, that although a council of inquiry, with iniquitous unanimity, has chosen to place him upon the retired list, is it none the less true that General Boulanger remains the only possible leader of the French armies in case war should break out.

In 1851, a period which some people affect to compare with this year of 1888 under the pretext that there is something of Bonaparte in Boulanger, we had no lost provinces to win back, and we did not hear night and day, upon our frontiers, the insulting rattle of those three million German rifles, with which Bismarck has threatened us in one of his last speeches. At present there is more than a chance — there is a probability — that the new German emperor will attack us without warning ; and it is with the prospect of this aggression before our eyes — an aggression continually held over us as a threat—that all Frenchmen who desire the safety of their country desire to see at the head of the army the one man who possesses their confidence, and whose qualities of resolute energy and patriotism constitute a guarantee which no other minister of war within the last ten years has been capable of giving. . . . *Dangers from Germany require a patriotic war minister*

Experience has proved beyond question the utter powerlessness of the parliamentary system of government as it exists to-day in France. The present *régime* is, properly speaking, nothing more nor less than a hunt for portfolios unrestrained by any close season. The guiding principle of all our politicians is the simple one, " Get out of that seat in order that I may sit there ! " Owing to the adoption of this principle no ministry is stable. A cabinet is at the mercy of any hostile coalition, and thus energies are paralyzed that might otherwise lead to some good result. . . . *Politics consists now in a scramble for offices*

What General Boulanger himself demands is the revision of the constitution by means of an assembly especially elected for that purpose. And yet the Radicals, Opportunists, and followers of M. Ferry, who make this demand a pretext for attacking General Boulanger, were themselves the first to start the cry for revision. Three years ago almost any Radical or Opportunist would have agreed with me in asserting that the safety of the Republic (I had almost said of France) depends upon this essential reform. The Republican party was then unanimous *The constitution needs revision* in declaring that the constitution of 1875, having been formed and elaborated by Monarchists, was the stumbling-block in the way of all possible projects of amelioration and progress. Our senate, based upon restricted suffrage, is invested with powers equal to those of the popular chamber. No upper house in Europe has such extensive rights. The House of Lords, for instance, is subordinated to the House of Commons in the most important point — the control of the public money. The French senate, on the other hand, is placed upon exactly the same footing as the Chamber of Deputies. And the constitution is so constructed that if a conflict between the two chambers took place, there would be no possible solution of the difficulty but by a *coup d'état*. Properly speaking, this constitution of 1875 is nothing more nor less than organized anarchy. One cannot expect those who profit by an abuse to abolish it ; the present senate, it is evident, will never commit suicide. Yet the constitution must be changed ; our institutions must evidently be made as democratic as is public opinion in France.

From 1875 to 1885 the Republican party in the chamber was unanimous in recognizing the abuses inherent in our constitution. Why, then, do these men accuse General Boulanger of aiming at a dictatorship because he sees what they saw and advocates the change which they themselves were the first to propose? The explanation is simple. They know well that General Boulanger is earnest in his demand, whereas in the last ten years they have got a liking for the spoils of office, and are now content with the abuses of an institution which they have learnt how to turn to their own personal profit.

The Boulanger episode was shortly followed by a still more disturbing affair growing out of the arrest and imprisonment of Captain Alfred Dreyfus on the charge of having betrayed military secrets to the German government. Believing that Dreyfus was an innocent man condemned in the first place on false charges and then further denounced by high army officials to prevent the revelation of scandal in high places, Zola, the distinguished novelist, braved a storm of public opinion and the penalties of the law by publishing in a Parisian newspaper, *L'Aurore*, on January 13, 1898, his famous denunciation of the parties concerned. This article was largely instrumental in securing a new trial for Dreyfus and ultimately his freedom and restoration to rank in the army.

Mr. President:

Will you permit me, in my gratitude for the kindly welcome that you once extended to me, to show my regard for the glory that is rightfully yours, and to say to you that your honor, so bright hitherto, is threatened with the most shameful, the most indelible of stains? You have emerged from base calumnies safe and sound; you have conquered our hearts. You seem radiant in that patriotic *fête* which the Russian alliance has been for France, and you are preparing to preside at the solemn triumph of our Universal Exposition, which will crown our great century of labor, truth, and liberty. But what a mud stain on your name — I was going to say on your reign — is this abominable Dreyfus affair! A council of war has just dared to acquit an Esterhazy in obedience to orders, — a final blow at all truth, at all justice. And now it is done! France has this stain upon her cheek; it will be written in history that under your presidency it was possible for this social crime to be committed.

285. Zola's open letter to Felix Faure, President of the French Republic, on the Dreyfus affair (January 13, 1898)

Since they have dared, I too will dare. I will tell the truth, for I have promised to tell it, if the courts, once regularly appealed to, did not bring it out fully and entirely. It is my duty to speak; I will not be an accomplice. My nights would be haunted by the specter of the innocent man who is atoning, in a far-away country, by the most frightful of tortures, for a crime that he did not commit.

Zola haunted by the wrong to Dreyfus

And to you, Mr. President, will I proclaim this truth, with all the force of an honest man's revolt. Your honor convinces me that you are ignorant of it. To whom, indeed, should I denounce the malevolent gang of the really guilty, if not to you, the first magistrate of the country?

First, the truth as to the trial and conviction of Dreyfus.

Paty de Clam principally responsible for the injustice

A calamitous man has managed it all, has done it all — Colonel du Paty de Clam, then a simple major. He is the entire Dreyfus case; it will be fully known only when a sincere investigation shall have clearly established his acts and his responsibility. He appears as the most heady, the most intricate, of characters, haunted with romantic intrigues, delighting in the methods of the newspaper novel, — stolen papers, anonymous letters, meetings in lonely spots, mysterious women who convey overwhelming proofs by night. It is he who conceived the idea of dictating the *bordereau* to Dreyfus; it is he who dreamed of studying it in a room completely lined with mirrors; it is he whom Major Forzinetti represents to us armed with a dark lantern, trying to gain access to the accused when asleep, in order to throw a sudden flood of light upon his face, and thus surprise a confession of his crime in the confusion of his awakening. And I need not say more. I simply claim that Major du Paty de Clam, intrusted as a judicial officer with the duty of preparing the Dreyfus case, is, in the order of dates and responsibility, the leading person among those guilty of the fearful judicial error that has been committed. . . .

The war office afraid of the truth

The Dreyfus case was a case for the war office, — a staff officer accused by his staff comrades, convicted under the pressure of the chiefs of staff. Accordingly he cannot come back innocent unless all the staff is proved guilty. Consequently the war offices, by all imaginable means, by press campaigns, by communications, by influence, have protected Esterhazy only to ruin Dreyfus a second time. Ah! with what a sweep should the republican government clear away this band of Jesuits, as General Billot himself calls them! Where is the truly strong and wisely patriotic minister who will dare to reshape and renew all? How many of the people I know are trembling in view of a possible war, knowing in what hands lies the national defense! And what a nest of base intrigues, gossip, and corruption has this sacred protector, intrusted with the fate of the country, become! We are frightened by the terrible light thrown upon it by the Dreyfus case, this human sacrifice of an unfortunate man, of a "dirty Jew." Ah! what a mixture of madness and folly, of crazy fancies, of low police practices, of inquisitorial and tyrannical customs, the good pleasure of a few persons in gold lace, with their feet on the neck of the nation, cramming back into its throat its cry of truth and justice under the lying and sacrilegious pretext of the *raison d'état!*

Another of their crimes is that they have accepted the support of the filthy press, have suffered themselves to be championed by all the knavery of Paris, so that we now witness knavery's insolent triumph in the downfall of right and simple probity. It is a crime to accuse of troubling France those who wish to see her generous, and place her at the head of free and just nations. It is a crime to mislead public opinion, to rouse it to a delirium with a view of compassing this man's death. It is a crime to poison the minds of the lowly and the humble, to exasperate the passions of reaction and intolerance, while seeking shelter behind odious anti-Semitism, which, if not suppressed, will destroy the great liberal France of the Rights of Man. It is crime to exploit patriotism for works of hatred, and, finally, it is a crime to make the sword the modern god, when all human science is at work on the coming temple of truth and justice. . . . *The "yellow journals" responsible for stirring up popular ignorance*

Such, then, is the simple truth, Mr. President, and it is frightful. It will remain a stain upon your presidency. I suspect that you are powerless in this matter, — that you are the prisoner of the constitution and of your environment. You have none the less a man's duty, upon which you will reflect, and which you will fulfill. Not indeed that I despair of triumph. I repeat with more vehement certainty, truth is now in motion, and nothing can stop it. To-day sees the real beginning of the affair, since not until to-day have the two opposing parties met face to face : on one hand, the guilty, who do not want the light ; on the other, the doers of justice, who will give their lives to get it. When truth is buried in the earth it accumulates there, and assumes so mighty an explosive power that, on the day when it bursts forth, it hurls everything into the air. We shall see whether its enemies have not merely prepared the way for the most appalling disaster yet to come. *An appeal to the President as a man of honor*

But this letter is too long, Mr. President, and it is time to finish.

I accuse Lieutenant Colonel du Paty de Clam of having been the diabolical author of judicial error, — unconsciously, I am willing to believe, — and of having then defended his fatal work, for three years, by the most guilty machinations.

I accuse General Mercier of having made himself an accomplice, at least through feebleness of mind, in one of the greatest iniquities of the century.

I accuse General Billot of having had in his hands certain proofs of the innocence of Dreyfus, and of having suppressed them; of having rendered himself guilty of this crime of *lèse-humanité* and *lèse-justice* for a political purpose, and to save the compromised staff.

I accuse General de Boisdeffre and General Gonse of having made themselves accomplices in the same crime, one undoubtedly through clerical passion, the other perhaps through that *esprit de corps* which makes of the war office the unassailable ark of the covenant.

I accuse General de Pellieux and Major Ravary of having conducted a rascally inquiry, — I mean by that, a monstrously partial inquiry, of which we have, in the report of the latter, an imperishable monument of naïve audacity.

I accuse the three experts in handwriting, Belhomme, Varinard, and Couard, of having made lying and fraudulent reports, unless a medical examination should prove them to be afflicted with diseases of the eye and of the mind.

I accuse the war office of having carried on in the newspapers, particularly in *L'Éclair* and in *L'Écho de Paris*, an abominable campaign, to mislead opinion and cover up their faults.

I accuse, finally, the first council of war of having violated the law by condemning an accused person on the strength of a secret document, and I accuse the second council of war of having covered up this illegality, in obedience to orders, in committing in its turn the judicial crime of knowingly acquitting a guilty man.

In preferring these charges I am not unaware that I lay myself liable under Articles 30 and 31 of the press law of July 29, 1881, which punishes slander. I consciously expose myself to the provisions of the law.

As for the people whom I accuse, I do not know them ; I have never seen them ; I entertain against them no feeling of revenge or hatred. They are to me simple entities, enemies of the social welfare. And the act that I perform here is nothing but a revolutionary measure to hasten the triumph of truth and justice. I have but one passion, the passion for the light, in the name of humanity which has suffered so much, and which is entitled to happiness. My vehement protest is simply the cry of my soul. Let them dare, then, to bring me into the court of assizes, but let the investigation take place in the open day. I await it.

It is not a personal question but one of humanity

Accept, Mr. President, the assurance of my profound respect.

ÉMILE ZOLA

Section 77. Separation of Church and State

One of the most important tasks which had confronted Bonaparte was the settlement of the relations between Church and State, which had been sadly disturbed in 1790 by the National Assembly when it not only reorganized the Church in France but also took possession of ecclesiastical property, at the same time binding the government to support the clergy. Accordingly Bonaparte sought to come to terms with the Pope, and in 1801 an agreement was reached between France and the Holy See. This agreement, or *Concordat* as it was called, supplemented by special acts on the part of the French government, remained the basis of union between Church and State until 1905, when the entire system was revolutionized by act of the French parliament. The historical importance of this document, therefore, warrants a careful study of its main provisions.

286. The Concordat of 1801 between Napoleon and the Pope

The government of the Republic acknowledges that the Roman Catholic and Apostolic religion is professed by the great majority of the people of France.

His Holiness, in view of the neglect of the rites of this religion, feels that its restoration at this time, with its impressive ceremonies, under the auspices of the Consuls of the Republic, will be generally approved and conduce to the welfare of the people.

Hence, in view of these considerations, mutually admitted, alike for the good of religion and of domestic tranquillity, it is agreed that :

1. The Roman Catholic and Apostolic religion shall be freely exercised in France. Its worship shall be free in conformity with such regulations of the police as the government may deem necessary for public tranquillity. . . .

The appointment of archbishops and bishops

4. The First Consul of the Republic, before the expiration of the three months following the publication of the bull of His Holiness, shall nominate the archbishops and bishops for the newly created sees. His Holiness shall confer the canonical institution, according to the forms existing in France before the change of government.

5. Nominations to sees which may subsequently become vacant shall also be made by the First Consul, and canonical institution shall be conferred by the Holy See in conformity with the preceding article.

The civil oath taken by the clergy

6. The prelates, before assuming their functions, shall take direct to the First Consul the oath of fidelity customary in times prior to the change of the government, in the following terms :

I swear and promise before God, upon the holy gospels, to render obedience and fidelity to the government established by the constitution of the French Republic. I promise also to have no understanding, to attend no council, to join no league, either within or without the country, which may endanger public tranquillity ; and if in my jurisdiction it should come to my knowledge that evil designs are meditated to the prejudice of the State, I shall make the same known to the government.

7. Ecclesiastics of the second order shall take a similar oath to the civil authorities designated by the government.

8. The following form of prayer shall be recited at the close of the divine offices in all Catholic churches in France :

"*Domine, salvam fac rempublicam. Domine, salvos fac consules.*" . . .

10. The bishops shall appoint the parish priests. They shall, however, select only such persons as shall be acceptable to the government. . . . .

12. All metropolitan churches, cathedrals, parochial residences or other buildings for religious use, which have not been confiscated, shall be placed at the disposition of the bishops.

13. His Holiness, for the peace, welfare, and happy reëstablishment of the Catholic religion, declares that neither he nor his successors will molest in any way the purchasers of confiscated church property; and consequently the possession and titles to such property, and the revenues appertaining thereto, shall remain permanently in the hands of those having legal titles thereto. *Owners of former church property reassured*

14. The government assures a suitable salary to the bishops and priests whose dioceses and parishes shall be included within the bounds of the newly established ecclesiastical territory. *Payment of salaries*

15. The government shall also arrange that French Catholics may, should they so wish, establish foundations for the benefit of the churches.

16. His Holiness acknowledges and concedes to the First Consul of the Republic of France the same rights and prerogatives exercised by the old government in its relations with the Holy See.

17. It is mutually agreed between the contracting parties that, in case any of the successors of the present First Consul should not be a Catholic, the rights and prerogatives named in the preceding articles, as well as the nomination of bishops, shall be regulated, in so far as he may be concerned, by a new convention.

PARIS, the 26 *Messidor*, the ninth year
 of the Republic of France.

From its very establishment the Third Republic came into collision with the clergy, who for the most part desired a restoration of either the empire or the monarchy. The Republicans passed measure after measure designed to break the power of the clergy. Education was made free and compulsory and placed strictly under government supervision. Certain monastic orders were dissolved and their property taken by the State. At length in December, 1905, the parliament passed a law separating Church and State by suppressing all appropriations to the clergy and expressly declaring the Concordat abrogated. On February 11, 1906, Pope Pius X, in a letter to the bishops of France, enumerated the measures which the Third Republic had passed against the Church and denounced the Separation law in strong terms. Considerable portions of the Pope's protest are printed here, since it affords an excellent idea of the attitude of the Roman Curia toward the modern State.

287. Pius X's denunciation of the Law of Separation, February, 1906 (condensed)

Venerable brethren, beloved sons, salutation and apostolic benediction :

Our soul is full of tender solicitude and our heart is wrung with anguish as our thoughts dwell upon you. And how, indeed, could it be otherwise on the morrow of the promulgation of the law which, in breaking violently the ancient ties by which your nation was united to the Apostolic See, places the Catholic Church in France in a situation unworthy of her and forever lamentable. This event is unquestionably of the gravest character, for it is as fatal to civil society as to religion. Nevertheless it cannot be a matter of surprise to any one who has given any attention to the religious policy pursued in France in these later years. To you, venerable brethren, it will come neither as an innovation nor a surprise, witnesses as you have been of the numerous and powerful blows unnecessarily inflicted on religion by the public authority.

You have seen the sanctity and inviolability of Christian marriage attacked by certain legislative provisions ; the schools and hospitals put under the control of the laity ; pupils torn from their studies and from ecclesiastical discipline and forced into military schools ; the religious congregations dispersed and plundered and their members commonly reduced to the last stages of destitution. Other legal measures have followed, all of which you know : the abrogation of the law ordering public prayers at the opening of each parliamentary session and of the courts ; the suppression of the signs of mourning on Good Friday, traditional on board of the ships ; the elimination from the judiciary oath of all that gave to it religious character ; the banishment from the courts, schools, army, navy, and finally from all public establishments, of every act or emblem which could recall religion in any way. These measures and others still, which little by little separated Church and State, were only the landmarks placed with the view of arriving at a complete and official separation ; their promoters themselves did not hesitate to acknowledge it proudly and often.

Review of anticlerical legislation

The Apostolic See, on the contrary, has spared no pains in warding off so great a calamity. On the one hand, it has never tired of warning those who were at the head of French affairs, and has implored them repeatedly to consider well the enormity of the evils which their separatist policy would inevitably bring ; on the other hand, it has multiplied striking evidences of its condescending affection toward France. It had the right to hope, therefore, in consideration of the obligations of gratitude, that it might be able to restrain these politicians from their wayward course and induce them at last to renounce their projects.

Rome has warned France of the coming dangers

But attentions, good offices, efforts, as much on the part of our predecessor as on our own part, have all been without avail. The violence of the enemies of religion has ended in their carrying into execution plans which were for a long time merely aspirations, — plans opposed to your rights as a Catholic nation and contrary to all which the wise desire. Accordingly, in an hour so grave for the Church, we, conscious of our apostolic duty, have considered it an obligation to lift our

Duty requires Pius to speak

voice and open our soul to you, venerable brethren, and to your clergy and your people, — you whom we have always surrounded with a protecting solicitude and whom we properly love at this moment more tenderly than ever.

Necessity of separation denied

That it is necessary to separate Church and State is a thesis absolutely false, — a most pernicious error. Based in fact upon the principle that the State ought not to recognize any religious faith, it is, to begin with, deeply insulting to God ; for the creator of man is also the founder of human societies, and he maintains them as he does us. We owe him, therefore, not only private worship, but also a public and social worship in his praise.

Moreover, this thesis is clearly the negation of the supernatural order. It limits the action of the State to the sole pursuit of prosperity during this life, which is only the secondary reason for political societies; and it does not recognize in any manner the highest object of the State, namely, eternal bliss offered to man at the close of this present life, so short in duration, but regards it as foreign to the concerns of State. This thesis reverses the order very wisely established by God in the world, the order which requires a harmonious concord between the two societies.

Governments cannot regard religion with indifference

The Roman Pontiffs have not ceased, according to circumstances and times, to refute and condemn the doctrine of the separation of Church and State. Our illustrious predecessor, Leo XIII, notably, has often and splendidly expounded what ought to be the relation between the two societies according to Catholic doctrine. "Between them," he said, "there must necessarily be a wise union, a union which can be compared with propriety to that which in man joins the soul and the body." He added : "Human societies cannot, without becoming criminal, conduct themselves as if God did not exist, or refuse to occupy themselves with religion as if it were a foreign matter or of no importance to them. . . . As for the Church, which has God himself for its author, to exclude it from the active life of the nation, from the laws, the education of the youth, from domestic society, is to be guilty of a great and pernicious error."

And if in separating itself from the Church, any Christian State commits an act eminently baleful and censurable, how much is such action to be deplored in the case of France above all nations! France, we say, which during the course of centuries has been the object of such great and peculiar favor on the part of the Holy See; France whose fortune and glory have always been intimately united with the practice of Christian virtues and respect for religion! The same Pontiff, Leo XIII, had good reason for saying: "France should never forget that her providential destiny has united her to the Holy See with bonds too close and too ancient for her ever to wish to break them. From this union, indeed, have come forth her true greatness and her purest glory. . . . To disturb this traditional union would be to take from the nation itself a part of its moral strength and high mission in the world." *France the object of special favors from Popes*

The bonds that consecrate this union ought, moreover, to be doubly inviolable on account of the sworn faith which treaties exact. The Concordat agreed upon by the sovereign Pontiff and the French government, like all similar treaties that States conclude between themselves, was a bilateral contract which was binding on both sides. The Roman Pontiff, on the one part, the head of the French nation on the other, agreed then solemnly, both for themselves and for their successors, to maintain inviolable the compact they had signed. The French government has not hesitated to ignore, with reference to the Holy See, the ordinary considerations and the courtesy with which even the smallest States do not dispense in dealing with each other. And its agents who were, moreover, the representatives of a Catholic nation, have not feared to treat with brutal disrespect the dignity and power of the Pontiff, supreme head of the Church, for whom they should have shown a respect superior to that which all political powers inspire, — all the more because this Pontiff labors for the eternal good of souls. *The Concordat cannot be broken by one party to the contract*

If we now examine the law itself which has just been promulgated we shall find a fresh reason to complain still more loudly. Since the State, breaking the bonds of the *The Church oppressed by the new law*

Concordat, separates itself from the Church, it was due the
latter naturally to let it enjoy its independence and rights in
peace and in the liberty ostensibly conceded to it. Now
nothing has been further from the facts : we note in the law
several exceptional measures which are odiously restrictive
and place the Church under the dominion of the civil power.
It has indeed been a source of bitter sorrow to us to see the
State thus invade the exclusive province of the ecclesiastical
power ; and we grieve the more, since, forgetful of equity and
justice, it has thus placed the Church in France in a critical
situation, subversive of its most sacred rights.

The law is contrary to the constitution of the Church   The provisions of the new law are, in effect, contrary to the
constitution on which the Church was founded by Jesus Christ.
The Scriptures teach us and the traditions of the fathers confirm it, that the Church is the mystic body of Christ, a body
ruled by pastors and teachers, — hence a body of men in the
midst of whom are found those leaders who have full power
to govern, teach, and judge.[1]

The refusal to pay the clergy is unjust   The law suppressing the appropriations for public worship
frees the State from the obligation of providing for the ex-
penses of religious worship, but it at the same time repudiates
an engagement contracted in a diplomatic agreement, and
seriously violates the principles of justice. On that point there
can indeed be no possible doubt, and historical documents
themselves bear witness to the fact in the clearest fashion. If
the French government assumed in the Concordat the burden
of assuring to the members of the clergy a salary which would
enable them to provide in a suitable fashion for themselves
and religious worship, it did not make this as a gratuitous
concession ; it pledged itself to do this by way of indemnification, partial at least, to the Church whose property the
State had appropriated during the Revolution. On the other
hand also, when the Roman Pontiff in the same Concordat
and for the sake of peace engaged in his own name and that
of his successors not to disturb the holders of property which

[1] Here the Pope enumerates his objections to the associations of
laymen (*associations cultuelles*), in whose hands the Law of Separation
placed the administration of the various local churches.

had been thus taken from the Church, it is certain that he only made that promise on one condition : that is, that the French government should agree for all time adequately to pay the clergy and provide for the expenses of divine worship.

Finally — and how can we well be silent on this point ? — aside from the interests of the Church which have been injured, the new law will be most fatal to your country. There can be no doubt that it will in reality destroy the union and harmony of souls, and without that union and harmony no nation can live and prosper. That is why, especially in the present situation in Europe, this perfect harmony is the most ardent wish of all those in France who, truly loving their country, have its welfare at heart. As for us, following the example of our predecessor and inheriting his very special partiality for your nation, we are unquestionably compelled to maintain the religion of your ancestors in the full possession of all its rights among you ; but at the same time, and always having before our eyes that fraternal peace of which religion is certainly the strictest bond, we have labored to strengthen all in unity.

The law disastrous to France

Accordingly we, remembering our Apostolic charge and bound to defend against every attack and to maintain in their absolute integrity the inviolable and sacred rights of the Church, by virtue of the supreme authority which God has conferred upon us, we, for the reasons given above, reject and condemn the law passed in France for the separation of the Church and State, as profoundly insulting to God whom it officially denies by making it a principle that the Republic recognizes no religion. We reject and condemn it as violating natural law, the law of nations, and the public faith due to treaties, as contrary to the divine constitution of the Church, to its fundamental rights, and to its liberty, as overturning justice and trampling under foot the property rights which the Church has acquired by manifold titles and especially by virtue of the Concordat. We reject and condemn it as grievously offensive to the dignity of this Apostolic See, to our person, to the episcopacy, to the clergy, and to all the French Catholics.

Sweeping condemnation of the law

An appeal to
the faithful in
France
Consequently we protest solemnly and with all our strength
against the proposal, the passage, and the promulgation of
this law, declaring that it could never be impleaded so as
to annul the imprescriptible and immutable rights of the
Church.[1] . . .

As for the defense of religion, if you desire to undertake it
in a worthy manner, to carry it on without error and with
success, two things above all are important : you should conduct yourselves according to the precepts of the Christian
law, so faithfully, that your acts and your entire life may be an
honor to the religion which you profess. You should also remain
in strict union with those to whom it properly belongs to
guard religion here below, — with your priests, your bishops,
and especially with the Apostolic See, which is the center of
Catholicism and of everything which may properly be done in
its name. Thus armed for the struggle, advance without fear
to the defense of the Church, taking care that your confidence
rests entirely in God whose cause you uphold, and in which
he will help you. Implore him without ceasing.

As for us, as long as you may have to struggle against
danger, we shall be heart and soul in your midst ; labors,
pains, sufferings, we shall share all with you ; and, addressing
ourselves at the same time to the God who has established
the Church and who heeds our humblest and most earnest
prayers, we supplicate him to look down on France with com-
passion, to rescue her from the billows raging around her,
and to give calm and peace to her soon through the inter-
cession of Mary the Immaculate.

As a sign of these divine favors, and in order to assure you
of our very especial good will, we most affectionately grant
our apostolic benediction to you, venerable brethren, to your
clergy, and to the entire French nation.

Given at Rome near Saint Peter's, February 11, 1906, the
third year of our pontificate.

PIUS X

[1] In the passages which follow, omitted here, the Pope encourages
French Catholics to be steadfast in the midst of their adversity, trust-
ing in Jesus Christ and their own faith.

Section 78. Political Parties in France

In the early years of the Third Republic the principal political parties were the Republicans, and their monarchical opponents, the Legitimists, the Orleanists, and the Bonapartists; but gradually the monarchists diminished in number, while the Republicans broke up into many groups on questions of social reform. The Radicals and Socialists have become especially prominent, and in 1906 the former came to power under the leadership of M. Clémenceau, who early stated his cardinal doctrines in a long debate with the socialist leader, M. Jaurès. An extract from M. Clémenceau's argument is given here.

The Socialist party has issued a programme for the use of all its candidates. Nothing could be more natural. This programme contains two sections : a declaration of principles, and a statement of immediate reforms which may and ought to be demanded from this present legislature. . . . It would be well if each one in this assembly should set himself to inquire what are the topics which it is his duty first to bring before this tribunal. I find in this manifesto, in the first place, a statement of doctrine : "There is only one way of emancipating yourselves ; it is to substitute collective property for capitalist property." I find no explanation of the consequences of this statement, no suggestion of the means of carrying it out. But at least it contains an affirmation of principle. What reforms, then, are to follow from it? Here they are :

288. The Radical programme contrasted with socialism

" Limitation of the working day to eight hours.

" Extension to all employees of the State, the Department, and the Commune of the right to form unions.

" General insurance against sickness and unemployment.

" Progressive income tax and death duties.

" Restoration to the nation of the monopolies in which capital has its strongest fortresses.

"General election tickets, with proportional representation."

The practical
demands of
socialists
accepted
by Radicals
What a terribly *bourgeois* programme. When M. Jaurès, after
expounding his programme, challenged me to produce my own,
I had great difficulty in resisting the temptation to reply : "You
know my programme very well ; you have it in your pocket, you
stole it from me." I am in principle for the eight-hour day.
I do not suppose that any of you would run the risk of an
economic crisis by suddenly changing the eleven-hour day to
eight. I could not; but I am ready to put things in train as
quickly as possible for an ultimate eight-hour day. I am in
favor of a progressive income tax. But M. Jaurès, you voted
against it in 1885 ; and it is in the name of this shifting infallibility of yours that you are surprised at my remaining true to
my convictions ! Truly that will not bear examination. I affirm,
then, that this practical programme is ours ; I am for the restoration to the nation of the great monopolies which are now in
the hands of private industry. But we must understand each
other. I do not want you to put into my words a sense they do
not bear. If you think I mean to say that I am prepared to
bring in a bill to-morrow for the restoration of all these monopolies, you deceive yourselves ; that is not my idea. What I mean
is, that I am quite ready to begin the work this very day, for
example, by the repurchase of certain of the railways. I have
no authority from the Cabinet to make that statement. I must
avow it in loyalty to the Chamber ; but you must not make
much of it ; only I know the opinion of most of my colleagues,
and I know that they will not contradict me. . . .

Socialism
too dogmatic
in spirit
Having said so much, I am bound to recognize that you have
set up an organization from the principle of which my bourgeois soul recoils. I mean what you call *unification*. Unification to my eyes is nothing but a kind of *catholization* of socialism. It is the heavy hand of a governing oligarchy laid on a
democracy of workmen who are struggling for freedom. It is
the introduction of that ancient state of mind, which, in order
to secure the triumph of the gospel, has turned a message of
liberty into a most terrible instrument of authority over the
free expansion of the individual. But it is not only the Pope
of Catholicism who was beaten at the last election ; it was the
spirit of oppression, the dogmatic spirit, in all fields of human

activity. The dogmatic spirit has been banished from the purely intellectual sphere, and we will have nothing to do with reëstablishing it in the sphere of economics. We are for liberty everywhere and in everything ; and we will allow no organization to set up an authority which, according to a saying of Ernest Renan, aptly quoted this morning by M. Gerault-Richard, would put us into the position of doing our thinking through an agent. . . .

M. Jaurès, there are only two hypotheses before the Chamber, — the existing form of society and the one you propose ; but between these two extremes there are an infinite number of social schemes which might come to pass. You make the task too easy. Even if we were to admit that your criticisms are well founded, that our existing society is as bad as you say, — and I am not one of those who say that it is very good, as you know, — even if we admit that the society you describe is really possible, still you have left out the one point which is worthy of consideration. We are not obliged to choose between the society you promise and the society we have. There are countless other hypotheses ; presently when I come to speak of the schemes of social order which this Republican bourgeoisie of which you speak so ill has succeeded in bringing about, I can easily show you that the social régime of to-day is not that of twenty years ago, and that it rests in fact upon quite different principles. I cannot, therefore, permit you to limit us to a choice between these two plans and to wind up with the challenge, "Beware of not accepting my plan, for otherwise the human mind is bankrupt." . . .

We are not bound to choose between socialism and inaction

After all, is this type of an ideal society which you offer us really so new? Who has not dreamed of a society of the future? I myself am not incapable of dreaming of it along with you whenever you like. Only it is not yet proved — the demonstration is for you to effect by and by — that this dream is as yet in a condition to occupy the attention of a deliberative assembly. It was the everlasting object of the dreams of all Asia. Jesus, the last of a long line of prophets, proposed to renovate all mankind by his words ; but his disciples reëstablished under his name the society of violence and bloodshed against which he had protested. Your victory will not be greater

Socialism an ancient dream

than his. I do not think the day will come when you will have your temples throughout the civilized world, and that your words will be daily rehearsed to crowded audiences eager to hear them. You will have no greater success; and when you remember that the material success of Christianity has only ended in the moral bankruptcy of the words of Christ, — that is, in a state of things which has only reproduced the ancient conditions which he proposed to destroy, — you will permit me not to wish you a triumph of that kind. America is full of mystical societies which are endeavoring to realize the City of God on earth. I have heard in forests of New England predictions not appreciably different from yours. In 1848 the Republic thought itself on the eve of the Great Day, and we have seen many a builder of the cities of the future. Do you recall the sittings of the Constituent and Legislative Assemblies in which Pierre Leroux or Victor Considérant or Proudhon developed, as you are presently going to do, his plans of the new society? A great many people pronounced in favor of the suppression of private property. Even before them Sir Thomas More, at the beginning of the sixteenth century, condemned private property in terms more definite than you can employ. These men were not inferior to you. Where are they now? Look for them. You have taken their place, and others will by and by take yours. . . .

The Radical party is the party of action   The Radical party will baffle your tactics by remaining true to itself, — to the Radical policy of action. You need not remind us of our programme, or ask whether we are prepared to carry it out. Our only right to sit here lies in action, — action which clears up ambiguities, which carries forward the weak, which regulates and disciplines the will of the strong. It is by action that we have overcome the Church, by action that we shall put down economic oppression, the oppression of the existing privileged class. We have set free the mind, we shall set free the body.

Have confidence, man of little faith, you who distrust the work of the Revolution of which you were a good workman. If we do not think alike, is that a reason for enmity? That is a survival of religious animosity. So far as I am concerned, I have no condemnation to pronounce against you, and it matters little that you have this or that ideal conception of the future. If we understand one another, which is a necessary condition of common action in this assembly, we can work together, if only your aid be sincere and complete.

Section 79. The Expansion of France

A distinguished modern French historian, M. Rambaud, gives the following excellent summary of the chief steps in the colonial expansion of France, and indicates briefly the world problems involved in the administration of this vast colonial dominion.

The last thirty years of the nineteenth century are characterized by a fact of capital importance not only for our history but also for the history of the world ; this is the expansion of France in Africa and in Asia, the construction of a new French colonial empire to take the place of the colonial empires which the treaties of 1713, 1763, and 1814 lost for us. It will remain the glory of the Third Republic to have made reparation as far as possible for the errors of the ancient royal and imperial policy, and to have claimed the legitimate share of France in the partition of the world.

In northern Africa, Algeria has annexed the oases of Mzab and those of the Moroccan frontier ; to the east this extension has been completed by the conquest of Tunis ; in western Africa some posts and factories which England restored to us in 1814 have been the points of departure for an expansion which, crossing the watershed between the Senegal and the Niger, has extended to the limits of the Nile basin. Furthermore, from some scattered factories on the shores of Guinea the French dominion has extended to the Kong Mountains and the middle of the Niger, and the powerful kingdom of Dahomey has been conquered. Our insignificant colony of Gaboon has been given, by way of annexations, the immense territories of the Congo, those of Ubangi, and those which surround Lake Tchad for three fourths of its way. All of our African continental domains on the Mediterranean, as well as on the Atlantic

289. French colonial dominions

and the Gulf of Guinea, have been joined together. To the east of Africa the island of Madagascar, greater in area than France by sixty thousand square kilometers, was at first put under our protection and then annexed. The occupation of Obock and Jibuti have given us a strong position on the Red Sea. In the extreme Orient, Anam, Tonquin, and some districts on the Mekong have been added to the six provinces of Cochin China and the protectorate of Cambodia, which we inherited from the Second Empire. Having become the neighbors of China on a frontier of more than a thousand kilometers, we have been able to obtain important concessions from her.

Among the statesmen of the Third Republic who perceived most clearly the necessity of a colonial policy, the first place belongs to Jules Ferry. During his two terms as head of the ministry (1880–1881; 1883–1885) he effected the conquest of Tunis and Tonquin, imposed our protectorate on Anam and the kingdom of Madagascar, and made Europe recognize our rights on the Niger and the Congo. In his speech of October 31, 1882, he gave a very clear statement of the new tendency: "A colonial policy is necessary for France. Every particle of its colonial dominion, the smallest fragments, should be sacred for us. . . . It is not a question of the immediate future, but of the future of fifty or a hundred years, even of the destiny of the country itself."

The responsibilities of France as a world power By her colonial acquisitions France has become in Africa the neighbor not only of Morocco but of Turkish Tripoli, the Abyssinian Empire, Equatorial Egypt, and of the European colonial powers (England, Belgium, Germany, and Portugal); in Asia, of the kingdom of Siam, the Anglo-Indian Empire, China, and Japan. It is a situation which has its advantages, but it implies cares and expenses. From being almost purely European, the rôle of France tends to become universal — world-wide. This new character tends to influence, to dominate all her politics. France having assumed the responsibility of governing and civilizing so many African and Asiatic nations, the necessary adaptations must be effected in her military institutions, in her temper, in her conceptions, and even in her mentality, which will permit her to face so many new duties.

CHAPTER XXV

POLITICAL REFORMS IN ENGLAND

Section 80. Parliamentary Reforms

The agitation for the reform of the English House of Commons began before the French Revolution and continued intermittently during the long conflict with Napoleon. It became especially violent after his final overthrow, and in 1830 the Duke of Wellington, who shared with his friend Metternich a deep distrust of every kind of political change, was at last forced to resign his place as head of the Tory Ministry. A new cabinet in favor of reform then came into power, and a distinguished member, Lord John Russell, introduced the bill into Parliament embodying the proposed changes. In a lengthy speech he set forth some of the abuses that had long existed.

The ancient constitution of our country declares that no man should be taxed for the support of the State who has not consented, by himself or his representative, to the imposition of these taxes. The well-known statute, *de tallagio non comedendo*,[1] repeats the same language ; and, although some historical doubts have been thrown upon it, its legal meaning has never been disputed. It included "all the freemen of the land," and provided that each county should send to the Commons of the realm two knights, each city two burgesses, and each borough two members. Thus about a hundred places sent representatives, and some thirty or forty others occasionally

290. Lord John Russell's speech on parliamentary reforms

---

[1] A so-called statute of Edward I's reign, long supposed to have forbidden taxation without the consent of Parliament.

enjoyed the privilege, but it was discontinued or revived as they rose or fell in the scale of wealth and importance. Thus, no doubt, at that early period the House of Commons did represent the people of England ; there is no doubt, likewise, that the House of Commons as it now subsists, does not represent the people of England. Therefore, if we look at the question of right, the reformers have right in their favor. Then, if we consider what is reasonable, we shall arrive at a similar result.

The inequality of representation

A stranger who was told that this country is unparalleled in wealth and industry and more civilized and more enlightened than any country was before it, that it is a country which prides itself on its freedom, and that once in every seven years it elects representatives from its population to act as the guardians and preservers of that freedom, would be anxious and curious to see how that representation is formed, and how the people choose those representatives, to whose faith and guardianship they entrust their free and liberal institutions. Such a person would be very much astonished if he were taken to a ruined mound and told that that mound sent two representatives to Parliament ; if he were taken to a stone wall, and told that three niches in it sent two representatives to Parliament ; if he were taken to a park, where no houses were to be seen, and told that that park sent two representatives to Parliament ; but if he were told all this, and were astonished at hearing it, he would be still more astonished if he were to see large and opulent towns, full of enterprise and industry and intelligence, containing vast magazines of every species of manufactures, and were then told that these towns sent no representatives to Parliament.

Corrupt practices

Such a person would be still more astonished if he were taken to Liverpool, where there is a large constituency, and told, "Here you will have a fine specimen of a popular election." He would see bribery employed to the greatest extent and in the most unblushing manner ; he would see every voter receiving a number of guineas in a box, as the price of his corruption ; and after such a spectacle he would no doubt be much astonished that a nation whose representatives are thus chosen could perform the functions of legislation at all, or enjoy respect in any degree. I say, then, that if the question before the House is a question of reason, the present state of representation is against reason.

The confidence of the country in the construction and constitution of the House of Commons is gone. It would be easier to transfer the flourishing manufactures of Leeds and Manchester to Gatton and Old Sarum than to reëstablish confidence and sympathy between this House and those whom it calls its constituents. If, therefore, the question is one of right, right is in favor of Reform; if it be a question of reason, reason is in favor of Reform; if it be a question of policy and expediency, policy and expediency are in favor of Reform.

Popular confidence in the House of Commons is gone

I come now to the explanation of the measure which, representing the ministers of the king, I am about to propose to the House. Those ministers have thought, and in my opinion justly thought, that no half measures would be sufficient; that no trifling or paltering with Reform could give stability to the crown, strength to Parliament, or satisfaction to the country. The chief grievances of which the people complain are these: first, the nomination of members by individuals; second, the election by close corporations; third, the expense of elections.

With regard to the first, it may be exercised in two ways, either over a place containing scarcely any inhabitants, and with a very extensive right of election; or over a place of wide extent and numerous population, but where the franchise is confined to very few persons. Gatton is an example of the first, and Bath of the second. At Gatton, where the right of voting is by scot and lot, all householders have a vote, but there are only five persons to exercise the right. At Bath the inhabitants are numerous, but very few of them have any concern in the election. In the former case we propose to deprive the borough of the franchise altogether. In doing so we have taken for our guide the population returns of 1821; and we propose that every borough which in that year had less than 2000 inhabitants should altogether lose the right of sending members to Parliament, the effect of which will be to disfranchise sixty-two boroughs.

Certain boroughs to be deprived of representation in Parliament

Other bor-
oughs to lose
one member
each

But we do not stop here. As the honorable member for Boroughbridge would say, we go *plus ultra ;* we find that there are forty-seven boroughs of only 4000 inhabitants, and these we shall deprive of the right of sending more than one member to Parliament. We likewise intend that Weymouth, which at present sends four members to Parliament, should in future send only two. The total reduction thus effected in the number of the members of this House will be 168. This is the whole extent to which we are prepared to go in the way of disfranchisement. . . .

Those who have long been accustomed to the democratic notions of a widely extended suffrage and the distribution of representatives according to the population doubtless find it difficult to discover any reason why an intelligent Englishman should have favored the continuance of the glaring inequalities, verging in some instances on absurdity, which existed in the English parliamentary system at the opening of the nineteenth century. Nevertheless, the reform measure introduced by Lord John Russell was stoutly opposed at every point and at every stage in its passage through Parliament. One of the most characteristic and effective arguments against the proposed change was made by Sir Robert Inglis, member of Parliament for the University of Oxford, from whose speech the following extract is taken. It well illustrates the complacent, conservative spirit which dreads change and always finds abundant reasons for opposing all modifications in ancient institutions.

291. An argu-
ment against
parliamen-
tary reform

I know there are such men as Delolme and Montesquieu, who have taken on themselves to talk of representation being founded on the basis of population and taxation, but I can find no trace of such a principle in any of the ancient times of our constitution. If it can be shown that places were entitled to send members which were neither parishes nor market towns, I presume that it will be admitted that those places could not be very considerable. Now there are Haslemere and West Looe, which have never been one or the other and yet they have been called on to send representatives to Parliament. And not only have small towns been called on to send representatives, but large towns have been left unrepresented; and this is a most important point in answer to those who pretend that they only ask for the restoration of the Constitution.

Can the noble lord show that any town or borough has been called into parliamentary existence because it was large or populous, or excluded from it because it was small? The noble lord has tried to make much of the instance of Old Sarum. In one and the same year, the 23d Edward I, a writ was issued to both Old and New Sarum, and in neither case was it conferred on account of population or taxation. On the contrary, I believe it was given, in the first instance, to oblige some earl of Salisbury, by putting his friends into the House. And in an account of the borough it was stated that it had lately been purchased by Mr. Pitt, the possessor of the celebrated diamond of that name, who had obtained an hereditary seat in the House of Commons, as much as the earl of Arundel possessed one in the House of Peers by being the owner of Arundel Castle. How, then, can it be said that, according to the Constitution of the country, noblemen are not to be represented and their interests regarded in this House? *[Representation in Parliament not based on population]*

The cause of the creation of many boroughs is, I believe, obscure; but, on the other hand, some were as clear and as well ascertained as possible. It is known that two writs to return members were issued by Elizabeth, at the desire of one of her favorites, Sir Christopher Hatton; and Newport, in the Isle of Wight, had received its franchise to please Sir George Carew. This is the history of many of the small boroughs; and all the Cornish boroughs were formed in that manner. Fifteen Cornish boroughs had at one time received the right of representation, some of which were small villages, and none of them entitled to rank as considerable among the towns of England.

Condition of
affairs never
better than at
present

It is in vain, after this, to talk of the purity of representation in former times. I defy the noble lord to point out any time when the representation was better than it is at present. I say, therefore, that what is proposed is not restorative. The House and the country may judge what it is, but I will state, in one word, that it is Revolution, — a revolution that will overturn all the natural influence of rank and property. . . .

Parliament
now repre-
sents all
interests and
open to all
talents

The great benefit of the constitution of the House of Commons, as it now exists (though if the noble lord's plan is adopted, that benefit will cease), is that it represents all interests and admits all talents. If the proposed change takes place, it will be almost entirely confined to one interest, and no talent will be admitted but the single one of mob oratory. Many of those who sat for "close and rotten boroughs," as they have been designated for the first time by a member of the government, have constituted the chief ornaments of the House and the support of the country, but would, if this plan had been adopted in their days, never have been received into the House.

Great men get
into Parlia-
ment as
representa-
tives of
" rotten
boroughs "

I ask the noble lord by what means the great Lord Chatham came into Parliament. By the bye, the first borough for which that great man sat was Old Sarum itself. Mr. Pitt sat for Appleby. Mr. Fox came in for a close borough, and when rejected for a populous place, he again took refuge in a close borough. Mr. Burke first sat for Wendover ; and when, by that means, he became known, he was transposed in his glory to Bristol, as Mr. Canning, who also first sat for Wendover, was transposed to Liverpool. When their talents became known they were the honored representatives of large towns ; but would such places ever have thought of selecting Mr. Canning, Mr. Burke, or Lord Chatham, if they had not previously had an opportunity of showing their talents in the House? It is only by this means that young men, who are unconnected by birth or residence with large towns, can ever hope to enter this House, unless they are cursed — I will call it cursed — with that talent of mob oratory which is used for the purpose of influencing the lowest and most debasing passions of the people.

Extreme and revolutionary as the Reform Bill of 1832 appeared to Tories like the duke of Wellington and Sir Robert Inglis, it was regarded as wholly inadequate by the great mass of English workingmen, who were still excluded from voting by its provisions. Accordingly agitation for additional reform immediately began, especially in the great manufacturing districts, and some of the most advanced Radicals attacked practically every point in the English system of government. Although their demands were later reduced to six main points, — universal suffrage, secret ballot, annual Parliaments, payment of members of Parliament, abolition of property qualifications for members of Parliament, and equal electoral districts, — in order that they might be more effectively urged upon the House of Commons, the leaders of the Chartist movement really contemplated the most thoroughgoing reforms of every kind, some of which were set forth in a little pamphlet entitled *The People's Charter*, published in London in 1832, from which a few extracts are given here.

Precedent

The rejection of precedent and authority as a guide in legislation, jurisprudence, etc. — " the tolerating nothing ancient that reason does not sanction, and the shrinking from no novelty to which reason may conduct."

(The history of precedent is simply this : that when despotism had treated the people sufficiently ill, the past, under the name of precedent, was impudently erected into a guide for the future ; robbery, fraud, and oppression consequently became the law of the land, and antiquity was adduced to sanctify its character. Precedent, accordingly, will generally be found to be a base fraud, directly opposed to principle ; and, in most instances, it ought to be shunned instead of being imitated.)

292. Reforms demanded by the Radicals, as set forth in 1832 in a pamphlet called *The People's Charter*

Aristocratic Government

The abolition of aristocratic and exclusive, plundering and inefficient government, and the substitution of representative and liberal, cheap and efficient government.

(Government, on the old system, is an assumption of power for the aggrandizement of itself, and measures its prosperity by the quantity of taxes it extorts; on the new, it is a delegation of power for the benefit of society, and proves its excellence by the small revenue it requires.)

The adoption especially of universal suffrage (for the man excluded from this is a slave); of the [secret] ballot (for the man who cannot thus vote may be oppressed by the superior to whom he refuses his vote); and of annual Parliaments (for the man from whom this is withheld, is destined for sale during so many years).

Taxes on Knowledge

The abolition especially of all taxes on paper, printed and unprinted, and of all official embarrassment to the printing and publishing of newspapers, and to their cheap conveyance by post.

(Despotic administrations have heaped taxes upon paper, and in particular upon newspapers, for the purpose of placing political knowledge beyond the reach of the poorer classes, and of thereby rendering it easy to plunder the people without the danger of exposure.)

The establishment of a system of national education, unfettered and untainted by religious tenets.

Peerage

The abolition of hereditary peerage and hereditary legislation.

(The application of such a principle to the government of nations is an insult to common sense; and a hereditary legislator is a far greater absurdity than a hereditary poet. These legislators are, in fact, a few hundreds in number, and these unqualified to legislate, because, being entitled by the mere accident of birth to a monopoly of honors and indulgences, they need make no effort to obtain them, their intellectual powers are gradually lost, and their minds are at last utterly debased.)

Privileges

The abolition of privileged classes.

(A peer may send and receive all letters free, may frank those of his friends, and may send by post on Sunday as on other days. He may vote by proxy, though not present at a debate, and ignorant of its purport. He may give a verdict, not on oath, but honor, as if he alone were honorable, and other men were villains. He may not be arrested, made bankrupt, or have his estate sequestrated. He may, with perfect impunity, defraud his creditors, by borrowing, buying houses and lands, and leaving them to whom he pleases, as the lenders cannot touch his real estate. It is in his interest, and that of the aristocracy in general, that game laws have been made, so peculiarly replete with insult and cruelty.)

Titles

The abolition of hereditary nobility, titles, honors, and distinctions.

Kingship

The abolition of the evils with which kingship is accompanied.

(Mental or moral character, in hereditary kingship, must necessarily be a matter of perfect indifference, as by its means the very worst man may, and often does, succeed to the same power. Kings have every motive to remain ignorant; they generally are so in a degree that would surprise even a peasant; and the report of their having any sort of talent is always a mere flattery of courtiers.

The intellectual organs of kings are so small, and their faculties are so feeble, as always to border on fatuity. See this explained in "The Rights of Nations." Fatuity has, consequently, in all ages and countries, been the disease of hereditary royalty and of ancient dynasty.

A king will, therefore, be found to be in reality the most useless official person, and to be scarcely necessary in any single act of the government; while the members of his family — who, in England, are often low-minded, cunning, and tyrannically disposed Germans — are of just the same value to the State as any similar number of paupers to be found throughout the kingdom.)

Insolence

The interdiction of all insulting terms and slavish language, as "subjects," "humbly petitioning," "praying," etc.

(The imposing grandeur of the crown and their own profit are at once consulted, when the aristocracy meanly consent to Parliament being a grant or boon from kings, — to its being called "my Parliament," — and when they basely solicit the king to grant to the assembly the liberty of speech, as is the case with the House of Commons.)

The Church

The prevention of public plunder by the priesthood.

(The English are dupes to their priesthood in a degree that is quite incredible to strangers. There is actually no other nation, however debased by superstition, in which the clergy enjoy such prodigious wealth. There is no other nation in which such enormous Church property supports so unprincipled and immoral a priesthood.

Besides tithes, that tax on the produce of land, animals, and industry, that impost on labor and capital, that penalty on agriculture, and prohibition to improve inferior lands, the priestly order in England has enormous revenues, amounting in all to £9,459,565.

As about 2152 clergymen do all the duty, and as their average income is about £300 per annum each, it is evident that the total thus formed, namely £1,974,503, should have sufficed for the maintenance of all the clergy.)

Abolition of State Church and State religion, leaving priests, parsons, preachers, ministers, etc., to be paid by those who choose to employ them.

The cessation of every species of persecution for religious opinions, and the punishment of such persecution when exercised by the followers of any creed.

Quite inevitably the bitter attacks of the Chartists on the government and the clergy called forth equally bitter denunciations from their opponents. Indeed, the whole country was flooded with controversial literature of the most violent type, and the horror which Conservative clergymen felt at the progress of Chartism is well illustrated by a very popular tract entitled *Chartism Unmasked*, written by the Reverend Evan Jenkins.

That the Church of England and Chartism totally oppose each other, produce wholly different effects, and lead to widely and utterly different destinations, will appear if we just consider to what they each lead.

293. A clergyman's attack on Chartism

Chartism	*The Church of England*
Leads to *unholy* desires, wicked counsels, and unjust works.	Leads us to pray to that God from whom "all *holy* desires, all good counsels, and all just works proceed."
Leads to perils, dangers, evil, and mischief.	Leads us "to pray to be kept from all perils and dangers, from all evil and mischief.
Leads "to battle, murder, and sudden death."	Leads us to pray to be delivered "from battle, and murder, and from sudden death."
Leads us to curse and oppose the magistrates in the execution of their duties, in punishing wickedness and vice.	Leads us to beseech God "to bless and keep the magistrates, giving them grace to execute justice and to maintain truth."

Leads all nations to war, hatred, and discord.

Leads us to ask God "to give to all nations unity, peace, and concord."

Leads to the murder of fathers and husbands; and leaves the fatherless children and widows, desolate and oppressed.

Leads us to ask God "that it may please Him to defend and provide for the fatherless children and widows, and all that are desolate and oppressed."

Leads to the disturbance of public worship, to the immediate dispersion of the congregation when in the middle of their devotions, at the sight of the pike, pistol, scythe, gun, etc.

Lead us to pray thus: "Grant, O Lord, we beseech thee, that the course of this world may be so peaceably ordered by thy governance, that thy Church may joyfully serve thee in all godly quietness."

Leads to skepticism, infidelity, and disbelief of the Scriptures.

Leads us to pray God "to grant us grace to hear, read, mark, learn, and inwardly digest them."

Leads to anarchy; to disobey and rebel against the powers that be; and to the subversion of all good government.

Leads us and all subjects duly to consider whose authority the Queen hath, that we may "faithfully serve, honor, and humbly obey her."

Leads to poverty, misery, and transportation; the gallows, death, and hell.

Leads to wealth, peace, freedom, pardon; and beseeches the Lord in his boundless mercy and love to "deliver us from wrath and from everlasting damnation."

In view of the widespread discontent which the Reform Bill created, many eminent political leaders, like Cobden, Bright, and Gladstone, came to believe a further extension of the suffrage was both just and inevitable,

although they had no sympathies with the violent demonstrations of the Chartists, who continued their propaganda even after their organization went to pieces on
the refusal of Parliament, in 1848, to consider their
grand petition. At length, in 1865, Earl Russell, who,
as Lord John Russell, had led the fight for reform in
1832, came to power as the head of the Ministry and
selected as his representative in the House of Commons,
Mr. Gladstone. But while the new ministers were not
overardent in their advocacy for reform, they realized·
the possible advantage to be gained to the Liberal party,
which they led, by extending the right to vote to large
numbers of workingmen who were then excluded.
Accordingly Mr. Gladstone, in 1866, introduced the
second great Reform Bill, which, owing to party changes,
was to be successfully carried through by his famous
opponent, Disraeli, the Conservative leader. The most
celebrated and perhaps most powerful argument advanced against Mr. Gladstone's measure was made by
Mr. Lowe in a long speech in which he prophesied the
dire calamity which the new democratic measure would
bring upon England.

If the working classes, in addition to being a majority in
the boroughs, get a redistribution of the seats in their favor,
it will follow that their influence will be enormously increased.
They will then urge the House of Commons to pass another
Franchise Bill, and another Redistribution Bill to follow it.
Not satisfied with these, yet another Franchise Bill and another redistribution of seats will perhaps follow. No one
can tell where it will stop, and it will not be likely to stop
until we get equal electoral districts and a qualification so low
that it will keep out nobody. There is another matter with
which my honorable friend has not dealt. I mean the point

294. **Lowe's
speech
against
giving the
vote to
workingmen
(condensed)**

of combination among the working classes. To many persons there appears great danger that the machinery which at present exists for strikes and trade unions may be used for political purposes.

Workingmen elect demagogues

I come now to the question of the representatives of the working classes. It is an old observation that every democracy is in some respect similar to a despotism. As courtiers and flatterers are worse than despots themselves, so those who flatter and fawn upon the people are generally very inferior to the people, the objects of their flattery and adulation. We see in America, where the people have undisputed power, that they do not send honest, hard-working men to represent them in Congress, but traffickers in office, bankrupts, men who have lost their character and been driven from every respectable way of life, and who take up politics as a last resource.

Democracy a failure in Australia

In the colonies they have got democratic assemblies. And what is the result? Why, responsible government becomes a curse, instead of a blessing. In Australia there is no greater evil to the stability of society, to industry, to property, and to the well-being of the country, than the constant change which is taking place in the government, and the uncertainty that it creates and the pitting of rival factions against each other. . . .

Democracy tends to centralization

Now, Sir, democracy has yet another tendency, which it is worth while to study at the present moment. It is singularly prone to the concentration of power. Under it individual men are small and the government is great. That must be the character of a government which represents the majority, and which absolutely tramples down and equalizes everything except itself. And democracy has another strong peculiarity. It looks with the utmost hostility on all institutions not of immediate popular origin, which intervene between the people and the sovereign power which the people have set up.

Now, look what was done in France. Democracy has left nothing in that country between the people and the emperor except a bureaucracy which the emperor himself has created. In America it has done almost the same thing. You have there nothing to break the shock between the two great powers of the State. The wise men who framed the constitution tried to provide a remedy by dividing functions as much as possible. They assigned one function to the President, another to the Senate, a third to the Congress, and a fourth to the different States. But all their efforts have been in vain, and you see how two hostile camps have arisen, and the terrible duel which is now taking place between them.

Now, apply that to England, which, above all countries in the world, is the country of intermediate institutions. There are between the people and the throne a vast number of institutions which our ancestors have created. Their principle in creating them seems to have been this, that they looked a great deal to equality. If there were something to be done, they sought for some existing institution which was able to do it. If some change were required, they altered things as little as they could, and were content to go on in that manner. This is a country of privileges above all other countries, but the privileges have been given, not as in other countries — as in France before the Revolution, for instance — for the benefit of the privileged classes, but because our ancestors, in all moderation, believed this to be the best way to insure order and good government and stability. What do you suppose would become of a House of Peers in America? What has become of the House of Peers in France? The name alone remains; but where is the power of that brilliant aristocracy which surrounded the throne of the Louises and gave a glitter even to their vices?

Privileges established in England only to insure good government

And now let us come to ourselves. Our position, as I have remarked already, is much more honorable than that of the members of any other Legislative assembly in the world. Do you think democracy would look with a favorable eye upon that? Would it not judge by analogy that such a state of things ought in some degree to be altered, and that we should be made to approach nearer to the level of our constituents? Now, we have a privileged class of electors who hold houses above £10. That class is a humble one, but it has discharged its duty up to the present time in a manner which almost defies criticism.

Democracy means the establishment of institutions deriving their origin from the people

But now, without any reason, but merely on account of an abstract principle of right, we have an attempt made to sweep that class away and swamp it in the class below it. Without enlarging upon this topic, I must say it is manifest to me that if the House of Commons is democratized, it will not rest under such modified circumstances until it has swept away those institutions which at present stand between the people and the throne, and has supplied the place of them, as far as it can, by institutions deriving their origin directly from the people. . . .

England in danger of complete ruin

I have now, Sir, traced as well as I can what I believe will be the natural results of a measure which, it seems to my poor imagination, is calculated, if it should pass into law, to destroy one after another those institutions which have secured for England an amount of happiness and prosperity which no country has ever reached or is ever likely to attain. Surely the heroic work of so many centuries, the matchless achievements of so many wise heads and strong hands, deserve a nobler consummation than to be sacrificed at the shrine of revolutionary passion or the maudlin enthusiasm of humanity. But if we do fall, we shall fall deservedly. Uncoerced by any external force, not borne down by any internal calamity, but in the full plethora of our wealth and the surfeit of our too exuberant prosperity, with our own rash and inconsiderate hands, we are about to pluck down on our own heads the venerable temple of our liberty and our glory. History may tell of other acts as signally disastrous, but of none more wanton, none more disgraceful.

While the Reform Bill of 1867 gave the right to vote to a great majority of the workingmen of the towns, the peasants in the country were still excluded, and it was not until almost twenty years later that any English ministry believed it politically expedient to propose a new extension of the suffrage. Finally, in 1884, partly from principle and partly from a political design to ruin the Conservatives, the Gladstone Ministry decided to enfranchise the agricultural laborer, and thus retain the confidence of all Radicals and gain the support of the new country voters. On reading the signs in the political skies, as his colleague, John Morley, has put it, Mr. Gladstone determined that the new bill should be pressed on Parliament, and he introduced it himself in a studiously temperate speech.

I am not prepared to discuss admission to the franchise as it was discussed fifty years ago, when Lord John Russell had to state, with almost bated breath, that he expected to add in the Three Kingdoms 500,000 to the constituencies. It is not now a question of nicely calculated less or more. I take my stand on the broad principle that the enfranchisement of capable citizens, be they few or be they many, — and if they be many, so much the better, — gives an addition of strength to the State. The strength of the modern State lies in the representative system. I rejoice to think that in this happy country and under this happy constitution we have other sources of strength in the respect paid to various orders of the State, and in the authority they enjoy, and in the unbroken course which has been allowed to most of our national traditions; but still, in the main, it is the representative system which is the strength of the modern State in general, and of the State in this country in particular. . . .

295. Gladstone's defense of popular suffrage (1884)

Sir, the only question that remains in the general argument is, Who are capable citizens? and, fortunately, that is a question which, on the present occasion, need not be argued at length, for it has been already settled, — in the first place by a solemn legislative judgment acquiesced in by both parties in the State; and, in the second place, by the experience of the last more than fifteen years. Who, Sir, are the capable citizens of the State, whom it is proposed to enfranchise? It is proposed, in the main, to enfranchise the county population on the footing and according to the measure that has already been administered to the population of the towns.

What are the main constituents of the county population? First of all, they are the minor tradesmen of the country and

Character of
the county
population

the skilled laborers and artisans in all the common arts of life, and especially in connection with our great mining industry. Is there any doubt that these are capable citizens? You honorable gentlemen opposite [i.e. the Conservatives] have yourselves asserted it by enfranchising them in the towns; and we can only say that we heartily subscribe to the assertion. But besides the artisans and the minor tradesmen scattered throughout our rural towns, we have also to deal with the peasantry of the country.

The peasants
are capable
citizens

Is there any doubt that the peasantry of the country are capable citizens, qualified for enfranchisement, qualified to make good use of their power as voters? This is a question which has been solved for us by the first and second Reform Bills; because many of the places which, under the name of towns, are now represented in this House are really rural communities, based upon a peasant constituency. For my part, I should be quite ready to fight the battle of a peasant upon general and argumentative grounds. I believe the peasant generally to be, not in the highest sense, but in a very real sense, a skilled laborer. He is not a man tied down to one mechanical exercise of his physical powers. He is a man who must do many things, and many things which require in him the exercise of active intelligence.

The new
Reform Bill
not perfect
but practical

I say this is not a perfect bill with regard to the franchise. What are the questions we leave out? We do not aim at ideal perfection, and I hope gentlemen will not force us upon that line; it would be the "road to ruin." I have heard that there have been artists and authors who never could satisfy themselves as to the perfection of their picture or of their diction, as the case may be, and in consequence the diction and the picture have been wasted. I remember a most venerable archbishop — Archbishop Howley — who, with respect be it spoken, was the worst speaker in the House of Lords. And why? Because he was a man of inferior intellect? He was a man of remarkable intellect, remarkable education, remarkable refinement; but, unfortunately, he had a taste so fastidious that he could never satisfy himself that his terms were perfect and his phrases entirely beyond criticism, and in consequence of his fastidiousness between the one and the other, catastrophe befell him. No, Sir; ideal perfection is not the true basis of English legislation. We look at the attainable; we look at the practicable; and we have too much of English sense to be drawn away by those sanguine delineations of what might possibly be attained in Utopia, from a path which promises to enable us to effect great good for the people of England. . . .

What does it do, and what does it do in comparison with what has been done before? In 1832 there was passed what was considered a Magna Carta of British liberties; but that Magna Carta of British liberties added, according to the previous estimate of Lord John Russell, 500,000, while according to the results considerably less than 500,000 were added to the entire constituency of the three countries. After 1832 we come to 1866. At that time the total constituency of the United Kingdom reached 1,364,000. By the bills which were passed between 1867 and 1868 that number was raised to 2,448,000. And now, Sir, under the action of the present law the constituency has reached in round numbers what I would call 3,000,000. I will not enter into details; but what is the increase we are going to make? There is a basis of computation, but it is a basis which affords, I admit, ground for conjecture and opinion. That basis of computation is the present ratio in towns, between inhabited houses and the number of town electors. Of course we have availed ourselves of that basis for the purpose of computation. I have gone into the matter as carefully as I can, and the best results I can attain are these. The bill, if it passes as presented, will add to the English constituency over 1,300,000 persons. It will add to the Scotch constituency, Scotland being at present rather better provided for in this respect than either of the other countries, over 200,000, and to the Irish constituency over 400,000; or, in the main, to the present aggregate constituency of the United Kingdom, taken at 3,000,000, it will add 2,000,000 more, nearly twice as much as was added since 1867, and more than four times as much as was added in 1832. Surely, I say, that is worth doing, that is worth not endangering. Surely that is worth some sacrifice.

The number of new voters estimated

"Read your history in a nation's eyes," for you will have deserved it by the benefits you will have conferred. You will have made this strong nation stronger still; stronger by its closer union without; stronger against its foes, if and when it has any foes without; stronger within by union between class and class, and by arraying all classes and all portions of the community in one solid compacted mass round the ancient Throne which it has loved so well, and round a constitution now to be more than ever powerful and more than ever free.

Section 81. The English Cabinet

It is a cardinal principle of modern democracy that the government has, in the last analysis, but one function, — namely, carrying out the will of the people by making and executing the laws of which the people approve. This notion is realized in England not only through the power of the Parliament to make laws, but also through its power to control a cabinet which is, after all, merely a group of departmental heads, charged with the execution of the law in various directions. This fusion of the executive and legislative powers, the most striking characteristic of the English constitution, is well described in an article by Mr. Gladstone.

296. Gladstone's description of cabinet government (condensed)

The Federal Executive [in the United States] is born anew of the nation at the end of each four years, and dies at the end. But during the course of those years it is independent — in the person both of the President and of his ministers — alike of the people, of their representatives, and of that remarkable body, the Senate of the United States. On the contrary, a vote of the House of Commons, declaring a withdrawal of its confidence, has always sufficed for the purpose of displacing a Ministry; nay, persistent obstruction of its measures, and even lighter causes, have conveyed the hint, which has been obediently taken. But the people, how is it with them? Do not the people in England part with their power, and make it over to 'the House of Commons, as completely as the American people part with it to the President? They give it over for four years, we for a period which on the average is somewhat more ; they to resume it at a fixed time, we on an unfixed contingency and at a time which will finally be determined, not according to the popular will, but according to the views which a Ministry may entertain of its duty or convenience.

All this is true, but it is not the whole truth. In the United Kingdom the people as such cannot commonly act upon the Ministry as such. But mediately, though not immediately, they gain the end ; for they can work upon that which works upon the Ministry, namely, on the House of Commons. Firstly, they have not renounced, like the American people, the exercise of their power for a given time ; and they are at all times free, by speech, petition, public meeting, to endeavor to get it back in full by bringing about a dissolution. Secondly, in a Parliament with nearly 660 members, vacancies occur with tolerable frequency ; and as they are commonly filled up forthwith, they continually modify the color of the Parliament, conformably not to the past but to the present feeling of the nation, or at least of the constituency, which for practical purposes is different indeed, yet not very different. *How the English people influence the cabinet*

But besides exercising a limited positive influence on the present, they supply a much less limited indication of the future. Of the members who at a given time sit in the House of Commons, the vast majority, probably more than nine tenths, have the desire to sit there again, after a dissolution which may come at any moment. They therefore study political weather wisdom, and in varying degrees adapt themselves to the indications of the sky. It will now be readily perceived how the popular sentiment in England, so far as it is awake, is not meanly provided with the ways of making itself respected, whether for the purpose of displacing and replacing a Ministry, or of constraining it (as sometimes happens) to alter or reverse its policy sufficiently, at least, to conjure down the gathering and muttering storm. . . . *Members of Commons watch public opinion*

The cabinet
is responsible
for royal acts

In the ordinary administration of the government the sovereign personally is, so to speak, behind the scenes, performing, indeed, many personal acts by the sign manual or otherwise, but, in each and all of them, covered by the counter signature or advice of ministers, who stand between the august personage and the people. There is, accordingly, no more power, under the form of our constitution, to assail the monarch in his personal capacity, or to assail through him the line of succession to the crown, than there is at chess to put the king in check.

The powers
theoretically
enjoyed by the
sovereign

The sovereign in England is the symbol of the nation's unity, and the apex of the social structure; the maker (with advice) of the laws; the supreme governor of the Church; the fountain of justice; the sole source of honor; the person to whom all military, all naval, all civil service is rendered. The sovereign owns very large properties; receives and holds, in law, the entire revenue of the State; appoints and dismisses ministers; makes treaties; pardons crime or abates its punishment; wages war or concludes peace; summons and dissolves the Parliament; exercises these vast powers for the most part without any specified restraint of law, and yet enjoys, in regard to these and every other function, an absolute immunity from consequences.

The sovereign
cannot be
called to
account

There is no provision in the law of the United Empire, or in the machinery of the constitution, for calling the sovereign to account; and only in one solitary and improbable, but perfectly defined case, — that of his submitting to the jurisdiction of the Pope, — is he deprived by statute of the throne. Setting aside that peculiar exception, the constitution might seem to be founded on the belief of a real infallibility in its head.

How the
Ministry is
dismissed

There is, indeed, one great and critical act, the responsibility for which falls momentarily or provisionally on the sovereign; it is the dismissal of an existing Ministry and the appointment of a new one. This act is usually performed with the aid drawn from authentic manifestations of public opinion, mostly such as are obtained through the votes or conduct of the House of Commons. Since the reign of George III there has been but one change of Ministry in which the monarch acted without the support of these indications.

But this power of dismissing a Ministry at will, large as it may be under given circumstances, is neither the safest nor the only power which, in the ordinary course of things, falls constitutionally to the personal share of the wearer of the crown. He is entitled, on all subjects coming before the Ministry, to knowledge and opportunities of discussion, unlimited save by the iron necessities of business. Though decisions must ultimately conform to the sense of those who are to be responsible for them, yet their business is to inform and persuade the sovereign, not to overrule him. *The sovereign is entitled to know about public business*

Were it possible for him, within the limits of human time and strength, to enter actively into all public transactions, he would be fully entitled to do so. What is actually submitted is supposed to be the most fruitful and important part, the cream of affairs. In the discussion of them, the monarch has more than one advantage over his advisers. He is permanent, they are fugitive; he speaks from the vantage ground of a station unapproachably higher; he takes a calm and leisurely survey, while they are worried with the preparatory stages, and their force is often impaired by the pressure of countless detail. He may be, therefore, a weighty factor in all deliberations of State. Every discovery of a blot that the studies of the sovereign in the domain of business enable him to make strengthens his hands and enhances his authority. It is plain, then, that there is abundant scope for mental activity to be at work under the gorgeous robes of royalty. *The king may be a weighty factor*

This power spontaneously takes the form of influence, and the amount of it depends on a variety of circumstances, — on talent, experience, tact, weight of character, steady, untiring industry, and habitual presence at the seat of government. In proportion as any of these might fail, the real and legitimate influence of the monarch over the course of affairs would diminish; in proportion as they attain to fuller action, it would increase. It is a moral, not a coercive, influence. It operates through the will and reason of the Ministry, not over or against them. It would be an evil and a perilous day for the *The king's influence varies according to circumstance* monarchy, were any prospective possessor of the crown to assume or claim for himself final, or preponderating, or even independent power in any one department of the State. The ideas and practice of the time of George III, whose will in certain matters limited the action of the ministers, cannot be revived, otherwise than by what would be, on their part, nothing less than a base compliance, a shameful subserviency, dangerous to the public weal and in the highest degree disloyal to the dynasty. Because in every free State, for every public act some one must be responsible; and the question is, Who shall it be?

The minister alone is responsible The British constitution answers: The minister, and the minister exclusively. That he may be responsible, all action must be fully shared by him. Sole action, for the sovereign, would mean undefended, unprotected action; the armor of irresponsibility would not cover the whole body against sword or spear; a head would project beyond the awning and would invite a sunstroke.

The distinction between the sovereign and the crown The reader, then, will clearly see that there is no distinction more vital to the practice of the British constitution, or to a right judgment upon it, than the distinction between the sovereign and the crown. The crown has large prerogatives, endless functions essential to the daily action and even the life of the State. To place them in the hands of persons who should be mere tools in a royal will, would expose those powers to constant unsupported collision with the living forces of the nation, and to a certain and irremediable crash. They are therefore intrusted to men, who must be prepared to answer for the use they make of them.

The social influence of the king This ring of responsible ministerial agency forms a fence around the person of the sovereign, which has thus far proved impregnable to all assaults. The august personage who from time to time may rest within it, and who may possess the art of turning to the best account the countless resources of the position, is no dumb and senseless idol, but, together with zeal and very large means of influence upon policy, enjoys the undivided reverence which a great people feels for its head; and is likewise the first and by far the weightiest among the forces which greatly mold, by example and legitimate authority, the manners, nay the morals, of a powerful aristocracy and a wealthy and highly trained society. The social influence of a sovereign, even if it stood alone, would be an enormous attribute.

In the face of the country the sovereign and the ministers are an absolute unity. The one may concede to the other; but the limit of concessions by the sovereign is at the point where he becomes willing to try the experiment of changing his government; and the limit of concession by the ministers is at the point where they become unwilling to bear what in all circumstances they must bear while they remain ministers, — the undivided responsibility of all that is done in the crown's name.

The unity of the Ministry and sovereign

But it is not with the sovereign only that the Ministry must be welded into identity. It has a relation to sustain to the House of Lords, which need not, however, be one of entire unity, for the House of Lords, though a great power in the State, and able to cause great embarrassment to an administration, is not able by a vote to doom it to capital punishment. Only for fifteen years out of the last fifty has the Ministry of the day possessed the confidence of the House of Lords. On the confidence of the House of Commons it is immediately and vitally dependent. This confidence it must always possess. . . .

The cabinet and the House of Lords

I have said that the cabinet is essentially the regulator of the relations between king, Lords, and Commons; exercising functionally the powers of the first, and incorporated, in the persons of its members, with the second and the third. It is, therefore, itself a great power. But let no one suppose it is the greatest. In a balance nicely poised a small weight may turn the scale; and the helm that directs the ship is not stronger than the ship. It is a cardinal axiom of the modern British constitution, that the House of Commons is the greatest of the powers of the State. It might, by a base subserviency, fling itself at the feet of a monarch or a minister; it might, in a season of exhaustion, allow the slow persistence of the Lords, ever eyeing it as Lancelot was eyed by Modred, to invade its just province by baffling its action at some time propitious for the purpose.

The House of Commons the greatest power in the government

But no constitution can anywhere keep either sovereign, or assembly, or nation, true to its trust and to itself. All that can be done has been done. The Commons are armed with ample powers of self-defense. If they use their powers properly, they can only be mastered by a recurrence to the people, and the way in which the appeal can succeed is by the choice of another House of Commons more agreeable to the national temper. Thus the sole appeal from the verdict of the House is a rightful appeal to those from whom it received its commission. . . .

The House of Commons is watched by the people

The House of Commons is superior, and by far superior, in the force of its political attributes, to any other single power in the State. But it is watched ; it is criticised ; it is hemmed in and about by a multitude of other forces ; the force, first of all, of the House of Lords, the force of opinion from day to day, particularly of the highly antipopular opinion of the leisured men of the metropolis, who, seated close to the scene of action, wield an influence greatly in excess of their just claims ; the force of the classes and professions ; the just and useful force of the local authorities in their various orders and places.

The peculiar position of the prime minister

Nor can anything be more curiously characteristic of the political genius of the people than the present position of this most important official personage, the premier. Departmentally, he is no more than the first named of five persons, by whom jointly the powers of the lord treasurership are taken to be exercised ; he is not their master, or, otherwise than by mere priority, their head, and he has no special function or prerogative under the formal constitution of the office. He has no official rank except that of privy councilor. Eight members of the cabinet, including five secretaries of state, and several other members of the government take official precedence of him. His rights and duties as head of the administration are nowhere recorded. He is almost, if not altogether, unknown to the statute law.

The singular position of the cabinet

Nor is the position of the body over which he presides less singular than his own. Every one of its members acts in no less than three capacities, — as administrator of a department of State, as member of a legislative chamber, and as a confidential adviser of the crown. Two at least of them add to those three characters a fourth ; for in each House of Parliament it is indispensable that one of the principal ministers should be what is termed its " leader."

This is an office the most indefinite of all, but not the least important. With very little of defined prerogative, the leader suggests, and in a great degree fixes, the course of all principal matters of business, supervises and keeps in harmony the action of his colleagues, takes the initiative in matters of ceremonial procedure, and advises the House in every difficulty as it arises. *Prime minister as leader*

The head of the British government is not a grand vizier. He has no powers, properly so called, over his colleagues ; on the rare occasions when a cabinet determines its course by the votes of its members, his vote counts only as one of theirs, but they are appointed and dismissed by the sovereign on his advice. In a perfectly organized administration, such for example as was that of Sir Robert Peel in 1841–1846, nothing of great importance is matured, or would even be projected, in any department without his personal cognizance ; and any weighty business would commonly go to him before being submitted to the cabinet. He reports to the sovereign its proceedings, and he also has many audiences of the august occupant of the throne. He is bound, in these reports and audiences, not to counterwork the cabinet, not to divide it, not to undermine the position of any of his colleagues in the royal favor. If he departs in any degree from strict adherence to these rules, and uses his great opportunities to increase his own influence or pursue aims not shared by his colleagues, then, unless he is prepared to advise their dismissal, he not only departs from rule but commits an act of treachery and baseness. As the cabinet stands between the sovereign and the Parliament, and is bound to be loyal to both, so he stands between his colleagues and the sovereign, and is bound to be loyal to both. *The work of the prime minister*

As a rule, the resignation of the first minister, as if removing the bond of cohesion in the cabinet, has the effect of dissolving it. A conspicuous instance of this was furnished by Sir Robert Peel in 1846, when the dissolution of the administration, after it had carried the repeal of the Corn Laws, was understood to be due not so much to a united deliberation and decision as to his initiative. The resignation of any other minister only creates a vacancy. In certain circumstances the balance of forces may be so delicate and susceptible that a single resignation will break up the government; but what is the rule in the one case is the rare exception in the other. The prime minister has no title to override any one of his colleagues in any one of the departments. So far as he governs them, unless it is done by trick, which is not to be supposed, he governs them by influence only. But upon the whole, nowhere in the wide world does so great a substance cast so small a shadow; nowhere is there a man who has so much power, with so little to show for it in the way of formal title or prerogative.

Section 82.   Reform of Local Government in England

The great changes in the constitution of the House of Commons are certainly the most striking features in the political history of England during the nineteenth century. But it may be doubted whether they are really more important than the less spectacular laws by which the ancient systems of city and county government have been thoroughly remodeled. For it will be remembered that about four fifths of the English people live in towns, and accordingly the citizens are more directly affected by their respective municipal governments than by Parliament at Westminster. It is now a well-known fact that English cities are among the most honestly governed municipalities in the world, and the revolutionary character of the changes which have come about during the nineteenth century will be apparent to any one who takes the trouble to examine the reports of the commissioners charged with investigating municipal government before the first great municipal reform of 1835, from which a brief extract is made here.

The most common and most striking defect in the constitution of the Municipal Corporations of England and Wales is,
that the corporate bodies exist independently of the communities among which they are found. The Corporations look
upon themselves, and are considered by the inhabitants, as
separate and exclusive bodies; they have powers and privileges within the towns and cities from which they are named,
but in most places all identity of interest between the Corporation and the inhabitants has disappeared. . . .

297. Abuses
in municipal
government
before the
reform of
1835

Some Corporations are occasionally spoken of as exercising
their privileges through a popular body; but in the widest
sense in which the term "popular body" is used in regard to
corporate towns, it designates only the whole body of freemen; and in most towns the freemen are a small number,
compared with the respectable inhabitants interested in their
municipal government, and possessing every qualification, except a legal one, to take a part in it. In Plymouth, where the
population, including Davenport, is more than 75,000, the
number of freemen is only 437, and 145 of these are non-
resident. In Norwich the great majority of the inhabitant
householders and ratepayers are excluded from the corporate
body, while paupers, lodgers, and others, paying neither
rates nor taxes, are admitted to the exercise of the functions
of freemen, and form a considerable portion of the Corporation.

The "free-
men" of
the towns

In Ipswich, containing more than 20,000 inhabitants, the
resident freemen form about $\frac{1}{55}$ part of the population. Of
these, more than $\frac{1}{3}$ are not rated; and of those who are rated,
many are excused the payment of their rates. About $\frac{1}{9}$ of the
whole are paupers. More than $\frac{11}{12}$ of all the property assessed
in this borough belong to those who are excluded from the
corporation. All the inhabitants whose rent exceeds £4 per
annum are taxed under a local act for municipal purposes.
Of those who are so taxed, less than $\frac{1}{15}$ are freemen. The
assessed taxes paid in the borough exceed £5000 per annum.
The amount paid by all the corporate body is less than $\frac{1}{20}$ of
the whole. The condition of these freemen exposes them to
bribery and undue influence, and advantage is taken of that
condition to establish the most demoralizing practices. . . .

The freemen
and the
taxpayers

The power of
Corporations
to choose
members of
Parliament

The importance which the privilege of electing members of Parliament has conferred upon Corporate Towns, or rather upon the governing bodies there, and the rewards for political services, which are brought within the reach of the ruling corporators, have caused this function to be considered in many places as the sole object of their institution. In some boroughs this right has survived all other traces of municipal authority. The custom of keeping the number of corporators as low as possible may be referred to this cause rather than to the desire of monopolizing the municipal authority, which has been coveted only as the means of securing the other and more highly prized privilege. . . .

Mismanage-
ment of city
property

The evils which have resulted from mismanagement of the corporate property are manifold and of the most glaring kind. Some Corporations have been in the habit of letting their lands by private contract to members of their own body, upon a rent and at fines wholly disproportionate to their value, and frequently for long terms of years. Others have alienated in fee much of their property for inadequate considerations. At Cambridge practices of this kind have prevailed to a very great extent. In large towns such malversations are less frequent, the most striking defects in those places not being the clandestine appropriation of the corporate property, but carelessness and extravagance in the administration of the municipal funds, and an exclusive distribution of patronage among friends and partisans.

Bribery in
elections

In some towns large sums have been spent in bribery and the other illegal practices of contested elections. During the election of 1826 the Corporation of Leicester expended ten thousand pounds to secure the success of a political partisan, and mortgaged some of their property to discharge the liabilities incurred. In Barnstaple and Liverpool the funds of the Corporation have been wasted in defending from threatened disfranchisement a body of freemen, who have been proved guilty of bribery.

Corporate
funds are
wasted

In general, the corporate funds are but partially applied to municipal purposes, such as the preservation of the peace by an efficient police, or in watching or lighting the town, etc.;

but they are frequently expended in feasting, and in paying the salaries of unimportant officers. In some cases in which the funds are expended on public purposes, such as building public works or other objects of local improvement, an expense has been incurred much beyond what would be necessary if due care had been taken. This has happened at Exeter, in consequence of the plan of avoiding public contract and of proceeding without adequate estimates. These abuses often originate in the negligence of the corporate bodies, but more frequently in the opportunity afforded to them of obliging members of their own body, or the friends and relations of such members.

Some Corporations consider that their property has been vested in them solely as trustees for the public; but in most cases this truth is acknowledged only when forced on their attention, is received with difficulty and qualification, and is continually forgotten. Few Corporations admit any positive obligation to expend the surplus of their income for objects of public advantage. Such expenditure is regarded as a spontaneous act of private generosity rather than a well-considered application of the public revenue, and the credit to which the Corporation, in such a case, generally considers itself entitled, is not that of judicious administrators, but of liberal benefactors. Even in these cases party and sectarian purposes often prevail in its application.

CHAPTER XXVI

SOCIAL REFORMS IN ENGLAND

Section 83. Freedom of Discussion and Religious Tolerance

298. Bulwer Lytton's plea for cheap newspapers in England (much condensed) Although censorship of the press was abolished in England as early as 1695, the government, on occasions of serious popular agitation, passed special measures designed to control the newspapers. Even when there was no direct governmental interference with publications, the establishment of cheap and popular newspapers was seriously hampered by the combined action of a stamp duty, an impost on advertisements, and a tax on paper. About the same time that the agitation for the first Reform Bill was being carried forward, a movement was started for the purpose of urging Parliament to repeal these obnoxious "taxes on knowledge." Political reformers who wanted a cheap means of spreading their doctrines, and educational reformers who wanted cheaper means for the diffusion of knowledge, joined in this agitation. In 1832 Bulwer Lytton, the celebrated novelist, made a powerful argument in Parliament against these taxes, and in favor of a free press.

He should proceed at once [the speaker said] to call the attention of the House to certain facts which would tend to show why it was our duty and our policy to diffuse cheap instruction amongst the people, and he should then show in what manner that instruction was, by the existing taxes, checked and obstructed. From an analysis, carefully made, of the cases of those persons who were committed for acts of incendiarism, etc., in 1830 and the beginning of 1831, it appeared that in Berkshire, of 138 prisoners only twenty-five could write, and only thirty-seven could read; at Abingdon, of thirty prisoners six only could read and write; at Aylesbury, of seventy-nine prisoners only thirty could read and write; of fifty prisoners tried at Lewes one individual only could read well! The same connection between crime and ignorance existed in France. In 1830 it appeared that in the French Courts of Assize there were 4519 entirely ignorant of reading and writing, and only 129 had received a superior education.

If, then, it was true, as the facts he had stated seemed to him sufficient to prove, that there was an inseparable connection between crime and ignorance, it followed as a necessary consequence, that it was their duty to remove all the shackles on the diffusion of knowledge. He thought it would be scarcely necessary for him to contend that newspapers were among the readiest and most effectual instruments of diffusing that instruction. *Newspapers the best means for popular education*

And now mark the interdict laid on the newspapers: the present taxes upon newspapers consisted, first, of a duty of 3*d.* per pound weight on the paper, or about a farthing a sheet; second, of a duty, nominally 4*d.*, but subject to a discount of twenty per cent; and third, a tax of 3*s.* 6*d.* upon every advertisement. The whole duties, with the price of printing and the news agency, amounted to 5½*d.* for every sevenpenny copy of a London paper. *The heavy taxes on newspapers*

Now let them glance rapidly at some of the consequences of the high prices at which newspapers sold. In the first place, owing to that price, the instruction they contained did not travel extensively among the poor; in the second place, as only the higher and the middling orders could afford, in general, the luxury of these periodicals, so it was chiefly to the tastes and interests of those wealthier orders that these journals addressed themselves. The poorer people are driven almost inevitably to those illegitimate, those dangerous productions, *Cheap literature at present tends to be pernicious* cheaper in price and adapted almost exclusively to themselves. It was thus that the real political education of the people was thrown into the hands of the wildest and sometimes the most pernicious teachers, some of whom struck at the root of all property, talked of the injustice of paying rents, insisted upon a unanimous seizure of all the lands in the kingdom, declared that there was no moral guilt in any violation of law, and even advocated assassination itself. Thus, then it was clear that the stamp duty did not prevent the circulation of the most dangerous doctrines.

Removal of stamp duty would reduce price of papers to twopence

His proposition was not at present to touch the paper duty; it was a tax which, in the present state of the revenue, might be fairly spared, and which, though a grievance, did not fall nearly so heavily on the public as the two taxes he would abolish; the first of these was the stamp duty, the second the advertisement duty. Take away the stamp duty and the $7d.$ paper would fall at once to $3\frac{3}{4}d.$; but he was inclined to believe, and in this he was borne out by many impartial, practical men on the subject, that, owing to the great increase of sale which the cheapness of the article would produce, the newspapers would be enabled to sell at a much lower rate than $3\frac{3}{4}d.$, and would probably settle into the average of $2d.$ each.

Cheap papers would be bought, not rented

To him it seemed equally evident that when newspapers were so cheap as to be within the reach of almost any man, there would be an enormous addition to the present number of readers; that many who hired a paper now would purchase it, — in short, when a weekly paper cost only $2d.$, there would scarcely be, in this great political community, a single man who could read who would not be able and willing to purchase one.

Newspapers in the United States

But besides these proofs that the cheapness of periodicals will incalculably increase their sale, we have the experience of other countries that it does; in America a newspaper sells on the average for $1\frac{1}{2}d.$ What is the result? Why, that there is not a town in America with 10,000 inhabitants that has not its daily paper. Compare Boston and Liverpool: Liverpool has 165,175 inhabitants; Boston had, in 1829, 70,000 inhabitants. Liverpool puts forth eight weekly publications; and Boston, with less than half the population, and with about a fourth part of the trade of Liverpool, puts forth eighty weekly publications. In 1829 the number of newspapers published in the British Isles was 33,050,000, or 630,000 weekly, which is one copy for every thirty-sixth inhabitant. In Pennsylvania, which had only in that year 1,200,000 inhabitants, the newspapers amounted to 300,000 copies weekly, or a newspaper to every fourth inhabitant.

From all these facts they had a right to suppose, that if newspapers were as cheap as they would be if his object were carried, the number of copies would be prodigiously increased. Thus information would circulate far more extensively; thus matters connected with trade, science, and law would become more familiar; thus there would be a thousand opportunities for removing those prejudices among the poor, which now so often perplexed the wisdom and benevolence of legislators. We have heard enough in this House of the necessity of legislating for property and intelligence; let us now feel the necessity of legislating for poverty and ignorance! At present we are acquainted with the poorer part of our fellow-countrymen only by their wrongs, their murmurs, their misfortunes and their crimes; let us at last open happier and wiser channels of communication between them and us. *Advantages of cheap newspapers*

We have made a long and fruitless experiment of the gibbet and the hulks; in 1825 we transported 283 persons, but so vast, so rapid has been our increase in this darling system of legislation, that three years afterwards (in 1828) we transported as many as 2449. During the last three years our jails have been sufficiently filled; we have seen enough of the effects of human ignorance, — we have shed sufficient of human blood. Is it not time to pause? Is it not time to consider whether the printer and his types may not provide better for the peace and honor of a free State than the jails and the hangman? Whether, in one word, cheap Knowledge may not be a better political agent than costly Punishment? *Ineffectual harshness of the criminal law*

At the opening of the nineteenth century the members of the Anglican Church enjoyed a monopoly of practically all the civil and military positions in England, although a limited freedom of worship had been granted to Catholics and Dissenters. Dissenters, however, were allowed to become members of Parliament, but Catholics were excluded from this privilege. This supremacy of the Anglicans was stoutly resisted in England by the Dissenters who had been steadily increasing, especially after the rise of the Methodist movement, and more particularly by the Catholics in Ireland, where an intense Irish patriotism added bitterness to the struggle. Among the many distinguished men who advocated a repeal of the repressive laws against Catholics and Dissenters was the witty man of letters, Rev. Sydney Smith, who advanced the arguments for his belief in an able speech which was widely circulated as a pamphlet shortly before the passage of the Catholic Emancipation Act in 1829.

299. Sydney Smith demands religious freedom for Catholics in Ireland (condensed)

What right have you to continue these rules, Sir, these laws of exclusion? What necessity can you show for it? Is the reigning monarch a concealed Catholic? Is his successor an open one? Is there a disputed succession? Is there a Catholic pretender? If some of these circumstances are said to have justified the introduction, and others the continuation of these measures, why does not the disappearance of all these circumstances justify the repeal of the restrictions? If you must be unjust, if it is a luxury you cannot live without, reserve your injustice for the weak and not for the strong; persecute the Unitarians, muzzle the Ranters, be unjust to a few thousand Sectaries, not to six millions; galvanize a frog, don't galvanize a tiger.

The fruits of intolerance in Ireland

We preach to our congregations, Sir, that a tree is known by its fruits. By the fruits it produces I will judge your system. What has it done for Ireland? New Zealand is emerging, Otaheite is emerging. Ireland is not emerging; she is still veiled in darkness; her children, safe under no law, live in the very shadow of death. Has your system of exclusion made Ireland rich? Has it made Ireland loyal? Has it made Ireland free? Has it made Ireland happy? How is the wealth of Ireland proved? Is it by the naked, idle, suffering savages, who are slumbering on the mud floor of their cabins? In what does the loyalty of Ireland consist? Is it in the eagerness with which they would range themselves under the hostile banner of any invader for your destruction and for your distress? Is it liberty when men breathe and move among the bayonets of English soldiers? Is their happiness and their history anything but such a tissue of murders, burnings, hanging, famine, and disease as never existed in the annals of the world? This is the system which, I am sure, with very different intentions and different views of its effects, you are met to uphold. These are the dreadful consequences which those laws your petition prays may be continued, have produced upon Ireland.

I have seen within these few weeks a degree of wisdom in our mercantile law, such superiority to vulgar prejudice, views so just and so profound, that it seemed to me as if I was reading the works of a speculative economist rather than the improvement of a practical politician, agreed to by a legislative assembly, and upon the eve of being carried into execution for the benefit of a great people. I rejoice that I have lived to see such an improvement in English affairs; that the stubborn resistance to all improvement, the contempt of all scientific reasoning, and the frigid adhesion to every stupid error, which so long characterized the proceedings of this country, is fast giving way to better things, under better men, placed in better circumstances. *Some of the exclusive trade laws have been recently repealed*

I confess it is not without severe pain that in the midst of all this expansion and improvement I perceive that in our profession we are still calling for the same exclusion, still asking that the same fetters may be riveted on our fellow-creatures, still mistaking what constitutes the weakness and misfortune of the Church for that which contributes to its glory, its dignity, and its strength. Sir, there are two petitions at this moment in this House, against two of the wisest and best measures which ever came into the British Parliament, — against the impending Corn Law and against the Catholic Emancipation; the one bill intended to increase the comforts, and the other to allay *Religious monopoly should be abolished also*

the bad passions of man. Of the Catholic Emancipation Bill
I shall say that it will be the foundation stone of a lasting religious peace; that it will give to Ireland not all that it wants,
but what it most wants, and without which no other boon will
will be of any avail.

The proposition to free Catholics and Dissenters from
the old restrictions of the law was warmly opposed at
the time by many eminent Englishmen, and especially
by the Anglican clergy. One of the most temperate and
reasonable statements of the Anglican party was made
by Sir Robert Inglis, a member of Parliament for the
University of Oxford, in a speech made in the House of
Commons against the proposal to remove the religious
tests imposed on Dissenters.

300. An argument in favor of religious tests for civil officers (condensed)

Some established opinions every government, in every age
and in every country, with one single and late exception, has
recognized and enforced. Some established form of religion
there has ever been in every other civilized State; all reason,
all experience, all history, ancient and modern, the United
States of America alone excepted, justify such a measure on
the part of every government. Now the very idea of an authorized religion implies some preference. I cannot conceive how
an establishment can exist without some special protection and
preference. The question then follows, What preference of those
belonging to that establishment, what exclusion of others, may
be necessary to its preservation? I am very willing to admit
that the least degree of exclusion, the lightest restraint, which
can meet and satisfy that object ought to be imposed. But
some exclusion, some restraint, is inseparable from the idea of
the public and recognized establishment of a Church.

No question of separation of Church and State

The question, in the present case, is not — let it ever be
recollected — whether this connection of Church and State be
or be not desirable in the abstract; with us that question is
already decided. We are not legislating for a new country; we
are not forming a constitution for New Zealand. We possess a

Church establishment inseparably connected with our State; and that establishment and that union we are bound to maintain.

I am to consider, then, whether, in the view of preserving the Church, more grievous restraints are imposed on those who dissent from it, than the necessity of the case requires. And here I cannot but remark the extraordinary fact, that for thirty-six or thirty-seven years there has hardly been uttered one complaint to Parliament on the subject of these restraints. The silence of the Dissenters may safely be considered as a proof that the grievances under the Test and Corporation Laws were not much felt; were not, in degree, so excessive as they are now described to be.

I come, then, to the mode, the particular test, applied by these laws for the purpose of securing the Church. Receiving the Sacrament is not the qualification, but the evidence of qualification, namely, the evidence of being a member of the Church of England. The Church requires all her members to receive the Holy Communion three times every year; and the law requires only that you should give evidence of having done that which your own Church has already required you to do, whether you take office or not; the constitution assuming that you are a member of the Church, or, at least, not so hostile to it as to refuse communion with it. *Receiving the sacrament only an evidence of fitness for office*

The original laws are kept in existence, to be enforced only when some great necessity shall arise; no one wishes to enforce them on the one side, and no great body of men, I should have thought, felt them a grievance on the other. They are at the same time the power which the constitution of England keeps in her own hand to protect the Church and herself, whenever such a combination of circumstances shall again arise as that which, two centuries ago, overthrew the altar and the throne, the Church and the State, in one common destruction. *The laws protect the constitution and the Church*

Against the recurrence of these dangers the laws in question were framed. Something has been said by the noble lord, and still more by the honorable member who seconded the motion, and something also by the honorable gentleman who has just sat down, on the "wisdom of our ancestors," — a topic often introduced, on late occasions, with a sneer. It seems, *The wisdom of our ancestors is good enough for us* indeed, the best, because it is the most frequent, joke of those who use it. Now, Sir, I am willing to admit that in physical science new and improved views are every day opening on mankind; but in moral science, and even in the arts of governing men, I am yet to learn that we are superior to our ancestors. The foundations of all moral truth were laid in a revelation not of yesterday. The principles of political government are to be found in the great authors of antiquity. Nowhere can you find more intimate knowledge of human nature in society than in the ten first books of Livy, in Tacitus, and in Thucydides; and in respect to the institutions of our own country, I am content with the principles of the constitution as established at the Revolution [of 1688]. . . .

The adoption of this reform will only lead to new demands
The Dissenters of the present day enjoy the fullest rights of conscience; and I am willing to admit that there is nothing in their overt acts from which I apprehend any danger. With some of them I am intimate, for many more I have the highest respect; but it is perfectly clear that the principles of Dissenters conscientiously opposed to the Church can never give the same undivided allegiance to the constitution in Church and State which a churchman does. The principles, if carried to the same extent as formerly, would produce the same results. The laws which restrain Dissenters are, and will ever be, left inoperative, so long as those principles slumber also; but I think that they should be retained. In fact, a richly endowed Church, with all its privileges and immunities, will always be an object of jealousy to those who differ from it; but, connected as it is with the constitution, the State is bound to protect it against any dangers from any quarters. Dangers will always exist; and if the present disabilities were removed, and Dissenters placed on the fullest equality as to power with the Church, some new question, perhaps of property, would immediately be started, on which new struggles and new dangers would arise. The question of tithes would probably come; and as we should have followed the example of America in giving no preference to any Church, we should be called upon to follow it further, and to enact that no man should pay anything to any pastor but his own [cries of hear! hear!].

Section 84. Humanitarian Legislation

The English criminal law at the opening of the nineteenth century prescribed the death penalty for about two hundred and fifty different offenses, and it was only the humane spirit of the jurors which prevented hundreds of persons guilty of minor offenses from being hung. In other words, jurors would often declare guilty persons innocent of crime in order to save them from the gallows, and thus there was great uncertainty in the enforcement of the law, although at times it was carried out with shocking cruelty. As we have seen, Beccaria, the celebrated Italian publicist, protested in the eighteenth century against the barbarity of criminal law in Europe; his protest was taken up in England by many eminent reformers, who urged that the number of capital offenses should be reduced to one or two, that punishment should be meted out according to the nature of each crime, and that only those laws should be retained which could actually be enforced. Among these eminent reformers was Sir Samuel Romilly, who, in a speech made in favor of repealing some of the old laws, described the most objectionable features of the criminal code, including flogging in the army.

Sir Samuel Romilly moved for leave to bring in bills to repeal the Acts 10 and 11, William III; 12 Anne; and 24 Geo. II (which make the crimes of stealing privately in a shop, goods of the value of *five* shillings; or in a dwelling house or on board a vessel in a navigable river, property of the value of *forty* shillings, capital felonies); and spoke to the following effect:

There is probably no other country in the world in which so many and so great a variety of human actions are punishable with loss of life as in England. These sanguinary statutes,

301. Sir Samuel Romilly attacks the cruel criminal law of England (condensed)

Harsh laws not really executed

however, are not carried into execution. For some time past the sentence of death has not been executed on more than a sixth part of the persons on whom it has been pronounced, even taking into the calculation crimes the most atrocious and the most dangerous to society, — murders, burning of houses, coining, forgeries, and attempts to commit murder. If we exclude these from our consideration, we shall find that the proportion which the number executed bears to those convicted is, perhaps, as one to twenty; and if we proceed still further, and, leaving out of the account burglaries, highway robberies, horse stealing, sheep-stealing, and returning from transportation, confine our observations to those larcenies unaccompanied with any circumstance of aggravation, for which a capital punishment is appointed by law, such as stealing privately in shops and stealing in dwelling houses and on board ships, property of the value mentioned in the statutes, we shall find the proportion of those executed reduced very far indeed below that even of one to twenty.

The law unequally administered

Not a great many years ago, upon the Norfolk Circuit, a larceny was committed by two men in a poultry-yard, but only one of them was apprehended ; the other, having escaped into a distant part of the country, had eluded all pursuit. At the next assizes the apprehended thief was tried and convicted ; but Lord Loughborough, before whom he was tried, thinking the offense a very slight one, sentenced him only to a few months' imprisonment. The news of this sentence having reached the accomplice in his retreat, he immediately returned and surrendered himself to take his trial at the next assizes. The next assizes came ; but, unfortunately for the prisoner, it was a different judge who presided ; and still more unfortunately, Mr. Justice Gould, who happened to be the judge, though of a very mild and indulgent disposition, had observed, or thought he had observed, that men who set out with stealing fowls generally end by committing the most atrocious crimes ; and, building a sort of system upon this observation, had made it a rule to punish this offense with very great severity ; and he accordingly, to the astonishment of this unhappy man, sentenced him to be transported. While one was taking his departure for Botany Bay, the term of the other's imprisonment had expired ; and what must have been the notion which that little public, who witnessed and compared these two examples, formed of our system of criminal jurisprudence? . . .

One of the greatest objections to the present system of military punishment is, that there exists no limit to it but the mercy or discretion of courts-martial. They may order the infliction of five or five thousand lashes, without control. But it is most important that they should in future know what they ought to do.

The great commentator on the laws of England has said that the rack and the knout are unknown amongst us, — that death, simple death, unattended with any circumstance of torture, is the severest infliction which the constitution allows. And yet we tolerate this species of punishment, — this refinement of cruelty; we permit a fellow-creature to be driven to the very verge of existence, a surgeon standing by to feel the pulse of the sufferer, and to pronounce at what moment exhausted nature can bear no additional infliction. Then, when his soul is about to forsake his tortured body and leap into eternity, then, indeed, the poor wretch is taken down from the halberts and removed into an hospital, where he is left, his body more at ease, but his mind still upon the rack, reflecting that the faster his wounds heal, the nearer he is to the renewal of his sufferings, and that his life is thus cherished by his tormentors, only that it may be again subjected to their torments.

When the Industrial Revolution brought the great factories into England, thousands of little boys and girls, sometimes not more than five or six years old, were employed in tending the machines. Their wages were often merely a pittance, and their hours of work long enough to have worn out even strong adults. Even before the close of the eighteenth century the attention of philanthropists was drawn to the miserable condition of mill workers, and reformers began to urge upon Parliament the necessity of making special provisions to safeguard the health and welfare of the children. In order to learn the real state of affairs, Parliament from time to time appointed commissioners, whose voluminous reports revealed the actual condition of the little workers in the mills.

Charles Harris, a boy working in the carding room of Mr. Oldacres's mill for spinning worsted yarn, testified as follows:

302. Extracts from a parliamentary report on child labor

I am twelve years old. I have been in the mill twelve months. I attend to a drawing machine. We begin at six o'clock and stop at half past seven. We don't stop work for breakfast. We do sometimes. This week we have not. Nothing has been said to me by Mr. Oldacres or the overlooker, or anybody else, about having any questions asked me. I am sure of that. The engine always stops for dinner. It works at tea time in the hot weather; and then we give over at half past seven instead of eight, which is the general time. We have generally about twelve hours and a half of it. On Saturdays we begin at six and give over at four. I get 2s. 6d. a week. I have a father and mother, and give them what I earn. I have worked overhours for two or three weeks together about a fortnight since. All the difference was, we worked breakfast time and tea time, and did not go away till eight. We are paid for such overhours at the rate of 2d. for three hours. I have always that for myself.

What do you do with it?

I save it for clothes sometimes. I put it into a money club for clothes. I have worked nine hours over in one week. I got for that 5½d. I gave it my mother, and she made it up to 6d. and put it into the money club. She always puts by 6d. a week from my wages for that.

Then your mother gets what you earn by the overhours, don't she?

No; I gets it for myself.

Do you work overhours or not, just as you like?

No; them as works must work. . . .

If overhours are put on next week, shall you be glad or sorry?

It won't signify. I shall be neither glad nor sorry. Sometimes mother gives me a halfpenny to spend.

What do you do with it?

I saves it to buy shoes. Have never saved above a shilling for that; mother put more to it, and bought me a pair. . . .

Don't you play sometimes after work's over?

Yes, sometimes.

Well, are you not sorry to lose that?

No, I don't mind about it. I am quite sure I don't. I am sometimes tired when I have been at work long hours. I am not tired now; I have been at work all day except dinner; it is now five o'clock. I am sure I had rather work as I do than lose any of my wages. I go to school of a Sunday sometimes. I went first about a month ago. I have been every Sunday since. I can only read in the alphabet yet. I mean to go regular. There is no reason why I should not. I wants to be a scholar.

The father of two children in a mill at Lenton deposed as follows:

My two sons (one ten, the other thirteen) work at Milnes's factory at Lenton. They go at half past five in the morning; don't stop at breakfast or tea time. They stop at dinner half an hour. Come home at a quarter before ten. They used to work till ten, sometimes eleven, sometimes twelve. They earn between them 6s. 2d. per week. One of them, the eldest, worked at Wilson's for two years, at 2s. 3d. per week. He left because the overlooker beat him and loosened a tooth for him. I complained, and they turned him away for it. They have been gone to work sixteen hours now; they will be very tired when they come home at half past nine. I have a deal of trouble to get 'em up in the morning. I have been obliged to beat 'em with a strap in their shirts, and to pinch 'em, in order to get them well awake. It made me cry to be obliged to do it.

Did you make them cry?

Yes, sometimes. They will be home soon, very tired; and you will see them.

I [i.e. the government inspector] preferred walking towards the factory to meet them. I saw the youngest only, and asked him a few questions. He said, " I'm sure I shan't stop to talk to you; I want to go home and get to bed; I must be up at half past five again to-morrow morning."

A family in the same town of Lenton gave the following evidence :

The boy. I am going fourteen; my sister is eleven. I have worked in Milnes's factory two years. She goes there also. We are both in the clearing room. I think we work too long hours; I 've been badly with it. We go at half past five; give over at half past nine. I am now just come home. We sometimes stay till twelve. We are obliged to work over-hours. I have 4s. a week; that is for staying from six to seven. They pay for overhours besides. I asked to come away one night lately, at eight o'clock, being ill; I was told, if I went I must not come again. I am not well now. I can seldom eat any breakfast; my appetite is very bad. I have had a bad cold for a week.

Children beaten in the mill

Father. I believe him to be ill from being overworked. My little girl came home the other day cruelly beaten. I took her to Mr. Milnes; did not see him, but showed Mrs. Milnes the marks. I thought of taking it before a magistrate, but was advised to let it drop. They might have turned both my children away. That man's name is Blagg; he is always strapping the children. I shan't let the boy go there much longer; I shall try to apprentice him; it 's killing him by inches; he falls asleep over his food at night. I saw an account of such things in the newspapers, and thought how true it was of my own children.

Mother. I have worked in the same mills myself. The same man was there then. I have seen him behave shocking to the children. He would take 'em by the hair of the head and drag 'em about the room. He has been there twelve years. There 's many young ones in that hot room. There 's six of 'em badly now, with bad eyes and sick headache. This boy of ours has always been delicate from a child. His appetite is very bad now; he does not eat his breakfast sometimes for two or three days together. The little girl bears it well; she is healthy. I would prefer their coming home at seven, without additional wages. The practice of working overhours has been constantly pursued at Milnes's factory.

Beginning in 1802, measure after measure was passed regulating factories and mines. In 1847 a bill was enacted by Parliament limiting the hours of work for women and children to ten per day. It was championed especially by the landowners and bitterly opposed by a large number of manufacturers, who found their spokes- man in John Bright, who argued that the manufacturers, if left to themselves, would do much for their employees.

No one [the speaker said] would accuse him of a want of sympathy with the working classes; but this he would tell the House, that if they went on, at the bidding of the working classes, to legislate against the capitalists, they would find a very different feeling engendered among the latter towards the operatives, from that which they now exhibited. . . . [In his own factory] they had a large infant school, together with a reading room and news room, and a school for adults, where the workmen attended after working hours. They had also a person employed, at a very considerable expense, who devoted his whole time to investigating the concerns of the workmen, and who was a kind of missionary among them. Not a few hundreds of pounds per annum were expended in promoting in this manner the interests of the workmen, and that, too, wholly independent of any act of the legislature. This was the case at many other wealthy factories; but he would warn the House that if they now armed the workmen against the capitalists by fixing by law ten hours, or any other number of hours for the duration of labor, and thus interfered with the established custom of the kingdom, he believed it would be impossible that the feeling which hitherto existed on the part of the manufacturers towards the operatives would continue, should the workmen think that by coming to that

303. John Bright's opposition to the ten- hour bill

House they could fix the time of work and the amount of wages. He thought, if such a result took place, that it would be the duty of the manufacturers — nay, that it would be absolutely necessary for them — to take such steps as would prevent the ruin from coming upon them which must result from the passing of this measure.

The bill a delusion practiced on working classes

He would not detain the House farther; but believing, as he did in his heart, that the proposition was most injurious and destructive to the best interests of the country; believing that it was contrary to all principles of sound legislation, that it was a delusion practiced upon the working classes, that it was advocated by those who had no knowledge of the economy of manufactures; believing that it was one of the worst measures ever passed in the shape of an act of the legislature, and that, if it were now made the law, the necessities of trade and the demands alike of the workmen and of the masters would compel them to retrace the steps they had taken; believing this, he felt compelled to give the motion for the second reading of this bill his most strenuous opposition.

Section 85. Free Trade

It had long been the policy of England to protect her farmers, manufacturers, and shippers from foreign competition by high duties on grain and manufactured goods, and by navigation laws restricting the carrying trade to English ships. After the Industrial Revolution, when English manufacturers in possession of the new and marvelous machines had nothing to fear from the competition of continental hand workers, they began to denounce all forms of protective tariffs, and especially those on grain, which, they argued, raised the price of the bread of the workingman. In 1838 the manufacturers, under the leadership of Cobden and Bright, formed the Anti-Corn Law League, which carried on an extensive campaign for the repeal of the "Corn Laws," as those measures which imposed tariffs on grain were called. A few extracts are here given from one of the hundreds of speeches in which Cobden denounced the working of the grain laws.

With all sincerity I declare that I am for the total repeal of those taxes which affect the price of bread and provisions of every description, and I will not allow it to be said without denying it, that the three millions of people who have petitioned the House for the total repeal of those taxes are not sincere in their prayer. What are those taxes upon food? They are taxes levied upon the great body of the people, and the honorable gentlemen opposite, who show such sympathy for the working classes after they have made them paupers, cannot deny my right to claim on their behalf that those taxes should be a primary consideration.

304. Cobden's denunciation of the Corn Laws

I have heard them called protections; but taxes they are, and taxes they shall be in my mouth, as long as I have the honor of a seat in this House. The bread tax is a tax primarily levied upon the poorer classes; it is a tax, at the lowest estimate, of 40 per cent above the price we should pay if there were a free trade in corn [i.e. grain]. The report upon the hand-loom weavers puts down 10s. as the estimated weekly earnings of a family, and states that in all parts of the United Kingdom that will be found to be not an unfair estimate of the earnings of every laborer's family. It moreover states, that out of 10s. each family expends 5s. on bread. The tax of 40 per cent is therefore a tax of 2s. upon every laboring man's family earning 10s. a week, or 20 per cent upon their earnings. How does it operate as we proceed upwards in society? The man with 40s. a week pays an income tax of 5 per cent; the man of £250 a year pays but 1 per cent; and the nobleman or millionaire with an income of £200,000 a year, and whose family consumes no more bread than that of the agricultural laborer, pays less than one halfpenny in every £100. . . .

The Corn Laws impose a bread tax on the poor

I will state generally, that, from both the manufacturing and agricultural districts, there was the most unimpeachable testimony that the condition of the great body of her Majesty's

Condition of
the working
classes
deteriorating laboring subjects had deteriorated woefully within the last ten years, and more especially so within the three years last past ; and furthermore, that in proportion as the price of the food of the people had increased, just so had their comforts been diminished. When they who sit in high places are oppressive and unjust to the poor, I am glad to see that there are men amongst us who, like Nathan of old, can be found to come forward and exclaim, " Thou art the man ! " The religious people of the country have revolted against the infamous injustice of that bread tax, which is condemned by the immutable morality of the Scriptures. They have prepared and signed a petition to this House, in which they declare that these laws are a violation of the will of the Supreme Being, whose providence watches over his famishing children.

In the following speech Mr. Cobden shows how the Anti-Corn Law League carried on its agitation for free trade.

305. The
Anti-Corn
Law
League's
" campaign
of education " We propose, — we, the League, propose a plan. And don't suppose that means a few men from Manchester. The League is composed, I hope, of this meeting to begin with. It contains a great majority of the electors in the great towns and cities I have mentioned. This is the League, and before long I hope it will comprise every man in the country, unless he either believes that he has an interest in monopoly, or because the marks of stupidity are so strongly imprinted on his countenance as to hold out a continual running invitation, " Come, rob me." We propose to provide a copy of every registration list for every borough and county in the United Kingdom, as soon as the present registration shall have been completed. We intend to bring these registers to a central office in London. We then propose to open a correspondence the most extensive that ever was contemplated, and that ever, I am sure, was undertaken. Those electors amount to 800,000 ; but I will take 300,000, excluding those in the already safe boroughs, as forming the number necessary to constitute the returns of a majority in the House of Commons.

We propose to correspond with these 300,000 to begin with.
We propose to keep people well informed as to the progress of
our question by means of the penny postage (which has not yet
been sufficiently used), inclosing the useful information connected with the question, and tracts bearing the most recent
illustrations of it together. What could be more desirable than
to-morrow to send to those 300,000 electors copies of the newspapers containing the best reports of this meeting? But we
propose to send them one letter a week, and that will cost twopence for the stamp and the inclosure. That will be £2500.
I mention this by way of illustration and preface to what I am
going to tell you before I conclude.

Besides this correspondence we intend to visit every borough
in the kingdom; not by agents, — we will go ourselves, because
we want the thing well done. We will specially invite the electors
to meet such deputations without distinction of party, — we know
nothing of party in this agitation, — and having met the electors
we shall have a little business to transact with them. In the
first place we shall urge upon our friends to organize themselves, and to commence a canvass of their boroughs to ascertain the number of free traders, and, in every case where it is
possible, to obtain a majority of the electors in favor of free
trade, — that majority to memorialize their members in Parliament where they have not voted rightly. Besides that, the
deputation will urge the electors to have a free-trade candidate ready to supplant every monopolist who still retains a
seat for a borough; and the League will pledge itself, where
a borough constituency finds itself at a loss for a candidate, to
furnish it with one.

Section 86. *Educational Reform*

By slow steps England has been gradually working
toward a free and secular educational system, supported
at public expense but in some cases under control of the
clergy. Until 1833 education had been entirely left to
private associations, but in that year the government

made a grant of money to aid private schools in their work. This government aid was steadily increased, and in 1870 was supplemented by a measure allowing the erection and equipment of schools at the public expense. The notion, however, of separating education entirely from religious instruction is steadily resisted by a large portion of all the religious people in England, although they cannot agree as to the exact nature of the religious instruction to be given. Naturally the members of the Established Church have been slow to relinquish their ancient authority over education, and in 1902 the Conservative government strengthened their control by a law which was designed to give uniformity to the whole system, and at the same time to put the burden of maintaining religious schools (of which the Anglican Church has the large majority) principally upon the government. This measure aroused heated opposition upon the part of the other sects, and carried the educational question into politics. A recent writer briefly sums up the situation as follows :

306. The controversy over popular education (condensed and adapted)

The history of modern education may not unfairly be represented as a gradual process of transfer from Church to State, from clerical to lay hands. And unless modern history is about to reverse its course, democracy to fall into the background, and government to revert to the hands of the unchosen few, there is no reason to doubt that this process will go on, and education will become the affair of State and municipal departments.

Progress in England, if equally certain, has been more gradual and less logical than in most countries ; and the course of national education, like everything else, has been tardy, partial, and the subject of continual compromise. Still, if we look at its conditions a century ago and its position to-day, we cannot fail to trace in it the general tendency, and to forecast with some confidence its future. Sooner or later, education, at least primary and secondary, is destined to be conducted by the government of this country, assisted by local authorities, but removed from the jurisdiction of ecclesiastical bodies. . . .

Up to 1870 the churches, for the most part, ran the schools, with large government aid. In olden times the Church held the management of other great departments of public life, — hospitals, relief of the poor, administration of wills, etc., long since transferred to lay hands. The clergy, who worked on the whole honestly and well, nevertheless proved unequal to the task of education. But at last the State took up the matter and established in many cities school boards with power to erect buildings, employ teachers, and conduct free elementary schools. At the same time the State permitted the Anglican, Catholic, and Nonconformist churches to do what they could, and increased the amount of public money granted to them. The board system, being public and energetic, has had an enormous success, and its energy has also improved, by example, the rival system. Nevertheless the dual arrangement has never worked without friction ; the clericals often went on to the board with the main intention of protecting their own schools from competition, and there are few large boards which have not witnessed a perpetual conflict — at least at election times — between the ecclesiastical and civil ideas which were at work.

The new law is governed by two main ideas. The first is to transfer the local administration from the school boards to bodies supervised and partly nominated by the county and town councils, and to confide to these bodies secondary as well as primary education. Unification is the alleged principle. Unification may be a good object — in the end. But to remove from office at a stroke all those persons who have shown themselves capable and enthusiastic in the promotion of primary education in recent years is a strange way of advancing it. To put primary teaching into the hands of city and county councils, whose purposes, thoughts, and traditions are occupied with wholly different matters, seems a hazardous experiment. And to give to such bodies the control and organization of secondary education, now in a very imperfect and chaotic state, is more dangerous still.

Marginal notes:

The State comes to the aid of the clergy in the work of education

Establishment of local school boards

Education taken from the school boards and put in the hands of county and town councils

The government must support the clerical schools

The second idea which led to the framing of the law is the permanent fortification of the clerical schools, by throwing almost the last penny of their financial burden on to public funds, while leaving them under ecclesiastical management; for the appointment by the public authority of one third of the managers is practically insufficient either to secure fair play to the Nonconformist children in the rural districts, or to check the enslavement to the clergy of about half the teaching profession.

The Dissenters about to refuse to pay taxes

No wonder that proposals like these have roused the most determined hostility amongst all Liberals, and especially amongst the Nonconformists, who, usually the most pronounced and hard working of Liberals, are in this case fighting a special battle of their own. So strong is the hostility that many Dissenters of eminence and influence are proposing to meet the rate which the law imposes for the support of the clerical schools with a refusal to pay, — a passive resistance on the lines of that which destroyed the old Church rates. People smile at this plan, as if it were a mere explosion of political hatred, an idle threat, which would not survive a few sales of furniture by auction. They are much mistaken. The matter is under the careful consideration of six hundred local councils of the Nonconformist churches, and if the plan be adopted it will probably be done deliberately, as a definite mode of warfare, and carried on by men who know how to organize it and are tenacious in temper.[1]

Section 87. The Irish Question

Among the many questions which have confronted the British Parliament in its government of Ireland during the nineteenth century, the religious issue has been most prominent. After the Catholic "emancipation" of 1829, which admitted Catholics to Parliament and to

[1] Many Dissenters did refuse to pay taxes, but they finally gave up that line of resistance and began an agitation against the new educational law, which contributed greatly in 1906 to the defeat of the Conservatives, the party which had passed the measure.

civil and military offices, Irish reformers concentrated their attention upon the special privileges enjoyed by the English Church, which had been established in Ireland at the time of the Protestant Reformation. By law the Irish were compelled to pay tithes to support a church whose doctrines they did not believe. Quite naturally they openly resisted the payment of tithes ; the measures which they adopted are described in the parliamentary reports.

Testimony of Colonel Sir John Harvey

On the 3d of March I moved into Graigue with 120 men of the county of Kilkenny constabulary, and remained a period of two months, during which time the police were indefatigable in their exertions, out every day, and frequently twice a day, and traversing a great extent of country upon every excursion ; the whole population was constantly on the watch, and signals made announcing the approach of the drivers and police ; the cattle were driven home by the farmers whenever it was possible, and placed under lock and key ; and as the law did not permit doors to be broken, the seizures made were not so numerous as would otherwise have been the case.

Question. What has been the mode of opposition which has been adopted by the people to the enforcement of the rights of the clergyman under the Composition Act?

Answer. I have described some of them, in the evasion of the law, by removing their cattle. The cattle that are distrained under the Composition Act must be seized between sunrise and sunset. The law does not empower the driver to force a door or a bolt, and I am doubtful whether it authorizes him to raise a latch ; so that the means of evasion are quite within the reach of the people. By doing what we did at Graigue, employing an overwhelming force, and applying that force to one particular parish for a period of two months, we were enabled, at the end of that two months, to collect about one third of the arrears due to the clergyman ; and by that period another arrear of half a year had become due ; so that, with all the force the

307. How tithes for Protestant clergy were collected in Ireland

Tithes hard to collect even when soldiers are used

government could bring to bear in the county of Kilkenny, not a tithe of the tithe of the clergy was collected in the course of two months, but only one third of one parish.

Q. Suppose you had succeeded in distraining the cattle to the full amount of the tithe, was there any possibility of finding purchasers?

Ans. Certainly not.

No one will buy cattle taken for tithes

Q. Supposing purchasers had been found, had they any means of disposing of the cattle which they had purchased?

Ans. Certainly not; they must be still protected through the whole country; they must find food in the country, where every individual was denounced who ventured to furnish that food. The cattle were invariably branded with the word " tithe," so that they were not saleable wherever they were seen; and it was reported, I do not know with what truth, that even when they were brought over to this country there was a difficulty in effecting a sale.

Q. By whom is that brand affixed to the cattle?

Ans. By the people themselves. Previous to the sale the word " tithe " is either painted or branded upon the animal.

Testimony of Joseph Green

Question. Have you been employed in assisting to serve tithe processes?

Answer. I have.

Q. What has occurred on those occasions?

Crowds assemble to prevent the collection of tithes

Ans. Almost every time that I have been out there has been an assemblage of people, evidently for the purpose of preventing the service of law processes, or of taking any steps for the recovery of tithes. The people assembled by signals principally, such as horns sounding, shouting, or whistling, and latterly by the ringing of the chapel bells. When assembled they have not fire arms, that I have ever seen, but they have forks and sticks and scythes; the forks evidently sharpened for the purpose of giving opposition.

Q. How many of the police and how many soldiers had you engaged to serve the law-processes?

Ans. I think fifty-five police, with the chief constable and a company of the 70th Regiment.

Q. Have any inflammatory publications been circulated in the county of Kilkenny?

Ans. Many, exciting the people not to pay tithes.

Q. Are you aware from whence those came?

Ans. I cannot say from my own knowledge; but since that unfortunate catastrophe near Knoctopher there was a notice posted on the chapel of Kells, which I will read to the Committee:

Notice. Brave hurlers of the county Kilkenny hold up your courage and persevere. There are 40,000 men well prepared and firmly determined to join you in the counties of Wexford and Carlow. Send notices to New Ross and Graigue, and they shall be with you in twenty-four hours. Any man that pays tithes, or does not join you to defeat the supporters of that damnable imposition, is a traitor and an enemy to the country, and you ought to pour the vial of your vengeance immediately upon him.

Men who pay tithes are traitors

INNISCORTHY, January 4, 1832

Mr. John Bright was a leader among the Englishmen who sympathized with the Irish Catholics in their struggle to be relieved from the payment of tithes to the Anglican Church, which had been forcibly established in their midst. In a public address he briefly summed up the reasons which impelled him to demand the disestablishment of the English Church in Ireland.

In Ireland, notwithstanding the vast emigration which has taken place from its shores, there is a population now of little under 6,000,000 of persons. Of those 6,000,000, 4,500,000 belong to the Roman Catholic Church. Half a million, or little more, — I doubt whether more than a very little more, — belong to the Protestant Episcopal Church, and about half a million belong to the Presbyterian Church. The census gives us under 700,000 of Church Protestants, but we know that when a Catholic is asked what is his Church by census enumerators,

308. John Bright's plea for the disestablishment of the Anglican Church in Ireland (much condensed)

The Catholics
greatly out-
number the
Protestants
he knows at once that the Presbyterian will state that he
is a Presbyterian, and that a Catholic calls himself so, but
that the other small sects who do not really belong to either
make this kind of answer, "Whenever we go anywhere, we go
to church [i.e. the established church]," and therefore they
swell the number of churchmen to a point higher than it would
reach if the census were taken in the same strict manner with
regard to them both, — with regard to Catholics on the one
hand and Presbyterians on the other.

The enormous
revenues paid
to Protestant
clergy
Now, if we knew, being these four and a half millions, that
this little Church of half a million was planted among us by
those who had conquered our fathers; if we knew also that
this little Church was associated with everything that had been
hostile to our national interests and our national prosperity;
and if we knew, further, that it absorbed incomes amounting
to not less than £700,000 or £800,000 sterling per year,
these incomes being derived from national property amounting to probably £13,000,000 or £14,000,000 sterling; I
say, that if we were of those four and a half millions, let me
ask every man of you whether we should not feel that we
have a just cause of complaint, and that there is a national
grievance in our country that requires to be speedily redressed.

The Church here in England is not to us a symbol of conquest, and although we may think that the institution is not
very useful in this country, and least of all useful to those who
are most attached to it; although we may think this, yet we
feel that we can wait for whatsoever changes in regard to the
Church time may bring forth, — changes which will be indicated by the growth of intelligence and wisdom in the nation
of which we form part. On the other hand, I believe a majority of the people of England, of the people of Wales, of the
people of Scotland, and, we know, a great majority of the people
of Ireland, nay, I believe every thoughtful and intelligent man
in the civilized world outside of these islands, emphatically
condemns this Church of Ireland.

The second Irish question has been the land problem.
In the wars which in past centuries the English waged

in Ireland vast estates were taken away from the Irish and bestowed upon landlords who, in many instances, resided in England, and were principally interested in securing the largest possible rents from their tenants, who were generally promptly evicted if they did not pay. Now as the great majority of the Irish people depended upon agriculture for their existence, and low rents and security of tenure were necessary to make the peasants prosperous, Irish reformers persistently carried the land question into English politics. In 1879 they formed a Land League, and since that time their agitations have secured many important measures improving the condition of the peasantry. Reasons for the formation of the Land League are set forth as follows by one of the original members.

The Land Leaguers, therefore, in asking the consideration of their case, have a right to make it a primary demand that their judges shall be possessed of the events and lessons of the Great Famine. The famine did not begin till 1846 ; the population accordingly had gone on with the natural increase until 1846 ; and when the famine began the population would be about 8,750,000. Again, without the intervention of the famine, and allowing for natural increase, the population in 1851 would have been something above nine millions. The work of the famine, then, was that a country which should have had a population of nine millions in 1851, had, in reality, a population of six millions and a half. The loss in population was two millions and a half.

And now for a few of the incidents of the time. There were 174 deaths in Cork workhouse in a single week, being at the rate of more than one death an hour. Mr. James H. Tuke tells of an inspector of roads who caused no less than 140 bodies to be buried, which he found scattered along the highway in Clifden, county Galway. It was quite a usual thing to find entire families swept away ; and the dead and the dying

309. The demand for land reform in Ireland (condensed)

Results of the Great Famine

Horrors of famine in Ireland

often lay together for days in the same cabin. At a place called Cooldorahey a young fellow named Manley was found dying, with his brother and sister lying close beside him, the last of a large family; the sister had been dead for five, the brother for three, days. Lord George Bentinck, in a speech in the House of Commons, mentioned a case in which, in one cabin, ten corpses were found out of a family of eleven; and another case in which seven putrid corpses were found in the same hovel. The supply of coffins proved utterly unequal to the demand.

In Roscommon, where whole families retiring to rest at night alive, were found all dead in the morning, sixty bodies were, within a short time, buried without coffins. A newspaper correspondent, writing from Dingle, in Kerry, speaks of a parish of three thousand souls, of whom five hundred had perished in six months. Three fourths of them were interred coffinless: "scores of them thrown beside the nearest ditch, and there left to the mercy of the dogs, which have nothing else to feed on." In other parts of the country the difficulty was met by a singular expedient: coffins were made with a slide or hinged bottom, and so did duty for several corpses in succession.

The evictions of the poor and starving

These few incidents, selected out of many thousands, are sufficient to give the reader an idea of what the Great Famine in Ireland meant to the Irish tenants; the next point to be considered is the action of the landlords during that period. In the year 1847, according to a report drawn up by Captain Larcom, afterwards Under Secretary for Ireland, 70,000 occupiers were evicted, — that is to say, about 300,000 persons. In 1849 there were, according to the late Mr. Kaye, 50,000 evictions; and in the four years following the famine — from 1849 to 1852 — there were, according to a table in Mr. J. C. Morison's excellent pamphlet, *Irish Grievances*, 221,845 evictions. These proceedings had almost depopulated whole districts. Mr. O'Rorke quotes a placard, posted in the town of Cahir in April, 1846, to the effect that if "all rent and arrears of rent due to the 25th of March" were not paid on the 12th of May, "the most summary steps will be taken to recover the

same." This is signed by "John Chaytor," agent to the Earl
of Glengall.

"Symptoms of a widespread systematic extermination," says
another authority, "are just beginning to exhibit themselves."
. . . The potato cultivation being extinguished, at least for
a time, the peasant cultivators can pay no rents; sheep and
horned cattle *can* pay rents, and smart rents too; therefore
the sheep and cattle shall have the lands, and the peasants
shall be ousted from them, — a very simple and most inevitable
conclusion, as you will see. . . . Cattle raising
ousts the
peasants

There was one case of eviction, however, which exceeded
all the rest in the harshness of its circumstances, and which
excited the greatest attention. This was the eviction in the
village of Ballinglass, county Galway. The landlords were a
Mr. and Mrs. Gerard. In this case no rent at all was actually
due, and the tenants had over and over again offered to come
to terms. Fixed in their determination to be rid of the villagers,
Mr. and Mrs. Gerard refused all offers; and on Friday, the 13th
of March, the sheriff, accompanied by a large force of the 49th
Regiment, and by a heavy body of police, carried out the
decree. Sixty houses were destroyed; one was left standing in
which were lying a man and woman who were ill of the fever,
and they shortly afterwards were served with notice to leave
the place within fifteen days, "or the house would be tumbled
on top of them." Only a portion of the walls were pulled down
in the first instance; and the villagers, pitching a few poles
slantwise against these walls, took shelter there. The next day
the bailiffs came, pulled down all the walls, and rooted up the
foundations. The tenants then took refuge in the ditches,
"where they slept in parties from ten to fifteen each. A description
of an eviction
scene

One other point must be noticed. The emigration between
the years 1842 and 1851, both inclusive, amounted to 1,436,862.
Quoting the *Irish Crisis*, by Sir Charles Trevelyan, Father
O'Rorke calculates that the deaths on the voyage to Canada
rose from five in the thousand (the ordinary rate) to about
sixty in the thousand, and whilst the ships were in quarantine
they rose from one to forty in the thousand; so that, instead of
six emigrants in the thousand dying on the voyage and during The emigra
tion from
Ireland

quarantine, one hundred died, "besides still larger numbers who died at Quebec, Montreal, and elsewhere in the interior." Out of 89,738 emigrants who embarked for Canada in 1847, Father O'Rorke calculates that 15,330 died on the voyage or afterwards in the hospital. Of 493 passengers who sailed in the *Erin Queen*, 136 died on the voyage ; of 552 in the *Avon*, 246 died ; of 476 in the *Virginius*, 267 died on the voyage ; and Mr. William Henry Smith, C.E., an English gentleman, in a pamphlet entitled *Twelve Months' Residence in Ireland during the Famine and the Public Works*, states that of 600 who emigrated in one vessel, not 100 survived. Lord Lansdowne, grandfather of the present peer, was one of the most ardent supporters of the system of forced emigration. So many of his tenants whom he sent abroad in these times perished, that a portion of a hospital in America was known by the name of the Lansdowne Ward.

One fact, finally, by way of showing the combined results of famine, pestilence, and evicting landlords during the famine years. The number of peasant cabins in 1841 was 491,278 ; in 1851 the number was 135,589. In Connaught, where famine, pestilence, and eviction raged most severely, the number of cabins fell from 121,346 in 1841 to 31,586 in 1851.

The third problem in Irish politics has arisen from the demand of Ireland for a parliament of her own, and for practical independence from the English government in all domestic matters. It will be remembered that Ireland once had a separate parliament, which was suppressed in 1801 cn the union of the island with Great Britain. While demanding the disestablishment of the English Church and the reform of the law, the more radical Irish leaders advocated Home Rule. At length, in 1886, they were able to induce Mr. Gladstone to take up the question, and in that year he introduced a Home Rule Bill in a long speech from which the following extract is taken,

The principle that I am laying down I am not laying down exceptionally for Ireland. It is the very principle on which, within my recollection, to the immense advantage of the country, we have not only altered, but revolutionized our method of governing the colonies. I had the honor to hold office in the Colonial Department — perhaps I ought to be ashamed to confess it — fifty-one years ago. At that time the colonies were governed from Downing Street. It is true that some of them had legislative assemblies; but with these we were always in conflict. England tried to pass good laws for the colonies at that period; but the colonies said, "We do not want your good laws; we want our own."

310. Gladstone's plea for Home Rule (condensed)

We admitted the reasonableness of that principle, and it is now coming home to us from across the seas. We have to consider whether it is applicable to the case of Ireland. Do not let us disguise this from ourselves. We stand face to face with what is termed Irish nationality. Irish nationality vents itself in the demand for local autonomy, or separate and complete self-government in Irish, not in imperial, affairs. Is this an evil in itself? Is it a thing that we should view with horror or apprehension? I hold that there is such a thing as local patriotism, which, in itself, is not bad, but good. Englishmen are eminently English; Scotchmen are profoundly Scotch; and, if I read Irish history aright, misfortune and calamity have wedded her sons to her soil. The Irishman is more profoundly Irish; but it does not follow that, because his local patriotism is keen, he is incapable of imperial patriotism.

Local patriotism not to be condemned

I say that the Irishman is as capable of loyalty as another man. I say that if his loyalty has been checked in its development, why is it? Because the laws by which he is governed do not present themselves to him, as they do to us in England and Scotland, with a native and congenial aspect. Have you a braver or a more loyal man in your army than the Irishman, who has shared every danger with his Scotch and English comrades, and who has never been behind them, when confronted by peril, for the sake of the honor and safety of his empire? Compare this case with that of an ordinary Irishman in Ireland. The Irish soldier has voluntarily placed himself under military

Irishmen are loyal

law, which is to him a self-chosen law, and he is exempted from that difficulty which works upon the population in Ireland, namely, that they are governed by a law which they do not feel has sprung from the soil.

Generous concession will pacify Ireland

Looking forward, I ask the House to assist us in the work which we have undertaken. I ask you to show to Europe and to America that we, too, can face political problems which America twenty years ago faced, and which many countries in Europe have been called upon to face, and have not feared to deal with. I ask that in our own case we should practice, with firm and fearless hand, what we have so often preached, namely, that the concession of local self-government is not the way to sap or impair, but the way to strengthen and consolidate, unity. I ask that we should apply to Ireland that happy experience which we have gained in England and Scotland, where the course of generations has now taught us that the best and surest foundation we can find to build upon is the foundation afforded by the affections, the convictions, and the will of the nation; and it is thus, by the decree of the Almighty, that we may be enabled to secure at once the social peace, the fame, the power, and the permanence of the empire.

In the following extracts from an address of Lord Randolph Churchill the arguments against Home Rule in Ireland are clearly set forth. They are largely based upon the assumption that Ireland is now so well off, owing to the considerate treatment she has received during the last few decades at the hands of the British Parliament, that she should be well satisfied with the existing system.

311. An English argument against Home Rule (condensed)

I will ask you to consider the practical aspect of the Irish question. You would suppose, from the language which is used and the arguments which are put forward by those who advocate the repeal of the Union, — you would naturally suppose that Ireland is being treated by Britain as a conquered country, and that the Irish people are being governed as if they were an enslaved people. You would suppose that the government in Ireland is decidedly despotic, responsible to no one, that every day or every month or every year innocent persons are either hanged or sent to prison for years or for life, that no political freedom of any sort or kind existed there. More than that, you would suppose that the occupiers of the soil, the great mass of the peasantry, the cultivators, are ground down and tyrannized over in the most barbarous fashion by every imaginable engine of landlord tyranny and oppression.

If that were the case, if there were any portion of truth in that statement of the case of Ireland, I would be a Home Ruler to-morrow. But what are the facts? The Irish people are as free for all practical purposes as you in this townhall. You do not enjoy one bit more of individual freedom than they do under the constitution. They enjoy the most perfect political equality with you. With them, mind you, no State Church disturbs the symmetry of religious liberty. With them no interference of any sort or kind by the government in the exercise of their political rights ever occurs. They have 103 representatives in Parliament, — more than they are entitled to by population. These representatives are elected by the great mass of the people just as your own representatives are elected. The elections in Ireland take place under the secrecy and protection of the ballot, and no one interferes with that secrecy or protection unless it be Roman Catholic priests or members of the National League. Any public meeting which has even a semblance of legality can be held in Ireland without interference; any speech, no matter how violent, as long as it does not obviously and openly incite to crime, can be delivered without notice by the government. *The Irish as free as the English*

But, more than that: the Irish peasantry, the cultivators of the soil, are surrounded and protected by an invulnerable, an impregnable wall of legislative fortification, on the strength of which has been concentrated for years all the skill of your most able and experienced public men. More than that: the Irish cultivators, by the free use of British credit and British resources, can transform themselves from occupiers into absolute owners, and they enjoy for that purpose privileges and *Irish peasants favored by land laws* facilities which, I can tell you, from a treasury point of view, are hardly financially sound, and which hitherto have been denied by Parliament to our own people.

Now this is the position of Ireland. I defy anybody to contradict that statement of the position, or to assert that there is a single word which is contrary to fact in what I have said ; and I say that the position of Ireland at the present moment is one of perfect political freedom. I do not know any country in the world, not even America, where political freedom has reached to greater lengths or is contained within larger and broader limits than it is in Ireland.

England concedes reasonable demands

If Ireland has suffered in the past, as she has, — suffered from British ignorance, British neglect, British apathy, — we have made amends in recent years, and we will make yet more. "There is nothing," we say, "which you Irish can reasonably demand either to increase your prosperity or to secure your happiness, which we will not do our utmost and our best to accord. Nor will we scrutinize too closely or too narrowly the reasonableness of any of your demands, but for your sakes and for our sakes and for the common interest, and for the sake, and for the safety, and for the honor, and for the power, aye, even for the life of this vast and varied empire, we ask, and we insist, and we will that you shall live peaceably and amicably with us under one Parliament, one government, and one throne." Now this is to be remembered : out of a population in Ireland of 4,800,000 people, nearer 3,000,000 than 2,000,000 are prepared to respond amicably to that appeal.

The Irish agitators reject all compromise

But there is a section of the Irish people, combined and consolidated and organized into a National League, with its sympathizers and supporters, who make us, the Unionists, this reply. They say, "We care nothing for your boasted civil and religious liberties. We care nothing for, and we do not recognize, any of your efforts to increase Irish prosperity or to raise the condition of the Irish people in recent years. We do not recognize them. We will not obey your laws, for they are foreign laws. We will not share in your Parliament, for it is to us an alien Parliament. We will not be governed by your government. We will have our own Parliament, our own government, and our own laws, no matter what may be the effect either upon us, or upon you, or upon the empire at large." That is their reply, and they say further : " If you English will not grant us this demand, we will carry disorder and destruction into your ancient Parliament ; we will ruin Irish society by terror and intimidation ; the queen's courts of justice shall be brought into general contempt and ridicule throughout the land ; and crime, outrage, robbery, and wrong — all undetected, all unpunished — shall turn Ireland into a howling wilderness, and shall make the name and the fame of the British people stink in the nostrils of the nations."

That is the reply of the National League to the demand and the appeal of the Unionist party, and it is with that reply Mr. Gladstone has identified himself. It is to encounter and nullify the effect of that most formidable menace, which with Mr. Gladstone's assistance they at the present moment have some power to carry into effect, that we Unionists call upon the British people to support the government which is carrying out their decision, to come to the back of the Parliament which they created only a few months ago.

CHAPTER XXVII

THE BRITISH EMPIRE IN THE NINETEENTH CENTURY

Section 88. The Extension of British Dominion in India

The following agreement imposed in 1849 by the British upon the ruler of the Punjab, Maharajah Dulleep Sing Bahadoor, illustrates the manner in which they treated the Indian princes whom they deposed and whose territories they one after another annexed.

312. How the English deposed the ruler of the Punjab Terms granted to the Maharajah Dulleep Sing Bahadoor, on the part of the Honorable East India Company, by Henry Meirs Elliot, Esq., Foreign Secretary to the Government of India, and Lieutenant Colonel Sir Henry Montgomery Lawrence, K.C.B., Resident, in virtue of full powers vested in them by the Right Honorable James, Earl of Dalhousie, Knight of the Most Ancient and Most Noble Order of the Thistle, one of her Majesty's Most Honorable Privy Council, Governor General appointed by the Honorable East India Company to direct and control all their affairs in the East Indies, and accepted on the part of his Highness the Maharajah, by Rajah Tej Sing, Rajah Deena Nath, Bhaee Nidhan Sing, Fukeer Noorooddeen, Gundur Sing, Agent of Sirdar Shere Sing Sindhanwalla, and Sirdar Lall Sing, Agent and son of Sirdhar Uttur Sing Kaleanwalla, Members of the Council of Regency, invested with full power and authority on the part of His Highness.

1. His Highness the Maharajah Dulleep Sing shall resign for himself, his heirs, and his successors, all right, title, and claim to the sovereignty of the Punjab, or to any sovereign power whatever.

2. All the property of the State, of whatever description and wheresoever found, shall be confiscated to the Honorable East India Company, in part payment of the debt due by the State of Lahore to the British government, and of the expenses of the war.

3. The gem called the Koh-i-noor, which was taken from Shah Shooja-ool-Moolk by Maharajah Runjeet Sing, shall be surrendered by the Maharajah of Lahore to the queen of England.

4. His Highness Dulleep Sing shall receive from the Honorable East India Company, for the support of himself, his relatives, and the servants of the State, a pension not less than four and not exceeding five lakhs of the Company's rupees per annum.

5. His Highness shall be treated with respect and honor. He shall retain the title of Maharajah Dulleep Sing Bahadoor, and he shall continue to receive, during his life, such portion of the above-named pension as may be allotted to himself personally, provided he shall remain obedient to the British government, and shall reside at such place as the Governor General of India may select.

Granted and accepted at Lahore, on the 29th of March, 1849, and ratified by the Right Honorable the Governor General on the 5th of April, 1849.

In a lengthy document dispatched by Lord Dalhousie, Governor General of India, to the king of Oudh in 1856, he describes the general conditions of the native kingdom as they appeared to the English officers, and sets forth the reasons why the kingdom of Oudh was summarily annexed.

. . . It has been my anxious and earnest desire, ever since I assumed the government of India, to uphold the honor and dignity of your Majesty's exalted station, to see the country, over which you rule, prosperous and flourishing, and the people, who are your subjects, happy and contented, in the enjoyment of peace and of all the blessings which flow from

313. English reasons for annexing Oudh (condensed)

a wise, liberal, and beneficent administration. For eight years I have watched with much solicitude the progress of affairs in your Majesty's kingdom, in the hope that the unceasing warnings and remonstrances addressed to your Majesty by my predecessors and by myself, and earnestly pressed upon your Majesty by the able and zealous officers who have held the office of Resident at your court, might have the effect of awakening your Majesty to a sense of the duties and responsibilities of your royal station, and of the solemn engagements imposed upon your Majesty's government by the treaty of 1801.

The British will not tolerate misrule

It has now become my most painful duty to inform your Majesty that the British government, influenced by a regard for its reputation among the nations, and still more by the obligations which, many years ago, it took upon itself in relation to the people of Oudh, can no longer lend its countenance and support to a government whose existence is the fruitful source of misrule, oppression, and misery to all who live under its control. . . .

Financial corruption

There is a strong body of concurrent testimony to prove that corruption reigns paramount in the fiscal department of your Majesty's administration, even from the highest functionary to the lowest subordinate, and that, though your Majesty's revenue receipts have been diminished, this has brought no relief to the Ryot, who is crushed by the weight of the exactions levied upon him to satisfy the arbitrary demands of your Majesty's dishonest and unscrupulous servants. The same advices further tend to confirm the impression which has long rested on my mind, that your Majesty's finances are in the last degree disordered and embarrassed. . . .

Inefficient police

Turning from the revenue administration and the financial condition of the kingdom, to the administration of civil and criminal justice, I find even a darker picture,—a state of things even more discreditable and injurious. Life and property are insecure on the roads and rivers, in the towns and villages. With the exception of the frontier police, which is under the direction of British officers and under the immediate control of the Resident, hardly any police force is maintained throughout your Majesty's extensive dominions, and such establishments as do exist are, in the last degree, inefficient and corrupt; apt to seize and mulct the poor and the weak under false and frivolous pretexts, but powerless to restrain bad characters or to check the universal prevalence of heinous crime. . . .

The corruption and servility of what are called courts of justice in your Majesty's kingdom were flagrantly exemplified in the case of the murder of Ramdut Banday by Mahomed Husein, the Nawab of Bharaitch, who, in the face of the clearest proofs of his guilt, was acquitted by your Majesty's court at Lucknow. . . . The courts will not convict murderers

At the present day the police management and the administration of criminal justice are as inefficient as ever. Criminals escape the penalty of their misdeeds; crime and violence of every complexion reign unrepressed throughout the length and breadth of the kingdom; and neither life nor property is secure. Week after week I receive reports of atrocious murders, of the wholesale destruction of villages by fire, and the enormous sacrifice of human life which attends such calamities; of daring and open robberies; of violence uncontrolled in every shape; and I am overwhelmed with sentiments of sorrow and commiseration for the people, who thus suffer from the weakness and the venality of your Majesty's administration.

Not less corrupt, I grieve to add, are the courts of civil justice. These exist only in the capital, and there justice is openly bought and sold. Notwithstanding the earnest expostulations of the Resident, and notwithstanding your pledge to exclude singers and fiddlers from offices of trust and responsibility, your Majesty is known to have placed one of this obnoxious class in a position of actual authority over the civil courts. . . . Civil courts are corrupt

Wherefore, having maturely considered the course of events in Oudh since the treaty of 1801, and more particularly since your Majesty's accession; having seen that every means of persuasion have been tried without effect; and having observed that advice, remonstrance, and warning have been exhausted in vain, I feel that the government of India, which I represent, would be guilty, in the sight of God and man, if it were any longer to aid in sustaining, by its countenance and power, an administration fraught with suffering to millions. . . . Warnings have been in vain

I have charged Major General Outram, the Resident at your court (by whose hands this letter will be delivered to your Majesty), to declare the treaty of 1801 at an end. I have communicated to him my instructions relative to the course which, under the circumstances above explained to your Majesty, I deem it my indispensable duty to adopt for the purpose of restoring order to your kingdom, and thus vindicating the character of the British government in the eyes of the nations, as well as in the eyes of the suffering people of Oudh. . . .

If your Majesty should, unfortunately, determine to refuse these proposals, Major General Outram is charged to set before your Majesty the immediate and inevitable consequences which will follow upon your shortsighted and ill-advised determination.

DALHOUSIE

For a hundred years after the battle of Plassey the English steadily extended their power, but in 1857 the terrible mutiny broke out in which the native troops (Sepoys) turned upon their masters. After a fierce struggle the English put down the revolt and banished the last Mogul emperor, who had become a mere figurehead. An English officer who witnessed the mutiny thus describes the conditions which the English faced in extending their control over the motley hordes of India.

314. Review of the English progress in India from 1757 to 1857 (by Lieutenant General Innes)

The great convulsion known as the Indian Mutiny broke out in May, 1857, consequent directly on the excitement and ill feeling engendered in the Bengal army by the well-known cartridge incident.[1] Any such military outbreak would naturally cause much civil disturbance and find numerous supporters outside the army, but the wide range and virulence of the general commotion that ensued were exceptional, and the rising was throughout marked by a variety of phases and by singular

[1] The troops objected, on religious grounds, to handling a cartridge smeared with animal grease.

episodes, for which the disaffection of the troops and the cartridge incident do not of themselves adequately account. . . .

Up to the year 1856, the year before the outbreak, there had been for a whole century a continuous, aggressive advance of the British power, till it completed the ring fence of the empire by the annexation of Oude. During all that time it had either been engaged in actual conflict or had been forming dominant relations with the several races of the country, and had reduced them one after another to subjection; some provinces being brought under its direct administration and others being left as feudatory or vassal states under their native rulers. At the start the old Mogul dominion had been in a hopeless state of decay, leading to all the horrors of internecine war, and some of the native principalities had gladly turned for safety to the shelter of English protection and supremacy. But the great mass of the people had been brought under our rule by conquest or forcible annexation.

With ruling dynasties thus set aside, reduced, or crushed, with great races humiliated, and bitterness and misery spread broadcast by the loss of power and place and property, it would be an outrage on common sense to doubt that we had created a host of enemies. . . . The benefits of civilized rule, of the *Pax Britannica*, were felt only skin-deep, and the old fierce instincts, the outcome of centuries of strife and oppression, were still in the ascendant. The memory of injuries was still keen and vivid, the newer cases helping to recall the old ones, and to reopen sores that might otherwise have been getting healed; so that, briefly, the mood and temper which prevailed were those of a conquered people who had wrongs and humiliations to remember, and were chafing at having to endure the sway of aliens in race and creed. There existed, in fact, a mass of constant disaffection, and whole hosts of malcontents. *The natives cherish resentment for wrongs done*

Of these the most powerful and dangerous were the Mussulmans. The entire Mohammedan population were as a body rebels at heart, and resented the Christian supremacy, if only on religious grounds and from fanatical pride; and the Moguls of the Upper Provinces had in addition a natural longing to revive their old predominance and restore their old empire. *The Mussulmans*

The Mah-
rattas

Next may be mentioned the Mahrattas, a warlike and unscrupulous Hindu race, who, though now split up into rival
States, had been most powerful as a confederacy, and felt that
but for the British they would have been the masters of India.

Another extensive body of malcontents consisted of those
who were actual sufferers from British conquests or annexation,
or from the action of British land policy.

And a fourth group, especially dangerous from their spirit
and energy, was formed by those who fretted at the closing of
those outlets for ambition, and the loss of those opportunities
for aggrandizement, through political intrigue or military
prowess, that had been current of old.

Such a mass of disaffection, however latent or suppressed,
was obviously a standing menace to the tranquillity of the country, constituting a solid basis, and providing a powerful agency
for the rousing of evil passions and the promotion of seditious
enterprise, — a sure factor in any movement or question involving the peace or security of the state.

In 1858, after the suppression of the great mutiny, the
English government withdrew the political authority
hitherto enjoyed by the East India Company, and assumed direct administration of the territories which had
been under that company's control. This radical change
in Indian affairs was announced to the princes, chiefs,
and people of India in a solemn proclamation issued by
the queen and council.

315. Procla-
mation estab-
lishing the
direct gov-
ernment of
India by
the English
crown (1858)
(condensed)

Victoria, by the grace of God, of the United Kingdom of
Great Britain and Ireland, and of the colonies and dependencies
thereof in Europe, Asia, Africa, America, and Australia, Queen,
Defender of the Faith.

Whereas, for divers weighty reasons, we have resolved, by
and with the advice and consent of the Lords Spiritual and
Temporal, and Commons, in Parliament assembled, to take
upon ourselves the government of the territories in India heretofore administered in trust for us by the Honorable East India
Company.

Now, therefore, we do by these presents notify and declare that, by the advice and consent aforesaid, we have taken upon ourselves the said government; and we hereby call upon all our subjects within the said territories to be faithful, and to bear true allegiance to us, our heirs and successors, and to submit themselves to the authority of those whom we may hereafter, from time to time, see fit to appoint to administer the government of our said territories, in our name and on our behalf.

And we, reposing especial trust and confidence in the loyalty, ability, and judgment of our right trusty and well-beloved cousin and counselor, Charles John, Viscount Canning, do hereby constitute and appoint him, the said Viscount Canning, to be our first Viceroy and Governor General in and over our said territories, and to administer the government thereof in our name, and generally to act in our name and on our behalf, subject to such orders and regulations as he shall, from time to time, receive from us through one of our principal secretaries of State. *The first viceroy named*

And we do hereby confirm in their several offices, civil and military, all persons now employed in the service of the Honorable East India Company, subject to our future pleasure and to such laws and regulations as may hereafter be enacted.

We desire no extension of our present territorial possessions; and while we will permit no aggression upon our dominions or our rights to be attempted with impunity, we shall sanction no encroachment on those of others. We shall respect the rights, dignity, and honor of native princes as our own; and we desire that they, as well as our own subjects, should enjoy that prosperity and that social advancement which can only be secured by internal peace and good government. *The rights of natives to be respected*

Firmly relying ourselves on the truth of Christianity, and acknowledging with gratitude the solace of religion, we disclaim alike the right and the desire to impose our convictions on any of our subjects. We declare it to be our royal will and pleasure that none be in any wise favored, none molested or disquieted by reason of their religious faith or observances, but that all shall alike enjoy the equal and impartial protection of the law; and we do strictly charge and enjoin all those who may be in *Religious tolerance assured* authority under us that they abstain from all interference with the religious belief or worship of any of our subjects, on pain of our highest displeasure.

Offices open to natives

And it is our further will that, so far as may be, our subjects, of whatever race or creed, be freely and impartially admitted to offices in our service, the duties of which they may be qualified, by their education, ability, and integrity duly to discharge.

Clemency for offenders

We deeply lament the evils and misery which have been brought upon India by the acts of ambitious men, who have deceived their countrymen by false reports and led them into open rebellion. Our power has been shown by the suppression of that rebellion in the field; we desire to show our mercy by pardoning the offenses of those who have been thus misled, but who desire to return to the path of duty. Our clemency will be extended to all offenders, save and except those who have been or shall be convicted of having directly taken part in the murder of British subjects. With regard to such the demands of justice forbid the exercise of mercy.

To all others in arms against the government we hereby promise unconditional pardon, amnesty, and oblivion of all offenses against ourselves, our crown and dignity, on their return to their homes and peaceful pursuits.

When, by the blessing of Providence, internal tranquillity shall be restored, it is our earnest desire to stimulate the peaceful industry of India, to promote works of public utility and improvement, and to administer its government for the benefit of all our subjects resident therein. In their prosperity will be our strength, in their contentment our security, and in their gratitude our best reward. And may the God of all power grant to us, and to those in authority under us, strength to carry out these our wishes for the good of our people.

316. India and her people to-day

An English census commissioner in India gives the following brief account of India and of the varied character of its enormous population.

Of all the general features of India the most striking is not its size or even its vast population. Its area is scarcely greater than that of Arabia. Comparing it with a standard with which we are familiar, we may call it about twenty-five times that of England and Wales, a mere speck on the map by the side of the great peninsulas of Africa or South America. More respect is due certainly to its population, which is not less than one fifth of the estimated number of inhabitants of the world and ten times that of this country. But in this respect again, what is most worth notice is not the mass, but the extraordinary variety found within the country.

Looking at the range of climate, the different geographical features, the number of different races inhabiting India, and the babel of languages they speak, we can well say that India is not so much a country as a small continent. As regards physical differences, though all India is either tropical or subtropical, in the south and along the coasts the people are certain of a hot but equable climate, with a more or less heavy rainfall once or at most twice a year. In the north, on the other hand, there is a fiercely hot season divided from a piercingly cold one by a few months of rain of uncertain intensity and duration. *Climate*

One part of India consists of vast plains of rice, another of small patches of arable land cleared out of the forest or terraced out of the steep hillside. Here we find acre after acre of wheat, there long stretches of prairie upland producing little but scanty crops of millet. In one tract nothing will come up except under canal irrigation; in another, canal water brings to the surface latent stores of alkaline matter which sterilize the soil. *Agriculture*

The life and customs of the people vary accordingly. In the matter of race, too, we range from the comparatively high type represented by the martial tribes of upper India and by the Brahmins and chieftains of the central tracts, to the dark colored denizens of the hills and forests which divide the continental part of the country from the peninsula. All along the mountain belt again, which bounds India on the north, and in the lower ranges which separate it from China on the east, the predominant type is that of the yellow or Mongolian races, which is slow in blending with any of the rest. A very brief *The racial differences* study of these types will serve to indicate the wide gaps which exist between the different sections of the community in their original purity of race. . . .

The variety of languages A further cause of the want of unity in the population is the extraordinary variety of language, which, of itself, is a serious obstacle to the obliteration of social distinctions. In the census of 1891 no less than 150 different tongues were sifted out of the number returned as current in India and recognized as worthy of individual mention in the tables. . . . What with real differences of language and local dialects of peculiar vocabulary or pronunciation, the native of any part of India cannot go many miles beyond his birthplace without finding himself at a loss in communicating with his fellows.

Religious differences Finally, India lacks that important factor in human cohesion, — community of religion. It is true that on paper, at all events, three fourths of the people are nominally of one creed, — that which we call Hinduism. This, however, is but a convenient term covering any amount of internal difference, which deprives it of its most material weight as a " nation-making " characteristic. Then again the remaining quarter of the population left outside the general designation is not confined to certain localities except in the case of the Buddhists, who affect Burma and the Himalayas, and Sikhs, who remain in the Punjab, their birth province. The bulk of those who are not Hindus acknowledge the creed of Islam and are scattered all over the country to the number of nearly sixty millions. Our Empress accordingly owns the allegiance of the largest Mussalman population in the world.

Section 89. *The Dominion of Canada*

The adjustment of the relations between the original French population of Canada and the British subjects who immigrated there was for a long time one of the most serious problems in the government of the colony. During the first half of the nineteenth century the more radical among the French cherished hopes of throwing off British rule, and sought to achieve their end by an insurrection in 1837. The revolt failed, however, but it led the English government to attempt to establish more sympathetic relations with their French subjects. Immediately after the rebellion Lord Durham was sent out to examine the situation in Canada, and in his report he gives the following account of the antagonism between the two races, especially in Quebec.

The two races thus distinct have been brought into the same community, under circumstances which rendered their contact inevitably productive of collision. The difference of language from the first kept them asunder. It is not anywhere a virtue of the English race to look with complacency on any manners, customs, or laws which appear strange to them ; accustomed to form a high estimate of their own superiority, they take no pains to conceal from others their contempt and intolerance of their usages. They found the French Canadians filled with an equal amount of national pride, — a sensitive but inactive pride, which disposes that people not to resent insult, but rather to keep aloof from those who would keep them under.

317. Extracts from Lord Durham's account of Anglo-French rivalry in Canada

The French could not but feel the superiority of English enterprise ; they could not shut their eyes to English success in every undertaking in which they came into contact, and to the constant superiority which the English were acquiring. They looked upon their rivals with alarm, with jealousy, and finally with hatred. The English repaid them with a scorn which soon also assumed the same form of hatred. The French complained of the arrogance and injustice of the English ; the English accused the French of the vices of a weak and conquered people, and charged them with meanness and perfidy. The entire mistrust which the two races have thus learned to conceive of each other's intentions induces them to put the worst construction on the most innocent conduct ; to judge every word, every act, and every intention unfairly ; to attribute the most odious designs ; and to reject every overture of kindness or fairness as covering secret designs of treachery and malignity.

The English treat the French as inferiors

Religious
differences   Religion formed no bond of intercourse and union. It is,
indeed, an admirable feature of Canadian society that it is entirely devoid of any religious dissensions. . . . But though the
prudence and liberality of both parties has prevented this fruitful source of animosity from imbittering their quarrels, the
difference of religion has, in fact, tended to keep them asunder.
Their priests have been distinct; they have not met even in
the same church.

There is no
common edu-
cational
system   No common education has served to remove and soften the
differences of origin and language. As they are taught apart,
so are their studies different. The literature with which each
is the most conversant is that of the peculiar language of each;
and all the ideas which men derive from books come to each
of them from perfectly different sources. Those who have
reflected on the powerful influence of language on thought will
perceive in how different a manner people who speak in different languages are apt to think; and those who are familiar
with the literature of France know that the same opinion will
be expressed by an English and French writer of the present
day, not merely in different words, but in a style so different as
to mark utterly different habits of thought.

The four provinces of Ontario, Quebec, New Bruns-
wick, and Nova Scotia were federated into the Dominion
of Canada by an act of Parliament in 1867. In November of that year the first governor general of the new
federation, Lord Monck, delivered the following speech
at the opening of the Canadian Parliament at Ottawa.

*Honorable Gentlemen of the Senate and Gentlemen of the House
of Commons:*

318. The
opening of
the first
Dominion
parliament
(1867)   In addressing you for the first time, parliamentary representatives of the Dominion of Canada, I desire to give expression to my own deep feelings of gratification that it has been
my high privilege to occupy an official position which has made
it my duty to assist at every step taken in the creation of this
great confederation. I congratulate you on the legislative

sanction which has been given by the Imperial Parliament to the Act of Union, under the provisions of which we are now assembled, and which has laid the foundation of a new nationality that I trust and believe will, ere long, extend its bounds from the Atlantic to the Pacific oceans.

In the discussions which preceded the introduction of this measure in the Imperial Parliament, between the members of her Majesty's Government on one side, and delegates who represented the provinces now united on the other, it was apparent to all those who took part in those conferences that while her Majesty's ministers considered and pressed the principle of union as a subject of great imperial interest, they allowed to the provincial representatives every freedom in arranging the mode in which that principle should be applied. In a similar spirit of respect for your privileges as a free and self-governing people, the Act of Union, as adopted by the Imperial Parliament, imposes the duty and confers upon you the right of reducing to practice the system of government which it has called into existence, of consolidating its institutions, of harmonizing its administrative details, and of making such legislative provisions as will secure to a constitution in some respects novel, a full and unprejudiced trial. *Federal unity and states rights*

With the design of effecting these objects, measures will be laid before you for the amendment and assimilation of the laws existing in the several provinces relating to currency, customs, excise, and revenue generally; for the adoption of a uniform postal system; for the proper management and maintenance of the public works and properties of the dominion; for the adoption of a well-considered scheme of military organization and defense; for the proper administration of Indian affairs; for the introduction of uniform laws respecting patents of invention and discovery; for the naturalization of aliens and the assimilation of criminal law, and the laws relating to bankruptcy and insolvency. *New federal laws to be enacted*

A measure will also be submitted to you for the performance of the duty, imposed upon Canada under the terms of the Union Act, of immediately constructing the Intercolonial Railway. This great work will add a practical and physical connection to *The Intercolonial Railway* the legislative bond which now unites the provinces comprising the Dominion, and the liberality with which the guarantee for the cost of its construction was given by the Imperial Parliament is a new proof of the hearty interest felt by the British people in your prosperity. . . .

In a speech delivered in the Canadian Parliament in 1888 Sir Wilfred Laurier advocated the establishment of trade reciprocity with the United States, and the following extracts illustrate his attitude toward Canadian independence and his view of loyalty to Great Britain.

319. Sir Wilfred Laurier's attitude toward Great Britain

Sir, the one great objection which we have heard from all quarters on the other side of the House has been the cry of disloyalty. That cry came as a lugubrious knell in all the speeches we have heard on this question. The objection was taken that to admit importations from the United States free of duty while we tax the importations from Great Britain would be disloyal. . . .

Loyalty to England does not demand business sacrifices

Sir, if this objection means anything, it simply means that if we find it to be to our advantage to adopt reciprocal free trade with the United States, we should forego the advantage because we are a colony of England. That is the proposition made by gentlemen on the other side. I denounce such a proposition; I repudiate it; I denounce it as unmanly, as anti-Canadian, and even anti-British. To pretend, Sir, that our colonial allegiance demands from us that we should be deterred from the spirit of enterprise, that we should refuse to extend our trade and to increase our prosperity according to the best methods which commend themselves to our judgment, to pretend that this is loyalty, I deny; and if I were to characterize the sentiment in the only language in which it ought to be characterized, I would say this is not loyalty, but that it is mere flunkeyism. We are a colony of England, it is true; but we are a colony not by force, but by choice; and if we are a colony to-day, it is because we are convinced that at the present day our colonial dependence is quite compatible with the largest measure of national advancement and material prosperity. . . .

The objection of the honorable gentlemen opposite would have been a much stronger one, at least in my eyes, if it had been made from a different standpoint. If instead of telling us that we have not the right to propose to discriminate against England, they had said it would not be generous to England to discriminate against her, the objection, to my mind, would have been far stronger; and if I am not trespassing beyond the limits of good taste in speaking my own individual sentiments, I would say that this is a consideration which gave me much concern. . . . *Discrimination against England may not be generous*

Sir, I am a subject of French origin, and, as I have often stated, — and you, Mr. Speaker, agree with me, — there is no more loyal race of men under the British crown on the American continent than her Majesty's subjects of French origin; loyalty is natural to you, men of British origin; it flows in your blood; you have inhaled it from the hearts of your mothers. But I tell you that gratitude has worked in the hearts of my countrymen feelings of the same nature which are implanted in your hearts by your origin or your birth. With all my soul I say, let my tongue adhere to the roof of my mouth if it were ever to speak an unkind word of England; let my right hand wither if it participated in anything which would be unfair to England. But this is not a question of sentiment. This is a question of duty, and if you put it in the light that I have to choose between the duty I owe to England and the duty I owe to my native land, I stand by my native land. And there is not an Englishman with an English heart in his bosom that will not say the same if he is a true-born Briton. *Loyalty to Canada comes first*

Sir, England would treat us with contempt if we were to act otherwise than we are acting. England expects from us that we will do the best we can for ourselves, and she will take care of herself without any assistance from Canadian Tories. I am quite sure of one thing. It is quite possible that John Bull may grumble, but in his grumbling there will be as much pride as anger, and John Bull will feel flattered if there is an offspring of his so much like the old gentleman that he will *England approves shrewd business methods*

not lose any occasion to earn an honest penny. John Bull
will feel flattered if he finds that scion of his a true chip of
the old block.

Section 90.   The Australasian Colonies

The English people in the Australasian colonies have
long been making radical experiments in social reform,
and in some of the colonies the labor parties actually control the government. A sympathetic American observer
gives the following summary of what he regards the leading principles of the labor-reform policy in New Zealand.

320. The
principles of
social reform
in New
Zealand

The following principles [are now established] as the basis
of New Zealand civic life :

1. That the taxing power is to be used not merely for
revenue but to advance the public good, by encouraging enterprise, breaking down monopoly, aiding the diffusion of
wealth, etc.

The land

2. That the people have a right to the increased value of
land resulting from public improvements and the development
of the country, and that every individual has a right to the use
and a share in the ownership of the earth, — the land and all
its wealth belongs to the people.

3. That the gradual nationalization of the soil, through
resumption and leasing of land with limitation of area, and
rents and taxes to take the unearned increment for the public
use, is a just and practicable method of dealing with the land
problem.

Labor

4. That government should guard the interests of labor even
more carefully than those of capital, for the hours and conditions of labor mold manhood and citizenship, and determine
the vitality of the people and their leisure for intellectual and
civic development.

5. That the law should recognize the principle of the living
wage, and secure to every worker a fair day's pay for a fair
day's work.

6. That the right to work is a clear corollary from the right to life, liberty, and the pursuit of happiness, the latter privileges being of questionable value without the former, and the State must open the way to employment for those in need of it.

7. That direct employment is more just and economical, and better for the workers, than the contractor system; wherefore the latter must be abolished from public work.

8. That coöperative methods have proved superior and shall be established in public work and fostered in private business.

9. That the substitution of judicial decision in place of settlement by conflict shall be extended to disputes between labor and capital; industrial peace and the administration of justice in labor difficulties belonging with the other objects of judicial procedure. *Peaceful settlement of labor disputes*

10. That industrial power is a public trust, and the public interest is the dominant interest in business as in politics.

11. That the control of industry should be in a body representing all three parties in the production and distribution of wealth, — labor, capital, and the public, — the principles of democracy, partnership, and majority rule applying to industrial life as well as to political life, and aristocratic and arbitrary control being as bad in one case as the other.

12. That economic freedom and independence are essential to full political liberty.

13. That veterans of industry shall have pensions as well as veterans of war; any orderly person who has put years of labor into the development and enrichment of the country having a right to a reasonable subsistence after his days of work are done. *Old-age pensions*

14. That public utilities should be constructed, owned, and operated by the people. *Public utilities*

15. That public railways shall be run for service, not for profit, and the management kept in touch with the people.

16. That the fundamental test of a railway system or any other institution, industrial or political, is not its financial results, but its human results, — its effect on the public good, its relation to manhood, morals, government, civilization, and progress.

17. That farmers and workingmen have a right to use the government in which they are partners, to get loans at low interest; and that government lending abolishes usury, prevents oppression, and aids the diffusion of wealth.

Monopolies   18. That banking and credit shall not be left to private manipulation, speculation, and monopoly, but shall be controlled by the State in the interest of all; the nationalization of credit being as important as the nationalization of the soil.

19. That private monopoly of vital interests is contrary to the public welfare, and the State is in duty bound to manage banks, take railways, operate coal mines, buy up patents, and do all other acts necessary to prevent it.

Right to limit immigration   20. That a nation as well as a family has a right and a duty to keep itself sweet and clear of contamination, a right to keep its soil and its civic partnership for those who are fit to be free and self-governing, and who will not lower its intellectual and spiritual level or dilute its civilization.

21. That the question of license or prohibition shall be left to local option under the referendum, and that taxation of land values for local purposes shall also be left to local option through the initiative and referendum.

Woman's suffrage   22. That sex has no essential relation to the right of self-government, wherefore women shall have the franchise on the same terms as men.

23. That equity demands political equality and self-government in municipal affairs as well as national.

24. That in politics and industry, as in science, experiment is the best method of arriving at truth, guiding the experiments by the light of the principles evolved from past experience.

Fundamental aims of legislation   25. That one object of the law should be to remove all needless barriers and artificial disabilities.

26. That accident and misfortune should not be left to fall with crushing weight on innocent individuals, but that burdens not resulting from the wrong conduct of those affected should be spread over the community like taxes, in proportion to ability to bear them.

27. That legislation should be in the interest of the whole people, not of a special class or party.

28. That the diffusion of wealth, comfort, intelligence, and virtue, and the equalization of opportunity are prime objects of political and industrial institutions.

29. That the government should be kept close to the people through short terms for legislators, direct nominations and a ballot that favors individual thought and judgment in voting, good civil service rules, and the use of the referendum in one or another of its many forms.

30. That the government is simply the people's agent to manage any business or do any act for the public good.

Every one of these principles has been established as the result of practical efforts to deal with actual problems and existing conditions. Confronted with specific difficulties and dangers, an earnest, open-minded, common-sense, true-hearted people have sought for remedies, and naturally found them in laws and institutions based on principles that accord with the public good. Moving in this way from a concrete evil to its logical remedy, progress has not been the carrying out of a preconceived programme, but a series of adaptations to present need, the recognition of the principles on which the adaptations rest, accompanying or following, but rarely much preceding, the original application. . . .

After the vast continent of Australia and the neighboring island of Tasmania had been laid out into six separate colonies, each with its own constitution and system of government, it was only natural that they should finally be federated into a single union. Five of these colonies, by legislative enactment and direct vote of the people, expressed their desire for a federal union, and accordingly the British Parliament, in July, 1900, passed a law constituting a commonwealth of five colonies, and providing at the same time for the admission of the sixth, — Western Australia, — which shortly afterwards acceded to the union. The chief clauses relating to the government are given in the following extracts from the constitution.

63 & 64 Vict., Ch. 12. An act to constitute the Commonwealth of Australia

9th July, 1900

321. An extract from the constitution of the Australian Commonwealth

Whereas the people of New South Wales, Victoria, South Australia, Queensland, and Tasmania, humbly relying on the blessing of Almighty God, have agreed to unite in one indissoluble Federal Commonwealth under the crown of the United Kingdom of Great Britain and Ireland, and under the constitution hereby established ; and whereas it is expedient to provide for the admission into the Commonwealth of other Australasian colonies and possessions of the queen : be it therefore enacted by the Queen's Most Excellent Majesty, by and with the advice and consent of the Lords Spiritual and Temporal, and Commons, in this present Parliament assembled, and by the authority of the same, as follows : . . .

1. The legislative power of the Commonwealth shall be vested in a Federal Parliament, which shall consist of the queen, a Senate, and a House of Representatives, and which is hereinafter called "The Parliament," or "The Parliament of the Commonwealth."

The governor general

2. A governor general appointed by the queen shall be her Majesty's representative in the Commonwealth, and shall have and may exercise in the Commonwealth during the queen's pleasure, but subject to this constitution, such powers and functions of the queen as her Majesty may be pleased to assign to him. . . .

5. The governor general may appoint such times for holding the sessions of the Parliament as he thinks fit, and may also from time to time, by proclamation or otherwise, prorogue the Parliament, and may in like manner dissolve the House of Representatives.

After any general election the Parliament shall be summoned to meet not later than thirty days after the day appointed for the return of the writs.

The Parliament shall be summoned to meet not later than six months after the establishment of the Commonwealth.

6. There shall be a session of the Parliament once at least in every year, so that twelve months shall not intervene between

the last sitting of the Parliament in one session and its first
sitting in the next session. . . .

7. The Senate shall be composed of senators for each State, The Senate
directly chosen by the people of the State, voting, until the
Parliament otherwise provides, as one electorate.

But until the Parliament of the Commonwealth otherwise
provides, the Parliament of the State of Queensland, if that
State be an original State, may make laws dividing the State
into divisions and determining the number of senators to be
chosen for each division, and, in the absence of such provision,
the State shall be one electorate.

Until the Parliament otherwise provides there shall be six
senators for each original State. The Parliament may make
laws increasing or diminishing the number of senators for each
State, but so that equal representation of the several original
States shall be maintained, and that no original State shall
have less than six senators.

The senators shall be chosen for a term of six years, and the
names of the senators chosen for each State shall be certified
by the governor to the governor general. . . .

24. The House of Representatives shall be composed of The House of
Representa-
tives
members directly chosen by the people of the Commonwealth,
and the number of such members shall be, as nearly as practicable, twice the number of the senators.

Section 91. Growth of the British Empire in Africa

During the war with Napoleon, Great Britain seized
Cape Colony, then in the possession of his allies, the
Dutch, and after a few years the English government
in South Africa came into collision with the sturdy Boers,
as the Dutch farmers were called. Resenting all interference in their affairs, the Dutch migrated north and
eastward beyond the Orange and Vaal rivers, where they
founded two little States, the Orange River Colony and the
Transvaal Colony. In 1852 Great Britain acknowledged

the independence of the Boers in the Transvaal, later known as The South African Republic, and two years later the independence of the Orange River Colony, which became known as the Orange Free State. But nevertheless, some thirty years later, in April, 1887, Great Britain formally annexed the Transvaal and issued the following proclamation setting forth the reason for this action.

Proclamation by his Excellency Sir Theophilus Shepstone, Knight Commander of the Most Distinguished Order of St. Michael and St. George, her Majesty's Special Commissioner for certain purposes in South Africa:

322. British proclamation annexing the Transvaal republic (1877)

Whereas at a meeting held on the 16th day of January, in the year of our Lord 1852, at the Sand River, between her Majesty's assistant commissioners, Major Hogge and C. M. Owen, Esquire, on the one part, and a deputation from the emigrant farmers then residing north of the Vaal River, at the head of which was Commandant General A. W. J. Pretorius, on the other part, the said her Majesty's assistant commissioners did "guarantee in the fullest manner on the part of the British government to the emigrant farmers north of the Vaal River, the right to manage their own affairs and to govern themselves according to their own laws, without any interference on the part of the British government."

Why independence was granted in 1852

And whereas the evident objects and inciting motives of the assistant commissioners in granting such guarantee or permission to persons who were her Majesty's subjects were "to promote peace, free trade, and friendly intercourse" with and among the inhabitants of the Transvaal, in the hope and belief that the territory which a few years afterwards, namely in February, 1858, became known by the style and title of "The South African Republic," would become a flourishing and self-sustaining State, a source of strength and security to neighboring European communities, and a point from which Christianity and civilization might rapidly spread towards central Africa.

And whereas the hopes and expectations upon which this mutual compact was reasonably and honorably founded have been disappointed, and the circumstances as set forth more at length in my address to the people, of to-day's date, hereunto attached, show that increasing weakness in the State itself on the one side, and more than corresponding growth of real strength and confidence among the native tribes on the other, have produced their natural and inevitable consequences. . . . Transvaal government is weak

And whereas the ravaging of an adjoining friendly State by warlike savage tribes cannot for a moment be contemplated by her Majesty's government without the most earnest and painful solicitude, both on account of the miseries which such an event must inflict upon the inhabitants of the Transvaal, and because of the peril and insecurity to which it would expose her Majesty's possessions and subjects in South Africa, and seeing that the circumstances of the case have, from the inherent weakness of the country already touched upon, become so grave that neither this country nor the British colonies in South Africa can be saved from the most calamitous circumstances except by the extension over this State of her Majesty's authority and protection, by means of which alone oneness of purpose and action can be secured, and a fair prospect of peace and prosperity in the future be established. There is great danger from warlike natives

And whereas I have been satisfied by numerous addresses, memorials, and letters which I have received, and by the abundant assurances which personal intercourse has given me, that a large proportion of the inhabitants of the Transvaal see, in a clearer and stronger light than I am able to describe them, the urgency and imminence of the circumstances by which they are surrounded, the ruined condition of the country, and the absence within it of any element capable of rescuing it from its depressed and afflicted state, and therefore earnestly desire the establishment within and over it of her Majesty's authority and rule ; and whereas the government has been unable to point out or devise any means by which the country can save itself. . . . Many inhabitants of the Transvaal implore protection

Now therefore I do, in virtue of the power and authority conferred upon me by her Majesty's Royal Commission, dated

The Transvaal territory is now British

at Balmoral, the 5th day of October, 1876, and published herewith, and in accordance with instructions conveyed to me thereby and otherwise, proclaim and make known, that from and after the publication hereof, the territory heretofore known as The South African Republic, as now meared and bounded, subject, however, to such local modifications as may hereafter appear necessary, and as may be approved of by her Majesty, shall be and shall be taken to be British territory, and I hereby call upon and require the inhabitants of the Transvaal, of every class and degree, and all her Majesty's subjects in South Africa, to take notice of this my proclamation and to guide themselves accordingly.

And I hereby further proclaim and declare that I shall hold responsible all such persons who, in the Transvaal, shall venture opposition, armed or otherwise, to her Majesty's authority hereby proclaimed, or who shall by seditious and inflammatory language or exhortations or otherwise incite or encourage others to offer such opposition. . . .

The Transvaal government will remain separate

And I further proclaim and make known that the Transvaal will remain a separate government, with its own laws and legislature, and that it is the wish of Her Most Gracious Majesty that it shall enjoy the fullest legislative privileges compatible with the circumstances of the country and the intelligence of its people. That arrangements will be made by which the Dutch language will practically be as much the official language as the English; all laws, proclamations, and government notices will be published in the Dutch language; in the Legislative Assembly members may, as they do now, use either language; and in the courts of law the same may be done at the option of suitors to a cause. The laws now in force in the State will be retained until altered by competent legislative authority. Equal justice is guaranteed to the persons and property of both white and colored; but the adoption of this principle does not and should not involve the granting of equal civil rights, such as the exercise of voting by savages, or their becoming members of a legislative body, or their being entitled to other civil privileges which are incompatible with their uncivilized condition.

The native tribes living within the jurisdiction and under the protection of the government must be taught due obedience to the paramount authority, and be made to contribute their fair share towards the support of the State that protects them. . . .   GOD SAVE THE QUEEN

Given under my hand and seal at Pretoria, in The South African Republic, this 12th day of April, in the year of our Lord 1877.

T. SHEPSTONE, *Her Majesty's Special Commissioner*

By command of his Excellency,
M. OSBORN, *Secretary*

The Boers in the Transvaal protested against this high-handed annexation of their territory, and finally revolted, defeating the small detachment of English troops at Majuba Hill. In 1881 Mr. Gladstone, who was then in office, not thinking the territory worth a war, concluded a treaty with the Transvaal government, giving it autonomy under the suzerainty of the English crown. A short time afterward another treaty was concluded with the Boers, giving them complete independence, subject to the provision that they should conclude no treaty with any other nation without the approval of the crown. Shortly after the signature of this treaty (1885) gold was discovered in the Transvaal, and thousands of miners, prospectors, and settlers quickly poured into the region, and before long outnumbered the Boers. Within a short time these *Uitlanders*, as they were called, began to protest against the policy of the government of the Transvaal, in which they had no share, and which they declared to be benighted and oppressive. Their point of view is well expressed by one of their sympathizers as follows :

The Uitlanders, seven eighths of whom belong to the English-speaking race, outnumber the Boers by more than two to one.

323. English
grievances
against the
Boers
They own half the land and contribute nineteen twentieths of the public revenue. It is through their brains and energy that the Transvaal has been raised from bankruptcy into its present prosperity. They are citizens of the most progressive countries in the world, accustomed to self-government and intolerant of any encroachments upon their liberty.

The Boers have altered little, if at all, since the days when the Dutch East India Company planted them at the Cape, except to add some of the vices of the nineteenth century to the ignorance of the seventeenth. "In some of the elements of modern civilization," says Mr. Bryce, a witness of inspired impartiality, "they have gone backward rather than forward." A half-nomad people of sullen and unsocial temperament, severed from Europe and its influences for over two hundred years, living rudely and contentedly on the vast, arid holdings where their sheep and cattle are pastured, — each man as far as may be from his neighbor, — disdaining trade, disdaining agriculture, ignorant to an almost inconceivable degree of ignorance, without music, literature, or art, superstitious, grimly religious, they are in all things, except character and stubbornness of character, the very antithesis of the strangers settled among them. The patriarch Abraham in Wall Street would hardly make an odder contrast.

The Uitlanders have even a greater share of the intelligence of the country than of its wealth. Nevertheless they are kept in complete subjection to their bucolic taskmasters. They are not allowed to vote; they have no voice in the spending of the money taken from their pockets; they see millions of dollars lavished on the secret service and fortifications at Pretoria, while Johannesburg remains a pesthole; their language is proscribed in the schools and law courts of a city where not more than one man in a thousand speaks anything but English; and their children are forced to learn geography and history from Dutch text-books after passing the elementary standards.

It is grotesque to think of Englishmen and Americans being treated in this fashion, and it is quite beyond imagination that they should rest passive in such a house of bondage.

In June, 1900, President Kruger sent the following letter to his commandant general and officers in the field fighting the "war of independence" against the British.

Flinch not and fall not into unbelief; for the time is at hand when God's people shall be tried in the fire. And the Beast shall have power to persecute Christ, and those who fall from faith and their Church will know him not, nor shall they be allowed to enter the Kingdom of Heaven. But those who are true to the faith and fight in the name of the Lord, wearing their glorious crown of victory, they shall be received in the Church of a thousand years and enter into glory everlasting. Brothers, I beseech you abandon not your faith, but hold fast by it, and so go forth and fight in the name of the Lord. Look well into your hearts. If Cowardice, hiding there, whispers to you, "Fly," you are blasphemers; for listening to the Tempter you deny your God; your faith is dead. Believe as you would be saved that nothing happens here below without the will of God. Victory and the sword are in his hands and he gives both to those who fight in his name. Is not our God the same God who led Israel under the power of his miracles out of the land of Pharaoh? Did he not lead them safely through the Red Sea? Did he not hide them in the thick cloud which was darkness to the enemy but light to his children; for the column of cloud was built upon the word of the Lord, and if we trust him as they trusted him, it shall be our guide also through the darkness, leading our feet safely to the light. But he who ceases to believe the word of the Lord shall perish in the dark prison of his unbelief. Is not our God the same God who made water flow from a rock, refreshing all Israel? Was he not the father of those three youths who chose death rather than deny him? He is the same God who guarded Daniel in the lions' den. The lions harmed him not, but when the king commanded that Daniel's persecutors be thrown into the den, the lions devoured them. Is he not the same God who walked upon the waves of the sea, and when he commanded Peter to come to him, did not Peter in his faith obey? But when the strength of his faith left him and he became afraid of the water, he sank, and the

324. **Kruger encourages the Boers in the fight with the British** (condensed)

Lord took his hand and saved him and admonished him for his want of faith. . . .

God will not
fail the Boers

And this same God, our lord and Savior, who has brought us here from our distant home and given us our liberty and performed miracles on our behalf, dare we doubt that he who commenced this work will finish it? No, what he has raised up, he will not allow to fall to the ground. Dear brothers, dear brothers, I beseech you, lose not your faith. Depend each one upon himself and fight in the name of the Lord. Let everybody fight where he happens to be, under whatever officer he finds himself; be courageous, firm, obedient, loyal, for that means victory. . . . Salisbury and Chamberlain stand convicted by their own words: "They shall not exist." But the Lord says, "This people shall exist," and Christ is our commander in chief, who leads us with his word. Dear brothers, once more I pray you, let us not fall from faith but follow his commands. He often leads his children through the barren desert where it seems as if they could never get through. But if we will only trust him, I assure you he will be our guide. He who trusts in God's guidance is under the protection of the King of Kings and safe through the darkest night. His word is everlasting. See Psalm 92. Let this be read to all officers and burghers, for our present sufferings are nothing compared with everlasting glory. Let us obey our Savior.

To Cecil Rhodes, more than to any other man, belongs the bold idea of securing for Great Britain all of the inhabitable and valuable regions of southern Africa. The following is a sympathetic account of this great financier and imperialist by a friend and admirer.

325. A
sympathetic
appreciation
of Cecil
Rhodes

Cecil Rhodes was the appointed instrument to preserve for and present to England the most permanently valuable because the most habitable portion of the last great continent that waited to be annexed; and his love of the excitement of money-making and his remarkable genius for finance were to supply the first of the two necessary instruments by which the realization of the dream of empire to the north might be made practicable, — the instrument of money and the command of moneyed men.

Cecil Rhodes never cared for money for itself, to hoard it or to spend it in luxury or ostentation. His wants remained perfectly simple, and the possession of riches did not make him change his mode of life or spend more upon himself. At first he cared for money making because he enjoyed the excitement of success, as a marksman enjoys bringing down a difficult shot, or a fox hunter enjoys taking a stiff fence; but gradually his financial schemes all centered round and were undertaken to advance his one dominant idea, the expansion and consolidation of Greater Britain in South Africa, the occupation for England of the seemingly illimitable and unexplored regions to the north up to and beyond the Zambesi. This one paramount idea which had at an early date begun to possess the mind of young Cecil Rhodes is certainly to be found unmistakably behind all his great financial schemes.

Little did his fellow-miners think as they passed the dreamy youth with impassive face gazing into vacancy, that the building of an empire, the occupation of the last unoccupied continent, was gradually assuming form under the shaping power of that youthful diamond digger's imagination. The paramount idea in his mind — the expansion of our empire and its supremacy in South Africa — was of course developed, and gained shape and consistency under the influence of the study of history and the experience of life. An enlightened patriotism has gradually become the one paramount sentiment of the great South African's life; and putting one's self in his place and looking with his eyes upon the world, one can understand his far-reaching saying that territory is everything, — that is to say, territory fit to support and breed a fine race of men. He sees with his mind's eye the vicious weaklings of our overcrowded English cities, and compares with them the magnificent race of Englishmen that might be reared on the fertile soil and in the fine air of the uplands of Rhodesia, and, as he reflects, the great need for England seems to be territory. England can supply the men in ever-increasing numbers to colonize it, but suitable land for them to colonize is strictly limited, and therefore to

Rhodes's paramount idea

England such territory for her expansion is all-important. "Having read the histories of other countries," to quote Rhodes upon himself, "I saw that expansion was everything, and that the world's surface being limited, the great object of present humanity should be to take as much of the world as it possibly could."

Future generations will appreciate his work

To the judgment of the future Cecil Rhodes may appeal with the certainty that it will applaud the unrivaled achievements of his energy and estimate justly the whole patriotic purpose of his life. The expansion of which he will be the acknowledged author will then be seen to have been not only an expansion of the empire but an expansion of the race, an expansion of English ideas and English principles. Men of that time who stand on the verge of the twenty-first century, as we on the verge of the twentieth, will wonder at the shortsighted judgment and narrow spirit that failed to recognize the greatness and the patriotism of the statesman, and the man that caviled at his methods and lightly esteemed the value of his accomplished work.

Section 92. *Imperial Federation*

326. The constitution of the British Empire League

For a long time after the adoption of free trade in Great Britain it was believed by a large number of the leading statesmen that each of the English-speaking colonies should be allowed to go its own way, making its own laws and regulating its own commerce, and ultimately, perhaps, becoming entirely independent. During the last quarter of the nineteenth century, however, since the new means of rapid communication have bound all parts of the empire closely together, a movement designed to form a closer union has developed and led to the formation, in 1895, of a British Empire League, the objects of which are set forth in its constitution.

1. The Association to be called The British Empire League.
2. It shall be the primary object of the League to secure the permanent unity of the empire.

3. The following to be among the other principal objects of the League :

(*a*) To promote trade between the United Kingdom, the Colonies, and India, and to advocate the holding of periodical meetings of representatives from all parts of the empire for the discussion of matters of general commercial interest, and the consideration of the best means of expanding the national trade.

(*b*) To consider how far it may be possible to modify any laws or treaties which impede the freedom of action in the making of reciprocal trade arrangements between the United Kingdom and the colonies, or between two or more British colonies or possessions.

(*c*) To promote closer intercourse between the different portions of the empire by the establishment of cheaper and, where required, more direct steam, postal, and telegraphic communication, preference being given to routes not traversing foreign territory.

(*d*) To develop the principles on which all parts of the empire may best share in its general defense ; endeavoring to bring into harmony public opinion at home and in the colonies on this subject, and to devise a more perfect coöperation of the military and naval forces of the empire with a special view to the due protection of the trade routes.

(*e*) To assimilate as far as local circumstances permit the laws relating to copyright, patents, legitimacy, and bankruptcy throughout the empire.

4. The League shall use every constitutional means to bring about the objects for which it is established, and shall invite the support of men of all shades of political opinion throughout the empire.

5. The League shall advocate the establishment of periodical conferences to deal with such questions as may appear ripe for consideration, on the lines of the London Conference of 1887 and the Ottawa Conference of 1894.

CHAPTER XXVIII

THE RUSSIAN EMPIRE IN THE NINETEENTH CENTURY

Section 93. Reigns of Alexander I and Nicholas I

Alexander I, who ruled the Russian Empire during the first quarter of the nineteenth century, had received a most liberal education in his youth; and during the early years of his reign he devoted his attention to devising numerous plans of reform for his people. His character and the leading reforms which he cherished are described in the Memoirs of the distinguished Polish prince, Adam Czartoryski (1770–1861), from which the following passages are taken. Czartoryski knew Alexander as a young man, and thus describes his ideals before his accession to the throne.

327. Alexander I and his plans for reforms (condensed) As soon as I came in the Grand Duke Alexander took me by the hand and proposed that we should go into the garden. We walked about in every direction for three hours, keeping up an animated conversation all the time. He declared that he did not in any way share the ideas and doctrines of the cabinet and the court; and that he was far from approving the policy and conduct of his grandmother, whose principles he condemned. He had wished for the success of Poland in her glorious struggle and had deplored her fall. Kosciuszko, he said, was, in his eyes, a man who was great by his virtues as well as owing to the cause which he had defended, — the cause of humanity and of justice. He added that he detested despotism everywhere, no matter in what way it was exercised; that he loved liberty, to which all men had a right; that he had taken the strongest interest in the French Revolution, and that while condemning its terrible excesses, he wished the French Republic success and rejoiced at its establishment.

I was deeply moved, and could hardly believe my ears. That a Russian prince, Catherine II's successor, her grandson and her favorite child, whom she would have wished to see reigning after her instead of her son, and of whom it was said that he would continue her reign, should disavow and detest his grandmother's principles, should repel the odious policy of Russia, should be a passionate lover of justice and liberty, should pity Poland and wish to see her happy, — all this seemed incredible. And that such noble ideas and great virtues should be able to grow and flourish in such an atmosphere and with such surroundings was surely little less than a miracle. *(Alexander a lover of liberty)*

It should be remembered that at that time so-called liberal opinions were much less prevalent than they are now, and had not yet penetrated into all the classes of society or even into the cabinets of sovereigns. On the contrary, everything that had the appearance of liberalism was anathematized in the courts and salons of most of the European capitals, and especially in Russia and at St. Petersburg, where all the convictions of the old French régime were grafted in an exaggerated form on Russian despotism and servility. *(Liberal ideas not popular in European courts)*

Alexander's opinions were indeed those of one brought up in the ideas of 1789, who wishes to see republics everywhere, and looks upon that form of government as the only one in conformity with the wishes and the rights of humanity. He held, among other things, that hereditary monarchy was an unjust and absurd institution, and that the supreme authority should be granted not through the accident of birth but by the votes of the nation, which would best know who is most capable of governing it. I represented to him the arguments against this view, the difficulty and the risks of an election, what Poland had suffered from such an institution, and how little Russia was adapted to or prepared for it. I added that now, at any rate, Russia would not gain anything by the change, as she would lose the man who, by his benevolent and pure intentions, was most worthy of succeeding to the throne. . . . *(Alexander declares hereditary monarchy absurd)*

Baptism of Nicholas I

During the year 1796 an event occurred which had vast consequences for Europe and terrible ones for Poland. The Grand Duchess Maria gave birth to a son. The baptismal ceremony took place in the chapel of Tsarskoe-Selo; the whole court attended in full dress in the spacious hall which leads to the chapel. The ceremony, as was to be expected, was a most sumptuous one. The ambassadors were present, and some of them held the child at the baptismal font as the representatives of their respective sovereigns. He was named Nicholas ! Looking at him then in his swaddling clothes as he moved about impatiently while the long baptismal ceremony of the Russian Church was being performed, I little thought that this weak and pretty child would one day become the scourge of my country....

Alexander's dreams difficult to realize in practice

As years went on, Emperor Alexander's vague and floating ideas were consolidated into a practical shape. All the eccentric views which were mere fireworks were abandoned, and he had to restrict his wishes to the realities and possibilities of the moment. He consoled himself by indulging in his hours of leisure, which were daily becoming more rare, in hopes of progress, which permitted him to retain some, at least, of the dreams of his youth. These seemed to me like a tree transplanted into a dry and arid soil and deprived of its exuberant vegetation, whose despoiled trunk puts forth a few weak branches and then perishes.

Alexander's reforms

The emperor's first step was to issue an ukase or manifesto to restore the authority and dignity of the Senate. Although every order of the emperor, whether written or spoken, had the force of law, such orders had all to be addressed to the Senate, which was intrusted with the task of publishing them and seeing to their due execution. It was at the same time laid down that all the ministers should make detailed reports of their acts, which the emperor would send to the Senate for its opinion. This, it was hoped, would be a first step in the direction of national and representative government.

Separate administrative departments created

After laying the first stone of the edifice of a regulated legislative power, and devising a limit to the autocratic power, the emperor turned his attention to the organization of his government, so as to make its action more enlightened, more just, and more methodical. The government machine was irregular and intermittent in its action, and the administration was a chaos in which nothing was regulated or clearly defined.

The object of the reform was to establish a system somewhat similar to those adopted in most other European States, by separating the governmental departments, defining their limits, assigning to each all the business of a particular kind, centralizing their management, and thereby augmenting the responsibility of the principal functionaries of State. It was hoped, among other things, that this would be an efficacious means of checking the numberless abuses and frauds which are the curse of Russia. The emperor accordingly created for the first time ministries of the Interior and of Police, of Finance, of Justice, of Public Instruction, of Commerce, of Foreign Affairs, of War, and of the Navy.

These changes, which anywhere else would seem the very A B C of politics, seemed at that time to the Russians novel and immense. The manifesto made much noise in the whole empire, and especially in the salons of St. Petersburg and Moscow; each man had his own opinion of it, and the majority judged it not by its intrinsic merits or the benefits it might confer on the State, but by the effect it would be likely to have on his own particular advancement. Those who obtained places approved it, while those who were left out in the cold criticised the juvenile infatuation that wished to change the old and venerable institutions under which Russia had become great. The personages high in office who had not been consulted, vented their disappointment by smiling with pity at the young men who were trying to reform the empire, and at the foolishness of some older men who consented to be the instruments of a servile and awkward imitation of foreign institutions. *How this reform was received*

Alexander also reconstituted the commission for the revision of the law. This had been formed by the Empress Catherine, who thereby gained the flattering appreciation of Voltaire and the Diderots; but the only result was the publication of the philanthropic and philosophical instructions addressed by Catherine to the commission. It was dissolved soon after, and its proceedings were never made public. The new commission was *Plans for the revision of the law* organized with the assistance of a German jurist, Baron Rosenkampf, on a vast and well-conceived plan. It was directed to codify all the existing Russian laws, which were very numerous and often contradicted each other, classifying them according to subjects, omitting such as were obsolete and adding new ones when necessary, but taking care to retain in the new codes all that had for many years entered into the life of the Russian people.

The backward state of learning

The creation of a Ministry of Public Instruction was a remarkable innovation in Russia which was fruitful of great and salutary results, and posterity will owe gratitude both to Alexander and to the young men, then so much criticised, who supported him in his plans. Nothing could be more wretched or insufficient than public instruction in Russia up to the reign of Alexander. There was an academy of sciences at St. Petersburg, which owed its only celebrity to the presence of some learned men whom the government had brought to the Russian capital from abroad. The transactions of this academy were for the most part written in the French and German languages; it had no relations whatever with the country, and exercised no influence on its progress. At Moscow there was a university which was equally isolated. The only other educational establishments in Russia proper were the so-called "national schools." The teaching in these was bad and extremely meager; the teachers were poor wretches whom idleness and ennui had rendered drunkards, and no respectable person sent his children to them.

University reforms

The establishment of the Ministry of Public Instruction completely changed all this. The existing universities of Moscow, Wilna, and Dorpat were better endowed, and three new ones were created, — those of St. Petersburg, Kharkoff, and Kazan, — each forming an educational center for a definite region in which it directed all educational matters.

By shrewd negotiations at the Congress of Vienna Alexander I was able to secure possession of the grand duchy of Warsaw, which Napoleon had created from the old Polish territories. Alexander transformed the duchy into the "kingdom of Poland" and assumed the crown himself. He gave the restored kingdom an elaborate constitution, guaranteeing self-government to the Poles, liberty of the press, religious toleration and equality of all citizens before the law. It was not long, however, before the Poles began to complain that the Tsar's agents observed neither the letter nor the spirit of the constitution, and, in 1830, encouraged by the example of the French, the Poles revolted against the rule of Alexander's successor, Nicholas I. The Tsar was able by great cruelty and harshness to suppress the Polish insurrection. He then abolished their constitution in 1832, and forced upon them in its stead a so-called "organic statute." This reduced Poland to the status of a Russian province. Nicholas strove to justify his conduct in the following proclamation:

When, by our manifesto of the 25th of January of last year, we announced to our faithful subjects the entrance of our troops into the kingdom of Poland, which had been for a moment withdrawn by rebellion from the rule of its lawful sovereign, we at the same time declared our intention of establishing the future state of that country on a solid basis, in accordance with the wants and welfare of our whole empire. An end having now been put, by force of arms, to the disturbances by which the kingdom of Poland was agitated, and the nation, which had been led away by factious men, having been once more brought back to its duty and restored to tranquillity, we consider that the proper moment has come for carrying our intentions into execution, and for laying the foundation of a solid and lasting order of things, by which the peace and the indissoluble union of the two nations committed by Divine Providence to our care may be secured against every new attack.

328. Nicholas I's proclamation on the abolition of the Polish constitution (1832)

The kingdom of Poland, once earlier conquered by the victorious arms of Russia, not only recovered, in 1815, its existence as a nation, but obtained rights of its own, and a constitutional charter, a monument to the magnanimity of our august

The Poles have abused the favors granted by the Tsar

predecessor, the Emperor Alexander of glorious memory. This charter did not, however, satisfy men who were the enemies of all order and legitimate power, and who, persevering in their guilty projects, and meditating the separation of the two nations subject to our scepter, abused the favors which they derived from the regenerator of their country by employing the very laws and institutions which his sovereign will had generously conferred upon them for the subversion of his great work.

Future insurrections to be prevented by strong government

Torrents of blood have been shed. The tranquillity and happiness which the kingdom of Poland enjoyed in a degree that it had never before known, have been succeeded by the horrors of civil war and general desolation. But these misfortunes are now past. The kingdom of Poland, again restored to our dominion, is now at peace, and will again breathe under the auspices of a protecting government. But our paternal solicitude for our faithful subjects imposes upon us the duty of preventing, by all the means in our power, the return of similar disasters, by henceforward depriving the evil-disposed of the means which they have openly employed to disturb the public peace.

It is nevertheless our will that our subjects in the kingdom of Poland should at the same time enjoy all the advantages essential to their own well-being and for the prosperity of their country; that persons and property, liberty of conscience and municipal franchises should be respected; that our said subjects should possess a distinct administration adapted to their wants, in such manner, however, that the kingdom of Poland shall never cease to be an integral part of our empire; and that they shall henceforth form with the Russians one single nation, one fraternal people. For these reasons we have deemed it necessary to determine, by an organic statute issued this day, the future mode of organization of the said kingdom, in conformity with the intentions herein set forth.

Given at St. Petersburg the 14th (26th) February, in the year of our Lord 1832, and the seventh year of our reign.

(Signed)   NICHOLAS

(Countersigned)   COUNT STEPHEN GRABOWSKI

Section 94. The Freeing of the Serfs and Growth of the Spirit of Revolution

In all the long list of personal recollections by distinguished Europeans, there is none more charming in spirit or fuller of interesting information than *Memoirs of a Revolutionist*, by Prince Kropotkin (born in 1842), who, as a youth, had an excellent opportunity of observing every aspect of Russian life from the highest to the lowest. He describes the old régime in Russia with striking fidelity, and traces in the most entertaining style the progress of the revolutionary spirit in Russia during the last half of the nineteenth century. The following picture of domestic life in a Russian noble's family, and of serfdom in the old days, is taken from the pages of this eminent revolutionist.

329. Domestic life in the family of a Russian noble (condensed)

Wealth was measured in those times by the number of " souls " that a landed proprietor owned. So many " souls " meant so many male serfs ; women did not count. My father, who owned nearly twelve hundred souls, in three different provinces, and who had, in addition to his peasants' holdings, large tracts of land which were cultivated by these peasants, was accounted a rich man. He lived up to his reputation, which meant that his house was open to any number of visitors, and that he kept a very large household.

Fifty servants for a family in town

We were a family of eight, occasionally of ten or twelve ; but fifty servants at Moscow and half as many more in the country were considered not one too many. Four coachmen to attend a dozen horses, three cooks for the masters and two more for the servants, a dozen men to wait upon us at dinner time (one man, plate in hand, standing behind each person seated at the table), and girls innumerable in the maidservants' room, — how could any one do with less than this? Besides, the ambition of every landed proprietor was that everything required for his household should be made at home, by his own men.

To maintain such numbers of servants as were kept in our
house in town would have been simply ruinous, if all provisions
had to be bought at Moscow; but in those times of serfdom
things were managed very simply. When winter came, father sat
at his table and wrote the following to the manager of his estate :

" On receipt of this, and as soon as winter communication is
established in the city of Moscow, twenty-five peasant sledges,
drawn by two horses each, one horse from each house, and one
sledge and one man from each second house, are to be loaded
with (so many) quarters of oats, (so many) of wheat, and (so
many) of rye, as also with all the poultry and geese and ducks,
well frozen, which have to be killed this winter, well packed
and accompanied by a complete list, under the supervision of a
well-chosen man " ; — and so it went on for a couple of pages,
till the next full stop was reached. After this there followed an
enumeration of the penalties which would be inflicted in case
the provisions should not reach the house situated in such a
street, number so and so, in due time and in good condition.

Some time before Christmas the twenty-five peasant sledges
really entered our gates, and covered the surface of the wide
yard. . . .

Serfdom was then in the last years of its existence. It is
recent history, — it seems to be only of yesterday ; and yet,
even in Russia, few realize what serfdom was in reality. There
is a dim conception that the conditions which it created were
very bad ; but those conditions, as they affected human beings
bodily and mentally, are not generally understood. It is amazing, indeed, to see how quickly an institution and its social
consequences are forgotten when the institution has ceased to
exist, and with what rapidity men and things change. I will
try to recall the conditions of serfdom by telling, not what I
heard, but what I saw.

Uliana, the housekeeper, stands in the passage leading to
father's room, and crosses herself ; she dares neither to advance
nor to retreat. At last, having recited a prayer, she enters the
room and reports, in a hardly audible voice, that the store of
tea is nearly at an end, that there are only twenty pounds of
sugar left, and that the other provisions will soon be exhausted.

"Thieves, robbers!" shouts my father. "And you, you are in league with them!" His voice thunders throughout the house. Our stepmother leaves Uliana to face the storm. But father cries, "Frol, call the princess! Where is she?" And when she enters he receives her with the same reproaches. The master in a rage

"You also are in league with this progeny of Ham; you are standing up for them"; and so on, for half an hour or more.

Then he commences to verify the accounts. At the same time he thinks about the hay. Frol is sent to weigh what is left of that, and our stepmother is sent to be present during the weighing, while father calculates how much of it ought to be in the barn. A considerable quantity of hay appears to be missing, and Uliana cannot account for several pounds of such and such provisions. Father's voice becomes more and more menacing; Uliana is trembling; but it is the coachman who now enters the room, and is stormed at by his master. Father springs at him, strikes him, but he keeps repeating, "Your highness must have made a mistake."

Father repeats his calculations, and this time it appears that there is more hay in the barn than there ought to be. The shouting continues; he now reproaches the coachman with not having given the horses their daily rations in full; but the coachman calls on all the saints to witness that he gave the animals their due, and Frol invokes the Virgin to confirm the coachman's appeal.

But father will not be appeased. He calls in Makár, the piano tuner and sub-butler, and reminds him of all his recent sins. He was drunk last week, and must have been drunk yesterday, for he broke half a dozen plates. In fact, the breaking of these plates was the real cause of all the disturbance; our stepmother had reported the fact to father in the morning, and that was why Uliana was received with more scolding than was usually the case, why the verification of the hay was undertaken, and why father now continues to shout that "this progeny of Ham" deserve all the punishment on earth.

Of a sudden there is a lull in the storm. My father takes his seat at the table and writes a note. "Take Makár with this note to the police station, and let a hundred lashes with the A hundred lashes for a serf birch rod be given to him." Terror and absolute silence reign in the house.

Yet father was not among the worst of landowners. On the contrary, the servants and the peasants considered him one of the best. What we saw in our house was going on everywhere, often in much more cruel forms. The flogging of the serfs was a regular part of the duties of the police and of the fire brigade.

When Alexander came to the throne in 1855 Russia was suffering from a great crisis in the government and in industry, resulting from the disasters of the Crimean War. The new Tsar was quick to see that many radical reforms were demanded for his empire, and after due deliberation upon the state of the serfs in his dominions, he issued in March, 1861, a decree emancipating the peasants from their galling bondage. A careful examination of this famous document, which assumes in Russian history the place which the proclamation emancipating the slaves assumes in American history, will reveal the provisions which were later destined to be the source of terrible oppression to the peasants. It will be observed that the Tsar treats the noble landlords throughout with the most distinguished consideration.

330. Declaration of the Tsar emancipating the serfs (March 3, 1861) (condensed)

We, Alexander II, by the grace of God Tsar and Autocrat of all the Russias, King of Poland, Grand Duke of Finland, etc., make known to all our faithful subjects :

Summoned to the throne of our ancestors by Divine Providence and the sacred law of heredity, we have promised ourselves with heartfelt sincerity to extend our affection and imperial solicitude to all our faithful subjects, whatever their rank or condition, from the soldier who nobly bears arms in the defense of his country to the humble artisan who faithfully carries on his industry ; from the functionary who occupies a high office in the State to the laborer whose plow furrows the fields.

As we consider the various classes of which the State is composed, we are convinced that the laws of our empire which have wisely provided for the upper and middle classes, and have fixed with precision their rights and obligations, have not reached the same degree of success in relation to the peasants bound to the soil, who, either through ancient laws or custom, have been hereditarily subjected to the authority of the landlords. Indeed, the rights of landowners over their serfs have hitherto been very extensive and very imperfectly defined by the laws, which have been supplemented by tradition, custom, and the good will of the landlords. Laws inadequate in the case of the serfs

This system has at best established patriarchal relations based upon the fairness and benevolence of the landowners and an affectionate docility on the part of the peasants; but as manners have lost their simplicity, the paternal ties between the landlords and the peasants have been weakened. Furthermore, as the seigniorial authority falls into the hands of those exclusively intent on their own selfish advantage, those relations of mutual good will have tended to give way and open the door to arbitrariness, burdensome to the peasants and hostile to their prosperity. This has served to develop in them an indifference to all progress. How serfdom had lost its patriarchal character

These facts did not fail to impress our predecessors of glorious memory, and they took measures to improve the lot of the peasants; but these measures have had little effect, since they were either dependent for their execution on the individual initiative of such landlords as might be animated by a liberal spirit or were merely local in their scope, or adopted as an experiment. Former Tsars have striven to improve the lot of the serfs

We became convinced, therefore, that the work of fundamentally ameliorating the condition of the peasant was for us a sacred heritage from our ancestors, a mission which in the course of events Divine Providence had called us to fulfill. We have commenced this work by demonstrating our imperial confidence in the nobility of Russia, who have given us so many proofs of their devotion and their constant disposition to make sacrifices for the well-being of the country. It was to the nobility themselves that, in conformity to their own wishes, we reserved the right of formulating the provisions for the new organization The nobles formulate the law fixing the new conditions for the serfs

of the peasants,—provisions which involve the necessity of limiting their own rights over the peasants, and of accepting the
responsibilities of a reform which could only be accomplished
with some material losses to them. Our confidence has not
been deceived. We have found the nobility, united in committees in the various governments, ready to make, through
agents who enjoyed their confidence, the voluntary sacrifices
of their rights so far as the personal servitude of the peasants
is concerned.

Propositions
of the land-
lords taken as
a basis of
reform

The propositions of the local committees of the nobility —
which varied greatly, as might be expected from the nature of
the problem — have been collated, compared, and reduced to a
regular system, then adjusted and supplemented by a higher
committee appointed for the purpose. The new provisions thus
formulated relative to the peasants and the domestic serfs of
the landholders have been submitted to the Council of the
Empire. After having invoked divine assistance we have resolved to carry out the work according to the regulations thus
drawn up.

Conditions on
which peasant
families hold
their cottages
and gardens
and rent the
land neces-
sary for their
support

The peasants now bound to the soil shall, within the term
fixed by the law, be vested with the full rights of freemen. The
landed proprietors, while they shall retain all the rights of ownership over all the lands now belonging to them, shall transfer to
the peasants, in return for a rent fixed by law, the full enjoyment of their cottages, farm buildings, and gardens. Furthermore, in order to assure to the peasants their subsistence and
enable them to meet their obligations toward the State, the
landlords shall turn over to the peasants a quantity of arable
and other land provided for in the regulations above mentioned.
In return for these allotments the peasant families shall be
required to pay rent to the landlords, as fixed by the provisions
of the law. Under these conditions, which are temporary, the
peasants shall be designated as "temporarily bound."

Peasants with
money may
buy land out-
right

At the same time the peasants are granted the right of purchasing their cottages and gardens, and, with the consent of
the landlords, they may acquire in complete ownership the arable
lands and other lands allotted to them as a permanent holding.
By the acquisition of a complete title to the land assigned them,

the peasants [1] shall be freed from their obligations toward the landlords for land thus purchased, and thus enter definitively into the class of free peasants and landowners.

Since the new organization, owing to the unavoidable complexity of the changes which it involves, cannot immediately be put into execution, a lapse of time is necessary, which cannot be less than two years or thereabouts; to avoid all misunderstanding and to protect public and private interests during this interval, the system actually existing on the estates of landowners will be maintained up to the moment when the new system shall have been instituted by the completion of the required preparatory measures.

Serfdom to continue until the new system is established

Aware of all the difficulties of the reform we have undertaken, we place our trust in the goodness of Divine Providence, who watches over the destinies of Russia. We also count upon the generous devotion of our faithful nobility, and we are happy to testify to that body the gratitude it has deserved from us, as well as from the country, for the disinterested support it has given to the accomplishment of our designs. Russia will not forget that the nobility, actuated solely by its respect for the dignity of man and its love for its neighbor, has spontaneously renounced the rights it enjoyed in virtue of the system of serfdom now abolished, and has laid the foundation of a new future for the peasants. We also entertain the firm hope that it will also direct its further efforts to carry out the new regulation by maintaining good order, in a spirit of peace and benevolence.

Praise for the nobles

In order to render the transactions between the landlords and the peasants easier, so that the latter may acquire in full proprietorship their houses and the adjacent lands and buildings, the government will grant them assistance, according to a special regulation, through loans of money or a transfer of mortgages encumbering an estate.

The government agrees to advance money to the peasant to enable him to buy his homestead

When the first rumors of this great reform contemplated by the government spread among the country people who were scarcely prepared for it, it gave rise in some instances to misunderstandings among individuals more intent upon liberty than

Reforms at first misunderstood

[1] This does not mean the *individual* peasants, but the village community, which was perpetuated under the new law.

mindful of the duties which liberty imposes. But generally the good sense of the country has asserted itself. It has been understood that the landlords would not be deprived of rights legally acquired, except for a fit and sufficient indemnity, or by a voluntary concession on their part; that it would be contrary to all equity for the peasants to accept the enjoyment of the lands conceded by the landlords without at the same time accepting equivalent charges.

It is hoped that the serfs will appreciate the generosity of the nobles

And now we confidently hope that the freed serfs, in the presence of the new future which is opened before them, will appreciate and recognize the considerable sacrifices which the nobility has made on their behalf. They will understand that the blessing of an existence based upon full ownership of their property, as well as the greater liberty in the administration of their possessions, entails upon them, with new duties towards society and themselves, the obligation of justifying the new laws by a loyal and judicious use of the rights which are now accorded them. For if men do not themselves endeavor to insure their own well-being under the ægis of the laws, the best of those laws cannot guarantee it to them. Only by assiduous labor, a rational expenditure of their strength and resources, a strict economy, and, above all, by an upright life, — a life constantly inspired by the fear of the Lord, — can they hope for prosperity and progress.

And now, my orthodox and faithful people, make the holy sign of the cross and join thy prayers to ours, invoking the blessing of the Most High upon thy first free labors, for this alone is a sure pledge of private well-being and the public weal.

Given at St. Petersburg, the nineteenth day of February [March 3, new style], of the year of grace 1861 and the seventh of our reign.   ALEXANDER

In addition to emancipating the serfs, Alexander II gave many of the provinces of his empire local representative bodies, — known as *Zemstvos*, — with power to conduct much of the local government, so that many Russian liberals began to hope that the Tsar would next

establish a national representative parliament on the model
of these miniature parliaments. Alexander, however, declared that he would not surrender any of the autocratic
power which he enjoyed, and many earnest reformers,
despairing of securing an enlightened government for
Russia, joined the ranks of the Nihilists. This name,
which was applied to the reformers who declared their
contempt for Russia's autocratic traditions and for her
State religion, was derived from the following passage in
one of Turgenief's most famous novels, *Fathers and
Children.*

"Well, and what sort of person is Mr. Bazároff himself?"
he asked, with pauses between the words.

"What sort of person is Bazároff?" Arkády laughed. "Would
you like to have me tell you, my dear uncle, what sort of
person he is?"

"Pray do, my dear nephew."

"He is a Nihilist."

"What?" asked Nikolai Petróvitch; and Pavel Petróvitch
elevated his knife, with a bit of butter sticking to the blade,
in the air, and remained motionless.

"He is a Nihilist," repeated Arkády.

"A Nihilist," said Nikolai Petróvitch.

"That comes from the Latin *nihil*, "nothing," so far as I
can judge; consequently that word designates a man who —
who recognizes nothing."

"Say, ' who respects nothing,' " put in Pavel Petróvitch, and
devoted himself once more to his butter.

"Who treats everything from a critical point of view,"
remarked Arkády.

"And isn't that exactly the same thing?" inquired Pavel
Petróvitch.

"No, it is not exactly the same thing. A Nihilist is a man
who does not bow before any authority whatever, who does
not accept a single principle on faith, with whatever respect
that principle may be environed."

331. Turgenief's definition of Nihilism

"And dost thou think that is a good thing?" interrupted Pavel Petróvitch.

"That depends on who it is, dear uncle. It is all right for one man and very bad for another."

"You don't say so. Well, I see that that is not in our line. We people of the old school assume that without principles it is impossible to take a step or breathe. . . . We shall content ourselves, therefore, with admiring these gentlemen — what do you call them?"

"Nihilists," replied Arkády, with distinctness.

In the seventies a large number of young Russian men and women began to go out among the peasants to educate them in political economy and kindred subjects, with the hope that in time the Russian people might be prepared for those liberal institutions which had been won by the nations in western Europe. The Russian government met this "go-to-the-people" movement with the utmost severity, and banished to Siberia, on the slightest pretext, those who did not yield explicit obedience to the autocratic power of the Tsar. The methods of the Russian government and the sufferings of those who were exiled to Siberia are illustrated in the following extract from the well-known work by George Kennan, *Siberia and the Exile System.*

332. Suffering caused by system of Siberian exile (slightly condensed)   The two things that are most exasperating to a liberal and warm-hearted young Russian are, first, official lawlessness, and second, the suffering brought by such lawlessness upon near relatives and dear friends. The suffering of a loved wife or the loss of an affectionate child is hard enough to bear when it comes in the ordinary course of nature and seems to be inevitable ; but when it comes as the direct result of unnecessary causes, such as injustice, tyranny, and official caprice, it has more than the bitterness of death, and it arouses fiercer passions than those that carry men into the storm of battle.

In the year 1879 there was living in the town of Ivángorod a skillful young surgeon named Dr. Biéli. Although he was a man of liberal views, he was not an agitator nor a revolutionist, and had taken no active part in political affairs. Sometime in the late winter or early spring of 1879 there came to him, with letters of introduction, two young women who had been studying in one of the medical schools for women in St. Petersburg, and had been expelled and ordered to return to their homes in central Russia on account of their alleged political "untrustworthiness." They were very anxious to complete their education and to fit themselves for useful work among the peasants; and they begged Dr. Biéli to aid them in their studies.

As they were both in an "illegal" position, — that is, were living in a place where, without permission from the authorities, they had no right to be, — it was Dr. Biéli's duty as a loyal subject to hand them over to the police, regardless of the fact that they had come to him with letters of introduction and a petition for help. He happened, however, to be a man of courage, independence, and generous instincts; and, instead of betraying them, he listened with sympathy to their story, promised them his aid, introduced them to his wife, and began to give them lessons. . . .

On the 10th of May, 1879, both they and the young surgeon were arrested and exiled by administrative process to Siberia. Dr. Biéli eventually was sent to the Arctic village of Verhoyánsk, latitude 67.30°, in the province of Yakútsk. At the time of Dr. Biéli's banishment, his wife, a beautiful young woman twenty-four or twenty-five years of age, was expecting confinement, and was therefore unable to go to Siberia with him. As soon as possible, however, after the birth of her child, and before she had fully recovered her strength, she left her nursing baby with relatives and started on a journey of more than six thousand miles to join her husband in a village situated north of the Arctic Circle and near the Asiatic pole of cold. She had not the necessary means to make such a journey by rail, steamer, and post, and was therefore forced to ask permission of the Minister of the Interior to travel with a party of exiles.

The case of Dr. Biéli

He teaches some political offenders

He is sent to Siberia and his young wife follows him

The terrible
privations of
the journey
As far as the city of Tomsk in western Siberia both political and common-criminal exiles are transported in convict
trains or barges. Beyond that point the common criminals
walk, and the politicals are carried in *telégas*, at the rate of
about sixty miles a week. At this rate of progress Mrs. Biéli
would have reached her husband's place of exile only after
sixteen months of incessant hardship, privation, and suffering.
But she did not reach it.

For many weeks her hope, courage, and love sustained her,
and enabled her to endure without complaint the jolting, the
suffocating dust, the scorching heat, and the cold autumnal
rains on the road, the bad food, the plank sleeping benches,
the vermin, and the pestilential air of the stations where
they stopped; but human endurance has its limits. Three or
four months of this unrelieved misery, with constant anxiety
about her husband and the baby that, for her husband's sake,
she had abandoned in Russia, broke down her health and her
spirit. She sank into deep despondency and eventually began
to show signs of mental aberration. After passing Krasnoyársk
her condition became such that any sudden shock was likely
completely to overthrow her reason,—and the shock soon came.

There are two villages in eastern Siberia whose names are
almost alike,—Verholénsk and Verhoyánsk. The former is
situated only 180 miles from Irkútsk, while the latter is nearly
2700 miles. As the party with which she was traveling approached the capital of eastern Siberia, her hope, strength,
and courage seemed to revive. Her husband, she thought, was
only a few hundred miles away, and in a few more weeks she
would be in his arms. She talked of him constantly, counted
the *verst* posts which measured her slow progress towards
him, and literally lived upon the expectation of speedy reunion
with him.

The wife be-
comes insane
A few stations west of Irkútsk she accidentally became
aware, for the first time, that her husband was not in Verholénsk, but in Verhoyánsk; that she was still separated from
him by nearly three thousand miles of mountain, steppe, and forest; and that in order to reach his place of banishment that
year she would have to travel many weeks on dog or reindeer

sledges, in terrible cold, through the arctic solitudes of north-eastern Asia. The sudden shock of this discovery was almost immediately fatal. She became violently insane, and died insane a few months later in the Irkútsk prison hospital, without ever seeing again her husband for whose sake she had endured such mental and physical agonies.

The actual experiences of the Russian revolutionists exiled to Siberia by the government are minutely and graphically described by a very active revolutionist Leo Deutsch, in a volume entitled *Sixteen Years in Siberia*, from which the following data are obtained.

A fortnight after my arrest I was informed that a party of convicts would start for Moscow that evening. I was to accompany them, and accordingly must assume the convict garb. After eighteen years I think of that day with a shudder.

333. The narrative of a Siberian exile (condensed)

First of all, I was taken into a room where was stored everything necessary to the equipment of a convict under sentence. On the floor lay piles of chains ; and clothes, boots, etc., were heaped on shelves. From among them some were selected that were supposed to fit me ; and I was then conducted to a second room. Here the right side of my head was shaved, and the hair on the left side cut short. I had seen people in the prison who had been treated in this fashion, and the sight had always made a painful impression on me, as indeed it does on every one. But when I saw my own face in the glass a cold shudder ran down my spine, and I experienced a sensation of personal degradation to something less than human. I thought of the days — in Russia not so long ago — when criminals were branded with hot irons. A convict was waiting ready to fasten on my fetters. I was placed on a stool, and had to put my foot on an anvil. The blacksmith fitted an iron ring round each ankle, and welded it together. Every stroke of the hammer made my heart sink, as I realized that a new existence was beginning for me.

The mental depression into which I now fell was soon accompanied by physical discomfort. The fetters at first caused

The discomfort of being in chains

me intolerable pain in walking, and even disturbed my sleep. It also requires considerable practice before one can easily manage to dress and undress. The heavy chains, about thirteen pounds in weight, are not only an encumbrance, but are very painful, as they chafe the skin round the ankles; and the leather lining is but little protection to those unaccustomed to these adornments. Another great torment is the continual clinking of the chains. It is indescribably irritating to the nervous, and reminds the prisoner at every turn that he is "deprived of all rights." I hardly knew myself as I looked in the glass and beheld a fully attired convict. . . .

My own clothes I gave away to the warders, and any possessions of value — watch, ring, cigarette case — I sent by post to relations. I kept only my books. I had been given a bag in which to keep a change of linen; and into it I also put a few volumes of Shakespeare, Goethe, Heine, Molière, and Rousseau, thus completing my preparations for traveling. . . .

General character of the exile's companions

We were taken straight to the railway carriage engaged for us by the organizers of the convoy. I asked my companions the reason of their banishment, and learned from them that — as in many other instances described to me by people who had similarly been exiled to Siberia — they had simply been accused by the police of being "untrustworthy." This word has become classical in Russian police affairs, and has a conveniently vague signification. Literally it means "of whom nothing good can be expected." A young man or girl associates with So-and-so, reads such and such books; this is enough to awaken suspicion that the said young man or girl is "untrustworthy." The police

Meaning of "untrustworthy" in Russian official parlance

or the gendarmerie pay a domiciliary visit, find a suspicious letter or a prohibited book, and then the course of events is certain, — arrest, imprisonment, Siberia. It may be scarcely credible that people languish for years in prison, without any pretense of legal procedure against them, simply by decree of an officer of the gendarmerie; and that at the good pleasure of these officers — most of them fabulously ignorant men — people are banished to the wilds of Siberia. Even those familiar with Russian affairs are often shocked and staggered by some fresh case of this kind.

As we were nearing a large station the officer informed us that we should be joined here by some more political exiles; and when the train came to a standstill, two quite young girls — at the most eighteen to twenty years of age — and two youths were brought into our carriage. We three who came from Kiev were by no means aged, but we might almost have been called old folks by these children. We received the newcomers cordially, and of course begged for their story, which was as follows:

In the district of Poltava the chief town is a small place called Romny, and in this little town there is a girls' school. Two or three of the scholars hit upon the idea of lending one another books, and making notes on them, — not books that were in any way forbidden, but that were accessible to all. Soon a few young men joined them; and thus a small reading society was formed, such as might help to pass away the long winter evenings in the dull little provincial town. As these young people had no idea that they were committing any offense, they naturally never dreamed of keeping their proceedings secret. But the eye of the law is sleepless! The officer commanding the gendarmerie in that place saw and triumphed.

A reading circle formed

For years he had been vegetating in this obscure corner of the empire, and had never unearthed the least little conspiracy nor brought to light a secret society; now was his chance. He could at last make manifest his burning zeal, his devotion to his country and his Tsar; and recognition by his superiors, perhaps an order or promotion, shone before him. One night the gendarmerie paid domiciliary visits to the dwellings of the young ladies of the school. Certainly nothing suspicious was found, but the frightened girls "confessed" that they had "held meetings," and that they read books in a "society." This was enough for the brave sergeant; here were grounds for the State to take action against the "secret society of Romny." The girls and their friends were arrested and imprisoned; a report was sent to St. Petersburg about the discovery of a secret society, in which such and such persons had taken part, and discussed "social questions" together; the officer was of the opinion that these evil doers should be sent to Siberia, and the thing was done. . . .

The members arrested as suspects

Leo Deutsch gives the following vivid description of one of the most famous of the women revolutionists, Vera Figner.

Vera Figner and the "go-to-the-people" movement

I had come to know Vera Figner personally in St. Petersburg during the year 1877, at a time when she had already adopted the idea of going "among the people." Twenty-two years of age, slender and of striking beauty, she was even then a noteworthy figure among the other prominent women socialists. Like so many other girls, she had thrown heart and soul into the cause of the Russian peasants, and was ready and willing to sacrifice everything to serve the people. In the summer of 1879 I again came repeatedly in contact with her. As I have previously said, this was a time of hot discussion as to our future programme. Some held the opinion that the whole strength of our party should be concentrated on the terrorist struggle to overthrow the existing machinery of State by attempting the lives of the Tsar and the lesser representatives of despotism. Others contended that revolutionary propaganda ought still to be tried and carried further than hitherto; that revolutionists should work among the people, colonize the villages, and instruct the peasants in the manner adopted by the organization called "Land and Freedom." Vera Figner was one of the most strenuous supporters of the former view.

The misery and ignorance of the peasants

I remember well, how once, when our whole circle had met together at Lesnoye, a summer resort near St. Petersburg, we were arguing hotly with her as to how propaganda among the peasantry might be made to yield the most fruitful results. She had just returned from a small village on the Volga, where she had been living as a peasant for purposes of propaganda. The impressions she had received there had stirred her deeply, and she described in graphic language the fathomless misery and poverty, the hopeless ignorance of the provincial working classes. The conclusion she drew from it all was that under existing conditions there was no way of helping these people.

"Show me any such way; show me how, under present circumstances, I can serve the peasants, and I am ready to go back to the villages at once," she said. And her whole manner left no doubt of her absolute sincerity and readiness to keep her word. But her experience had been that of many others who had idealized "the people," and also their own power of stirring them; and we were none of us prepared with any definite counsel that could deter her from the new path she had determined to tread — simply because she could see no other leading to the desired end.

When I went to Odessa in the late autumn of the same year I found Vera Figner there. In conjunction with Kibaltchitch, Frolenko, Kolotkevitch, and Zlatopolsky she was busy with preparations for an attempt on the life of Alexander II, who was about to return to St. Petersburg from Livadia. The dynamite was stored in her house; she had now put aside all doubt, and devoted herself with her whole soul to terrorist activity.

Vera Figner turns to terrorist methods

She belonged to the Russian aristocracy; her grandfather had won a name for himself in the guerrilla warfare against Napoleon's invasion. Inflexible determination and tireless perseverance were her most prominent qualities; she was never contented with a single task, even the most enthralling, but would carry on work in all sorts of different directions simultaneously. While engaged in making ready for this attempt on the Tsar's life she was at the same time organizing revolutionary societies among the youth of the country, doing propaganda work in the higher ranks of society, and helping us in Odessa with a secret newspaper that we were starting for South Russia.

But Vera Figner was still only in the developing stage of her strength and capacities. She was already highly esteemed by all who came near her, winning their sympathy and confidence; yet even her greatest friends could hardly suspect the depth of character possessed by this radiantly beautiful girl. It was fully shown in 1882, when nearly all her comrades were in prison, and the few who had escaped capture had fled into foreign countries; she resolutely declined to entertain the idea of flight, though the danger of arrest menaced her at every turn. In 1883 she fell a victim to the treachery of Degaiev, and was sentenced to death; but "by favor" this was altered to lifelong penal servitude, and she was immured in the living grave of the Schlüsselburg fortress, where she still is (1902).

Her imprisonment

Finding that his cruel police system and manifold precautions against the spread of revolutionary ideas were
without avail in checking the opposition to his autocratic
system, Alexander II at last consented to summon a
deliberative assembly which his more liberal advisers
hoped would readily be transformed into a permanent
national parliament. But in March, 1881, before the
Tsar's resolution was made known to his people, he was
assassinated. The following description of this terrible
episode is taken from the memoirs of Prince Kropotkin,
mentioned above (p. 345).

334. The
assassina-
tion of Alex-
ander II

In February, 1881, Melikoff reported that a new plot had
been laid by the Revolutionary Executive Committee, but its
plan could not be discovered by any amount of searching.
Thereupon Alexander II decided that a sort of deliberative
assembly of delegates from the provinces should be called.
Always under the idea that he would share the fate of Louis XVI,
he described this gathering as an assembly of notables, like the
one convoked by Louis XVI before the National Assembly in
1789. The scheme had to be laid before the Council of State,
but then again he hesitated. It was only on the morning of
March 1 (13), 1881, after a final warning by Loris Melikoff,
that he ordered it to be brought before the council on the following Thursday. This was on Sunday, and he was asked by
Melikoff not to go out to the parade that day, there being
danger of an attempt on his life. Nevertheless he went. He
wanted to see the Grand Duchess Catherine, and to carry her
the welcome news. He is reported to have told her, "I have
determined to summon an assembly of notables." However, this
belated and half-hearted concession had not been made public,
and on his way back to the Winter Palace he was killed.

The bombs
are thrown

It is known how it happened. A bomb was thrown under his
iron-clad carriage to stop it. Several Circassians of the escort
were wounded. Rysakoff, who flung the bomb, was arrested on
the spot. Then, although the coachman of the Tsar earnestly
advised him not to get out, saying that he could drive him still

in the slightly damaged carriage, he insisted upon alighting. He felt that his military dignity required him to see the wounded Circassians, to condole with them as he had done with the wounded during the Turkish war, when a mad storming of Plevna, doomed to end in a terrible disaster, was made on the day of his fête. He approached Rysakoff and asked him something; and as he passed close by another young man, Grinevetsky, the latter threw a bomb between himself and Alexander II, so that both of them should be killed. They both lived but a few hours.

There Alexander II lay upon the snow, profusely bleeding, abandoned by every one of his followers ! All had disappeared. It was cadets, returning from the parade, who lifted the suffering Tsar from the snow and put him in a sledge, covering his shivering body with a cadet mantle and his bare head with a cadet cap. And it was one of the terrorists, Emeliánoff, with a bomb wrapped in a paper under his arm, who, at the risk of being arrested on the spot and hanged, rushed with the cadets to the help of the wounded man. Human nature is full of those contrasts. Terrorists aid the wounded Tsar

Thus ended the tragedy of Alexander II's life. People could not understand how it was possible that a Tsar who had done so much for Russia should have met his death at the hands of revolutionists. To me, who had the chance of witnessing the first reactionary steps of Alexander II, and his gradual deterioration, who had caught a glimpse of his complex personality, — that of a born autocrat whose violence was but partially mitigated by education, of a man possessed of military gallantry, but devoid of the courage of the statesman, of a man of strong passions and weak will, — it seemed that the tragedy developed with the unavoidable fatality of one of Shakespeare's dramas. Its last act was already written for me on the day when I heard him address us, the promoted officers, on June 13, 1862, immediately after he had ordered the first executions in Poland. Character of Alexander II

Here follows the letter sent by the Revolutionary Executive Committee to Alexander III, after the assassination of Alexander II.

Your Majesty: March 10, 1881

335. Letter
of the Revo-
lutionary
Committee to
Alexander III
(1881)
(condensed)   Although the Executive Committee understands fully the
grief that you must experience at this moment, it believes that
it has no right to yield to the feeling of natural delicacy which
would perhaps dictate the postponement of the following explanation to another time. There is something higher than the
most legitimate human feeling, and that is, duty to one's country, — the duty for which a citizen must sacrifice himself and
his own feelings, and even the feelings of others. In obedience
to this all-powerful duty we have decided to address you at
once, waiting for nothing, as will wait for nothing the historical
process that threatens us with rivers of blood and the most
terrible convulsions. . . .

Hanging will
not destroy
the Revo-
lution   You are aware, your Majesty, that the government of the
late Tsar could not be reproached with a lack of energy. It
hanged the innocent and the guilty, and filled prisons and
remote provinces with exiles. Scores of so-called "leaders"
were captured and hanged, and died with the courage and
tranquillity of martyrs; but the movement did not cease, — on
the contrary it grew and strengthened. The revolutionary movement, your Majesty, is not dependent upon any particular individuals; it is a process of the social organism; and the scaffolds raised for its more energetic exponents are as powerless to
save the outgrown order of things as the cross that was erected
for the Redeemer was powerless to save the ancient world from
the triumph of Christianity. The government, of course, may
yet capture and hang an immense number of separate individuals, it may break up a great number of separate revolutionary
groups; but all this will not change, in the slightest degree,
the condition of affairs. . . .

Terrorist
deeds will
increase   A dispassionate glance at the grievous decade through which
we have just passed will enable us to forecast accurately the
future progress of the revolutionary movement, provided the
policy of the government does not change. The movement will
continue to grow and extend; deeds of a terroristic nature will
increase in frequency and intensity. Meanwhile the number of
the discontented in the country will grow larger and larger;
confidence in the government, on the part of the people, will

decline; and the idea of revolution — of its possibility and in-
evitability — will establish itself in Russia more and more
firmly. A terrible explosion, a bloody chaos, a revolutionary
earthquake throughout Russia, will complete the destruction of
the old order of things. Do not mistake this for a mere phrase.
We understand better than any one else can how lamentable is
the waste of so much talent and energy — the loss, in bloody
skirmishes and in the work of destruction, of so much strength
which, under other conditions, might have been expended in
creative labor and in the development of the intelligence, the
welfare, and the civil life of the Russian people. Whence proceeds this lamentable necessity for bloody conflict?

It arises, your Majesty, from the lack in Russia of a real Cause of the
government in the true sense of that word. A government, in disturbances
the very nature of things, should only give outward form to the
aspirations of the people and effect to the people's will. But
with us — excuse the expression — the government has degenerated into a mere coterie, and deserves the name of a usurping
" gang " much more than does the Executive Committee.

Whatever may be the *intentions* of the Tsar, the *actions* of The govern-
the government have nothing in common with the popular wel- ment robs
fare or popular aspirations. The government has brought Russia the people
to such a pass that, at the present time, the masses of the
people are in a state of pauperism and ruin; are subjected to
the most humiliating surveillance, even at their own domestic
hearths; and are powerless even to regulate their own com-
munal and social affairs. The protection of the law and of
the government is enjoyed only by the extortionist and the
exploiter, and the most exasperating robbery goes unpunished.
But, on the other hand, what a terrible fate awaits the man
who sincerely considers the general good! You know very
well, your Majesty, that it is not only socialists who are exiled
and prosecuted.

These are the reasons why the Russian government exerts
no moral influence and has no support among the people.
These are the reasons why Russia brings forth so many revolutionists. These are the reasons why even such a deed as killing
a Tsar excites in the minds of a majority of the people only

gladness and sympathy. Yes, your Majesty! Do not be deceived by the reports of flatterers and sycophants; Tsaricide is popular in Russia.

Voluntary
surrender
alone will save
the Tsar from
revolution

From such a state of affairs there can be only two modes of escape: either a revolution, — absolutely inevitable and not to be averted by any punishments; or a voluntary turning of the supreme power to the people. In the interest of our native land, in the hope of preventing the useless waste of energy, in the hope of averting the terrible miseries that always accompany revolution, the Executive Committee approaches your Majesty with the advice to take the second course. Be assured, so soon as the supreme power ceases to rule arbitrarily, so soon as it firmly resolves to accede to the demands of the people's conscience and consciousness, you may, without fear, discharge the spies that disgrace the administration, send your guards back to their barracks, and burn the scaffolds that are demoralizing the people. The Executive Committee will voluntarily terminate its own existence, and the organizations formed about it will disperse, in order that their members may devote themselves to the work of promoting culture among the people of their native land.

We address your Majesty as those who have discarded all prejudices, and who have suppressed the distrust of you created by the actions of the government throughout a century. We forget that you are the representative of the authority that has so often deceived and that has so injured the people. We address you as a citizen and as an honest man. We hope that the feeling of personal exasperation will not extinguish in your mind your consciousness of your duties and your desire to know the truth. *We* also might feel exasperation. You have lost your father. We have lost not only our fathers, but our brothers, our wives, our children, and our dearest friends. We are nevertheless ready to suppress personal feeling if it be demanded by the welfare of Russia. We expect the same from you.

We set no conditions for you; do not let our proposition irritate you. The conditions that are prerequisite to a change from revolutionary activity to peaceful labor are created, not by us, but by history. These conditions are, in our opinion, two.

1. A general amnesty to cover all past political crimes; for the reason that they were not crimes but fulfillments of civil duty.

2. The summoning of representatives of the whole Russian people to examine the existing framework of social and governmental life, and to remodel it in accordance with the people's wishes.

We regard it as necessary, however, to remind you that the legalization of the supreme power, by the representatives of the people, can be valid only in case the elections are perfectly free. We declare solemnly, before the people of our native land and before the whole world, that our party will submit unconditionally to the decisions of a National Assembly elected in the manner above indicated, and that we will not allow ourselves, in future, to offer violent resistance to any government that the National Assembly may sanction.

And now, your Majesty, decide! Before you are two courses, and you are to make your choice between them. We can only trust that your intelligence and conscience may suggest to you the only decision that is compatible with the welfare of Russia, with your own dignity, and with your duty to your native land.

THE EXECUTIVE COMMITTEE

Section 95. *The Industrial Revolution in Russia*

In an elaborate work of many volumes, giving statistical accounts of the recent development of the chief industries, the Russian government summarizes the reasons for the backward economic condition of the country, and shows how the beginnings of an industrial revolution were made during the latter part of the nineteenth century. This work, translated into English for the World's Fair at Chicago, is one of the best sources available to English-speaking students on the early stages of the industrial transformation in Russia.

336. The rise
of Russian
industries
(slightly
condensed)

The Russian branch of the Slavonic peoples, occupying as colonists from immemorial times the western half of the immense plain stretching for twenty-five hundred kilometers, from the rocks of Finland to the mountains of the Caucasus, and from the Carpathians to the Urals, from necessity, from the rapidity of its natural increase, from its inclination to peaceful domestic occupations, and finally from its habit of struggling against the difficulties presented by nature, has ever been mainly occupied with agricultural pursuits.

How industry
was checked
in the Middle
Ages

Trade relations were assisted by the vast rivers and the winter sledge roads, but were long hindered by the lack of seacoast, by the extensive forests, and by the raids of the tribes of Finnish and Mongolian descent. The division [during the Middle Ages] of the country into many separate principalities, the warring of the princes, the imposition for two centuries of the Mongol yoke, the ceaseless defensive wars undertaken against the Swedes and the Teutonic knights pressing in from the northwest, against the Poles who had deprived Russia of her western and southwestern territories, and against the Tartars who attacked her from the east and southeast, — all this occupied the Russian people even in the fourteenth, fifteenth, and sixteenth centuries to such an extent that there was little possibility of beginning any lasting industrial development.

Only in the seventeenth century the Moscovite Tsars, after uniting the people and strengthening their authority with the aid of the most enterprising inhabitants of the Moscow region, were in a position to present stout resistance to the west, and, having finally broken the force of their eastern enemies, were able to begin to think about the development of Russian trade and industry.

Reforms of
Peter the
Great offset
by wars

Opening with the great reforms of Peter the Great, the eighteenth century already brings Russia into the circle of nations with a trading and industrial organization. But these efforts were opposed by the wars with the Swedes, ending with the occupation of the Baltic provinces, the wars in the south for pushing back the Turks who had succeeded in seizing the northern shores of the Black Sea and the territories of the related Slavs, and the ceaseless extension to the east, where unorganized Asiatic hordes long prevented the establishment of peace and order toward which the Russian people have ever striven, and which they attained so recently.

The beginning of the nineteenth century bears the same character in consequence of the invasion by Napoleon, the Turkish wars, and the forcible introduction of an orderly rule in the Caucasus and the Central Asiatic territories, where it was impossible to permit the constant raids upon the country and the seizure of the inhabitants by petty Asiatic rulers. At this time relations with the west began to develop principally in agricultural raw materials, the production of which visibly increased in proportion as order was established, and to such an extent that the surplus grain, hemp, flax, timber, and wool began to be sent in abundance to the markets of western Europe, and furnished grounds for regarding Russia as an exclusively agricultural country, — a view justified by the whole record of Russia's past history. *Russia regarded as exclusively agricultural*

Although the government and a few enlightened people made great efforts to establish in Russia various forms of mining and manufacturing industry, and although the rapid development of certain works and manufactories — for example, the metallurgical works in the Urals, the factories around Moscow, the beet industry near Kiev, the petroleum industry in Baku — demonstrated the existence of the conditions in Russia essential to industrial progress, nevertheless, the economic development of the empire moved very slowly. In fact, it did not keep pace with the other features in Russian advance, for example, the development of science, the advances of literature, music, and painting, the multiplication of the implements of war, and increasing demands for articles of foreign production.

The chief cause of the feebleness of the development of the home manufacturing consisted for a long time in the whole organization of Russian life, which was centered in the peasantry, which directed all its energies to agricultural production, and employed for the attainment of this object only the resources which lay immediately at hand, such as the replacement of lands exhausted by cultivation by fresh lots, homemade implements, and the felling of forests. *Peasants supply nearly all their own wants*

Habits of the rural gentry and their serfs

The rural gentry, or large landholders, having serf laborers bound to them, employed them also mainly in the cultivation of the land, and, like the peasants, strove to satisfy their wants as far as possible from their domestic resources, only having recourse to the productions of manufacturing industry as a luxury. Thus houses were built chiefly of wood from their own estates by their own carpenters, who had attained extraordinary skill in their trade. Clothing also was, in the main, woven from home-grown flax and wool or made from home furs and skins. In the matter of food the people confined themselves so strictly to their domestic resources that the preparation for winter of various preserves, beginning with salted and soured vegetables and ending with the making of confectionery and sparkling drinks, formed part of the business of every well-to-do household. This patriarchal state of domestic economy, preserved with due reverence for the old order of things here and there to this day, prevailed over the whole country, even in the middle of the present century.

Mills spring up where the patriarchal system breaks down

There was thus little chance for a demand for the products of manufacture, — a fact which till now serves as the chief explanation of the feeble development of the latter in the empire. All that there is in this respect is almost entirely new. Mills and manufactories first appeared in those places where, from the growth of the population and from the exhaustion of the soil or the want of land, the conditions permitting of the indefinite preservation of the beloved patriarchal system were disappearing. Particularly, and earlier than anywhere else, was this the case in localities situated near Moscow, where there is already a very dense population. In that province, for example, more than 2,250,000 inhabitants live upon an area of 33,300 square kilometers, or about 68 inhabitants to the square kilometer. At the same time the dwellers in the central or Moscow region of Russia have been distinguished in all respects from the earliest times by their greater enterprise, and have always been to the fore in seeking out new expedients for the permanent development and strengthening of their country.

With the increase of population in this heart of Russia, for a long time, and even to-day, the surplus has been colonizing the more distant districts of the empire, but notwithstanding this, here earlier than elsewhere, appeared the conditions necessary for the springing up of mills and manufactories requiring such labor as was not employed in agriculture. Accordingly the neighborhood of Moscow, from ancient times the center of Russia's trade relations not only with the interior but with foreign countries, especially with Asia, has become the center for the free and independent growth of many kinds of manufactories and works.

Section 96. Struggle for Liberty under Nicholas II

Among the terrible incidents of recent Russian history nothing could exceed in horror the massacres of the Jews, one of the most notorious of which occurred at Kishenef (in Bessarabia) in the spring of 1903. The following atrocious proclamation appeared in a journal— *Bessarabetz* — on the eve of the massacre, urging all faithful Christians to destroy the Jews. They are not only accused of every species of atrocity, just as they were in the Middle Ages in western Europe, but are declared to be the real fomenters of all revolutionary disturbances which they are promoting in their own interests.

Fellow-Christians:

Our great festival of the Resurrection of Christ draws near. It is many years since, put to death by the Jews, Our Lord expiated by his blood our sins and those of all the world, pouring out in his mercy his holy blood for the salvation of all the nations of the earth, of us Christians as well as the adherents of other religions.

337. A proclamation inciting a massacre of the Jews, Easter, 1903

But the vile Jews are not content with having shed the blood of our Savior, whom they crucified, and who suffered for them. Every year they shed the innocent blood of Christians. They shed it and use it in their religious rites.

You have doubtless been told that at Dubossari they crucified a Christian youth, whose blood they offered in sacrifice.

The story is quite correct. The authorities know it too, though they do not breathe a word in order not to excite our anger against these miserable, bloodthirsty men who should have been driven out of our country long ago. A similar case has just occurred at Kief, where they bled to death an innocent child and afterwards threw its body into the street.

At the present moment, whilst we are preparing to celebrate the Passion of our Lord, they are drinking Christian blood among themselves. Brothers, we are overcome with horror when we think of the number of Christian souls lost through them for many years.

They aspire to seize our beloved Russia. They issue proclamations in order to incite the people against the authorities, even against our Little Father, the Tsar, who knows them for a cowardly, vile, rapacious people, and will not give them liberty. They try, therefore, to provoke disturbances by which they hope to obtain more liberties for themselves. Now, if liberty is granted to the Jew, he will speedily become master of Holy Russia, lay his greedy hands on everything, and there will no longer be a Russia, but only a Jewry left.

Brothers, in the name of our Savior who gave his blood for us, in the name of our very pious Little Father, the Tsar, who watches over the wants of his people, and alleviates their lot by generous manifestoes, let us join on Easter Day in the cry, " Down with the Jews ! " Let us massacre these sanguinary monsters who slake their thirst with Russian blood !

Act in such a manner that they will remember the *pogrom* [i.e. massacre] of Odessa, where the troops themselves assisted the people. This time they will again aid us, inspired as they are, like ourselves, with the love of Christ.

Brothers, lend us your aid. Let us massacre these vile Jews. We are already numerous.

THE PARTY OF THE WORKINGMEN
WHO ARE TRUE CHRISTIANS

P. S. Make your visitors read this, or else your establishment will be sacked. We shall be kept informed of this by those of us who go amongst you.

The correspondent of the London *Times* sent the following account (here much condensed) to London of the occurrences on Bloody Sunday, January 22, 1905.

A more perfect and lovely day never dawned. The air was crisp and the sky almost cloudless. The gilded domes of the cathedrals and churches, brilliantly illuminated by the sun, formed a superb panorama. I noticed a significant change in the bearing of the passers-by. They were all wending their way, singly or in small groups, in the direction of the Winter Palace. Joining in the stream of workingmen, I proceeded in the direction of the Winter Palace. No observer could help being struck by the look of sullen determination on every face. Already a crowd of many thousands had collected, but was prevented from entering the square by mounted troops drawn up across the thoroughfare. Presently the masses began to press forward threateningly. The cavalry advanced at a walking pace, scattering the people right and left.

Event has succeeded event with such bewildering rapidity that the public is staggered and shocked beyond measure. The first trouble began at 11 o'clock, when the military tried to turn back some thousands of strikers at one of the bridges. The same thing happened almost simultaneously at other bridges, where the constant flow of workmen pressing forward refused to be denied access to the common rendezvous in the Palace Square. The Cossacks at first used their knouts, then the flat of their sabers, and finally they fired. The strikers in the front ranks fell on their knees and implored the Cossacks to let them pass, protesting that they had no hostile intentions. They refused, however, to be intimidated by blank cartridges, and orders were given to load with ball.

The passions of the mob broke loose like a bursting dam. The people, seeing the dead and dying carried away in all directions, the snow on the streets and pavements soaked with blood, cried aloud for vengeance. Meanwhile the situation at the Palace was becoming momentarily worse. The troops were reported to be unable to control the vast masses which were constantly surging forward. Reënforcements were sent,

338. Accounts of Bloody Sunday, January 22, 1905, by eye-witnesses

and at 2 o'clock here also the order was given to fire. Men, women, and children fell at each volley, and were carried away in ambulances, sledges, and carts. The indignation and fury of every class were aroused. Students, merchants, all classes of the population alike were inflamed. At the moment of writing, firing is going on in every quarter of the city.

Father Gapon wounded

Father Gapon, marching at the head of a large body of workmen, carrying a cross and other religious emblems, was wounded in the arm and shoulder. The two forces of work-men are now separated. Those on the other side of the river are arming with swords, knives, and smiths' and carpenters' tools, and are busy erecting barricades. The troops are apparently reckless, firing right and left, with or without reason. The rioters continue to appeal to them, saying, " You are Russians ! Why play the part of bloodthirsty butchers? "

Dreadful anxiety prevails in every household where any members are absent. Distracted husbands, fathers, wives, and children are searching for those missing. The surgeons and Red Cross ambulances are busy. A night of terror is in prospect.

Still more horribly detailed is the account of the massacre telegraphed to the Paris newspaper, *Le Matin,* by its correspondent.

Report of a French news-paper corre-spondent

The soldiers of the Preobrazhensky regiment, without any summons to disperse, shoot down the unfortunate people as if they were playing at bloodshed. Several hundred fall; more than a hundred and fifty are killed. They are almost all children, women, and young people. It is terrible. Blood flows on all sides. At 5 o'clock the crowd is driven back, cut down and repelled on all sides. The people, terror-stricken, fly in every direction. Scared women and children slip, fall, rise to their feet, only to fall again farther on. At this moment a sharp word of command is heard and the victims fall *en masse.* There had been no disturbances to speak of. The whole crowd is unarmed and has not uttered a single threat.

As I proceeded, there were everywhere troops and Cossacks. Successive discharges of musketry shoot down on all sides the terrorized mob. The soldiers aim at the people's heads and the victims are frightfully disfigured. A woman falls almost at my side. A little farther on I slip on a piece of human brain. Before me is a child of eight years whose face is no longer human. Its mother is kneeling in tears over its corpse. The wounded, as they drag themselves along, leave streams of blood on the snow.

The terrible struggle between the Russian people and their government, combined with the reverses of the war with Japan, finally led the Tsar, whose empire appeared to be on the point of collapsing, to issue a manifesto in August, 1905, summoning a representative assembly which should participate with him thereafter in the government.

339. The manifesto calling the first Duma (August, 1905) (slightly condensed)

The empire of Russia is formed and strengthened by the indestructible union of the Tsar with the people and the people with the Tsar. This concord and union of the Tsar and the people is the great moral force which has created Russia in the course of centuries by protecting her from all misfortunes and all attacks, and has constituted up to the present time a pledge of unity, independence, integrity, material well-being, and intellectual development in the present and in the future.

The Duma to be formed as a consultative body

In our manifesto of February 26, 1903, we summoned all faithful sons of the fatherland in order to perfect, through mutual understanding, the organization of the State, founding it securely on public order and private welfare. We devoted ourselves to the task of coördinating local elective bodies [*zemstvos*] with the central authorities, and removing the disagreements existing between them, which so disturbed the normal course of the national life. Autocratic Tsars, our ancestors, have had this aim constantly in view, and the time has now come to follow out their good intentions and to summon elected representatives from the whole of Russia to take a constant and active part in the elaboration of laws, adding for this purpose to the higher State institutions a special consultative body intrusted with the preliminary elaboration and discussion of measures and with the examination of the State Budget. It is for this reason that, while preserving the fundamental law regarding autocratic power, we have deemed it well to form a *Gosoudarstvennaia Duma* (i.e. State Council) and to approve regulations for elections to this Duma, extending these laws to the whole territory of the empire, with such exceptions only as may be considered necessary in the case of some regions in which special conditions obtain. . . .

Arrangements for elections

We have ordered the Minister of the Interior to submit immediately for our approbation regulations for elections to the Duma, so that deputies from fifty governments, and the military province of the Don, may be able to assemble not later than the middle of January, 1906. We reserve to ourselves exclusively the care of perfecting the organization of the *Gosoudarstvennaia Duma*, and when the course of events has demonstrated the necessity of changes corresponding to the needs of the times and the welfare of the empire, we shall not fail to give the matter our attention at the proper moment.

The Duma to coöperate with existing powers

We are convinced that those who are elected by the confidence of the whole people, and who are called upon to take part in the legislative work of the government, will show themselves in the eyes of all Russia worthy of the imperial trust in virtue of which they have been invited to coöperate in this great work ; and that in perfect harmony with the other institutions and authorities of the State, established by us, they will contribute profitably and zealously to our labors for the well-being of our common mother, Russia, and for the strengthening of the unity, security, and greatness of the empire, as well as for the tranquillity and prosperity of the people.

In invoking the blessing of the Lord on the labors of the new assembly which we are establishing, and with unshakable confidence in the grace of God and in the assurance of the great historical destinies reserved by Divine Providence for our beloved fatherland, we firmly hope that Russia, with the help of God Almighty, and with the combined efforts of all her sons, will emerge triumphant from the trying ordeals through which she is now passing, and will renew her strength in the greatness and glory of her history extending over a thousand years.

Given at Peterhof on the nineteenth day of August, in the year of grace 1905, and the eleventh year of our reign.

NICHOLAS

The Duma was solemnly opened on May 10, 1906, but owing to the large number of revolutionary and radical representatives which it contained, it was unable to come to any amicable arrangements with the Tsar, and immediately began to devote its attention to the consideration of innumerable liberal reforms. The Tsar soon got out of patience with his new assembly, and on July 21, 1906, issued the following manifesto, dissolving the Duma and promising at the same time to call a new assembly.

We summoned the representatives of the nation by our will to the work of productive legislation. Confiding firmly in divine clemency and believing in the great and brilliant future of our people, we confidently anticipated benefits for the country from their labors. We proposed great reforms in all departments of the national life. We have always devoted our greatest care to the removal of the ignorance of the people by the light of instruction, and to the removal of their burdens by improving the conditions of agricultural work.

340. The dissolution of the first Duma (July, 1906)

A cruel disappointment has befallen our expectations. The representatives of the nation, instead of applying themselves to the work of productive legislation, have strayed into spheres beyond their competence, and have been making inquiries into the acts of local authorities established by ourselves, and have been making comments upon the imperfections of the fundamental laws, which can only be modified by our imperial will. In short, the representatives of the nation have undertaken really illegal acts, such as the appeal by the Duma to the nation.

The representatives have meddled in affairs reserved for the Tsar

Good order
necessary to
reforms

The peasants, disturbed by such anomalies, and seeing no hope of the amelioration of their lot, have resorted in a number of districts to open pillage and the destruction of other people's property, and to disobedience of the law and of the legal authorities. But our subjects ought to remember that an improvement in the lot of the people is only possible under conditions of perfect order and tranquillity. We shall not permit arbitrary or illegal acts, and we shall impose our imperial will on the disobedient by all the power of the State.

An appeal to
the people to
maintain
order

We appeal to all well-disposed Russians to combine for the maintenance of legal authority and the restoration of peace in our dear fatherland. May calm be reëstablished once more in Russia, and may God help us to accomplish the chiefest of our tasks, the improvement of the lot of the peasant. Our will on this point is unalterable. The Russian husbandman, in case his land is too small to maintain him, shall be supplied, without prejudice to the property of others, with legitimate and honest means for enlarging his holdings. The representatives of the other classes will, at our request, devote all their efforts to the promotion of this great undertaking which will be given a definitely legal form by a future Duma.

A new Duma
promised

In dissolving the Duma we confirm our immutable intention of maintaining this institution, and in conformity with this intention we fix March 5, 1907, as the date of the convocation of a new Duma by a ukase addressed to the Senate. With unshakable faith in divine clemency and in the good sense of the Russian people, we shall expect from the new Duma the realization of our efforts and their promotion of legislation in accordance with the requirements of a regenerated Russia.

Faithful sons of Russia, your Tsar calls upon you as a father upon his children to unite with him for the regeneration of our holy fatherland. We believe that giants in thought and action will appear, and that, thanks to their assiduous efforts, the glory of Russia will continue to shine.

NICHOLAS

The following extracts from the Russian imperial constitution promulgated April 23, 1906, show that the Tsar, while retaining his title of "Autocrat of all the Russias," has granted a constitution resembling in its form and provisions those of western Europe, establishing a legislature consisting of two houses and guaranteeing the ordinary rights of citizens, including freedom from arbitrary imprisonment, religious liberty, and freedom of the press. Although these provisions have been frequently violated by himself and his officials during the last two years, their actual observance would serve to introduce constitutional government into Russia.

341. Extracts from the Russian Constitution of April 23, 1906

ART. 4. The supreme autocratic power is vested in the Tsar of all the Russias. It is God's command that his authority should be obeyed not only through fear but for conscience' sake.

The autocratic powers of the Tsar

ART. 5. The person of the Tsar is sacred and inviolable.

ART. 7. The Tsar exercises the legislative power in conjunction with the Council of the Empire and the imperial Duma.

ART. 8. The initiative in all branches of legislation belongs to the Tsar. Solely on his initiative may the fundamental laws of the empire be subjected to a revision in the Council of the Empire and the imperial Duma.

ART. 9. The Tsar approves the laws, and without his approval no law can come into existence.

ART. 10. All governmental powers in their widest extent throughout the whole Russian empire are vested in the Tsar. . . .

ART. 17. The Tsar appoints and dismisses the president of the council, the ministers themselves, and the heads of the chief departments of administration, as well as all other officials where the law does not provide for another method of appointment and dismissal.

ART. 25. The imperial throne of all the Russias is hereditary in the present beneficent ruling imperial house.

ART. 59. The full title of His Imperial Majesty is as follows : We, ———— by the grace of God, Emperor and Autocrat of all the Russias, of Moscow, Kiev, Vladimir, Novgorod, Tsar of Kasan, Tsar of Astrakhan, Tsar of Poland, Tsar of Siberia, Tsar of Tauric Khersones, Tsar of Grusia, Lord of Pskov, and Grand

Full title of the Tsar

Duke of Smolensk, Lithuania, Volhynia, Podolia, and Finland, Prince of Esthonia, Livonia, Courland and Semgallia, Samogitia, Bielostok, Korelia, Tver, Jugor, Perm, Vyatka, Bulgaria, and other territories; Lord and Grand Duke of Novgorod, Chernigov; Ruler of Ryazan, Polotsk, Rostov, Jaroslav, Bieloöero, Udoria, Obdoria, Kondia, Vitebsk, Mstislav, and all northern territories; Ruler of Iveria, Kartalinia, and the Kabardinian lands and Armenian territories; hereditary Ruler and Lord of the Tcherkess and Mountain Princes and others; Lord of Turkestan, Heir to the throne of Norway, Duke of Schleswig-Holstein, Stormarn, Ditmarsch, Oldenburg, and so forth, and so forth, and so forth.

Religion   ART. 62. The established and ruling faith of the Russian Empire is the Christian, Orthodox Catholic, Eastern faith.

ART. 63. The Tsar who sits upon the throne of all the Russias may confess none but the orthodox faith.

ART. 64. The Tsar as Christian ruler is the supreme defender and upholder of the doctrines of the ruling faith, the protector of the true belief, and of every ordinance in the holy Church.

ART. 65. In the administration of the Church the autocratic power acts through the Holy Directorial Synod, which it has created.

ART. 66. All those subjects of the Russian State who do not belong to the ruling Church, natives as well as the inhabitants of annexed districts, foreigners in the Russian service, or temporary sojourners in Russia, enjoy the free exercise of their respective faiths and religious services according to their particular usages.

ART. 67. Religious freedom is granted not only to Christians of foreign faiths, but to Jews, Mohammedans, and heathen. May all the people residing in Russia praise God Almighty in their various tongues according to the law and faith of their forefathers, while they glorify the rule of the Russian monarch and pray to the Creator of the Universe for an increase of the public welfare and a strengthening of the power of the Tsar.

ART. 70. The defense of the throne and of the fatherland is the sacred duty of every Russian subject. The male population, without distinction of class, is subject to military service according to the provisions of the law.

ART. 71. Russian subjects are in duty bound to pay the imposts and taxes legally imposed, and to fulfill all additional obligations according to the provisions of the law.

ART. 72. No one can be prosecuted for an offense except according to the process established by law.

ART. 73. No one shall be arrested except in the cases determined by law.

ART. 74. No one shall be brought into court or punished for an offense which was not a crime according to the law when committed.

ART. 75. The dwelling of every one is inviolable.

ART. 76. Every Russian subject is entitled freely to choose his residence and occupation.

ART. 77. Property is inviolable. Property shall be taken only for public use and after just compensation.

ART. 78. Russian subjects are entitled to meet peaceably and without arms for such purposes as are not contrary to law.

ART. 79. Within the limits fixed by law every one may express his thoughts by word or writing and circulate them by means of the press or otherwise.

ART. 84. The Russian Empire shall be governed by laws passed according to a fixed and regular proceeding.

ART. 86. No new law shall go into force without the sanction of both the Council of the Empire and the Duma and the ratification of the Tsar.

ART. 98. The Council of the Empire and the Duma shall be convoked annually by imperial decree.

ART. 99. The length of the annual sessions of the Council of the Empire and the Duma, and the limits of the recesses during the year, shall be determined by imperial decrees.

ART. 100. The Council of the Empire shall be composed of persons appointed by his Majesty the Tsar, and elected persons. . . .

ART. 101. The Duma shall be composed of members chosen by the inhabitants of the Russian Empire for five years, according to regulations established by law.

CHAPTER XXIX

TURKEY AND THE EASTERN QUESTION

Section 97. The Greek War of Independence

It was in the latter half of the seventeenth century that the Turks made their last serious invasion into central Europe. In 1683 the grand vizier, Kara-Moustafa, determined to march straight upon Vienna, to which he laid siege with an immense army. The town was upon the point of falling into the enemy's hands, when the king of Poland, John Sobieski, accompanied by some of the German princes, arrived. In the following letter, dated September 13, Sobieski describes to his wife the memorable defeat of the Turks, which was the beginning of their rapid expulsion from their western conquests.

342. How Sobieski defeated the Turks before Vienna (1683) Praised be our Lord God forever for granting our nation such a victory and such glory as was never heard of in all times past! The whole camp of the enemy, with their artillery and untold treasure, has fallen into our hands. They are now retreating in great confusion, and the approaches to the town, the camp, and the open fields are covered with their corpses.

The camels and other beasts of burden, the cattle, and the sheep belonging to the enemy were captured to-day by our troops and the captive Turkish shepherds driven off. . . .

What the Turks lost in powder and ammunition alone is worth a million. Some of our camp followers foolishly set off the powder in several places, and it made a fearful noise, but there was no further harm done. The grand vizier lost all his rich treasure and barely escaped, on horseback, with nothing but the coat on his back, and I have become his heir and successor.

It all came about in this way. Having forced my way into the enemy's camp, I was pressing forward in pursuit of the vizier when one of his chamberlains surrendered to me and afterwards showed me his leader's tent, which was so large it might have contained within its circumference the city of Warsaw or of Lemberg. The standard that the grand vizier always had carried before him with great ceremony fell into my hands, along with the Mohammedan banner presented to him by the Sultan for this campaign, which I have sent by post to his Apostolic Holiness in Rome. There are quantities of the most beautiful gold-mounted sabers and other rare Turkish accouterments to be seen in our army.

The coming on of night prevented us from continuing the pursuit. It cannot be denied that they defended themselves bravely, especially the companies of janizaries who guarded the approaches to the camp and so bore the brunt of the battle. The daring and courage of these people were such that while part of them fought with us in the field the rest undertook to storm the fortifications, which with their great numbers they were well prepared to do.

The Turks fought valiantly

I estimate the number of the besieging army at three hundred thousand, not counting the Tartars; others believe there were three hundred thousand tents and reckon three men to a tent; but that would make the number too great to be believed. However, there must have been at least one hundred thousand tents, and from these the conquerors take away what they like. The townspeople, too, are rushing out to get their share. I believe that it will take them a week to gather in all the booty.

A number of Austrian people — women folk especially — whom the Turkish army had taken captive, but could not carry away with them in their hasty flight, they cut down with their sabers; but many of them can be healed of their wounds.

This morning I went into the town and found that it could not have held out five days longer. Never have the eyes of men beheld so great damage done in so brief a time; great masses of stone and rock have been broken up and tossed about in heaps by the enemy's mines, and the imperial castle is riddled with holes and ruined by their cannon balls. . . .

Sobieski greeted as the savior of Vienna

The governor of Vienna, accompanied by a great crowd of people of both high and low degree, came out to greet me, all kissing and petting me and calling me their savior. Later I visited two churches, where again I found crowds of people who tried to kiss my hands, and even my feet and clothing; most of them had to content themselves with touching my coat. All around one heard them crying, " Let us through to kiss the valorous hand ! "

There is a huge pile of captured flags and tents; in short, the enemy has departed with nothing whatever but his life. Let Christendom rejoice and thank the Lord our God that he has not permitted the heathen to hold us up to scorn and derision and to ask, " Where, now, is your God ? "

It was apparent to the statesmen who refashioned the map of Europe at the Congress of Vienna that the power of the Sultan over his European dominions was steadily declining, and they had grave apprehensions of the serious troubles which were bound to arise in those regions. Within two years the Servians, who had long been in revolt against the Turks, secured their practical independence by establishing themselves as a tributary principality, and in 1821 the Greeks began an insurrection in Morea. On January 27, 1822, the Greek National Assembly issued the following proclamation of independence.

343. Proclamation of independence issued by the Greek National Assembly (January 27, 1822)

We, descendants of the wise and noble peoples of Hellas, we who are the contemporaries of the enlightened and civilized nations of Europe, we who behold the advantages which they enjoy under the protection of the impenetrable ægis of the law, find it no longer possible to suffer without cowardice and self-contempt the cruel yoke of the Ottoman power which has weighed upon us for more than four centuries, — a power which does not listen to reason and knows no other law than its own will, which orders and disposes everything despotically and according to its caprice. After this prolonged slavery we have determined to take arms to avenge ourselves and our country against a frightful tyranny, iniquitous in its very essence, — an unexampled despotism to which no other rule can be compared.

The war which we are carrying on against the Turk is not that of a faction or the result of sedition. It is not aimed at the advantage of any single part of the Greek people; it is a national war, a holy war, a war the object of which is to reconquer the rights of individual liberty, of property and honor, — rights which the civilized people of Europe, our neighbors, enjoy to-day; rights of which the cruel and unheard-of tyranny of the Ottomans would deprive us, — us alone, — and the very memory of which they would stifle in our hearts. *The war is a holy war*

Are we, then, less reasonable than other peoples, that we remain deprived of these rights? Are we of a nature so degraded and abject that we should be viewed as unworthy to enjoy them, condemned to remain crushed under a perpetual slavery and subjected, like beasts of burden or mere automatons, to the absurd caprice of a cruel tyrant who, like an infamous brigand, has come from distant regions to invade our borders? Nature has deeply graven these rights in the hearts of all men; laws in harmony with nature have so completely consecrated them that neither three nor four centuries — nor thousands nor millions of centuries — can destroy them. Force and violence have been able to restrict and paralyze them for a season, but force may once more resuscitate them in all the vigor which they formerly enjoyed during many centuries; nor have we ever ceased in Hellas to defend these rights by arms whenever opportunity offered.

Building upon the foundation of our natural rights, and desiring to assimilate ourselves to the rest of the Christians of Europe, our brethren, we have begun a war against the Turks, or rather, uniting all our isolated strength, we have formed ourselves into a single armed body, firmly resolved to attain our end, to govern ourselves by wise laws, or to be altogether annihilated, believing it to be unworthy of us, as *Liberty or death* descendants of the glorious peoples of Hellas, to live henceforth in a state of slavery fitted rather for unreasoning animals than for rational beings.

Victories in
spite of
obstacles

Ten months have elapsed since we began this national war; the all-powerful God has succored us; although we were not adequately prepared for so great an enterprise, our arms have everywhere been victorious, despite the powerful obstacles which we have encountered and still encounter everywhere. We have had to contend with a situation bristling with difficulties, and we are still engaged in our efforts to overcome them. It should not therefore appear astonishing that we were not able from the very first to proclaim our independence and take rank among the civilized peoples of the earth, marching forward side by side with them. It was impossible to occupy ourselves with our political existence before we had established our independence. We trust these reasons may justify, in the eyes of the nations, our delay, as well as console us for the anarchy in which we have found ourselves. . . .

EPIDAURUS, January $\frac{15}{27}$, 1822:
the First Year of Independence

344. Letter of
Lord Byron
on the mod-
ern Greeks
(somewhat
condensed)

The appeal of the revolutionists in the name of ancient Greece to the nations of western Europe met with immediate response. Meetings were held everywhere on behalf of the Greek cause; great sums of money were raised; thousands of soldiers and private citizens volunteered to aid the Greeks in winning their independence. However, the Europeans who went to Greece found that the revolutionists were not the ideal Greeks of the age of Pericles, and Lord Byron, who gave his life to their cause, in a letter written two years after the Declaration of Independence, thus describes the situation.

February 26, 1824

The present state of Greece is perhaps different from what has been represented both by friends and enemies. The foreigners in Greece have, with few exceptions, never been in the country before, and of those exceptions still fewer have visited these regions before the revolution. Those who have will be rather surprised that the disorganization is not still greater, although in any other country it would appear unbounded.

The Greeks have been downright slaves for five centuries, and there is no tyrant like a slave. Men whose fathers' fathers, farther than they can reckon, were absolute vileins, without property, even of their own persons, still move as if they were in fetters, or, in many instances, may seem only to have exchanged the chains of the prisoner for the freedom of the jailer. This is a hard truth; but we fear that it is one. We are not here to flatter, but to aid, as far as in our power, to a better order of things.

The number of pamphlets which have been published in Europe on the subject of the Greek contest has, of course, been sufficient. The narratives of travelers, military and civil, may not have been less numerous. Without entering into their merits or demerits, *one* thing it is essential to remark, namely, that hitherto *no* stranger has succeeded in Greece, either in doing much for the natives or for himself. French, Germans, Italians, English, Poles; men of all nations, ages, and conditions; military and naval, rich and poor, good and evil, speculative and practical; merchants, officers, tars, generals, German barons and bankers, English gentlemen and adventurers, and surely some men of talent and good intention amongst them, — have in the course of the last three years run the gantlet of Greece, and, of the survivors of fever, famine, fatigue, and the sword, the greater part of those who have not gone back in disgust remain in misery.

Discouraging circumstances in Greece

Owing to the general anarchy that prevailed in southeastern Europe as the result of the Greek insurrection, the great powers — England, France, and Russia — decided to intervene, and at length forced the Sultan to recognize the independence of Greece under Prince Otto of Bavaria, whom they selected as a king for the new State. In 1832 the powers announced to Greece, in the following proclamation, the selection of the new sovereign, and bade the Greeks receive him with affection.

Greeks :

345. Declaration of the courts of France, Great Britain, and Russia (1832) recognizing the independence of the kingdom of Greece

Your new destinies are about to be fulfilled ! The courts of France, Great Britain, and Russia have decided upon the choice of a sovereign, whose election the Greek nation had committed to their charge. Their coöperation, equally active and disinterested, had contributed to the independence of Greece. By the choice which they have now made, that independence will be consolidated under the scepter of Prince Otto of Bavaria. Greece is raised to the dignity of a kingdom, and obtains the alliance of one of the most ancient and illustrious of the royal houses of Europe,—one which has supported Greece in her struggles, assisted her in her misfortunes, and encouraged her in her regeneration.

The king of Greece will hasten, in person, to bind himself to the nation by the most sacred ties. He brings with him the best-founded hopes for territorial boundaries of increased extent and security, of great financial resources, every means of attaining gradually a high degree of civilization, all the elements of an enlightened administration, of a good military organization, and, consequently, every pledge for the peace and happiness of his new country. The three courts are persuaded that they would mistake the character of the Greek nation, if they could doubt the sentiments which the nation will, with one voice, proclaim on this event.

Greeks, indulge these feelings with confidence ! Encircle your new sovereign with gratitude and affection. Faithful subjects ! rally round his throne ; aid him with true devotion in the work of giving to the State a definitive constitution, and of securing to it the double blessing of peace abroad, of tranquillity, the observance of the laws, and of order, at home. This is the only recompense which the three courts require of you for the services which they have had the means of rendering to you.   (Signed)   TALLEYRAND
                                                                    PALMERSTON
                                                                    LIEVEN, MATUSZEWIC

Section 98. The Crimean War

From the days of Peter the Great the rulers of Russia have looked with longing eyes upon the dominions of the Sultan which lay on the west shore of the Black Sea, and from time to time they have gained territory at his expense. After the settlement of the Grecian question in 1832, Tsar Nicholas I hinted to England that the time had come for a partition of European Turkey. But England opposed any expansion of Russia to the south, and in 1853, when the Tsar, under the color of protecting Christians in Turkey, began to interfere in Turkish affairs, she opened negotiations with France with a view of resisting Russia's policy. The situation, as it appeared to the English prime minister, Lord Palmerston, is revealed in the following letter:

My dear Sidney Herbert,　　BALMORAL, September 21, 1853

The question between Russia and Turkey seems, as you say, to be in an unsatisfactory and unpromising state, and yet it lies in a nutshell, and its solution depends upon honest intentions and plain dealing on the part of Russia. What is it the emperor [of Russia] wants? Why will he not plainly tell us what it is? Does he want merely what all of us want, namely, that the Christians in the Turkish Empire shall be safe from oppression, vexation, and injury? If that is what he wants, let him begin by setting himself the example, and let him, by evacuating the Principalities,[1] relieve the Christian inhabitants of that part of the Turkish Empire from the complicated and various miseries which the occupation of their country by a Russian army inflicts upon them. Beyond that, let him be satisfied, as we all are, with the progressively liberal system of Turkey, and let him keep his remonstrances till some case or occasion arises which calls for them.

346. Lord Palmerston on the relations of Russia and England in respect to the Turkish question (condensed)

[1] The so-called Danubian Provinces, Moldavia and Wallachia, which now form Roumania.

The Tsar himself encourages persecution

At present he has not been able even to allege any oppression of the Christians, except that which he himself practices in the Principalities. I believe the real fact at the bottom of all these unintelligible pretenses is, that what he really wants is that the Sultan should not, by liberal measures and progressive improvement, interfere with the arbitrary and tyrannical powers which the Greek clergy now too often exercise, whether by right or by assumption, to the cruel oppression of the Greek communities. But if the emperor wants no more than what I have said, he ought to be satisfied with the declarations which the Sultan is ready to make.

Let the Tsar say frankly what he wants

If, on the other hand, the emperor wants to become acknowledged protector of the Greek subjects of the Sultan, and to be allowed to interfere between the Sultan and the Sultan's subjects, why, then I say let him manfully avow this pretension, and let us manfully assist Turkey in manfully resisting it, and let the fortune of war decide between the emperor's wrongs and the Sultan's rightful cause. I believe that what I have last stated is what the emperor really means and wants, and therefore I am coming reluctantly to the conclusion that war between him and Turkey is becoming inevitable. If such war shall happen, upon his head be the responsibility of the consequences.

Christians in Turkey may well dread Russian rule

I by no means think with you that he will have an easy victory over the Turks. On the contrary, if the betting is not even, I would lay the odds on the Turks. . . . The fact is, that the Christian subjects in Turkey know too well what a Russian régime is, not to be aware that it is of all things the most to be dreaded, and the oftener Russian troops enter Turkish territory the stronger this conviction is impressed upon the people ; Russia ought not to forget that she has weak points, — Poland, Circassia, Georgia. My wish is that England should be on friendly terms with Russia ; it is desirable that this should be, for the sake of both countries and for the sake of Europe. Neither country would gain anything by war with the other.

Brunnow has often said to me that, however different the internal organization of England and Russia, and however opposite their respective views as to the theory of government, they have, nevertheless, so many great interests in common that there is nothing to prevent them from working well together *so long as no difference arises between them in regard to the affairs of Turkey or of Persia*. Brunnow is a *wise* man, but matters seem to have been lately managed at Petersburg by men who are *otherwise*. . . . Yours sincerely,

PALMERSTON

Nicholas I, finding that he could hope to gain his ends in no other way, invaded Turkish territory. Thereupon England and France came to the Sultan's assistance and declared war on the Tsar in 1854. In the autumn of that year English and French troops landed in the Crimea, and after the battles of Alma, Balaklava, and Inkermann they concentrated their efforts upon the capture of the great fortress of Sebastopol. This was defended by two powerful batteries, the Malakoff and the Redan. After a long bombardment it was arranged that on September 8 the French should attack the Malakoff and the English the Redan. The former were so successful that the Russians blew up their magazines and evacuated the city. The English attack on the Redan had however failed, after a terrible loss of men. A celebrated war correspondent, Mr. Russell, gives the following picture of these awful September days.

On the 9th September Sebastopol was in flames ! The fleet, the object of so much diplomatic controversy, and of so many bloody struggles, had disappeared in the deep ! One more great act of carnage was added to the tremendous but glorious tragedy, of which the whole world, from the most civilized nations down to the most barbarous hordes of the East, was the anxious and excited audience.

347. Scenes in the storming of Sebastopol (much condensed)

Amid shouts of victory and cries of despair — in frantic rejoicing and passionate sorrow — a pall of black smoke, streaked by the fiery flashings of exploding fortresses, descended upon the stage, on which had been depicted so many varied traits of human misery and of human greatness, such high endurance and calm courage, such littleness and weakness.

A dull, strange silence, broken at distant intervals by the crash of citadels and palaces as they were blown into dust, succeeded to the incessant dialogue of the cannon which had spoken so loudly and so angrily throughout an entire year. Tired armies, separated from each other by a sea of fires, rested on their arms, and gazed with varied emotions on all that remained of the object of their conflict.

The bom-
bardment
The last and decisive cannonade had been commenced on the morning of Wednesday, September 5, by the French; it was continued with great vigor and effect, and was followed at night by a devastating bombardment, in which all the allied batteries joined. On the morning of the 6th the English and French together opened the cannonade, beneath which the Russian batteries were almost broken to pieces, and to which they could not answer. In the evening the bombardment was renewed, and kept up all night; a fire appeared behind the Redan, and the enemy seemed, by their constant signaling, to be in much uneasiness. On the 7th the cannonade was continued in salvos, as before, and it was remarked that the town began to present, in a most unmistakable manner, traces of the terrible effects of the nightly bombardment. Nearly every house within range was split or in ruins. The bridge between the north and south side was much crowded all day with men and carts passing to and fro, and large convoys were seen leaving the town.

In the middle of the day there was a council of the allied generals, and at two o'clock it became generally known that the allies would assault the place at noon on the 8th, after a vigorous cannonade and bombardment. The hour was well selected, as it had been ascertained that the Russians were accustomed to indulge in a siesta about that time.

The weather changed suddenly on the 7th September, and on the morning of the 8th it became bitterly cold. A biting wind right from the north side of Sebastopol blew intolerable clouds of harsh dust into our faces. The sun was obscured, and the sky became of a leaden, wintry gray.

The French were reënforced by five thousand Sardinians, The French attack the Malakoff who marched up from the Tchernaya. It was arranged that the French should attack the Malakoff at noon, and, as soon as their attack succeeded, we were to assault the Redan. At five minutes before twelve o'clock, the French, like a swarm of bees, issued forth from their trenches close to the Malakoff, scrambled up its face, and were through the embrasures in the twinkling of an eye. They crossed the seven meters of ground which separated them from the enemy at a few bounds; they drifted as lightly and quickly as autumn leaves before the wind, battalion after battalion, into the embrasures, and in a minute or two after the head of their column issued from the ditch the tricolor was floating over the Korniloff Bastion. The musketry was very feeble at first, — indeed, our allies took the Russians by surprise, and very few of the latter were in the Malakoff; but they soon recovered themselves, and from twelve o'clock till past seven in the evening the French had to meet and repulse the repeated attempts of the enemy to regain the work, when, weary of the fearful slaughter of his men, who lay in thousands over the exterior of the works, and despairing of success, the Muscovite general withdrew his exhausted legions, and prepared, with admirable skill, to evacuate the place.

As the alarm of the English assault on the Redan circulated, The English assault the Redan the enemy came rushing up from the barracks in the rear of the Redan, increasing the force and intensity of their fire, while our soldiers dropped fast. The Russians were encouraged to maintain their ground by the immobility of our soldiers and the weakness of a fusillade, from the effects of which the enemy were well protected. In vain the officers, by voice and act, by example and daring valor, tried to urge our soldiers on to clear the works. The men, most of whom belonged to regiments which had suffered in the trenches and were acquainted with the traditions of June 18, had an impression that the Redan was extensively mined, and that if they advanced they would all be blown up; yet, to their honor be it recorded, many of them acted as became the men of Alma and Inkermann, and, rushing confusedly to the front, were swept down by the enemy's fire.

A bloody hand-to-hand combat

Every moment our men were diminishing in numbers, while the Russians were arriving in swarms from the town, and rushing down from the Malakoff, which had been occupied by the French. The struggle that ensued was short, desperate, and bloody. Our soldiers, taken at every disadvantage, met the enemy with the bayonet too, and isolated combats occurred, in which the brave fellows who stood their ground had to defend themselves against three or four adversaries at once. In this mêlée the officers, armed only with their swords, had but little chance; nor had those who carried pistols much opportunity of using them in such a close and sudden contest. They fell like heroes, and many a gallant soldier with them. The bodies of English and Russians inside the Redan, locked in an embrace which death could not relax, but had rather cemented all the closer, were found next day as evidences of the terrible animosity of the struggle.

A terrible scene in the ditch

The scene in the ditch was appalling, although some of the officers have assured me that they and the men were laughing at the precipitation with which many brave and gallant fellows did not hesitate to plunge headlong upon the mass of bayonets, muskets, and sprawling soldiers, — the ladders were all knocked down or broken, so that it was difficult for the men to scale the other side, and the dead, the dying, the wounded, and the uninjured were all lying in piles together. . . .

Section 99.   Revolts in the Balkan Peninsula

Some twenty years after the Peace of Paris which closed the Crimean War, an insurrection against the Sultan's rule broke out in Boznia and Herzegovina, and set all of the Sultan's dominions in Europe in a state of unrest. The Turks met this revolt by the most cruel atrocities, especially in Bulgaria, and the powers failing to agree upon any way of meeting the difficulties, the

Tsar, Alexander II, determined, in 1877, to act alone. He accordingly dispatched his troops across the Danube, and issued the following proclamation to the Bulgarians on June 28, 1877.

My troops, having crossed the Danube, will to-day enter your territory upon which they have already fought more than once for the amelioration of the condition of the Christian inhabitants of the Balkan Peninsula. My ancestors, faithful to their ancient and historical traditions, ever gathering fresh strength from the intimate union which had for centuries united them to the orthodox population, succeeded, by their influence and their arms, in securing the present position of the Servians and the Roumanians by summoning them to a new political existence. Time and circumstances have not altered the sympathies of Russia for her co-religionists in the East. She nourishes ever the same affection, the same solicitude towards all the members of the great Christian family of the Balkan Peninsula. . . .

348. Alexander II's proclamation to the Bulgarians (1877)

Inhabitants of Bulgaria! The aim of Russia is to build up, not to destroy. She is called by the decrees of Providence to pacify and conciliate all races and all denominations in the Bulgarian territory, which is inhabited by people of various origin and belief. Henceforward the arms of Russia will protect all Christians against violence of all kind; no attack will be made by any one with impunity upon either their persons or their property; every crime will be followed by punishment; the life, liberty, honor, and property of every Christian will be equally guaranteed, to whatever sect he may belong. Vengeance will not guide our actions; a sentiment of strict equity will alone preside over them, as well as the firm intention of developing order and law in regions where disorder and despotism are now rampant.

Protection offered to the Christians

And to you, Mussulmans of Bulgaria, I address a salutary warning. It is painful for me to evoke the memory of the crimes and violence of which many of you have been guilty toward defenseless Christians. These horrors cannot be forgotten, but the Russian authorities do not wish to hold all

Warning to the Mohammedans

responsible for the crimes of a few. A regular and impartial administration of justice will overtake only the criminals who have remained unpunished, although their names were perfectly well known to our government. Recognize to-day that it is the justice of God which overtakes you; bend before his will; submit yourselves to the lawful demands of the authorities who will be appointed whenever my troops appear; become peaceful citizens of a society which is ready to accord to you the benefits of a regular organization. Your religion will remain to you intact; your existence, your property, the life and property of your families, will be held sacred by us.

Christians of Bulgaria! You are passing through a memorable period. The hour of deliverance from Mussulman despotism has at length struck. Give the world an illustration of Christian love; forget former internal dissensions, and respect scrupulously the legitimate rights of each nationality; unite yourselves, as brothers in religion, in a sentiment of concord and brotherly love, which alone offers foundations for a solid and lasting edifice; gather closely under the shadow of the Russian flag, whose victories have so often resounded upon the Danube and among the Balkans. As the Russian troops advance into the interior of the country, the Turkish rule will be replaced by a regular organization, the native inhabitants will be at once summoned to take an active part therein under the supreme direction of special and newly appointed authorities. Obey the Russian authorities. Follow their directions faithfully. Therein lies your strength and your safety.

With humility I beseech the Lord to grant us the victory over the enemy of the Christians, and to send down his blessing upon our just cause.   ALEXANDER

349. Extracts from the Treaty of Berlin (1878)   After the Russians had defeated the Turks in the war of 1877–1878 and brought the Sultan to terms, the other powers of Europe intervened and convoked a great congress at Berlin for the purpose of settling all the questions arising out of the war. This congress embodied its conclusions in the Treaty of Berlin, bearing the date of July 13, 1878, which remained the "fundamental law for southeastern Europe" until the revolutionary events of 1908. The following are some of the most important articles of the treaty.

ART. 1. Bulgaria is constituted an autonomous and tributary principality under the suzerainty of his Imperial Majesty the Sultan; it shall have a Christian government and a national militia. *Bulgaria is made a tributary principality*

ART. 3. The prince of Bulgaria shall be freely elected by the population and confirmed by the Sublime Porte with the assent of the powers.

ART. 4. An assembly of notables of Bulgaria, convoked at Tirnovo, shall, before the election of the prince, draw up the organic law of the Principality.

ART. 9. The amount of the annual tribute which the Principality of Bulgaria shall pay to the Suzerain Court — such amount being paid into whatever bank the Porte may hereafter designate — shall be fixed by an agreement between the powers signatory of the present treaty at the close of the first year of the working of the new organization.

ART. 13. A province shall be formed south of the Balkans which shall take the name of "Eastern Roumelia," and shall remain under the direct political and military authority of his Imperial Majesty the Sultan, under conditions of administrative autonomy. It shall have a Christian governor general. *Eastern Roumelia*

ART. 25. The provinces of Bosnia and Herzegovina shall be occupied and administered by Austria-Hungary. *Bosnia and Herzegovina*

ART. 26. The independence of Montenegro is recognized by the Sublime Porte and by all of those high contracting parties who have not hitherto admitted it. *Montenegro*

ART. 34. The high contracting parties recognize the independence of the Principality of Servia, subject to the conditions set forth in the following article [on civil and religious liberty]. . . . *Servia*

ART. 43. The high contracting parties recognize the independence of Roumania subject to the conditions set forth in the two following articles [on civil and religious liberty]. . . . *Roumania*

Cessions to
Russia

ART. 58. The Sublime Porte cedes to the Russian emperor in Asia the territories of Ardahan, Kars, and Batum, together with the latter port, as well as all the territories comprised between the former Russo-Turkish frontier and the following line [drawn roughly about forty miles to the south of the old Russian boundary].

Reforms
promised by
the Sultan

ART. 62. The Sublime Porte having expressed the intention to maintain the principle of religious liberty [1] and give it the widest scope, the contracting parties take note of this spontaneous declaration. In no part of the Ottoman Empire shall difference of religion be alleged against any person as a ground for exclusion or incapacity as regards the discharge of civil and political rights, admission to the public employments, functions, and honors, or the exercise of the various professions and industries. All persons shall be admitted without distinction of religion to give evidence before the tribunals. The freedom and outward exercise of all forms of worship are assured to all. . . .

As a result of the steady decline of the Sultan's power in Europe there remains under his direct administration only a narrow strip of territory — less in extent than the state of Missouri — reaching from the Black Sea to the Adriatic, to which the name of Macedonia is generally given. Though relatively small in extent, this territory is inhabited by many different peoples who are in constant trouble with one another as well as with the Turkish officials. The racial question and the antagonism to Turkish government, especially in the matter of taxation, are the most fruitful sources of trouble in Macedonia.

An excellent idea of a state of affairs more or less chronic in Macedonia can be secured from the following statements contained in a dispatch of February 28, 1903, from the English consul general in Salonica, on the southern coast, to the English ambassador in Constantinople.

[1] In a decree issued in 1856.

Sir:

About ten days ago I received a somewhat alarming report from a Christian, in whose statements I considered I could place faith, regarding the exasperation among the Moslems, and the possibility of their retaliating on the local Rayahs for the murders, etc., committed on their co-religionists by the Bulgarian bands in some of the neighboring cazas of this vilayet.

350. A brief account of the disorders prevalent in Macedonia

I therefore lost no time in sending a confidential agent to Doiran, Stroumnitsa, Gevgeli, Yenijé, Vardar, and Vodéna, and have now the honor to submit to your Excellency the contents of his report to me.

The following are the murders of Moslems already reported by me during the last four months:

In November, two Coldjis of the Régie; in December, one of two Albanians shot at; in January, two Albanian shepherds and two rural guards (whose heads, according to my agent's report, were thrown to the dogs to eat); in February, Mehmed Aga, the gendarme, — giving the total of eight Moslems killed by the bands without provocation.

My agent adds to these the murder by three Greco-Vlachs of a renegade in January, and gives details of the disgusting desecration and mutilation of his corpse. The three murderers joined a Bulgarian band, but the beys have not allowed their co-religionists to avenge the death of their comrade.

On the 16th February, Ali, servant of Deli Ahmed, of Veleusa, was beheaded with an ax, near the village, and his head thrown at a distance from the body.

The same day the bands carried off from Nisi — a farm belonging to an Albanian named Seifoullah Bey — the Soubashi Nasif Aga, also an Albanian, who has not been heard of since. He had more than once denounced the bands to the local authority.

And yet the feeling of the Moslem population towards the Christians is not represented to me as indicating danger. The Turks, in fact, appear to be cowed, and I hear from different quarters that they have dropped the obnoxious tone which they used to adopt toward the Christians, and have become very much quieter and more considerate. . . . In other parts of the country the Moslem population, especially that of the villages, is so uncertain of what is in store for them that, in spite of what is said to the contrary, there is no chance of their molesting the Christians; and even if a few hot-headed young Turks were to attempt anything, the authorities would stop them.

As I was writing the present report, a foreigner living in the country told me of a case in which about thirty young Moslems suddenly took up their rifles and made for the nearest Christian village with the intention of burning it down. They had got within a few minutes' walk of their object when the hastily summoned troops arrived and enjoined them, with loaded rifles, to retire, which they did.

Section 100.   The Independent Balkan States

After remaining in the position of a tributary State under the sovereignty of the Sultan for thirty years, Bulgaria, on October 5, 1908, announced her complete independence. Her ruler, Prince Ferdinand, read the following manifesto before a great assembly of dignitaries at the ancient capital of Tirnovo.

351. The Bulgarian proclamation of independence (1908)

By the will of our never-to-be-forgotten liberator and the great kindred Russian nation, aided by our good friends and neighbors, the subjects of the king of Roumania, and by the Bulgarian heroes, on February 18, 1878, the chains were broken which had for so many centuries enslaved Bulgaria, once a great and glorious power.

From that time until to-day, full thirty years, the Bulgarian nation, still cherishing the memory of those who had labored for its freedom, and inspired by its traditions, has worked incessantly for the development of its beautiful country, and, under my guidance and that of the late Prince Alexander, it has become a nation fit to take a place as an equal among the civilized States of the world, and has shown itself capable of progress in science, art, and industry. While advancing along this path nothing should arrest the progress of Bulgaria, nothing should hinder her success. Such is the desire of the nation, such is its will. Let that desire be fulfilled. The Bulgarian nation and its chief can have but one sentiment, one desire. Practically independent, the nation was impeded in its normal and peaceful development by certain illusory·and formal limitations which resulted in a coldness in the relations of Turkey and Bulgaria. I and the nation desire to rejoice in the political development of Turkey. Turkey and Bulgaria free and entirely independent of each other may exist under conditions which will allow them to strengthen their amicable relations and devote themselves to peaceful internal development.

Inspired by the sacred purpose of satisfying national requirements and fulfilling national desires, I proclaim, with the blessing of the Almighty, Bulgaria, united since September 6, 1885, an independent kingdom.

In conjunction with the nation I believe that this act will meet the approbation of the great powers.[1]

On October 7, two days after the Bulgarian declaration of independence, the emperor of Austria formally announced the annexation of the provinces of Bosnia and Herzegovina, which, although nominally Turkish territories, had been under Austria's protection and administration since 1878. The proclamation follows :

We, Francis Joseph, Emperor of Austria, King of Bohemia, and Apostolic King of Hungary, to the inhabitants of Bosnia and Herzegovina :

352. The annexation of Bosnia and Herzegovina

When a generation ago our troops crossed the borders of your lands, you were assured that they came not as foes, but as friends, with the firm determination to remedy the evils from which your fatherland had suffered so grievously for many years. This promise given at a serious moment has been honestly kept. It has been the constant endeavor of our government

[1] After the prince of Bulgaria had read the above proclamation, the president of the Bulgarian parliament tendered him, on the part of the representatives of the nation, the kingly crown. The prince thereupon accepted the title of first Bulgarian king with "pride and thanksgiving."

to guide the country by patient and systematic activity to a happier future.

To our great joy we can say that the seed then scattered in the furrows of a troubled soil has richly thrived. You yourselves must feel it a boon that order and security have replaced violence and oppression, that trade and traffic are constantly extending, that the elevating influence of education has been brought to bear in your country, and that under the shield of an orderly administration every man may enjoy the fruits of his labors.

A share in the government promised

It is the duty of us all to advance steadily along this path. With this goal before our eyes, we deem the moment come to give the inhabitants of the two lands a new proof of our trust in their political maturity. In order to raise Bosnia and Herzegovina to a higher level of political life we have resolved to grant both of those lands constitutional governments that are suited to the prevailing conditions and general interests, so as to create a legal basis for the representation of their wishes and needs. You shall henceforth have a voice when decisions are made concerning your domestic affairs, which, as hitherto, will have a separate administration. But the necessary premise for the introduction of this provincial constitution is the creation of a clear and unambiguous legal status for the two lands.

For this reason, and also remembering the ties that existed of yore between our glorious ancestors on the Hungarian throne and these lands, we extend our suzerainty over Bosnia and Herzegovina, and it is our will that the order of succession of our House be extended to these lands also. The inhabitants of the two lands thus share all the benefits which a lasting confirmation of the present relation can offer. The new order of things will be a guarantee that civilization and prosperity will find a sure footing in your home.

Inhabitants of Bosnia and Herzegovina :

Among the many cares of our throne, solicitude for your material and spiritual welfare shall not be the last. The exalted idea of equal rights for all before the law, a share in the legislation and administration of the provincial affairs, equal protection for all religious creeds, languages, and racial differences, all these high possessions you shall enjoy in full measure. The freedom of the individual and the welfare of the whole will be the aim of our government in the two lands. You will surely show yourselves worthy of the trust placed in you, by attachment and loyalty to us and to our House. And thus we hope that the noble harmony between the prince and the people, that dearest pledge of all social progress, will ever accompany us on our common path.

FRANCIS JOSEPH

After Russia became, at least legally, a constitutional monarchy in 1906, Turkey alone remained an example of an old-fashioned despotism. While an effort was made in 1876 to establish a constitution in Turkey, it failed, but in July, 1908, the dead constitution was revived and now promises to admit the people to a share in the government. December 17, 1908, the parliament, consisting of a senate and house of representatives, was opened at Constantinople. The following account of the event and of the Sultan's speech are taken from the New York *Evening Post* of December 17 and the *New York Times* of December 18, 1908.

The Sultan opened parliament in person, with elaborate ceremony, fashioned after the customs of older similar assemblies. The new legislature met in the same chamber where the short-lived parliament of 1876 assembled, — a moderate-sized hall in a building facing the Square of St. Sophia. The scene was, perhaps, one of the most remarkable in the political history of the world. All the creeds and races of the Turkish Empire sent their duly elected representatives, and the varied costumes of the delegates, some in flowing silk robes and others in the modern frock coat, formed a multicolored picture never before witnessed in a legislative gathering in Europe. Albanians, Syrians, and Arabs were among the Moslem representatives, while Greeks, Armenians, and Bulgars represented the Christian

353. Opening of Turkish parliament, December 17 1908

nationalities. Members from Jerusalem and Mecca rubbed shoulders with their colleagues from the European provinces.

Enthusiasm
of the people

Abdul Hamid, the Sultan, who granted the constitution providing for this assembly, rode in a state coach through the city to-day at the head of a procession to open the first session of the body. Everywhere he was greeted with loud cheering, and there was no semblance of disorder. The entire line of march of the imperial party, a distance of five miles, had been swept and spread with fresh sand for the passage of the Sultan.

Every regiment in Constantinople was out under arms, and lined up along the route of the procession to guard the progress of the Sultan. Triumphal arches spanned the streets, and as the occasion had been made a public holiday, the city was crowded with people. Thousands came in from surrounding towns and villages as well as from more remote parts of the empire, and almost the entire local population turned out to witness the ceremonies.

In his speech, which was read by Ali Bjevad Bey, the Sultan condemned the action of Austria-Hungary in declaring the annexation of Bosnia and Herzegovina. On this point the speech said:

Sultan
deprecates
independence
of Bulgaria

" I regret to be compelled to announce to the representatives of the nation that the prince of Bulgaria and the governor general of Eastern Roumelia have deviated from the path of loyalty and proclaimed the independence of those provinces.

and the loss
of Bosnia and
Herzegovina

" I also regret to announce that Austria-Hungary has made the illegal move of proclaiming the annexation of Bosnia and Herzegovina, temporarily occupied by her, contrary to international good faith and treaty stipulations.[1] My ministers are occupying themselves with these grave questions, and I hope they will receive the assistance of parliament.

" Our relations with all the powers are excellent, and I anticipate that with the good offices of the great friendly nations all these questions will be peacefully and favorably settled."

Restoration of
constitutional
government

" When I first proclaimed a constitution thirty-two years ago there were many difficulties in the way of its execution, and I

[1] Turkey accepted in January, 1909, Austria's offer of £2,500,000 (Turkish) as an indemnity for the provinces of Bosnia and Herzegovina.

was advised to suspend it momentarily. In the interval great efforts were made toward popular education and for the establishment of institutions of a nature calculated to increase the public enlightenment. I am now happy to know that the people are more able to appreciate the benefits of a constitution, and I was heartily glad to restore it, notwithstanding influential advice to the contrary. My will is definite and unalterable, and henceforth the constitution will regulate the affairs of the nation. The cabinet, which Kiamil Pasha has formed, will fulfill our decision.

"The budget of the empire will be presented to you, the financial situation being the chief matter for your considera- Budget to be submitted tion. Public instruction and the strengthening of the army and navy will also occupy the most serious attention of my government.

" I am hopeful that your labors will prove fruitful to the good of the empire and the people, and with this hope I hereby proclaim the formal opening of the new parliament.

" I am happy to see assembled here the representatives of the people, and heartily salute them, it being my will that the constitution be faithfully observed and jealously guarded. I pray that God bless your labors and grant divine assistance."

The Sultan's address was greeted with an outburst of great applause.

CHAPTER XXX

THE EXPANSION OF EUROPE IN THE NINETEENTH CENTURY

Section 101. The Growth of International Trade and Competition

The invention of cheap and rapid means of communication was one of the chief causes of that quest for markets which has led European nations to establish protectorates, spheres of influence, and colonies in all of the available parts of the world. The revolution in navigation was begun in 1807, when Robert Fulton made his famous journey from New York to Albany and back in his steamboat, the *Clermont*. In the following letter to the editor of the *American Citizen*, Fulton briefly describes his wonderful experiment.

Sir :

NEW YORK, September 15, 1807

354. Robert Fulton's account of the *Clermont's* first trip from New York to Albany and return

I arrived this afternoon, at four o'clock, in the steamboat from Albany. As the success of my experiment gives me great hopes that such boats may be rendered of great importance to my country, to prevent erroneous opinions and give some satisfaction to the friends of useful improvements, you will have the goodness to publish the following statement of facts :

I left New York on Monday at one o'clock, and arrived at Clermont, the seat of Chancellor Livingston, at one o'clock on Tuesday, — time, twenty-four hours ; distance, one hundred and ten miles. On Wednesday I departed from the chancellor's at nine in the morning, and arrived at Albany at five in the afternoon, — distance, forty miles ; time, eight hours. The sum is one hundred and fifty miles in thirty-two hours, equal to near five miles an hour.

On Thursday, at nine o'clock in the morning, I left Albany, and arrived at the chancellor's at six in the evening; I started from thence at seven, and arrived at New York at four in the afternoon, — time, thirty hours; space run through, one hundred and fifty miles, equal to five miles an hour. Throughout my whole way, both going and returning, the wind was ahead; no advantage could be derived from my sails; the whole has therefore been performed by the power of the steam engine.

I am, sir, your obedient servant,

ROBERT FULTON

In a letter to his friend, Mr. Barlow, Fulton adds the following observations :

The power of propelling boats by steam is now fully proved. The morning I left New York there were not perhaps thirty persons in the city who believed that the boat would ever move one mile an hour, or be of the least utility ; and while we were putting off from the wharf, which was crowded with spectators, I heard a number of sarcastic remarks. This is the way in which ignorant men compliment what they call philosophers and projectors.

Having employed much time, money, and zeal in accomplishing this work, it gives me, as it will you, great pleasure to see it fully answer my expectations. It will give a cheap and quick conveyance to the merchandise on the Mississippi, Missouri, and other great rivers, which are now laying open their treasures to the enterprise of our countrymen ; and although the prospect of personal emolument has been some inducement to me, yet I feel indefinitely more pleasure in reflecting on the immense advantage my country will derive from the invention. . . .

As soon as Fulton thoroughly demonstrated the possibility of using steam for driving ships, inventors set to work on the problems of increasing the size of boats and improving the old crude and wasteful steam engine. The result has been a marvelous reduction in the amount of coal consumed, and consequently passengers and goods can be carried to all parts of the world at rates which would have astounded Fulton. A glimpse at these marvelous achievements is afforded by the following extract from a work by David A. Wells, written several years ago before the recent triumphs of the turbine engine.

355. Improvements in methods of transportation

The result of the construction and use of compound engines in economizing coal has been illustrated by Sir Lion Playfair, by the statement that " a small cake of coal that would pass through a ring the size of a shilling, when burned in the compound engine of a modern steamboat, would drive a ton of food and its proportion of the ship two miles on its way from a foreign port." Another calculator, says the London *Engineer*, " has computed that half a sheet of note paper will develop sufficient power, when burned in connection with a triple-expansion engine, to carry a ton a mile in an Atlantic steamer." How, under the circumstances, the charge for sea freights on articles of comparatively high value has been reduced, is shown by the fact that the ocean transport of fresh meat from New York to Liverpool does not exceed one cent per pound. . . .

Transportation on land

Great, however, as has been the revolution in respect to economy and efficiency in the carrying trade upon the ocean, the revolution in the carrying trade on land during the same period has been even greater and more remarkable. Taking the American railroads in general as representative of the railroad system of the world, the average charge for moving one ton of freight per mile has been reduced from about two and one-half cents in 1869 to about a cent in 1887. To grasp fully the meaning and significance of these figures, their method of presentation may be varied by saying that two thousand pounds of coal, iron, wheat, cotton, or other commodities can now be carried on the best-managed railways for a distance of one mile for a sum so small that, outside of China, it would be difficult to find a coin of equivalent value to give to a boy as a reward for carrying an ounce package across the street, even if a man or boy could be found in Europe or the United States willing either to give or accept so small a compensation for such a service.

Smiles, in his story of the *Life of George Stephenson*, gives the following account of the formal opening of the railway line between Liverpool and Manchester.

At length the line was completed and ready for the public ceremony of the opening, which took place on September 30, 1830. This important event attracted a vast number of spectators from all parts of the country. Strong palings were erected for miles along the deep cuttings near Liverpool, to keep off the pressure from the multitude and prevent them from falling over in their eagerness to witness the passing trains. Constables and soldiers were there in numbers to assist in keeping the line clear. The completion of the railway was justly regarded as an important national event, and the ceremony of the opening was celebrated accordingly. The duke of Wellington, then prime minister, Sir Robert Peel, secretary of state, Mr. Huskisson, one of the members for Liverpool and an earnest supporter of the project from the commencement, were amongst the number of distinguished public personages present.

356. The opening of the Liverpool and Manchester railway in 1830

Eight locomotives constructed at the Stephenson works had been delivered and placed upon the line, the whole of which had been tried and tested weeks before with perfect success. The various trains of carriages accommodated in all about six hundred persons. The "Northumbrian" engine, driven by George Stephenson himself, headed the procession; then followed the "Phœnix," driven by Robert Stephenson; the "North Star," by Robert Stephenson, senior (brother of George); the "Rocket," by Joseph Locke; the "Dart," by Thomas L. Gooch; the "Comet," by William Allcard; the "Arrow," by Frederick Swanwick; and the "Meteor," by Anthony Harding.

Eight locomotives in line

The procession was cheered in its progress by thousands of spectators, — through the deep ravine of Olive Mount, up the Sutton incline, over the great Sankey viaduct, beneath which a multitude of persons had assembled, carriages filling the narrow lanes and barges crowding the river; the people below gazing with wonder and admiration upon the trains which sped along far above their heads at the rate of some twenty-five miles an hour.

Crowds cheer the procession

The sad accident to Mr. Huskisson

At Parkside, about seventeen miles from Liverpool, the engines stopped to take water. Here a deplorable accident occurred to one of the most distinguished of the illustrious visitors present, which threw a deep shadow over the subsequent proceedings of the day. The "Northumbrian" engine, with the carriage containing the duke of Wellington, was drawn up on one line, in order that the whole of the trains might pass in review before him and his party on the other. Mr. Huskisson had unhappily alighted from the carriage and was standing on the opposite road along which the "Rocket" engine was observed rapidly coming up. At this moment the duke of Wellington, between whom and Mr. Huskisson some coolness had existed, made a sign of recognition and held out his hand. A hurried but friendly grasp was given, and before it was loosened there was a general cry from the bystanders, "Get in, get in." Flurried and confused, Mr. Huskisson endeavored to get around the open door of the carriage, which projected over the opposite rail; but in so doing was struck down by the "Rocket," and, falling with his leg doubled across the rail, the limb was instantly crushed. His first words on being raised were, "I have met my death," which unhappily proved too true, for he expired that same evening in the neighboring parsonage of Eccles. It was cited at the same time as a remarkable fact that the "Northumbrian" engine conveyed the wounded body of the unfortunate gentleman a distance of about fifteen miles in twenty-five minutes, or at the rate of thirty-six miles an hour. This incredible speed burst upon the world with the effect of a new and unlooked-for phenomenon. . . .

The speed of the first trains

It was anticipated that the speed at which the locomotive could run upon the line would be about nine or ten miles an hour; but the wisest of the lawyers and the most experienced engineers did not believe this to be practicable, and they laughed outright at the idea of an engine running twenty miles in an hour. But very soon after the railway opening for traffic, passengers were regularly carried the entire thirty miles between Liverpool and Manchester in little more than an hour. Two Edinburgh engineers who went to report on the railway expressed their wonder at the traveling being smoother and easier than any they had hitherto experienced, even on the smoothest turnpikes of Mr. M'Adam. "At the highest speed of twenty-five miles an hour," they said, "we could observe the passengers, among whom a good many were ladies, talking to gentlemen with the utmost *sang-froid*."[1]

The desire for markets in which to sell their surplus products, and for secure investments for their surplus capital, has impelled all the industrial nations of Europe to enter an intense competition for trading privileges and for territory, especially in Africa and the Orient. An excellent example of the way in which this struggle for foreign trade and colonies influences politics at home is afforded by the following speech delivered by that able champion of Imperialism, Mr. Chamberlain, to an audience in Birmingham composed principally of manufacturers and workingmen.

We must look this matter in the face, and must recognize that in order that we may have more employment to give we must create more demand [hear, hear]. Give me the demand for more goods and then I will undertake to give plenty of employment in making the goods; and the only thing, in my opinion, that the government can do in order to meet this great difficulty that we are considering, is so to arrange its policy that every inducement shall be given to the demand;

357. A plea for Imperialism

[1] The official figures for the world's railway mileage in 1901 were Europe, 180,708; Asia, 41,814; Africa, 14,187; North America, 226,503; South America, 33,067; Australia, 15,649.

In commemoration of the great revolution inaugurated by George Stephenson, the officials of the Roman railways set up some years ago the following tablet:

"In this City of Rome from which wondrous roads once radiated for the governing of the world, the officials of the Roman Railway fitly commemorate the hundredth anniversary of the birth of George Stephenson, on June 9, 1789, who revealed still more wondrous roads for the brotherhood of nations. With his example before us great achievements shall never fail."

that new markets shall be created, and that old markets shall be effectually developed [cheers].

You are aware that some of my opponents please themselves occasionally by finding names for me [laughter], and among other names lately they have been calling me a Jingo [laughter]. I am no more a Jingo than you are [hear, hear]. But for the reasons and arguments I have put before you to-night I am convinced that it is a necessity as well as a duty for us to uphold the dominion and empire which we now possess [loud cheers]. For these reasons, among others, I would never lose the hold which we now have over our great Indian dependency [hear, hear], by far the greatest and most valuable of all the customers we have or ever shall have in this country. For the same reasons I approve of the continued occupation of Egypt, and for the same reasons I have urged upon this government, and upon previous governments, the necessity for using every legitimate opportunity to extend our influence and control in that great African continent which is now being opened up to civilization and to commerce ; and, lastly, it is for the same reasons that I hold that our navy should be strengthened [loud cheers] until its supremacy is so assured that we cannot be shaken in any of the possessions which we hold or may hold hereafter.

New markets give employment to workingmen

Believe me, if in any one of the places to which I have referred any change took place which deprived us of that control and influence of which I have been speaking, the first to suffer would be the workingmen of this country. Then, indeed, we should see a distress which would not be temporary, but which would be chronic, and we should find that England was entirely unable to support the enormous population which is now maintained by the aid of her foreign trade. If the workingmen of this country understand their own interests, they will never lend any countenance to the doctrines of those politicians who never lose an opportunity of pouring contempt and abuse upon the brave Englishmen, who, even at this moment, in all parts of the world are carving out new dominions for Britain, and are opening up fresh markets for British commerce and laying out fresh fields for British labor [applause].

If the " Little Englanders " had their way, not only would they refrain from taking the legitimate opportunities which offer for extending the empire and for securing for us new markets, but I doubt whether they would even take the pains which are necessary to preserve the great heritage which has come down to us from our ancestors [applause]. The " Little Englanders " who oppose Imperialism

When you are told that the British pioneers of civilization in Africa are filibusters, and when you are asked to call them back, and to leave this great continent to the barbarism and superstition in which it has been steeped for centuries, or to hand over to foreign countries the duty which you are unwilling to undertake, I ask you to consider what would have happened if, one hundred or one hundred and fifty years ago, your ancestors had taken similar views of their responsibility? Where would be the empire on which now your livelihood depends? We should have been the United Kingdom of Great Britain and Ireland, but those vast dependencies, those hundreds of millions with whom we keep up a mutually beneficial relationship and commerce would have been the subjects of other nations, who would not have been slow to profit by our neglect of our opportunities and obligations [applause]. . . . What a century and a half of anti-imperialism would have done

An English writer, J. A. Hobson, gives the following summary of the astounding acquisitions of territory made by the imperial powers of the world during very recent times.

Since 1884 some three and three-quarter millions of square miles have been added to the British Empire. Nor does Great Britain stand alone in this enterprise. The leading characteristic of modern imperialism, the competition of rival empires, is the product of this same period. The close of the Franco-German War marks the beginning of a new colonial policy in France and Germany, destined to take effect in the next decade. 358. Present extent of European colonies (from J. A. Hobson)

It was not unnatural that the newly founded German Empire, surrounded by powerful enemies and doubtful allies, and perceiving its more adventurous youth drawn into the United States and other foreign lands, should form the idea of a colonial Small extent of German colonies empire. During the seventies a vigorous literature sprang up in advocacy of the policy, which took shape a little later in the powerful hands of Bismarck. The earliest instance of official aid for the promotion of German commerce abroad occurred in 1880. But the definite advance of Germany upon its imperialistic career began in 1884 with a policy of African protectorates and annexations of oceanic islands. During the next fifteen years she brought under her colonial sway about a million square miles, with an estimated population of fourteen millions. Almost the whole of this territory is tropical, and the white population forms a total of a few thousands.

French colonies

Similarly, in France a great revival of the old colonial spirit took place in the early eighties. The extension of empire in the Senegal and Sahara in 1880 was followed the next year by the annexation of Tunis; and France was soon actively engaged in the scramble for Africa in 1884, while at the same time she was fastening her rule upon Tonquin and Laos in Asia. Her acquisitions since 1880 (exclusive of the extension of New Caledonia and its dependencies) amount to an area of over three and one-half million square miles, with a native population of some thirty-seven million; almost the whole territory is tropical or subtropical, inhabited by lower races, and incapable of colonization.

Italian colonization

Italian aspirations took similar shape from 1880 onwards, though the disastrous experience of the Abyssinian expedition has given a check to Italian imperialism. Her possessions in East Africa are confined to the northern colony of Eritrea and the protectorate of Somaliland.

Of the other European States two only, Portugal and Belgium, enter directly into the competition of the new imperialism. Spain may be said to have definitely retired from imperial competition. The large and important possessions of Holland in the East and West Indies, though involving her in imperial politics in some degree, belong to older colonialism; she takes no part in the new expansion.

Russia

Russia, the only active expansionist country of the north, stands alone in the character of her imperial growth, which differs from other imperialism in that it has been principally

Asiatic in its achievements, and has proceeded by direct extension of imperial boundaries, partaking to a larger extent than in the other cases of a regular colonial policy of settlement for purposes of agriculture and industry.

The recent entrance of the powerful and progressive nation of the United States of America upon imperialism by the annexation of Hawaii and the taking over of the relics of the ancient Spanish Empire, not only adds a new formidable competitor for trade and territory, but changes and complicates the issues. As the focus of political attention and activity shifts more to the Pacific States, and the commercial aspirations of America are more and more set upon trade with the Pacific islands and the Asiatic coast, the same forces which are driving European States along the path of territorial expansion seem likely to act upon the United States, leading her to a virtual abandonment of the principle of American isolation which has hitherto dominated her policy.

The United States

The manner in which the Christian missionaries, especially the women, are able, by tact, patience, and example, to change the habits of the people among whom they work, and to introduce Western ideas, is well illustrated by the policy of a member of the American Presbyterian mission in Canton, China, Dr. Mary H. Fulton, who writes as follows:

I am doing what little I can in my small sphere to show an applied Christianity. In the first place, I try always to be neat in dress. This invariably calls out complimentary remarks. The Chinese women at once compare my pretty and fresh, though cheap, dress with their silken (and generally soiled) robes. Then they notice my clean, short finger nails, and contrast them with their long ones, — often a finger in length, — which indicate that they are ladies of leisure. They at once want to know *why* I dress so differently from them. It is an easy step to tell them that God, who made us, has put women into the world for *use*, and not merely to live to adorn our bodies, and that there are many poor suffering children and

359. **Manner in which the missionaries spread Western ideas and customs throughout the world** (from Dennis's *Christian Missions and Social Progress*)

others who need our help. If we have such long nails and bound feet, we cannot go about to help them.

They all assent to this, and generally there is an inquiry on the part of some one present if she cannot have her feet unbound. Then you should hear the clamor! A dozen will admonish the one who has been so bold as to propose such a thing. Had she lost all her modesty that she wanted to go about like a man? Now you will laugh, but all my arguments are as nothing compared with showing them a well-fitting, pretty foreign boot or shoe. I have always thought, since feet are such a momentous question in this land, that we should be very careful to make our own as presentable as possible. To see us start off quickly and gracefully and go through the streets so independently often makes them desirous of imitating us, especially when they see women hobbling along painfully, or being carried on the backs of others.

The same is true of our homes. I try to make mine attractive in its simplicity. I have a weekly prayer meeting here just because I want to show my home to these women who have never seen cleanliness and order in their dark, damp, crowded quarters. I give them, after the meeting, tea and sponge cake, served in pretty cups and plates. Simple as all this is, it lifts them up and out of their sordid surroundings, for the time being, at least, and, I hope, will lead them to make their own houses more homelike. I always urge those coming under my influence to try and be as clean as possible, and I am happy to say that I observe year by year an increasing tendency to the use of foreign soap and handkerchiefs.

The two following extracts show what can be done among far less highly civilized peoples than the Chinese.

360. How Rev. Mr. Williams revolutionized a town in the Society Islands

It was in 1818 that Mr. Williams settled at Raiatea, in the Society Islands, under the famous chief Tamatoa. The inhabitants welcomed them with every demonstration of delight, and provided a great feast, which included five hogs for Mr. Williams, five hogs for Mrs. Williams, and five hogs for the baby! With characteristic energy and practical common sense Mr. Williams devoted himself to stimulating the people to all kinds of good works. Apparently there was nothing that he could not make, from a house to a constitution; and even the notorious indolence of the Raiateans gave way under his energetic leadership.

The main settlement of the natives lay in an exposed position, which resulted in their huts and crops being frequently destroyed by storms. Largely at Mr. Williams's instigation there was an exodus of the entire settlement. A new town was formed in a more healthy and sheltered position. Good houses were built, wells were sunk, a beautiful place of worship erected, gardens planted, until the whole place was a monument to Mr. Williams's genius and industry.

In 1844 Rev. Charles Hardie with Rev. G. Turner, who in the previous year had been obliged to flee for his life from the island of Tanna in the New Hebrides, established a self-supporting boarding school for higher education at Malua, on the island of Upolu. They purchased three hundred acres of land covered with wild jungle and bordering on a lagoon, erected buildings, and enrolled one hundred students, in classes of twenty-five, for a four years' course of study. With the aid of the students the land was cleared of brush and planted with ten thousand breadfruit and cocoanut trees, thousands of bananas and yams, taro, maize, manioc, and sugar cane; and a road was made in circuit around the tract, and shaded by cocoanut palms. Besides cultivating the soil and catching fish from the lagoon, the students learned useful mechanical arts. The produce of the land and the fish of the lagoon supplied all their wants. In this school pupils were received from the New Hebrides, New Caledonia, and the Savage Islands as well as from the Samoa Islands.

A mission school in the New Hebrides

In few fields have the missionaries been more strikingly successful than in carrying throughout the world modern scientific ideas of the nature, treatment, and prevention of disease. Rev. James S. Dennis, in his important *Christian Missions and Social Progress*, published in 1899, gives the following information:

361. Medical
missionaries
and mission-
ary hospitals

The total of medical missionaries at present is 680; of this number 470 are men and 210 women. There are 45 medical schools and classes with 382 male and 79 female students, making a total of 461. There are 21 training schools for nurses, with 146 pupils. Neither of these statements includes 240 female medical students now in training as physicians, nurses, and hospital assistants, under the care of the Lady Dufferin Association of India. There are 348 hospitals and 774 dispensaries. . . . The sum total of those annually treated will not be far from 2,500,000. There are 97 leper asylums, homes, and settlements, with 5453 inmates. There are 227 orphan and foundling asylums, with 14,695 inmates. The statistics of temperance-reform and rescue societies have not been obtained with sufficient exactness to report at present. The same may be said of children's aid societies, prison-reform movements, and less prominent charities.

How Chris-
tian benevo-
lence stimu-
lates the
founding of
charitable
institutions
by the heathen
(Rev. T. W.
Pearce of
Hongkong,
quoted by
J. S. Dennis)

Missionary hospitals have led to the founding of native societies, in order that Christianity may be met on its own grounds and conquered with its own weapons. The Chinese Benevolent Society of Canton is a most noteworthy institution. . . . There are four native doctors in attendance at the central building. These men prescribe for all comers. Their diagnosis is, of course, from a Western point of view, incomplete and often absurd. There is, however, the fact of an institution known throughout China, with a yearly expenditure amounting to thousands of dollars, and with branches in different parts of the suburbs of Canton and in country districts.

Here again is an indirect result of Christianity manifest in the alleviation of suffering through heathen benevolence brought into play by the opposing force of Christian missions. Before missions were established in the south of China private benevolence was no doubt exercised by many of the wealthy Chinese. Some of these may have combined to heal the sick, to help the destitute and famine-stricken, and to bestow coffins as gifts when deserving families among their neighbors were found without the means to bury their dead. But anything in the nature of a public society organized for the express purpose of systematic and regular benevolence, one may affirm, was an unheard-of project.

Section 102. Relations of Europe with China

From time to time during the eighteenth century and the early years of the nineteenth, the English sought in vain to obtain from China larger trading privileges than those afforded at the single port of Canton under the vigilant eye of Chinese officials. The commercial advantages which they thus tried to secure by negotiation were at last obtained as the result of the conflict known as the "Opium War." Traffic in opium had been long forbidden by the Chinese government, but the English, finding the business exceedingly profitable, continued to smuggle the drug into China. In 1839 the Imperial High Commissioner, Lin, was charged with suppressing the traffic at all hazards, and, after warning the foreigners in the following proclamation to deliver up the opium which they held illegally, he seized and burned many thousand chests of the drug, thus precipitating a serious conflict.

First. You ought to make haste and deliver up the opium, by virtue of that reason which Heaven hath implanted in all of us. I find that during the last several tens of years, the money out of which you have duped our people by means of your destructive drug amounts I know not to how many tens of thousands of myriads. Thus, while you have been scheming after private advantage, with minds solely bent on profit, our people have been wasting their substance and losing their lives; and if the reason of Heaven be just, think you that there will be no retribution? If, however, you will now repent and deliver up your opium, by a well-timed repentance you may yet avert judgment and calamities; if not, then your

362. Reasons for the proclamation ordering foreigners to deliver up opium smuggled into China (1839) (condensed)

wickedness being greater, the consequences of that wickedness will fall more fearfully upon you !

You are distant from your homes many tens of thousand miles; your ships, in coming and going, cross a vast and trackless ocean; in it you are exposed to the visitations of thunder and lightning and raging storms, to the dangers of being swallowed up by monsters of the deep; and under such perils, fear you not the retributive vengeance of Heaven? Now our great emperor, being actuated by the exalted virtue of Heaven itself, wishes to cut off this deluge of opium, which is the plainest proof that such is the intention of high Heaven ! . . .

Secondly. You ought to make immediate delivery of this opium, in order to comply with the law of your own countries, which prohibits the smoking of opium, and he who uses it is adjudged to death ! thus plainly showing that you yourselves know it to be an article destructive to human life. If, then, your laws forbid it to be consumed by yourselves, and yet permit it to be sold that it may be consumed by others, this is not in conformity with the principle of doing unto others what you would that they should do unto you.

Now you foreigners, although you were born in an outer country, yet for your property and maintenance do you depend entirely upon our Chinese Empire; and in our central land you pass the greater part of your lives, and the lesser portion of your lives is passed at home; the food that you eat every day, not less than the vast fortunes you amass, proceeds from naught but the goodness of our emperor, which is showered upon you in far greater profusion than upon our own people. And how is it, then, that you alone do not tremble before and obey the sacred majesty of the laws?

Our great emperor looks upon the opium trade with the most intense loathing, and burns to have it cut off forever; and I, the high commissioner, looking up to the great emperor, and feeling in my own person his sacred desire to love and cherish the men from afar, do mercifully spare you your lives. I wish nothing more than that you deliver up all the opium you have got, and forthwith write out a duly prepared bond, to the effect that you will henceforth never more bring opium to

China, and, should you bring it, agreeing that the cargo be confiscated and the people who bring it, put to death.

Thirdly. You ought to make immediate delivery of this opium, by reason of your feelings as men. You come to this market of Canton to trade, and you profit thereby full threefold. Every article of commerce that you bring with you, no matter whether it be coarse or fine, in whole pieces or in small, there is not one iota of it that is not sold off and consumed ; and of the produce of our country, whether it be for feeding you, for clothing you, for any kind of use, or for mere sale, there is not a description that we do not permit you to take away with you ; so that not only do you reap the profit of the inner land by the goods which you bring, but, moreover, by means of the produce of our central land, do you gather gold from every country to which you transport it. Supposing that you cut off and cast away your traffic in the single article of opium, then the other business which you do will be much increased, and you will thereon reap your threefold profit comfortably.

Fourthly. You ought to make a speedy delivery of your opium by reason of the necessity of the case. You foreigners from afar, in coming hither to trade, have passed over an unbounded ocean ; your prospect for doing business depends entirely on your living on terms of harmony with your fellow-men, and keeping your own station in peace and quietness. Thus may you reap solid advantage and avoid misfortune ! But if you will persist in selling your opium, and will go on involving the lives of our foolish people in your toils, there is not a good or upright man whose head and heart will not burn with indignation at your conduct ; they must look upon the lives of those who have suffered for smoking and selling the drug as sacrificed by you ; the simple country folk and the common people must feel anything but well pleased, and the wrath of a whole country is not a thing easily restrained : these are circumstances about which you cannot but feel anxious.

The importance of the foreigners being on good terms with the Chinese

I, the high commissioner, as well as the governor and lieutenant governor, cannot bear the idea of being unnecessarily harsh and severe ; therefore it is that, though I thus weary my mouth, as it were, entreating and exhorting you, yet do I not shrink from the task! Happiness and misery, glory and disgrace, are in your own hand! Say not that I did not give you early warning thereof! A special proclamation, to be posted before the foreign factories.[1]

TAOUKWAN, 19th year, 2d month, 12th day
[March 26th, 1839]

The Taiping rebellion was put down, thanks largely to the "Ever Victorious Army" which the Englishman, Gordon, organized. As he was completing his work of reducing the rebels in 1863–1864 he became acquainted with the consul at Shanghai, Sir Harry Parkes, from whose letters we get some idea of Gordon and of the conditions in which they both worked. Sir Harry writes to his wife, July 4, 1863:

363. Some reminiscences of " Chinese Gordon "

I am closing my mail after such a day of work, heat, thunder, lightning, rain, and *row*. Being Independence Day, all the American ships through the night and through the day have been firing cannon until everybody is ill with the perpetual shocks. I have protested to the American consul general, and he has sent out a circular to stop it. I have just come from my last business chat with Sir F. Bruce [the British minister]. He is mighty civil to me in word and most complimentary on the work I have done since I have been here. He dines with me to-night. We sit down twelve [including Gordon].

[A year later Sir Harry writes to his wife] Gordon has been up to Nanking, and further on to see Tsang Kwo-fan, who is the highest authority out of Peking that the Chinese have, and he has been back a week. He stays with me whenever in Shanghai, and is a fine, noble, generous fellow, but at the same time very peculiar and sensitive,—exceedingly impetuous,—full

[1] China has recently become a leader in the abolition of the opium trade throughout the world. In September, 1906, the Chinese emperor issued a decree ordering the gradual restriction of its use until it should, within ten years, be wholly prohibited in China. Two years later the Chinese government announced that all the powers had agreed to prohibit the importation of morphia except for medicinal purposes.

of energy, which just wants judgment to make it a very splendid type. We see a good deal of each other when he is here, for, as he is very shy, I try as much as possible to dine alone, and we then tattle on Chinese affairs all to ourselves.

[November 20, 1864] Gordon goes home by this mail and will make a point of seeing you. He had grown tired of his last job of forming a Camp of Instruction, which is far too *slow* an occupation to be suited to his active and somewhat erratic tastes, and, being unsuited, he has not made a very good job of it. He had not received assistance enough either from our government or the Chinese, and what is now arranged must be regarded still as experimental.

I trust that we may secure from it the organization of such a force as will keep rebels from this neighborhood. They are to be met with elsewhere, however. Amoy and Swatow have been thrown into alarm, and Hankow also, by the approach of marauding hordes, and it will be some time before China loses the pest altogether; in fact, without a reformed government she will not part with them, — and that again is a very great question. Perhaps years hence we may have a divided empire — a North and South — in the oldest country in the world as in the youngest.

Continued dangers from the Taiping rebels

Reference to the American Civil War

I was writing [November 24] when Gordon came in to wish me good-bye, and he has just left me to go on board. Of course we closed in round the fire and had a chat and a cigar, — or rather *he* smoked, for *I* am off my tobacco just now, as I have caught cold and am out of sorts. . . . I told him that he has reason to be thankful that he has been permitted to leave this country alive, or with a whole skin. He is a very shy man, and when at Shanghai will not call upon a soul. He has re-fused money whenever it has been offered to him, and has served throughout on a very low rate of pay. I have no doubt he will find you out, for he is not a man to spare himself trouble, and he will not allow himself to be involved in a Lon-don whirl, which will possess little fascination for him. He is a reserved, retiring man, and avoids glitter and bustle of all kinds. I hope he may recover his health before he reaches England, for he left us very poorly and much shaken.

Section 103. How Japan became a World Power

From the early part of the seventeenth century until 1853 Japan remained in haughty isolation from other countries, tolerating practically no commercial intercourse with European nations. In that year the United States dispatched Commodore Perry to Japan for the purpose of securing certain privileges to American citizens. On this memorable expedition Commodore Perry carried the following very interesting letter from President Fillmore to his Majesty, the Emperor of Japan.

Millard Fillmore, President of the United States of America, to his Majesty, the Emperor of Japan

Great and Good Friend :

364. President Fillmore's letter to the emperor of Japan (1852)

I send you this public letter by Commodore Matthew C. Perry, an officer of the highest rank in the navy of the United States, and commander of the squadron now visiting your imperial majesty's dominions.

I have directed Commodore Perry to assure your imperial majesty that I entertain the kindest feelings towards your majesty's person and government, and that I have no other object in sending him to Japan but to propose to your imperial majesty that the United States and Japan should live in friendship and have commercial intercourse with each other.

The constitution and laws of the United States forbid all interference with the religious or political concerns of other nations. I have particularly charged Commodore Perry to abstain from every act which could possibly disturb the tranquillity of your imperial majesty's dominions.

The mutual advantages of trade

The United States of America reach from ocean to ocean, and our territory of Oregon and State of California lie directly opposite to the dominions of your imperial majesty. Our steamships can go from California to Japan in eighteen days. Our great State of California produces about sixty millions of dollars in gold every year, besides silver, quicksilver, precious stones, and many other valuable articles. Japan is also a rich and fertile country, and produces many very valuable articles. Your imperial majesty's subjects are skilled in many of the arts. I am desirous that our two countries should trade with each other, for the benefit both of Japan and the United States.

We know that the ancient laws of your imperial majesty's government do not allow of foreign trade except with the Chinese and the Dutch ; but, as the state of the world changes, and new governments are formed, it seems to be wise, from time to time, to make new laws. There was a time when the ancient laws of your imperial majesty's government were first made. *It is sometimes wise to change old laws*

About the same time America, which is sometimes called the New World, was first discovered and settled by the Europeans. For a long time there were but a few people, and they were poor. They have now become quite numerous ; their commerce is very extensive ; and they think that if your imperial majesty were so far to change the ancient laws as to allow a free trade between the two countries, it would be extremely beneficial to both.

If your imperial majesty is not satisfied that it would be safe altogether to abrogate the ancient laws, which forbid foreign trade, they might be suspended for five or ten years, so as to try the experiment. If it does not prove as beneficial as was hoped, the ancient laws can be restored. The United States often limit their treaties with foreign States to a few years, and then renew them or not, as they please. *An experiment at least might be tried*

I have directed Commodore Perry to mention another thing to your imperial majesty. Many of our ships pass every year from California to China, and great numbers of our people pursue the whale fishery near the shores of Japan. It sometimes happens, in stormy weather, that one of our ships is wrecked on your imperial majesty's shores. In all such cases we ask, and expect, that our unfortunate people should be treated with kindness, and that their property should be protected till we can send a vessel and bring them away. We are very much in earnest in this. *Protection for ship-wrecked Americans asked*

Commodore Perry is also directed by me to represent to
your imperial majesty that we understand there is a great
abundance of coal and provisions in the empire of Japan. Our
steamships, in crossing the great ocean, burn a great deal of
coal, and it is not convenient to bring it all the way from
America. We wish that our steamships and other vessels
should be allowed to stop at Japan and supply themselves
with coal, provisions, and water. They will pay for them in
money, or anything else your imperial majesty's subjects may
prefer ; and we request your imperial majesty to appoint a
convenient port, in the southern part of the empire, where
our vessels may stop for this purpose. We are very desirous
of this.

These are the only objects for which I have sent Commodore Perry, with a powerful squadron, to pay a visit to your
imperial majesty's renowned city of Yedo : friendship, commerce, a supply of coal and provisions, and protection for our
shipwrecked people.

A few pres-
ents for the
emperor We have directed Commodore Perry to beg your imperial
majesty's acceptance of a few presents. They are of no great
value in themselves, but some of them may serve as speci-
mens of the articles manufactured in the United States, and
they are intended as tokens of our sincere and respectful
friendship.

May the Almighty have your imperial majesty in his great
and holy keeping !

In witness whereof I have caused the great seal of the
United States to be hereunto affixed, and have subscribed the
same with my name, at the city of Washington, in America,
the seat of my government, on the thirteenth day of the
month of November, in the year one thousand eight hundred
and fifty-two.

Your good friend,

[Seal attached]   MILLARD FILLMORE

By the President : EDWARD EVERETT, Secretary of State

Early in 1868 the young Mikado, who had assumed
the powers previously in the hands of the shogun, invited

the representatives of the chief foreign powers to visit him in his sacred city of Kyoto. An Englishman wrote the following account of the incident, which appeared in the London *Times*, May 20, 1868.

You are aware that the newly formed government of the Mikado, anxious to establish foreign relations on the most friendly footing, invited the foreign ministers to Kyoto to have an audience with the Mikado. Three of the representatives, those of England, France, and Holland, accepted the invitation. We left Osaka on the 20th of March and reached Kyoto the following day toward noon. The temple of Chion-in, a residence of the princes of the blood, had been set aside for the English legation, and more splendid quarters it is difficult to imagine. The 22d was spent by Sir Harry Parkes[1] in paying official visits to the high officers of the Mikado's court and to two or three of the daimios. The 23d was fixed by the Mikado for his reception of the foreign ministers. Up to that time everything had gone off most satisfactorily, and every one was highly pleased with the frank and friendly manner in which we had been treated by high and low. With such confidence did we set out on our way to the palace that I did not even carry my revolver.

Down a straight street nearly facing our temple the front men passed without let or hindrance, but as they turned the corner of the street, two, or perhaps more, ruffians sprang out upon them with naked swords and attacked them. Nakai leaped from his horse and engaged one, but, catching his foot, stumbled and received a severe cut in the head. At this moment Goto Shojiro, who, with the minister [Sir Harry Parkes], had not yet turned the corner, perceiving from the backing of the horses and the scuffle in front that there was mischief ahead, dismounted, and, rushing forward, came to Nakai's rescue, and between them, fighting like brave men, they killed and decapitated the villain on the spot. The other scoundrel, crouching like a tiger, ran swiftly down our line, brandishing his sword like lightning and cutting right and left in his blind rage. I,

[1] See above, p. 422.

who was in the rear, saw a disturbance, but at first thought that it was only caused by restive horses, until I heard the cry of " Kill him ! " " Stop him ! " " Cut him down ! " Then I saw the inspector of the escort canter down the street and fire his pistol, and some one said, " We are attacked ! "

I jumped out of my palanquin just as the pistol went off close to me. I saw a man rush into the house next me, pursued by the inspector and the two officers commanding the infantry guard. I drew my sword and ran to the front, not knowing the extent of the danger and anxious to see whether all our party were safe. As I ran up the street I met one man after another of the mounted escort coming down, streaming with blood from their wounds, but not a single man complained. I found the minister at the angle of the street with the headless body of one of our enemies at his feet, and ascertained that he was unhurt as well as all our officers. I then ran back to look after the man who had fled into the house. Finding him still alive, I stayed by him, in order, if possible, to protect him and revive him sufficiently to subject him to an examination. Never shall I forget that little yard with the Japanese murderer lying in a pool of his own blood; for, besides being shot in the head, he had received several wounds from sword, bayonet, and lance.

Of course going on to the court was out of the question. We had twelve men wounded, including Nakai. My special care was for our prisoner, for of course his evidence was all-important; all the coolies that could be got were wanted for our own men, so literally at the point of the sword I pressed in two honest shopkeepers to carry him, much to their disgust. And so we got home, — a most dismal return. Our beautiful temple was turned into a ghastly hospital. My duty lay with the prisoner, whom we thought to be dying. The following is his statement :

The statement of a Japanese priest who took part in the riot

" My name is Ichikawa Samuro; I am a priest from the temple called Jorenji Hegurigori, near Osaka. I left the castle this morning determined to kill all the foreigners that I might meet. I came to Kyoto on the second day of this month to form one of the Mikado's bodyguard and put up at the temple called Hommanji in the Temple Street. I left it the day before yesterday and went to the castle. I was in the First Regiment at the castle, but could not agree with my companions, so determined to regulate my conduct according to my own ideas. I set out to kill all foreigners." At a second examination he said : " I had an accomplice, one Hayashida ; I forget his other name. He is the son of a village doctor, not belonging to the samurai class, from a village near Kyoto. He belonged to the First Regiment of the guards. I heard last night from the servants that foreigners were going to court, and waited to see them pass. Did not know to what nation they belonged. It was the first time I had seen foreigners. I repent of my crime. It was a sudden thought on the part of both of us. I had no previous hate for foreigners."

In the evening the Mikado, whose court had been shocked, as we can well imagine, by the news, sent several of his highest ministers to present his condolences and regret for what had occurred ; this, taken in conjunction with the gallant behavior of his officers and with the prompt punishment inflicted for recent outrages, could leave no doubt of the horror which was expressed. They inquired with great solicitude after our wounded. The next afternoon the Mikado sent his ministers a second time, bringing with them a dispatch conveying in writing the apologies they had delivered orally the night before, and offering a full reparation. Nothing could be more noble, nothing more unlike the government with which we have hitherto had to deal, than the language of the Mikado's ministers. Sir Harry Parkes had made no complaint and had demanded no reparation. The spontaneity of the Japanese action was complete, and a great relief from the bullying and endless disputing which we have had to adopt hitherto. *The Mikado expresses regret for the outbreak*

The reason of the attack was perfectly irrational, and to us unintelligible. As a French officer said, there is a party in Japan to whom the sight of a foreigner is as a red rag to a bull. They believe in the assertion of a priest of Isé, who lived one hundred years ago and wrote a pamphlet to prove that the children of Japan are gods and the rest of the world cats and dogs. Should cats and dogs be permitted to defile the city, the court, and the sacred presence of the Son of Heaven?

A Japanese official gives the following brief summary of the remarkable advance in commerce and industry which has transformed Japan during the last thirty years into one of the world's great industrial nations.

366. A review of Japan's economic advance (condensed)

The first line of railway was constructed between Tokyo and Yokohama, eighteen miles, in 1872. Since that time the government railroads have been yearly extended at a varying rate of increase. The first private line was built in 1883, and covered sixty-three miles. After that, the railroad construction was somewhat slow, but recently, with national progress, it has been advancing very rapidly. In 1890 we had 551 miles of government lines and 896 miles of private lines, — total, 1447 miles. Since the war with China marked development has been made, and in 1901 there were 1059 miles of government lines and 2966 miles of private lines, — a total of 4025 miles.

Navigation

Navigation in Japan began to develop about 1884 or 1885, but until the war in 1895 it did not make any considerable progress. In 1890 there were only 1450 vessels constructed after the European pattern, the tonnage of which was 145,692 tons. But since the promulgation of the Navigation Encouragement Subsidy Law and Shipbuilding Encouragement Subsidy Law of March, 1896, the work has developed remarkably. New lines to Europe, America, and Australia have been founded. Thus we find that in 1901 Japan owned 5415 vessels of the Western pattern, the tonnage of which was 919,968 tons.

Foreign trade

Since the Restoration the foreign trade of Japan has made wonderful strides. In 1877 the total trade with foreign countries, exports and imports, amounted to only 50,000,000 yen,[1] but in 1890 the amount had risen to 138,330,000 yen. Ten years later, in 1900, it went up again to 491,690,000 yen, having quadrupled during one decade. In 1902 it reached 530,044,324 yen.

Weaving

In 1890 or 1891 the weaving industry did not show any marked development, and the value of goods woven was about 30,000,000 or 40,000,000 yen. But recently, aided by the progress of applied chemistry, and also of technology, the industry

[1] A *yen* is about fifty cents.

has made considerable progress, and in 1899 its product was valued at 150,000,000 yen. During ten years the increase has been more than fourfold. Now, with the manufacture of cotton-yarn, it has become one of the principal industries of the empire.

The cotton-spinning industry had its origin in 1880 or 1881, and developed gradually until, in 1890, the total number of spindles reached 277,895, producing 5,132,588 kwan [about 42,000,000 pounds] of cotton yarn. But since, in 1894, the duty on exports of cotton yarn, and in April, 1896, that on the import of raw cotton, were removed, the industry made marked progress, and in 1901 the number of spindles in use daily reached 1,181,762, and the productive capacity had increased to 33,323,770 kwan [nearly 275,000,000 pounds]. To-day cotton spinning has become the chief industry of the country. *Cotton spinning*

With the progress of Japan in trade, industry, and general enlightenment, there came inevitably a demand for a more liberal government. After sending a commission to Europe for the purpose of studying representative institutions there, the Japanese drafted a Constitution of their own (issued in 1889), from which the following clauses are taken. It well illustrates the eagerness of Japan to follow European example in organizing its government.

Chapter I. The Emperor

Art. 1. The Empire of Japan shall be ruled over by Emperors of the dynasty which has reigned in an unbroken line of descent for ages past. **367. Some extracts from the Japanese Constitution (February 11 1889)**

2. The succession to the throne shall devolve upon male descendants of the Imperial House, according to the provisions of the Imperial House Law.

3. The person of the Emperor is sacred and inviolable.

4. The Emperor being the Head of the Empire, the rights of sovereignty are vested in him, and he exercises them in accordance with the provisions of the present Constitution.

5. The Emperor exercises the legislative power with the consent of the Imperial Diet.

6. The Emperor gives sanction to laws, and orders them to be promulgated and put into force.

7. The Emperor convokes the Imperial Diet, opens, closes, and prorogues it, and dissolves the House of Representatives. . . .

9. The Emperor issues, or causes to be issued, the ordinances necessary for the carrying out of the laws, or for the maintenance of the public peace and order, and for the promotion of the welfare of his subjects. . . .

10. The Emperor determines the organization of the different branches of the administration ; he fixes the salaries of all civil and military officers, and appoints and dismisses the same. Exceptions specially provided for in the present Constitution or in other laws shall be in accordance with the respective provisions bearing thereon.

11. The Emperor has the supreme command of the army and navy.

12. The Emperor determines the organization and peace footing of the army and navy.

13. The Emperor declares war, makes peace, and concludes treaties. . . .

Chapter II. Rights and Duties of Subjects

18. The conditions necessary for being a Japanese subject shall be determined by law.

19. All Japanese subjects shall be eligible equally for civil and military appointments, and any other public offices, subject only to the conditions prescribed by laws and ordinances.

20. Japanese subjects are liable to service in the army or navy, according to the provisions of law.

21. Japanese subjects are subject to taxation, according to the provisions of law.

22. Subject to the limitations imposed by law, Japanese subjects shall enjoy full liberty in regard to residence and change of abode.

23. No Japanese subject shall be arrested, detained, tried, or punished, except according to law.

24. No Japanese subject shall be deprived of his right of being tried by the judges determined by law.

25. Except in the cases provided for by law, the house of no Japanese subject shall be entered or searched without his permission.

26. Except in the cases provided for by law, the secrecy of the letters of Japanese subjects shall not be violated.

27. The rights of property of Japanese subjects shall not be violated.

Such measures, however, as may be rendered necessary in the interests of the public welfare shall be taken in accordance with the provisions of the law.

28. Japanese subjects shall, within limits not prejudicial to peace and order, and not antagonistic to their duties as subjects, enjoy freedom of religious belief.

29. Japanese subjects shall, within the limits of law, enjoy liberty in regard to speech, writing, publication, public meetings, and associations. . . .

Section 104. War between Japan and China and its Results

In the war which Japan began against China in 1894, she gave evidence of her determination to advance her commercial and industrial interests on the mainland at all costs, and at the same time demonstrated her ability to wage war with all the modern devices known to military science. Japan's official reasons for going to war with China are set forth in the following proclamation:

We, by the grace of Heaven, Emperor of Japan, seated on a throne occupied by the same dynasty from time immemorial, do hereby make proclamation to all our loyal and brave subjects as follows:

368. The Japanese declaration of war against China (1894)

We hereby declare war against China, and we command each and all of our competent authorities, in obedience to our wish, and with a view to the attainment of the national aim, to carry on hostilities by sea and by land against China, with all the means at their disposal, consistent with the law of nations.

During the last three decades of our reign our constant aim has been to further the peaceful progress of our country in civilization ; and, being sensible of the evils inseparable from complications with foreign States, it has been our pleasure to instruct our ministers of State to labor for the promotion of friendly relations with our treaty powers. We are gratified to know that the relations of our empire with those powers have yearly increased in good will and fellowship. Under the circumstances we were unprepared for such a conspicuous want of amity and of good faith as has been manifested by China in her conduct toward this country in connection with the Korean affair.

China interferes with Korea's independence

Korea is an independent State. She was first introduced into the family of nations by the advice and under the guidance of Japan. It has, however, been China's habit to designate Korea as her dependency, and both openly and secretly to interfere with her domestic affairs. At the time of the recent civil insurrection in Korea, China dispatched troops thither, alleging that her purpose was to afford succor to her dependent State. We, in virtue of the treaty concluded with Korea in 1882, and looking to possible emergencies, caused a military force to be sent to that country. Wishing to procure for Korea freedom from the calamity of perpetual disturbance, and thereby to maintain the peace of the East in general, Japan invited China's coöperation for the accomplishment of that object. But China, advancing various pretexts, declined Japan's proposal.

China interferes with Japanese reforms in Korea

Thereupon Japan advised Korea to reform her administration so that order and tranquillity might be preserved at home, and so that the country might be able to discharge the responsibilities and duties of an independent State abroad. Korea has already consented to undertake the task, but China has secretly and insidiously endeavored to circumvent and thwart Japan's purpose. She has further procrastinated, and endeavored to make warlike preparations both on land and at sea. When those preparations were completed she not only sent large reënforcements to Korea, with a view to the forcible attainment of her ambitious designs, but even carried her arbitrariness and insolence to the extent of opening fire upon our ships in Korean waters.

China's plain object is to make it uncertain where the responsibility rests of preserving peace and order in Korea, not only to weaken the position of that State in the family of nations, — a position obtained for Korea through Japan's efforts, — but also to obscure the significance of the treaties recognizing and confirming that position. Such conduct on the part of China is not only a direct injury to the rights and interests of this empire, but also a menace to the permanent peace and tranquillity of the Orient. Judging from her actions, it must be concluded that China from the beginning has been bent upon sacrificing peace to the attainment of her sinister object. In this situation, ardent as is our wish to promote the prestige of this country by strictly peaceful methods, we find it impossible to avoid a formal declaration of war against China. It is our earnest wish that, by the loyalty and valor of our faithful subjects, peace may be soon permanently restored, and the glory of the empire be augmented and completed.

China injures Japanese interests

Section 105. The Boxer Uprising. The Russo-Japanese War

The latest attempt of the conservatives in China to drive out the foreigners by open violence was made during the summer of 1900 by an organization known as the "Boxers," who regarded with horror the innovations which were being made in their country. All of the great Western powers, including the United States, took part in the military expedition which suppressed the Boxer uprising, and in the arrangements for securing to foreigners "their rights" in China. The following account of the incident is from the message which President McKinley laid before the Congress of the United States in December, 1900.

369. An account of the Boxer uprising in China (much condensed)

The recent troubles in China spring from the antiforeign agitation, which for the past three years has gained strength in the northern provinces. The Taiping rebellion and the opening of Chinese ports to foreign trade and settlement disturbed alike the homogeneity and the seclusion of China. Meanwhile foreign activity made itself felt in all quarters, not alone on the coast, but along the great river arteries and in the remoter districts, carrying new ideas and introducing new associations among a primitive people which had pursued for centuries a national policy of isolation. The telegraph and the railway spreading over their land, the steamers plying on their water ways, the merchant and the missionary penetrating year by year farther to the interior, became to the Chinese mind types of an alien invasion, changing the course of their national life and fraught with vague forebodings of disaster to their beliefs and their self-control.

For several years before the present troubles all the resources of foreign diplomacy, backed by moral demonstrations of the physical force of fleets and arms, have been needed to secure due respect for the treaty rights of foreigners. The posting of antiforeign placards became a daily occurrence, which the repeated reprobation of the Imperial power failed to check or punish. These inflammatory appeals to the ignorance and superstition of the masses, mendacious and absurd in their accusations and deeply hostile in their spirit, could not but work cumulative harm. They aimed at no particular class of foreigners; they were impartial in attacking everything foreign.

The Boxer movement grows with the secret approval of the Chinese government

Hostile demonstrations towards the stranger gained strength by organization. The sect, commonly styled the Boxers, developed greatly in the provinces north of Yangtsze, and, with the collusion of many notable officials, including some in the immediate councils of the Throne itself, became alarmingly aggressive. No foreigner's life, outside of the protected Treaty ports, was safe. No foreign interest was secure from spoliation.

The diplomatic representatives of the powers in Peking strove ·in vain to check this movement. Protest was followed by demand, and demand by renewed protest, to be met with perfunctory edicts from the palace, by evasive and futile assurances from the Tsung-li Yamên. The circle of the Boxer influence narrowed about Peking, and while nominally stigmatized as seditious, it was felt that its spirit pervaded the capital itself, that the Imperial forces were imbued with its doctrines, and that the immediate counselors of the empress dowager were in full sympathy with the antiforeign movement.

The Chinese government proved unable to check the rising strength of the Boxers, and appeared to be a prey to internal dissensions. In the unequal contest the antiforeign influences soon gained the ascendency under the leadership of Prince Tuan. Organized armies of Boxers, with which the Imperial forces affiliated, held the country between Peking and the coast, penetrated into Manchuria up to the Russian borders, and through their emissaries threatened a like rising throughout northern China.

Attacks upon foreigners, destruction of their property, and slaughter of native converts were reported from all sides. At this critical juncture, in the early spring of this year, a proposal was made by the other powers that a combined fleet should be assembled in Chinese waters as a moral demonstration. The United States, while not participating in the joint demonstration, promptly sent from the Philippines all ships that could be spared for service on the Chinese coast. A small force of marines was landed at Taku, and sent to Peking for the protection of the American Legation. Other powers took similar action, until some four hundred men were assembled in the capital as Legation guards.

An armed demonstration by the powers meets with resistance

Still the peril increased. The Legations reported the development of the seditious movement in Peking and the need of increased provision for defense against it. While preparations were in progress for a larger expedition to strengthen the Legation guards and keep the railway open, an attempt of the foreign ships to make a landing at Taku was met by a fire from the Chinese forts. The forts were thereupon shelled by the foreign vessels, the American admiral taking no part in the attack.

Two days later the Taku forts were captured after a sanguinary conflict. By the 19th June the Legations were cut off. An identical note from the Yamên ordered each

The murder
of Baron von
Ketteler
(June 20)
minister to leave Peking, under a promised escort, within twenty-four hours. To gain time they replied, asking prolongation of the time, which was afterwards granted, and requesting an interview with the Tsung-li Yamên on the following day. No reply being received, on the morning of the 20th the German minister, Baron von Ketteler, set out for the Yamên to obtain a response, and on the way was murdered. An attempt by the Legation guard to recover his body was foiled by the Chinese. Armed forces turned out against the Legations. Their quarters were surrounded and attacked. The Mission compounds were abandoned, their inmates taking refuge in the British Legation, where all the other Legations and guards gathered for more effective defense. Four hundred persons were crowded in its narrow compass. Two thousand native converts were assembled in a near-by palace under protection of the foreigners. Lines of defense were strengthened, trenches dug, barricades raised, and preparations made to stand a siege, which at once began.

The attack on
the Legations
"From the 20th June until the 17th July," writes Minister Conger, "there was scarcely an hour during which there was not firing upon some part of our lines and into some of the Legations, varying from a single shot to a general and continuous attack along the whole line." Artillery was placed around the Legations and on the overlooking palace walls, and thousands of three-inch shot and shell were fired, destroying some buildings and damaging all. So thickly did the balls rain that, when the ammunition of the besieged ran low, five quarts of Chinese bullets were gathered in an hour in one compound and recast.

Attempts were made to burn the Legations by setting neighboring houses on fire, but the flames were successfully fought off, although the Austrian, Belgian, Italian, and Dutch Legations were then and subsequently burned. With the aid of the native converts, directed by the missionaries, to whose helpful coöperation Mr. Conger awards unstinted praise, the British Legation was made a veritable fortress.

During the siege the defenders lost 65 killed, 135 wounded, and 7 by disease, — the last all children.

Mr. Conger's letter to the Secretary of State at Washington, dispatched from Peking on the 18th July, afforded to the outside world the first tidings that the inmates of the Legations were still alive and hoping for succor. This news stimulated the preparations for a joint relief expedition in numbers sufficient to overcome the resistance which for a month had been organizing between Taku and the capital. Reënforcements sent by all the coöperating governments were constantly arriving. The United States contingent, hastily assembled from the Philippines or dispatched from this country, amounted to some 5000 men, under the able command first of the lamented Colonel Liscum and afterwards of General Chaffee.

Preparations for relief of the Legations

Towards the end of July the movement began. A severe conflict followed at Tien-tsin. The city was stormed and partly destroyed. Its capture afforded the base of operations from which to make the final advance, which began in the first days of August, the expedition being made up of Japanese, Russian, British, and American troops at the outset. Another battle was fought and won at Yang-tsun. Thereafter the disheartened Chinese troops offered little show of resistance. A few days later the important position of Ho-si-woo was taken. A rapid march brought the united forces to the populous city of Tung Chow, which capitulated without a contest.

The movement on to the capital

On the 14th August the capital was reached. After a brief conflict beneath the walls the relief column entered and the Legations were saved. The United States soldiers, sailors, and marines, officers and men alike, in those distant climes and unusual surroundings, showed the same valor, discipline, and good conduct, and gave proof of the same high degree of intelligence and efficiency, which have distinguished them in every emergency. The Imperial family and the government had fled a few days before. The city was without visible control. The remaining Imperial soldiery had made, on the night of the 13th, a last attempt to exterminate the besieged, which was gallantly repelled.

Peking taken by the foreign troops

The policy of the United States through all this trying period was clearly announced and scrupulously carried out. A circular note to the powers, dated the 3d July, proclaimed our attitude.

The policy of the United States

Our declared aims involved no war against the Chinese nation. We adhered to the legitimate office of rescuing the imperiled Legation, obtaining redress for wrongs already suffered, securing wherever possible the safety of American life and property in China, and preventing a spread of the disorders or their recurrence. As was then said, "The policy of the government of the United States is to seek a solution which may bring about permanent safety and peace to China, preserve Chinese territorial and administrative entity, protect all rights guaranteed to friendly powers by treaty and international law, and safeguard for the world the principle of equal and impartial trade with all parts of the Chinese Empire."

The Chinese government was compelled by the powers to pay heavy indemnities for the damage done to foreigners and their property during the Boxer outbreak, and also to punish the most conspicuous leaders in the revolt. The imperial edict of November 13, 1900, ordering the punishment of certain offenders, is given here.

370. Imperial Chinese edict ordering the punishment of offenders in the Boxer uprising

The present troubles are to be attributed to the leniency shown towards, and the protection afforded to, the Boxer rebels by various officers of State. These troubles have caused us to become embroiled with friendly powers, and have proved a source of grief to the spirits of our ancestors.

We have already published edicts on this subject, decreeing punishments for the guilty, but we are extremely vexed and annoyed to find that in the districts round about the capital the Boxer rebels have not yet been completely exterminated, with the result that the country has been completely devastated and the populace plunged into a state of abject misery.

Unless, therefore, some severe and additional punishments are meted out, we cannot conciliate popular feeling nor appease the resentment of the friendly powers. We accordingly ordain as follows :

Tsai I, Prince Tuan, is deprived of his rank and offices, and is, together with Tsai-hsün, Prince Chuang, who has already been degraded, to be temporarily handed over to the Imperial Clan Court for incarceration. When hostilities shall have ceased they are to be sent to Mukden, and there imprisoned for life. Pu Ching, Prince of I, already degraded, Tsai Ying, a prince of the Fourth Order, likewise already degraded, are also to be handed over to the Imperial Clan Court for incarceration.

Tsai Lien, a prince of the Fourth Order, who has been deprived of his rank and offices, is directed to shut his door and reflect on his misdeeds.[1]

Kang Yi, former Assistant Grand Secretary and President of Civil Office, when sent on a mission to discover how to deal with the Boxer rebels, returned to Peking and submitted a report largely screening and extenuating their offenses. He ought, properly speaking, to have been most severely punished, but as he has since died a natural death, he is left out of account.

Yü Hsien, while officiating as governor of Shansi, in that he protected and encouraged the Boxer rebels and killed missionaries and Christian converts, was guilty of having acted in a most arbitrary and reckless manner. The circumstances of the case are peculiarly grave, and he is accordingly sentenced for life to hard labor on the remotest parts of the frontier.

371. The educational revolution in China The reform of the old system of education in China is one of the most important events in the world's history in modern times.[2] Since the year 627 the Chinese have required all candidates for the higher offices in the government to pass elaborate examinations on the Chinese classics, for which years of preparation were necessary. The students learned little or nothing, however, which

---

[1] Equivalent apparently to confinement in his own house.

[2] On August 27, 1908, the constitution, promised the year before, was published, modeled in a general way on that of Japan. A representative parliament is to be established. Accompanying the constitution are a bill of rights and an elaborate programme of reforms, political, social, and economic, which the Chinese government proposes to put into force gradually, year by year, until they shall be all in effect ten years hence.

bore on their practical duties. After the unsuccessful and humiliating war with Japan, the emperor issued the first order directed toward bettering the educational system, January 17, 1898. In this he said: "We have been compelled to issue this decree because our examinations have degenerated to the lowest point, and we see no way of remedying matters except by changing entirely the old methods of examination for a new system of competition. Let us all try to reject empty and useless knowledge which has no value in the crisis we are now passing through." The Dowager Empress blocked the reform for the moment, but after the Boxer rising she issued a decree in 1901 ordering that the topics of the examinations should consist in the main of questions relating to China, its history and government, and to the government, arts, and sciences of other lands. Dr. Charles Keyser Edmunds, of the Christian College of Canton, gives the following interesting examples from the old examination papers and the new.

From the old lists of topics on which the candidates were to comment:

Topics from the old style of examination papers

To possess ability, and yet defer to those who do not; to know much and yet inquire of those who know less; to possess and yet appear not to possess; to be full and yet appear empty.

He took hold of things by the two extremes, and in his treatment of the people maintained the golden mean.

A man from his youth studies right principles, and when he arrives at manhood he wishes to reduce them to practice.

Write in pentameters on, The sound of the oar and the green of the hills and of the water.

In the Han Dynasty there were three commentators on the *Yih King*, whose explanations and divisions into chapters and sentences were all very difficult. Can you give an account of them?

The following topics were assigned, among others, to the students taking the examination in 1903 under the new rules.

Western commerce depends essentially upon a knowledge of animals and plants. Cattle and sheep are raised by regulated methods ; climates suitable for the various kinds of cattle are distinguished ; soils and their particular qualities are studied. China should find out the best way to promote industry and commerce in like fashion. Discuss this. Examples of topics on the new examination papers of 1903

Metternich and Bismarck greatly aided in the advance of their countries. Tell briefly what they did.

The English scholar, Herbert Spencer, says that it is good for a people to form societies, and that through wars a people are compacted. When the people are more a unit, progress is easier and a higher civilization will be attained. And again he says that among those people who like to fight wars, civilization will decline or be retarded. What does he really mean by these seemingly contradictory statements?

Since the government has allowed the presence and work of foreign missionaries, many foolish people have sought refuge from the law of the land under the protection of the missionary by becoming converts; and some anti-Christians make a great deal of trouble throughout the empire. Because of this, for-eigners look down on China and declare that she is a country without education and without religion. But foreign scholars who are familiar with the literature of China say that five hun-dred years hence Confucianism will be spread over the whole world. The trouble at present is that we do not know how properly to propagate Confucianism, and not that the foolish people who are false Christians can injure our religion. If we want our religion to grow and the people to progress, what shall we do, what is the best plan to follow?

Western countries have established commercial centers and subsidized and protected great enterprises, — railroad and steamship lines for transportation ; banks and newspapers as a key to unlock the country's resources ; postal routes and telegraph lines to spread news very quickly ; and schools for education. In what order as to importance should we establish these things in China, according to the Western principle?

The war which broke out in February, 1904, between Russia and Japan was preceded by long and tedious negotiations between the two powers, in which attempts at a definition of the rights of the respective countries were made without avail. As early as July, 1903, Japan sent to her ambassador at St. Petersburg the following protest against the operations of Russia in Manchuria, and proposed negotiations looking toward an adjustment of the matter.

TOKIO, July 28, 1903

372. The grievances of Japan against Russia which led to war in 1904

The Japanese government has observed with close attention the development of affairs in Manchuria, and it views with grave concern the present situation there. So long as there were grounds for hope that Russia would carry out her engagement to China and her assurances to other powers on the subject of the evacuation of Manchuria, the Japanese government maintained an attitude of watchful reserve. But the recent action of Russia in formulating new demands in Peking, and in tightening rather than relaxing her hold on Manchuria, compels belief that she has abandoned the intention of retiring from Manchuria, while her increased activity along the Korean frontier is such as to raise doubts regarding the limits of her ambition. The unrestrained permanent occupation of Manchuria by Russia would create a condition of things prejudicial to the security and interest of Japan. Such occupation would be destructive of the principle of equal opportunity and an impairment of the territorial integrity of China.

Russian occupation of Manchuria is against Japan's interests

Russia seeks predominance in Korea

But, what is of still more serious moment to the Japanese government, Russia stationed on the flank of Korea would be a constant menace to the separate existence of that empire, and in any event it would make Russia the dominant power in Korea. Korea is an important outpost in Japan's line of defense, and Japan consequently considers the independence of Korea absolutely essential to her own repose and safety.

Japan possesses paramount political as well as commercial and industrial interests and influence in Korea, which, having regard to her own security, she cannot consent to surrender to, or share with, any other power. The Japanese government has given the matter its most serious consideration and has resolved to approach the Russian government in a spirit of conciliation and frankness, with a view to the conclusion of an understanding designed to compose questions which are at this time the cause of just and natural anxiety ; and, in the estimation of the Japanese government, the moment is opportune for making the attempt to bring about the desired adjustment.[1]

The following extracts are from a long official report by Admiral Togo to the emperor of Japan, describing in detail the great naval battle in the Sea of Japan, May 26–27, 1905.

The head of the enemy's column, when our main squadron bore down upon it, changed its course a little to the starboard, and at eight minutes past two o'clock they opened fire. We did not reply for some time, but when we came within six thousand meters' range we concentrated heavy fire on two of their battleships. The *Oslyabya*, which headed the left column, was soon seriously injured, burst into strong conflagration, and left the fighting line. The fire of both our squadrons becoming more and more effective as the range decreased, the flagship *Kniaz Suvaroff*, and the *Emperor Alexander III*, which was the second in line, burst into roaring flames and left the fighting line, so that the enemy's order became still more deranged.

373. Admiral Togo's description of the battle in the Sea of Japan (condensed)

[1] Russia agreed, through her representative, December 12, 1903, to respect the independence of Korea, to recognize Japan's preponderating interests there, and not to oppose Japan's industrial and commercial activities there or the presence of Japanese troops for promoting such interests. These propositions seemed reasonable to the Russian government and to many outside observers, but Japan was not satisfied with the concessions. Nothing was said of the evacuation of Manchuria, and Japan had good reason to suspect that the Russians might not fulfill their engagements ; accordingly she broke off diplomatic relations with Russia, February 5, 1904, and opened hostilities.

Several of the ships following also took fire, and the smoke carried by the westerly wind quickly swept over the face of the sea, combining with the fog to envelop the enemy's fleet so that our principal fighting squadrons ceased firing for a time.

On our side also the ships had suffered more or less. The *Asama* had been struck by three shells near the water line, her steering gear had been injured, and she was leaking badly; but she effected temporary repairs, and was very soon able to resume her place. Such was the state of the main fighting forces on each side at 2.45 P.M. Already the fate of the battle had been decided. . . .

Losses in the battle   The above are the results of the battle which continued from the afternoon of the 27th to the afternoon of the 28th. About thirty-eight of the enemy's vessels had attempted to pass the Sea of Japan, and I believe that the ships that escaped destruction or capture at our hands were limited to a few cruisers, destroyers, and special-service steamers. Our own losses in the two days' fight were only three torpedo boats. Some others of our vessels sustained more or less injuries, but not even one of them is incapacitated for future service. Our casualties throughout the whole fleet were 116 killed and 538 wounded, officers included.

Spirits of Imperial ancestors won the fight   There was no great difference in the strength of the opposing forces in this action, and I consider that the enemy's officers and men fought with the utmost energy and intrepidity on behalf of their country. If, nevertheless, our combined squadrons won the victory and achieved the remarkable success recorded above, it was because of the virtues of His Majesty the Emperor, and not owing to any human prowess. It cannot but be believed that the small number of our casualties was due to the protection of the spirits of the Imperial ancestors. Even our officers and men who fought so valiantly and so stoutly, seeing these results, found no language to express their astonishment.

After the disastrous defeat of the Russian fleet in the Sea of Japan, President Roosevelt, believing that the opportune moment had come for the establishment of peace between Russia and Japan, dispatched, on June 8,

1905, the following note to the Tsar and Mikado, urging them to open those negotiations which ultimately led to the Treaty of Portsmouth, New Hampshire.

The President feels that the time has come when, in the interest of all mankind, he must endeavor to see if it is not possible to bring to an end the terrible and lamentable conflict which is now being waged. With both Russia and Japan the United States has inherited ties of friendship and good will. It hopes for the prosperity and welfare of each, and it feels that the progress of the world is set back by the war between these two great nations. The President accordingly urges the Russian and Japanese governments, not only for their own sakes, but in the interest of the whole civilized world, to open direct negotiations for peace with one another.

374. President Roosevelt's peace proposals to Russia and Japan

The President suggests that these peace negotiations be conducted directly and exclusively between the belligerents; in other words, that there may be a meeting of Russian and Japanese plenipotentiaries or delegates, without any intermediary, in order to see if it is not possible for these representatives of the two powers to agree to terms of peace. The President earnestly asks that the Russian and Japanese governments do now agree to such a meeting.

While the President does not feel that any intermediary should be called in, in respect to the peace negotiations themselves, he is entirely willing to do what he properly can, if the two powers concerned feel that his services will be of aid in arranging the preliminaries as to the time and place of the meeting. But if these preliminaries can be arranged directly between the two powers or in any other way, the President will be glad, as his sole purpose is to bring about a meeting which the whole civilized world will pray may result in peace.

Section 106. Occupation of Africa by the Powers

An eminent French writer prefaces his account of the partition of Africa since 1880 by the following brief survey of the situation.

375. The partition of Africa (adapted from the *Histoire générale*)

By about 1880 the political geography of Europe was fixed; the attempt of any country to acquire territory at the expense of a neighbor would have precipitated an instantaneous armed conflict. Moreover, Europe had recovered from the fatigues which had accompanied the wars for the unification of the great nations, and regained its spirit of action; but its desire for expansion could now be satisfied only outside of Europe. All the continents, however, were occupied, except Africa, until then despised. The powers threw themselves upon that continent, so long scorned, and fairly dashed into the work of partition. The rivalry and the haste of the competitors was so great that one might well speak of "the great African hunt." Within twenty years almost everything was appropriated in Africa, and when the rivals wished to extend their borders further, they could only do so at the expense of the weaker among themselves.

History of native Africa of slight importance

The annals of Africa for twenty years (1880–1900) are practically limited to the story of the partition of the continent to its very heart. Its improvement and civilization have hardly begun; it has not yet passed out of the most rudimentary industrial state; and its development, of which there can be no question, will serve as a subject for the investigation of future historians. In itself the history of native Africa offers, with some few exceptions, no events of general interest. One may say, however, that the numberless African races have been happy because they have had no history. Some of them have had a little, but it is so confused that it cannot be told. Torrents of blood, which still flow in Africa, have been caused by the exploits of slave hunters, and by internecine pillages resulting from the general anarchy prevailing on a large scale; but the details of these horrors are so microscopic that they must be passed by with this general mention. The real object of our study should be the partition of Africa among the civilized nations.

The work of Stanley

One man epitomizes the political evolution of Africa, — Stanley. He began as an explorer and ended a conqueror and organizer. His geographical revelations attracted the attention of the covetous powers of Europe and led them to hurl themselves on Africa. The great journey of Stanley and the published accounts of his exploits were immediate causes of "the great African hunt." The passion which they aroused led to a grand attempt, at the Congress of Berlin in 1885, to institute an African public law. Through the stories of Stanley's discoveries, the enterprise of the king of Belgium, and the efforts of the Congress of Berlin a new State was created. That State, the Congo Free State, is at the present time the most advanced model of the methodical exploration, occupation, and industrial improvement of a great intertropical African country.

Stanley, the famous African explorer, set out in 1869 on a long and perilous journey into the heart of Africa in search of Livingstone, the missionary, who, it was feared, had lost his way or had been killed by the natives. Stanley thus describes his meeting with the veteran explorer after a trying journey of many months.

We push on rapidly. We halt at a little brook, then ascend the long slope of a naked ridge, the very last of the myriads we have crossed. We arrive at the summit, travel across, and arrive at its western rim, and Ujiji is below us, embowered in the palms, only five hundred yards from us ! At this grand moment we do not think of the hundreds of miles we have marched, of the hundreds of hills that we have ascended and descended, of the many forests we have traversed, of the jungles and thickets that annoyed us, of the fervid salt plains that blistered our feet, of the hot suns that scorched us, nor the dangers and difficulties now happily surmounted. Our hearts and our feelings are with our eyes, as we peer into the palms and try to make out in which hut or house lives the white man with the gray beard we heard about on the Malagarazi.

We are now about three hundred yards from the village of Ujiji, and the crowds are dense about me. Suddenly I hear a voice on my right say, " Good morning, sir ! "

Startled at hearing this greeting in the midst of such a crowd of black people, I turn sharply around in search of the man, and see him at my side, with the blackest of faces, but animated and joyous, — a man dressed in a long white shirt, with a turban

376. Stanley's meeting with Livingstone (condensed)

of American sheeting around his woolly head, and I ask, "Who the mischief are you?"

"I am Susi, the servant of Dr. Livingtone," said he, smiling, and showing a gleaming row of teeth.

"What! Is Dr. Livingstone here?"

"Yes, sir."

"In this village?"

"Yes, sir."

"Are you sure?"

"Sure, sure, sir. Why, I leave him just now."

Stanley wild with joy at the good news that Livingstone was near

In the meantime the head of the expedition had halted, and Selim said to me: "I see the Doctor, sir. Oh, what an old man! He has got a white beard." My heart beats fast, but I must not let my face betray my emotions, lest it shall detract from the dignity of a white man appearing under such extraordinary circumstances.

So I did that which I thought was most dignified. I pushed back the crowds, and, passing from the rear, walked down a living avenue of people until I came in front of the semicircle of Arabs, in the front of which stood the white man with the gray beard. As I advanced slowly toward him I noticed he was pale, looked wearied, had a gray beard, wore a bluish cap with a faded gold band round it, had on a red-sleeved waistcoat and a pair of gray tweed trousers. I would have run to him, only I was a coward in the presence of such a mob, — would have embraced him, only, he being an Englishman, I did not know how he would receive me; so I did what cowardice and false *Stanley greets Livingstone* pride suggested was the best thing, — walked deliberately to him, took off my hat, and said, "Dr. Livingstone, I presume?"

"Yes," said he, with a kind smile, lifting his cap slightly.

I replace my hat on my head and he puts on his cap, and we both grasp hands, and I then say aloud, "I thank God, Doctor, I have been permitted to see you."

He answered, "I feel thankful that I am here to welcome you."

Then, oblivious of the crowds, oblivious of the men who shared with me my dangers, we — Livingstone and I — turn our faces towards his tembe. He points to the veranda, or, rather, mud platform, under the broad overhanging eaves; he points to his own particular seat, which I see his age and experience in Africa has suggested, namely, a straw mat, with a goatskin over it, and another skin nailed against the wall to protect his back from contact with the cold mud. I protest against taking this seat, which so much more befits him than me, but the Doctor will not yield: I must take it. . . .

Conversation began. What about? I declare I have forgotten. Oh! we mutually asked questions of one another, such as: "How did you come here?" and "Where have you been all this long time? — the world has believed you to be dead." Yes, that was the way it began; but whatever the Doctor informed me, and that which I communicated to him, I cannot correctly report, for I found myself gazing at him, conning the wonderful man at whose side I now sat in Central Africa. Every hair of his head and beard, every wrinkle of his face, the wanness of his features, and the slightly wearied look he wore, were all imparting intelligence to me, — the knowledge I craved for so much ever since I heard the words, "Take what you want, but find Livingstone."

I called "Kaif-Halek," or "How-do-ye-do," and introduced him to Dr. Livingstone, that he might deliver in person to his master the letter bag he had been intrusted with. This was that famous letter bag marked "November 1, 1870," which was now delivered into the Doctor's hand 365 days after it left Zanzibar! How long, I wonder, had it remained at Unyanyembe had I not been dispatched into Central Africa in search of the great traveler? The Doctor kept the letter bag on his knees, then presently opened it, looked at the letters contained there, and read one or two of his children's letters, his face in the meantime lighting up.

The letter bag delivered and Livingstone reads his children's letters

He asked me to tell him the news. "No, Doctor," said I, "read your letters first, which I am sure you must be impatient to read."

"Ah," said he, "I have waited years for letters, and I have been taught patience. I can surely afford to wait a few hours longer. No, tell me the general news. How is the world getting along?"

"You probably know much already. Do you know that the Suez Canal is a fact, — is opened, and a regular trade carried on between Europe and India through it?"

"I did not hear about the opening of it. Well, that is grand news! What else?"

Stanley tells the news of the civilized world

Shortly I found myself enacting the part of an annual periodical to him. There was no need of exaggeration, — of any penny-a-line news, or of any sensationalism. The world had witnessed and experienced much the last few years. The Pacific Railroad had been completed; Grant had been elected President of the United States; Egypt had been flooded with savants; Prussia had humbled Denmark and annexed Schleswig-Holstein, and her armies were now around Paris; the "Man of Destiny" was a prisoner at Wilhelmshöhe; the Queen of Fashion and the Empress of the French was a fugitive; and the child born in the purple had lost forever the imperial crown intended for his head; the Napoleon dynasty was extinguished by the Prussians, Bismarck and Von Moltke; and France, the proud empire, was humbled to the dust.

What could a man have exaggerated of these facts? What a budget of news it was to one who had emerged from the depths of the primeval forests of Manyuema! The reflection of the dazzling light of civilization was cast on him while Livingstone was thus listening in wonder to one of the most exciting pages of history ever repeated. How the puny deeds of barbarism paled before these! Who could tell under what new phases of uneasy life Europe was laboring even then, while we, two of her lonely children, rehearsed the tale of her late woes and glories?

The Congo Free State government, to wit, King Leopold of Belgium, has energetically sought to develop the natural resources and especially the rubber industry of the region, but it is alleged that in this process of opening up the country the natives have been treated with horrible brutality by the officials. The charges have been indignantly denied by the parties concerned, and an

American writer, Professor Starr, who recently visited the regions, sums up his impressions of the controversy in the following manner :

Why should we pick out the Congo Free State for our assault. Atrocities occur wherever the white man with his thirst for gold comes into contact with "a lower people." He is ever there to exploit; he believes that they were created for exploitation. If we want to find cruelty, atrocities, all kinds of frightful maltreatment, we may find them in almost every part of negro Africa. They exist in the French Congo, in German Africa, in Nigeria, even in Uganda. If we insist on finding them, we may find cruelty, dispossession, destruction of life and property, in all these areas. The only ruthless act involving the death of a black native that we really saw was in French territory. If there were any object in doing so, we could write a harrowing story of British iniquity in Africa, but it is unnecessary; every one who stops to think and who reads at all knows the facts. Wherever British trade finds native custom standing in its way, we shall find cruelty. . . .

377. The treatment of natives in the Congo region

To me the real wonder is that there are any of the Congo peoples left. Think of the constant drain due to the foreign slave trade, continued from an early date until after the middle of the last century. Think of the continuous losses due to the barbarism of native chiefs and demands of native customs, — to wars, cannabalism, execution, and ordeal. Think of the destruction caused by punitive expeditions, — towns burned, people killed. Think of the drafts made by the public works which the state has been forced to carry out. Think of the multitudes who have died from the diseases of the country and from pestilence introduced by the newcomers. Yet the population really shows signs of great vitality to-day, and the most discouraged missionary hesitates to give a real prediction for the future. . . .

The terrible losses of life among the natives

Returned from the Congo country and a year and more of contact with the dark natives, I find that a curious and most disagreeable sensation has taken possession of me. I had read often and heard that other peoples find the faces of white

The fierceness of the white man's face

men terrifying and cruel. The Chinese, the Japanese, and other peoples of Asia tell the same story. The white man's face is fierce and terrible. His great and prominent nose suggests the beak of some bird of prey. His fierce face causes babes to cry, children to run in terror, grown folk to tremble. I had been always inclined to think that this feeling was individual and trifling; that it was solely due to strangeness and lack of contact. To-day I know better. Contrasted with the other faces of the world, the face of the fair white is terrible, fierce, and cruel. No doubt our intensity of purpose, our firmness and dislike of interference, our manner in walk and action and in speech all add to the effect. However that may be, both in Europe and our own land, after my visit to the blacks I see the cruelty and fierceness of the white man's face as I never would have believed was possible. For the first time I can appreciate fully the feelings of the natives. The white man's face is a dreadful prediction; where the white man goes, he devastates, destroys, depopulates. Witness America, Australia, and Van Dieman's Land.

From the suppression of the Egyptian uprising against the foreigners in 1882 down to the present day, England has "occupied" Egypt, steadily maintaining, however, that the situation is only temporary. During this period many great improvements in government, finance, industry, and public works have been carried out under the direction of English advisers and officials. Lord Milner, at one time Undersecretary for Finance in Egypt, states his views of the problem of occupation and withdrawal as follows:

378. English occupation of Egypt (condensed)　If it be admitted that to guide Egypt in the direction of civilized independence and to protect the various foreign interests which are bound up with her peace and prosperity, it is desirable that she should remain for a time under the guardianship of some great power, then there are obvious reasons why England should remain her guardian. The position that we occupy in Egypt may be said to be the result of accident. But it has more than accidental justification. Alike by the nature of our interests, by the nature of our power, and by certain special qualities in our national character, we seem marked out for the discharge of this particular duty.

Our interests in Egypt are absolutely identical with those of the Egyptian people. We are their principal customers and they are also very important customers of Great Britain. With the deficiency of outlets which threatens our vast foreign trade, the great and growing market of Egypt is evidently not a thing which we can afford to despise. And if Egyptian prosperity is British interest, so is Egyptian independence. We have no desire to possess ourselves of Egypt, but we have every reason to prevent any rival power from so possessing itself.

The truth is that the idea of a definite date for the conclusion of our work in Egypt is misleading. The withdrawal of Great Britain, if it is not to end in disaster, can only be a gradual process. If British troops were to be withdrawn, it would be more than ever necessary that the position of the British officers in the Egyptian army should be maintained. And not only the position of the British officers, but that of a limited number of high British officials in the civil service. No doubt, in time, even these safeguards might gradually be dispensed with ; but that is looking forward to a more distant period than it is of any use trying to speculate about just at present. The circumstances must decide. *Withdrawal, if it comes, must be gradual*

As native governing capacity develops, as natives come forward who are fit for responsible posts now held by Englishmen, these posts should be resigned to them. Perhaps some British element in the government would always be necessary. Perhaps the British prime minister would always need to exercise some control on the most important questions of policy, but that control might be, in the end, very light and almost imperceptible.

Let us hope that there may be no more attempts to confuse the issue by antiquated tirades about bondholders. Financial swindling may have helped to produce the state of things which made our intervention necessary. But the interest of *England's great object is promotion of Egypt's welfare* the bondholder — though, like every other legitimate interest, it has been benefited by England's action — has never been the inspiring motive of our policy, least of all our policy during recent years. Nothing could be more false than any suggestion to that effect. The inspiring, the predominant motive of that policy is the welfare of the Egyptian people. We have done much to promote their welfare, but there is something yet to do. The desire to complete the work is surely a worthy one. It is an effort in which, if we would be true to ourselves, we are bound to persist as long as we have the power.

Soon after England assumed "temporary control" of Egypt a revolt began in the Soudan, under the leadership of the Mahdi. General Gordon, who had once helped the Chinese government to suppress the Taiping rebellion,[1] was in command of the British troops. He was surrounded in Khartum and besieged by the followers of the Mahdi. The following letter, sent to him by one of the Mahdi's officers, December, 1884, gives us some idea of the enemies with whom he had to deal, and of the situation in which the English found themselves in attempting to extend their control over the Soudan.

379. General Gordon warned by a letter from an officer of the Mahdi (1884)   *In the name of God the Merciful, the Compassionate. Praise be to the Bountiful God, and blessings be upon our Lord Mohammed and upon his family. We, the servant of God, Abdallah Mohammed Jifarah, one of the governors of the Mahdi, on whom be peace, on the East, to Gordon, the Pasha of Khartum.* You have paid no attention to the counsel and reasoning repeatedly sent to you, but have increased in folly; and the numerous kindly admonitions have only made you more haughty and wayward; since truth enlightens the breasts of Believers, but only increases the oppressors in their degeneration. Your letter has reached us, in which you deceived the population, saying that the British reënforcement

[1] See above, pp. 422 *sqq.*

is coming to you in three divisions, and that it will soon reach you and give you victory ; thus your letter betrays the greatness of your fear, and anxiety, and alarm, as in your deceit you have caught hold of spider-web ropes and have feared to die at our hands. Thou must inevitably die, O thou heathen !

These promises, — you have been holding them out since last year to the inhabitants of Khartum, and have been promising them that the English will come soon. Your promise has only increased their sorrows ; and now that you are in straits, and that evil is coming upon you, you are practicing deceit from the interior of your den in which God has imprisoned you, upon him who is in the land of peace and crowned with exceeding much honor, and who is able to get the news of riders arriving from the remotest regions. I ask, do the sounds, winged and free, unfettered, need news from the like of thee in the sea of billows covered by waves upon wave, above which are clouds of darkness piled one over the other. Know thou, O thou enemy of God, that the true news is with us and not with you, and that the news which has reached us contains nothing to cheer thy eye or uphold thy power; on the contrary, there is no escape for thee from death at our hands, and from death by lack of food. No relief will come

But it is no wonder that you deny the Mahdiship, for you did not believe in the apostleship of Mohammed ; but the wonder is that the learned men of wickedness, who are raised to prominent positions by you, and whom God has left to go astray, and whose hearts he has closed, whose ears he has sealed, and over whose eyes he has put a veil, since they have been satisfied with you as a leader, and have taken you as a teacher, have waged war against Believers, and seek victory for those who believe in more than one God, as though they had not heard the word of God. "If you wage war, war will come upon you, and if you end war, it is better for you, and if you return, God will return, and he is with the Believers." . . . God is with the true believers

It is strange how you frighten the people, saying the English are coming, and how you think that the Allies will be affected by your false rumors. No, by God ! even though swarms of English and others should come, this would only increase the faith of the Allies, and their steadfastness would grow in the labor of the siege until God shall make you taste confusion and destruction. Take warning by those who are like you, if you are children of intelligence. Before you the people of Obeid were longing for reënforcements, like the longing of the thirsty for water; and they too were writing deceitful and cheering letters, more than you have done; and, nevertheless, you have heard what befell them.

If you are content to remain as you are, then prepare for what shall come; but if you knock at the door of repentance, peradventure it may be opened unto you.

Peace be upon those who follow after the right way.

ABDULLAH MOHAMMED

[7th or 8th December, 1884]

Section 107. Influences favoring Universal Peace

The Quakers were perhaps the first to make opposition to war a part of their religious creed. William Penn, one of the most distinguished members of the sect, drafted a plan for a parliament of nations which should settle all disputes without recourse to arms. When Voltaire visited England in 1726 he found himself drawn to the Quakers by reason of their simple religion and manners and their detestation of war. In his *Letters on the English* he reports, in his amusing way, an interview with a representative of the Quaker faith.

380. The Quakers' view of war (Voltaire)

I was of opinion that the doctrine and history of so extraordinary a people as the Quakers deserved the attention of the curious. To acquaint myself with them, I made a visit to one of the most eminent Quakers in England, who, after having traded thirty years, had the wisdom to prescribe limits to his fortune and to his desires, and was settled not far from London. He was a hale, ruddy-complexioned old man, who had never been afflicted with sickness because he was a perfect stranger to intemperance. I never in my life saw a more noble or a more engaging aspect than his. He was dressed like those of his persuasion, in a plain coat, without plaits in the sides, or buttons on the pockets and sleeves; and he had on a beaver, the brims of which were horizontal, like those of our clergy. He did not uncover himself when I appeared, and advanced towards me without once stooping his body; but there appeared more politeness in the open, humane air of his countenance than in the custom of drawing one leg behind the other, and taking that from the head which is made to cover it. "Friend," says he to me, "I perceive thou art a stranger, but if I can do anything for thee, only tell me." "Sir," says I to him, bending forwards, and advancing as is usual with us, one leg towards him, "I flatter myself that my just curiosity will not give you the least offense, and that you'll do me the honor to inform me of the particulars of your religion." "The people of thy country," replied the Quaker, "are too full of their bows and compliments, but I never yet met with one of them who had so much curiosity as thyself. Come in, and let us first dine together." I still continued to make some very unseasonable ceremonies, it not being easy to disengage one's self at once from habits one has been long used to; and after taking part of a frugal meal, which began and ended with a prayer to God, I began to question my curious host. . . .

"We never war or fight in any case; but 't is not that we are afraid, for so far from shuddering at the thoughts of death, we, on the contrary, bless the moment which unites us with the Being of Beings; but the reason of our not using the outward sword is that we are neither wolves, tigers, nor mastiffs, but men and Christians. Our God, who has commanded us to love our enemies and to suffer without repining, would certainly not permit us to cross the seas, merely because murderers clothed in scarlet and wearing caps two foot high enlist citizens by a noise made with two little sticks on a tightly stretched ass's skin. And when, after a victory is gained, the whole city of London is illuminated; when the sky is in a blaze with fireworks, and a noise is heard in the air of thanksgivings, of bells, of organs, and of the cannon, we groan in silence, and are deeply affected with sadness of spirit and brokenness of heart, for the sad havoc which is the occasion of those public rejoicings."

The Quakers are no longer alone in their denunciations of war. A few years ago the well-known novelist, Maupassant, as he witnessed the target practice of a group of French soldiers, felt a great wave of horror and disgust sweep over him, and he penned the following terrible picture of the real character and effects of war :

381. Maupassant on the horrors of war

I have but to think of the word " war " and a paralyzing sense of horror creeps over me, as though I were listening to stories of witchcraft, or tales of the Inquisition, or of things abominable, monstrous, unnatural, of ages past. . . .

Civilization and " schools for murder "

War ! The fighting ! The murdering ! The slaughter of men ! And to-day — with all our wisdom and civilization, with the advancement of science, the degree of philosophy to which the human spirit has attained — we have schools where the art of murder, of aiming with deadly accuracy and killing large numbers of men at a distance, is actually taught ; killing poor, harmless fellows who have families to support, killing them without the pretext of the law.

It is stupefying that the people do not rise up in arms against the governments. What difference is there between monarchies and republics ? It is stupefying that society does not revolt as a unit at the very sound of the word " war."

Alas ! we shall never be free from the oppression of the hateful, hideous customs, the criminal prejudices, and the ferocious impulses of our barbarous ancestors, for we are beasts, and beasts we shall remain, moved by our instincts and susceptible of no improvement.

A clever expert in this business, a genius in the art of murder, Von Moltke, once made the following reply to a peace delegate :

Von Moltke's view of war

" War is sacred ; it is a divine institution ; it fosters every lofty and noble sentiment in the human heart, — honor, self-sacrifice, virtue, courage, — and saves men, so to speak, from settling into the grossest materialism."

Assembling in herds by the hundred thousand, marching night and day without rest, with no time for thought or for study, never to read, learning nothing, of no use whatsoever to any living being, rotting with filth, sleeping in the mud, living like a wild beast in a perennial state of stupidity, plundering cities, burning villages, ruining whole nations; then to encounter another mountain of human flesh, rush upon it, cause rivers of blood to flow, and strew the fields with the dead and the dying, all stained with the muddy and reddened soil; to have one's limbs severed, one's brain scattered as wanton waste, and to perish in the corner of a field while one's aged parents, one's wife and children are dying of hunger at home, — this is what it means to be saved from " settling into the grossest materialism."

Soldiers are the scourge of the world. We struggle against nature, ignorance, all kinds of obstacles, in the effort to make our wretched lives more endurable. There are men, scientists and philanthropists, who devote their whole lives to benefiting their fellow-men, and seeking to improve their condition. They pursue their efforts tirelessly, adding discovery to discovery, expanding the human intelligence, enriching science, opening new fields of knowledge, day by day increasing the well-being, comfort, and vigor of their country. *War destroys the results of civilization*

Then war comes upon the scene, and in six months all the results of twenty years of patient labor and of human genius are gone forever, crushed by victorious generals. And this is what they mean when they speak of man's rescue from materialism !

We have seen war. We have seen men maddened, — returning to the condition of brutes ; we have seen them kill in wanton sport, out of terror, or for mere bravado and show. Where right no longer exists, and law is dead, where all sense of justice has been lost, we have seen innocent men shot down on the highway because they were timid and thus excited suspicion. *War degrades the soldier*

To invade a country, to kill the man who defends his home, to burn the dwellings of starving wretches, to ruin or plunder a man's household goods, to drink the wine found in the cellars, to violate the women found in the streets, to consume

millions of francs in powder, and to leave misery and cholera
in their track, — this is what they mean by saving men from
the grossest materialism !

Tolstoi, the celebrated Russian philosopher and man of
letters, who quotes the passages from Maupassant given
above, adds his own denunciation of men like the German
emperor, who represent the old confidence in war and
the firm belief that it is a necessary part of human life.

382. Tolstoi attacks the warlike sentiments of the German emperor

In 1891 this same Wilhelm (who expresses what other
men only venture to think), in a talk with certain soldiers,
uttered publicly the following words, which were repeated the
next day in thousands of papers :

"Recruits ! You have given *me* the oath of allegiance before
the altar and the servant of the Lord. You are still too young
to comprehend the true meaning of what has been said here,
but, first of all, take care ever to follow the orders and instructions that are given you. You have taken the oath of allegiance to *me ;* this means, children of my guards, that you
are now *my* soldiers, that you have given yourselves up to me,
body and soul. But one enemy exists for you, — *my* enemy.
With the present socialistic intrigues *it may happen that I shall
command you to shoot your own relations, your brothers, even
your parents* (from which may God preserve us !), *and then
you are in duty bound to obey my orders unhesitatingly.*"

This man expresses what is known but carefully concealed
by all wise rulers. He says outright that the men who serve in
the army serve *him* and *his* advantage, and should be ready,
for that reason, to kill their brothers and fathers.

Roughly, but distinctly, he lays bare all the horror of the
crime for which men who become soldiers prepare themselves,
— all that abyss of self-abasement into which they fling themselves when they promise obedience.

Poor, sick, miserable man, intoxicated with power, who by
these words insults all that is sacred to men of modern civilization ! And we, Christians, Liberals, men of culture, so far
from feeling indignant at this insult, pass it over in silence.

Men are put to the final test in its rudest form ; but they hardly observe that it is a test, that a choice is put before them. It seems to them as if there were no choice, but only the one necessity of slavish submission. It would seem as if these insane words, offensive to all that a civilized human being holds sacred, ought to rouse indignation, — but nothing of the kind happens. Year after year every young man in Europe is subjected to the same test, and, with very few exceptions, they all foreswear what is and should be sacred to every man ; all manifest a readiness to kill their brothers and even their fathers, at the order of the first misguided man who wears a red and gold livery, asking only when and whom they are to be ordered to kill.

Not only the horrors of actual war, but the terrible burden of the modern standing army and the vast expense of modern arms and battle ships, which must be borne by all nations so long as disputes are settled by resort to arms, are impressing thoughtful men of all classes, from the socialistic reformer to the Autocrat of all the Russias. Indeed, it was the Tsar himself who issued the invitation to the powers to join with him in a conference to consider the possibility of reducing the armaments which now crush the European peoples. At the regular weekly reception of the diplomats held at the court of St. Petersburg, August 24, 1898, each visitor received from the Russian foreign minister the following lithographed letter :

The maintenance of general peace, and a possible reduction of the excessive armaments which weigh upon all nations, present themselves in the existing condition of the whole world, as the ideal towards which the endeavors of all governments should be directed.

383. The Tsar's rescript calling the first peace congress, August, 1898

The humanitarian and magnanimous ideas of His Majesty the Emperor, my august master, have been won over to this view. In the conviction that this lofty aim is in conformity with the most essential interests and the legitimate views of all powers, the Imperial Government thinks that the present moment would be very favorable for seeking, by means of international discussion, the most effectual means of insuring to all peoples the benefits of a real and durable peace, and, above all, of putting an end to the progressive development of the present armaments.

In the course of the last twenty years the longings for a general pacification have become especially pronounced in the consciences of civilized nations. The preservation of peace has been put forward as the object of international policy; in its name great States have concluded powerful alliances between themselves. It is the better to guarantee peace that they have developed, in proportions hitherto unprecedented, their military forces, and still continue to increase them without shrinking from any sacrifice.

All these efforts, nevertheless, have not yet been able to bring about the beneficent results of the desired pacification. The financial burdens following an upward trend strike the public prosperity at its very source.

The waste of military expenditure   The intellectual and physical strength of the nations, labor and capital, are, for the major part, diverted from their natural application and unproductively consumed. Hundreds of millions are devoted to acquiring terrible engines of destruction, which, though to-day regarded as the last word of science, are destined to-morrow to lose all value in consequence of some fresh discovery in the same field.

National culture, economic progress, and the production of wealth are either paralyzed or checked in their development. Moreover, in proportion as the armaments of each power increase, so do they less and less fulfill the object which the governments have set before themselves.

The economic crises, due in great part to the system of armaments *à l'outrance*, and the continual danger which lies in this massing of war material, are transforming the armed peace of our days into a crushing burden, which the peoples have more and more difficulty in bearing. It appears evident, then, that if this state of things be prolonged, it will inevitably lead to the very cataclysm which it is desired to avert, and the horrors of which make every thinking man shudder in advance.

To put an end to these incessant armaments and to seek the means of warding off the calamities which are threatening the whole world, — such is the supreme duty which is to-day imposed on all States.

Filled with this idea, his Majesty has been pleased to order me to propose to all the governments whose representatives are accredited to the Imperial Court, the meeting of a conference which should occupy itself with this grave problem. The Tsar invites a peace conference of the powers

This conference should be, by the help of God, a happy presage for the century which is about to open. It would converge in one powerful focus the efforts of all States which are sincerely seeking to make the great idea of universal peace triumph over the elements of trouble and discord.

It would, at the same time, confirm their agreement by the solemn establishment of the principles of justice and right, upon which repose the security of States and the welfare of peoples.

The first International Peace Conference was held at The Hague in 1899, and a second conference assembled in the same city in 1907. The most important results of the latter are thus summed up by Dr. James B. Scott, who was a technical delegate representing the United States.

The second International Peace Conference, like its predecessor of 1899, endeavored to humanize the hardships necessarily incident to war and to substitute for a resort to arms a pacific settlement of international grievances, which, if unsettled, might lead to war or make the maintenance of pacific relations difficult and problematical. The conference of 1907, no more than its immediate predecessor, satisfied the leaders of humanitarian thought. War was not abolished, nor was peace legislated into existence. Universal disarmament was as unacceptable now as then, and some few nations were still unwilling to bind themselves to refer all international disputes **384. The work of the second Hague Conference (1907)** not involving independence, vital interests, or national honor, to a court of arbitration.

The work of the Second Conference, for which the year 1907 will be memorable, was twofold. First, it revised and enlarged the conventions of 1899 in the light of experience, in the light of practice as well as of theory, and put them forth to the world in a new and modified form. In the next place, the Conference did not limit itself to these subjects. To the three conventions of 1899, revised in 1907, were added ten new conventions. This simple statement shows the enormous field covered and the positive results achieved by the Second Conference within the comparatively short period of four months. Tried by the standards of results, the Conference clearly justified its existence, but it would have been a success had it demonstrated nothing more than the possibility of the representatives of forty-four nations to live in peace and quiet during four months. If it had done nothing more than to bring these representatives into close contact, to learn to understand one another's needs by understanding one another, the conference would have been a success.

Leaving out minor matters, this Conference did four things of fundamental importance :

1. It provided for a meeting of the Third Conference within an analogous period, namely eight years, to be under the control of the powers generally, instead of the control of any one of them.

2. It adopted a convention for the nonforcible collection of contract debts, substituting arbitration and an appeal to reason for force and an appeal to arms.

3. It established a prize court to safeguard neutrals.

4. It laid the foundations of, if it did not put the finishing stone to, a great court of arbitration.

CHAPTER XXXI

SOME OF THE GREAT PROBLEMS OF TO-DAY

Section 108. The Responsibilities of Modern Government

Among the chief political questions of the nineteenth century were: How far should the king, nobility, and clergy retain the powers which they had so long enjoyed? what kind of a parliament should the constitution provide? what should be its powers? who should be permitted to vote for the representatives which composed it? and, lastly, how far should the old restrictions be removed so that every one should be free to say and write what he wished and hold such religious ideas as appealed to him? In the several European States there was a tendency for *four* main political parties to form, each representing its particular views of these questions. A French historian gives the following description of the party programmes:

385. Party issues in western Europe during the first half of the nineteenth century (from Seignobos)

1. The Absolutist Conservative party, formed by the high officials and landed aristocracy, desired to maintain absolute government, the authority of the Church, and the censorship of the press; it controlled all the central, eastern, and southern States of Europe. It no longer existed in England, for the former Absolutist party, the Jacobites, had not survived the century of political liberty.

The Absolutist party

2. The Liberal Conservative, or Constitutional party, sometimes called the Tory, or Right Center, composed of the upper middle class and the liberal officeholders, demanded that the parliament should control the administration of the government, particularly in financial matters. Its ideal was personal government by the sovereign, with a parliament of two houses, one

The Constitutional party, or Right Center

467

aristocratic, the other elective. It believed that the electoral body should be limited by a considerable property qualification, and that the parliament should vote the annual budget and leave the prince free in the choice of his ministers and in the direction of general policy. There should be no censorship of the press, but liberty should be restricted to the wealthy classes; the nation's rights should be guaranteed by a constitution. This party was in power in the States which had constitutions; in the absolute monarchies it demanded a constitution, a representative assembly, and the abolition of censorship.

The Parliamentary party, or Left Center

3. The Parliamentary Liberal party, sometimes called the Whig, or Left Center, recruited from the middle class, demanded not only control by the elective assembly but its supremacy over the sovereign, his ministers, and the aristocratic chamber. Its ideal was the parliamentary system, a ministry chosen from the party in majority in the lower house, governing in the prince's name, but according to the will of the elected representatives of the nation. It demanded a constitution which recognized the superior rights or sovereignty of the people, political liberties (such as liberty of the press, holding public meetings, and forming associations), and absolute religious liberty. . . . It would admit only property owners to vote, but tended to lower the qualifications for the franchise in order to include in the voting body the lower middle class.

The Radical Democratic party

4. The Democratic, or Radical party, formed by students, workingmen, writers, and lawyers, demanded, according to the motto of the French Revolution, the sovereignty and political equality of the people. It added to the demands of the Parliamentary party universal suffrage, remuneration of representatives, abolition of all political privileges of the wealthy classes, and separation of Church and State. Its ideal was a purely representative, democratic, and preferably republican government like that of the French Convention, or even a direct government by the people, in which they should themselves make the constitution. In 1815 this party, so far from being in power in any country, had not even the right to formulate its programme publicly, except in England, Sweden, and Norway.

The two extreme parties, Absolutist and Democratic, held diametrically opposite conceptions of government and society. The Absolutists wanted a society based on hereditary inequality. . . . They also demanded an established religion. The Democrats admitted neither political, hereditary, nor ecclesiastical authority.

A country might, however, pass from one of these extremes to the other gradually, for the four parties formed a continuous gradation. The Absolutist system became constitutional when the prince consented to grant a constitution, as in the South German States in 1816–1819. The constitutional system was insensibly transformed into the parliamentary system as the sovereign took more account of the wishes of the elective chamber, as in England after 1830. The parliamentary system became democratic with the extension of the suffrage and the assembly's acquisition of supremacy over all the other powers, as in Switzerland.

Before the nineteenth century was over, however, the purely political questions as to the suffrage, the form of government, and rights of the individual began to be superseded by new questions growing out of the demands of the mass of the people and their sympathizers for help from the government in improving the condition of the people, especially the workingmen, and in lessening ignorance, poverty, and disease. Accordingly governments began to interfere in the conduct of business, the education of the people, and many other matters which had once been deemed purely private concerns. Many writers of insight and ability opposed the extension of the powers of the government on the ground that it would curtail the liberty of the individual and lead to innumerable abuses, perhaps to downright tyranny. The views of these thinkers are fairly represented by the following extracts from Donisthorpe's work, *Individualism*.

386. An argument against government interference with private matters (condensed)

Turn now to the great question, What ought the government, however constituted, to do? What are the duties of the State, be it monarchical, republican, or mixed? And here again the politicians may be split up into two great parties. There are those who maintain the greatest possible liberty of the individual citizen compatible with the equal liberty of his fellows, and who disapprove, therefore, of all meddlesome legislation. They would restrict the functions of the State to the administration of justice, the maintenance of order, the defense of the country against foreign antagonism, and the collection and management of the revenue for these purposes, and leave other matters to take care of themselves. .

On the other hand, there are those who believe that a well-organized body like the State is, or might be made, the most highly efficient machine for the carrying out of many great and noble schemes for the improvement of the people and the amelioration of their lot. Such are the persons who support State education, State charities, State museums and galleries, State railways and telegraphs, State banks, State post offices, and even State censors and spies. Such are the persons who would close the public houses at ten o'clock or altogether, and who would convert drunkards by force, who would and do force their medical nostrums upon unbelievers and imprison those who resist. Such *were* the persons who took general charge of the eternal welfare of their fellow-creatures, and founded inquisitions to keep them in the right path.

Many matters are well regulated by private agreement

The radical papers teem with questions calculated to bring ridicule upon those who oppose State interference in general. It seems to be forgotten that other bodies make laws besides the State. The Stock Exchange and the Jockey Club at once present themselves as private bodies making laws which are virtually accepted by the whole country. The customs of the Lancashire cotton trade are the finest example of commercial law in the world. Every club, every society and association, makes its own laws, which are sufficiently sanctioned to meet with respect and obedience, quite as uniformly as the laws of the land.

And yet the prevailing impression seems to be that only the State can make laws having any binding effect, — that without

such State rules and regulations everything would be topsy- It is a false
turvy. Mine owners and miners would conspire to blow up the notion that
mines; shipowners would scuttle their ships, drown their crews, disorder
get up a glorious reputation for going to the bottom, and pay occurs when
double insurance; cabmen would charge at least a guinea a the State
mile; bankers would smother the country with worthless paper; does not
railway companies would smash up passengers and goods, charge regulate
prohibitive fares, and ruin their shareholders; theatrical managers would drive all the respectable and moneyed classes away
from theaters by exhibitions of bad taste; publicans would sit
up all night in order to sell a pint of ale; pawnbrokers would
charge sixty per cent a month and receive stolen goods with
alacrity; landlords would keep their farms unlet and uncultivated; farmers would pay more in rent than they could recoup
in profit; and everybody would work to death without taking
a holiday; in fine, society is accredited with suicidal mania and
must be kept in a straight waistcoat.

The first question asked is, "What! would you allow a Let private
thoughtless collier to light his pipe in the workings?" or persons regu
"Would you let railway companies charge what they like?" late their
or something equally irrelevant. Now the answer to all these own affairs
and similar questions is, that it is not the expediency or appro-
priateness of this or that regulation with which individualism
concerns itself. It may be an excellent provision that passenger
trains should not run at more than sixty miles an hour, or it
may not; if it is, let the companies make such a rule or let the
public refrain from traveling by lines which have no such rule;
but let not Parliament interfere in the matter. Again, as to
naked lights in a coal pit, is it really believed that colliers are
so absurdly reckless of their own lives as to imperil them for
the sake of a whiff of tobacco? And even granting that there
are a few such dangerous lunatics in the pits, as out of them,
is the mine owner so anxious himself for a meeting with his
creditors as to allow such doings if they can possibly be
prevented?

The plain fact is, apart from theory, that before the passing
of any acts relating to mines the most stringent regulations were
in force concerning the use of lights and lamps in workings,

— rules not so much imposed by the masters as agreed to alike by owners, managers, and men, for the common safety. It is the ability to make such rules and to obey them, and to enforce them, that makes the Anglo-Saxon race what it is, — a colonizing people, a people fit for self-government. And it is the weakening and supplanting of these contractual rules by rules emanating from a central legislature, which will some day, if persisted in, reduce the Englishman to the level of his continental neighbors.

Notwithstanding the warnings of individualists like the philosopher Herbert Spencer, Donisthorpe, and many others, governments are assuming new and larger tasks and responsibilities. Nowhere in the world has the government undertaken to do more for the people than in the comparatively new States of New Zealand and Australia. The vast change that has come about in this respect can be best illustrated, perhaps, by a comparison of the powers conferred on the federal Congress of the United States by the Constitution of 1787, with the following powers enjoyed by the federal parliament of the Australian Commonwealth under the constitution which went into effect in 1901.

387. Powers of the Australian parliament

The parliament shall, subject to this Constitution, have power to make laws for the peace, order, and good government of the Commonwealth with respect to

1. Trade and commerce with other countries, and among the States;

2. Taxation; but so as not to discriminate between States or parts of States;

3. Bounties on the production or export of goods, but so that such bounties shall be uniform throughout the Commonwealth;

4. Borrowing money on the public credit of the Commonwealth;

5. Postal, telegraphic, telephonic, and other like services;

6. The naval and military defense of the Commonwealth and of the several States, and the control of the forces to execute and maintain the laws of the Commonwealth;

7. Lighthouses, light-ships, beacons, and buoys;

8. Astronomical and meteorological observations;

9. Quarantine;

10. Fisheries in Australian waters beyond territorial limits;

11. Census and statistics;

12. Currency, coinage, and legal tender;

13. Banking, other than State banking; also State banking extending beyond the limits of the State concerned, the incorporation of banks, and the issue of paper money;

14. Insurance, other than State insurance; also State insurance extending beyond the limits of the State concerned;

15. Weights and measures;

16. Bills of exchange and promissory notes;

17. Bankruptcy and insolvency;

18. Copyrights, patents of inventions and designs, and trade-marks;

19. Naturalization and aliens;

20. Foreign corporations, and trading or financial corporations formed within the limits of the Commonwealth;

21. Marriage;

22. Divorce and matrimonial causes; and, in relation thereto, parental rights and the custody and guardianship of infants;

23. Invalid and old-age pensions;

24. The service and execution throughout the Commonwealth of the civil and criminal process and the judgments of the courts of the States;

25. The recognition throughout the Commonwealth of the laws, the public acts and records, and the judicial proceedings of the States;

26. The people of any race, other than the aboriginal race in any State, for whom it is deemed necessary to make special laws;

27. Immigration and emigration;

28. The influx of criminals ;

29. External affairs ;

30. The relations of the Commonwealth with the islands of the Pacific ;

31. The acquisition of property on just terms from any State or person for any purpose in respect of which the parliament has power to make laws ;

32. The control of railways with respect to transport for the naval and military purposes of the Commonwealth ;

33. The acquisition, with the consent of a State, of any railways of the State on terms arranged between the Commonwealth and the State ;

34. Railway construction and extension in any State with the consent of that State ;

35. Conciliation and arbitration for the prevention and settlement of industrial disputes extending beyond the limits of any one State.

While governments have been regulating more and more matters once left to private arrangement, they have at the same time been removing many restrictions formerly imposed upon the individual citizen. Some of the most noteworthy changes in the latter direction have been made on behalf of women by admitting them to educational advantages, to the enjoyment of full property rights, and sometimes to the suffrage. The celebrated English philosopher and political economist, John Stuart Mill (1806–1873), was much interested, in the latter years of his life, in freeing women from the old trammels which restricted their independence and placed them legally almost completely under the control of men. In his work, *The Subjection of Women*, published in 1869, he describes with ill-concealed indignation the attitude of the then existing English law towards women.

Originally women were taken by force, or regularly sold by their father to the husband. Until a late period in European history the father had the power to dispose of his daughter in marriage at his own will and pleasure, without any regard to hers. The Church, indeed, was so far faithful to a better morality as to require a formal "yes" from the woman at the marriage ceremony; but there was nothing to show that the consent was other than compulsory, and it was practically impossible for the girl to refuse compliance if the father persevered, except, perhaps, when she might obtain the protection of religion by a determined resolution to take monastic vows.

388. Former position of women under English law

After marriage the man had anciently (but this was anterior to Christianity) the power of life and death over his wife. She could invoke no law against him; he was her sole tribunal and law. For a long time he could repudiate her, but she had no corresponding power in regard to him. By the old laws of England the husband was called the *lord* of the wife; he was literally regarded as her sovereign, inasmuch as the murder of a man by his wife was called treason (*petty* as distinguished from *high* treason), and was more cruelly avenged than was usually the case with high treason, for the penalty was burning to death.

The husband called the "lord" of his wife

Because these various enormities have fallen into disuse (for most of them were never formally abolished, or not until they had long ceased to be practiced), men suppose that all is now as it should be in regard to the marriage contract; and we are continually told that civilization and Christianity have restored to the woman her just rights. Meanwhile the wife is the actual bond servant of her husband; no less so, as far as legal obligation goes, than slaves commonly so called. She vows a lifelong obedience to him at the altar, and is held to it all through her life by law. Casuists may say that the obligation of obedience stops short of participation in crime, but it certainly extends to everything else.

Woman a bond servant to her husband

She can do no act whatever but by his permission, at least tacit. She can acquire no property but for him; the instant it becomes hers, even if by inheritance, it becomes *ipso facto* his. In this respect the wife's position under the common law

The husband secures his wife's property

of England is worse than that of slaves in the laws of many countries; by the Roman law, for example, a slave might have his *peculium*, which, to a certain extent, the law guaranteed to him for his exclusive use. The higher classes in this country have given an analogous advantage to their women, through special contracts setting aside the law, by conditions of pin money, etc.; since, parental feeling being stronger with fathers than the class feeling of their own sex, a father generally prefers his own daughter to a son-in-law who is a stranger to him. By means of settlements the rich usually contrive to withdraw the whole or part of the inherited property of the wife from the absolute control of the husband; but they do not succeed in keeping it under her own control; the utmost they can do only prevents the husband from squandering it, at the same time debarring the rightful owner from its use. The property itself is out of the reach of both. . . . In the immense majority of cases there is no settlement, and the absorption of all rights, all property, as well as all freedom of action, is complete.

Husband and wife are "one person" in law

The two are called "one person in law," for the purpose of inferring that whatever is hers is his, but the parallel inference is never drawn, that whatever is his is hers; the maxim is not applied against the man, except to make him responsible to third parties for her acts, as a master is for the acts of his slaves or of his cattle. I am far from pretending that wives are, in general, no better treated than slaves; but no slave is a slave to the same lengths, and in so full a sense of the word, as a wife is. Hardly any slave, except one immediately attached to the master's person, is a slave at all hours and all minutes; in general he has, like a soldier, his fixed task, and when it is done, or when he is off duty, he disposes, within certain limits, of his own time, and has a family life into which the master rarely intrudes.

The power of husband over the children

While she is held in this worst description of slavery as to her own person, what is her position in regard to the children in whom she and her master have a joint interest? They are by law *his* children. He alone has any legal rights over them. Not one act can she do towards or in relation to them, except by delegation from him. Even after he is dead she is not their legal guardian, unless he by will has made her so. He could even send them away from her, and deprive her of the means of seeing or corresponding with them, until this power was in some degree restricted by Serjeant Talfourd's Act.

This is her legal state, and from this state she has no means of withdrawing herself. If she leaves her husband, she can take nothing with her, neither her children nor anything which is rightfully her own. If he chooses, he can compel her to return, by law or by physical force; or he may content himself with seizing for his own use anything which she may earn, or which may be given to her by her relations. It is only legal separation by a decree of a court of justice, which entitles her to live apart, without being forced back into the custody of an exasperated jailer, or which empowers her to apply any earnings to her own use without fear that a man whom perhaps she has not seen for twenty years will pounce upon her some day and carry all off. This legal separation, until lately, the courts of justice would only give at an expense which made it inaccessible to any one out of the higher ranks. Even now it is only given in cases of desertion or of the extreme of cruelty; and yet complaints are made every day that it is granted too easily.

Separation almost impossible

Surely if a woman is denied any lot in life but that of being the personal body servant of a despot, and is dependent for everything upon the chance of finding one who may be disposed to make a favorite of her instead of merely a drudge, it is a very cruel aggravation of her fate that she should be allowed to try this chance only once. The natural sequel and corollary from this state of things would be, that since her all in life depends upon obtaining a good master, she should be allowed to change again and again until she finds one. . . . Its refusal completes the assimilation of the wife to the slave, — and the slave under not the mildest form of slavery; for in some slave codes the slave could, under certain circumstances of ill usuage, legally compel the master to sell him.

If the authority of men over women, when first established, had been the result of a conscientious comparison between

different modes of constituting the government of society;
if, after trying various other modes of social organization, —
the government of women over men, equality between the
two, and such mixed and divided modes of government as
might be invented, — it had been decided, on the testimony
of experience, that the mode in which women are wholly
under the rule of men, having no share at all in public concerns, and each in private being under the legal obligation of
obedience to the man with whom she has associated her
destiny, was the arrangement most conducive to the happiness and well-being of both, its general adoption might then
be fairly thought to be some evidence that, at the time when
it was adopted, it was the best; though even then the considerations which recommended it may, like so many other
primeval social facts of the greatest importance, have subsequently, in the course of ages, ceased to exist.

Section 109. The War against Poverty

**389. Extracts
from More's
*Utopia***   During the past three or four hundred years men of
sympathetic and humane spirit, impressed by the poverty
and misery of a great portion of their fellow-creatures,
have imagined ideal societies where poverty and degradation could not exist. Among these ideal common-
wealths, that of Sir Thomas More is one of the most
celebrated. In his little work, bearing the name *Utopia*
(derived from a Greek word meaning "Nowhere"), printed
in 1516, he describes a land where plenty and happiness
abounded and where the chief sources of the misery of
Europe did not exist. The following extract is from the
chapter on the industries and manner of life of the
Utopians.

The chief and almost the only business of the magistrates is
to care that no man may live idle, but that every one may follow his trade diligently; yet they do not wear themselves out

with perpetual toil from morning to night, as if they were beasts A six-hour working-day in Utopia of burden, which, although it is a heavy slavery, is none the less everywhere the common course of life for mechanics except in Utopia. But the Utopians, dividing the day and night into twenty-four hours, appoint six of these for work, three of which are before dinner and three after. They then sup, and at eight o'clock counting from noon, go to bed and sleep eight hours. The rest of the time besides that taken up in work, eating, and sleeping is left to every man's discretion ; yet they are not to abuse that interval in luxury and idleness, but must employ it in some proper exercise according to their various inclinations, which is, for the most part, reading. It is quite common to have public lectures every morning before daybreak, at which none are obliged to appear except those who are marked out for literature, and yet a great many, both men and women of all ranks, go to hear lectures of one sort or another, according to their inclinations.

But if others that are not made for contemplation choose Diversions in Utopia rather to employ themselves at that time in their trades, as many of them do, they are not hindered, but rather commended as men that take care to serve their country. After supper they spend an hour in some diversion, in summer in their gardens, in winter in the halls where they eat, where they entertain one another with music or discourse. They do not so much as know dice or any such foolish and mischievous games. They have, however, two sorts of games not unlike our chess.

But the time appointed for labor is to be narrowly examined, The number of idle person under the system then existing in England otherwise you may imagine that since there are only six hours appointed for work, the people may fall under a scarcity of the necessary provisions. But it is so far from being true that this time is not sufficient for supplying every one with plenty of all things either necessary or convenient that it is rather too much ; and this you will easily apprehend if you consider how great a part of all other nations is quite idle. First, women generally do little, who are half mankind ; and if some few women are diligent, their husbands are idle. Then consider the great company of idle priests and of those that are called religious men.[1]

[1] That is, monks and friars.

Add to these all rich men, chiefly those who have estates in land, who are called noblemen and gentlemen, together with their families, made up of idle persons that are kept more for show than for use. Add to these all those strong and lusty beggars that go about pretending some disease, in excuse for their begging; and upon the whole account you will find that the number of those by whose labors mankind is supplied is much less than you perhaps imagined.

The great waste in foolish luxury

Then consider how few of those that work are employed in labors that are of real service; for we by measuring all things by money give rise to many trades that are both vain and superfluous and serve only to support riot and luxury. For if those who work were employed only in such things as the conveniences of life required, there would be such an abundance of them that the prices of them would so sink that tradesmen could not be maintained by their gains. If all those who labor about useless things were set to more profitable employments, and if all they that languish out their lives in sloth and idleness, every one of whom consumes as much as any two of the men that are at work, were forced to labor, you may easily imagine that a small proportion of the time would serve for doing all that is either necessary, profitable, or pleasant to mankind, especially while pleasure is kept within its due bounds. . . .

No poverty or misery in Utopia where communism prevails

In Utopia, where every man has a right to everything, they all know that if care is taken to keep the public stores full, no private man can want anything; for among them there is no unequal distribution, so that no man is poor, none in necessity. And though no man has anything, yet they are all rich, for what can make a man so rich as to lead a serene and cheerful life, free from anxieties, neither apprehending want himself nor vexed with the endless complaints of his wife. . . .

Existing governments mistreat and neglect the most useful persons

I would gladly hear any man compare the justice that is among them with that of all other nations, among whom, may I perish, if I see anything that looks either like justice or equity. For what justice is there in this, that a nobleman, a goldsmith, a banker, or any other man, that either does nothing at all, or at best is employed in things that are of no use to the public, should live in great luxury and splendor upon what is so ill acquired ; and a mean man, a carter, a smith, or a plowman, that works harder than even the beasts themselves and is employed in labors so necessary that no commonwealth could hold out a year without them, can only earn so poor a livelihood, and must lead so miserable a life, that the condition of beasts is so much better than his? . . .

Is not that government both unjust and ungrateful that is so prodigal of its favors to those that are called gentlemen, or goldsmiths, or such others who are idle, or live by flattery or by contriving the arts of vain pleasure ; and, on the other hand, take no care of those of a meaner sort, such as plowmen, colliers, and smiths, without whom it could not subsist?

Robert Owen (1771–1858), a successful English cotton manufacturer, devoted a great part of his life to plans for bettering the lot of the working classes. He believed that the world had so far improved that a millennium of prosperity and happiness was at hand, — that England and America could become Utopias. His reasons for thinking that at last "the wise, the good, and the happy existence of man" was not far away, are the following :

The almost miraculous decline of reverence for the priesthood over the world ; — their insane dissensions in opposition to each other, and, at this stage of society, their equally insane presumption over their more enlightened fellow-men ; — the progress of the temperance societies in Great Britain and America ; the daily advance of scientific discoveries ; the new passion for educating the masses ; the extraordinary disinclination to war among the British and other warlike nations ; the easy and rapid communication between the most distant countries ; the general adoption by civilized countries of scientific power to supersede the necessity for severe or injurious manual service ; and the friendly union of governments which until latterly have been in a great savage hostility to each

390. Robert Owen's reasons for expecting the speedy arrival of the millennium (1841)

other ; — all, with many other strange and extraordinary occurring events, indicate with unerring certainty that a great change is coming over the nations of the earth; and that the wise, the good, the happy existence of man approaches with gigantic strides; in fact, that the millennium is not far distant.

Nothing can stop progress toward the millennium

And shall irrational man, in any of his present puerile divisions of class, or sect, or party, or country, or color, set himself to oppose this great, magnificent, and glorious change for the benefit of the human race now and through the coming ages? Vain and useless will such attempts prove. The decree has gone forth from the almighty energies of the universe, that man shall be put in the right path now, to become good and wise and happy; and every obstacle in the way of his progress to this advent of his existence shall prove unavailing and powerless. . . .

Some changes which must be made before the millennium arrives

But to effect this great and glorious change, it must be made known to the world:

Evil influence of the lawyers

. . . That the necessary character of the profession of the law is to maintain the ignorant and most injurious laws of man in direct opposition to the wise and most beneficent laws of man's nature, evidently formed by the Supreme Creating Power of the universe, to insure man, when he shall understand and act upon them, health and enjoyment beyond the imaginings of poets; but that as long as the profession of the law, based on the principles on which all human laws have been founded, shall be maintained, it will prevent the period arriving when man shall be just to man, when he shall love his neighbor as himself, or when he shall understand his own interest or become a rational being. . . .

The military class perpetuates disorder

That the necessary character of the military profession is to generate a warlike spirit and a desire for war; . . . to perpetuate feelings of hostility among individuals and nations, that must immortalize immorality, continue to foster all the bad passions, create confusion and disorder throughout the world. . . .

That the necessary character of the individual buying-and-selling system is to train the human race to acquire the inferior mind of a peddler and dealer whose business of life is to endeavor to procure everything from others at the lowest price and to dispose of everything to others at the highest price, or in such a manner that he shall secure the greatest amount of money, profit, worldly honors, or individual considerations to himself. And in this sense, all, from the highest to the lowest, are now trained to become, by the individual competition system, mere peddlers, tradesmen, or dealers, who are constantly endeavoring to obtain the services and productions of others at the easiest rate, the lowest value, and to sell their own services at the highest, or to obtain all they can in exchange for them. The sovereigns, statesmen, legislators, professional men, military, merchants, bankers, manufacturers, tradesmen, workmen, and beggars are now all, under the individual competitive system which has hitherto prevailed over the world, engaged in this low, unjust, degrading traffic. . . . By these means the successful in this inferior and immoral course of conduct do not obtain a tithe, no, nor a fiftieth part of the permanent, substantial, healthy, enlightened, superior advantages, pleasures, and enjoyments that, under the united system, *all* may attain and securely possess without obstruction, competition, or contest.

> *Profit seeking makes the world wretched*

A French contemporary of Robert Owen, Charles Fourier (1772–1837), proposed to realize a Utopia by establishing coöperative colonies called "phalanxes." The general plan for one of these colonies he describes as follows:

It is necessary for a company of 1500 to 1600 persons to have a stretch of land comprising a good square league, not forgetting, however, that a third of that would suffice for the simpler system. The land should be provided with a fine stream of water; it should be intersected by hills and adapted to a varied cultivation; it should be near a forest and not far removed from a large city, but sufficiently so to escape intruders. A company should be collected consisting of from 1500 to 1600 persons of graduated degrees of fortune, age, and character, of theoretical and practical knowledge. Care

> *391. Fourier's scheme for communistic societies (condensed)*

should be taken to secure the greatest amount of variety possible, for the greater the number of variations either in the passions or the faculties of the members, the easier it will be to harmonize them all in a short space of time.

Special buildings required

The edifice occupied by a Phalanx does not in any way resemble our buildings whether of the city or country, and none of our buildings could be used to establish a large Harmony of 1600 persons, — not even a great palace like Versailles. The lodgings, plantations, and stables of a society conducted on my plan must differ vastly from our villages and country towns, which are intended for families having no social relations and which act in a perverse manner.

Instead of that class of little houses which rival one another in filth and ugliness in our little towns, a Phalanx constructs an edifice for itself which is as regular as the ground permits. The central part of the main building, or Phalanstery, ought to be appropriated to peaceful uses, and contain the dining halls, business offices, libraries, study, etc. In this central portion are located the places of worship, the telegraph, the post-office boxes, the chimes for ceremonials, the observatory, the winter court adorned with evergreen trees and situated in the rear of the parade court.

The workshops

One of the wings ought to combine all the noisy workshops, such as the carpenter shop, the forge, and all hammer work ; it ought to contain, also, all the industrial gatherings of the children, who are generally very noisy in industry, and even music. This combination would obviate a great annoyance of our civilized cities, where we find some man working with a hammer in every street, some dealer in iron, or tyro on the clarinet, who torture the ears of fifty families in the vicinity. The other wing ought to contain the hotel with its ballrooms and its halls appropriated to intercourse with outsiders, that these may not encumber the central portion of the building and embarrass the domestic relations of the Phalanx.

The savings effected by coöperation

An examination of the savings to be effected by coöperative associations shows them to amount always to three fourths, or nine tenths, or frequently to ninety-nine one-hundredths. We have found it so in case of markets, the sale and purchase of commodities. For example, three hundred families of an agricultural village send to the markets not once but twenty times in the course of a year. The peasant delights in loitering about the market places and taverns; though he have nothing but a bushel of beans, he spends an entire day in the city. And for the three hundred families this constitutes an average loss of 6000 days' labor, not including the cost of transportation, which is twenty times greater than in an association which sells its commodities in large quantities, since under coöperation purchases are made only for Phalanxes numbering about 1500 individuals. If a village is situated near a city, we find that the three hundred families will sometimes send a hundred milk women with a hundred cans of milk, the sale and transportation of which will cause these women to lose a hundred mornings. I have observed that they can be replaced by a small cart drawn by an ass and driven by a woman, — a gain of forty-nine fiftieths. There is nothing in which economy is recognized as more urgently needed than in fuel; this economy assumes vast proportions in the coöperative state; a Phalanx has only five kitchens in place of three hundred. The whole can be supplied by three great fires, which, compared to the 300 fires of a village, brings the economy in fuel to nineteenths.

The following statement of the principles of trade unionism is made by George Howell, who was for many years a prominent leader in the labor movement in Great Britain.

In their essence trade unions are voluntary associations of workmen for mutual assistance in securing generally the most favorable conditions of labor. This is their primary and fundamental object and includes all efforts to raise wages or resist a reduction in wages; to diminish the hours of labor or resist attempts to increase the working hours; and to regulate all matters relating to methods of employment or discharge and mode of working. They have other aims also, some of them not less important than those embraced in the foregoing definition, and the sphere of their action extends to almost every

392. The principles of trade unionism

detail connected with the labor of workmen and the well-being of their everyday lives. . . .

It must be conceded that every man has a perfect right for himself to fix the price at which he will give his labor, or to refuse to work if the terms offered him do not suit him. So equally has another man the right to accept or refuse either the work or the terms without molestation from his fellow-workmen or from his employer ; and that which one has the right to do singly, two or more have the right to do in agreement so long as they both individually and in combination do not interfere by unlawful means with the free action of a third party to refuse or accept the proffered terms. An employer has an equal right to say to the workman, " I will give only a certain price, or employ you on specified conditions ; if you don't like it you can go elsewhere." A good deal depends in all cases upon the manner in which these things are said and done ; the right, however, remains in theory and in fact.

The needy workingman not in a position of equality with his employer

An individual workman has but little chance of obtaining what he deems a fair day's pay for a fair day's work, or other equitable conditions of labor. His necessities often compel him to accept terms which he feels to be inadequate and even unjust, but the question with him is how to enforce higher wages or better terms. It is true that he wants work ; it is equally true that the employer wants his labor, but the latter can afford to wait until another man more needy than the first applies for employment, when perhaps he will be able to obtain the services of the last comer on his own (the employer's) terms. In any case he can but wait and see, and if he cannot procure workmen on the terms he has fixed, there is no great harm done ; he can only then agree to give the higher price and secure their labor. With the journeyman it is different ; he cannot wait, his means are exhausted and hunger compels him to accept any terms that may be offered.

Unions equalize conditions of bargaining

But if the workmen who are thus seeking employment have mutually agreed not to accept work below a stated price, or only upon specified conditions, and they have with others provided a fund which will enable them to withhold their labor until a better price is offered, they are justified in so doing, and they have by this arrangement placed themselves upon something like an equality with the employer, because they have the means of waiting and bidding for better terms.

Notwithstanding the dreams of the philosophers and Utopians and the varied activities of coöperative societies and trade unionists, there exists all over western Europe a vast mass of poverty and wretchedness. A distinguished English philanthropist, Mr. Rowntree, published in 1901 a careful survey of the amount and character of the poverty in York, an English city of about 78,000 population, and the following are his conclusions :

Having made an estimate, based upon carefully ascertained facts, of the earnings of practically every working-class family in York, the next step was to show the proportion of the total population living in poverty. Families regarded as living in poverty were grouped under two heads :

393. The extent of poverty in the English city of York (condensed)

(*a*) Families whose total earnings were insufficient to obtain the minimum necessaries for the maintenance of merely physical efficiency. Poverty falling under this head was described as "primary" poverty.

(*b*) Families whose total earnings would have been sufficient for the maintenance of merely physical efficiency, were it not that some portion of it was absorbed by other expenditure, either useful or wasteful. Poverty falling under this head was described as "secondary" poverty.

To ascertain the total number living in primary poverty it was necessary to ascertain the minimum cost upon which families of various sizes could be maintained in a state of physical efficiency. This question was discussed under three heads, namely, the necessary expenditure for (1) food, (2) rent, and (3) all else, and it was shown that for a family of father, mother, and three children, the minimum weekly expenditure upon which physical efficiency can be maintained in York is 21*s*. 8*d*. This estimate was based upon the assumption that the diet is selected with careful regard to the nutritive value

How the standard of living was measured

of various food stuffs, and that these are all purchased at the lowest current prices. It only allows for a diet less generous as regards variety than that supplied to able-bodied paupers in workhouses. It further assumes that no clothing is purchased which is not absolutely necessary for health, and assumes, too, that it is of the plainest and most economical description. No expenditure of any kind is allowed beyond that which is absolutely necessary for the maintenance of merely physical efficiency.

The total number in poverty in York

The number of persons whose earnings are so low that they cannot meet the expenditure necessary for the above standard of living, stringent to severity though it is, and bare of all creature comforts, was shown to be no less than 7230, or almost exactly 10 per cent of the total population of the city. [The investigators from a house-to-house investigation reported] 20,302 persons, or 27.84 per cent of the total population, as living in poverty. Subtracting those whose poverty is "primary," we arrive at the number living in "secondary" poverty, namely, 13,072, or 17.93 per cent of the total population. The figures will be clearer if shown in tabular form :

Number of Persons in Poverty in York	Per Cent of the Total Population
"Primary" poverty 7,230	9.91
"Secondary" poverty 13,072	17.93
Total. 20,302	27.84

The closing years of the nineteenth century were marked by the extraordinary growth of socialistic parties whose fundamental contention is that poverty is caused, first and foremost, by the ownership by private individuals of the land, mines, machinery, etc., necessary for production. This "bourgeois" system, as they call it, enables the capitalists to keep the workingmen in poverty by appropriating from their labor an inordinate amount of profit. Two of the founders of modern socialism, Karl

Marx and Friederick Engels, in the *Communist Manifesto* published in 1848, declared that the socialistic movement was simply part of a great historical process extending through a long period, and that the industrial revolution would inevitably create in each country a vast proletariat which in time was destined to overthrow the capitalist system just as the bourgeoisie had destroyed feudalism. This notion of socialism as a historical prophecy is stated in the following extracts :

The history of all hitherto existing society is the history of class struggles. In the earlier epochs we find almost everywhere a complicated organization of society into various orders. In ancient Rome we have patricians, knights, plebeians, slaves ; in the Middle Ages, feudal lords, vassals, guild masters, journeymen, apprentices, serfs.

394. Extracts from the Communist Manifesto *(much condensed)*

The modern bourgeois society, which has sprung from the ruins of feudal society, has not done away with class antagonisms. It has only established new classes, new conditions of oppression, new forms of struggle in place of the old ones. Our epoch, the epoch of the bourgeois, possesses, however, this distinctive feature : it has simplified the class antagonisms. Society as a whole is more and more splitting up into two great hostile camps, into two great classes directly facing each other, — Bourgeoisie and Proletariat.

New class struggles in our time

Bourgeoisie vs. Proletariat

The discovery of America, the rounding of the Cape, opened up fresh fields for the rising bourgeoisie. The East Indian and Chinese markets, the colonization of America, gave to commerce, navigation, and industry an impulse never before known. The feudal system of industry, under which industrial production was monopolized by close guilds, now no longer sufficed for the growing demands of the new markets. The manufacturing system (on a small scale) took its place. The guild masters were pushed to one side by the manufacturing middle class ; division of labor between the different corporate guilds vanished in the face of the division of labor in each single workshop.

How commerce helped to overthrow feudalism

The factories make millionaires

Meantime the markets kept ever growing, the demand ever increasing. Production by hand no longer sufficed. Thereupon steam and machinery revolutionized industrial production. The place of handwork was taken by that giant, Modern Industry; the place of the industrial middle class, by industrial millionaires, the leaders of whole industrial armies, — the modern bourgeoisie. We see, therefore, how the modern bourgeoisie is itself the product of a long course of development, of a series of revolutions in the modes of production and of exchange.

Mediæval notions rudely cast aside

The bourgeoisie, wherever it has got the upper hand, has put an end to all feudal, patriarchal, idyllic relations. It has pitilessly torn asunder the motley feudal ties that bound man to his "natural superiors," and has left no other tie between man and man than naked self-interest, callous "cash payment." It has drowned the heavenly ecstasies of religion, of chivalrous enthusiasm, of philistine sentimentalism, in the icy water of selfish business calculation. The bourgeoisie has stripped of its halo every occupation hitherto honored and looked up to with reverent awe. It has converted the physician, the lawyer, the priest, the poet, the man of science, into its paid wage laborers.

Constant change the watchword to-day

Constant revolutionizing of production, uninterrupted disturbance of all social conditions, everlasting uncertainty and agitation, distinguish the bourgeois epoch from all earlier periods. All fixed relations, with their ancient and venerable prejudices and opinions, are swept away; all new-formed ones become antiquated before they can solidify. All that is holy is profaned, and man is at last compelled to face with clear vision and without illusion his real conditions of life and his relations with his fellow-men.

Western industry conquers the world

The bourgeoisie, by the rapid spread of all instruments of production, by the immensely facilitated means of communication, draws even the most barbarous peoples into civilization. The low prices of its commodities are the heavy artillery with which it batters down all Chinese walls, with which it softens the barbarians' intensely obstinate hatred of foreigners. It compels all nations, on pain of extinction, to adopt the bourgeois mode of production; it forces them to introduce what it calls "civilization" into their midst, i.e. to become bourgeois themselves. In one word, it creates a world after its own image.

The bourgeoisie has subjected the country to the rule of the towns. It has created enormous cities, has greatly increased the urban population as compared with the rural, and has thus rescued a considerable part of the population from the stupidity of rural life. Just as it has made the country dependent on the towns, so it has made barbarian and semibarbarian countries dependent on the civilized ones, nations of peasants on nations of bourgeoisie, the East on the West.

Cities rule the country

The bourgeoisie, during its rule of scarce one hundred years, has created more colossal productive forces than have all preceding generations together. Subjection of Nature's forces to man, machinery, the application of chemistry to industry and agriculture, steam navigation, railways, electric telegraphs, clearing of whole continents for cultivation, — what earlier century had even a presentiment that such productive forces slumbered in the lap of social labor?

The arms with which the bourgeoisie felled feudalism to the ground are now turned against the bourgeoisie itself. It has not only forged the weapons for self-destruction; it has also called into existence the men who are to wield those weapons, — the modern working class, — the proletarians. In proportion as the bourgeoisie, i.e. capital, is developed, in the same proportion is the proletariat, i.e. the modern working class, developed, — a class of laborers, who live only so long as they find work, and who find work only so long as their labor increases capital. These laborers, who must sell themselves, are a commodity, like every other article of commerce, and are consequently exposed to all the vicissitudes of competition, to all the fluctuations of the market.

The bourgeoisie have created their own antagonists — the workingmen

Owing to the extensive use of machinery and to division of labor, the work of the proletarians has lost all individual character, and, consequently, all charm for the workman. He becomes an appendage of the machine, and it is only the most simple, most monotonous, and most easily acquired knack that is required of him.

The workman a machine

Workingmen are being organized

Modern industry has converted the little workshop of the patriarchal master into the great factory of the industrial capitalist. Masses of laborers, crowded into the factory, are organized like soldiers. Not only are they slaves of the bourgeois class, and of the bourgeois State; they are daily and hourly enslaved by the machine, by the overseer, and, above all, by the individual bourgeois manufacturer himself. The less skill and exertion of strength is implied in manual labor, in other words, the more modern industry becomes developed, the more is the labor of men superseded by that of women.

Conflicts of capital and labor

But with the development of industry the proletariat not only increases in number; it becomes concentrated in greater masses, its strength grows, and it feels that strength more. The unceasing improvement of machinery, ever more rapidly developing, makes their livelihood more and more precarious; the collisions between individual workmen and individual bourgeois take more and more the character of collisions between two classes. Thereupon the workers begin to form combinations (trades unions) against the bourgeoisie; they club together in order to keep up the rate of wages. Here and there the contest breaks out into riots.

How some of the intellectual among the bourgeoisie accept socialism

Just as, in an earlier period, a section of the nobility went over to the bourgeoisie, so now a portion of the bourgeoisie goes over to the proletariat, and, in particular, that portion of the bourgeois idealists who have raised themselves to the point of comprehending theoretically the historical movement as a whole.

The working class represent a vast majority

All previous historical movements were movements of minorities, or in the interest of minorities. The proletarian movement is the self-conscious, independent movement of the immense majority. The proletariat, the lowest stratum of our present society, cannot stir, cannot raise itself without the whole superincumbent strata of official society being blown into the air.

The bourgeoisie have failed to establish decent conditions for labor

It has become evident that the bourgeoisie is unfit any longer to be the ruling class in society and to impose its conditions of existence upon it. It is unfit to rule because it is incompetent to assure an existence to its slave in his slavery, because it cannot prevent his sinking into such a state that it has to feed him instead of being fed by him. Society can no longer live under this bourgeoisie; in other words, its existence is no longer compatible with society.

The essential condition for the existence and sway of the bourgeois class is the creation and increase of capital; the condition for capital is wage labor. Wage labor rests exclusively on competition between the laborers. The advance of industry, whose involuntary promoter is the bourgeoisie, replaces the isolation of the laborers, due to competition, by their revolutionary combination, due to association. The development of modern industry, therefore, cuts from under its feet the very foundation of capitalist production and distribution of wealth. What the bourgeoisie therefore produces, above all, are its own gravediggers. Its fall and the victory of the proletariat are inevitable. *The victory of the working class is inevitable*

The following political platform, drafted by the German Social-Democratic party at Gotha in 1875, illustrates the manner in which socialist parties have adopted the principles of Marx and Engels, and also indicates some of the practical reforms which they demand, and which they believe would abolish poverty.

1. Labor is the source of all wealth and of all civilization; and since it is only through society that generally productive labor is possible, the whole product of labor, where there is a general obligation to work, belongs to society, — that is, to all its members, by equal right, and to each according to his reasonable needs. *395. The socialist programme issued at Gotha (1875)*

In the society of to-day the means of production are a monopoly of the capitalistic class; the dependence of the working class, which results from this, is the cause of misery and servitude in all its forms.

The emancipation of labor requires the conversion of the means of production into the common property of society and the social regulation of all labor and its application for the general good, together with the just distribution of the product of labor.

The emancipation of labor must be the work of the laboring class itself, opposed to which all other classes are reactionary groups.

2. Proceeding from these principles, the socialist labor party of Germany endeavors by every lawful means to bring about a free State and a socialistic society, to effect the destruction of the iron law of wages by doing away with the system of wage labor, to abolish exploitation of every kind, and to extinguish all social and political inequality.

International nature of the socialist movement

The socialist labor party of Germany, although for the time being confining its activity within national bounds, is fully conscious of the international character of the labor movement, and is resolved to meet all the obligations which this lays upon the laborer, in order to bring the brotherhood of all mankind to a full realization.

The socialist labor party of Germany, in order to prepare the way for the solution of the social question, demands the establishment of socialistic productive associations with the support of the State and under the democratic control of the working people. These productive associations, for both industry and agriculture, are to be created to such an extent that the socialistic organization of all labor may result therefrom.

Immediate reforms demanded by the socialists

[In addition to the demand for universal suffrage for all above twenty years of age, secret ballot, freedom of the press, free and compulsory education, etc.,] the socialist labor party of Germany demands the following reforms in the present social organization : (1) the greatest possible extension of political rights and freedom in the sense of the above-mentioned demands ; (2) a single progressive income tax, both State and local, instead of all the existing taxes, especially the indirect ones, which weigh heavily upon the people ; (3) unlimited right of association ; (4) a normal working day corresponding with the needs of society, and the prohibition of work on Sunday ; (5) prohibition of child labor and all forms of labor by women which are dangerous to health or morality ; (6) laws for the protection of the life and health of workmen, sanitary control of workmen's houses, inspection of mines, factories, workshops, and domestic industries by officials chosen by the workmen themselves, and an effective system of enforcement of the same; (7) regulation of prison labor.

The Fabian Society in England, a socialist organization, maintains that the solution of the problem of poverty is government ownership of the means of production, but it does not believe with Marx that it involves a bitter struggle between workingmen and capitalists. The Fabians contend rather that the whole nation should be educated into socialistic doctrines, and two of their prominent leaders, Sydney and Beatrice Webb, advocate as the basis for all other reforms the adoption of a policy of a "national minimum," which they explain as follows:

The policy of the "national minimum" translates itself into four main branches of legislative and executive activity. There will have to be a national minimum of wages. The trusts, or the other employers, will be under no legal obligation to employ any person whatsoever. But if they do employ him or her, it will be a condition of every contract, not to be waived or ignored, that its terms shall not be such as will impair the efficiency of the citizen or diminish the vitality of the race. To engage labor at wages insufficient to repair the waste of tissue caused by the employment is demonstrably to injure the community as a whole, and will be prosecuted as such in the criminal courts. Those whose labor is not worth the national minimum — the aged, the crippled, and the blind; the mentally or morally deficient; the epileptic; and the chronically feckless and feeble-minded — will be maintained by the community, as indeed they are now. But of all the ways of maintaining those unable to earn a full livelihood, by far the most costly and injurious is to allow them to compete in the labor market, and thus to drag down by their infirmity those who are whole. There are still people, of course, who simply cannot imagine how a legal minimum wage could possibly be enforced, just as there were, sixty years ago, economists who demonstrated the impossibility of factory laws. As a matter of

[margin note:] 396. A Fabian programme of reform

Minimum of wages

fact, the legal minimum wage can be seen in force to-day in Victoria and New Zealand, South Australia, and New South Wales.

Leisure and recreation secured to every citizen

There will be a national minimum of leisure and recreation secured by law to every citizen. It will be an implied condition of every contract of employment, rigidly enforced by law, that it shall leave untouched sixteen hours out of each twenty-four for needful sleep, recreation, exercise of mind or body, and the duties of citizenship and family life. Any attempt by man or woman to sell for wages any part of the sixteen sacred hours will be blamed as virtual embezzlement, since this part of the twenty-four-hours day must be regarded as necessarily reserved for the purpose of maintaining unimpaired the efficiency of the race. Any employer purchasing them, or allowing them to be spent in his mill or mine, will be prosecuted and punished, as if he had incited to embezzlement or had received stolen goods.

The preservation of public health

There will be a national minimum of sanitation, enforced not merely on land or house owners or occupiers, but also on local governing authorities. The nation will find it preposterous that any city, merely out of stupidity or incapacity or parsimony, should foster disease, or bring up its quota of citizens in a condition of impaired vitality. The power of the community as a whole will, somehow or other, be brought to bear upon every backward district, compelling it to introduce pure water, to improve its drainage, and to take such action, even by municipal building if need be, that no family in the land shall have less than "three rooms and a scullery," as the minimum required for health and decency. Along with this must go the adequate provision of medical attendance, skilled nursing, and hospital accommodation for the sick. Within a generation of the adoption of such a policy the death rate and sickness experience would show a reduction of one third of what is at present endured as if it were the decree of Providence.

Adequate educational facilities

There will be a national minimum of education — not merely in the provision of schools, but in genuinely compulsory attendance at them. Besides schools and colleges of every grade, there will have to be an adequate "scholarship ladder," securing maintenance as well as free tuition, right up to the post-graduate course, for every scholar proving himself or herself fitted for anything beyond common schooling. And this provision will be enforced by the national power upon local school authorities as well as upon parents and employers. What right has any part of the community to allow any part of its quota of citizens to be reared in ignorance or to suffer even one potential genius to be lost to the community? The next few years will see not only a great improvement in common schooling but also the doubling or trebling of our expenditure on higher education.

Only by the enforcement of some such national minimum of subsistence, leisure, sanitation, and education will modern industrial communities escape degeneration and decay. Where life is abandoned to unfettered competition, what is known as Gresham's law applies, — the bad drives out the good. To prevent this evil result is, as both Europe and America are discovering in the twentieth century, the main function of government. *Reform to prevent decay*

There are a great number of earnest and thoughtful men, who recognize fully the many evils which accompany our present industrial system, but at the same time hold that socialism, instead of remedying things, would only make them worse. Professor John B. Clark, one of the most distinguished economists in America, in an address recently delivered before the Phi Beta Kappa Society in New York, fairly reviewed the excellent features of socialist theories, and then advanced the following important arguments against the socialist position.

The pursuit of wealth now furnishes the outlet for the overmastering ambition of many persons. In the new socialistic state the desire to rise in the world would have only one main outlet, namely *politics*. The work of governing the country, and that of managing its industries, would be merged in one great official body. The contrast between rulers and ruled would be enormously heightened by this concentration of power in the *397. Professor Clark's arguments against socialism (condensed)* hands of the rulers, and by the further fact that the ruled would never be able, by means of wealth, to acquire an offset for the advantages of officeholding. The desire for public position would therefore be intensified in a socialistic state.

Offices would be chief prizes under a socialistic régime

There would, it is true, be some prizes to be gained, in a worthy way, by other kinds of service, such as authorship, invention, and discovery; but the prizes which would appeal to most men would be those of officeholding. Is it in reason to suppose that the method of securing the offices would then be better than it is at present? Would a man, under the new régime, work quietly at his task in the shoe shop, the bakery, or the mine, waiting for the office to which he aspired to seek him out, or would he try to make terms with other men for mutual assistance in the quest of office? Would "rings" be less general than they are now? Could there fail to be bosses and political machines? Would the Tammanys of the new order, then, be an improvement on the Tammanys of the old order? Without making any dogmatic assertions, we may say that there would certainly have to be machines of some sort for pushing men into public offices, and that these would have very sinister possibilities. They would be opposed by counter machines, made up of men out of office and anxious to get in.

Difficulties of apportioning workmen among the various occupations

Furthermore, very nice adjustments would have to be made between agriculture, on the one hand, and manufactures and commerce on the other; and further adjustments would have to be made between the different branches of each form of business. All this would be done, not automatically as at present, by the action of demand and supply in a market, but by the voluntary acts of officials. Here is the field in which the wisdom of officials would be overtaxed. They might manage the mills of the steel trust, but it would trouble them to say how many men should be employed in that business and how many in every other, and, of the men in that particular branch, how many should work in Pittsburg and how many in the mines of Michigan and Minnesota.

Another grave objection to socialism is the check that it might impose on technical progress. At present we see a bewildering succession of inventions transforming the industries

of the world. Machine after machine appears in rapid succes- *Socialism*
sion, each displacing its predecessor, working for a time and *would check*
giving way to still better devices. The power of man over *progress in*
nature increases with amazing rapidity. Even in the relatively *inventions*
simple operations of agriculture, the reaper, the thresher, the
seeder, and the gang plow enable a man to-day to do as
much work as could a score of men in the colonial period of
American history. In manufacturing the gain is greater; and
in transportation it is indefinitely greater. The progress goes
on without cessation, since the thing which guarantees it is the
impulse of self-preservation. An employer *must* improve his
mechanism if his rivals do so. He must now and then get
ahead of his rivals if he is to make any profit. Conservatism
which adheres to the old is self-destruction, and a certain
audacity affords the nearest approach to safety. From this
it comes about, first, that forward movements are made daily
and hourly in some part of the field; and, secondly, that with
every forward movement the whole procession must move on
to catch up with its new leader.

Now, it is possible to suppose that under socialism an *Officials slow*
altruistic motive may lead men to make inventions and dis- *to adopt*
coveries. They may work for the good of humanity. The *improvements*
desire for distinction may also impel them to such labors, and
nonpecuniary rewards offered by the State may second this
desire. The inventive impulse may act even where no reward
is in view. Men will differ greatly in their estimates of the
amount of progress that can be gained in this way; but the
thing that may be affirmed without danger of denial is, that
the competitive race absolutely compels progress at a rate
that is inspiringly rapid, and that there is much uncertainty as
to the amount of progress that would be secured where other
motives are relied on. Officialdom is generally unfavorable to
the adoption of improved devices, even when they are presented; its boards have frequently been the graveyards of
inventions, and there is no blinking the uncertainty as to
whether a satisfactory rate of improvement could be obtained
where the methods of production should be at the mercy of
such boards.

The saving of capital for future improvements would be discouraged

In the socialistic State all the incomes of the year would be pooled. They would make a composite sum out of which every one's stipend would have to be taken. There would be no special and personal profit for any one. The gains that come from improved technique would not be distinguishable from those that come from other sources. Every one would be a laborer, and every one would get his daily or weekly stipend; and if capital had to be increased, — if the needs of an enlarging business had to be provided for at all, — it could only be done by withholding some part of that stipend. It would be an unwelcome way of making accumulations. It would mean the conscious acceptance by the entire working class of a smaller income than might otherwise be had. If one has heroic confidence in the far-seeing quality and in the generous purpose of the working class, he may perhaps think that it will reconcile itself to this painful self-denial for the benefit of the future; but it is clear that there are large probabilities in the other direction. There is danger that capital would not be thus saved in sufficient quantity, and that, if it were not so, no power on earth could prevent the earning capacity of labor from suffering in consequence. From mere dearth of capital the socialistic State, though it were more progressive than we think, would be in danger of becoming poorer and poorer.

398. Leo XIII on socialism and labor reforms (much condensed)

Socialism also has a stanch opponent in the Catholic Church, and in May, 1891, Pope Leo XIII, in a long encyclical, advanced his objections to the socialistic doctrines, while at the same time urging the importance of ameliorating the lot of the working classes.

> *To our venerable brethren, all Patriarchs, Primates, Archbishops, and Bishops of the Catholic world, in peace and communion with the Apostolic See. Venerable brethren, health and apostolic benediction.*

It is not surprising that the spirit of revolutionary change, which has so long been predominant in the nations of the world, should have passed beyond politics and made its influence felt in the cognate field of political economy. The elements of a conflict are unmistakable, — the growth of industry and the surprising discoveries of science, the changed relations of masters and workmen, the enormous fortunes of individuals and the poverty of the masses, the increased self-reliance and the closer mutual combination of the working population, and, finally, a general moral deterioration. The momentous seriousness of the present state of things just now fills every mind with painful apprehension ; wise men discuss it ; practical men propose schemes ; popular meetings, legislatures, and sovereign princes, — all are occupied with it, and there is nothing which has a deeper hold on public attention.

Therefore, Venerable Brethren, as on former occasions, when it seemed opportune to refute false teaching, we have addressed you in the interest of the Church and of the commonweal, and have issued letters on Political Power, on Human Liberty, on the Christian Constitution of the State, and on similar subjects, so now we have thought it useful to speak on the *Condition of Labor.*

All agree, and there can be no question whatever, that some remedy must be found, and quickly found, for the misery and wretchedness which press so heavily at this moment on the large majority of the very poor. The ancient workmen's guilds were destroyed in the last century, and no other organization took their place. Public institutions and the laws have repudiated the ancient religion. Hence, by degrees, it has come to pass that workingmen have been given over, isolated and defenseless, to the callousness of employers and the greed of unrestrained competition. The evil has been increased by rapacious usury, which although more than once condemned by the Church, is, nevertheless, under a different form, but with the same guilt, still practiced by avaricious and grasping men. And to this must be added the custom of working by contract, and the concentration of so many branches of trade in the hands of a few individuals, so that a small number of very rich men have been able to lay upon the masses of the poor a yoke little better than slavery itself.

To remedy these evils the socialists, working on the poor man's envy of the rich, endeavor to destroy private property, and maintain that individual possessions should become the

Some remedy must be found for existing misery

Socialist proposals are futile

common property of all, to be administered by the State or by municipal bodies. They hold that, by thus transferring property from private persons to the community, the present evil state of things will be set to rights, because each citizen will then have his equal share of whatever there is to enjoy. But their proposals are so clearly futile for all practical purposes, that if they were carried out the workingman himself would be among the first to suffer. Moreover, they are emphatically unjust, because they would rob the lawful possessor, bring the State into a sphere that is not its own, and cause complete confusion in the community.

Justice demands the right to own property

What is of still greater importance, however, is that the remedy they propose is manifestly opposed to justice, for every man has by nature the right to possess property as his own. This is one of the chief points of distinction between man and the animal creation. Man alone among animals possesses reason ; it must therefore be within his right to have things not merely for temporary and momentary use, as other living beings have them, but in stable and permanent possession ; he must have not only things which perish in the using, but also those which, though used, remain for use in the future.

Individual rights older than the State

Nor must we, at this stage, have recourse to the State. Man is older than the State ; and he holds the right of providing for the life of his body prior to the formation of any State. And to say that God has given the earth to the use and enjoyment of the whole human race is not to deny that there can be private property. For God has granted the earth to mankind in general ; not in the sense that all without distinction can deal with it as they please, but rather that no part of it has been assigned to any one in particular, and that the limits of private possessions have been left to be fixed by man's own industry and the laws of individual peoples.

Socialism against human nature

Let it be laid down, in the first place, that humanity must remain as it is. It is impossible to reduce human society to a level. The socialists may do their utmost, but all striving against nature is vain. There naturally exist among mankind innumerable differences of the most important kind ; people differ in capability, in diligence, in health, and in strength; an unequal fortune is a necessary result of inequality in condition. Such inequality is far from being disadvantageous either to individuals or to the community; social and public life can only go on by the help of various kinds of capacity and the playing of many parts; and each man, as a rule, chooses the part which peculiarly suits his case.

As regards bodily labor, even had man never fallen from "the state of innocence," he would not have been wholly unoccupied; but that which would then have been his free choice and delight became afterwards compulsory, and the painful expiation of his sin. "Cursed be the earth in thy work; in thy labor thou shalt eat of it all the days of thy life." In like manner, the other pains and hardships of life will have no end or cessation on this earth; for the consequences of sin are bitter and hard to bear, and they must be with man as long as life lasts. To suffer and to endure, therefore, is the lot of humanity; let men try as they may, no strength and no artifice will ever succeed in banishing from human life the ills and troubles which beset it. If any there be who pretend differently, — who hold out to a hard-pressed people freedom from pain and trouble, undisturbed repose, and constant enjoyment, — they cheat the people and impose upon them; and their lying promises will only make the evil worse than before. There is nothing more useful than to look at the world as it really is, — and at the same time to look elsewhere for a remedy to its troubles.

To suffer and endure is the lot of mankind

The great mistake that is made in the matter now under consideration, is to possess one's self of the idea that class is naturally hostile to class; that rich and poor are intended by nature to live at war with one another. So irrational and so false is this view that the exact contrary is the truth. Just as the symmetry of the human body is the result of the disposition of the members of the body, so in a State it is ordained by nature that these two classes should exist in harmony and agreement, and should, as it were, fit into one another, so as to maintain the equilibrium of the body politic. Each requires the other; capital cannot do without labor, nor labor without capital. Mutual agreement results in pleasantness and good order; perpetual conflict necessarily produces confusion and violence.

Rich and poor created to help each other

Christianity draws rich and poor together

Now, in preventing such strife as this, and in making it impossible, the efficacy of Christianity is marvelous and manifold. First of all, there is nothing more powerful than religion (of which the Church is the interpreter and guardian) in drawing rich and poor together, by reminding each class of its duties to the other, and especially of the duties of justice. Thus religion teaches the laboring man and the workman to carry out honestly and well all equitable agreements freely made; never to injure capital, or to attack the person of an employer; never to employ violence in representing his own cause, or to engage in riot or disorder; and to have nothing to do with men of evil principles, who work upon the people with artful promises, and raise foolish hopes which usually end in disaster and in repentance when too late.

Christianity upholds the dignity of labor

Religion teaches the rich man and the employer that their work people are not their slaves; that they respect in every man his dignity as a man and as a Christian; that labor is nothing to be ashamed of, if we listen to right reason and to Christian philosophy, but is an honorable employment, enabling a man to sustain his life in an upright and creditable way; and that it is shameful and inhuman to treat men like chattels to make money by, or to look upon them merely as so much muscle or physical power.

The labor of women and children should be regulated

If we turn now to things exterior and corporeal, the first concern of all is to save the poor workers from the cruelty of grasping speculators, who use human beings as mere instruments for making money. It is neither justice nor humanity so to grind men down with excessive labor as to stupefy their minds and wear out their bodies. Finally, work which is suitable for a strong man cannot reasonably be required from a woman or a child. And, in regard to children, great care should be taken not to place them in workshops and factories until their bodies and minds are sufficiently mature. For just as severe weather destroys the buds of spring, so too early an experience of life's hard work blights the young promise of a child's powers and makes any real education impossible.

The wages question

We now approach a subject of very great importance, and one on which, if extremes are to be avoided, right ideas are absolutely necessary. Wages, we are told, are fixed by free consent; and therefore the employer, when he pays what was agreed upon, has done his part, and is not called upon for anything further. The only way, it is said, in which injustice could happen would be if the master refused to pay the whole of the wages, or the workman would not complete the work undertaken; when this happens the State should intervene, to see that each obtains his own, — but not under any other circumstances.

This mode of reasoning is by no means convincing to a fair-minded man, for there are important considerations which it leaves out of view altogether. To labor is to exert one's self for the sake of procuring what is necessary for the purposes of life, and, most of all, for self-preservation. "In the sweat of thy brow thou shalt eat bread." The preservation of life is the bounden duty of each and all, and to fail therein is a crime. It follows that each one has a right to procure what is required in order to live; and the poor can procure it in no other way than by work and wages.

Workingmen have a right to ask employment

Section 110. *Progress and Effects of Natural Science*

The development and achievements of modern science have never been sketched with more enthusiasm and warmth than by Carl Snyder, who has given us a brilliant picture of "the world machine," or universe as now conceived.

From the infancy of the race there have been minds which, turning aside from the ordinary pursuits and passions of men, from the prizes of trade, from the clamor of war, have given their lives to the search for truth. Argonauts in quest of the golden fleece of knowledge, their voyages have penetrated to the remotest corners of the earth and reached out among the stars. Magicians and sorcerers they seemed to the tribal man; philosophers, the lovers of wisdom, when Hellenism rose; discoverers and men of science, — Galileos, Newtons now, — civilization is their work; the modern world is in some sense

399. The development of the modern scientific conception of a mechanistic universe (condensed)

their creation. Amid the destruction and decay that attends all else from human hands, their achievements remain.

Slow but tolerably steady advance of science

Thanks to five or ten thousand years, perhaps a still greater period, of tolerably connected and consecutive effort, there has been built up a considerable stock of knowledge which, deftly fitted together in an orderly way, has become our one sure guide. So it may be that some future historian, chronicling the stages of human development, will write:

The world conceived as a machine or mechanism

"It was at about the beginning of the twentieth century that man attained at last a true picture of the world, — came to know, in brief, the cosmos as it is. It was at about this time that he came to perceive the eternal round of matter in the universe, — the coalescence of vague and formless nebular masses into suns and satellites, their slow refrigeration into dark bodies, with the transient appearance of life, their dissipation again into primitive nebula. It was then that he came definitely to conceive the whole scheme of world formation as a mechanical process, following simple and well-understood laws. It was at about this time that he came to recognize that the varied life of these vast globes springs up under appropriate material conditions and in response to simple physical and chemical stimuli; that the races of intelligent beings, with all their attendant creations of civilization, — their art, literatures, sciences, institutions, — are part and parcel of this same mechanical or physical process. In a larger phase, it was at this period that the more instructed among men came definitively to regard the universe as an unceasing machine, with no beginning and without end."

Scientific progress a part of general evolution

We may now perceive that the development of a science of the earth and sun and stars, like human development in general, is an integral part of that vast scheme of evolution, of unfolding and becoming, which pervades the world. If life be universal, and of this we may little doubt, this growth of the race mind is a constant incident of the cosmic process. Doubtless in æons past other races upon infinitely distant planets have pursued the same difficult and devious way toward the light; doubtless in æons to come, when, by the chance collision with some dark sun or huge swarm of meteorites, our little earth and the system of which it is a part has been resolved again into chaos, the same process will be endlessly repeated within other systems possibly yet unborn.

This development of science in some sense forms the fairest possession of stumbling, groping humanity. In this it presents an inspiring contrast to the empty bubble of wars and dynasties, of conquests and crusades, that passes ordinarily for history : whole armies of men flung into a field to butcher one another for an envied province or an imagined slight ; arson and thievery, pillage and atrocious crimes applauded under the sounding name of conquest ; great cities sacked, the populations sold into degrading slavery, the women to shameful lives ; until a scant century ago, the lower classes lost in barbarism and ignorance ; the upper class — a privileged few — despising work, despoiling the poor ; heroes fed to slow fires for the preservation of the religion of God ; low intrigues and court scandal. *Striking contrast between political history as commonly written, and the history of science*

Set over against this tale full of sound and fury is the steady advance of civilization, often slow, often halted, but ever renewed ; the progress of invention, the amelioration of savage and brutal customs, the abolition of slavery, the wide diffusion of material comforts, of justice and of peace, — in larger phrase, the broadening of the human mind, the heightening of the human consciousness. Instead of the mood of Volney's *Ruins* we have that of Macaulay's pæan upon the Baconian philosophy ; instead of disheartenment, a buoyant and invigorating sense of things done, of progress, and of attainment.

Darwin's idea of evolution called forth innumerable attacks such as the following, taken from a pamphlet published in 1873, entitled *Darwinism Reproved and Refuted*.

Darwin's theory of the descent of man, the leading proposition of which is, that man is descended immediately from some species of monkey, and remotely from one of the lowest orders in the animal series, — from an Ascidian larva, — is so repugnant to every feeling of humanity, and so revolting to *400. Darwin's theory of evolution "reproved and refuted"* the common sense of the human mind, that on presentation to any unsophisticated intellect it is at once rejected and spurned with indignation. This proposition, so universally deemed insulting to humanity, forces upon us the conviction that it can be entertained only by a mind whose common sense has first been outraged and silenced by the deadening influence of a cunning sophistry, — a sophistry that, in this instance, has had a more general bearing on the human intellect from the fact that it has not been detected and exposed by scientists. The earnestness and seeming candor of the writer, in pressing and urging his peculiar views, have also exerted an influence over the minds of his readers that has had its effect in the adoption of this theory. A scientific proposition that to every unsophisticated mind appears manifestly absurd may be set down as being fallacious.

The true bearing and real tendency of Darwin's argument has not been suspected by scientists, not seen by himself. This tendency unquestionably is, to demonstrate, by the argument which logicians call a *reductio ad absurdum*, the fallacy of the whole system of European science. A system of science, on the principles of which a valid argument could be made in support of a proposition so utterly false as that of Darwin, stated above, must be radically and fundamentally wrong. . . .

Any one who has taken a correct view of nature in the light of true science at once sees that there are no grounds there for Darwin's principal positions, and becomes convinced that his main proposition, as stated above, is futile in the extreme, is unreliable and unfounded.

More natural to assume that the monkey is descended from man, than the contrary

Had Darwin contended that the monkey is descended from man, and that its present degraded form was the punishment inflicted for a neglect or nonobservance of an instinct of man's nature, he might have constructed a more plausible argument than he has done. He might have pointed to the condition of the Fuegian savage, — whose brutal appearance seems to have reconciled his mind to the notion of claiming the monkey as his progenitor, — as one of the stages of this degradation to which he had been brought by a perversion of his instincts, and, to some extent, by his inherited habits of reckless indulgence of passion, and also in some measure by the environment of savage life.

But this proposition, on reflection, would have appeared false ; for it must be admitted that the vast scheme of creation was planned in the will of an omniscient and omnipotent Creator, and that it is not allowed to his creatures to mar or to interfere materially with the details of " the work which God worketh from the beginning." He has endowed no creature with the power nor with the intelligence that would be required for such an undertaking. The world has all along been as God has appointed, and the course of nature will continue as he may direct, notwithstanding the shortsighted theories of would-be philosophers.

Let the ridiculous doctrine of evolution, which is founded on *materialism*, — that is another term for *atheism*, and which Darwin embraces and strenuously endeavors to bolster up in his false theory, — let this doctrine be compared with the Mosaic account of the creation, and then let the student of nature determine if he will choose for his progenitors Darwin's pair of ring-tailed monkeys, or " Adam, the comeliest man of men since born his sons," and " The fairest of her daughters, Eve." *Evolution is founded on "materialism" and is another term for "atheism"*

John Fiske, an eminent American philosopher and historian, not only enthusiastically accepted the theory of evolution but stoutly maintained (writing in 1884) that instead of its degrading mankind, as the writer just quoted declares, it serves to prove that the perfection of man is the object toward which all things have been working for untold æons. The discovery by Copernicus that the universe did not revolve about the earth served to alter profoundly men's views of themselves and their importance. *401. Argument of John Fiske that the theory of evolution elevates rather than degrades man (condensed)*

During the nineteenth century, however, a still greater revolution has been effected. Not only has Lyell enlarged our mental horizon in time as much as Newton enlarged it in space, but it appears that throughout these vast stretches of time and space with which we have been made acquainted there are sundry well-marked changes going on. Certain definite paths of development are being pursued, and around us on every side we behold worlds, organisms, and societies in divers stages of progress or decline. Still more, as we examine the records of past life upon our globe, and study the mutual relations of the living things that still remain, it appears that the higher forms of life — including man himself — are the modified descendants of lower forms. Zoölogically speaking, man can no longer be regarded as a creature apart by himself. We cannot erect an order on purpose to contain him, as Cuvier tried to do ; we cannot even make a separate family for him. Man is not only a vertebrate, a mammal, and a primate, but he belongs, as a genus, to the catarrhine family of apes. And just as lions, leopards, and lynxes — different genera of the cat family — are descended from a common stock of carnivora, back to which we may also trace the pedigrees of dogs, hyenas, bears, and seals, so the various genera of apes, including man, are doubtless descended from a common stock of primates, back to which we may also trace the converging pedigrees of monkeys and lemurs until their ancestry becomes indistinguishable from that of rabbits and squirrels. Such is the conclusion to which the scientific world has come within a quarter of a century from the publication of Mr. Darwin's *Origin of Species;* and there is no more reason for supposing that this conclusion will ever be gainsaid than for supposing that the Copernican astronomy will sometime be overthrown.

Revolutionary effects of the evolutionary theory

It is not strange that this theory of man's origin, which we associate mainly with the name of Mr. Darwin, should be to many very unwelcome. It is fast bringing about a still greater revolution in thought than that which was heralded by Copernicus ; and it naturally takes some time for the various portions of one's theory of things to become adjusted to so vast and sweeping a change. From many quarters the cry goes up, If this be true, then man is at length cast down from his high position in the world. "I will not be called a mammal, or the son of a mammal!" once exclaimed an acquaintance of mine who perhaps had been brought up by hand. It is urged that if man is physically akin to a baboon, as pigs are akin to horses, and cows to deer, then humanity can in nowise be regarded as occupying a peculiar place in the universe; it becomes a mere incident in the endless series of changes, and how can we say that the same process of evolution that has produced mankind may not by and by produce something far more perfect? In such case, why should we regard man as in any higher sense the object of divine care than a pig?

Still stronger does the case appear when we remember that those countless adaptations of means to ends which we have been accustomed to cite as evidences of creative design, have received at the hands of Mr. Darwin a very different interpretation. The lobster's powerful claw, the butterfly's gorgeous tints, the rose's delicious fragrance, are no longer explained as the results of contrivance. The simple but wasteful process of the survival of the fittest, through which such marvelous things have come into being, has little about it that is analogous to the ingenuity of human art. The infinite power which is thus revealed in the physical life of the universe seems nowise akin to the human soul. The idea of beneficent purpose seems for the moment to be excluded from nature, and a blind process, known as natural selection, is the deity that slumbers not nor sleeps. Reckless of good and evil, it brings forth at once the mother's tender love for her infant and the horrible teeth of the ravening shark. *[Natural selection]*

In spite of these appalling arguments the man of science, urged by the single-hearted purpose to ascertain the truth, be the consequences what they may, goes quietly on and finds that the terrible theory must be adopted; the fact of man's consanguinity with the dumb beasts must be admitted. To pursue unflinchingly the methods of science requires dauntless courage and a faith that nothing can shake; such courage and such loyalty brings its own reward. For when once the formidable theory really is understood, when once its implications are properly unfolded, it is seen to have no such logical consequences as were first ascribed to it. As with the Copernican astronomy, so with the Darwinian biology, we rise to a higher *[The creation and perfecting of man the goal of nature's work]* view of the workings of God and of the nature of man than was ever attainable before. So far from degrading humanity or putting it on a level with the animal world in general, the Darwinian theory shows us distinctly for the first time how the creation and perfecting of man is the goal toward which nature's work has all the while been tending. It enlarges tenfold the significance of human life, places it upon even a loftier eminence than poets and prophets have imagined, and makes it seem more than ever the chief object of that creative activity which is manifested in the physical universe. . . .

The cruel features of evolution being eliminated

As regards the significance of man's position in the universe, the gradual elimination of strife is a fact of unparalleled grandeur. It means that the wholesale destruction of life, which has heretofore characterized evolution ever since life began, and through which the higher forms of existence have been produced, must presently come to an end in the case of the chief of God's creatures. The coarser forms of cruelty are disappearing and the butchery of man has greatly diminished. But most people apply to industrial pursuits a notion of antagonism derived from ages of warfare, and seek in all manner of ways to cheat and overreach one another. And as in more barbarous times the hero was he who had slain his tens of thousands, so now the man who has made wealth by overreaching his neighbors is not uncommonly spoken of in terms which imply approval. Though gentlemen, moreover, no longer assail one another with knives and clubs, they still inflict cruel wounds with cruel words and sneers. Though the freethinker is no longer chained to a stake and burned, people still tell lies about him, and do their best to starve him by hurting his reputation.

Nevertheless, in all these respects some improvement has been made, along with the diminution of warfare, and by the time warfare has not merely ceased from the earth but has come to be the dimly remembered phantom of a remote past, the development of the sympathetic side of human nature will doubtless become prodigious. The manifestations of selfish and hateful feelings will be more and more sternly repressed by public opinion, and such feelings will become weakened by disuse, while the sympathetic feelings will increase in strength as the sphere for their exercise is enlarged.

And thus at length we see what human progress means. It means throwing off the brute inheritance. Man is slowly passing from a primitive social state in which he was little better than a brute, toward an ultimate social state in which his character shall have become so transformed that nothing of the brute can be detected in it. The ape and tiger in human nature will become extinct. Theology has had much to say of original sin. This original sin is neither more nor less than the brute inheritance which every man carries with him, and the process of evolution is an advance toward true salvation. *The brute inheritance being thrown off*

A distinguished English biologist, Dr. E. Ray Lankester, speaks of the question of the antiquity of man as follows :

There must be many here who remember, as I do, the astounding and almost sudden discovery some forty-five years ago of abundant and overwhelming evidence that man had existed in western Europe as a contemporary of the mammoth and rhinoceros, the hyena and the lion. The dispute over the facts submitted to the scientific world was violent and of short duration. The immense antiquity of man was established and accepted on all sides just before Mr. Darwin published his book on *The Origin of Species.* The palæolithic implements, though not improbably made 150,000 years ago, do not, any more than do the imperfect skulls occasionally found in association with them, indicate a condition of the human race much more monkey-like than is presented by existing savage races. The implements themselves are manufactured with great skill and artistic feeling. *402. The antiquity of man*

Within the last ten years much rougher flint implements, of peculiar types, have been discovered in gravels which are 500 feet above the level of existing rivers. These eoliths of the south of England indicate a race of men of less-developed skill than the makers of the palæoliths, and carry the antiquity of man at least as far back beyond the palæoliths as these are from the present day.

We have as yet found no remains giving the direct basis for conclusions on the subject; but judging from analogy (not by any means a conclusive method) furnished by the history of other large animals now living alongside of man, such as the horse, the rhinoceros, the tapir, the wolf, the hyena, and the bear, it is not improbable that it was in the remote period known as the lower Miocene — remote even as compared with the gravels in which eoliths occur — that natural selection began to favor that increase in the size of the brain of a large and not very powerful, semi-erect ape, which eventuated, after some hundreds of thousands of years, in the breeding out of a being with a relatively enormous brain case, a skillful hand, and an inveterate tendency to throw stones, flourish sticks, protect himself in caves, and in general to defeat aggression and satisfy his natural appetites by the use of his wits rather than by strength alone, — in which, however, he was not deficient. Probably this creature had nearly the full size of brain and every other physical characteristic of modern man, although he had not as yet stumbled on the art of making fire by friction, nor converted his conventional grunts and groans, his screams, laughter, and interjections into a language corresponding to (and thenceforth developing) his power of thought.

The well-known English zoölogist, Huxley, in a discourse delivered as early as 1868, gives a popular explanation of the cell and protoplasm.

403. Huxley on protoplasm (much condensed) What, truly, can seem to be more obviously different from one another, in faculty, in form, and in substance than the various kinds of living beings? Think of the microscopic fungus which finds space enough to multiply into countless millions in the body of a living fly; and then of the giant pine of California, towering to the dimensions of a cathedral spire, or the Indian fig, which covers acres with its profound shadow, and endures while nations and empires come and go around its vast circumference. Picture to yourself the great Finner whale, hugest of beasts that live, or have lived, disporting his eighty or ninety feet of bone, muscle, and blubber with easy roll, among waves in which the stoutest ship that ever left dockyard would flounder hopelessly ; and contrast him with the invisible animalcules — mere specks, multitudes of which could dance upon the point of a needle. With these images before your minds, you may well ask, what community of form or structure is there between the animalcule and the whale, or between the fungus and the fig tree?

If we regard substance or material composition, what hidden bond can connect the flower which a girl wears in her hair and the blood which courses through her youthful veins ; or what is common between the dense and resisting mass of the oak, or the strong fabric of the tortoise, and those broad disks of glassy jelly which may be seen pulsating through the waters of a calm sea? Nevertheless beast, fowl, reptile, and fish, mollusk, worm, polyp, are all composed of structural units of the same character, namely, masses of protoplasm with a nucleus. A nucleated mass of protoplasm turns out to be what may be termed the structural unit of the human body. As a matter of fact, the body in its perfect condition is a mere multiple of such units variously modified. What has been said of the animal world is no less true of plants. Traced back to its earliest state, the nettle arises as the man does, in a particle of nucleated protoplasm. Protoplasm is the formal basis of all life.

Thus it becomes clear that all living powers are cognate, Protein and that all living forms are fundamentally of one character. The researches of the chemist have revealed a no less striking uniformity of material composition in living matter. All the forms of protoplasm which have yet been examined contain the four elements, carbon, hydrogen, oxygen, and nitrogen, in a very complex union. To this complex combination, the nature of which has never been determined with exactness, the name of protein has been applied.

Science has not only revolutionized our ideas of animal and plant life but of the treatment of maladies. By means of the most delicately adjusted microscopes it has become possible to discover and study the minute plants known as bacteria, some of which are not over a hundred and fifty thousandth of an inch in diameter.

404. The beneficent bacteria (from Dr. William Osler)

The study of the life histories of these diminutive plants excites the wonder of those who make observations upon them. It is truly marvelous to know that these bacteria can accomplish, in their short lives of possibly a few hours or days, feats which would baffle the cleverest of chemists if given years of a lifetime to work upon. They give to the farmer the good quality of his crops, to the dairyman superior butter and cheese; they assist in large measure in freeing our rivers and lakes from harmful pollutions. Here it should be strongly emphasized that those bacteria which cause disease are only a few species, all others contributing to our welfare in countless ways.

Quite as astonishing is the discovery that within the root knobs of peas and beans live bacteria which, by splitting up mineral salts containing nitrogen and by absorbing nitrogen from the air, give it over to the plant, so that it is enabled to grow luxuriantly, whereas without their presence the tiller of the soil might fertilize the ground in vain. It is quite possible that not alone peas and beans but all grasses and plants and trees depend upon the presence of such germs for their very existence, which in turn supply man and animals with their means of existence. Hence we see that these nitrifying bacteria, as they are called, if swept out of existence, would be the cause of cessation of all life upon the globe.

The astonishing effects of scientific discovery in promoting the highly practical art of surgery are well described by Dr. Keen in the following passage:

405. Modern surgery (from Dr. W. W. Keen)

Great theologians, such as a Calvin or a Jonathan Edwards, were they recalled to life, could discourse as learnedly as ever of predestination and free will; great forensic orators, such as a Burke or a Webster, could convince us by the same arguments and arouse us by the same invectives that made our fathers willing captives to their silver tongues. But to-day, so

rapid had been our surgical progress that a Velpeau, a Sir
William Ferguson, or a Pancoast, all of whom have died within
the last thirty years, could not teach modern surgical principles nor perform a modern surgical operation. Even our
everyday surgical vocabulary — staphylococcus, streptococcus,
infection, immunity, antisepsis and asepsis, toxin and antitoxin
— would be unintelligible jargon to him ; and our modern operations on the brain, the chest, the abdomen, and the pelvis
would make him wonder whether we had all lost our senses,
until, seeing the almost uniform and almost painless recoveries,
he would thank God for the magnificent progress of the last
half century, which had vouchsafed such magical — nay,
almost divine — power to the modern surgeon.

The man of science is constantly impressed with the
fact that humanity is only at the very beginning of its
task of reaching an understanding of the world and its
multiform creatures. Science is as yet, as Carlyle declared, no more than a film on the infinitely deep sea of
our ignorance. The danger, not to say absurdity, of our
guesses about the origin and fate of the universe as a
whole is very prettily expressed by the scientist, Langley,
in a little parable.

We have read somewhere of a race of ephemeral insects   406. A para-
who live but an hour. To those who are born in the early   ble on the
morning the sunrise is the time of youth. They die of old age   ignorance
of man
while the sun's beams are yet gathering force, and only their
descendants live on to midday ; while it is another race
which sees the sun's decline from that which saw it rise.
Imagine the sun about to set, and the whole nation of mites
gathered under the shadow of some mushroom (to them ancient
as the sun itself) to hear what their wisest philosopher had to
say of the gloomy prospect.

If I remember aright, he first told them that, incredible as
it might seem, there was not once a time in the world's youth
when the mushroom itself was young, but that the sun in those

early ages was in the eastern, not in the western, sky. Since then, he explained, the eyes of the scientific ephemera had followed it, and established by induction from vast experience the great " law of nature " that it moved only westward ; and he showed that since it was now nearing the western horizon, science pointed herself to the conclusion that it was about to disappear forever, together with the great race of ephemera for whom it was created. What his hearers thought of this discussion I do not remember, but I have heard that the sun rose again the next morning.

In an essay dealing with the advance of science from 1881 to 1906, E. Ray Lankester, the English zoölogist, makes the following reflections :

407. Problems of scientific research

As one might expect, the progress of the knowledge of nature has consisted, in the last twenty-five years, in the amplification and fuller verification of principles and theories already accepted, and in the discovery of hitherto unknown things which either have fallen into place in the existing scheme of each science or have necessitated new views, some not very disturbing to existing general conceptions, others of a more startling and, at first sight, disconcerting character. Nevertheless I think I am justified in saying that exciting and of entrancing interest as have been some of the discoveries of the past few years, there has been nothing to lead us to conclude that we have been on the wrong path, — nothing which is really revolutionary ; that is to say, nothing which cannot be accepted by an intelligible modification of previous conceptions.

The enemies of science

Whilst some onlookers have declared to the public that science is at an end, its possibilities exhausted, and but little of the hopes it raised realized, others have asserted, on the contrary, that the new discoveries — such as those relating to the X rays and to radium — are so inconsistent with previous knowledge as to shake the foundations of science and to justify a belief in any and every absurdity of an unrestrained fancy. These two reciprocally destructive accusations are due to a class of persons who must be described as the enemies of science. Whether their attitude is due to ignorance or traditions of self-interest, such persons exist. It is one of the objects of our scientific associations and societies to combat those assertions and to demonstrate, by the discoveries announced at their meetings and the consequent orderly building up of the great fabric of "natural knowledge," that science has not come to an end of her work, — has, indeed, only as yet given mankind a foretaste of what she has in store for it, — that her methods and her accomplished results are sound and trustworthy, serving with perfect adaptability for the increase of true discovery and the expansion and development of those general conceptions of the processes of nature at which she aims. . . .

I would venture to allude to the relations of scientific progress to religion. Putting aside the troubles connected with special creeds and churches and the claims of the clerical profession to certain funds and employments to the exclusion of laymen, it should, I think, be recognized that there is no essential antagonism between the scientific spirit and what is called the religious sentiment. "Religion," said Bishop Creighton, "means the knowledge of our destiny and of the means of fulfilling it." We can say no more and no less of science. Men of science seek, in all reverence, to discover the Almighty, the Everlasting. They claim sympathy and friendship with those who, like themselves, have turned away from the more material struggles of human life and have set their hearts and minds on the knowledge of the Eternal.

BIBLIOGRAPHY

GENERAL

The best general bibliographies relating to the general history of ^{General} Europe since the Congress of Vienna will be found in the following bibliographies works: (a) *The Cambridge Modern History*, Vol. X, "The Restoration," 1907; Vol. XI, "The Growth of Nationalities," 1909; and Vol. XII, "The Latest Age" (in preparation). (b) *Histoire générale*, edited by LAVISSE et RAMBAUD, Vol. X, "Les Monarchies constitutionelles," 1898; Vol. XI, "Révolutions et Guerres nationales, 1848–1870," 1899; Vol. XII, "Le Monde contemporaine, 1870–1900," 1901. Each of these works gives elaborate lists of sources and writers for each chapter. *The Cambridge Modern History* is the more recent and the fuller of the two, but the *Histoire générale* is often the more helpful because the more discriminating. Excellent bibliographies, kept nearly up to date, are given in the *Statesman's Year-Book*. For Germany and the history bound up with hers one should consult the monumental and almost ideal work, DAHLMANN-WAITZ, *Quellenkunde der deutschen Geschichte*, 7th ed., 1905–1906, and supplementary volume, 1907.

For the annual historical bibliographies and the chief historical magazines which enable one to keep pace with current publications, see above, Vol. I, p. 389.

The best general accounts of the history of Europe during the nine- ^{General} teenth century, especially of the political events, to be had in English histories of are: ANDREWS, C. M., *The Historical Development of Modern Europe* ^{the nineteenth} (two volumes bound in one); FYFFE, *History of Modern Europe* (origi- century in nally in three volumes, now published in one); SEIGNOBOS, *A Political* English *History of Europe since 1814* (edited by Professor Macvane). A shorter narrative may be found in PHILLIPS, W. A., *Modern Europe, 1815–1899;* and a lively, journalistic review, especially of German history, in MÜLLER, *History of Recent Times.* Unfortunately none of these furnish an adequate account of the development of the past quarter of a century. This deficiency is in a measure remedied by Professor Andrews in his volume, "Contemporaneous Europe," in the great set, *The History of All Nations.* In due time Vol. XII of *The Cambridge Modern History* will bring the reader down to 1908 or 1909. The *Annual Register*, which has been appearing in England since 1758, gives an admirable sketch of Europe's history year by year, and is indispensable to one who wishes to be abreast of the developments of his time (see below, p. 540).

French and German works

In French and German the following general histories of the century are perhaps the best: BULLE, *Geschichte der neuesten Zeit*, 2d ed., 4 vols., 1886–1887, a careful work by one familiar with public questions in Germany; STERN, A., *Geschichte Europas seit den Verträgen von 1815 bis zum Frankfurter Frieden von 1871*, more recent and excellent (four volumes have appeared, 1894–1905, covering the period from 1815 to 1835); LAVISSE et RAMBAUD, *Histoire générale*, Vols. X–XII, clear and excellent, dealing with all the broader phases of European development; DEBIDOUR, *Histoire diplomatique de l'Europe, 1814–1891*, 2 vols.; BOURGEOIS, *Manuel historique de politique étrangère*, 3 vols. (down to 1878), 1905; HERTSLET, *Map of Europe by Treaty since 1814*, 4 vols., a remarkable collection of the chief treaties and agreements translated into English.

Annual histories

There are several convenient annual publications which sum up the history year by year and often give the texts of important documents. There is first and foremost the *Annual Register* mentioned above. For France, *Annuaire historique universel*, 1818–1860, and *L'Année politique*, since 1874; for Germany, Austria, etc., SCHULTHESS, *Geschichtskalender*, since 1860. The *British and Foreign State Papers*, annual since 1829, furnish important material for the history of Europe since the year 1812 (see below, pp. 540–541).

The voluminous reports of the proceedings in the various parliaments constitute an unwieldy but indispensable source for the political history.

Papal affairs

La Civiltà Cattolica, issued since 1850 in Rome (four volumes yearly), is the most natural place to look for all papal decrees, bulls, encyclicals, etc. They will be found there in both the original Latin and in Italian.

CHAPTER XVII

GENERAL POLITICAL HISTORY OF EUROPE FROM 1815 TO 1848

General

The Cambridge Modern History, Vol. X, and the works of ANDREWS, FYFFE, SEIGNOBOS, PHILLIPS, and MULLER (mentioned above, p. 521) all furnish good accounts of this period. They may be supplemented by the *Histoire générale*, Vol. X; STERN, *Geschichte Europas seit den Verträgen von 1815*, Vols. I–IV (to 1835); DEBIDOUR, HERTSLET, and BOURGEOIS, also mentioned above. A suggestive general review of the period is given in *The Cambridge Modern History*, Vol. X, chap. i; MALLESON, G. B., *Life of Prince Metternich*, 1888.

The Cambridge Modern History, Vol. X, chaps. ii, iii, and xv, are de- France,
voted to France from 1815 to 1848. On pages 792 and 845 one will find 1815–1848
enumerated the old voluminous histories of the Restoration for which
he is likely to find little time nowadays. *Histoire générale*, Vol. X,
chaps. iii, vii, x–xii. ANDERSON, *Constitutions and Other Select Documents Illustrative of the History of France, 1789–1901*, is useful but sometimes inaccurate in translation. DUVERGIER, *Collection complète des lois,
décrets*, etc. (1824–1875), 75 vols., gives a vast number of important
documents. TRIPIER, *Constitutions qui ont régi la France depuis 1789.*

For Belgium and Holland, *The Cambridge Modern History*, Vol. X, Belgium
chap. xvi; SEIGNOBOS, chap. viii; and *Histoire générale*, Vol. X, chap. ix,
all of which give ample bibliographies.

For the German Confederation, *The Cambridge Modern History*, Vol. Germany,
X, chap. xi. SYBEL, H., *Founding of the German Empire*, Vol. I, gives an 1815–1848
illuminating account of German history following the treaties of 1815.
Histoire générale, Vol. X, chap. xvii. TREITSCHKE, *Deutsche Geschichte*,
5 vols., 1886–1895, comes down to 1848 (by a very able but highly
Prussian writer). The *Allgemeine deutsche Biographie*, in 40 volumes, is
an admirable biographical dictionary in which an account can be found
of all the important public men in Germany.

The Cambridge Modern History, Vol. X, chaps. iv–v, deal with Italy Italy
and the Papal States. Much the best thing for English readers is THAYER,
W. R., *Dawn of Italian Independence*, 2 vols., 1893, scholarly and remarkably well written. See also CESARESCO, *Liberation of Italy*, and STILLMAN,
The Union of Italy, 1815–1895, both by writers who lived long in Italy.

For Spain, *The Cambridge Modern History*, Vol. X, chaps. vi–x, with Spain and
excellent bibliographies; SEIGNOBOS, chap. x; *Histoire générale*, Vol. X, her colonies
chap. xxiii; CLARKE, H. B., *Modern Spain, 1815–1898*, 1906; HUME,
MARTIN, A. S., *Modern Spain* (Story of the Nations Series); TEMPERLEY,
Life of Canning, 1905.

CHAPTER XVIII

THE INDUSTRIAL REVOLUTION

There is no history of the Industrial Revolution in Europe as a whole. The Indus-
GIBBINS, *Economic and Industrial Progress of the Century*, 1903, written trial Revolu-
for the general reader, contains chapters on France and Germany as well tion in general
as England. COCHRANE, *Modern Industrial Progress*, 1904, a popular
description of some of the most striking mechanical inventions of the
last century. MARSHALL, *Principles of Economics*, 1905, Book IV, chaps.
viii–xiii, contains an excellent study of modern industrial organization.

McVey, *Modern Industrialism*, 1905; *The Cambridge Modern History*, Vol. X, chaps. xxiii–xxiv.

General works on the Industrial Revolution in England
Cunningham, *Growth of English Industry and Commerce*, edition of 1903, Vol. II ; Cheyney, *Introduction to the Industrial and Social History of England*, 1901, especially full on the Industrial Revolution and the nineteenth century; Toynbee, Arnold, *Lectures on the Industrial Revolution of the Eighteenth Century*, 1902, not a connected account, but a collection of somewhat unrelated lectures bearing on the subject; Hobson, J. A., *The Evolution of Modern Capitalism*, 1904, 2d ed., full and excellent account of the origin and tendencies of modern industry; Warner, G. T., *Landmarks in English Industrial History*, 1899, contains clear and valuable chapters on the Industrial Revolution; Taylor, R. W. C., *The Modern Factory System*, 1891, a more or less cursory treatment, not very scientific in method but useful; Smiles, Samuel, *Lives of the Engineers*, 1905, contains brief and readable lives of Boulton and Watt; Thurston, R. H., *History of the Steam Engine*, 1878, an excellent popular account in the International Scientific Series. The lives of Kay, Arkwright, Hargreaves, Crompton, Newcomen, Watt, Stephenson, and the other great inventors may be studied in the *Dictionary of National Biography*. The best brief history of the Industrial Revolution in England is the recent French work, Mantoux, *La Révolution industrielle au XVIIIe siècle*, 1906.

France
For the industrial development of France consult the great work by Lavasseur, E., *Histoire des classes ouvrières et de l'industries en France de 1789 à 1870*, 2 vols., 1903–1904. For the condition of the working classes in France: Reybaud, *Rapport sur la condition des ouvriers qui vivent de la soie* (1860), *le coton* (1863), *la laine* (1867), *le fer et la houille* (1874); Blanqui, A., *Les Classes ouvrières en France en 1848–1849*, 1849; Leroy-Beaulieu, P., *La Question ouvrière au XIXe siècle*, 1872, *Le Travail des femmes au XIXe siècle*, 1873 ; Levasseur, *La Population française*, 3 vols., 1889–1891 ; Fontaine, A., *Lois sociales*, 1895, a collection of laws relating to social reforms.

Germany
There is no adequate account of the Industrial Revolution in Germany, but Sombart, *Die deutsche Volkswirtschaft im neunzehnten Jahrhundert*, 1903, and *Der moderne Capitalismus*, 2 vols., 1902, furnish a detailed account of the rise of the capitalistic method of production and its social results.

Guidance for advanced work
For technical articles on the great industries, the various encyclopedias in English, French, and German may be consulted with profit.

Practical guidance in the advanced study of industrial and economic questions is afforded by the various special encyclopedias : Palgrave,

Dictionary of Political Economy, 3 vols., 1894–1899; CONRAD, *Hand-wörterbuch der Staatswissenschaften,* 7 vols., 1898–1901.

The sources for the Industrial Revolution in every country are to be found in the voluminous government reports and statistical publications, such, for example, as the parliamentary inquiries into the state of commerce, industry, and labor published by the English government. The English papers are accessible through JONES, H. V., *Catalogue of Parliamentary Papers* (no date). Similar publications are available for all the other European governments.

CHAPTERS XIX–XX

THE REVOLUTION OF 1848

Perhaps the most skillfully arranged short account of the complicated events in all the countries affected is to be found in ANDREWS, *Historical Development of Modern Europe. The Cambridge Modern History,* Vol. XI, chaps. ii–vii; SEIGNOBOS, *Political Development of Europe since 1814,* chaps. v–vi, xii–xiv; MAURICE, C. E., *The Revolutionary Movement of 1848–1849,* 1887, useful for the events in Germany, Austria, and Italy. An interesting and vivid account of the revolutionary movement in Germany is given in the first volume of *The Reminiscences of Carl Schurz,* 3 vols., 1908. TREVELYAN, *Garibaldi's Defense of the Roman Republic,* 1907, is useful for the whole Italian situation about the middle of the nineteenth century and contains a good bibliography. JOHNSTON, R. M., *The Napoleonic Empire in Southern Italy and the Rise of the Secret Societies,* 1904. EVANS, T. W., *The Second French Empire,* 1905, is a very sympathetic account of Napoleon III. SENIOR, N., *Conversations with Thiers, Guizot, and Others,* 2 vols., 1878, is valuable for interesting glimpses of men and politics during the Second Empire. BLANC, L., *Historical Revelations,* 1858, contains a full account of the Revolution of 1848 in France from the point of view of a socialistic sympathizer. There is an English translation of some of the more valuable works of Louis Napoleon, *Life and Works of Louis Napoleon,* 2 vols., 1852. MARX, K., *Revolution and Counter Revolution,* 1894, is a socialistic interpretation of the Revolution of 1848. Works in English

The best work on the social aspects of the Revolution of 1848 in France is STEIN, *Geschichte der sozialen Bewegung in Frankreich,* 1850. ISAMBERT, G., *Les Idées socialistes en France de 1815 à 1848,* 1905. THOMAS, E., *Histoire des ateliers nationaux,* 1848, an account of the workshops experiment by the director. For the political side of the Revolution in France see SPULLER, E., *Histoire parlementaire de la 2ᵉ* Materials for advanced study
France

République, 1891. PIERRE, V., *Histoire de la République de 1848*, 2 vols., 1873–1878, is written from the conservative standpoint. The best and most recent work on the Second Empire, though with a conservative bias, is GORCE, P. DE LA, *Histoire du Second Empire*, 7 vols., 1896–1905. BERTON, H., *L'Évolution constitutionelle du Second Empire*, 1900; BOURGEOIS, É., et CLERMONT, E., *Rome et Napoléon III*, 1907.

Italy   LA FARINA, *Storia d'Italia dal 1815 al 1850*, 4 vols., 1850; FARINI, *Lo Stato Romano dall' anno 1815 al 1850*, to be had in English translation, *The Roman State from 1815 to 1850*, 4 vols., 1851; D'AZEGLIO, M., *L'Italie de 1847 à 1865*, 1867, a valuable collection of letters by an eminent Italian leader; PEPE, GENERALE GUGLIELMO, *Révolutions et Guerres d'Italie pendant 1847–1849*, 1850; OTTOLINI, V., *La Rivoluzione Lombarda del 1848–1849*, 1887.

Austria   SPRINGER, *Geschichte Oesterreichs*, 1863–1865; HELFERT, *Geschichte Oesterreichs vom Ausgange des Wiener Oktober-Aufstandes*, 1870–1876; RESCHAUER, *Das Jahr 1848*, 1870, contains important documents. For the social aspects, BACH, M., *Die Wiener Revolution 1848*, 1898, and ZENKER, E., *Die Wiener Revolution von 1848 in ihren sozialen Voraussetzungen*, 1897.

Germany   BULLE, *Geschichte der neuesten Zeit*, Vol. II. SYBEL, *Die Begründung des deutschen Reiches*, Vols. I and II, gives the official Prussian view to be had in English translation, *The Founding of the German Empire*, 7 vols., 1890–1897. BIEDERMANN, *Geschichte Deutschlands, 1815–1871*, 1891; BLUM, H., *Das deutsche Reich zur Zeit Bismarcks*, 1893. For the papers relating to the Frankfort Assembly, *Stenographische Berichte über die Verhandlungen der ersten Konstitutionale Nationalversammlung*, edited by Wigard, 9 vols., 1849. MATTER, P., *La Prusse et la Révolution de 1848*, 1903.

CHAPTER XXI

ITALY SINCE 1848

Treatments in English   *The Cambridge Modern History*, Vol. XI, chaps. xiv and xix; SEIGNOBOS, *Political History of Europe since 1814*, chap. xi.; STILLMAN, W. J., *The Unity of Italy, 1815–1895*, 1898, the best brief account in English, with a well-selected bibliography in the Appendix; KING, B., *A History of Italian Unity*, 2 vols., 1899, a full and readable history laying emphasis on the political aspects of Italian development from 1814 to 1871; MAZZINI, J., *Life and Writings*, 6 vols., 1890–1891; GARIBALDI, *Autobiography of Giuseppe Garibaldi*, 3 vols., 1889; KING, B., and OKEY, T., *Italy To-day*, 1901, an excellent study, especially good on the causes of emigration; COUNTESS CESARESCO, *Cavour* (Foreign Statesmen Series), and her *Liberation of Italy;* GODKIN, *Life of Victor Emmanuel II*, 2 vols.,1879; HOLLAND, R., *Builders of United Italy*, 1908. Essays on Gioberti, Mazzini, Garibaldi, Cavour, and others.

The Cambridge Modern History, Vol. X, chap. v, and Vol. XI, chap. xxv; *Histoire générale*, Vol. X, chap. xxi; Vol. XI, chap. xxvi; Vol. XII, chap. xvi; NIELSEN, F., *History of the Papacy in the Nineteenth Century*, 2 vols., 1906; D'AGEN, B., *Le Prélature de Léon XIII*, 1900; MATER, A., *L'Église Catholique, sa constitution, son administration*, 1906, an excellent description of the Church's organization. See also *La Civiltà Cattolica*, mentioned above, p. 522. — The papacy in the nineteenth century

CHAPTERS XXII–XXIII

GERMANY AND AUSTRIA-HUNGARY SINCE THE REVOLUTION OF 1848

The Cambridge Modern History, Vol. XI, chaps. xv–xvii; SEIGNOBOS, *Political History of Europe since 1814*, chaps. xii–xvi; SYBEL, *Founding of the German Empire by William I*, 7 vols., 1890–1898, perhaps the best of the extensive works in English, but only comes down to the opening of the Franco-Prussian War; HEADLAM, *The Foundation of the German Empire, 1815–1871*, 2 vols., 1897, and, by the same author, *Bismarck and the Founding of the German Empire*, 1899, a shorter account in the Heroes of the Nations Series. There is a good deal available in English in regard to Bismarck: SMITH, MUNROE, *Bismarck and German Unity*, 1898, excellent short account; LOWE, *Life of Prince Bismarck*, 2 vols., 1888, and, by the same writer, *The German Emperor, William II*, 1898; BUSCH (long Bismarck's secretary), *Bismarck: Some Secret Pages of his History*, 3 vols., 1898. Then from the statesman's own hand, *Bismarck, the Man and the Statesman: Reflections*, etc., by himself, 2 vols., 1898. — Germany

MOLTKE, *The Franco-German War, 1870–1871*, 1893; ELTZBACHER, *Modern Germany*, 1905; HOWARD, B. E., *The German Constitution*, 1906, a clear analysis of the German imperial government, which may be supplemented by ROBINSON, J. H., *The German Bundesrath*, 1891, in which the chief peculiarities of the federation are emphasized. — The German Constitution

In French and German perhaps the chief books are: ONCKEN, *Das Zeitalter des Kaiser Wilhelm*, 1888–1892, two stout volumes, fully illustrated; LORENZ, O., *Kaiser Wilhelm und die Begründung des Reiches, 1866–1871*, 1902; DENIS, *La Formation de l'empire allemand* — Books in French and German

1852–1871, 1906; LEBON, *Étude sur l'Allemagne politique*, 1898; MAT-
TER, *Bismarck et Son Temps*, 3 vols., 1905 *sqq.;* LEHAUTCOURT, *Histoire
de la guerre de 1870–1871*, 7 vols., 1901–1908, very detailed. Finally,
excellent chapters on Germany will be found in the *Histoire générale*,
Vol. XI, chap. viii, and Vol. XII, chap. x. A very convenient collection
of documents relating to the formation of the German Empire is edited
by HAHN, *Zwei Jahre preussisch-deutscher Politik, 1866–1867*, followed
by *Der Krieg Deutschlands gegen Frankreich, 1867–1871*.

Austria-
Hungary

SEIGNOBOS, *Political History of Europe since 1814*, chap. xvii;
WHITMAN, S., *Austria*, 1899, and, by the same author, *The Realm of the
Hapsburgs*, 1893; LEGER, *History of Austro-Hungary*, 1889, an English
translation of a French work which has gone into a fourth edition in
the original, 1895; ARNOLD-FORSTER, *Francis Deák, a Memoir*, 1880
(Deák was the leading Hungarian statesman during the formation of
the present dual union); *Histoire générale*, Vol. XI, chap. xiii, and
Vol. XII, chap. iv; BERTHA, *La Hongrie moderne, 1849–1901*, 1901;
EISENMANN, *Le Compromis austro-hungrois de 1867;* HELPERT, *Geschichte
Oesterreichs seit 1848 ;* SAYOUS, *Histoire générale des Hongrois*, 2d ed.,
1900; KRONES, *Geschichte der Neuzeit Oesterreichs*, 1879; AUERBACH,
Les Races et les Nationalités en Autriche-Hongrie, 1898.

CHAPTER XXIV

FRANCE UNDER THE THIRD REPUBLIC

Works in
English

SEIGNOBOS, *Political History of Europe since 1814*, chap. vii; COU-
BERTIN, *The Evolution of France under the Third Republic*, 1897;
HANOTAUX, *Contemporary France*, an interesting and full history of
the Third Republic (three volumes have now appeared, 1903–1907).
For the work of Thiers, SIMON, J., *The Government of M. Thiers*, 2 vols.,
1879; LISSAGARAY, *History of the Commune*, 1898, an interesting work
by a communard sympathiser. The government of France is well described in LOWELL, *Governments and Parties in Continental Europe*,
2 vols., 1897, Vol. I, chaps. i and ii.; BODLEY, J. E. C., *France*, 2 vols.,
1898; WENDELL, B., *The France of To-day*, 1907; SABATIER, P., *Disestablishment in France*, 1906.

General
works in
French

There are excellent chapters on France since 1870 in the last volume
(Vol. XII) of the *Histoire générale ;* ZEVORT, *Histoire de la Troisième
République*, 4 vols., covering the period from Thiers to Carnot; DANIEL,
L'Année politique, published annually since 1874, contains many im-
portant papers and extracts from noteworthy parliamentary debates;
DURET, T., *Histoire de France de 1870 à 1873*, 2 vols., 1901.

There is a large number of books on the Commune, but all of them Commune are seriously biased. DU CAMP, M., *Les Convulsions de Paris*, 5 vols., 1878–1879, is conservative in tone; LISSAGARAY, *Histoire de la Commune* (also in English translation; see above), favors the communards. The official acts of the Commune are to be found in CLARETIE, J., *Documents pour l'histoire de la Commune, 1871*.

WEILL, *Histoire du parti républicain en France de 1814 à 1870*, 1900, Social and *Histoire du mouvement social en France, 1852–1902*, 1905, — two valu- problems able works by a careful scholar.

VIGNON, L., *L'Expansion de la France*, brief and clear; GAFFAREL, Colonies P., *Les Colonies françaises*, 6th ed.; DUBOIS, M., et TERRIER, A., *Les Colonies françaises : un siècle d'expansion coloniale, 1800–1900*, 1902; DUVAL, J., *L'Algérie et les Colonies françaises;* GAISMAN, *L'Œuvre de la France au Tonkin;* LANESSAN, J., *L'Indo-Chine française;* WAHL, A., *L'Algérie*, 5th ed., 1908.

There is an enormous mass of literature on the Dreyfus affair, but Dreyfus nearly all of it is bitterly partisan in character. A satisfactory brief account of the conviction of Dreyfus is to be found in ANDREWS, *Contemporaneous Europe* (History of All Nations Series). There are two interesting books by DREYFUS himself, *Lettres d'un innocent*, 1898, and *Cinq années de ma vie*, the latter translated under the title of *Five Years of My Life*. The fullest account is REINACH, J., *L'Affaire Dreyfus*, 5 vols., 1898 *sqq.* (in course of publication). For a full list of materials see DESACHY, *Bibliographie de l'affaire Dreyfus* (no date).

The separation of Church and State in France is reviewed in two Church and valuable articles, "Die Trennung von Staat und Kirche in Frankreich," State by GEORGES FARDIS and DR. JOH. PROST in the *Jahrbuch des öffentlichen Rechts*, Vol. II, 1908, pp. 178–249 (containing in an Appendix a splendidly selected bibliography of materials on the subject), and "Church and State in France," by OTHON GERLAC, *Political Science Quarterly*, Vol. XXIII, June, 1908, pp. 259–296; DEBIDOUR, A., *L'Église Catholique et l'État sous la Troisième République*, 1906; BAUDRILLART, A., *Quatre cents ans de Concordat*, 1905, an excellent historical review of the relations between Church and State; BRIAND, A., *La Séparation des Églises et de l'État*, 1905, a historical review of the whole religious situation in France made to the Chamber of Deputies by M. Briand, the minister in charge of the law of separation; ODIN, G., et REMAUD, E., *La Loi du 9 décembre, 1905, concernent la séparation des Églises et de l'État*, 1906, a careful study giving the origin, nature, and interpretation of the law of separation, with a fine array of documents; RÉVILLE,

M., and ARMBRUSTER, L., *Le Régime des cultes*, 1906, a popular exposition of the law; FRANCE, A., *L'Église et la République*, 1904, a review of the relation between Church and State from 1897 to 1904. From the Catholic standpoint: *The Catholic Encyclopædia*, art. "Concordat"; FÈVRE, MGR., *Un Complot libéral contre la Sainte-Église*, 1906; LE DORE, A., *La Persécution: devoirs des Catholiques*, 1905. Valuable articles in the *Revue Catholique des institutions et du droit*, Vols. 64–68, *passim*.

CHAPTERS XXV–XXVII

ENGLAND AND THE BRITISH EMPIRE SINCE THE NAPOLEONIC WARS

General works

The Cambridge Modern History, Vol. X, chaps. xviii–xx, and Vol. XI, chaps. i, xi, xii, and xxvii; SEIGNOBOS, *Political History of Europe since 1814*, chaps. ii–iv. OMAN, *England in the Nineteenth Century*, 1900, is an excellent brief epitome. The period of the nineteenth century is covered by the last two volumes of HUNT and POOLE, *Political History of England*, 1906–1907, —Vol. XI, by BRODERICK, G., and FOTHERINGHAM, J. K., and Vol. XII, 1837–1901, by LOW, S., — neglects the fundamental economic and social questions and is often marred by a high Tory prejudice; PAUL, H., *A History of Modern England*, 5 vols., 1904–1906, deals with the period from 1846 to the present time, and is well written and Liberal in its interpretation of events. McCARTHY, J., *History of Our Own Times*, 4 vols., 1888; *England in the Nineteenth Century* (Story of the Nations Series); *Epoch of Reform, 1830–1850*, 1897; *History of the Four Georges*, 2 vols., 1885–1890, — all written in a popular style. The history from 1815 to 1880 is fully treated in WALPOLE, S., *History of England since 1815*, 5 vols., 1879–1886, and *History of Twenty-five Years*, 2 vols., 1904 (the author was a moderate Liberal); WHATES, *The Third Salisbury Administration, 1895–1900*, 1900.

Constitutional history

DICEY, A., *Lectures on the Relation between Law and Public Opinion in England during the Nineteenth Century*, 1905, a suggestive work by an eminent English publicist. For the constitutional history of the first half of the century, MAY, *Constitutional History of England* (several reprints), is still the standard treatise. ROBERTSON, C. G., *Select Statutes, Cases, and Documents*, 1904, contains some materials for the constitutional history of the nineteenth century.

The government of England

The great works on the government of England are LOWELL, A. L., *The Government of England*, 2 vols., 1908; ANSON, *Law and Custom of the English Constitution*, 2 vols., 2d ed., 1896; BAGEHOT, *The English Constitution*, 1886; LOW, S., *The Governance of England*, 1905. MORAN,

Theory and Practice of the English Government, 1903, is a useful, brief compendium. DICEY, *The Law of the Constitution*, 1885, is an invaluable discussion of the principles of the English constitution. BLAUVELT, M., *The Development of Cabinet Government in England*, 1902.

HOWARD, JOHN, *On Prisons*, 1777, the most exact and detailed **Prison reform** source for the subject. For an outline of the life and work of this great philanthropist see DIXON, HEPWORTH, *John Howard and the Prison World of Europe*, 1850. PIKE, LUKE OWEN, *A History of Crime in England*, 2 vols., 1876 (Vol. II gives a readable, reliable account of the development of crime and penal law in England from Henry VII to the present time).

The best history of the development of factory legislation is HUTCHINS, B. L., and HARRISON, L., *A History of Factory Legislation*, 1903. The principles of the legislation are discussed in WEBB, S. and B., *Problems of Modern Industry*, 1902; NICHOLSON, J. S., *The History of the English Corn Laws*, 1904. GAMMAGE, *History of Chartism*, 1854, is the only work of importance on the Chartist movement and is written by a sympathizer.

Among the most available and useful sources for the nineteenth cen- **Advanced** tury may be reckoned the *Annual Register*, the *Statesman's Year-Book*, **study** the various reviews, such as the *Contemporary Review*, the *Westminster Review*, the *National Review*, etc., the lives and speeches of public men like Gladstone, Cobden, Disraeli, John Bright, and others, and the files of the London *Daily* or *Weekly Times*. Among the many valuable biographies the following take high rank : MORLEY, J., *Life of Cobden*, 2 vols., 1881, and the *Life of William E. Gladstone*, 3 vols., 1903; CHURCHILL, *Lord Randolph Churchill*, 2 vols., 1906; FITZMAURICE, *Life of Earl Granville*, 2 vols., 1905; PARKER, *Life of Sir Robert Peel*, 3 vols., 1891–1899; MORRIS, *Wellington, Soldier and Statesman*, 1904. *Letters of Queen Victoria*, 3 vols., 1907, contain interesting characterizations of nearly all the prominent figures in Europe during the period covered.

Nearly all the literature on the Irish question is partisan in charac- **Ireland** ter. The following are perhaps the most useful : BRYCE, *Two Centuries of Irish History*, 1888; LECKY, *History of England and Ireland in the Eighteenth Century*, 8 vols., 1876–1890, and *Leaders of Public Opinion in Ireland*, 1872; SMITH, GOLDWIN, *Irish History and the Irish Question*, 1905; MCCARTHY, J., *Ireland and Her Story*, 1903. For Irish views the following may be cited : O'BRIEN, W. P., *The Great Famine ;* O'CONNER, *The Parnell Movement*. DAVITT, *The Fall of Feudalism in*

Ireland, 1904, is valuable for the land question. MURRAY, A. E., *History of the Commercial and Financial Relations between England and Ireland,* 1903, is indispensable. PLUNKETT, SIR H., *Ireland in the New Century,* 1905, gives a valuable account of the more recent reforms. Voluminous materials on the Irish question are to be found in the Parliamentary debates and in the numerous Parliamentary investigations.

The British Empire

On colonial policy and imperial federation in general: DILKE, *Problems of Greater Britain,* 2 vols., 1890; HOLLAND, B., *Imperium et Libertas,* 1901; *British Empire Series,* 5 vols., 1889–1902; PARKIN, G. R., *Imperial Federation,* 1892; JEBB, *Colonial Nationalism,* 1905. JENKYNS, *British Rule and Jurisdiction beyond the Seas,* 1902, classifies the colonies and discusses the relations among them and with the mother country. EGERTON, H., *A Short History of British Colonial Policy,* 1897 (Books III–V cover the period from 1830 to 1897). STORY, A. T., *The British Empire* (Story of the Nations Series). GRISWELL, *The Growth and Administration of the British Colonies, 1837–1897,* 1898, is a brief review of the constitutional development of Canada, Australia, and South Africa. PAYNE, E. J., *Colonies and Colonial Federations,* 1904; LUCAS, C. P., *Historical Geography of British Colonies,* 6 vols., new ed., 1906 *sqq.* (in course of publication), is indispensable.

Canada

BOURINOT, SIR JOHN, *Canada under British Rule, 1760–1900,* 1900, the best brief work, contains an excellent bibliography; by the same author, *A Manual of the Constitutional History of Canada,* 1901; KINGSFORD, *History of Canada,* 10 vols., 1887–1897, a full and standard work; MONTAGUE, E., and HERBERT, B., *Canada and the Empire,* 1904, written from the imperialist point of view; BRADSHAW, *Self-Government in Canada and How it was Accomplished,* 1903; HOUSTON, *Constitutional Documents of Canada,* 1891, contains, among other papers, the Quebec Act and the Act of Confederation in 1867.

South Africa

BRYCE, *Impressions of South Africa,* 1897, excellent for the conditions prevailing on the eve of the Boer War; THEAL, G. M., *Southern Africa* (Story of the Nations Series); *Briton and Boer,* a collection of papers by eminent men, giving both sides of the case; HOBSON, J. A., *The War in South Africa,* 1900, written from the anti-British standpoint. *The Memoirs of Paul Kruger,* 1902, gives an insight into the views of Kruger as well as the causes of the war.

Australia

JENKS, E., *The History of the Australasian Colonies,* 1895, an excellent brief work; TREGARTHEN, G., *Australasia* (Story of the Nations Series); GREY, J., *Australasia Old and New,* 1901, gives a good account of the development of representative government; *British*

Empire Series, Vol. IV, 1900, contains a collection of lectures on special topics by competent authorities; CLARK, *Studies in Australasian Constitutional Law*, 1905, useful for the new constitution of the Commonwealth. For recent developments in social reform: CLARK, V., *The Labor Movement in Australasia*, 1906; REEVES, W. P., *The Long White Cloud*, 1899; *State Experiments in Australia and New Zealand*, 2 vols., 1902; PARSONS, F., *The Story of New Zealand*, 1904.

FRASER, R. W., *British Rule in India* (Story of the Nations Series). India For the Indian Mutiny of 1857 the following are valuable: MALLESON, *The Indian Mutiny of 1857*, 1891; INNES, M., *The Sepoy Revolt*, 1897; STRACHEY, SIR JOHN, *India: its Administration and Progress*, 1903, an official view by a writer experienced in Indian affairs. DIGBY, *Prosperous British India*, 1901, is a bitter criticism of British administration. *The Imperial Gazetteer of India* (2d ed. in progress, to be in several volumes), is a comprehensive survey of all Indian interests.

CHAPTER XXVIII

THE RUSSIAN EMPIRE SINCE 1815

The Cambridge Modern History, Vol. X, chaps. xiii and xiv, and General Vol. XI, chaps. ix, xi, and xxii, relate to the period from 1815 to 1870 (with accounts bibliographies). SEIGNOBOS, *Political History of Europe since 1814*, in English chap. xix. Similar accounts are given in the *Histoire générale*, Vol. X, chap. iv; Vol. XI, chap. xiv; Vol. XII, chap. xi, and bring the story down to 1900. RAMBAUD, *History of Russia*, Vol. III (coming down to 1881), and, by the same author, *The Expansion of Russia*, a brief and suggestive sketch of Russian advance; SKRINE, *Expansion of Russia*, 1815–1900, a rather dry but reliable statement of facts; MORFILL, W. R. A., *History of Russia from the Birth of Peter the Great to the Death of Alexander II*, 1902; KRAUSSE, A., *Russia in Asia*, 1899, excellent.

These must all be supplemented by books describing the all-impor- Events of tant events of the past ten years. A few only of the best can be the last included here; for example, MILYOUKOV, *Russia and its Crisis*, 1905, ten years based on lectures delivered by this historian in the United States; ZILLIACUS, *The Russian Revolutionary Movement*, 1905, by a Finn of insight; WALLING, WM. E., *Russia's Message*, 1908, by an ardent American friend of the revolutionary movement who gained much of his information on the spot; SCHIERBRAND, *Russia, her Strength and her Weakness*, 1904, an account of modern conditions by a German; STEPNIAK, *Underground Russia*, by a prominent revolutionist who died in

1895; PERRIS, *Russia in Revolution*, 1905, journalistic; KOVALEWSKY, *La Crise russe*, 1906, by an eminent scholar.

The changes year by year can be followed in the *Annual Register*, the *Statesman's Year-Book* (with its useful bibliographies), or in one of the French or German annuals (see below, pp. 540–541).

Descriptions of Russian society and institutions

For general descriptions of Russian civilization, WALLACE, MAC-KENZIE, *Russia*, 2 vols., new ed., 1905, is perhaps the best. The elaborate work of LEROY-BEAULIEU, *The Empire of the Tsars* (English translation, 1893–1896), was published in the French original in 1882; but, while rather old, is nevertheless excellent in some respects, especially in dealing with religious matters and the position of the Russian church. KOVALEVSKY, *Russian Political Institutions*, 1902, brief and excellent.

Memoirs, etc.

CZARTORISKY, *Memoirs and his Correspondence with Alexander I*, English translation, 2 vols., 1888; and KROPOTKIN, *Memoirs of a Revolutionist*, 1899, are both charming and very instructive. LEO DEUTSCH, *Sixteen Years in Siberia*, 1905, must be supplemented by the classical work of the distinguished American traveler and journalist: KENNAN, GEORGE, *Siberia and the Exile System*, 2 vols., 4th ed., 1897, which gives a terrible but accurate description of the sufferings of the Russian political prisoners and exiles.

Detailed histories

A more detailed account of Russian history may be found in the following works: JOYNEVILLE, *Life and Times of Alexander I*, 3 vols., 1875; SCHIEMANN, *Geschichte Russlands unter Nikolaus I*, Vol. I, 1904, dealing with the reign of Alexander I (the work is in progress); SAMSON-HIMMELSTIERNA, *Russia under Alexander III* (from the German), 1893.

CHAPTER XXIX

TURKEY AND THE EASTERN QUESTION

General accounts

SEIGNOBOS, *Political History of Europe since 1814*, chaps. xx–xxi; ROSE, *Development of European Nations*, Vol. I, pp. 184–224; POOLE, STANLEY-LANE, *Turkey*, 1889; FREEMAN, E. A., *The Ottoman Power in Europe, its Nature, its Growth, and its Decline*, 1877; CURTIS, W. E., *The Turk and his Lost Provinces*, 1903; DAVEY, R., *The Sultan and his Subjects*, 2 vols., 1897; HOLLAND, *The European Concert in the Eastern Question; a Collection of Treaties*, etc., 1897; VILLARI (editor), *The Balkan Question*, 1905; MILLER, WM., *The Balkan States* (Story of the Nations Series); CREASY, *History of the Ottoman Turks* (based on the standard old German work of Von Hammer and continued to 1876),

1882. For Greece: PHILLIPS, *Greek War of Independence*, 1897, and FYFFE, *Modern Europe*, Vol. II, chap. iv.

Histoire générale, Vol. X, chap. xxvi; Vol. XI, chap. vi; Vol. XII, chaps. xii–xv; ENGELHARDT, *La Turquie et le Tanzimat: histoire des réformes depuis 1826*, 2 vols., 1882–1883; SCHOPOFF, *Les Réformes et la Protection des Chrétiens en Turquie, 1673–1904*, 1904; VERNEY et DAMBMANN, *Les Puissances étrangères dans le Levant*, 1900; CANUET, *La Question d'Orient dans l'histoire contemporaine, 1821–1905*, 1905. *Some works in French*

CHAPTER XXX

THE EXPANSION OF EUROPE IN ASIA AND AFRICA

The bibliographies relating to the Industrial Revolution and to the British Empire in the nineteenth century (pp. 523 *sq.* and 530 *sqq.*, above) contain a number of works on the development of means of communication, modern commerce, and imperialism. THURSTON, *A History of the Growth of the Steam Engine*, and SAMUELSON, *The Civilization of Our Day*, 1886, may be supplemented by WELLS, *Economic Changes*, 1899, and COCHRANE, *Modern Industrial Progress*, 1904 (see above, p. 523). DAY, CLIVE, *History of Commerce*, 1907, is a clear, recent manual of the whole subject; REINSCH, *World Politics at the End of the Nineteenth Century*, 1900, a suggestive and valuable work on the forces underlying imperialism, the Chinese question, and the reflex influence of Eastern developments on Western politics; by the same, *Colonial Government*, 1902, and *Colonial Administration*, 1905, containing analyses of the economic forces in imperialism and a discussion of the methods of colonial government, besides useful general and topical bibliographies; HOBSON, J. A., *Imperialism: a Study*, 1902, an indictment of British imperial policy on economic grounds. *Modern commerce and imperialism*

A useful but not exhaustive bibliography of materials on imperialism will be found in GRIFFIN, *List of Books relating to the Theory of Colonization, Government of Dependencies, Protectorates, and Related Topics*, 1900; LEROY-BEAULIEU, *De la colonisation chez les peuples modernes*, 1906, best account in moderate compass of recent European colonization; *The British Empire Series*, 5 vols., 1899–1902, a collection of lectures by specialists describing British possessions. Official materials are contained in the *British Parliamentary Papers* (" Blue Books"); RAMBAUD, *La France coloniale*, 1895, historical and descriptive; ARNAUD et MÉRAY, *Les Colonies françaises*, 1900, recent concise account; *Annuaire colonial*, since 1888, official French publication; HASSERT, *Deutschlands Kolonien*, 1898, brief historical and descriptive work. *Materials for advanced study*

Missions

There is an almost endless literature of foreign missions, a great part of which is not designed for the serious historical student. Rev. JAMES S. DENNIS has done the world a great service in his *Christian Missions and Social Progress*, 3 vols., 1897–1906, where the reader will find a vast amount of well-arranged and authentic information with an abundance of references to the literature of the subject. The missions of the Catholic Church will doubtless be well described in the *Catholic Encyclopædia*, 1907 *sqq.* (now in course of publication).

China and Japan

The best manual dealing with the relations of Europe with China and Japan is DOUGLAS, ROBERT J. K., *Europe and the Far East*, an altogether admirable work with an excellent list of books at the end. The same author deals with the history of China in his *China*, 1901 (Story of the Nations Series). KRAUSSE, *The Far East: its History and its Questions*, 1900, with appendix of documents; PARKER, E. H., *China, her History, Diplomacy, and Commerce from the Earliest Times to the Present Day*, 1901, an interesting book; GILES, *China and the Chinese*, a series of lectures, by an eminent authority. From these works one can easily proceed to others in the considerable range of literature on China. The United States Congressional Library has published a *Select List of Books relating to the Far East*, 1904.

The outline of Japanese history given by DOUGLAS in his *Europe and the Far East* may be supplemented by MURRAY, D., *Japan*, 1904 (Story of the Nations Series); KNOX, GEO. W., *Japanese Life in Town and Country*, 1905, a remarkable little book. GRIFFIS, W. E., *The Japanese Nation in Evolution*, 1907, deals with recent events.

Recent developments

MARTIN, W. A. P., *The Awakening of China*, 1907, by an American missionary who has lived in China for well-nigh fifty years and taken part in public life.

Histoire générale, Vol. X, chap. xxviii; Vol. XI, chap. xx; Vol. XII, chap. xxv.

VLADIMIR, *The China-Japan War*, 1905; ASAKAWA, *The Russo-Japanese Conflict*, 1904. THOMPSON, H. C., *China and the Powers*, 1902, relates to the Boxer rising.

CORDIER, H., *Histoire des relations de la Chine avec les puissances occidentales*, 3 vols., 1901–1902, covers the period from 1860 to 1902.

Africa

(For South Africa, see above, p. 532.) KELTIE, J. S., *Partition of Africa*, 1895; JOHNSTON, SIR HARRY, *History of the Colonization of Africa by Alien Races*, 1899, with bibliography; BROWN, ROBERT, *The Story of Africa*, 4 vols., illustrated, 1894–1895; ROSE, *Development of the European Nations*, Vol. II, pp. 269–298, for the Congo.

HUGHES, THOMAS, *David Livingstone*, 1889 (English Men of Action Exploration
Series); BLAIKIE, W. G., *Personal Life of David Livingstone*, 1885, and,
by LIVINGSTONE himself, *Missionary Travels and Researches in South
Africa*, 1857; also, *Last Journals in Central Africa from 1865 to his
death*, edited by Waller, 1875; STANLEY, H. M., *How I found Living-
stone: Travels, Adventures, and Discoveries in Central Africa*, 1872; also,
Through the Dark Continent, or the Sources of the Nile, 1878, and *In
Darkest Africa*, new ed., 1897.

ROSE, *Development of the European Nations*, Vol. II, pp. 143–227. Egypt
The best account of the English occupation of Egypt is now that of
CROMER, EARL OF, *Modern Egypt*, 2 vols., 1908, which traces the history
from the French and English intervention in 1876 to the present day, —
a masterly work; HOLLAND, *European Concert in the Eastern Question;*
BREHIER, L., *L'Egypte de 1789 à 1900*, 1901; ROUX, *L'Isthme et le Canal
de Suez*, 1901.

HOLLS, F. W., *The Peace Conference at the Hague*, 1900; SCOTT, Universal
JAMES B., *Texts of the Peace Conference, 1899 and 1907*, 1908; HULL, peace move-
W. I., *The Two Hague Conferences and their Contributions to Inter-* ment
national Law, 1908; FOSTER, *Arbitration and The Hague Court*, 1904.

For the events during the past three or four years one must turn to
the *Annual Register*, the *Statesman's Year-Book*, or some other of the
annuals mentioned below, pp. 540–541.

CHAPTER XXXI

POLITICAL, SOCIAL, AND ECONOMIC PROBLEMS OF TO-DAY

Scholarly treatises on the constitutions of the European states are to Political and
be found in MARQUARDSEN, *Handbuch des öffentlichen Rechts*, 1883 *sqq.*, constitutional
a series of volumes by specialists; BURGESS, *Political Science and Com-* matters
parative Constitutional Law, 2 vols., 1900, a remarkable comparative
study of the constitutions of France, Great Britain, Germany, and the
United States. For the administrative organization see GOODNOW,
Comparative Administrative Law, 2 vols., 1902. The leading authority
for England is ANSON, *Law and Custom of the Constitution*, 2 vols., 1892;
but compare BAGEHOT, *The English Constitution* (admirably written),
and DICEY'S suggestive *Law of the Constitution*, which has a chapter on
the contrast between the spirit of the English and of the French government. BODLEY, *France*, 2 vols., 1898; DODD, W. F., *Modern Constitutions*, 1909, a translation of the chief constitutions of the world.

Strong statements of the individualist position are to be found Social reforms
in SPENCER, H., *The Man versus the State*, 1894; DONISTHORPE,

Individualism, a System of Politics, 1889; *A Plea for Liberty* (edited by
Herbert Spencer), 1891. MEYER, H. R., *Government Regulation of Railway Rates in the United States, Germany, France*, etc., 1905, and *Municipal
Ownership in Great Britain*, severe attacks on public ownership. Both
works have been sharply criticised by reviewers on the score of inaccu-
racy and misrepresentation. MILL, J. S., *On the Subjection of Women*,
cheap edition, 1906, especially valuable for the description of woman's
position at the time the book was written, in 1869; WESTERMARCK, *A
History of Human Marriage*, 1891; PARSONS, E. C., *The Family*, 1906,
a study of the social position of women; STETSON-GILMAN, C. P., *Woman
and Economics*, a plea for the economic independence of women.

Municipal
problems

WEBER, A. F., *The Growth of Cities in the Nineteenth Century*, 1899
(Columbia University Studies), contains valuable statistical material
and important conclusions; BOOTH, C., *The Labour and Life of the
People*, 17 vols., 1892–1902, a truly monumental work, one of the greatest
contributions ever made to social science, — a detailed study of the
wages, homes, and general conditions of the masses in·London; ROWN-
TREE, S., *Poverty: a Study of Town Life*, 1901, and subsequent cheaper
editions, — a detailed study of the poverty in York, England; HOWE,
F. C., *The British City*, 1907, a readable description of present-day
conditions by a warm partisan of municipal ownership and reform.

Trade unions
and coöpera-
tion

WEBB, S. and B., *The History of Trade Unionism*, 2d ed., 1901, a
full and scholarly history of trade unionism in England. *Industrial
Democracy*, 1901, by the same authors, is a detailed analysis of the
aims and political economy of trade unionism. POTTER, B. (Mrs. Sydney Webb), *The Coöperative Movement in Great Britain*, 1899, an
interesting and brief account of the origin, development, and nature of
the coöperative movement.

Socialism

BLISS, W. (editor), *Encyclopædia of Social Reform*, new ed., 1907,
a large work containing articles on various problems of social reforms,
many of them by experts; BROOKS, J. G., *The Social Unrest*, 1903, a
serious and important study of labor and socialistic movements; SOM-
BART, *Socialism and the Social Movement*, 1898, popular lectures on
the subject by a distinguished German economist; SCHAEFFLE, *The
Quintessence of Socialism*, a brief and fair representation of socialism
by an opponent; SPARGO, *Socialism*, 1906, perhaps the best short
work by a socialist; ENSOR, R., *Modern Socialism*, 1904, a valuable collection of papers and programmes relating to socialism in England and
on the Continent.

MARX, K., *Capital: a Critique of Political Economy*, 1906–1907 (two
volumes of the three-volume work, *Das Kapital*, by one of the founders

of modern socialism, have now appeared, and the third is announced) ; Works by
DEVILLE, G., *The People's Marx*, 1900, a brief summary of the doc- advocates
trines to be found in the voluminous works of Marx ; ENGELS, F., of socialism
Socialism : Utopian and Scientific, 1892, a short presentation of the
Engels-Marxian theory of social evolution ; the *Fabian Essays*, originally published in London in 1889 (to be had in many subsequent editions), a collection of essays on the various aspects of socialism by
members of the Fabian Society ; WELLS, H. G., *New Worlds for Old*,
1908, a fair and attractive consideration of the leading objections
to socialism by the distinguished novelist ; HUNTER, R., *The Socialists
at Work*, 1908, a series of studies of the nature and influence of
socialism in various European countries.

SCHAEFFLE, *The Impossibility of Social Democracy*, a strong state- Criticism of
ment of the objections to socialism ; ELY, *Socialism : its Strength and* socialism
Weaknesses, 1894, an important and useful book ; CATHREIN, V.,
Socialism, 1904, a scholarly criticism from the Catholic standpoint ;
RAE, J., *Contemporary Socialism*, new ed., 1908, a full treatment of the
recent socialistic developments by an opponent of socialism ; SIMON-
SON, A., *A Plain Examination of Socialism*, a spirited denunciation of
socialist theories ; ARNOLD-FORSTER, *English Socialism To-day*, 1908, an
unfavorable examination of its aims and teachings ; LEROY-BEAULIEU,
P., *Collectivism*, 1908, a lengthy criticism of the whole socialist position ;
MALLOCK, W. H., *A Critical Examination of Socialism*, 1907 ; MASARYK,
T., *Die philosophischen und sociologischen Grundlagen des Marxismus*,
1899, a scholarly criticism of the fundamental doctrines of Marx, giving
a full bibliography.

QUACK, *De Socialisten*, 4 vols., 1887–1897, a voluminous history of Materials
socialism from Plato to the present time by a Dutch writer, especially for advanced
valuable for the biographical work ; PARETO, V., *Les Systèmes socialistes*, study of
2 vols., 1902–1903 ; MENGER, A., *Die neue Staatslehre*, 1905, an excel- socialism
lent statement of the socialist theories of political science by a distinguished Austrian scholar, a socialist ; BERNSTEIN, E., *Documente des
Socialismus*, 5 vols., 1902–1905, a valuable collection of papers relating to
socialism in the various European countries (translated into German);
MEHRING, F., *Gesammelte Schriften von Karl Marx und Friedrich Engels*, 4 vols., 1902, invaluable for the socialist movement from 1841 to
1862, and for the original socialistic doctrines.

WALLACE, A. R., and others, *Progress of the Century*, a series of Modern
clear and excellent articles of distinguished men, summing up the scien- science and
tific achievements of the nineteenth century ; KARL SNIDER, *The World* discoveries
Machine, 1907, a popular and not always wholly accurate history of

science, with a good bibliography. DUNCAN, *The New Knowledge*, a very clear statement in attractive form of the most recent discoveries in the field of physical chemistry; WILLIAMS, H. S. and E. H., *A History of Science*, 5 vols., 1904 (Vols. III–V deal with the nineteenth century and are very readable). OSBORN, H. F., *From the Greeks to Darwin*, 1894, a clear and scholarly account of the history of the theory of evolution. Those who wish a more profound treatment of the modern scientific spirit will find it in MERZ, J. T., *History of European Thought in the Nineteenth Century*, 2 vols., 1896–1903, a work more highly esteemed by men of science than any of the preceding contributions to the subject. COCHRANE, *Modern Industrial Progress*, 1904.

Works on French and German

Histoire générale, Vol. X, chap. xx; Vol. XI, chap. xxv; Vol. XII, chap. xvii, — very good; DENNERT, *Die Weltanschauung des modernen Naturforschers*, 1907; DANNEMANN, *Grundriss einer Geschichte der Naturwissenschaften*, 2 vols., 1896–1898 (Vol. I contains an interesting series of selections from the scientific writers of all nations and times).

General history of thought

BENN, A. W., *The History of English Rationalism in the Nineteenth Century*, 2 vols., 1906; ROBERTSON, J. M., *A Short History of Free Thought*, 2 vols., 2d ed., 1906 (the latter part of Vol. II deals with the nineteenth century); HÖFFDING, *History of Modern Philosophy*, 1900 (the latter part of Vol. II takes up some of the chief thinkers of the nineteenth century).

NOTE: ON KEEPING UP WITH THE TIMES

By clipping and arranging extracts on foreign matters from the daily papers and by watching the London *Weekly Times*, or American periodicals, like the *Independent*, the *Outlook*, or *Review of Reviews*, the alert teacher will have little difficulty in keeping fairly well informed on the important events in contemporary history.

For periodical summaries, the following are useful:

"Record of Political Events," published in the June and December issues of the *Political Science Quarterly*. This may be regarded as an index to current history.

The *Annual Register* gives an annual review of the history of the entire world.

The *Statesman's Year-Book*, an annual publication, while not primarily concerned with history, indicates the important changes made during the year in the governments of the respective countries; gives statistical information on the commerce, population, education, army and navy, and finances of each; and contains from time to time valuable maps illustrating geographical changes, such, for example, as followed the Russo-Japanese War.

VIALLATE, A. (editor), *La Vie politique dans les deux mondes*, 1907 *sqq.*, is a new French annual historical register prepared by competent scholars and written in a clear and concise style.

GLASER, F. (editor), *Wirtschaftspolitische Annalen*, 1906 *sqq.*, is a new German annual giving a clue to the social and economic history of all the countries of the world, and is especially useful for Germany.

SCHULTHESS, *Europaeischer Geschichtskalender*, published annually since 1860, is also a handy review of the world's history by years.

ROLOFF, *Staatsarchiv*, published from time to time since 1861, gives the important official papers and treaties relating to each important world event, such as the South African War or the Russo-Japanese War.

Jahrbuch des öffentlichen Rechts, first published in 1907, is a scholarly review of recent constitutional and legal developments.

ANNOUNCEMENTS

EUROPEAN HISTORY FOR COLLEGES

By JAMES HARVEY ROBINSON and CHARLES A. BEARD

PROFESSORS ROBINSON AND BEARD have long been recognized as representing the highest authority on European History. The volumes listed here are as well known as are the authors' other textbooks for sound historical perspective, fitting proportion, and narrative charm.

THE DEVELOPMENT OF MODERN EUROPE
By James Harvey Robinson and Charles A. Beard

VOLUME I   The Eighteenth Century : The French Revolution and the Napoleonic Period. xi + 362 pages, illustrated

VOLUME II   Europe since the Congress of Vienna. 448 + lxxx pages, illustrated

The aim has been to bring the past into relation with the present — to trace past events, conditions, politics, industries, and intellectual achievements of Europe in such a way that the student will recognize their results as they appear in the Europe of today.

READINGS IN MODERN EUROPEAN HISTORY
Edited by James Harvey Robinson and Charles A. Beard. In two volumes

HISTORY OF WESTERN EUROPE
By James Harvey Robinson. In one volume or two volumes

A textbook which has been the standard for many years. It covers the period from 378 A.D. to the present time.

READINGS IN EUROPEAN HISTORY
Edited by James Harvey Robinson. In two volumes or one volume abridged

SYLLABUS FOR THE HISTORY OF WESTERN EUROPE   94 pages
By Norman Maclaren Trenholme, University of Missouri

GINN AND COMPANY PUBLISHERS

TEXTBOOKS ON HISTORY

By Ephraim Emerton

Winn Professor of Ecclesiastical History Emeritus in Harvard University

---

INTRODUCTION TO THE STUDY OF THE MIDDLE AGES
From the battle of Adrianople to the death of Charlemagne (A.D. 378–814)
12mo, cloth, xviii + 268 pages

MEDIÆVAL EUROPE (814–1300)
12mo, cloth, 607 pages, illustrated

BEGINNINGS OF MODERN EUROPE
12mo, cloth, xiv + 550 pages, with maps

Professor Emerton's scholarly histories have taken a high place on account of their clearness, their accuracy in statement and conclusion, their interpretation of the reasons for great movements, and their reliance upon original sources.

The "Introduction to the Middle Ages" aims to give, in simple narrative form, an account of the settlement of the Germanic peoples on Roman soil, the gradual rise of the Frankish supremacy, the growth of the Christian Church and its expression in the monastic life and in the Roman Papacy, and, finally, the culmination of all in the Empire of Charlemagne.

"Mediæval Europe" is a continuation of the author's "Introduction." Its aim is to call the attention of students to the most important political, social, and religious institutions of Continental Europe during the Middle Ages proper.

"Beginnings of Modern Europe" emphasizes the distinctions between medieval and modern ways of thought and life, the increasing importance of individual activities, the growth of lay culture, and the rise of national sentiment.

GINN AND COMPANY Publishers

COLONIZATION

A STUDY OF THE FOUNDING OF NEW SOCIETIES

By ALBERT GALLOWAY KELLER

Professor of the Science of Society in Yale University

8vo, cloth, xii + 632 pages, with maps

COLONIZATION is unique in being the first history in the English tongue to describe the founding of new settlements and societies, and presents a wealth of information, hitherto widely scattered and disconnected, in a style at once logical and of absorbing interest.

In scope the book covers the whole history of colonization, excepting that of the English and French and of several of the most recent colonizing peoples. Information concerning these is reasonably easy of access. The several chapters treat of the colonies of the Orientals and ancients, mediæval and modern Italians, Portuguese, Spanish, Dutch, Scandinavians, and Germans.

The view point is in general that of the economist and sociologist ; such topics as emigration, colonial trade, race contact, and the like are given precedence over historical, administrative, and legal detail. The method is, above all, comparative ; the subject is treated topic-wise, and data are arranged as illustrative of general principles rather than in chronicle fashion. A constant effort has been made to attain simplicity and concreteness of both style and argument.

The book is written especially for American college students, but its style and content will also appeal to the intelligent general reader.

Especially adapted to college students of the junior or senior year

GINN AND COMPANY PUBLISHERS

REFERENCE BOOKS IN HISTORY

Abbott: Roman Political Institutions

Asser: Life of King Alfred

Brigham: From Trail to Railway through the Appalachians

Brigham: Geographic Influences in American History

Callender: Economic History of the United States, 1765–1860

Cannon: Reading References for English History

Channing, Hart, and Turner: Guide to the Study and Reading of
    American History (Revised and Augmented Edition)

Cheyney: Readings in English History

Dealey: Growth of American State Constitutions

Hayes: British Social Politics

Keller: Colonization

Muzzey: Readings in American History (Revised Edition)

Myers: History as Past Ethics

Priest: Germany since 1740

Reinsch: Readings on American Federal Government

Reinsch: Readings on American State Government

Richardson, Ford, Durfee, and Lutz: Syllabus of Continental
    European History (Revised Edition)

Robinson: Readings in European History, Volume I
    Volume II
    Abridged Edition

Robinson and Beard: Readings in Modern European History
    Volume I
    Volume II

Thallon: Readings in Greek History

Tuell and Hatch: Selected Readings in English History

Webster: General History of Commerce (Revised Edition)

GINN AND COMPANY PUBLISHERS